Before the War of 1866 the name of Helmuth von Moltke was scarcely known outside the Prussian army. His appointment as Chief of the General Staff was in many ways surprising, and he certainly did not himself expect it. He was thus put at the head of a military institution that was already to some extent superior to its counterparts elsewhere; he was to turn it into a formidable machine that became, in his hands, very nearly invincible. This was due to a number of factors which coincided with his appointment. Among these were the many advances in military technology and logistics on the one hand, and on the other the emergence of Otto von Bismarck as Minister-President of Prussia, with whom Moltke had a crucial, if occasionally uneasy, relationship.

This book follows Moltke's part in the course of the campaign at the end of which his name had become a household word. It traces his rise to the position of Chief of the General Staff, against the background of the political situation of Prussia in the middle of the 19th Century, and the way in which he developed the functions of the General Staff. Moltke's contribution to the allied campaign of Prussia and Austria against Denmark in 1864 was an important part of his own development, before the inevitable war between the successful allies in 1866. As the book shows, for that war Moltke prepared his plans in the minutest detail. The triumphant success of his strategy in Bohemia was supplemented by the boldness of his campaign in western Germany, in which a small Prussian army overcame a huge numerical disadvantage. By the end of the Seven Weeks' War Moltke had made Prussia the strongest military power in Europe. The Campaign of 1866 in Bohemia is covered in great detail, including the most extensive coverage of the Battle of Königgätz yet published in English.

The author's detailed text is accompanied by a large number of illustrations and maps.

Quintin Barry is a solicitor. He retired recently as an Employment Judge. Throughout his professional career he has maintained his lifelong interest in military and naval history. He has made a special study of the period 1848 – 1878, with particular reference to the Wars of German Unification. This is his second work for Helion, following publication in 2007 of a widely praised two-volume study of the Franco–Prussian War 1870–71. He is married and lives in Sussex.

THE ROAD TO KÖNIGGRÄTZ

Helmuth von Moltke and the Austro-Prussian War 1866

Quintin Barry

The commanders of the victorious Prussian army of 1866. (Rogers)

THE ROAD TO KÖNIGGRÄTZ

Helmuth von Moltke and the Austro-Prussian War 1866

Quintin Barry

Helion & Company Ltd

Helion & Company Limited
26 Willow Road
Solihull
West Midlands
B91 1UE
England
Tel. 0121 705 3393
Fax 0121 711 4075
Email: info@helion.co.uk
Website: www.helion.co.uk
Twitter: @helionbooks
Visit our blog http://blog.helion.co.uk

Published by Helion & Company 2010
This paperback reprint 2014

Designed and typeset by Farr out Publications, Wokingham, Berkshire
Cover designed by Farr out Publications, Wokingham, Berkshire
Printed by Lightning Source Ltd, Milton Keynes, Buckinghamshire

ISBN 978-1-909384-96-5

British Library Cataloguing-in-Publication Data.
A catalogue record for this book is available from the British Library.

Cover illustrations: Bismarck and Moltke at Königgrätz, July 3 1866, painting by Röchling (front cover); King William I of Prussia greets the Crown Prince on the field of Königgrätz, July 3 1866, painting by Röhling (rear cover). Note that despite the names, Carl Röchling, and Carl Röhling, they are two different artists.

CONTENTS

Appendices
Orders of Battle

List of Illustrations

Key to Sources

Album della Guerra del 1866 (Milan, 1867)
C.v.H. *Schießpulver und Feuerwaffen. Illustrirte Uebersicht aller auf diesen Gebiete gemachten Erfindungen und Entdeckungen, unter vorzugsweiser Berücksichtigung der gegenwartig bei den europäischen Heeren bestehenden Geschütze und Gewehre* (Leipzig, 1866)
Fontane *Der deutsche Krieg von 1866* (Berlin, 1871, 2 volumes)
Hofmann & Rohling *Otto von Bismarck. Ernstes und Heiteres aus dem Leben des Grossen Kanzler* (Berlin, 1897)
Hohenlohe-Ingelfingen *Aus meinem Leben* (Berlin, 1897-1907, 4 volumes)
Illustrirte Kriegs-Chronik. Gedenkbuch an den Feldzug von 1866 in Deutschland und Italien (Leipzig, 1867)
Lezius *Deutsche Uniformen Album III: Das Zeitalter der Deutschen Einigung 1864-1914 Band 1* (Dresden, 1933)
Lukeš *Militärischer Maria-Theresien-Orden. Neue Folge 1850-1890* (Vienna, 1891)
Mollinary *Sechsundvierzig Jahre im österreich-ungarischen Heere 1833-1879* (Zürich, 1905, 2 volumes)
Moltke *Letters of Field-Marshal Count Helmuth von Moltke to his mother and his brothers* (London, 1891, 2 volumes)
Priesdorff *Soldatisches Führertum* (Hamburg, 1936-42, 10 volumes)
Reimer *Bismarck. Das Jahrhundert der deutschen Einigung 1815-1915 in Wort und Bild* (Hamburg, 1915)
Regensberg *1866 – Von Dresden bis Münchengrätz* (Stuttgart, 1903)
Regensberg *1866 – Nachod-Wysokow* (Stuttgart, 1905)
Regensberg *1866 – Von Skalitz bis Königgrätz* (Stuttgart, 1906)
Regensberg *1866 – Königgrätz* (Stuttgart, 1903)
Regensberg *1866 – Letzte Kämpfe und Friedenschluss* (Stuttgart, 1908)
Regensberg *1866 – Der Mainfeldzug* (Stuttgart, 1908)
Rogers - original photographs and other material from private collection of Duncan Rogers
Voss *Illustrierte Geschichte der deutschen Einigungskriege 1864-1866* (Stuttgart, 1914)

List of Maps

Acknowledgements

As is always the case, this book could not have been produced without the encouragement and practical help of many people, to all of whom I wish to express my heartfelt gratitude. In particular, I greatly appreciate the help of Tim Readman and of the late Rob Mantle, both of whom cheerfully undertook to read the book in draft; to Jean Hawkes and Lindsey Cadle who once again patiently shouldered the heavy burden of turning my manuscript into an acceptable text; and to David Townsend for all his help in translating some difficult passages in a number of German texts.

Above all, I should like to express my particular thanks to Duncan Rogers and all his colleagues at Helion and Company. Duncan's help and encouragement in preparing the book for publication, and in particular the maps and illustrations, has been of immense value. I should also like to record my appreciation of his company during our tour of the Bohemian battlefields, during which our joint navigational skills ultimately always brought us to our intended destinations, albeit with the occasional inadvertent diversion, for which I accept all blame. I should mention in particular our adventurous assault on the Roskosberg. I should also thank Tomáš Kaláb and Jiří Jemelka, who enthusiastically showed us around the battlefield of Tobitschau. Finally, I am grateful to my wife and family for their tolerance and understanding while this book was being written.

It is dedicated to my brother Richard, who died before its publication. I hope that he would have been pleased with the result.

The publishers wish to acknowledge the following:

Cambridge University Press for permission to reprint an excerpt from *Supplying War* by Martin van Creveld, p. 108, published Cambridge: Cambridge University Press, 1978.

Cambridge University Press for permission to reprint an excerpt from *The Austro-Prussian War* by Geoffrey Wawro, p. 31, published Cambridge: Cambridge University Press, 1996.

The Orion Publishing Group for permission to reprint six excerpts from *The Battle of Königgrätz* by Gordon Craig, pp. 12, 13, 85, 95, 100 and 136, published London: George Weidenfeld and Nicolson Ltd, an imprint of the Orion Publishing Group, 1965.

The Orion Publishing Group for permission to reprint an excerpt from *A Military History of Germany from the Eighteenth Century to the present day* by Martin Kitchen, p. 103, published London: George Weidenfeld and Nicolson Ltd, an imprint of the Orion Publishing Group, 1975.

Pearson Education for permission to reprint two excerpts from *Austria, Prussia and Germany 1806-1871* by J. Breuilly, p. 91 and 92, published Harlow: Longman, 2002.

Random House, Inc. for permission to reprint five excerpts from *Moltke on the Art of War: Selected Writings* edited by Daniel J. Hughes, pp. 45, 48, 108, 184 and 235-236, published by New York: Presidio Press, an imprint of The Ballantine Publishing Group, a division of Random House, Inc, 1993, © Daniel J. Hughes.

University of Pennsylvania Press for permission to reprint an excerpt from *French Opinion on War and Diplomacy during the Second Empire* by L.M. Case, p. 199, published Philadelphia: University of Pennsylvania Press, 1954.

Introduction

The Times, which in the days immediately prior to the outbreak of the Austro–Prussian War had been relentlessly hostile to Prussia and in particular to its Minister President, had by September 22 1866 come round to an entirely different view. A leading article of that date recorded:

> Of all the victorious pageants that the ancient or modern world ever witnessed, none can compare with that wonderful Berlin procession, [the triumphant parade of the two previous days] none, at least, was made to celebrate deeds of equal magnitude … Well may the Prussian people enjoy their proud and happy day. The army … is part of them. It is "the Prussian nation in arms". That nation … did not go forth impelled by lust of conquest, or even by love of strife and adventure … They thought of nothing but what they owed to King and country.[1]

The battle of Königgrätz, as Professor Gordon Craig noted, was in terms of the numbers engaged the greatest encounter of the modern era up to that time. Between 440,000 and 460,000 troops took part in the battle, which was the first encounter between armies of the Great Powers to demonstrate the changes in warfare that had been wrought by the developments in technology. But, as again Professor Craig pointed out in what was, and remains, far and away the best work on the subject, it was not technology which decided the outcome, but the qualities of the Prussian troops and their leadership:

> The superiority of its infantry weapon was of undeniable importance in the victory of the Prussian Army at Königgrätz, explaining among other things the rapid deterioration of morale in some Austrian units. But this advantage was not decisive in itself, and it is important to note that such cool observers as the French military attaché Stoffel and the future German Chief of General Staff Alfred von Schlieffen insisted that the Zündnadelgewehr (needle gun) had less effect upon the battle than Austrian persistence in faulty tactics and failures of command.[2]

But it was not merely mistakes on the part of the Austrian leadership that led to the outcome; it was the calm and dispassionate judgment of the man who in practice led the Prussian troops that created the conditions for victory. Helmuth von Moltke, like the army which he managed so superbly in 1866, had come a long way since the year of his birth in 1800. That year had seen Napoleon take a long stride towards the mastery of Europe at Marengo. It was to be fifteen years before his final defeat at Waterloo, and in that time the Prussian army was humiliated at Jena and later reborn under Scharnhorst and Gneisenau. In the half century that followed before Prussia was again at war, Moltke's progress towards the top of his profession was steady and unremarkable, until he became Chief of the Great General Staff, and the stage was set for a series of events that changed the course of European history.

For as well as being an encounter on the largest scale, Königgrätz was a truly significant event both in its military outcome and in the events that followed it. To quote Professor Craig again:

> The political consequences of the battle of Königgrätz were so profound and so far-reaching that it is not difficult to understand why it has generally been considered one of the "decisive battles" of the modern era.[3]

The Prussian achievement was indeed extraordinary. Much of the credit must of course go to the brave and steadfast troops who outperformed every expectation. But it was Moltke's strategy that won the Austro-Prussian War. However, although Königgrätz was a stunning success, it could have been even more so. Alfred von Schlieffen was in no doubt of this:

> Twice could a Cannae have taken place. The idea of a complete surrounding and annihilation of the enemy was too foreign to the Prussian generals to allow Moltke's simple and grand plan to succeed. The enemy was only pushed back. It is true that he was entirely broken. But should he find some rest, he could regain strength, as was hoped, draw in reinforcements and regain capability of resistance, even of attack.[4]

A critical component of Moltke's success was his development of the General Staff. He started with the advantage of inheriting a system of military management that was well in advance of anything to be found among the other Great Powers. Professor Arden Bucholz has summarised Moltke's achievement in modern terms, pointing out that it was at an age when many of his contemporaries were already dead or retired that he 'developed and validated deep future-oriented war-planning processes.'[5]

Professor Bucholz quotes an apt comment by Peter Drucker to describe the efficiency of the military machine that was largely Moltke's creation: 'The Prussian army was as much a marvel of organisation for the world of 1870 as Henry Ford's assembly line was for the world of 1920.'[6] In seeking an explanation for the successes of the Prussian Army in the Wars of Unification, military commentators could not fail to be struck by the effectiveness of its organisation, with the result that all other armies sooner or later, and to a greater or lesser extent, sought to imitate it.

Moltke was a lucid exponent of his own military beliefs, and he left behind him a substantial body of work which set out his philosophy. After his death the Prussian General Staff edited and published his official writings; as Professor Hughes has pointed out 'although he wrote not a single integrated work on warfare, his views became the foundation of Prussian military thought, particularly in the areas of strategy and large-units operations.'[7]

The principles which he enunciated ensured that the so-called 'demigods' whom he trained had an instinctive appreciation of his intentions; but although Moltke had developed a mutual understanding with his General Staff officers, on which throughout the Wars of Unification he could absolutely rely, the same was not always true of his senior commanders. Not only in the course of the Königgrätz campaign, but also in 1864 and 1870-71, they failed on occasion to grasp the strategic concepts on which his plans were based. As a result, some of his victories were less complete than they might have been. No one, however, in Berlin on September 20 1866 was going to indulge in military perfectionism, apart perhaps from Moltke himself. When he rode down Unter den Linden in the victory parade beside Bismarck and Roon, Moltke received the public adulation about which he always felt uncomfortable but which he manifestly deserved. It had been a long road that he had travelled, and his journey was not yet at an end. For the moment, however, even Moltke could share in the celebration of his remarkable victory.

Part I
PRELUDE

1

Helmuth von Moltke

A few months before the outbreak of the Austro-Prussian War, King William's Adjutant-General, Lieutenant-General Leopold von Boyen, moaned to a friend: 'The King in command, at the age of seventy, with the decrepit Moltke at his side! What will come of it all?'[1] Certainly, in 1866 little was known of Moltke's ability to command large armies. His combat experience was slight, and most of his career had been spent in staff appointments, so Boyen's pessimism is perhaps not altogether surprising. But the events of that year were to demonstrate just how wide of the mark an apparently well-informed observer could be.

Helmuth Carl Bernhard von Moltke was born in Parchim in Mecklenburg on October 26 1800, into one of the families of the impoverished nobility that produced so many of the leading figures of the Prussian army in the 19th Century. His father Friedrich von Moltke had served in the Prussian army prior to his marriage in 1797. In 1805 he bought an estate in Holstein, and became a Danish citizen. His family remained in Lübeck while he was building a new house on his estate of Augustenhof. It was while this was going on that there occurred one of the defining incidents of the young Moltke's life. In October 1806, after Napoleon's crushing victory at Jena, the family had to endure the traumatic experience of heavy street fighting in Lübeck between Prussian and French troops, in the course of which there was extensive looting by the French. Among the houses plundered was the Moltkes' family home. All his life Helmuth von Moltke felt an enduring hostility towards the French nation, and although he seems not to have made much reference to it, his experience in Lübeck evidently left an indelible impression on him.

In Holstein, Friedrich von Moltke's farming career proved decidedly unsuccessful, and he returned to the military life, joining the Danish army and taking part in a number of its campaigns, including the storming of Stralsund in 1809. He rose ultimately to the rank of Lieutenant-General before he died in 1845. In 1811 he sent his sons Helmuth and Fritz to the military academy in Copenhagen. Years later Moltke looked back on his time there:

> I had no education but thrashing. I have had no chance of forming a character. I am often painfully conscious of it. This want of self-reliance and constant reference to the opinions of others, even the preponderance of reason over inclination, often gives me moral depressions, such as others feel through opposite causes.[2]

His later career, consistently marked by great strength of character, suggests that Moltke was inclined to overstate the effect of his upbringing, but there is no doubt that he was deeply unhappy there. He did, however, form a lifelong friendship with the family of General Hegermann-Lindencrone, three of whose sons went on to distinguish themselves in the Danish army. Moltke later wrote that this friendship 'with this noble, highly educated family has exercised the greatest influence on my development.'[3]

Moltke left the academy in 1819, and entered the Danish army as a Second-Lieutenant. However, a visit to Berlin kindled the idea of entering the Prussian Army, and in 1822 he passed the examination for a commission, being posted as a Second-Lieutenant to an infantry regiment before, in the following year, commencing his studies at the Allgemeine Kriegsschule in Berlin. The Commandant of the Academy at this time was Carl von Clausewitz, who was a remote and rather severe figure rarely seen by his students. Moltke graduated in 1827; his final certificate, signed by Clausewitz and others, recorded that he had 'written good essays on the practical military subjects given. The result of his scientific studies has been very good. His conduct was blameless.'[4] When he emerged from the Academy, however, he was not at all well off, noting years later that 'as my father's fortune had been dissipated by wars and his many misfortunes, I had no addition to my pay from home, and was compelled to be very economical.'[5] His poverty compelled him a few years later to embark on the translation into German of Gibbon's 'Decline and Fall of the Roman Empire', a monstrous task for which he was ill rewarded, the publisher going bankrupt while Moltke was engaged on the eleventh of the twelve volumes.

After leaving the Kriegsschule, he returned to his regiment where he served for some time as Commandant of the Divisional Cadet School, before being appointed to a topographical survey in Silesia and Posen, on which he was engaged for three years. He was evidently a good map maker; one of his ordnance surveys still makes up part of one of the modern German ordnance survey maps for the area.[6] In 1832 he was appointed to the General Staff. Promotion was normally very slow, but Moltke was made First-Lieutenant in 1833. In 1834 he was sent on two secret missions, first to the Italian Riviera and then to Copenhagen, for which he was rewarded with the Order of St John. In the following year he was unusually fortunate to be promoted to Captain. His economic situation was still very precarious; in his voluminous correspondence with his family, and in particular with his mother, who helped him out from time to time, there are frequent references to his financial difficulties. But his military career as a quiet and thoughtful staff officer, if giving no hint of what was to come, was clearly progressing satisfactorily.

Taking extended leave in 1835, he made his way eastwards, stopping in Vienna before exploring the Balkans *en route* to Constantinople. There, he attracted the attention of the Sultan's Minister of War, Chosref Pasha. In the course of a series of meetings, the Minister formed a very high opinion of Moltke's professional ability, and applied to the Prussian Government for his leave to be extended, so that he might serve as an adviser to the Turkish Government. What had begun as a short holiday trip became an extended assignment of four years' duration, for it was not until 1839 that he finally returned to Prussia.

In that period Moltke had gained a very broad practical military awareness. He wrote of his experiences fully and regularly to his family, and on his return to Prussia published them as *Letters on the Conditions and Events in Turkey in the years 1835 to 1839*. During this time, Moltke served as adviser to Chosref Pasha, producing schemes for the reorganisation of the Turkish army and the introduction of Prussian military systems, carrying out topographical surveys, and preparing many reports on fortifications and other engineering works. The Sultan himself was vastly impressed, and soon a military mission comprising four other Prussian officers was sent to support Moltke. In 1838 he went with a colleague, Captain von Muhlbach, to serve on the staff of Hafiz Pasha, who was commanding an army of observation some 30,000 strong on the Syrian border, which had been assembled because of the threat of war with Mehemet Ali. Moltke reconnoitred the surrounding country and accompanied a number of expeditions against rebel forces. He had by now been joined at headquarters by another Prussian officer, Captain von Vincke. By April 1839 the Egyptian army, under Ibrahim Pasha, was at Aleppo, from which point it was feared it might either march directly on Constantinople or attack the army of Hafiz Pasha. In one of history's remarkable ironies, Ibrahim had on his staff a French officer, Captain Beaufort d'Hautpoul, who occupied much the same position as Moltke. Just over three decades later they were to come face to face at the end of the Franco Prussian War, when the unfortunate Frenchman was part of Jules Favre's negotiating team at Versailles. Beaufort d'Hautpoul was to put up an undistinguished performance during the negotiations, evidently so hampered by his emotion that uncharitable German observers concluded that he was drunk.

Moltke believed that of the options open to Ibrahim an advance on the capital was more probable, and recommended that in order to prevent this, Hafiz should prepare an entrenched camp at Biradschik, which would threaten the right wing of any advance which Ibrahim might make. Although its flanks were protected by a winding river, the

Moltke in Turkey 1837, a contemporary drawing. (Moltke)

position was in one respect not ideal, as there was no bridge over the river at the rear of the Turkish army. Moltke's view of the effectiveness of the Turkish army can be judged from his comment that 'a bridge would only be useful for deserters, but as matters now stand every man must hold his ground or perish.'[7]

Hafiz might have taken Moltke's sound advice to remain in the excellent position at Biradschik but for an incident arising from a chance skirmish on the Syrian border between a few of his cavalrymen who were attacked by Egyptian cavalry. Enraged, Hafiz summoned a council of war, announcing that he had consulted the mullahs who accompanied the army and that they had advised that the incident justified the commencement of hostilities. Moltke was asked for his views, but he firmly declined to give political advice in the absence of information about the international consequences of going to war.

Hafiz, evidently still moved by what he regarded as a personal affront, resolved to advance his whole force from the entrenched position at Biradschik to Nisib; Ibrahim finally moved to attack him on June 20, by way of a march around the left flank of the Turkish army. By ignoring Moltke's advice that he should launch a pre-emptive strike at Ibrahim while he was manoeuvring, Hafiz let slip an excellent opportunity to defeat the Egyptian army in detail, and in turn left himself much exposed. Moltke now strongly advised an immediate retreat to Biradschik, but apparently out of pride Hafiz hesitated, even though Ibrahim's advance now threatened him on both flanks. Moltke was extremely angry, believing that in consequence Hafiz had 'thrown away Syria.' He later wrote to Captain von Vincke to describe what happened: 'Hafiz Pasha had absolutely refused to go back to Biradschik, because he said it was "aib" (a shame), when we were suddenly surrounded from the left (strategically) at Nisib. Whereupon I asked for my discharge and for passports to Constantinople, just before the battle began.'[8]

Moltke grimly warned Hafiz that 'by tomorrow at sundown you will know what it is to be a commander without an army.'[9] On June 23, this was exactly what occurred. Soon after the battle commenced, the Turkish left collapsed and precipitately retreated, leaving the rest of the army hopelessly exposed. Panic set in. In spite of all that Moltke and his fellow Prussians could do, in particular in directing the artillery, the army rapidly disintegrated. Leaving the chaotic battlefield, Moltke and his colleagues rode away from the scene through the crowds of fleeing Turkish soldiers retreating in complete disorder. Two years later on the evening of the anniversary of the battle he set down his recollections of his adventures in a letter to his fiancée:

> After the battle, we were riding till sunset towards Aintab, where I arrived dead tired, ill, and dispirited. But at this hour we were again in the saddle, and continued riding all night over the mountains, and also all the next day, with nothing to eat but half a biscuit, two onions and a glass of water. Today, I was riding the same horse, and was thinking all the time that, next to God, I owe it to his legs that I am still moving about in the world.[10]

Later, when they rejoined Hafiz, the Prussian officers learned both of the death of the Sultan and of their own recall to Prussia. For Moltke, it was the end of a remarkable and very valuable phase of his military education in the course of which, notwithstanding the disaster at Nisib, he had done very well. Hafiz wrote a reference for Moltke recording that he had

> done his duty as a faithful and brave man from the beginning of his commission to this moment, performing all his tasks perfectly. At the same time I have been a witness that this officer has given proofs of bravery and courage and has served the Ottoman Government with fidelity, and even to the hazard of his life.[11]

On his way back through Constantinople Moltke interceded with Chosref Pasha on behalf of the unfortunate Hafiz, pointing out the impossibility of the task set him:

> It was hardly his fault if instead of giving him 80,000 men he was allowed only half that number, and the various corps were not placed under one general, as we had repeatedly advised in our despatches. Nor could the faulty arrangement of the army, formed as it was of two thirds Kurdish troops, be set down to him – troops who were loath to remain in the service and who turned tail and fled when it came to the point.[12]

Vincke wrote to Major-General Fischer to comment on Moltke's performance, remarking that he had

> behaved on every occasion as *un chevalier sans peur et sans reproche* and an able, active and a discreet officer of the General Staff. Even when he was ill and when he had better have stayed in bed, he was at his post.... The Pasha had always valued his opinion and advice, though on the most important point he did not listen to him. He now sees, only too clearly, how wrong he was not to do so.[13]

Back home, after a journey during much of which he was seriously ill, Moltke was assigned to the staff of the IV Corps commanded by Prince Charles of Prussia. In 1842 he was promoted to Major, and in the same year was married to the sixteen year old Marie Burt, stepdaughter of his sister Augusta. In spite of the considerable gap in their ages, it was to be a marriage of unreserved happiness, and to his wife, from whom he was frequently separated over the next twenty five years, he wrote regularly in a series of letters minutely descriptive of the events he witnessed and full of loving tenderness.

Moltke had meanwhile been working on his history of the Russo-Turkish War of 1828-9, which was published at about this time. In it he offered a penetrating analysis of the performance of the Russian commanders and of the organisation of the Russian army. He was especially critical of the failure of the Russians to make effective use of the large amount of siege artillery at their disposal, as well as their reliance on an army very much weaker than was really required.

> The preparations were insufficient, the campaign begun too late, and the direction of the main army not likely to ensure a successful result. But all these faults were atoned for by the innate excellence of the Russian troops.[14]

A translation of Moltke's work was published in England in 1854; two years later, visiting London, Moltke was amused to see a copy of his book at the publishers John Murray, and to read in the translator's preface that it was by a 'Baron von Moltke, who is now dead.'[15]

Very much to his surprise, in late 1845 Moltke was appointed ADC to the King's elderly uncle, Prince Henry, who lived in Rome. The duties were not onerous; Moltke, his wife and his brother spent an agreeable time in Rome until the Prince's death in the following year. He returned to active duty on the staff of the VIII Corps in December 1846 and it was in this post that he was still serving in the Rhineland during the 'March Days' of unrest in Berlin. These he watched mournfully, writing to his brother Adolf in August 1848:

> The poor Fatherland! The better sort of the nation are silent, the scum come to the top and govern… It must all end in war, and it is some comfort to think that the first gun shot will put an end to the part of all these praters.[16]

Moltke was next promoted to the position of Chief of Staff of the IV Corps, in Magdeburg, a position which he had come to regard as the likely pinnacle of his career. Writing from Magdeburg in 1850, he noted that as a result of the rising tension in Germany 'the peace of Europe no longer depends on the conferences of ministers, but on the action of a patrol of hussars', and he was soon deeply involved in all the practical problems for his corps arising from the order for the mobilisation of the Prussian army. The anticlimax of the Convention of Olmütz brought him to despair. On January 29 1851 he wrote to his wife, as the ensuing demobilisation came to an end:

> That our whole policy has been so perverted that we must now accept many humiliations, that we must give up everything we have claimed and attempted during the last three years, I quite understand. But that we should muster five hundred thousand men to yield at all points, and help the Austrians over the Elbe on Frederick the Great's birthday, that is difficult to understand. What disasters a single day has brought upon us![17]

Next month to his brother Adolf he wrote:

> A more disgraceful peace was never signed…But the worst Government cannot ruin this nation; Prussia will stand yet at the head of Germany… Still it must be true that a more pitiable nation than the Germans does not exist on earth.[18]

Although much had gone wrong with the mobilisation of the Prussian Army and a great number of reforms were going to be necessary before it achieved an acceptable standard of efficiency, Moltke had found that in Magdeburg the operation had gone reasonably well, commenting soon afterwards to his brother that 'mobilisation and demobilisation have given me much to do, but the result was satisfactory;' nonetheless, he was very much aware that there were many lessons to be learned from the experience.

Moltke continued to perform his duties at Magdeburg in his usual quiet and unobtrusive manner, and took part in the annual staff rides, to which he attached great

Moltke in 1866. (Rogers)

importance. Among the staff and those who knew and were familiar with the staff, his reputation was rising. For his part, he was forming professional opinions about many of those who would have a part to play in the future, noting for instance of the military capacity of Prince Frederick Charles in 1854 that he 'has an absolute passion for the business, which is very creditable to his powers of insight. He does his work very well. I believe he is the man who will some day restore the ancient glory of the Prussian arms.'[19] In later years there were occasionally days when he would not perhaps have thought quite so well of the Red Prince.

On June 2 1855 occurred a crucial turning point in Moltke's career, when he was suddenly summoned to King Frederick William IV to be told of the royal wish that he should take up the post of Adjutant to the King's nephew, Prince Frederick William. For the next two years Moltke lived the life of a courtier, attending the young Prince on all his considerable travels, not the least important of which were his visits to England, which culminated in his engagement to the Queen's eldest daughter, the Princess Victoria. In the course of his duties as the Prince's Adjutant, Moltke was in close and regular contact with the Prince's father, Prince William, as well as meeting most of the great and the good, both in Germany and abroad. He wrote to Marie with lengthy descriptions of his experiences. In December of 1856 he went with the Prince to Paris, noting that Napoleon III looked better on horseback than on foot, and was, in society, not imposing. 'In conversation he seems even slightly embarrassed. He is all an Emperor, but never a King.'[20]. He liked the Empress Eugénie, who herself also took passing note of Moltke:

> A General called Moltke or some such name is in attendance on the Prince; this gentleman who talks but little is nothing but a dreamer; nevertheless he is always interesting, and surprises one by his apt remarks. The Germans are an imposing race. Louis says they are the race of the future. Bah![21]

By now, Moltke's various appointments had made him a well-known and well-respected figure in Court circles. He was a tall, spare, ascetic man; prematurely bald, he habitually wore a wig, not from vanity, but to keep his head warm. Profoundly intellectual, he had become an extremely accomplished linguist. He was also, however, as Eugénie had noted, reserved to the point of taciturnity; it was famously said of him that he could be silent in seven languages. His Court life was, however, drawing to a close. In October 1857 Karl von Reyher, the Chief of the General Staff, died. Although Moltke noted to his wife that 'Reitzenstein, from Frankfurt, may very likely be put into Reyher's place, and it would be a good choice', it was in fact Moltke who was asked to take over the duties of the Chief of the General Staff on a provisional basis. The principal responsibility for making such an appointment lay with the recently appointed Chief of the Military Cabinet, Major General Edwin von Manteuffel, whose personality and very considerable ability exercised a major influence on Prussian military policy.

Manteuffel was born in 1809. In March 1848 he was serving as aide-de-camp to Prince Albrecht of Prussia, and found himself at the centre of the confused situation surrounding Frederick William IV, as that bewildered monarch struggled to cope with the 'March Days' in Berlin. By the force of his personality he took a prominent part in the anxious discussions among the King's advisers, always counselling fierce resistance to the incipient revolution. When the crisis abated, he was appointed the King's 'Flügeladjutant', and he was thereafter never far from the levers of power in the military establishment. He had considerable diplomatic skills, and was sent on a number of important missions abroad, especially during the Crimean War. He held the most extreme reactionary views, from which he never departed; throughout the struggle over army reform he argued violently against making any concessions to the Landtag. In May 1860 he wrote on the subject of army reform; 'I consider the state of army morale and its inner energy and the position of the Prince Regent compromised, if these regiments are not established definitively at once.'[22] He was perpetually alert to the possibility of a royalist coup d'état which would put paid to any dangerous advance towards democracy on the part of the Landtag, and in January 1862 King William was to adopt, on the basis that it was purely a precautionary measure, a plan for action to be taken in the event of a further rising in Berlin, which Manteuffel had drafted in conjunction with Lieutenant General Hiller von Gärtringen.

Professor Craig has described Manteuffel as an 'incurable romantic':

> His imagination was captured by figures like Epaminondas and Hannibal and Wallenstein, men who had combined in their persons both military and political genius. It is not difficult to infer, from his own correspondence, that he sought to model his career after these giants of the past and to become the greatest soldier and the greatest statesman of his own age.[23]

Such a personality was always likely to be at odds with any statesman aiming to achieve change by a complex and subtle set of policies that paid some regard to constitutional propriety; and in due course Manteuffel came into conflict with Bismarck, especially after the latter became Minister President. That lay in the future; for the moment, however, in 1857 his post as Chief of the Military Cabinet gave Manteuffel, now a Major General, the opportunity to make a major contribution to the development of the Prussian Army as a fighting machine by undertaking a comprehensive rejuvenation of the officer corps, weeding out the elderly and incompetent. This, which he always, and rightly, regarded as his greatest military achievement, was in due course to entitle him to a not inconsiderable share of the credit for the rapid improvement in the effectiveness of the Prussian army, as well as its becoming a more reliable instrument of royal power.

His views were widely known, and he became identified in the minds of liberals with the most extremist elements of the army, supportive of the most unpopular elements of Landwehr reform. When in 1861 a City Councillor named Carl Twesten published a pamphlet in which he accused Manteuffel of seeking to separate the army from the Prussian people, Manteuffel demanded an immediate withdrawal. In the alternative, he challenged Twesten to a duel. The latter refused to withdraw; the outcome of the duel was that Twesten was shot in the arm, and Manteuffel was briefly imprisoned in a fortress, to King William's dismay but to his own considerable satisfaction. When he emerged, his position was, if anything, more influential than ever, and he continued his work of strengthening the role of the Military Cabinet to considerable effect at the expense of the War Ministry. This, in turn, would bring him in due course into conflict with the War Minister Albrecht von Roon. Opinion within the Prussian military hierarchy had already polarised, Manteuffel and the members of the 'Camarilla' being opposed to those such as the former War Minister Edouard von Bonin and his supporters who sought to resist the increase in the power of the Military Cabinet. It has been suggested that when the time came to find a replacement for Reyher as Chief of the General Staff, Moltke was in effect a compromise candidate, acceptable to both of the factions. His indisputable technical competence, and his obvious discretion and unwillingness to engage in the internal political struggle, made him an entirely suitable choice.[74]

Military matters were, of course, always of central concern to the members of the Prussian royal family; for many of them, the army was their natural career. In 1814 Prince William, the second son of King Frederick William III of Prussia, had accompanied his father and the other allied monarchs on the campaign in France that led to the overthrow of Napoleon I. He was not, however, merely an onlooker; by then aged 17 and always destined for a military career, he already held the rank of Captain. During the campaign he distinguished himself by his courage under fire, earning from the Czar the decoration of the Order of St George, and from his father the Iron Cross. Thereafter he led the orthodox life of a royal prince and career soldier, dutifully forsaking the love of his life, the Princess Radziwill, because she was not of the blood royal and hence was an inappropriate match. By 1829, when he married the entirely suitable Princess Augusta of Weimar, he was a Lieutenant-General commanding an army corps. In 1840, his father's death made him heir-presumptive, for his brother had no children, and he took the title Prince of Prussia.

During the troubled times of 1848 William became identified with the forces of reaction, and was so much the target of the violent hostility of the Berlin mobs that he was ordered by the King to leave the city. For two months he spent a not disagreeable exile in England until, with the gradual restoration of order in Prussia, he was able to return to Berlin. There, carefully avoiding controversy, he lived quietly in his palace at Babelsberg.

In May 1849, however, he was placed in command of the army sent by the German Confederation to put down the insurrection in Baden. Campaigning in the Palatinate, he won victories at Kirchheim Bolanden on June 14, Upstadt on June 23 and Durlach on June 25, on which day he entered Karlsruhe. Closely pursuing the retreating insurgent forces commanded by Mieroslawski and Franz Sigel, he soon dispersed them in the hill country of the Black Forest.

Returning to Berlin, he resumed the ceremonial and uncontroversial life of the heir to the throne, as well as his military career, being promoted to the rank of Field Marshal in 1854. Much of his time was spent at his headquarters at Koblenz. His experiences in Baden, however, and the serious defects that had become apparent during the mobilisation of 1850, confirmed in his mind the need for the substantial reform of the Prussian Army.[25] In particular, he believed that the term of service in the army should be extended from two years to three, and that the Landwehr should be integrated with the regular army. Both of these objects were likely to bring him into serious political conflict with the majority of liberal politicians.

William's single-minded devotion to the army continued all his life; as the French Military Attaché, Colonel Stoffel, noted, he had 'such a passionate love for the military profession, to the exclusion of everything else, that his subjects, even those most devoted to him, reproach him with it.' And Moltke himself commented on this narrow outlook to Stoffel, after they had been shown around Paris during the exhibition of 1867:

> I am very glad that the King has seen the magnificence of Paris; he occupies himself almost entirely with the army. He can today see that a monarch may, without neglecting the army (for yours is excellent), interest himself in all that contributes to the greatness of the nation. I, perhaps, may be allowed more than anyone else to speak thus, for I have no cause to complain of the King's love for the army.[26]

In 1855 William chaired the Military Commission that reviewed the important question of what infantry weapon should be adopted by the Prussian Army. The Dreyse needle gun, which had been used with some success during the Baden campaign, was chosen. It was a decision which was to have enormous and far reaching consequences, and William thus made a major military contribution to the future history of his country. Another important influence over Prussia's future arose from William's close personal friendship with General Albrecht von Roon, which had developed during the early 1850s when they were both stationed at Coblenz. In Roon he found powerful intellectual support for his belief in the need for army reform.

In 1848 Roon, then a Major, had been invited by Princess Augusta to become military tutor to the young Prince Frederick William, an offer which he declined on the grounds of his political differences with her, regarding himself as altogether too conservative to take the post. He held strong views about those with liberal tendencies, and had been outraged at what he saw as King Frederick William IV's capitulation to the Berlin mob. Gloomily, he wrote to his wife that 'the army is now our fatherland, for there alone have the unclean and violent elements who put everything into turmoil failed to penetrate.' It was a view widely shared in the Prussian Army, but Roon was not simply an unthinking reactionary. He was an intelligent and thoughtful man who had a clear sight of the future role of the army, and the political influence it could exert. The situation seemed to him to be

> as if the Prussian National Army was nothing but a homeless rabble of bought mercenaries which must remain without rights and subordinate to the sovereign

> will of philistines and proletarians. But the Army shall and must play a role in the evolutionary process in which we are involved; it has a right to that.[27]

Roon was born in 1803, his family being originally of Dutch descent, and had been educated at military academies, first at Kulm and then at Berlin. He was commissioned in 1821 and was attached to the General Staff in 1834. Appointed as a lecturer at the Kriegsschule, his subjects were geography and tactics, and he published a number of text books. He was taken seriously ill in 1841, but recovered to be promoted to the rank of Major in 1842; in the following year he was appointed instructor to Prince Frederick Charles, the nephew of the King and of the Prince of Prussia, which gave him a substantial opportunity to catch the eye of the Prussian royal family. In May 1848, after witnessing the March Days in Berlin, he became Chief of Staff of the VIII Corps in the Rhineland; in the following year he served in the same capacity in von Hirschfeld's corps in the Baden campaign, under William's leadership. The command first of an infantry regiment and then a brigade followed, before in 1858, by now a Major-General, he was appointed to command the 14th Division.

The close friendship between William and Roon had given powerful impetus to the Prince of Prussia's determination to bring about substantial army reforms. It was evidently a frequent subject of discussion between them; when Roon was posted for a while in 1846 to Posen, William wrote to him to regret that he had been sent so far away 'for it puts an end to our intimate conversations, and that is a great loss to me.' But they kept closely in touch, and it was not long before their relationship was to lead to important consequences for the course of German history.

There was at least one other aspect of Prussian military development over which William exercised an influence that was to prove of enormous significance, and that was in the equipment of the artillery. On a number of occasions William was prepared to override more cautious professional opinion in the placing of orders for new weapons, and in this way ensured the success of a crucial development in technology that would ultimately play a key role in the events of 1870-71. William is often portrayed as an irresolute or ineffectual ruler, perpetually manipulated by powerful advisers; but a glance at the decisions he made for himself belies such a judgment. He picked Roon, and Moltke, and Bismarck; he chose the needle gun; and he backed Alfred Krupp's cast steel artillery. Not many monarchs could claim such a record.

2

Moltke and the General Staff

The institution which Moltke joined as a Lieutenant in 1832 had already developed to a point where it provided the Prussian army with an organisational resource substantially more efficient that than of its potential opponents. When, 25 years later, the leadership of the Prussian Great General Staff was placed in his hands, he was given the opportunity to build on the already solid foundations of its historical development, and to create an administration that was unique in its corporate military ethos.

The first traces of an evolving Prussian General Staff were to be seen under the Great Elector, in the middle of the seventeenth century. During the hundred years that ensued the vestigial organisation then established, with very limited functions, changed little. It was Frederick the Great who provided the next significant impetus to its development; commenting on the lack of specially trained officers during the Seven Years War, he wrote:

> The Army has stood the test of many campaigns, but the want of a good Quartermaster General's Staff was often felt at headquarters. The King being anxious to create a body of officers of this description, selected twelve officers who showed special aptitude for these duties.[1]

During the closing years of the eighteenth century, the size of the General Staff fluctuated between fifteen and twenty four officers. In 1783 came the first major influence on its development, when Christian von Massenbach was appointed to the staff. By 1800 the duties of the General Staff extended not only to the laying out of camps, fortification, and reconnaissance, but also to the leading of columns on the march, intelligence gathering, and the giving of advice to commanders. Massenbach's authority steadily increased, and in 1802 he devised a set of 'Instructions' intended to define the duties and responsibilities of the General Staff. The first part dealt with the 'order and rules by which we are to draw up a detailed plan of any military undertaking.'[2] It led, in the following year, to the adoption of a scheme of organisation based on Massenbach's proposals. Of these, perhaps the most important, apart from the planned increase in the size of the General Staff, was the creation of three sections to be responsible for the military affairs of Prussia to the south, west, and east respectively. Another important innovation was the requirement that young candidates for appointment to the staff should take an examination covering surveying, fortification, tactics and military art and history. In addition, they would be required to display integrity, reliability and a thorough knowledge of regimental duty. The further development of Massenbach's ideas saw additions to the permanent strength of the staff, as well as the adoption of some of his more detailed proposals. In this way he succeeded in getting a number of his pet theories accepted as the correct military doctrine, of which one example was his scheme for 'several large central fortresses and scattering broadcast an enormous number of smaller ones.'[3].

Massenbach was thus in many ways one of the true parents of the modern German General Staff; his influence on its further development ceased abruptly, however, when as its principal historian observed, his 'military career came to such an untimely end at Prenzlau.'[4] But although the military reputation of its first designer was destroyed as a result of the disastrous Jena campaign, the task of shaping the future of the staff was almost at once taken up by Gerhard von Scharnhorst as part of the root and branch reorganisation of the Prussian Army after its shattering defeat by Napoleon.

Scharnhorst decreed that there should be a staff comprising twenty six officers led by a Quartermaster-General, whose rank was to be that of Major-General. He also prescribed a fresh set of Special Instructions, which were not to be confined to the staff, but circulated to all General Officers,

> so that every officer of the former, on the one hand, should know exactly what he had to do and what was expected of him, and on the other, that the latter should be cognisant of the duties of a General Staff Officer, so that misunderstandings, overlapping, wrong expectations, or accusations might be avoided.[5]

In this way, the consistency of thought on which all commanders could depend became a central tenet of staff training, and was a crucially important factor in the subsequent success of the Prussian army.

Scharnhorst also extended the peace time training of the officers of the General Staff in troop handling and in familiarity with the terrain over which the army might be expected to operate. Summer tours were henceforth to include foreign countries which might become future theatres of war; and the study of military history was to be linked to practical geography. Three military schools were established to provide a continuous supply of officers with scientific training, and a military academy was set up in Berlin; all these were supervised by a Central Office for Military Education.[6] He missed no opportunity of enlarging the experience of his officers, and arranged for a top heavy contingent of General Staff officers to accompany the Prussian corps that served in Napoleon's Russian campaign, in order that as many as possible might have practical experience of all the subjects they had studied theoretically.

The process of educating the Prussian army in the essential nature of an efficient staff system took time to evolve. In the early days of its development, the fundamental importance of the work of the general staff work was only gradually understood. It was the vast increases in the size of the armies in the Napoleonic era that made the role of its Quartermaster-General so significant:

> With huge forces dispersed over considerable areas, armies needed better management than the old organisation could supply. The staff needs of a commander of a concentrated army of 40,000 men differed markedly from those of 200,000 spread over a wide area.[7]

It was the good fortune of Prussia that its evaluation of an effective staff system was much further advanced than even that of the French army under Napoleon.

After Scharnhorst's death he was succeeded by the very influential August Neidhardt von Gneisenau. He once described himself as Scharnhorst's St Peter; a man of very different temperament, he nonetheless made a major contribution to the development of Scharnhorst's ideas. One particular concept for which he was responsible was that of the joint responsibility of chiefs of staff for decisions taken by army commanders. Gneisenau continued in post until the end of the Napoleonic Wars. Thereafter there was a further reorganisation, separating what was to become the Great General Staff in Berlin, reporting to the War Ministry, from the rest, distributed as 'Truppengeneralstab' among operational units. The term of office of Gneisenau's successor Carl von Grolmann marked another crucial stage in the development of the General Staff:

> His character was marked by pride, firmness and a strong sense of independence. He was at one with Boyen in demanding a reform of head and members. Under his leadership, the intellectual and scientific eminence of the General Staff made it a discernibly anti-feudal element in feudal Prussia.'[8]

In 1816 Grolmann restored the previous organisation based on three geographical sections, east, south and west, covering the potential theatres of war, later adding a fourth section expressly responsible for the study of military history. It was Grolmann who, with Boyen's support, translated Scharnhorst's original concepts into an enduring reality, with a pronounced emphasis on continuing education and high intellectual standards. He also ensured that there was regular rotation of officers between line regiments and the General Staff, as well as within the General Staff itself. In this way the progress and particular attributes of promising officers could be carefully monitored.

The independence of the Great General Staff from the War Ministry came, more or less accidentally, with the appointment of Karl von Müffling as Chief of the General Staff, and was due to the seniority of his rank. The General Staff had hitherto been part of the second department of the War Ministry, of which the head was Major-General Rühle von Lilienstern; the appointment of Lieutenant-General von Müffling created problems of seniority, as a result of which his post was revised to extend its authority, thus bringing about the partial autonomy of the General Staff. As Bronsart von Schellendorff noted before the end of the century, this separation was a critical factor in the development of the Prussian General Staff: 'We may regard this circumstance as one of the most important causes of the splendid achievements of the General Staff in recent campaigns'. Bronsart went on to observe that in other countries where the Chief of the General Staff was subordinate to the War Minister, the latter would assume the key responsibilities on the outbreak of war. This was, he thought, 'a terrible mistake'; the necessary qualifications for the two posts were quite different, and even if someone with all the required skills could be found,

> he could not possibly fill both appointments referred to in wartime. It would be impossible even for the most talented man…. The Chief of the General Staff of the army must hold, in peace, a separate and independent position.[9]

Müffling's reputation and authority ensured the subsequent independent development of the General Staff, even though its peace time size was reduced on the

General der Infanterie Johann Wilhelm von Krauseneck, head of the Prussian General Staff from 1829 until 1848. (Priesdorff)

grounds of economy to twenty eight officers serving with the Great General Staff and eighteen more with the army general staffs; the total of forty six was to be increased to one hundred and one on the outbreak of war. Müffling's rank of Lieutenant-General was in future to be the rank held by the Chief of the General Staff, providing a further recognition of its growing authority.

In 1828 Müffling produced his instructions for the reorganisation of the staff which contained, it has been suggested,

> all of the essential elements of a modern staff system. There was an educational system to train staff officers in the execution of their duties. Authority to issue orders in the name of the commanding officer had been delegated to the Chief of Staff. All matters coming to headquarters were canalised through the proper staff section by fixed procedure. There was a strong inference that General Staff Officers possessed authority to check and supervise the manner in which subordinate units executed orders issued by higher headquarters.[10]

And certainly by this time, when Clausewitz came to review the role of the General Staff, its duties were clearly defined. It was, he wrote:

> intended to convert the ideas of the General Commanding into Orders, not only conveying the former to the troops, but also working out all matters of detail.... It is only the General who commands and is responsible. The officers of the General Staff must be his devoted and confidential counsellors.[11]

During the second and third quarters of the nineteenth century, there was an informal allocation of responsibilities that gave to the Second (or Central) Department

General der Kavallerie Karl Friedrich Wilhelm von Reyher, Moltke's immediate predecessor as head of the Prussian General Staff, occupying this position from 1848 until his death in 1857. (Priesdorff)

of the General Staff the task of overseeing organisation, training, mobilisation and deployment, as a result of which it became the core of the staff's operational planning system. It also had, until a separate Department was set up, responsibility for railway affairs.

After Müffling, only two men held the post of Chief of the General Staff before Moltke; Johann von Krauseneck from 1829 until 1849, and Karl von Reyher from 1848 until his death in 1857. The latter, like Krauseneck a commoner who had risen through the ranks, continued the development of the training of General Staff officers, but was handicapped to some extent by peacetime economies. During the eventful years of 1848-50 these economies were found, particularly at the time of Olmütz, to have caused many deficiencies. As a result Reyher embarked on a further reorganisation which increased the peacetime establishment to sixty four officers.

After Reyher's death Moltke was at first only provisionally appointed to his post, and the temporary nature of this appointment was due both to his rank – he was still only a Major-General – and to the fact that at that time William, who made the appointment on his brother's behalf due to the latter's ill health, expected the King to recover and reassume his authority. Moltke explained his new position in a letter to his brother Adolf in December 1857:

> As this position is properly that of a General of Division, and I hold only the rank of Major-General, this appointment can only be temporary. I still wear the scarlet collar of the Infantry uniform; my salary too is 800 thalers less than that due to the position in the Staff. Otherwise, I have all the functions and attributes of the Chief; an official residence, general orders, and so forth. My force consists of sixty four men, among the fifty of the so called "Great", but in reality very small, General

Staff, and the Staff of the nine army corps and eighteen divisions. The funds appropriated to the department amount to 26,000 thalers for general purposes, over which I have full control, out of which I have to pay for the trigonometrical and topographical survey of the country. In this I have at my command a corps of thirty officers, drawn from the army; I have also 10,000 thalers for travelling expenses. At the beginning I was obliged to work very hard in order to acquaint myself with the duties of my office; with the business and the personnel. This last is of great importance, not only for the good of the corps itself, but especially for that of the Army.[12]

William, of course, knew Moltke well. Years of service at the Prussian Court had given Moltke an opportunity to become well acquainted with the Royal family and the senior officers of the Army, so it was not surprising that he should be trusted in such a responsible post, albeit at first on a temporary basis. In 1858 Moltke was confirmed in his position, as he laconically reported to his wife at the conclusion of the annual manoeuvres:

While on the battlefield at the close of the last day's doings, Waldersee was promoted by the prince in the name of the king to the position of General ... I too, received a blue letter:

"I very gladly take the opportunity at the close of the general practices of the Vth and VIth Corps to give you a proof of my entire satisfaction with your services by promoting you to the post of Chief of the General Staff of the army. By order of his Majesty the King.
(Signed) Prince of Prussia Leignitz 18 September 1858."

In consequence of this I shall wear again the uniform of the Staff. Today I had a first conference with my officers. Tomorrow is a holiday and then we start on our staff ride. There is a very neat little theatre here, light and pleasantly arranged, and with very passable actors. My rheumatism went almost as quickly as it came.[13]

Thus modestly began the momentous term of office in the course of which Moltke was to lead the armies of Prussia and then of all Germany to victory in the wars of unification.

Moltke's appointment brought with it a strange echo of Scharnhorst's tenure of office. Reyher, in an appraisal of Moltke made in the early 1850s, noted of him that 'lastly he lacks the force and vitality without which a troop commander cannot in the long run maintain his authority.'[14] An American historian of the history of general staffs has compared the 'curiously similar.... negative manner' in which Moltke and Scharnhorst impressed their superiors early in their careers:

Scharnhorst, scholarly almost to the point of being unmilitary, seemed foreign to the stiff smartness of his fellow officers. There is a story to the effect that one of them once observed that every non commissioned officer he knew was superior to Scharnhorst in military matters. One of Moltke's commanders remarked "that man will never make a soldier."[15]

The truth about Moltke, though, was that he was very much more than a soldier:

No Prussian officer was ever less confined within the limits of technical military expertise. In a certain sense, he must be considered the great exception, in any event an absolutely unique figure in the ranks of German generals, an astonishingly talented and versatile man, infinitely curious and open minded.[16].

It was this breadth and depth of ability that enabled him to bring to his task a calm authority and confidence which, in a commander with almost no experience of actual combat command, was astounding.

Moltke at once embarked on a number of important changes in the organisation of the General Staff. Krauseneck had abandoned Grolmann's system of organising staff into sections on a geographical basis, replacing it with a function-based system. Moltke now restored Grolmann's structure, creating four departments responsible for planning and strategic analysis. The Eastern Department was concerned with Russia, the Habsburg Empire, Sweden and Turkey. The German Department was responsible for Germany, Denmark, Switzerland and Italy, and the Western Department covered France, Spain, Great Britain, the Low Countries and the USA. Crucially important was the creation of a Railways Department, which had the overall responsibility for the organisation of the railways, with General Staff officers working with officials of the Ministry of Commerce and the railway companies; it also had a key role in co-ordinating mobilisation and planning and maximising the utilisation of the railway network. To back up these operational departments there was a support unit in the shape of the Military History Department.[17]

Moltke's arrival brought about immediate changes in the culture as well as the structure of the General Staff. It led to an immediate expansion of its role and the acceptance by its members of their wider responsibility. Their contact with the life of the army as a whole was increased by the regular assignment to regimental duty; and the more abstract aspects of their work such as military history, statistical analysis and map making were augmented. Above all, the tactical and strategical training of General Staff officers was systematically enhanced.[18]

It was the breadth of his understanding of the huge changes that had come over the battlefield that enabled Moltke to refashion the General Staff into an instrument capable of meeting the challenge. Renewed demands made on the staff by the widespread employment of railways for troop movements, and the use of the telegraph for their direction, significantly enhanced the role and responsibility of the staff officer. Despite the growth in size of the armies with which he had to deal, these technological advances had provided Moltke with the means for their effective employment. This went some way towards neutralising the essentially disadvantageous nature of Prussia's geographical position:

It was part of Moltke's genius that he was the first to grasp the extraordinary possibilities opened by these new means of communication for the conduct of

> operations and the changes they were inevitably going to introduce into strategy. He was quick to realise the greater speed at which campaigns would be conducted, and that this would make it almost impossible to make good any mistakes in the original concentration of forces; it would also greatly increase the importance of careful preparation for the mobilisation and particularly for the exploitation of the available railways.[19]

One of his earliest biographers summed up Moltke's reform of the General Staff as it was seen by his contemporaries:

> Moltke added to the number of his subordinates, superintended their education with incessant care, and spared no pains in selecting the officers; and, in a word, steadily laboured to make the Prussian staff, what it has been aptly called, the Brain of the Army, the source and centre of its intellectual force. The complete instruction of the staff officer was naturally, indeed, an ideal sought by one who excelled in the learning of war.[20]

This meticulous care in the training of his staff officers did not prevent Moltke from ensuring their regular contact with practical realities. In 1858, in his comments on the staff rides during the first year of his acting tenure as Chief of the General Staff, he was at pains to emphasise the need for straightforward solutions to the problems posed that fitted their particular circumstances, rejecting anything that was purely artificial or detached from reality. The war games, staff rides and annual manoeuvres were always designed to simulate different scenarios that might actually materialise in the event of war, and the conclusions to be drawn were carefully analysed by Moltke and his officers, and plans made accordingly.

Moltke's reforms were entirely consistent with the earlier development of the General Staff. The process by which it came to assume a central role in Prussian military affairs was a gradual one, and came about not because its leaders were constantly asserting jurisdiction or ambition, but because, in practice, they (and Moltke in particular) provided a source of calm, dispassionate and authoritative advice. And of course above all in Moltke's case this increase in authority came because he was almost uniformly militarily successful. But for the staggering victories of the Prussian Army in 1864-71, and the fact that the sovereign was first and foremost a soldier, the steady accretion of power by the General Staff would hardly have occurred.

In the early part of Moltke's tenure of office, that power was very limited indeed and there were still many aspects of military policy about which the General Staff was not formally consulted. It took no part, for instance, in the planning of the great army reorganisation of 1860, which was exclusively carried out under the control of the War Minister, who acted only upon the expert advice of a few senior officers. Moltke kept himself and the staff firmly out of the limelight as the political controversy raged and took no public part in it, although he strongly endorsed Roon's view of the need for the army reforms; and similarly Moltke was never directly or indirectly involved with any of Edwin von Manteuffel's extravagant ideas about a *coup d'état*. Again, in 1862 it was only in the form of a casual enquiry that Moltke was asked for his advice about possible economies in the military budget. Even Moltke's reorganisation of the staff itself and the training programme that he proposed had to be accomplished under the aegis of the War Ministry, although in 1859 Moltke was given the right of direct access to the War Minister rather than through officials of the Ministry.[21]

Moltke's first opportunity to monitor the effectiveness of his reforms came with the mobilisation of the Prussian army during Austria's war against France and Sardinia in 1859. The staff itself performed well; but the speed of mobilisation was disappointing in a number of respects, and many lessons were learned from that, as well as from the detailed analysis that was subsequently undertaken of the campaign in Northern Italy. Research of this kind was central to Moltke's conception of the role of the General Staff. The Military History Department had a vitally important part in the training of the staff and the planning process. The history of the war of 1859 that was produced came from Moltke's own pen, based on the reports of Major von Redern, the Prussian military attaché in Vienna, who gave lectures to the staff on Magenta and Solferino; and also on the appreciations prepared by other officers such as Major von Strantz, who toured the battlefields to obtain a clear and impartial insight into the actual course of events.

This exercise gave Moltke an opportunity to reflect on the role of the commander and those around him in the decision making process:

> Some commanders have no need of counsel. They study the questions which arise, themselves decide them, and their entourage has only to execute their decisions. But such generals are stars of the first magnitude, who appear scarcely once in a century. In the great majority of cases the head of an army cannot dispense with advice. This advice may in many cases be the outcome of the deliberations of a small number of men qualified by abilities and experience to be sound judges of the situation. But in this small number, one, and only one opinion must prevail.

Moltke went on to comment on one category of advisers who were particularly harmful:

> In every headquarters are always to be found people who with great sagacity can see the difficulties of every undertaking. The moment things go wrong they have no difficulty in proving that everything was foreseen by them. They are always right, for since their criticism is never constructive they can never be confounded by the result. Such men are a positive calamity.[22]

In looking at the role of the staff and of the command structure generally in the war of 1859, Moltke went on to draw a number of conclusions:

> During the Austrian advance from the Mincio to Solferino the high command issued orders directly and in excessive detail to the corps, paying no attention to the field army headquarters. If the high command wished to allow the headquarters of the armies to function in their necessary role it should have ordered nothing for that advance other than the general direction to be taken, the roads assigned each army, and the objectives of the movement. But this was not done… It would have been much better under these conditions to abolish the army Headquarters … [which] proved to be not only superfluous at Solferino but actually dangerous to a

> great degree. During the battle the high command did not bypass them, but rather adhered to the regular military channels... The old experience again proved true that not only rapidity of transmission of orders, but also their clarity, diminishes in proportion to the number of headquarters through which they have to pass.[23]

From the analyses made of other campaigns, and from his own observations, Moltke arrived at a number of settled convictions about the desirability of limiting the extent to which the high command should intervene, which he embodied in a set of 'Instructions for Higher Commanders' published in 1869.

> The advantage which the commander believes to achieve through continuous personal intervention, is mostly only an apparent one. He thereby takes over functions for whose fulfilment other persons are designated. He more or less denigrates their ability ...In general one does well to order no more than is absolutely necessary and to avoid planning beyond the situations one can foresee. These change very rapidly in war. Seldom will orders that anticipate far in advance and in detail succeed completely to execution. This shakes the confidence of the subordinate commander and it gives the units a feeling of uncertainty when things develop differently.[24]

Moltke faithfully followed these principles during the Wars of German Unification, always giving his subordinate commanders the widest latitude possible consistent with his objectives, and thus ensuring that they felt ready and able to take independent decisions when these were demanded by the situation.

Moltke's belief in the importance of the study of military history, and the lessons to be learned from it, was, however, largely confined to recent European experience. It is probably untrue that, as has often been suggested, he dismissed the American Civil War as offering no useful experience for those concerned with the conduct of European war, or that he described it as an affair of 'two armed mobs chasing each other around the country'; it would, of course, have been an understandable reaction to the conduct of the first battle of Bull Run, but it would have been an uncharacteristically superficial statement from so thoughtful a student of war.[25] What he did derive in particular from the American experience was the further valuable guidance it offered as to the military use of railways under war time conditions. In 1864 the addition of the Railways Section to the General Staff was based on events in the United States, and two years later the creation of the 'Feldeisenbahnabteilung' was directly modelled on the Construction Corps of the Union Army. A close study was made of the military use of railways during the Civil War, and the conclusions drawn from it were put into practice in 1866.[26]

The first crucial test of the lessons learned by Moltke and his staff from their analysis of the 1859 mobilisation came in 1862. That year the annual manoeuvres were held in North Germany, and were based on the possibility of war against Denmark; they took the form of a railway mobilisation and deployment exercise. On this occasion there was a marked improvement in the efficiency of the mobilisation, and it was clear to Moltke that he was proceeding on the right lines.

As a result of Moltke's approach to the duties and organisation of his staff, there was a profound difference between the products of his system and Napoleon's Marshals.

One historian has noted that Napoleon demanded blind obedience, and was indifferent to an individual's particular abilities. As a result, when on their own, the Marshals performed badly. Moltke's subordinates, on the other hand, were trained to act on their own initiative. Moltke, confident in himself, had complete confidence in them; this produced 'a generation of General Staff officers distinguished by a very high standard of morals and great simplicity of life.'[27]

The natural consequence of this patient attention to the training and development of his staff officers soon showed itself on the battle field; with the strong imprint of Moltke's personality upon them throughout their training, they could be relied on almost invariably to take decisions consistent with Moltke's own philosophy. One of his biographers has observed that

> it must have been of considerable assistance to Moltke that the executive power of the various subordinate headquarters was in the hands of officers trained in one and the same school, and the school of which he was the head.[28]

This is something of an understatement; frequently the success of Moltke's plans depended entirely to the extent to which he could rely on the staff officers he had so thoroughly trained.

3

The New Technology

By the 1840s, spurred on by the impetus of the industrial revolution and the consequent rapid enlargement of the German economy, the rate of development of the German railway system was accelerating, growing from 469km in 1840 to 5,856km in 1850, at which point it was over three times the size of the French network. It was still, however, not generally perceived as offering any decisive military advantage. In part, this was because the development of the system followed commercial opportunity rather than any strategic thinking:

> For military purposes, the network was still thin. Most lines were single tracked. Railway companies, public or private, lacked experience in large-scale, rapid movement of men and freight. Connections and switches were primitive, road beds inadequate to support heavy traffic...specialised systematic training for railwaymen was a decade away.[1]

As with many technological innovations, the innate conservatism of the military was resistant to arguments that the railways might have major strategic significance. One of the first proponents of their military application was Friedrich Harkort, a clear sighted Westphalian, who wrote that 'in the wars of the future there slumbers the seeds of great developments in railways, the results of which it is as yet, quite beyond the powers to foresee'. He published in 1834 *Die Eisenbahn von Minden nach Köln*, pointing out the defensive advantages of such a line:

> Let us suppose we had a railway on the right bank of the Rhine, from Mainz to Wesel. Any crossing of the Rhine by the French would then scarcely be possible, since we should be able to bring a strong defensive force on the spot before the attempt could be developed.[2]

Harkort was far ahead of his time, and his arguments received little support, and aroused little response from the military.

The great economist Friedrich List was also one of the earliest to argue that the existence of a comprehensive rail network would confer enormous military advantages on the defence, which was thereby enabled to concentrate rapidly from all directions to meet an attacker with a force that would arrive fresh and fully equipped. He drew the optimistic conclusion that this

> meant that wars would be confined to frontier areas, and once the nations of Europe discovered the impossibility of following up their victories, they would conclude that it would be better – and more profitable – for all to live in peace. Thus the railroad would be the instrument which destroyed war itself.[3]

List argued his case tenaciously, putting forward arguments for railways all over Prussia, and gradually began to have some limited impact on military thinking, even though the report of a special commission in 1835 tended to emphasise negative aspects of the practical problems of the rail network. This led the then Chief of the General Staff, Krauseneck, who was looking for ways to improve troop movement, to conclude that the construction of a rail network was not a military necessity.[4]

Elsewhere in Germany, however, others were developing List's conclusions. Carl Pönitz, a captain in the Saxon army, published in 1842 a comprehensive survey of the development of railways and the strategic possibilities which they offered. Struck by the far sightedness of Belgium in having 'taken in hand a scheme for the construction of a network of railways designed to extend over the entire country', he observed that 'in this way King Leopold has raised up for himself a memorial the full value and significance of which may, perhaps, be appreciated only by generations yet to come.'[5] The Belgian rail network would, he thought, increase both Belgium's prosperity and her security, and it stood as an example to Germany. He put forward a programme for a network of railways that would serve to protect Germany against invasion from East or from West:

> We have to look to these two fronts; and, if we want to avoid the risk of heavy losses at the outset, we needs must – also at the outset – be prepared to meet the enemy there with an overwhelming force. Everyone knows that the strength of an army is multiplied by movements which are rapid in themselves and allow of the troops arriving at the end of their journey without fatigue.[6]

But while agreeing with List that rail power gave huge advantages to the defence, he also suggested that a line along the west bank of the Rhine would make possible a rapid concentration of German troops for a sudden advance deep into France. Pönitz was in many ways another writer far ahead of his time, calling for progress in railway development that was only realised by a later generation, as Professor Showalter has pointed out:

> At a time when thinking on the subject of troop movement by rail had scarcely advanced beyond the concept of loading everyone onto trains at one end of the line and unloading them at the other, Pönitz presented a sophisticated analysis of the use of transport echelons as the only way to move the masses of men necessary for modern war.[7]

In 1841 Moltke was invited to join the board of the company promoting a new railway between Berlin and Hamburg. He threw himself wholeheartedly into the venture, investing his savings and rapidly mastering the technical and economic intricacies in running a railway company. It was the start of a life long belief in the possibilities, political, economic and military, that railways offered to Germany:

> During the three years he served as a director, his desk was constantly full of articles, papers and memoranda on railroads. He studied the projected right of way, inspected the site of the Berlin terminal, talked with surveyors and engineers.[8]

He took an active part in the commercial and legal negotiations crucial to the company's future, and his pen was constantly employed in the writing of articles and essays in support of the venture. In 1843 he published a comprehensive essay on the choice of railway routes, displaying a profound technical understanding of all aspects of railway management and economics.

The experience he thus gained was invaluable, demonstrating clearly to him the military opportunity which a fully developed network offered Prussia. While believing that in general the commercial routes that were developed would correspond with military needs, he also believed that the Prussian government must itself invest in railways, in order to ensure that less profitable lines, essential in time of war, should be built and maintained. The peculiar strategical problems of Prussia, split into two parts, made railway development of particular significance, and he gradually succeeded by his persistence in ensuring that military considerations played a important part in Prussian, and later German, railway planning. A twentieth century biographer of Moltke, paraphrasing an earlier writer, has observed:

> It is hardly too much to say that from 1857 until his death, not only was no important railway construction entered upon without reference to Moltke, but even the details likely to be of strategical importance – e.g. bridges, tunnels, and crossing places, were invariably submitted for his consideration and approval.[9]

Moltke served for three years on the board of the Berlin Hamburg Railway Company, leaving in 1844; but he could feel some satisfaction that railway development in Germany was beginning to go the right way, writing to his mother in that year: 'While the French Chambers are still engaged discussing the matter, we have laid down three hundred miles of railway, and are working at two hundred more.'[10] And during that decade, between 1840 and 1850, German railway development was at twice the rate of that in France, although the network itself was still patchy and incapable of supporting heavy traffic, while railway staff lacked the training and experience to cope with the sudden demands of military necessity. However, some practical military experience was being gained. Prussian troops were, for instance, moved by rail to the Silesian frontier in 1846, during political disturbances in Cracow; and the railways were used elsewhere as well. But not all of Prussia's military leaders were swift to grasp the military potential of the rail network. Hermann von Boyen, for instance, who was reappointed War Minister in 1841, and whose operational ideas had been heavily conditioned by his experiences in the Wars of Liberation, feared that too heavy a reliance on the railways could make mobilisation inflexible.

In 1848-9 there were a number of instances of rapid troop movement by rail to deal with sudden revolutionary crises all over Germany. An example of the use of railways to defeat orthodox military forces occurred in Baden, where the Federal corps led by the Prince of Prussia was frequently frustrated by the insurgents' use of the railway to escape after being beaten in the field. Roon, serving in the campaign, wrote irritably that 'this frustrating war' would only end when the entire railway was in their hands, necessitating an advance on Freiburg. But it was the humiliation of the Convention of Olmütz that was to give the General Staff the clearest evidence of the scope of railway assisted mobilisation, and of the penalty for getting it wrong. By now, the General Staff had in Reyher a chief who was deeply interested in the use of railways for military purposes; it fell to him, however, to preside over a mobilisation that was an absolute shambles, and which

> made the continuing weakness of the link between the military and the railroads in Prussia painfully clear to even a casual observer. Men, animals and supplies piled up at loading centres and shuttled aimlessly from station to station on trains whose destination was a mystery... Units in their regular stations often had their mobilisation equipment stored at central depots, and bringing the two together brought even more confusion to the already overstrained railway system.[11]

Austria, on the other hand, succeeded in moving by rail 75,000 men, 8,000 horses and 1,000 vehicles to Olmütz very much more efficiently, and in much better order than the Prussian forces would have been if hostilities had broken out. Moltke, in Magdeburg, reflected on the experience of the mobilisation, writing to an old friend, von Gliszinski, on February 13 1851 to remark that

> the instructions for the mobilisation were all vague, and numerous special orders had to be given. I hope we shall have learnt some lessons for our 40 millions! We have gained one experience, and that is that the way in which business is at present conducted is utterly useless during the mobilisation; this refers especially to the audit system. We have had more than a thousand letters every month at the office of the Commander in Chief.[12]

It was an experience which remained in Moltke's mind when he came in due course to be responsible for the mobilisation of the whole of the army.

Reyher, for his part, called for the railways to pass under military control in time of war. William, after his experiences in Baden, and smarting under what, like all soldiers, he regarded as the disgrace of Olmütz, was by now a strong advocate of new railway construction. The able and energetic von der Heydt, who had been Minister of Commerce in 1848, had always been a keen exponent of railway development, and during the next decade there was a substantial expansion of the state owned railway network.

When in 1857 Moltke came to assume the duties of the Chief of the General Staff, the military had had two decades of experience in the use of railways to speed the mobilisation process. Tentatively at first, and with as many frustrating setbacks as successes, the new system of communications was beginning to dominate mobilisation theory, and Moltke's own interests and experiences ideally fitted him to exploit the potential of the railway network. From the outset he pressed for the closer collaboration between the military and the railway companies on which efficient mobilisation depended, and for this he needed political clout in the support not only of the Minister of War, but also of the Minister of Commerce. He was soon to discover that the problem was even more urgent than he had realised, when in 1859 a further comparison between the effectiveness of Prussian mobilisation and that of a potential enemy again demonstrated the extent of Prussian shortcomings. This time it was France, whose laggard development of railways had afforded him so much satisfaction fifteen years earlier, which showed just how much things had changed since then.

Mobilising for war with Austria, the French army shifted 604,381 men and 129,227 horses by rail, utilising the whole of the French rail network, between April 16 and July 15, and of these 227,649 men and 36,357 horses were transported to the battle front in Northern Italy:

> It was estimated that the 75,996 men and 4469 horses transported by rail from Paris to the Mediterranean or to the frontiers of the Kingdom of Sardinia between April 20 and April 30 would have taken sixty days to make the journey by road... and this again was about double as fast as the best achievement recorded up to that time on the German railways.[13]

It was a vivid illustration of the scope of railways not only to move troops very much more quickly than on foot, but also to deliver them to their destination fresh and ready for immediate operations. In Prussia, even before the French movement began, Moltke was advising the Minister of War of the importance of the rail network since 'in the case of war with France...the greatest emphasis must be placed on the concentration of the Prussian army on and across the Rhine as soon as possible.'[14] Mindful of the deficiencies of the existing rail system, Moltke advocated the doubling of existing single track lines and the building of new lines, in a bid to reduce the total time required for mobilisation; but however persuasive might be his memoranda from a military point of view, they received no support from either the Minister of War or the Minister of Commerce. It was not until May that a mixed commission to investigate the question was established, and it was the end of June before it had determined the routes to be taken for the deployment of the Prussian army. By then, events in Northern Italy had moved on, and the decisive phase of the campaign was approaching. Six Prussian corps had been mobilised in the middle of June, and by July 1, the projected date for the forward movement of the army, the rail network was ready. Then the Regent lost his nerve, and cancelled the operation. By the time William changed his mind again on July 4, the assembled rolling stock had been dispersed, which imposed a further delay of eleven days before the troops could move. Since it would take six weeks to complete the concentration, which Moltke wished should be as far forward as possible, the potential consequence was obvious.

In the event the swift victories of the Allies over the Austrians, and the resulting armistice, meant that Moltke need have no further concern for the conduct of a campaign that would have been so needlessly hampered both by political irresolution as well as by the material inadequacy of the railway system; but he was determined to make the best use he could of the experience at second hand. As has been seen, in order to derive the most reliable information about what had actually happened, he put in hand thorough research, sending officers to France to assess the capacity of its rail network. In addition, a careful review was undertaken of the works published in both France and Austria dealing with the war and the contribution made by the respective railway systems.[15] The comparison with France left Moltke in no doubt that in Prussia there was a lot of work still to do, not least by bringing about the central co-ordination or control over the dozens of different railway companies that existed for which he had always argued.[16] The

Austrians, on the other hand, did not appear to have progressed substantially in the nine years since Olmütz:

> Little or no real attempt at organisation in the time of peace had been made, and, in the result, trains were delayed or blocked, and stations got choked with masses of supplies which could not be forwarded. At Vienna there was such a deficiency of rolling stock – accelerated by great delays in the return of empties – that many of the troop trains for the South could not be made up until the last moment.[17]

For all that, the Austrians had moved many units far faster by rail than they could have done on foot, and on both sides reinforcements were frequently brought up to the front line by rail in the nick of time. The 1859 campaign was thus an extremely valuable field of study, since it represented a major step forward in the utilisation of the railways for military purposes. It also demonstrated that the Prussian mobilisation system still fell far short of what was required, due not only to the priority still being afforded to civilian traffic, but also to inadequate preparation at regimental and brigade levels.

In 1861 Moltke set down his own thoughts on the importance of railways in an essay in which he reviewed some of the arguments arising from railway construction and its effect on national security:

> Railways acquire special importance where they cross large rivers. There, not only the railroads, but also the bridges are of great importance. The defence of Prussia to the east and west is based upon the four large rivers flowing through the country from south to north, along which our main fortresses are situated... Railroads must cross the larger rivers only at fortresses because we must preserve the bridges for our use. Thus it is necessary to enlarge almost all our fortresses, such as those at Cologne, Coblenz and Mainz, and to construct new ones at Marienburg and Breslau, since these are limited by financial means and garrisons, new railroads must cross rivers at existing fortresses. A conflict between military and political/economic/commercial interests can, therefore, exist only at the frontiers and at large rivers. At all other points, full freedom of construction should not be denied.[18]

By the time that Moltke wrote these words, the German rail network had in technical matters come a long way towards effective integration for military purposes. A standard gauge existed, and most rolling stock was now interchangeable. Many railway companies had become used to co-operation and, if not always as successfully as hoped, had on occasion shifted large numbers of men and equipment. Military co-operation, however, between members of the German Confederation had not kept pace, and in 1861 a military commission was set up to look into the question. Together with members from Bavaria and Hanover, the four man commission included two particularly talented officers with an outstanding reputation in railway matters – Gründorf von Zerbégeny from Austria and Captain Hermann von Wartensleben from Prussia.[19]

The commission's comprehensive report contained few surprises. It found that there were still problems of co-ordination between the large number of state railways and those in the private sector. The lack of experience in military transport, already well known, meant that the process required close supervision. The military traffic should move as quickly as possible, in regular sequence; civilian traffic should be suspended during the process; there should be a central co-ordinating authority. And the report endorsed Moltke's call for the provision of double track lines. The report went on to apply the principles it had identified to a plan for a mobilisation on the Rhine frontier.

In Prussia, the process of developing co-ordination between the military and the railway authorities accelerated with the provision of training in railway duties for infantry NCOs and the establishment of Field Railway Detachments, and the evolution of standing orders covering rail transport. These instances of the military taking increasing responsibility for their own transport were in part prompted by the gradual retreat of the Prussian Government from state ownership of railways.[20]

Railways were by no means the only product of a rapidly developing technology which contributed to the process of change in the application of the basic principles of strategy and tactics. Although his age might have suggested that he was approaching the end of a career in what was a decidedly conservative profession, Moltke in fact recognised much more clearly than many of his younger colleagues the revolutionary extent of this change and the way in which the Prussian General Staff must respond.

Among the advances which contributed to the development of military communications was a vastly improved road system. It was obviously preferable to stick to the roads for as long as possible; but this meant that the march column of an army corps if confined to a single road was extremely long; with all its artillery, equipment, baggage and trains, an army corps might be spread over a distance that was effectively a day's march. But in spite of this, the existence of decent roads meant that, once away from the railheads, combat units could move faster, and still remain in contact with their support services to a greater extent than hitherto. It should also have ensured, although in practice it frequently did not, that victualling the army was much more effectively undertaken.

It was also immediately evident to Moltke that the electric telegraph would have an enormous effect on the central direction of a campaign. He grasped, as he later put it, that 'the ability to send reports quickly to even the most distant points and by circuitous routes offers the means to direct separated parts of the army according to a single will toward a common goal.'[21] Given the necessity for the widely scattered deployment in 1866 which political considerations and the mobilisation timetable had forced on Moltke, the use of the telegraph was of much greater value to him in Bohemia than to his opponent, even if at times the breakdown of the facility was extremely frustrating to him. Nonetheless, his ready acceptance of the major influence that the telegraph would exert was a further instance of Moltke's farsighted and innovative approach to the conduct of war.

In the early stages of its development, the telegraph suffered not only from the suspicion of conservative soldiers, but also from the practical difficulties of establishing and maintaining the system. The equipment itself was awkward and vulnerable, and prolonging the telegraph lines to keep pace with advancing troops proved in practice to be a constant headache. Nonetheless Prussia, like all the Great Powers, had by the time Moltke took office made considerable progress in setting up an effective organisation for the use of the telegraph in war:

Johann Dreyse, inventor of the needle gun. *(Illustrirte Kriegs-Chronik)*

> The construction of lines at two to three miles per hour was regarded as practicable, as was a transmission over them of messages at the rate of eight to ten words per minute. For the transmitters to function, however, the wagons on which they were mounted had to be stationary, a limitation which meant that service would be interrupted whenever headquarters moved.[22]

An even greater limitation was the concern that the direct contact between the army commander and the supreme headquarters might shackle the former and thus stifle initiative; an Austrian view was that

> a commander who is tied down in this way is really to be pitied; he has two enemies to defeat, one in front and another in his rear…everything combines to rob the commander of his force and independence, partly by accident, partly by design.

And the same writer saw serious drawbacks in the use of the telegraph under operational conditions:

> In most cases, i.e. in the presence of the enemy, the telegraph can never replace personal messages…the telegraph, like the railway, will only be of use to the tactician in the most exceptional of cases.[23]

But the greatest technological change of all to which military leaders were obliged to respond was presented by the new weapons with which the wars of the second half of the century were to be fought. In this, as in so much else, the change had begun, and quickly accelerated, in the first half of the century; and Moltke, like his opponents, had at first little to go on in evaluating its effect. The most dramatic development was in the weapons used by the infantry.

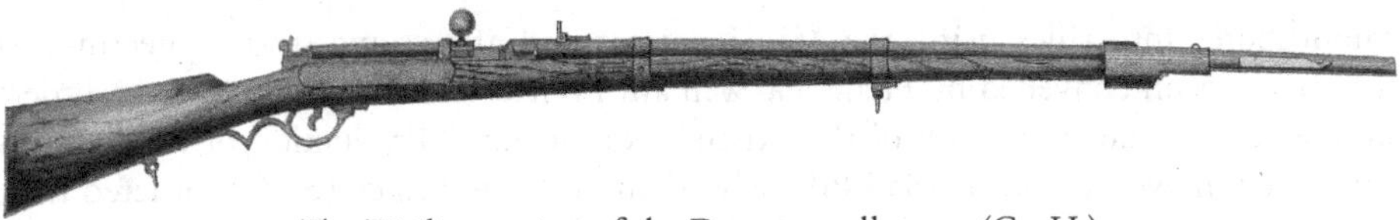

The Füsilier version of the Dreyse needle gun. (C.v.H.)

In the 1820s Johann Dreyse began to develop a gun based on the principle of a needle which, when the gun was fired, was driven forward and ignited the cartridge. At this stage of its development, the needle gun was a muzzle-loading weapon. Attempts to market this to various German war ministries were at first decidedly unsuccessful. However, in Prussia, after the Crown Prince, later to become King Frederick William IV, and his brother Prince William had been impressed by sporting guns produced by Dreyse on the same principle, the gunsmith began to make progress, and in 1832 a test was undertaken of sixty of the latest pattern of needle guns. This led to the placing of a larger order, as a result of which two Prussian fusilier battalions were equipped with the weapon in 1835. That year, convinced that the age of the muzzle loader was nearing its end, Dreyse constructed his first breech loading rifle; the design was patented in 1838 and in the following year a prolonged series of tests proved sufficiently successful to lead in December 1840 to an order for sixty thousand needle guns. Their potential was seen as enormous – so much so that they were not immediately served out to infantry units, but were kept secretly in store against a moment when they might be decisively employed.[24]

In the meantime, a fierce debate raged within the Prussian army as to the future use of the needle gun. The dispute really revolved around the position of the elite Jäger units, which hitherto had alone been equipped with rifles, and who believed that the needle gun was neither accurate enough nor had a sufficient range for their purposes. Apart from this, there were doubts whether ordinary infantry of the line, equipped with a weapon that could be loaded and fired more than three times as fast as the existing muzzle loaders, could be trusted not to waste ammunition by constant firing. One possibility considered was that only a number of special battalions of light infantry, trained in skirmishing and marksmanship, should have the needle gun.

The upheavals of 1848 led to the immediate issue of the needle gun to all fusilier battalions. The lack of preparation and training for this step meant that there were still disputes as to the employment of the new weapons. Reyher, as Chief of the General Staff, was sharply opposed to the suggestion that the whole of the Guard Corps should be issued with needle guns, on the grounds that the weapon was untested in battle; and he believed that if to equip the Guard Corps meant taking the needle guns from the fusiliers, the morale of the latter would be badly affected.[25] In the event, battle experience in the fighting with insurgents in Saxony and in Prince William's campaign in Baden soon validated the effectiveness of the needle gun. As a result, in 1851 it was decreed that all new weapons issued to the Prussian infantry should be Dreyse needle guns.

During the following years, the re-equipment of the infantry proceeded apace, though the debate over whether a proportion only of the army should have the new weapon still continued. An alternative means of improving the infantry's equipment also appeared at this time in the shape of the muzzle loading Minié rifle, used to good effect in the Crimea by the French and British armies. It was possible to convert existing smoothbores into rifles using the Minié design, and after some stormy meetings of the commission convened by Frederick William IV had looked into the matter, orders were given for the conversion of the existing equipment.[26] Production of needle guns continued, however, and in 1858 Prince William, by now Prince Regent, ordered their issue to all those units not already equipped with them.

It still remained of crucial importance that the effectiveness of the new weapons be maximised by the application of correct techniques, and this required a careful analysis of the changes needed both to tactical doctrines and also to strategic considerations. Much attention was paid to the infantry tactics employed during the Italian campaign of 1859. Here, in spite of the superiority of the Austrian infantry weapons, the French appeared to have succeeded by relying on shock tactics. A number of successful French bayonet charges, usually in battalion columns, seemed to demonstrate that in this way the technological improvements of the rifle, and the consequent increases in the stopping power of the defence, might be nullified. At Solferino, Marshal Niel noted the effectiveness of shock action: 'When the combat was a firefight… I lost ground…Then I formed a column of attack with one of the battalions of my reserve, and the bayonet gave us more than we had lost with the fusillade.'[27]

Moltke's own review of the Italian campaign, based on the detailed reports of his staff officers, drew a number of conclusions that went behind the simple acceptance of the superiority of shock action:

> Not French bayonet charges, but Austrian passivity, their inability to use either the terrain or their rifle properly, their failures of generalship and leadership, had brought about Magenta and Solferino. Bayonets had not crossed in 1859 any more than they had in the eighteenth century or in the days of Napoleon. What the French had done in fact was to advance close enough to be able to use their own inferior weapons effectively; they had fired as many rounds as the Austrians in the course of the war.[28]

The tactical strength given to the defensive by the new weapons had already led Moltke to conclude, in 1858, that 'the goal of future commanders must be a defensive battle ending in a counter-attack.'[29] Strategically, the most effective way to overcome the firepower of the defence was by manoeuvre; by employing an offensive strategy which was nonetheless based on the tactical defensive, Prussia could make the best use of the new firepower of the needle gun. Moltke put it this way:

> On the whole, the offensive is not only tactical. Skilful leadership will in many cases succeed in selecting defensive positions, which are strategically of such an offensive nature that the opponent will be forced to attack them. We will then take the tactical offensive only after casualties, loss of cohesion, and exhaustion have weakened him. Thus is the strategic offensive united with the tactical defence.[30]

The range of the needle gun made it extremely effective up to six hundred yards, which with its much higher rate of fire meant that it could be used to break up infantry assaults long before they could reach the riflemen. Firing from a stationary position, selected with an eye to the advantages of the terrain, tipped the balance heavily in favour of the defensive. Bravery would be of no avail in such circumstances. Moltke's firm belief was that

> a good horseman did not drive even the boldest steed against a barrier it cannot hurdle, whether that barrier was a six foot water filled ditch or an open front which gave the firearm a chance to work its full effect.[31]

But, as a leading American historian of the period has gone on to point out, the tactical doctrines still in force at the commencement of the Wars of Unification continued to be based on the proposition that the use of shock tactics was the ultimate means of attaining a decisive result:

> Closed formations might be dangerous, but official Prussian opinion still considered them necessary... The needle gun's firepower was utilised to reduce the strength of skirmish lines...Moltke himself recommended that skirmish lines be used to deliver bayonet charges. Properly executed, not only would they neutralise the enemy's skirmishers but, by drawing in his reserves they would render him more vulnerable to the attack of the closed formations in which the real power of decision rested.[32]

It is certainly true that the passage from Moltke's memorandum quoted above went on to note that

> when we are absolutely compelled to advance offensively against a hostile position, the advantage of stationary firing may be fully utilised if we know how to bring our battalions up to the range most suited for that...The advance with the bayonet is the means finally to overcome the enemy. No army can do without the bayonet.[33]

In spite of the additional firepower provided by the needle gun and the tactical flexibility advocated by Moltke and others, the old convictions died hard. In the manoeuvres of the early 1860s the Prussian army performed so badly as to attract sharp criticism from both their own commanders and from foreign observers; one French observer in 1861 went so far as to comment that the Prussians were compromising the entire military profession.[34] This can have done nothing to have increased the awareness of, for instance, the Austrians of the extent to which the Prussian army had developed.

Such comments by observers might be forgiven; it was not immediately obvious that behind the stiffly conventional officers who still held much of the apparent authority in the Prussian army, a new generation of more thoughtful and intelligent military thinkers led by Moltke was making the maximum use of the learning points afforded by every development, whether an apparent set back or a success.

The history of artillery during the nineteenth century also reflected the enormous technological advances made by manufacturing industry. The process of development was however extremely complex, and generated fierce professional dispute. In terms of the guns themselves, there were three fundamental issues – between muzzleloaders and breechloaders, between smoothbore and rifled barrels, and between bronze and cast steel as the material for their construction.

Alfred Krupp (Wikipedia)

Prussia enjoyed one important advantage in the assessment of such technical questions, and it was a legacy of Scharnhorst, himself originally a gunner. This was the 'Artillerie Prüfungs Kommission', which examined with painstaking care the many and varied questions referred to it. In 1816 uniform designs of field guns and howitzers had been adopted for the Prussian army; but twenty years later demands for increased mobility led to the examination by the APK of new designs. The objective was achieved in the 1840s,with the issue of a new pattern of six and twelve-pounder field guns and seven-pounder howitzers, which weighed very much less than those they replaced.[35] The new guns were entirely traditional in their fundamental design, being smoothbore muzzle loaders, manufactured of bronze. By the time of their introduction, however, advances in industrial technology were opening an era of rapid development in artillery design.

Bronze had been the favoured material for gun makers in spite of its cost, because it was more reliable than cast iron. The development by Alfred Krupp of a process for producing cast steel of sufficient reliability offered an alternative material that was only slightly costlier than bronze; and his assiduous salesmanship finally led the War Ministry to take delivery of a cast steel three-pounder, which the APK tested to destruction in 1849 with strikingly successful results.

Meanwhile practical experience was demonstrating that the range of smoothbore cannon was no longer sufficient to put them safely beyond the range of infantry equipped with rifles; clearly it might also be necessary for the artillery to use rifled barrels as well. This was a question that led to prolonged disputes between the APK, now led by Lieutenant General Encke who believed passionately in the need for rifles, and the Inspector General of Artillery, General von Hahn, who strongly favoured smoothbores. At the same time the experimental development of breechloading cannon was held up by the difficulty of producing a gas-tight breech mechanism. What was becoming evident, however, was that bronze might in any case not be a reliable enough material for breechloaders.

Krupp attracted much publicity, but no orders, as a result of his display of a six-pounder steel gun at the Great Exhibition in London of 1851; two years later, William was a rare official visitor to the Krupp works. For years, however, Krupp's frustration continued, as in spite of all his efforts no orders came from the Prussian government. But the tide was about to turn. By 1857, APK experiments with rifled steel barrels were proving extremely satisfactory. It was also concluded that new weapons should be breechloaders. Finally, after a demonstration of Krupp steel six-pounders at Berlin in 1859 attended by William, now Prince Regent, the latter personally ordered that three hundred should be purchased.[36]

Hahn, though, was still determined to maintain the army's dependence on smoothbore weapons. Even the evident success of the French rifled artillery in the 1859 campaign (the French army was the first to go over entirely to rifled cannon, albeit muzzle loaders) did not cause him to change his mind, and he held to his view until his retirement at the end of 1864. Earlier that year, William had appointed Gustav von Hindersin as Second Inspector-General of the artillery – another of William's far-reaching and well-judged appointments – and, during the Danish war he was further to demonstrate his commitment to Krupp steel guns by placing an additional order for three hundred barrels.

4

Army Reform

William had taken up the reins of royal authority under the terms of a temporary vice regency in October 1857, as a result of the serious illness of the King, soon after which he had appointed Moltke to be acting Chief of the General Staff. At the same time he took the first steps towards achieving his long-held ambition for a major reform of the army, when he asked the War Ministry to put forward detailed proposals, which he received in February 1858. He had also remained in continuous contact with Roon on the subject, particularly with regard to his unalterable conviction that the minimum period of service should be three years, and that there should also be an extensive reform of the Landwehr. A quarter of a century earlier William had written of the need to instil the right spirit in the army, in order to resist what he described as

> the tendencies of the revolutionary or liberal party in Europe…Discipline, blind obedience, come into being and endure only by long habituation and require a longer term of service so that the monarch can count on his troops in the hour of danger. It is precisely this blind obedience that the revolutionaries find most troublesome.[1]

Such views were, of course, certain to drive him into a direct confrontation with the Landtag.

Meanwhile Roon had been working on his own proposals for the extensive reform of the Prussian army, and on July 21 1858 he published his own paper on the subject, which closely reflected William's views. In this document he pulled no punches. He turned his back entirely on the concept of the Landwehr as it had been established by Hermann von Boyen in 1813:

> The Landwehr was no more than a stop-gap. Its practical achievements in the field were for the most part grossly overestimated. Yet this overestimate left its mark, as did the after dinner speeches and phrase-mongering of journalists in that spirited and over-stimulated time. They spread the wrong idea that a nation in arms was irresistible, and thus what was a makeshift became the corner stone of the whole system.[2]

Instead, Roon proposed that the Landwehr should be amalgamated with the reserve units of the regular army, which would increase military control of these forces, improve their training, and above all massively increase the size of the reserve available in time of war.

The size of the standing army should, he proposed, be significantly increased. The annual call up under the existing arrangements produced 40,000 men; but this was based on the population of 12,000,000 at the time that the scheme was introduced

Minister of War Albrecht von Roon. (Rogers)

in 1833. The population of Prussia was now half as large again; an annual intake of 63,000 would remove the considerable sense of injustice created by the partial call up, and would increase the standing army by about 40%, to about 200,000 men, and, of course, would also increase the number of trained reserves. This increase in numbers would necessitate a doubling in the number of infantry battalions, while the cavalry and artillery would be increased by 25%.

During 1858, William widely discussed these plans. Although the concept of a larger, better-trained army was likely to appeal to most Prussian military leaders, there were certainly some who felt concern about the suggested root and branch reform of the Landwehr. Among these was the Minister for War, General Edouard von Bonin. He believed that a reform such as was proposed would have the effect of totally alienating the army from the general population, creating the kind of public indifference that had existed before 1806.[3] In this view, Bonin reflected the immediate reaction of most liberal politicians to Roon's proposals. He was an admirer of Boyen, and in any case could see all too clearly the kind of political uproar that would result from the introduction of the necessary legislation. In the hope of being able to persuade William not to adopt the politically disagreeable aspects of Roon's plans, he went out of his way to reassure the Landtag that the Government regarded itself as bound by the existing Landwehr legislation, which there were no plans to amend. 'Nothing will be changed in the basic principles and forms on which the Landwehr system rests, nor in the basic ideas of our entire army system, for line and Landwehr alike.'[4]

Not surprisingly this greatly annoyed William. It also gave Manteuffel, who was a bitter opponent of Bonin, both on general political grounds and because the War Minister sought to restrict the power of the Military Cabinet, an effective stick with which to beat him. Manteuffel and Gustav von Alvensleben, the Adjutant General, formed a powerful bloc at William's elbow urging Bonin's removal from office. William dealt with the matter in September 1859 by appointing Roon to head a special military commission

King William of Prussia. (Rogers)

charged with the task of drafting an army reform bill, which was to be produced solely by reference to military considerations. Bonin objected furiously; prodded by Manteuffel, William told him bluntly in November 1859 that 'in a monarchy like ours, the military point of view must not be subordinated to the financial and economic, for the European position of the State… depends on it.'[5] Bonin at once resigned; and in due course Roon was appointed in his place.

He accepted office as War Minister on the basis that he would be a technical and professional adviser, and he at once set about the task of introducing the necessary legislation for army reform. He was scornful of 'all of this constitutional business', and if William's requirement was for a minister of the 'right constitutional perfume' he would not, he said, be suitable. His job was to get army reforms through the Landtag, and he was not going to compromise in order to achieve this.

The reform bill was submitted to the Landtag in February 1860. Its outlines accorded with Roon's original proposals of July 1858, calling for an increase in the annual intake to 63,000 with a three year term of service (four years in the cavalry) followed by five years in the reserve and eleven years in the Landwehr. The size of the standing army would be approximately doubled. All of this was, of course, extremely costly, requiring an increase in the annual military budget of nine and a half million thalers.

This huge increase in public expenditure, as well as the political implications of what was proposed for the Landwehr, and also of the three year service term, predictably aroused strong popular hostility to the bill, which was remitted on February 15 to the Military Committee. There, it did not immediately encounter out and out opposition. The rapporteur of the Military Committee, General von Stavenhagen, carried most of its members with him in trying to find a way both to moderate the detail of the bill and to meet the Government's realistic military objectives. Some aspects of the reform were seen as perfectly acceptable. The requirement, for instance, that all men fit for service should be called up was self-evidently fair, and would produce an immediate accession of strength to Prussian national power. On the other hand, the proposed reduction in the independence of the Landwehr was an issue on which liberal politicians were bound to take a firm stand, as was the increase in the term of service to three years. The liberals on the Committee hoped to find a half way house at which their views and those of the Government might meet, but in this they were soon disappointed.

The proposal put forward by the Committee provided for a reduction of the Landwehr from one half to one third of the total mobilised forces. The net effect of this was not great, since about the same number of troops classified as Landwehr would see active service, while the independent organisation of the force was effectively ended by the linking of the Landwehr battalions to their parent line regiments. This acceptance by the liberals of the real core of the bill, while tinkering with it superficially, came as a surprise to the government; Roon derisively told Gerlach that it was due to 'soft hearted humanitarianism.'

It was not, therefore, the Landwehr issue on which ultimately the confrontation with the government was to be based, but the issue over the requirement for a three year term of service. Here the liberal position did reflect sharply held views in the population as a whole:

> People saw the country in danger of being smothered in countless new barrack buildings, a vast increase in professional officers and non coms trained at military and cadet schools – the growth, in other words, of a machine staffed with men known to oppose the liberal spirit of the time and resolved upon fighting that spirit by every possible means, including nationwide military indoctrination.[6]

In suspecting that this was the primary objective of Manteuffel and his colleagues on the Right, who were quite happy to treat it as a useful *casus belli* for a head-on clash with the Landtag, popular opinion was certainly correct. But behind Roon, who argued for the adoption of the three year service term on technical grounds, and sought to persuade the liberals of the need for it, stood the Regent, who was adamant that he would entertain no changes whatever to the form of the bill. What was particularly striking, in the evolution of a reform that was of critical importance to the future of the Prussian army, was that Moltke and the General Staff played no part in it, and were not formally consulted about the proposals.[7]

It was always clear that the Landtag would accept the report of the Committee. To general surprise, the Government on May 5 withdrew the bill, substituting a persuasive request for an addition of 9,000,000 thalers to the army budget, to enable the army to be strengthened. Von Patow, the Finance Minister, promised that the money could be voted without prejudice to any later debate on army reform, and would be used only for units already legally authorised. On May 15, the request was approved. It was a decision which gave the Regent and those around him the chance to push forward a large part of their plans if, but only if, they were prepared to operate in a manner that was outside the law.

In anticipation of the reform bill, William had in early 1860 authorised the creation of new units intended to replace Landwehr units. Having regard to Patow's promises to the Landtag, the raising of these new regiments should have been discontinued. Under the powerful influence of Manteuffel, William did not do this. Manteuffel went further; he urged Roon that the new regiments should be organised in the teeth of the parliamentary opposition, writing to him: 'I consider the state of army morale and its inner energy imperilled and the position of the Prince Regent compromised if these regiments are not established definitively at once.'[8]

William's accession to the throne, on the death of his brother in January 1861, brought about no change in the constitutional situation, but it gave him the opportunity to mark the commencement of his reign with a further provocative gesture to the Landtag, when he announced that he would, on January 18, dedicate the standards of the new regiments in a ceremony at Frederick the Great's tomb. In spite of this, however, the Landtag gave the Government a grant to cover the military budget, although calling for a new military service bill to be presented to the next session. In the circumstances, this was a very conciliatory gesture; but it fell on stony ground.

The crisis deepened as a result of a pronounced swing to the Left in the outcome of the elections for the Landtag held in December 1861. The success of the Progressive Party, now the single largest bloc, seemed to Manteuffel and Roon to indicate that a final confrontation over the military question could not be avoided. It was as a result of this that planning was begun for a military *coup d'état*, by which the constitution would be suspended. Manteuffel's close friend General Hiller von Gärtringen, later to die a hero's death at Königgrätz, prepared a scheme for the massive strengthening of the garrison at Berlin, and for the seizure of control of the city by the carefully planned operations of 50,000 men and 100 guns moving outwards from the royal palace in co-operation with other units moving on the city from outside.[9] It was beginning to look very much as if the necessary preconditions for Manteuffel's long sought counter revolution had finally arrived.

In fact, however, the newly elected members of the Landtag behaved most circumspectly and the next casualty of the confrontation turned out to be the 'New Era' Cabinet, which William had appointed. It was not only its domestic policy that had got it into difficulties. The mounting pressure for some effective step towards German unity demanded a meaningful Prussian response, but von Schleinitz, the Foreign Minister, had not succeeded in making any impression on Austria, whose intransigence over power sharing in Germany remained undiminished. As a result Schleinitz had been replaced by Count Albrecht von Bernstorff, the Prussian Ambassador in London, who took office very reluctantly indeed in July 1861. By March 1862, again very much at Manteuffel's urging, William was ready to dispose of the rest of the New Era ministry. Since the Landtag had rejected not only a bill for the introduction of the three year service term, but also the Government's request for funds, he also determined on dissolution in the hope that fresh elections would produce a better result. Rumours abounded that army units were, in Berlin, preparing for action.

Pondering the options open to him for the appointment of a new Cabinet, William began to toy with the idea of grasping the nettle very firmly indeed and choosing as his Minister President an individual whose appointment would send the most uncompromising message possible. He had in mind his ambassador to St Petersburg, Otto von Bismarck. He drew back, however, and for the moment confined himself to the formation of a conservative Cabinet, as a result of which Bernstorff remained in office, as did Roon and von der Heydt, who had succeeded Patow as Finance Minister. Five of the liberal ministers in the previous Cabinet, however, left office; the new ministry was headed by Prince Hohenlohe. William, however, had not entirely abandoned the project of appointing Bismarck to his Cabinet, and in May he returned to the notion. Summoned to Berlin early that month, Bismarck chafed at being made to kick his heels while William dithered. The prospect of appointing a man of such extravagantly reactionary views was all a bit too much for the King. Bernstorff, who would not at all have regretted giving up his post and returning to London, promised Bismarck that he could go next to Paris, subject to William's decision as to the composition of the ministry. William continued to vacillate. Bismarck wrote to his wife on May 21 to describe the uncertain situation in Berlin and its effect on his future:

> No decision has yet been made here. Perhaps Heydt's ambition will save me; he wants to be Prime Minister himself; I do not wish for this position unless I have the Foreign Office with it; and then Bernstorff wants to stay, or to hold London open for himself. On Saturday I shall have been here a fortnight; then I shall explode, and demand either a post or permission to resign.[10]

His threat evidently did the trick and he was duly appointed to Paris, for the time being at any rate; he had himself no doubt of the considerable likelihood that he would before long be called upon to form a ministry.

The summer of 1862 wore on, with the deadlock unbroken. Secret discussions between Heydt and representatives of the Progressive Party suggested the possibility of a deal, based on the Government's withdrawal of the three year term in exchange for military budget approvals. Manteuffel was exceedingly anxious about the signs of possible compromise and wrote on August 1 to Roon that

> any further reduction would endanger army strength, not only in terms of effectives, but of morale as well. Once the King, in the eyes of both the army and the nation, ceases to be the supreme arbiter the very foundations of the army will be shaken.[11]

The members of the Cabinet, however, including Roon, grasped this as a solution to the constitutional crisis. The real need for a three year term of service was in fact extremely doubtful. In April 1862, a special commission set up to study the problem, among whose fifteen members was Moltke himself, concluded that two and a half years would be enough, with leave during the winter; indeed it was conceded that two years might even be sufficient. This was one of the few occasions that Moltke had himself got involved in the issues that had occasioned the prolonged constitutional struggle, although it cannot be doubted that he generally supported the aims of the reformers. He was not himself devoid of strong political views. Like most Prussian senior officers, he saw France, not Austria, as the ultimate enemy; in 1861, as one of the Prussian delegates to a conference on the reform of the Federal army, he had supported a proposed Prussian guarantee of Austria's possession of Venetia, seeing this highly sensitive issue as being principally a military question. He had a dim view of politicians that he had always held and frequently expressed privately, especially to his brother Adolf, to whom he wrote for instance in 1852: 'Our diplomats have always hurled us into misfortune, our generals have always saved us.'[12] But although prepared to make orthodox military noises of this

A rare photograph of Bismarck, Roon and Moltke. (Reimer)

kind, Moltke was always extremely careful not to be overtly involved in political issues and throughout the crisis kept both himself and the General Staff out of the conflict.

On September 17 Roon publicly hinted that a deal such as Heydt had been discussing might be acceptable to the Government; but later that day William dug his heels in, refusing to agree to any reduction in the three year term of service and threatening to abdicate rather than give way. Two days later, therefore, Roon was obliged to retract his public suggestion of the possible compromise. Although this was apparently a humiliating climb down imposed on him by his obstinate King, it may well be that Roon was playing a longer game than appeared, having in mind a new plan to postpone the final crisis. It was his firm intention to do all he could to get Bismarck appointed to lead the Government, and in the Cabinet crisis, which followed William's announcement of his unshakable commitment to the three year term, Roon kept his eye constantly on the *moment d'appui*. He lobbied the King constantly on Bismarck's behalf, to the extent of suggesting, quite incorrectly, that Bismarck would accept office without a portfolio. Meanwhile, in the face of the rejection by the Landtag of the military budget, the Cabinet lost its nerve completely. It had previously warned William that if the budget was rejected, the Government would lose its constitutional legitimacy. In Berlin the immediate result of this was that Heydt, Bernstorff and Holzbruck all resigned on September 19. The disputants were, therefore, as far apart as ever. Although Manteuffel happened to be away when the crisis broke, the reactionary view continued

Count Otto Eduard Leopold von Bismarck-Schönhausen. (Rogers)

to be strongly asserted in his absence by Alvensleben, the Adjutant General. To Roon it looked very much as if Bismarck's hour had come and he sent his famous message to Bismarck, at that time relaxing in South Western France. Over a prearranged code name the telegram read: '*Periculum in mora.* Dépechez vous.' The urging of the need for haste was unnecessary. Bismarck was already on his way, arriving in Berlin on September 20 where he went at once to see Roon, to be briefed on the situation and to prepare the way for his interview with the King.

This finally took place on September 22. William complained that he could not find ministers willing to stand up to the majority; Bismarck responded confidently that he had been willing since May to enter the ministry, that Roon would stand by him and that other suitable ministers would be found. William went on to ask the questions that were at the heart of the crisis. Would Bismarck press through the army programme? And would he do so notwithstanding the opposition's majority? Bismarck's firm and positive response was enough for William. It was his duty, he said, with Bismarck's help, to continue the battle. By the end of this meeting, in the gardens of Babelsberg, Prussia had found a new Minister President.

Within a few days of taking office, a characteristic moment of incautious frankness on Bismarck's part created a political furore, and confirmed the worst fears of those who had criticised his appointment. It was in his speech to the Budget Committee of the Landtag on September 29, that he famously observed that 'the great questions of the time will be decided, not by speeches and resolutions of majorities, but by iron and blood.' These were words which even Roon, his closest ally, described as 'witty digressions' which were unhelpful in the delicate state of Prussian politics.[13] However, in the first of many such encounters with his sovereign, Bismarck was able to overcome the deep alarm felt by William at the public response to the speech by a firm appeal to his Prussian spirit: 'Your Majesty is faced with the necessity of fighting. You cannot capitulate. You must oppose tyranny, even if you incur bodily danger.'

In the ensuing months Bismarck fought the Landtag at every turn in his efforts to push through the army budget. He was not himself persuaded of the absolute necessity for a term of military service longer than two years, but he was committed to the King's plans for army reform. When the Lower House sought to excise the army estimates from the budget, he adjourned the Landtag; the army expenditure, although unauthorised, continued by virtue of what he claimed was a gap in the constitution. When in 1863 the Lower House proposed a compromise whereby the enlargement of the army and the three year term would be agreed if the reform of the Landwehr was abandoned, he overruled Roon, who was prepared to agree, and acted in such a way as to make sure that the compromise was abandoned. For the moment, his intention was by foreign policy successes to overwhelm liberal opposition at home. He was unmoved by the popular hostility to the support which he gave to the Russian suppression of the Polish uprising in 1863; the Alvensleben Convention which he concluded with Russia provided for cross-border military co-operation, and ensured continuing sympathy for his foreign policy objectives from Russia in the years that followed. When Franz Joseph seemed to have outflanked him over the question of German Federal reform later in the year by his proposed 'Congress of Princes' at Frankfurt, he had another sharp tussle with his reluctant monarch. 'Thirty Princes sending an invitation and the courier, a King! How can one refuse?' was William's anguished response. But Bismarck was having none of it. Reform of the Confederation was the last thing he wanted and in a prolonged argument he overcame William's resistance, although after it he felt 'so weak and exhausted that I could scarcely stand... So nervous and unhinged that in closing the outer door I tore off the handle.' It was perhaps the most stressful of all the disputes between Bismarck and the King. In his memoirs he wrote:

> Not until midnight did I succeed in obtaining the King's signature to a refusal to the King of Saxony. When I left my master, both he and I were ill and exhausted by the nervous tension of the situation; and my subsequent verbal communication with the Saxon minister, von Beust, bore the stamp of this agitation.[14]

The poor King felt no better after this titanic conflict, writing to the King of Saxony that he could not see him as he was retiring at once to bed with 'twitching nerves.' The Congress of Princes continued its deliberations and struggled to reach an agreement, but without Prussia, its discussions were rendered meaningless.

5

Strategic Planning

The first practical experience of the Prussian army in mobilising on a large scale under modern conditions had come in 1850 and this, as has been seen, proved calamitously unsuccessful. The political confrontation with Austria which led to this had come to the boil as early as May 1850. At that time no clear cut plan of operations existed, and the use of the railway system for the first time on this scale was itself unplanned, and under the direction not of the army, but of the Ministry of Commerce. Supply and hospital units had to be improvised; there were insufficient horses for both artillery and cavalry. As Chief of Staff of the IV Corps in Magdeburg, Moltke had been involved at first hand in the problems involved in mobilising; while he thought that from the perspective of his own corps the result had been satisfactory, other observers were uninhibited in their critical comments; Alfred von Waldersee, one day to succeed Moltke as Chief of the Great General Staff, but at that time a regimental artillery officer, observed that train columns found themselves in a 'tragic situation', while supply officers 'fell all over themselves.'[1]

A recent historian has observed that during the first six years of his tenure of office

> the war planning processes evolved slowly and haltingly. Moltke tried to transform the Great General Staff, but neither he nor the Great General Staff had sufficient prestige or independence, and the task environment was not urgent, but only indirectly and unclearly supported change.[2]

But given the fact that the existing power structures within the Prussian army, particularly in peace time, did not focus any particular attention on the work of the General Staff or its Chief, Moltke was nevertheless building on the strong foundations of its tradition in the reforms he was quietly introducing. Effective organisation of the process by which the nation's soldiers were mobilised to fight, and thorough advance planning of the campaigns in which they would do so, were of course the primary tasks of any general staff organisation. In Prussia a lot more thought had been given to these tasks from the earliest days of the existence of the General Staff, and it was accordingly better prepared to cope with the vastly increased demands made by population increase and technological advance.

By the time of his appointment as Chief of the General Staff, all Moltke's previous convictions about the efficacy of rail power had been effectively confirmed. It meant that mobilisation and deployment must be planned accurately and swiftly executed:

> From his first weeks in office, Moltke emphasised his conviction that the best of operations plans could not be executed by the greatest of generals if the mobilisation was slow or the initial development faulty. It was at the very beginning that the machine must be in the most perfect order.[3]

The experiences of the 1859 mobilisation, and his planning for a campaign over the Rhine, reinforced Moltke's determination to ensure that on the next occasion the whole mobilisation process and the plans for the army's deployment would be ready for any eventuality. Although culturally sympathetic to Austria, he was profoundly conscious of the relationship of this forward planning to the international political situation; and the events of 1859 had outraged his professional and personal pride. After Villafranca he wrote to his brother Adolf to comment on Austrian arrogance and the way in which Prussian help had been rejected. He reflected on Prussia's exposed position, having no allies; even if they could be obtained as allies, England had no army and Russia's help would be too late to be effective. On the other hand the 1859 mobilisation had not weakened his confidence in the Prussian army. He recorded his belief:

> Prussia missed a great opportunity. Only four weeks ago we might have placed ourselves at the head of all Germany... Now we are left entirely to ourselves and I am convinced that we shall prepare for coming events with all possible skill and diligence. But that our situation will soon be more favourable in a political and military sense than in the immediate past I very much doubt.

Moltke went on to express also his belief in the need for strong leadership. 'A bold revolution can only be the act of one man... It needs a Frederick the Great to take no advice and to act solely on his own responsibility.'[4]

The principal contingency for which the staff must prepare was of course that of war with France. Given the prevailing political situation, Moltke did not see Austria as an immediate threat. In an essay on the importance of fortresses in 1861-2 he noted that:

> Probably no one will deny that Russia (which is engaged in domestic reconstruction), and Austria are presently (and will probably be for decades to come) far less dangerous neighbours for us than is France...the fortresses along the Rhine will have a greater initial influence than those situated along the Vistula or the Silesian Mountains.[5]

With this in mind, in all the earliest deployment plans he produced, Moltke had envisaged a purely defensive war.

In a memorandum of November 1857, he contemplated a French assault along the line Strasbourg-Ulm, since the line of the Rhine to the north was such a serious obstacle, quite apart from the protection afforded by neutral Belgium. To the south, however, protected initially by the VII and VIII Federal Corps, the French were offered a temptingly weak objective. In these circumstances Prussia must quickly mobilise two corps to

> dispute the left flank of the Rhine until the main Prussian army and X Federal Corps are collected between Kulm and Mainz. Then with 200,000 men Jülich and Saarlouis can be relieved, and an attack on the French on either bank of the Rhine would stop their advance into South Germany.[6]

A French attack, he thought, would be based on surprise; in this plan he assumed that Austria would be fighting alongside the rest of Germany; the delayed mobilisation of the Austrian army would mean that the principal concentration of the allied German forces could not be as far west as a position between Rastatt-Germersheim and Stuttgart. He added the comment that 'if they consider the subject coolly the South German Governments will see that help can reach them soonest from Prussia, and that their line of retreat must be not to the east but to the north, to the Main.'[7]

In his plans produced in October 1858 he was still assuming the alliance with Austria, and he repeated his concerns about the speed of Austrian mobilisation and the fact that the Federal forces must, in the event of a French advance, concentrate well to the east, choosing between Ulm and Würzburg. A neutral Belgium protected a large part of the Prussian front, so that four corps on the lower Rhine would probably suffice to defend that area, while four more concentrated on the Main and thereby protected the assembly of the Federal forces at Würzburg. Two corps would be concentrated on the Saale in reserve. Practical considerations would, in Moltke's opinion, effectively solve the next political question, which was who should command the combined Federal forces. The late arrival of the Austrians would, if the South German states caused their forces to retire eastwards, mean that their nations would be the scene of the fighting:

> But if they unite all their forces at Würzburg with Prussia's no French army can get far into South Germany. They may not see this in peace time discussions, but in the hour of need they will see how they stand and the question of the command in chief will settle itself.[8]

In February 1859, much the same scheme was proposed, although this memorandum now contained the significant and somewhat surprising statement that Moltke did not yet know whether Prussia would take the French or the Austrian side. Two weeks later, a more offensive plan was prepared contemplating an advance into Alsace and Lorraine, if possible in conjunction with the Belgian army.[9]

By May 1859, however, the plans for an advance were based on the assumption that, after all, Belgium would be neutral. Since the objective was to gain Alsace and Metz, two alternative strategies were contemplated – either an immediate advance to Paris, or first the occupation of Alsace. The plan aimed to reach the line of the Saar by the forty-seventh day of mobilisation. In all these plans, there were, of course, other crucial areas of uncertainty, such as the intentions of Russia and the possibility that measures would need to be taken simultaneously against Denmark.

During the years following 1859, Moltke continued to refine his basic plan of operations against France. This assumed an army of three corps on the lower Rhine, and another of three corps on the Main, with a powerful central reserve. Even Moltke's defensive schemes, however, assumed that the ultimate objective was the acquisition of Alsace-Lorraine. In meeting a French offensive, Moltke wrote that 'we must have all the force we can at Mainz and as soon as possible. The French cannot go as in 1806 for Prussia (Berlin) so long as we have a strong army at Mainz. Our army there will draw them as a magnet…Mainz, though not Prussian, is Prussia's most important fortress – her shield and sword.'[10] His plans still contemplated the possibility that France would not respect Belgium's neutrality, and that the strength of the Prussian fortresses close to the frontier was not sufficient to delay the French advance for long; it was the speed of mobilisation of the field army that would be decisive, since 'if the French invade the Rhine province on the left bank they have not secured it until they have beaten our army.' By 1863, however, Moltke had reverted to the idea that France would not invade Belgium, and that therefore the thrust would be across the upper Rhine into Southern Germany. Once again, he saw Mainz, and the line of the Main, as crucial if the French advance was to be speedily halted.

Although during this period Moltke regarded France as the most obvious adversary that Prussia might expect to face, he naturally also considered the possibility of war against Austria, and wrote a series of memoranda in which his ideas for the conduct of such a war gradually matured. In these, of course, he was not operating in a political vacuum, and the papers he produced are of absorbing interest as disclosing his own thoughts on the wider political situation. As early as the Spring of 1860 he set these out in a lengthy memorandum on the deployment of the army in the event of an Austrian war, in which he analysed the help that Prussia could expect in a conflict that would affect all the powers in Europe. It was of course written on the basis of the political situation as it then existed, and some of his assumptions proved ill-founded, not least in the way he underestimated the reluctance of the Great Powers to get involved in a shooting war where their own interests were not immediately threatened. He was, though, perfectly aware of the difficulty of forecasting with any accuracy the way in which individual states would behave:

> To no human intelligence can it be given to trace in advance the course of such great political events, upon which not only the permanent interest of States, but also the sympathies and antipathies of rulers, the insight and energy of Cabinets at the critical moment, and internal disturbances or popular risings often exercise an effective, though incalculable, impulsion.[11]

Having made the assumption that a war between Prussia and Austria would draw all Europe into the conflict, he went on to calculate that Prussia might expect help from Russia and probably England as well; that Denmark would be neutral, but that Belgium, Holland and Italy would be on Prussia's side; that France would be hostile, aiming at the conquest of the Rhineland; that North Germany, apart from Saxony, must cooperate with Prussia, while the South German states might remain neutral. Whichever side won, he reckoned, Germany might be united, but at the expense of provinces in both east and west. He based the Prussian deployment upon the assumption of a defensive war; if on the other hand an aggressive war against Austria was intended, the Prussian Army would assemble in Silesia. But he was dubious about the prospect of sustained success:

> Possibly Austria might be completely surprised, but it would be well to consider whether, in opposition to the power of the Empire, which increases for resistance with time, Prussia would be able to maintain her initial success, for it must be remembered that the strategical offensive, differing in this from the tactical offensive, undoubtedly presupposes a far greater development of force than the strategical defensive.[12]

Even a defensive campaign required an advance to occupy Dresden, the possession of which must seriously threaten any Austrian line of advance; while Berlin could be better secured by a defensive position along the rivers Nuthe and Notte than by fortifications around the city itself. 'The main decision must take place south of Berlin, and it is therefore of the greatest importance to be as strong as possible there.'[13]

Moltke examined the question of a campaign against Austria in another memorandum of June 3 1862; in this he considered the question of acting against the Confederation. Prussia must, he wrote, make herself master of the small states. 'To draw back would be more dangerous for us than lost battles – it would be political death. Any middle course leads to destruction, only the most absolute offensive to the goal.'[14] In this paper he proceeded on the basis that not only Austria and Bavaria, but also France, and maybe England and Denmark, might be hostile. What would be vital would be for Prussia to seize the initiative, which was entirely possible as a result of her ability to put her forces more rapidly into the field than Austria or the rest of the German states. Once again he saw swift action against Saxony as a key element of Prussian strategy.

These plans, which already reflected Moltke's fundamental ideas for the strategy to be pursued, formed the basis of all his subsequent planning for a war against Austria and we shall return to them when considering the final version of his scheme.

Meanwhile, Roon's request dated November 28 1862 for a formal appreciation of possible military operations against Denmark came as no surprise to Moltke. In his response of December 6 Moltke wrote:

> The eventuality of a military solution to the dispute so long pending with Denmark has not for an instant been lost sight of here. Already the concentration of a Prussian army around Hamburg and Lübeck has been by my orders examined by the General Staff in a work study of its movements by rail.[15]

He went on to warn Roon that while identifying the immediate objective was in itself not easy, bringing about a definitive result presented especial difficulties. Since the Danes had command of the sea, operations must be confined to the occupation of Jutland which, to be effective in bringing Denmark to heel, must be prolonged, increasing the risk of foreign interference. However, applying basic principles, Moltke was clear that the true objective, if the occupation of the enemy's capital was not possible, must be the Danish army. Merely driving it back would not bring about the end of the war; it was necessary to aim at its destruction.

In his paper Moltke pointed out that the first issue would be the strong Danish fortified position in Schleswig. The Dannewerk rested on the inundations of the Treene to the west, and upon the arm of the sea of the Schlei in the east; only in winter, if the ice on its flanks froze to a sufficient depth, would it become indefensible. A winter campaign would therefore be best; but it was always possible that the Danish army would retreat, in order to avoid encirclement, and by taking up positions in Alsen and Fünen avoid a decisive result. It was essential therefore that sufficiently strong forces be employed for the operation, to enable these positions at Düppel and Fredericia respectively to be masked, while Jutland was completely occupied by the rest of the army. Although the province must be evacuated as part of a peace settlement, its occupation would be a sufficiently effective bargaining counter in the peace negotiations to enable an acceptable outcome to be achieved. This, of course, was a political question; Moltke's readiness to advocate it was the first indication of his willingness to put forward a suggestion that fell squarely into Bismarck's sphere of decision, and proposals of this kind would in due course become an important area of dispute between the Minister President and the military.

Analysing the likely strength of the opposition, Moltke put the strength of the Danish army at 32,560 men in thirty-seven battalions. For the operation to succeed, therefore, he suggested the employment of four full strength divisions: the total force would comprise 50 battalions, with 37 squadrons and 24 batteries, with three engineer battalions, a total of 61,000 men. The staff mobilisation exercise carried out earlier in the year had indicated that he could put a strength of twelve battalions with eight squadrons and six batteries into the Hamburg area by the seventeenth day to deal with the existing Danish garrison of Holstein which amounted to five battalions with four squadrons and four batteries, while another three battalions and four squadrons occupied Schleswig. The exercise had shown that the Prussians could build up their force more quickly by using the rail network than the Danes could by moving reinforcements by sea.[16]

In his paper Moltke again raised the question of building a railway line to connect Hamburg to Altona. If the Senate of Hamburg approved this, it would be possible to remove the rolling stock of the Holstein railways and prevent it falling into the hands of the Danes; it could be used to accelerate the Prussian advance to the line of the Eider, which he hoped could be reached by the twentieth day of mobilisation; behind the leading troops, the rest of the army could be within one day's march of the enemy by the twenty eighth day. In this way, by the time the Danes got sufficient forces into line in the Dannewerk, they would be opposed by a Prussian army of superior numbers.

Moltke's memorandum to Roon had only been a general outline of his proposals for the operation. Later that month he prepared a much more detailed plan aimed at the destruction of the Danish army. To achieve this, it was necessary that the Danes should commit themselves fully to the defence of the Dannewerk position and, once they were pinned down there, to get around their flank in order to cut them off from a retreat northwards, to Düppel. This plan required that the forces available should out number the enemy by two to one. There were of course plenty of troops available for the operation; but bearing in mind the need to maintain strong forces along the French and Russian borders, he proposed to employ units which in peacetime were based in the centre of Prussia. Accordingly, he designated the III Corps, together with the 7th and 11th Infantry Divisions as comprising the invading force. In this paper he drew out detailed march tables for the advance to the line of the Eider, and went on to set out in considerable detail the way in which he intended operations to be conducted thereafter. Much was known about the strength and weaknesses of the Dannewerk; after reviewing the position he identified the main point of attack as being Fortress No. 11. He emphasised, however, that to achieve success it was essential that absolute secrecy be observed in order to maintain the maximum advantage of surprise.[17]

Somewhat later Moltke sent a copy of this paper to Prince Frederick Charles, who was likely to be given the command of the invading army, and from whom he received on February 5 1863 a lengthy series of comments. In his turn, Moltke annotated this response with a number of observations of his own to clarify his intentions. Broadly speaking, however, Frederick Charles accepted Moltke's plan of operations; in particular, he accepted that the sole objective must be the Danish army. However, he somewhat misunderstood Moltke's intentions as to the envelopment of the Danish Army. In his comments on Frederick Charles' paper, Moltke noted that it was not his intention to operate against both flanks simultaneously, but to choose whichever flank was found to offer the best prospect of achieving this.[18] The seriousness with which they both addressed the matter and their attention to detail was demonstrated by the fact that their consideration extended to identify not only each of the individual units to be employed, but even the extent of the particular responsibilities of von Zastrow, the commander of the 11th Division, whom Frederick Charles saw as the ideal man for the tasks he was set. Of course, at the time Moltke prepared this plan it was far from clear as to what the overall political situation would actually be if war broke out, so that at this stage he could make provision only for operations by the Prussian Army, making no assumptions about the involvement of Austria.

Moltke's approach to war planning always depended heavily on a most thorough review of all the guidance afforded by a study of military history and current field operations. If experience is the best of teachers, the experience of others provides the most cost effective education of all, and Moltke drew on all aspects of the information available. In the course of preparing himself for all eventualities, he personally researched and lectured on the campaign in Bavaria of 1809; on the basis of the reports from various members of his staff of the French mobilisation and demobilisation of 1859, and of the conduct of operations in northern Italy, he prepared a detailed account of that campaign, which he both published and lectured on to his staff.[19] He drew important conclusions as to mobilisation and troop movements from the American Civil War, in which for the first time operations had been conducted over great distances by the use of the railways, and it was this, as has been seen, which led him to add a Railways Section to the General Staff. The validation of the schemes proposed was always extremely thorough; they were tested in war games, staff rides and in the annual manoeuvres of the Prussian army.

From the moment that he took office, the process by which campaign planning was developed was continuous. The frequent revisions arose not only from the ceaselessly changing kaleidoscope of international relations, but also from the growing strength of the Prussian army and Moltke's increasing confidence in the outcome of any war. The permutations of international politics were endless. He could, for instance, never be sure that the French might not strike through Belgium or even Holland, but if they did, the armies of other nations might be available for the ensuing campaign, (for what they were worth; in 1861 he assumed that the 'Belgians will be shut up in Antwerp…and England helpless') and although France was the most probable enemy, he was also obliged at all times to consider the possibility of war with Austria. The growing seriousness of the Schleswig-Holstein problem, however, made it increasingly likely during 1863 that the first campaign Moltke would have to fight would be against Denmark, and it was to this task that he now began to address himself.

6

Schleswig-Holstein

The tangled history of the Schleswig-Holstein problem had stretched over four centuries of increasing complexity. The intricate issues are remembered today more for Palmerston's famous joke than for themselves; he remarked that only three people had ever understood the problem; the Prince Consort, who was dead, a German professor who had gone mad and Palmerston himself, who had forgotten all about it.

The Convention of Ribe in 1460 had purported to settle the difficult issues of succession, and had pronounced that the Duchies should be perpetually undivided. They had, however, subsequently had a very different history, not least due to the difference in the make-up of their populations; Schleswig, much closer to Denmark in terms of religion, language and ethnic origin, was a fief of the Danish crown whilst Holstein, a fief of the Holy Roman Empire, was very largely German. The relationship of the two Duchies to each other, to the Kingdom of Denmark and to the German Confederation had not been conclusively resolved by the post-Napoleonic settlement. In 1815 Holstein was incorporated in the Confederation while remaining under the Danish Crown; Schleswig continued to be part of the Danish King's possessions, which apart from Denmark itself also included the tiny rural Duchy of Lauenburg which was entirely German. As the 19th Century wore on, forces far stronger than dynastic rights of succession were at work, as the rising tide of nationalism focused attention on the Duchies. Holstein was still solidly German, and southern Schleswig predominantly so, while German influence in north Schleswig was also increasing. Denmark's population was about 1.5m; Schleswig had about 400,000 inhabitants, Holstein 500,000 and Lauenburg 50,000. In the three Duchies, the nationalist party sought the establishment of an independent German state; on the other hand Danish nationalists, who became known as the 'Eider Danes', wished to absorb Schleswig into the Kingdom of Denmark, thus restoring the River Eider as its southern boundary. The growing bitterness of the dispute was expressed in complex and legalistic arguments over the respective rights of succession under the Danish Lex Regia and the Salic Law respectively, the latter excluding succession through the female line.

While the Diet of the Confederation at Frankfurt was still pondering how to respond to King Christian VIII's 'Open Letter' asserting that the Lex Regia applied, the chain reaction of revolutions of 1848 turned European politics upside down. In Denmark, where a new King, Frederick VII had just ascended the throne, the Eider Danes gained the upper hand, and promulgated a new constitution to bring Schleswig under direct control. On March 18 a meeting of leading Schleswig-Holsteiners countered this by calling among other things for Schleswig to join the Confederation, a demand that the new Danish government abruptly rejected. On March 24 a provisional government of the Duchies was proclaimed at Kiel, while on the same day in a separate development the Duke of Augustenburg obtained Prussian backing for his claim to the throne.

Events moved rapidly. While the provisional government seized the fortress of Rendsburg, pro-Danish demonstrations in north Schleswig led to violence, and Danish forces crossed the Konge Aa and occupied that part of the Duchy. On April 4 Prussian troops under the veteran General von Wrangel moved into Holstein. The respective forces both headed for the line of the Eider, and conflict could hardly be avoided. The Prussian action was enthusiastically supported by the 'Vorparliament' in Frankfurt and the Federal Diet organised a force to cooperate with the Prussians.

The ensuing operations were later to be the subject of a detailed review by Moltke and the Prussian General Staff. The recommendations which he put forward in December 1862 were based on the lessons learned by the events of 1848-1850. Then, lacking in any clear war aims, the Prussian and Federal forces engaged put up a disappointing performance. The confused situation in Frankfurt, and the ultimate irresolution of the Prussian government meant that the numerical superiority of the German forces, and the enormous resources which lay behind them, were of no avail against the single-minded Danish leaders. During the various campaigns a number of engagements were fought at points that were again to be important in 1864, and from them Moltke drew some valuable conclusions.

In 1850 Moltke, like the rest of Germany, had watched with mounting gloom as the developments in the Duchies unfolded. By the end of the year it was clear to him that the game was up for the army of Schleswig-Holstein, by now under the command of a prominent military theoretician, the Prussian General von Willisen. Moltke considered the latter's dispositions to be defective; Willisen told him that he 'did not consider the qualities of the Holstein troops sufficient to guarantee success'. Moltke wrote to his wife in January 1851: 'that the Holsteiners must lay down their arms is imperative; but that Prussia and Austria will then, if necessary, take up arms for them in defence of their real right, must be taken for granted'.[1]

Flushed with their success in 1848 to 1850, the Danes pursued an arrogant and high-handed policy in Schleswig, prompting protests from both Prussia and Austria, and tension increased progressively both in Schleswig and in Germany as a whole. A threat by the Diet of a 'Federal Execution', and a public commitment by King William I to Prussia's duty to solve the problem led to nothing more than a brisk exchange of diplomatic notes. In September 1862 Earl Russell, the British Foreign Secretary, put forward in his 'Gotha Despatch' a plan to settle the issue; perceived as pro-German, it was immediately rejected by Denmark and Sweden. Although both Prussian and Austrian Governments sought to prevent the situation again reaching crisis point, this aim was increasingly undermined by the growing strength of German public opinion, as a leading historian of the issue has noted: 'The sad truth was that the time for compromise had passed. Nationalism was on the march in Denmark as well as in Germany; Eider Danism was growing rapidly in 1861 and 1862 in Denmark and also in Schleswig'. [2]

Things were about to change; on September 24 1862 there had arrived on the front of the European stage a man who would fundamentally alter the course of international politics, and the Schleswig-Holstein question was one of the most pressing issues with which he had to deal. Otto von Bismarck's appointment as Minister-President of Prussia had been a direct consequence of the conflict over army reform, but he soon began to show that his approach to foreign policy was very different from that of his predecessors. During his years as Prussia's ambassador to the Diet at Frankfurt he had made no secret of his sustained hostility to Austria's pretension to pre-eminence in Germany; now, soon after taking office, he bluntly spelled out his position in a conversation with Count Karolyi, the Austrian ambassador in Berlin. Austria must, he said, accept Prussia as having equal status in Germany, and should in return for Prussian support for her crucial interests shift her own centre of gravity eastwards. Prussia must be free to act in North Germany, and must have 'enough air to keep alive'. If Austria did not follow these precepts, she would invite catastrophe; Bismarck would prefer a partnership with her, but if not would seek allies where he could find them, including an accommodation with Napoleon III. His relationship with the Emperor was complex; certainly at times Napoleon III found Bismarck difficult to read, remarking after the latter's farewell audience at the end of his short term as ambassador in Paris: 'Il n'est pas un homme sérieux', a misjudgment he would live to regret. In fairness to Napoleon, however, it should be said that at that time a lot of other leading European statesmen would have expressed a similar view.

In January 1863 Bismarck outraged liberal opinion when he sent General von Alvensleben to conclude the convention with the Russian Government providing for cooperation against the Polish insurgents in their common frontier districts. Napoleon, pushed by French public opinion to come out in sympathy with the Polish uprising, led international protests against the Russian actions, a step which, ensuring the estrangement of France and Russia, was to be significant when the Schleswig-Holstein crisis came to the boil. When it did, it directly resulted from the publication of a Danish royal ordinance, the 'March Patent', which decreed a separate constitution for Holstein and stripped the Estates of that Duchy of the right to vitiate legislation for the rest of the Danish monarchy. In July, the Federal Diet demanded the revocation of the March Patent, on pain of a Federal Execution. In Prussia, the Liberal Party denounced the Government, claiming that Bismarck's policies had led to the country's isolation and the destruction of its power to wage war on Schleswig-Holstein's behalf. Even if it should try to go to war, declared one speaker in the Landtag, the Liberals would oppose it, 'because in the present state of things we cannot regard the present conditions as those in which even a successful outcome of the war would allow us to expect a satisfactory solution of the question'. Bismarck gave this sort of thing short shrift: 'If we find it necessary to wage war, we will do so with or without your sanction'.[3]

Abroad, the Danes had been strengthened in their intransigence by British support. Palmerston, somewhat rashly, told the House of Commons that anyone trying to disturb the *status quo* 'would find, in the result, that it would not be Denmark alone with which they would have to contend.' Privately, he observed that it was important that 'the gentlemen in Frankfurt and the crazy minister at Berlin' should have impressed on them that aggression against Denmark would have catastrophic results especially for Prussia: 'the Prussian provinces would at once be occupied by France and in the present state of the Prussian Army… the first serious encounter between it and the French would be little less disastrous to Prussia than the battle of Jena'.[4] Buoyed up by foreign support of this kind, the Danish Government's reply to the Diet failed to meet the German demands and in October a resolution that the Diet's decrees be enforced by Federal Execution was finally passed. Hanover and Saxony were to carry it into effect, with Prussia and Austria providing a reserve. Unmoved, the Danish Parliament passed the new constitution into law. Two days after this, King Frederick VII died suddenly, leaving his successor the

King Christian IX of Denmark. (Voss)

responsibility for signing the new constitution. Christian IX was a German prince, and popular opinion in Denmark was suspicious of his loyalties; advised by Hall, the Prime Minister, that he should sign the document, he did so on November 18.

Bismarck, anxious to keep control of the developing situation, had done his best to avert the Federal Execution; the Duke of Augustenburg had renounced his claims in favour of his eldest son Prince Frederick, and Bismarck certainly did not wish to see the Duchies gain their independence under a new Grand Duke. For the moment he could shelter behind Prussia's commitment contained in the Treaty of London to recognise Christian IX.

Meanwhile Moltke had been closely monitoring the situation ever since his appreciation of the military situation written for Roon in December 1862. He had never supposed that an occupation of Holstein would suffice; he had noted in a memorandum of June 8 that what was at issue was the future of Schleswig, which lay outside the boundary of the Confederation:

> An Execution that has as its result the occupation of Holstein, without being able to penetrate into Schleswig, can only have an indirect effect in compelling the restoration of the union between the two Duchies.

He went on to estimate the size of the force necessary, and pointed out that fifteen thousand troops occupied for a year in carrying out the Federal Execution would cost the same as a campaign of sixty thousand men for three months which would suffice to overrun the whole of Jutland.[5] Later that month he prepared for Roon a further assessment of the Danish Army and the positions which it currently occupied. He went on to analyse the strength of the defensive works, and explained the lines of advance open to an invading army. While Denmark had not yet made any direct preparations for war, she was nonetheless preparing herself for an eventual conflict with Germany. There were now seventy separate works along the defence line, which ran from Friedrichstadt to Eckernförde. This, Moltke noted, was the real front line; the fortress of Rendsburg and the works south of the river at Friedrichstadt had merely a political purpose, as a trip wire to identify an aggressor to the rest of Europe.[6]

Moltke wrote another lengthy paper for Roon on June 30 stressing the need to occupy Schleswig, and again noting the object of the Danes in holding Rendsburg and the bridgehead at Friedrichstadt. What did concern him was that if only a weak Federal force entered Holstein, it would encounter sufficient Danish forces at Rendsburg and Friedrichstadt, consisting of the units retreating from Holstein, together with the troops at Schleswig and Eckernförde, to expose it to the risk of a humiliating defeat. Observing the slow progress at Frankfurt, he reckoned that the delay would prove advantageous. It would be desirable, he wrote,

> to begin hostilities when our merchant shipping were to return to port, when the Danish fleet will hesitate to come out and when the transport of troops across the Belts will have become difficult. In the case of severe frost, not only will it become possible to cross the Schlei and the Treene to turn the strong central position Schleswig-Rheide, but we can also carry the war to the islands, and achieve a rapid and decisive result if we operate with a sufficient force.

He reckoned that this must be of the order of 50,000 men; William, in a marginal note which he made on July 16, regarded 70,000 men as the minimum number with which to embark on war.[7] The focus of attention now switched to Frankfurt, where the technical discussions as to how the Federal Execution was to be effected were now under way. At the end of November Moltke went there to attend the meeting of the military committee. His presence in Frankfurt, in the fevered atmosphere surrounding the deliberations of the Federal Diet, did not pass unnoticed, as he reported to his wife; it was a clear indication that Prussia was beginning to take the matter very seriously indeed.[8] But things were moving on, and the picture was already beginning to change. The huge popular excitement, and the calls for the deliverance of the Duchies, did not impress Moltke very much; Schleswig-Holstein could not, he told his wife be 'be liberated by filibusters, but only by a strong regular army; and even if the troops of the German Bund enter it, it does not necessarily follow that the formation of the Holstein battalions will be proceeded with'. The immediate problem was that the terms of the Treaty of London precluded direct action by the Prussian army, so for the moment Moltke's concept of a swift military solution was frustrated.

Having used the Hamburg-Lübeck area as the location of the first General Staff rail transport exercise in 1863, Moltke went to Frankfurt with the ground work for the logistical planning for intervention in Schleswig-Holstein already laid. Captain von Wartensleben, who had masterminded the exercise, was chosen by Moltke to accompany him to Frankfurt to join the Federal Diet's commission to plan the operation. Later, when the detailed planning was assigned to the more junior staff officers, Wartensleben was the Prussian representative at a meeting the following month at Leipzig. His Austrian colleague was Captain Gründorf von Zerbégeny, with whom he had worked in 1861 on the Federal commission which had reviewed the military suitability of the German railway system.[9] These two officers enjoyed a very considerable reputation as soldiers who actually understood the practical and technical aspects of railway management, and worked very well together. It was as a result of this that the move of Federal troops into Holstein went so smoothly. Later, when the time came to move forward the very much larger forces from Prussia and Austria, it was the efficient Wartensleben who presided over an exercise that was remarkable for its punctual operation, considering the unfamiliarity of the techniques involved. It was later estimated that the journeys to the concentration area that would have taken sixteen days by road were completed within six days by rail, and this in spite of appalling weather conditions and the fact that the rail systems in and approaching the Duchies had by no means been designed for military use.[10]

Before he went to Frankfurt, Moltke had attended a briefing meeting with the King, Roon and Manteuffel, and minuted the instructions given to him, which he subsequently endorsed with the note of the steps which he had taken to carry them out. In this, he estimated the potential size of the enemy force at up to 68,000 men, made up as to 43,000 Danish troops and a possible 25,000 reinforcement from Sweden. 12,000 Federal troops should be joined by 35,000 each from Austria and Prussia, which would give a clear margin of superiority.[11] Once at Frankfurt Moltke sent a series of reports to the King. On November 29, he raised the question of the commander of the Federal forces engaged in the Execution, which, with the Prussian and Federal reserves, would amount to a total of 22,000 men. Moltke was dubious about putting Prussian troops under foreign command; the Saxon contingent being the largest, it seemed that state should provide the commander, which was at least better than having an Austrian. The King shared his doubts, minuting that 'the reasons seem in favour of choosing a Saxon general, but will he be man enough to command a corps of 22,000 men? Nobody knows.'[12] It was a matter that soon became of academic interest, as the two Great Powers concerted their own plans for joint action, and by December 1 Moltke was reporting that the Austrians were putting together a force of some 20,000 to operate alongside a Prussian corps of 31,000. Next day Moltke wrote to Bismarck that, with agreement on the military contribution of the states involved, the work of the commission could be completed within two days. He added that he and his Austrian counterpart had already given their consent to a Saxon commander of the Federal forces involved in the first phase of the operation; much more significantly, he wrote that it was his impression that Austria would not have any serious objection in due course to a Prussian commander in chief.[13] And back in Berlin, he was able to report back to Roon on his ensuing audience with the King:

> The Minister President read to me a despatch from Vienna in which the Austrian Government declared itself ready to place its army corps under the orders of Prince Frederick Charles. I explained, in His Majesty's presence, my advice that it would be wise to seize on this consent by the Austrians, and that it seemed by no means certain that they necessarily agreed that the command should go to a general officer who was not a prince of the blood. Fresh discussions would in any case be necessary.[14]

Bismarck's pressure for speedy action on the Execution had the desired effect, and on December 24 Federal troops entered Holstein and Lauenburg. With Austrian support, Bismarck endeavoured to take matters one stage further. On December 28 the Prussian representative proposed to the Federal Diet that Schleswig should also be occupied, as a guarantee of the Danes' fulfilment of their treaty obligations, but it soon became evident from this point the two Great Powers had no hope of getting a majority. From that point onwards unilateral action by Prussia and Austria became inevitable, and Moltke had

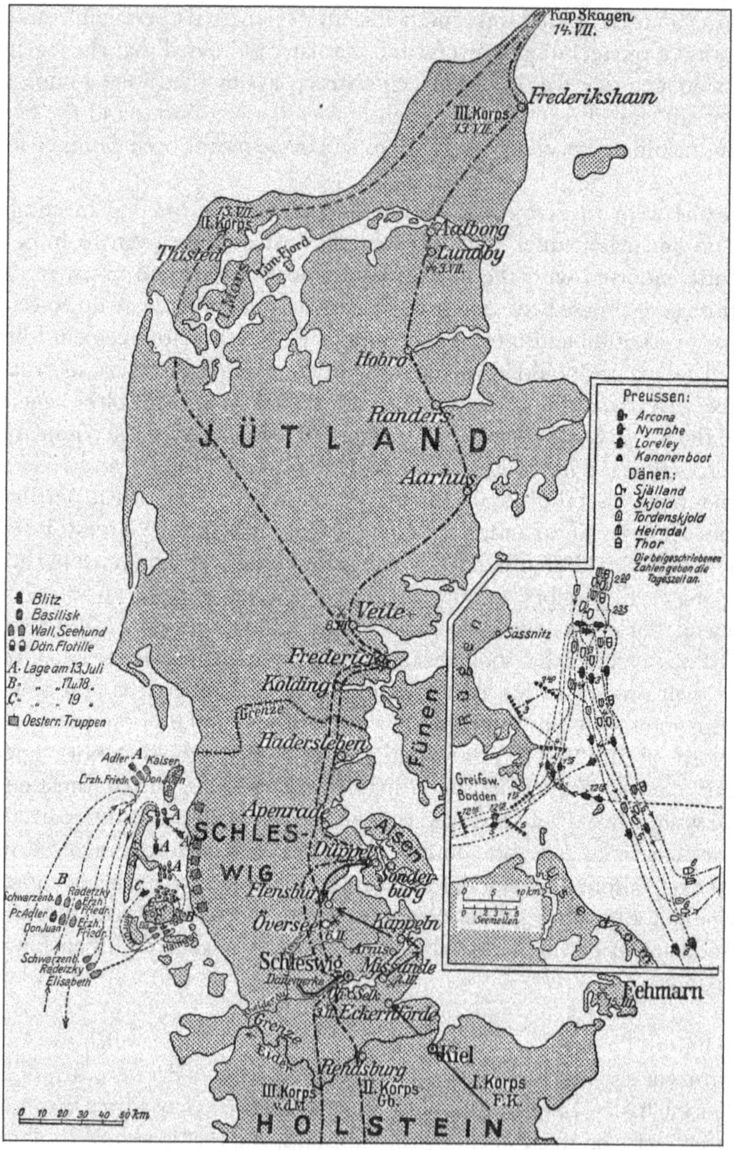

Map 1 – Overview of the theatre of war in Schleswig-Holstein 1864. The detail on the left shows the capture of the North Frisian islands, the inset to the right the naval action of Jasmund, March 17 1864.

Field Marshal Friedrich von Wrangel. (Rogers)

been hard at work to complete his preparations and the military steps which must now be taken. One of the ironies of the situation was that his good friend the Danish General Hegermann-Lindencrone would shortly became an adversary; nevertheless such was their relationship that, hearing that his old friend was in Berlin, Moltke told his wife that the Dane might perhaps call on her there.[15] In fact, Moltke was back in Berlin in time to see Hegermann himself. In the light of the deepening political crisis, Moltke asked him whether, if their sovereigns were to quarrel, their friendship would come to an end. Hegermann's reply was emphatic: 'I answered that our mutual relations would under any circumstances remain unchanged, even though we should appear to the outside world to be separated in such a case as the one that he mentioned.'[16] He was right; they corresponded for the rest of their lives, often on the subject of the war in which they were to fight on opposite sides.

Following the rejection by the Diet on January 14 of the joint motion put forward by Austria and Prussia, their ministers in Copenhagen presented an ultimatum to the Danish Government requiring the withdrawal of the November Constitution within forty-eight hours. The Danes immediately refused, and diplomatic relations were broken off. Ignoring the presence of the Federal troops there, the leading Allied units at once marched into Holstein and began to move up to the Schleswig frontier.

Moltke's previous concern that the Austrians would only place themselves under the command of a royal prince proved unfounded. A suitable candidate was found in the aged Field Marshal von Wrangel, on the basis that his experience of the previous war would come in useful. Born in 1784, Wrangel had taken part in the later stages of the Jena campaign, and in the battle of Leipzig. To his lasting disappointment the dragoon regiment which he was by then commanding took no part in the Waterloo Campaign. By 1823 he had already reached the rank of Major General; in 1848, as a senior corps commander, he was appointed to the command of the Prussian forces in the campaign against Denmark. He was promoted to Field Marshal in 1856. It had been a long and distinguished career, but as Sybel observed, he 'had not, as was soon to be seen, gained with age in breadth of view and keenness of insight, in sureness of judgment, nor in evenness of temper and will.'[17]

These deficiencies were not made good by the selection of General Ernest Vogel von Falckenstein as Wrangel's Chief of Staff, who matched his commander in wilfulness to the point of irresponsibility. He too, born in 1797, was old enough to have taken part in the Wars of Liberation, and in the course of a hard working but unremarkable career also participated in the 1848 campaign in Holstein. In spite of Manteuffel's ruthless pruning of the Prussian officer corps, the upper echelons on the military establishment still contained a number of officers whose quality was debatable. Appointments such as those in the war against Denmark were made largely on the basis of Manteuffel's advice; not for the last time in his career Moltke had relatively little influence on the selection but had to manage the consequences.

To Wrangel's staff was attached the thirty two year old Crown Prince Frederick William, in order that he might gain some first hand military experience. His situation was somewhat equivocal, since he had strongly opposed the action against Denmark, not least because his brother-in-law, the Prince of Wales, was married to Christian IX's daughter Alexandra. His influence was not great, but at least he was a source of sensible comment on events at Headquarters.

Command of the Prussian I Corps was given to the King's nephew Prince Frederick Charles. Still only thirty-six years of age, his military education had been carefully supervised. In 1849, with the rank of Major, he had been wounded in the Baden campaign when on his uncle's staff; during the lengthy period of his recovery he devoted himself to an intensive study of military history. By 1859 he had reached the level of corps commander, and was with good reason regarded as a safe pair of hands. Moltke had a high regard for him; his later career, however, was to show that he generally erred on the side of caution, sometimes with serious consequences. As Chief of Staff he was assigned the able if very egocentric Colonel Karl von Blumenthal, of whom Moltke had the highest opinion. Marooned in Berlin, as he was to be for much of the campaign, Moltke was largely dependent on Blumenthal for information as to its progress, which the latter provided in a series of comprehensive letters. In 1864 Blumenthal was already fifty-four years old; for a long time like many others in the Prussian service his career had moved very slowly, with seventeen years spent in the rank of Second Lieutenant. He was now, however, one of those upon whom Moltke could confidently rely, as the rest of his career was to demonstrate. The I Corps consisted of two infantry divisions, the llth Division commanded by Lieutenant General von Manstein, based in Brandenburg, and the 13th Division by Lieutenant General von Wintzingerode, based in Westphalia. In addition there was a Combined Cavalry Division, led by Major General Count Münster. The corps comprised a total of 24,950 men, with seventeen batteries and ninety-six guns. The rest of the Prussian contingent was designated as the III Corps, consisting of two Guard Brigades and a regiment of Guard Hussars; it was commanded by Lieutenant General von der Mülbe. This force was 10,100 men strong, with two batteries of fourteen guns. The Austrian component of the Allied Army was designated as the II Corps, commanded by Lieutenant Field Marshal von Gablenz; it comprised four infantry brigades and a cavalry brigade, and included six batteries of forty eight guns.[18]

Bismarck owed his success in getting the war he needed to the obstinacy of the Danes in sticking to their position in spite of most of the foreign advice they received to the contrary. As the final rupture approached, the Danish hopes of external assistance gradually melted away. Fleury, Napoleon III's special envoy, made it plain that France had no intention whatsoever of intervening militarily. In St. Petersburg, Gorchakov, who was above all anxious to maintain the solidarity of the other Great Powers against France in the face of Napoleon's call for a Congress to set aside the terms of the Vienna settlement of 1815, strongly advised the Danish Government not to resist. In Britain, despite a fiercely pro-Danish press and public opinion, the attraction of naval intervention by despatching the Channel Fleet to Copenhagen soon began to fade. On January 2 the peace party in the Cabinet gained the upper hand; Palmerston, notwithstanding his previous bombastic statements, was obliged to be privately emphatic in a letter read to the Danish minister in London that Denmark 'mustn't imagine that for its sake England will wage war with the whole of Germany.'[19]

Palmerston's stern warning to the Danes did not reflect any change in his personal views. As recently as December he had expressed these in a letter to Russell:

> Schleswig is no part of Germany, and its invasion by German troops would be an act of war against Denmark, which would in my clear opinion entitle Denmark to our active military and naval support. But you and I could not announce such a determination without the concurrence of the Cabinet and the consent of the Queen.[20]

Apponyi, the Austrian Ambassador, correctly noted Palmerston's frustration:

> The key to the Premier's irritation is his impotence. He senses the fact that the direction of general policy is escaping him and that in the isolation in which he finds himself, unable to count on any of the Great Powers and not even supported by the Queen and the majority of his colleagues, he can undertake nothing.[21]

Finally, and most disappointingly of all for the Danes, the help looked for from Sweden failed to materialise. Although King Charles was still determined to offer military support, his Cabinet, apart from Manderström the Foreign Minister, was firmly opposed to this, unless one of the Great Powers moved first. As the Prussian forces moved forward to Holstein, therefore, the Danes found themselves at the last entirely on their own.

In Berlin the concerns were whether Hanover would order its troops in Holstein to stand aside and let the Allies march unhindered to the Eider. On January 17 Moltke advised the King of the possible strength of Hanoverian opposition to the movement of the 13th Division by rail through Holstein. He reckoned the total strength of the Hanoverian Army to be 26,000 men, of which 7,000 were in Holstein. It would take Wintzingerode two days to enter the city of Hanover where no more than 6,000 men could be concentrated against him: 'if these troops wish to offer an effective resistance, they will be crushed.' Since it would be necessary to occupy all the stations along the line into Holstein, there should be no delay in mobilising the IV Corps to relieve the

General C.J. de Meza, commander of the Danish Army December 1863 until February 28 1864. (Voss)

13th Division as soon as possible. He recognised that no part of the force intended for operations against Denmark should be diverted to deal with any Hanoverian resistance.[22]

In the event no such resistance was forthcoming and the Hanoverian and Saxon troops in Holstein resentfully stood back and made no attempt to interfere with the Allied operations. Hake, the Federal commander there, received an enquiry from Roon as to whether he would now place his troops under Wrangel's command, a suggestion which he indignantly rejected. Even without Federal opposition, Moltke was soon becoming anxious about the speed of the advance; reporting to the Military Cabinet on January 18, he recommended that orders should go to Frederick Charles without delay, pending Wrangel's assumption of the overall command on January 20.[23] Thanks, however, to the efficient and pre-planned use of the railway lines at their disposal, the Allied troops were able to make their way to their concentration points without difficulty and by January 31 were poised to enter Schleswig, the move that marked the formal commencement of hostilities.

Moltke was well informed of the strength of the opposition, which he had outlined in the memorandum of January 13, and which four days later was sent to Wrangel as the basis upon which he should conduct his operations. The Danish Army in Schleswig consisted, he wrote, of 36,500 men. Of these, Gerlach's lst Division, Steinmann's 3rd Division and the 4th Division (of cavalry), commanded by his old friend, Hegermann-Lindencrone, together with the reserve artillery, were concentrated in the Dannewerk position; these accounted for 22,000 men. Du Plat's 2nd Division was in front of them, with a brigade on the right at Freidrichstadt and a brigade on the left, covering Missunde, Eckernförde and the Eider Canal. The rest of the army, comprising a reserve of 5,000 men in seven battalions, was strung out to the North as far as the Jutland frontier.[24] By concentrating all his available troops, including the garrison at Rendsburg, in the

Dannewerk, de Meza, the Danish Commander in Chief, could await attack there with 33,000 men.

In calculating the total Allied strength available to deal with them, Moltke was still at this stage taking into account the 12,900 Hanoverian and Saxon troops, although it should have been already evident that this was an extremely optimistic view.

In the final draft of the plan he produced for the forthcoming campaign Moltke adopted the principles of his memoranda of 1862. The document was intended for Wrangel's guidance in the conduct of the war but it was, unfortunately, as was soon to become apparent, couched only in those terms and not in the form of direct and binding instructions. Before it went to Wrangel, however, it was first to be considered at a high level meeting called by the King on January 20. The meeting produced an immediate and violent dispute between Bismarck and the generals. The Minister President particularly objected to the proposal to occupy the whole of Jutland, a suggestion which he believed would cause the Austrians to take fright; having only four days previously finally coaxed them to sign up to the terms of an effective Austro-Prussian alliance, he wanted to take no risks that they might be alarmed into withdrawing from the joint project. Roon and the King firmly supported Moltke's plan; a campaign in which the German armies were confined to Schleswig would be meaningless and inconclusive, with little prospect of destroying the Danish Army, which would simply withdraw northwards out of harm's way.

Roon was all for pushing the Austrians to the limit, arguing that if they were not to be trusted it would be better to find out sooner rather than later. But Bismarck was adamant. His concern was solely with the diplomatic situation: 'We learnt in 1849 that it is bad to fight one against four; two against three is better.'[25] The dispute was ultimately resolved only by a blunt threat to resign on Bismarck's part, which shocked Roon sufficiently to look about for a compromise. This took the form of simply omitting from the instructions to Wrangel any reference to the possible occupation of Jutland, while stressing the importance of cutting off the enemy's retreat to Düppel if at all possible.[26] The giving of instructions in the form of a bland statement of the military obvious was certainly not an adequate substitute for the firm directions that were necessary to keep a commander as headstrong as Wrangel in check. But the sense of the instructions was, or ought to have been, entirely plain, particularly the stress laid upon turning the Dannewerk from its left by crossing the Schlei before the Danes became alarmed and fell back to the north. In particular Moltke believed that the Danish position around Missunde was too strong for a frontal assault; instead, he proposed to mask it, to develop feint attacks against the Dannewerk, and across the Schlei further East, and head north to Flensburg. However, when Wrangel called a conference of his commanders to decide on the operations to be undertaken, he brushed aside suggestions that it would be unwise to attack the Missunde position directly, and insisted that Frederick Charles launch his corps in a frontal assault. Frederick Charles and Blumenthal tried to talk him out of this, but could do nothing to shift the obstinate Wrangel, and orders went out for the advance into Schleswig to commence on February 3.

7

The Dannewerk

The Dannewerk, for nine hundred years the traditional barrier against invasion from the south, had in recent times been massively strengthened; so much so that Napoleon III, for instance, believed that the Germans might be held up before it for two years. It consisted of three sections. The western end of the position, which began as Friedrichstadt on the North Sea, extended to Hollingstedt. In the central part of the Dannewerk, behind the Rheide Aa, the fortifications extended to Schleswig, while the easternmost position, which was less heavily fortified, reached the Baltic at Eckernförde. In all it comprised seventy forts, strengthened by outworks to the south and also by inundations of the Treene and Rheide Aa. The position was certainly a strong one; but its length was such that it really required more troops to man it than the able commander of the Danish army, Lieutenant General Christian De Meza, had at his disposal for its effective defence. He was reputed to have said that he would be confident of holding it with 100,000 men; as it was he would only have about a third of this number immediately available.

Much of the terrain over which an invader must pass was very unfavourable, as a result of which the Danes were able to concentrate the bulk of their forces in the centre of the position. Another advantage enjoyed by the Danes was their command of the sea, which had proved so crucial in 1848-50. These two factors went some way to offset the numerical superiority of the Allies. The Danish army itself, if lacking in basic training and short of junior officers, was composed of first class troops upon whose courage and dependability their competent leaders could rely with confidence. Its peacetime strength was as low as 7,500, but the calling up of the reserves of trained troops could produce an additional 54,000 men.

However, at sea, the infant Prussian Navy, although very small, proved sufficiently active to occupy the attention of a large part of the Danish fleet, while the potential arrival of the Austrian Fleet would challenge Danish maritime supremacy. The weather, too, was on the side of the big battalions; the depth of ice over the marshes in the west made them partially at any rate able to bear the passage of troops, to some extent depriving the Danes of one of the advantages on which they counted. The optimism with which they went to war, remembering the victory of 1848-50 rather than the underlying reasons for it, led them into error in investing so heavily in strengthening the Dannewerk; it had been their strong flank positions of Düppel and Fredericia, coupled with command of the sea, which had been decisive. But their fundamental aim, to prolong the war as long as possible, was obviously correct; only thus could they hope for foreign intervention, either militarily or diplomatically.

On February 1 the Allies crossed the Eider at various points between Kiel and Rendsburg, meeting little or no opposition from the Danish outposts apart from a brief skirmish at Eckernförde when the advancing Prussian troops got closer to the retreating Danes than intended. In the town, the Prussian troops received an enthusiastic welcome.

General G.D. Gerlach, commander of the Danish Army February 29-July 1864. (Voss)

Next day, in raw cold weather, the Prussians pushed on towards the fortifications at Missunde, occupied by the Danish 1st Division under General Gerlach. With his artillery in place, Frederick Charles bombarded the position for three hours with seventy-eight guns; neither side was able to get any very clear idea as to its effect. The keenness of the leading Prussian infantry brought them into contact with the enemy, and a brisk skirmish developed in the course of which the Prussians lost 33 men killed and 187 men wounded, the Danes losing 38 dead and 103 wounded.[1] Nothing at all had been achieved, except to show de Meza the strength of the movement on his left, and Frederick Charles had no hesitation in breaking off the action. Unknown to him, a spectator on the Danish side of these events was King Christian IX. He was accompanied by Monrad, now his Prime Minister, and had come down to visit the Danish army in its defence of Schleswig. He was no doubt cheered by what he had seen, and went off next day to visit de Meza.

This inconclusive outcome was, of course, exactly what Blumenthal and Frederick Charles had expected, and it emboldened the former to try again to obtain some sensible instructions from Wrangel. This he attempted on February 3, with no success, and the I Corps remained in position before Missunde. At this point, however, Edwin von Manteuffel arrived at the corps headquarters, and Blumenthal prevailed on him to go to Wrangel and to persuade that stubborn octogenarian to change his mind and allow a crossing further down the Schlei, at Arnis or Kappeln where Moltke had originally intended the crossing to be made. Manteuffel was successful; Wrangel at last relented, and fresh orders were issued on the night of February 4 which might give some chance that Moltke's original conception could be realised:

> The serious attack on the Dannewerk is not to take place before a report has been received that the I Corps has succeeded in crossing the Schlei and that they have advanced as far as Missunde, which will probably not take place until the afternoon of February 6.[2]

The orders went on to deal with the possibility of Danish attacks from either Missunde or Schleswig, or alternatively a retreat from the Dannewerk. In the light of this, the Austrian brigades of Gondrecourt and Nostitz were to deploy on as broad a front as possible. Wrangel now had a total of thirty-five battalions, with fourteen squadrons and seventy-four guns, in front of the Danish positions, while Frederick Charles prepared to move against their flank and rear with twenty-four battalions, twenty-one squadrons and ninety guns. This was more like it; if de Meza stayed where he was, and the Prussians moved quickly across the Schlei, Moltke's plan might after all come off.

On February 5, in a heavy snowstorm, Frederick Charles' corps moved to its right, passing with great difficulty over the icy roads towards Arnis. During the evening of that day he called his senior commanders together to give oral instructions for the crossing of the Schlei. Manteuffel attended this briefing, during which plans for the crossing of the Schlei were confirmed; it was expected that it would be fiercely opposed. Once across the river, the corps cavalry, ten squadron strong, was to push on north towards Rendsburg. During the day Blumenthal had again personally reconnoitred the crossing points, 'and had found conditions for the success of the enterprise very favourable.'[3] At midnight, however, it was clear that the Danes were pulling back from the line of the Schlei; Röder's Brigade and the advanced guard began to cross in boats and on the following morning a pontoon bridge was thrown across the river, over which the rest of the corps advanced. Pursuing the Danes northward, the corps was, however, unable to make any contact at all with the enemy.

To the west the Austrians with the Prussian Guard Battalion had encountered stiffer opposition. The traveller and writer Laurence Oliphant, who had accompanied the Prince of Augustenburg to Holstein, and who had at first moved with the Prussian troops in front of Missunde, had on February 3 set off to join the Austrian forces, where more action was to be expected. He came upon Gondrecourt leading his brigade to the

The Battle of Missunde, February 2 1864. (Voss)

front, which gave him a good opportunity to compare the Austrian troops with the Prussian troops which he had accompanied the previous day:

> The difference was sufficiently marked. The youthful light-hearted Prussian seemed to go into action as a new experience, but did not inspire much confidence in his steadiness; the Austrian, on the other hand, worn and rugged, often brutalised in expression, plodded on like a machine. The Prussian looked intelligent enough to understand the Schleswig Holstein question; the Austrian looked as if brandy and tobacco constituted the sum total of his ideas; but he was every inch a "professional", the others looked like amateurs.[4]

South of the Dannewerk the Danes took up a strong position at Oberselk; driven back after a stiff fight by a bayonet charge, they retreated to the Königshügel, a hill within range of the Dannewerk's artillery. The Austrians again attacked and notwithstanding considerable losses, stormed the position, supported by Prussian artillery. To the west von der Mülbe's leading troops met strong opposition at Jagel, which they overcame with an immediate attack. Losses in these exchanges were not inconsiderable, the Allies losing 430 dead and wounded and the Danes 413.[5]

Christian IX and Monrad had set off back to Copenhagen reasonably encouraged by what they had seen; de Meza, however, was by no means as sanguine as he seems to have appeared. It was becoming clear to him that to remain on the Dannewerk was to remain in precisely the trap that Moltke intended. The frost which deprived him of the protection of the inundations, the considerable effect on his raw troops of the Allied artillery, and the inevitable crossing by Frederick Charles of the Schlei all convinced him by nightfall on February 4 that he must retreat, notwithstanding the political consequences. With a heavy heart, he that evening convened a Council of War. The issue was straightforward, as Sybel described it:

> The Council of War recognised the fact that the organisation and training of the troops were by no means what is required in a well prepared army. The prospect was therefore not very favourable either for defensive or offensive action; and nothing remained but to evacuate the Dannewerk immediately, in order to preserve for Denmark the army and with it the possibility of continuing the struggle, as well as to gain time for the friendly Foreign Powers to interfere. The whole Council, with the exception of General von Lüttichau, adopted this view.[6]

During the night of February 5/6 the retreat, unobserved by the Allied troops, began in bitter weather. By midnight the works were untenanted save for the fixed artillery, which was abandoned. In a heavy snow storm the infantry trudged north along the icy roads. The speed of the retreat took the Allies entirely by surprise; first news of the withdrawal was received with incredulity, both by the leading units and then by Headquarters. When Waldeck, commanding the Austrian advanced guard, sent a report to Gablenz, to the effect that he was in Schleswig, the Austrian commander turned to his staff and cried: 'What a pity! Waldeck has gone mad!'[7] The Austrian official historian, reviewing de Meza's decision to pull out of the Dannewerk, was at some pains to assert that it was a concern with the strength of the enemy in his immediate front that was his principal reason. 'The bulk of the Prussian Corps given the task of outflanking the enemy began to move towards the lower Schlei only once the withdrawal of the Danes had been decided.'[8] While literally true, this statement ignores the fact that the Allied intention to cross the Schlei had already been apparent.

The hardships endured by the Danes in their retreat were graphically described by Antonio Gallenga, the *Times* correspondent:

> The snow thickened and hardened on the ground; the road became smooth and as bright as glass; horses and men slipped dreadfully and fell at almost every step… It was not long before our march began to exhibit, on a small scale, some of the horrors of the famous retreat of the French from Moscow.[9]

It took nine hours to cover the first seven miles, but the need to get as far as they could from their possible pursuers kept the Danes moving, and the bulk of the army reached Rendsburg, twenty-two miles north, after a march of eighteen hours. There was a brisk rear guard action at Sankelmark, in which Brigade Muller, attacked by Austrian cavalry, suffered heavy casualties. However, by the end of the second day the retreat reached Gravenstein, in spite of chaotic traffic conditions on the roads; fortunately the Danes had got well clear of their pursuers and by nightfall on February 7 the divisions of Gerlach, du Plat and Steinmann were safely in the lines of Düppel, while the cavalry of Hegermann-Lindencrone's 4th Division, accompanied by some infantry, were retreating north to Jutland and had reached Apenrade.

On each side the retreat from the Dannewerk was greeted with dismay. For the Allies it meant that Wrangel's obstinate incompetence had cost them the chance of a quick end to the fighting, which Moltke had planned. Blumenthal, in a letter to Moltke, expressed his disgust:

> There are but few men, indeed, who can execute a simple plan in a simple way. The Danish army does us the kindness of so placing itself that by making a detour we can bring it into the greatest possible embarrassment; instead of this, we run so violently at their strongest position and produce such terror there, that an early opportunity is taken by them to sound a retreat. The Danes on February 4 were wiser than we; we made our detour two days too late.[10]

Much more violent was the Danish reaction. Having been confident of the supposedly impregnable strength of the Dannewerk, the public reaction to its abandonment was one of furious indignation, and Copenhagen was plunged into political turmoil. Dotézac, the French Ambassador, reported on the events that followed Monrad's return to the capital:

> He was wise enough to quit the train at the station before the terminus and drive to the capital in a carriage which was awaiting him. The King's return had also been announced and his baggage had already arrived, but a telegram from the Queen warned him that the loss of the Dannewerk could not fail to provoke riots in Copenhagen. He halted, therefore, in Sønderborg. The nation's grief and

indignation were extreme, especially the old officers'. Hardly a dry eye was to be seen.[11]

In the course of the stormy Cabinet meeting that followed Monrad's return, Lundbye, the War Minister, was especially loud in his denunciation of de Meza. However, Monrad had almost succeeded in pacifying his angry colleagues when Lundbye precipitated a crisis by threatening to resign if de Meza was not at once sent for to come to Copenhagen to explain himself. Monrad could resist no longer; de Meza was recalled and Lüttichau, the Commander of the artillery, temporarily put in command of the army. It was an ill reward for a capable general who had by his brave decision saved the only army that Denmark had.

The unexpectedly early fall of the Dannewerk aroused immediate international reaction. Napoleon found that his hope that Prussia's involvement in the war would cause a breach with Austria had been disappointed; while in London Palmerston was greatly shocked by the news. Although privately now very doubtful that Britain would go to war over the Duchies, he offered as a substitute some characteristically violent language, telling Bernstorff, the Prussian Ambassador, that Prussia's action was the most unjust aggression and most outrageous action known to history and that 'in the spring England would not fail to assist the Danes.'[12] While the news was enthusiastically received by the German public the governments of the lesser states were dismayed by the open discussion of the possible annexation of the Duchies, and contemplated ways in which the Augustenburg claim might be supported. One consequence was that Wrangel began to encounter difficulties with the Confederation troops in Holstein who, it was said, refused quarters to the Allied troops, delayed supplies and hampered telegraphic communication. In response to Bismarck's demands, through his envoy at Frankfurt, an instruction to cease this conduct was sent to Hake, the commander of the Confederation force. Bismarck next insisted that key communication centres such as Rendsburg, Neumünster, Kiel and Altona must be occupied by Prussian troops. When these arrived Hake refused to admit them; Wrangel sent them in anyway, provoking a further outcry in Frankfurt.

Militarily, the position which had now developed had been exactly what Moltke had foreseen, if the Allies had failed to pin down and destroy the Danish army on the Dannewerk. The Danes were now securely entrenched in what was known to be a strong fortified position at Düppel, and Moltke was still firmly of the view that a frontal assault there would occasion quite unjustifiable losses. It was an opinion shared by Wrangel and his staff and senior commanders, who preferred the course, always advocated by Moltke, of overrunning the whole of northern Schleswig and Jutland. In making this the basis of his strategic plan, Moltke believed that this was the only way of bringing effective pressure to bear on the Danish Government. Not surprisingly the suggestion caused considerable unease in Berlin in the light of the possible political consequences, and on February 11 Moltke was ordered by the King to visit the front and report back as to the future conduct of operations.

Wrangel was already beginning to exhibit signs of extreme irritability, and his anger was particularly aroused by what he saw as improper political interference with his freedom of action. At Allied Headquarters the Crown Prince recorded in his diary on

February 9 that 'at certain moments Wrangel is really half foolish, and the energy and vigour with which he was once filled shows itself now only in stubbornness and vanity.'[13]

Moltke set off on his mission at once, reaching Flensburg on February 12 after an exhausting journey. From there he wrote to Mary:

> Fearfully slow journey from Rendsburg. Ten times delayed, wind and snow storms, so heavy that there was danger of our being snowed up; hungry, completely frozen, without any place to shelter, I wandered about with Wartensleben for over an hour in a frightful snow storm, combined with thaw, from inn to inn with all our baggage. Every place was full.[14]

Eventually, he found some quarters and went to pay his respects to Wrangel and his headquarters staff.

Next day he received a letter from Roon asking his advice as to the steps to be taken to make sure the conquered territory could be securely held. In his reply of February 16 from Apenrade, Moltke recommended that the fortifications of the Dannewerk be immediately razed. As to the crucially important fortress of Rendsburg, he had sent for the archive material on the existing fortifications in order to review what further work was needed. Friedrichstadt, at the western end of the Dannewerk was, he considered, in its existing state perfectly defensible even against an attack from the north; little was needed to be done there. At the other end of the line he regarded the small fortress of Friedrichsort as essential to the protection of Kiel and its important harbour; he recommended the placing of a battery of twenty-four guns there, and construction of two outlying works. Rendsburg created greater difficulty; where to locate a fortified line must depend on the outcome of the campaign, although he favoured a position at Blau.[15]

Two days later Moltke made his first acquaintance with the redoubtable armoured turret ship *Rolf Krake* which was to prove a thorn in the side of the Prussian troops attacking Düppel. He had gone from Rendsburg to Holnis where artillery exchanges had been reported, but arrived after the firing had died down. At 8.30am, however, the *Rolf Krake* appeared; the German batteries allowed her to approach within two thousand yards before opening fire. Moltke described the action in a report to Wrangel:

> This vessel…lay in the water almost to the water line. I saw no one on deck. Suddenly it got up steam and moved towards the battery and fired six or eight shots. One shell fell just in front of the battery on the slope where it was stationed; another fell nearby without exploding. Although several projectiles from the battery hit the vessel, they had no effect.[16]

Moltke remained at the scene as the engagement continued. A large warship, which he thought was probably not an ironclad, joined the *Rolf Krake*, but kept well out of range; the *Rolf Krake* itself continued to endure the fire of the batteries, until perhaps sixty or eighty shots had been fired.

Moltke, after visiting Prince Frederick Charles at his headquarters at Gravenstein, some six miles from the lines of Düppel, returned to Berlin, where he found that there was consternation about Wrangel's latest move. On February 14 Wrangel had written to the effect that, unless he received orders to the contrary, he proposed to commence an invasion of Jutland on February 17. Bismarck reacted promptly, telegraphing explicit instructions to Wrangel not to cross into Jutland until further orders, coupled with the request that he take no further political decisions concerning Holstein without consultation with Bismarck. Clearly, however, the present situation was untenable, and it would lead Manteuffel, currently visiting Dresden and Hanover in order to calm the injured feelings there, to go to Vienna, to reach agreement as to future conduct of the campaign. It was a wise move; Gablenz had already received orders directly from Vienna that he was not on any account to take part in an invasion of Jutland, while Franz Joseph wrote personally to William to express his concern.

On the ground, however, events were moving faster than the political processes. Both Gablenz and von der Mülbe had been moved up towards the Jutland border. On February 18 a unit of Guard Hussars from von der Mülbe's III Corps had clashed with a Danish force near Kolding and in following up the retreating enemy had occupied that town. This was a clear breach of the instructions received by Wrangel, who seemed not to have passed on the order, and Bismarck was furious; his hand had been forced since he could not order the troops in Kolding to retreat without disclosing the policy differences between Berlin and Vienna. Von der Mülbe was, however, ordered to halt at Kolding, and Bismarck returned to the task of persuading his jittery Allies to agree to an advance into Jutland. A further explicit order was sent to Wrangel expressly prohibiting any further advance. Bismarck had by now come around to Moltke's way of thinking; the occupation of Jutland was militarily correct, and he was quite prepared to face international outrage so long as he had Austria firmly in tow. Only then could Wrangel be let off the leash or, as he put it to Roon, could he give 'the old baby new boots to paddle in the water with.'[17] To Werther, in Vienna, Bismarck wrote on February 16 that 'the storming of Düppel and the crossing to Alsen would involve enormous sacrifices. Why make them, if we can gain the same results by a pressure put to bear upon Jutland?'[18]

When on February 19 Wrangel got the latest order, he was beside himself with rage. He at once fired off a lengthy personal telegram of protest to the King, containing what Bismarck later described as 'the coarsest insults' against him. In the course of this communication in which he said that he awaited with 'reverent expectation' further instructions to resume his advance, he told the King:

> To recall the Prussians from their career of victory is quite impossible for me, for the curse of the fatherland would strike even my grandchildren. The diplomats may counsel such a thing, but they may be sure that their name will be affixed to the gallows.[19]

Bismarck had had more than enough of Wrangel's erratic and insubordinate behaviour, and it took him a long time to put this latest affront to one side.

While the decision about an advance northward hung in the balance, Frederick Charles had in the meantime taken a step that was in due course to prove of vital significance. On February 18 he seized the Broagerland peninsula, the northern shore of which looks across the Wemmingbund to the Düppel position. From Gammelmark, the Danish forts were well within range of modern rifled guns, as had not been the case in 1852. The establishment of batteries there meant that the Düppel forts could now be enfiladed by the German artillery, significantly weakening their ability to resist an assault if one were mounted.

Back in Berlin Moltke had for the time being still to endure the frustration of watching from the sidelines. With no formal responsibility for the conduct or future planning of the campaign, he was not always kept fully informed of its detailed progress. He still had, however, one reliable source of intelligence in the form of his regular correspondence with Blumenthal. And Moltke's indirect influence was considerable; he enjoyed regular access to the King, and to Roon, to each of whom he gave frequent advice as to the strategy to be pursued. In the course of this he did not hesitate to address some of the key political issues arising from the developing situation.

In his letter to Blumenthal of February 21, Moltke dealt with some of the most pressing questions. After reviewing the course of operations thus far, he commented on the current view prevailing at Allied headquarters:

> As to what is happening now, the idea dominating the headquarters staff, absolutely correctly from the military point of view, is to occupy Jutland while observing Fredericia and Düppel. This conquest could be completed before the end of the month, if it were not for obstacles. The halt previously ordered decided me to return here, my special mission having ended. But, in the meantime, the frontier has been crossed, and the measures taken here have only been such as most carefully to meet our confederate's scruples... If insurmountable political difficulties prevent an

Prussian troops on the march in Schleswig-Holstein, February 1864. (Voss)

> invasion of Jutland, it will then only remain, certainly, for us to concern ourselves seriously with Düppel.[20]

As he had told Blumenthal, Moltke had returned to the capital as a result of the stop order issued to Wrangel, and on February 27 he set out in a memorandum to the King in very strong terms the reasons why Kolding could not be given up. It would expose the embarrassing policy split between the Allies, while the possession of the town was necessary to cover the troops echeloned to the south. He went on to deal with the question of what should happen next:

> As for the ultimate occupation of Jutland, this measure is from the military viewpoint the most correct of all. The capture of the fortified position of Düppel cannot, unless there is a complete collapse of the morale of the Danish Army, be achieved without a siege of several weeks. On the other hand, we can overrun Jutland within a few days, merely observing Fredericia.[21]

It was in Jutland, he suggested, that compensation could be obtained for all the losses sustained by Prussia as a result of the Danish blockade of its ports.

Meanwhile Manteuffel had concluded his visits to Saxony and Hanover and had succeeded in winning over those states so that a confrontation with their troops had been avoided. A more demanding task now faced him in Vienna. Prussian policy was now urgently to put some backbone into her reluctant ally, and both William's letter of February 21 to Franz Joseph and Bismarck's instructions to Manteuffel were couched in militant terms. To Franz Joseph, William wrote:

> Our policy would be abortive if we did not follow it out to a satisfactory conclusion. I place great value upon England's friendship; but do not believe that England or any other Power will find it in their interest to attack us, so long as we remain united. And even if the danger lay nearer than is in my opinion the case, there are still circumstances in which I do not think it would be possible to yield to the fear of it. Therefore, I believe that nothing could be more likely to make this danger imminent than such conduct on our part as would betray any anxiety about it.[22]

In the brief to Manteuffel, Bismarck was emphatic:

> The occupation of Jutland is indispensable as reprisal for the capture of German ships and the blockade of our ports, which must be expected; and it is very clear that we cannot take such reprisals in Schleswig. We owe it to public opinion in the army and among the people to carry out our programme resolutely and completely, to assert our power and influence in Germany, and not to yield to any direct attacks from the Lesser States.[23]

Bismarck was now entirely of one view with Moltke as to the strategy to be adopted, and was feeling confident enough to tackle the issue head on. Nor was he willing to pay too high a price for Austrian acquiescence; Manteuffel was privately instructed to keep off the subject of any permanent alliance between the two countries if he possibly could, and to be extremely circumspect if Rechberg brought the subject up. In this Bismarck may have had in mind the willingness of the Prussian military to contemplate a guarantee of Venetia in exchange for Austrian support, an idea which had been around for sometime. In 1861, for instance, when the suggestion had been raised in the course of military discussions over the reform of the Confederation's army, Moltke had irritably observed after the failure of these talks: 'If people would only leave military-political matters to regulation by a few clever and reliable officers, without diplomats, they would get together to everyone's satisfaction.'[24]

Manteuffel was personally well received in Vienna, but it soon became apparent that the Austrians were beginning to repent of their adventure in Schleswig-Holstein, raising all kinds of difficulties. Both diplomatic and military objections were put forward to an actual advance out of Schleswig; the occupation of disputed territory was one thing, but a formal invasion of Denmark proper was quite another. General Hess claimed that the advance to the north was strategically unsound, extending too far the lines of communication and exposing the armies to the risk of Danish counter-attacks.

All the Austrian objections were embodied in the lengthy memorandum written by General Huyn, which was put before Moltke for comment. He had little difficulty in disposing of Huyn's arguments, both in a report to Roon of February 28 and in the letter he wrote to Blumenthal on the same day. To Roon, he pointed out that the Danes had some 34,000 men in the field, of which no more than 27,000 would be available to launch a counter offensive from Fredericia or Düppel. There were presently 29,500 Allied troops in front of Düppel while at Kolding, facing Fredericia, there were 31,000, more than enough to deal with any Danish counter-attack. The only alternative to the conquest of Jutland was a frontal attack on Düppel, the difficulties of which he did not need to repeat. As for Huyn's suggestion that they had faced a still tougher task in front of the Dannewerk he retorted:

> This is true, and we would have been held up there if we had not turned the position. But Düppel cannot be turned. If the cabinet in Vienna could not be persuaded to agree to the invasion of Jutland, then the siege guns must be mobilised and sent to the front; it would take fifteen days to assemble the siege guns and other materiel.[25]

To Blumenthal, Moltke repeated these arguments, and dismissed Huyn's views still more contemptuously:

> It is a pure masterpiece of staff pedantry. The temporary occupation of Schleswig is presented as the object of the war, where it is only a means to force Denmark to accept certain conditions relating to the Duchies, the means that have obviously proved insufficient. On this false base has been erected an enormous strategic dissertation throwing light on what has never been in dispute, that the Danes as masters of the sea can concentrate their forces at Düppel or Fredericia in order to take the offensive against us.[26]

Moltke went on to review the course to be followed if the Prussians were obliged to attack Düppel. He favoured an attack on the south end of the line of forts; an attack at the other end, on Fort No. 10, could be taken in flank. Moltke ended his letter by repeating his hope that these considerations would prove academic. 'Please God, however, that we can exchange Alsen for Jutland. Meanwhile, I will be very happy if you would continue to keep me informed confidentially.'[27]

In Vienna, Manteuffel had his work cut out to make any impression on his timid and half-hearted Austrian colleagues, who were fearful of the possible reaction in Paris and London, but he kept at the task. After five days of talks, since nothing much seemed after all to be materialising from the Western Powers, Manteuffel's persuasive arguments for an invasion of Jutland finally won the day. By February 29 not only Rechberg but also Franz Joseph accepted the position and next day the deal was struck; Düppel and Alsen were still to be treated as the principal military objective, but Wrangel was to be allowed over the border to prevent Danish interference with these operations. Assurances would be given to the Great Powers that the proposed operation changed nothing in the Austro-Prussian policy, and that a conference or an armistice would still be accepted on appropriate terms. Perhaps the most important term of the agreement, however, was the provision that since the outbreak of war had rendered the Treaty of London null and void, the two Powers would reach an understanding in the future as to the position of the Duchies within the Danish monarchy – a provision intended to block the Augustenburg claim. The agreement arrived at Berlin for signature on March 6, although not before Wrangel had nearly scuppered it by a further breach of his instructions by permitting a body of troops to move north from Kolding. Bismarck was understandably furious, and at his request Roon sent Wrangel a strong rebuke for an action which was

> contrary to the very precise royal orders, on the exact observation of which the Ministry of Foreign Affairs bases its statements to foreign cabinets… Under different circumstances, and in order to direct our foreign affairs safely and without the appearance of ambiguity, I must consider it absolutely imperative that the renewal of such steps be prevented by resolute measures.[28]

In anticipation of Austrian agreement to an advance into Jutland, Moltke prepared on March 4 a draft of the instructions to be given to Wrangel. Allowing for Danish mastery of the sea, he reckoned that no more than 20,000 to 25,000 men would be available to them to launch a counter-attack, unless they abandoned Fredericia or Alsen completely. They might attempt a combined operation against the north German ports, or against the eastern coast of Schleswig-Holstein, but this would not affect the outcome of the campaign. He calculated that even if it was felt necessary to leave one brigade in Holstein, there would be 38,000 Allied troops available to overrun Jutland. Of these 20,000 to 25,000 would cover Fredericia, which in the absence of the necessary artillery and other material should not be seriously attacked. That would leave 10,000 to 15,000 troops to conquer the rest of Jutland, where they would at most face Hegermann's 4th Division, unless that also retreated into the lines of Fredericia. He was confident that he could resist any counter-attack:

> In case of the unexpected appearance of Danish forces, either from Fredericia or Düppel, although the forces in the rest of Jutland would arrive too late, the detachments in front of these places would be strong enough to deal with the enemy.

If, when siege artillery arrived, an assault was launched on Düppel, this would have the effect of preventing a Danish offensive from that position.[29]

On the same day Moltke wrote to Blumenthal, to bring him up to date with international developments and their effect on thinking in Berlin. He was still sorry that it was necessary for Frederick Charles and his corps to be pinned down at Düppel, and asked Blumenthal to tell the Prince how much he regretted

> not to see him at the head of the expedition into Jutland instead of being in charge of such a difficult and thankless task as an artillery assault on Düppel. But this attack is considered in high places as an inevitable necessity.[30]

Once political sanction had been obtained, the advance into Jutland began at once, von der Mülbe's III Corps heading for Fredericia, led by units of Prussian Guard at William's express request. The advance was supported by Gablenz, whose II Corps moved on to Veile where after a brief action he compelled Hegermann's 4th Division there to retreat. Composed largely of mounted troops, the Danish forces slipped away to the north, and Gablenz lost touch with them. Meanwhile on March 19 von der Mülbe advanced on the immensely strong Danish position at Fredericia. Next day the German artillery commenced a heavy bombardment; but, lacking siege guns, it was soon clear that it would be ineffective. The obvious difficulty of launching an immediate assault, and the need for all available siege artillery, when it arrived, to go to Düppel, led to the decision that von der Mülbe should go back to reinforce Frederick Charles, leaving Gablenz to mask the fortress of Fredericia.

8

Düppel

As early as March 4 Moltke had gloomily accepted the inevitability of an assault on the Düppel position, but at Allied headquarters the mood was still highly unfavourable; it was regarded as an unnecessary and potentially very expensive operation. Wrangel had got himself into more hot water by interfering in civil administration in the Duchies, and William was finally obliged to clip his wings by directing him to make no disposition without first consulting the Crown Prince.[1] It was, however, the Düppel issue which principally occupied Wrangel, who had pointed out to William that bringing up siege artillery would take a long time and that in any case 'the conquest of that little corner of earth would be of no real gain.'[2] This view was shared by Frederick Charles, who grumbled to the King about the projected assault: 'Is it supposed to be a political necessity to take the bulwarks? It will cost a lot of men and money. I don't see the military necessity.'[3]

Blumenthal shared this view, and determined to do something more than protest. In a letter of March 4 he put before Moltke a plan for a seaborne assault on the island of Alsen from Ballegaard. Moltke's response was immediate; the project deserved, he said, mature consideration. There were, as he pointed out in his reply of March 8, a number of conditions precedent which must be fulfilled before launching such an operation. It would require careful consideration; if it was to go ahead soon it would have to be without the siege artillery; and above all the cooperation of the navy was essential. The *Rolf Krake* was a serious threat; by itself it could bring the assault to an end before half of the troops had crossed over. The key to all the operations was the artillery, and Moltke regretted a press leak on the subject:

> It is unfortunate that today's newspapers have spoken of your observation post at Broager. As for the batteries at this point, I hope that they will not only interdict the Wemmingbund, but that they will also inflict heavy losses on the large bodies of troops that must, immediately after an attack, be established behind the entrenchments.[4]

Frederick Charles, to whom Blumenthal submitted his plans, was at first dubious because of the risks entailed, but gradually became more enthusiastic, embracing the chance of avoiding any costly assault on the Düppel forts; and on March 10 he put forward a plan for approval.

In Berlin, Moltke shared the view of the commanders on the ground as to the unwisdom of a direct assault on Düppel; but he was very much a lone voice there. The King, Bismarck, Roon and Manteuffel were determined on an attack; and Manteuffel pointed out bluntly to Frederick Charles their views:

> If your Royal Highness goes on demanding more weapons, if you go on postponing the attack, then doubts will arise in people's minds concerning your Royal Highness's determination; and I should not desire, for the sake of the army and of the person of your Royal Highness and of the hope which I place in it, that an armistice should be concluded while our troops were still standing *in front of* Düppel. This is a matter markedly not of the importance of the position, not of the question whether it can be held without Alsen, whether Alsen should be captured, whether without Alsen's capture the taking of Düppel is not worthless – this is a matter of the renown of the Prussian army and the position of the King in the councils of Europe. The prize is worth streams of blood, and for its sake that blood will be spilled with joy by everyone from the highest officer down to the drummer boy.[5]

Manteuffel was dismissive of the plan to cross to Alsen, telling Roon that it would be vulnerable both to weather and to the Danish fleet. To make sure that the views held in Berlin were firmly understood, Manteuffel was sent off to Frederick Charles' headquarters.

On March 14 Moltke had a meeting with the King and Roon, at which he put forward his initial thoughts on an assault on Düppel; he was at pains to stress that there should be no interference with the conduct of the operation. He was still unenthusiastic:

> The attack on Düppel having been prescribed, this intention having been openly confirmed by the despatch of siege artillery, and Prince Frederick Charles having received the resources he has requested, the attack must now be carried out. It is the Prince upon whom falls all responsibility for its execution, and from now on he must be given the full freedom of action.

Moltke went on to consider the proposal to cross to Alsen, which, without the cooperation of the fleet, he did not consider practicable. Prince Adalbert, the commander of the fleet, had considered that it was impossible for it to operate effectively at Alsen; on the other hand, it might be able to do so elsewhere, a reference to a landing on Fünen, which Moltke preferred:

> This operation would provide an effective diversion for Düppel and will be, so far as Denmark is concerned, the most effective means of coercion that could be employed. In any case, the commander of the fleet must be heard on the subject of the plan submitted by Prince Frederick Charles.[6]

Prussia's relative weakness at sea was always of concern to Moltke in the operations against Denmark, but it so happened that a brilliantly successful operation on March 16 suggested that perhaps the dangers of a seaborne landing had been overstated. A battalion of Prussian troops had succeeded in landing on the island of Fehmarn off the Holstein coast after rowing across for a mile during the night and in the middle of a storm; once ashore they quickly overran the island, taking the whole garrison prisoner. Next day another episode suggested that perhaps the power of the Danish fleet had also been overrated, or that its leaders were not disposed to handle it as boldly as in the previous war. On March 17 a naval action was fought off Rügen, which was a source of great inspiration to the infant German navy. Jachmann, the commander of a small Prussian force consisting of the two screw corvettes *Arcona* and *Nymphe* and the paddle wheeled despatch boat *Lorelei*, had a strong conviction of German naval potential, and was prepared to act boldly to demonstrate it. He sailed from Swinemünde to investigate the activities of the Danish fleet of six ships under Rear Admiral Dockum, which was operating off Rügen. Jachmann could oppose only forty-three guns to the one hundred and eighty three guns of the Danes. Nonetheless he closed to attack the Danish fleet and after a brisk but indecisive engagement which lasted for two hours had the satisfaction of being able to break off the action without losing any ships. He had gained a valuable moral advantage, which encouraged the Prussian high command to believe that the defence of the Baltic coast against the vastly superior Danish fleet was not, after all, as impossible as had appeared. It was, of course, in military terms an engagement of trifling significance; and the lavish praise accorded to it by the German press was the subject of particular derision on the part of British diplomats in Berlin.

In the days following the final decision to launch an assault on Düppel, and also to attempt a seaborne landing on Alsen, an operation that was finally approved on March 25, Moltke was kept extremely busy. He produced detailed papers on the proposed crossing to Alsen, and the alternative option of a descent on Fünen, for the King's consideration. In the first of these, he concluded that in spite of the serious risks involved in the crossing to Alsen,

> during the course of the siege, the removal for instance of all the war ships from the Alsen Sund, the transports available at Apenrade, the demoralisation caused to the enemy and finally all other fortunate circumstances, make possible this operation, which will always be dangerous.[7]

William sent a copy of his paper to Frederick Charles; evidently mindful of Moltke's insistence that the Prince should be given a free hand, he included a slightly apologetic passage explaining why so much advice and explanation was being offered. 'If we thus do not send you any orders prescribing the manner in which you must operate, we must, however, explain our views, which you must take account of if circumstances permit their application.'

Moltke's second paper, of March 16, set out in some detail the possibilities of a landing on Fünen, which he believed would provide the most effective pressure on Denmark if the occupation of Jutland and the attack on Düppel did not do the trick. It was, of course, an option which might involve further lengthy and wearisome negotiations with the Austrians, since it was outside the agreed terms of reference for the campaign. But it would take the Danes by surprise, and it was an operation in which the cooperation of the Prussian navy could be counted on. The Danish forces in the island could not be, Moltke reckoned, more than 7,000 strong.[8]

Meanwhile he continued to offer advice and support to Blumenthal. As for Alsen, he explained on March 17 that it was not going to be possible to despatch the navy to an area in which it must encounter the bulk of the Danish fleet. Negotiations to strengthen the Prussian navy by purchase had, he told Blumenthal, been unfortunately managed, and it was going to be necessary to accept the help of the Austrian navy. Even without the fleet, however, he hoped that the project would not be abandoned. On the subject of Düppel, he made plain his continuing reservations:

> Any sensible soldier must see that one cannot hope for an immediate solution before Düppel and that it must take time; have no concern about this. I would like also to believe that the Prince will not be given too narrow instructions. One cannot respond positively to the boldest hopes, and a good rider does not attempt, even on his best horse, a jump that will break its back. Our troops will certainly show what they are capable of, but it is necessary that the assault is properly prepared.[9]

Moltke also kept in close touch with Prince Adalbert, discussing with him not only the arrangements for the landing on Alsen, but also the prospects of his own scheme for an assault on Fünen. To Roon he confirmed that, even without the fleet, the Alsen operation would proceed; but the presence of Prussian war ships for no more than six hours would make a crucial difference to the chances of success. To Blumenthal, he sent reassurance on March 21:

> Most people now clearly understand that a premature assault, insufficiently prepared [should not be undertaken] in spite of the most pressing hints. I have told the King, the War Minister and General von Manteuffel that …it would be unjustifiable not to wait for the artillery, still on its way, and this has had effect.[10]

Writing on March 22 to his nephew Henry, who was serving with the troops in front of Düppel, Moltke was naturally more encouraging:

> The service may be fatiguing, but the greatest vigilance is requisite at this juncture, for the position of affairs prompts the Danes to act at once on the offensive. If once their line is broken the game is up; but it will last a few days longer. All the batteries have not yet been brought up, and we must wait to see what effect they have before proceeding to storm the place. Düppel must be taken; and it will be, by one way or the other; it cannot hold out much longer.[11]

Moltke was still deeply anxious about the attack on Alsen and he wrote regularly to Blumenthal with suggestions as to ways in which the operation might be carried out. On March 27 he wondered whether the establishment of a battery to the east of Rackebüll, opposite the narrowest part of the Sund, might be possible without giving the game away, since it would suggest only to the Danes an attack on their right. But it was the naval support about which he was most concerned, and he ended his letter expressing the hope that Blumenthal would learn before him of the arrival of the warships. Without them, he could envisage all too clearly the devastation that could be caused by Danish naval superiority.

Blumenthal, meanwhile, had been pressing on with his plans for the operation, which were bold in the extreme, and designed to take the Danes completely by surprise. He proposed to cross the northern end of the Alsen Sund; although it was twice as wide here the Danes had concentrated most of their forces on the southern part of the island, and Blumenthal reckoned that he could get enough troops ashore to secure the landing before the Danes knew what was afoot. Ballegaard was therefore chosen as the jumping off point. The number of boats available limited him to crossing with 1500 men in each wave, some ninety minutes apart. He transferred a large part of the heavy artillery that had arrived in front of Düppel to cover the crossing and in particular to deal with the *Rolf Krake*, whose arrival on the scene was regarded as potentially the most dangerous threat to the landing. Finally satisfied with his preparations, Blumenthal now fixed the night of April 2/3 for the crossing.

At first all went well. The weather seemed fair, and there was a calm sea. A force totalling 26 battalions had been concentrated around Ballegaard, ready for the embarkation. Suddenly, however, the weather changed; and it soon became clear that, as conditions deteriorated further, the assault must be called off. Blumenthal was profoundly disappointed. Subsequent events were to suggest that, with the benefit of surprise, his chances of success were good; the Danes would have been unable to concentrate any large force to meet the first three waves of the landing force, and by then Blumenthal would have got enough men ashore to give him a force too strong to be overcome. Most importantly there had been no sign of the *Rolf Krake*. As reinforcements had continued to cross, Blumenthal would soon have had sufficient strength to overrun the whole of Alsen.

Moltke was quick to sympathise with Blumenthal, and to emphasise that the prospective benefits of the operation must not be lost sight of:

> I see from your letter of yesterday that God did not wish the operation so long prepared by you to be carried out. I believe, however, that even now there is no case for it to be definitively abandoned, for only in this way could the war be brought to an end, since this would have led to the destruction of the enemy army. Even a successful assault on Düppel may not achieve this result; it will result in the retreat of the Danish troops to Fünen where they will confront us anew in that insular position.[12]

News of the abandonment of the assault was soon public knowledge and caused great disappointment in Berlin, from where the British Ambassador reported:

> Marshal Wrangel and Prince Frederick Charles were greatly annoyed at the failure of what they had hoped would have proved a feat highly creditable to the army of Prussia, and it is said that the affair has caused great dissatisfaction at Berlin, and that orders have been given to abandon a prospect of doubtful success and of extreme hazard, the preparations for which have hitherto retarded the regular operations of the siege.[13]

For the moment, of course, the essential element of surprise having been lost, there was no choice but to press on with the siege and the eventual assault of Düppel; and Frederick Charles and Blumenthal were accordingly resigned to winning the required victory the hard way.

The reluctance of Frederick Charles to commit himself to an assault on the Düppel position was due to more than his conviction that it was a militarily pointless exercise. As noted previously, caution was always a most pronounced trait in the professional character of the 'Red Prince' as he was popularly known. Early in his education his father, Prince Charles, had selected the then Major Albrecht von Roon as his tutor, and a close friendship developed between them. He brought to his chosen career the advantages and disadvantages of his birth; rapid advancement was inevitable, but his assertive manner, and his insistence on the prerogatives of his position, made him difficult at times to deal with. Nonetheless he was a brave and determined soldier who was by no means without ability, and he had devoted himself to a tireless study of the intellectual aspects of his calling. His reputation as well as his royal blood had meant that the resistance he had put up against the projected operations at Düppel had had to be taken very seriously. He was familiar with the terrain over which he was operating, having served as a Captain on Wrangel's staff during the first Schleswig-Holstein war. By the time he was thirty three he had reached the rank of General of Cavalry, and his appointment to command the I Corps had been more or less inevitable once the Austrians had been persuaded to accept Wrangel as commander in Chief.

The commander of the Danish forces at Düppel was now the sixty six year old Lieutenant General Georg Daniel Gerlach, in succession to Lüttichau who had briefly taken over after the supersession of de Meza. Edward Dicey, the *Daily Telegraph* correspondent, supposed that Gerlach's appointment was because 'he happened, unlike General Lüttichau, not to be present at the Council of War which decided on the evacuation of the Dannewerk. He is free, therefore, from the responsibility of that most unpopular step.'[14] Gerlach had commanded a battalion in the last war, greatly distinguishing himself at Fredericia and Idsted, and much impressed the English observers accompanying the Danish army.

In the first weeks of the Düppel campaign those observers were puzzled by the failure of the Prussian forces to take more direct action as they moved up to the Danish lines after the retreat from the Dannewerk. Skinner, the correspondent of the *Daily News*, believed that in this they had missed their chance. He explained the reasons for this:

> The roads were so bad that heavy artillery could scarcely be taken along, and the Prussian troops had suffered much from cold. Thus far in excuse of the hesitating strategy which neglected its one great opportunity of charging in upon the Düppel works and ending the business at a blow.[15]

Frederick Charles never contemplated an attempt to seize the position by *coup de main*; the Düppel lines had a formidable reputation, and those on the Danish side were not to know of the lengthy negotiations between their enemies as to how best to proceed or, once the invasion of Jutland was decided upon, of the resistance put up by Frederick Charles against the potentially costly assault. The position was a powerful one, having been strengthened in recent years, although not perhaps as strong as one nineteenth century historian described it: 'the redoubts of Düppel formed such a formidable line of defence as had rarely, if ever, before opposed the advance of an invading army in the open field.'[16]

Nonetheless, having arrived in front of the position, the Prussians began cautiously to feel its strength. On February 22, early in the morning, the Prussian troops attacked the Danish outposts; after quite a sharp encounter the Danish advanced positions west of Düppel village were taken, and their defenders driven back with losses of 62 killed, 233 wounded and 87 prisoners; the Prussians only lost 6 killed and 27 wounded. The great disparity in the casualties was largely due to the Danes having occupied much too forward a position; it was probably just as well for them that Wrangel never had any intention of developing this successful reconnaissance in force into a major assault.

As the armies settled down to what was evidently going to be a prolonged campaign at Düppel, the Danes set particular store on the prospective influence on the fighting of the operations of the *Rolf Krake*. The ironclad's sortie on February 18, which Moltke had witnessed, had been an effort to nullify the effect of the Prussian occupation of Broagerland by attacking the pontoon bridge at Egernsund which was an essential link in the Prussian lines of communications. The attempt failed because she could not bring her guns to bear at close range; ramming the bridge would have been altogether too risky, so the operation was confined to a prolonged exchange of fire with the Prussian batteries at Gammelmark.

If the lines of Düppel were not perhaps as formidable as their reputation, their importance in terms of Danish national morale was immense. With the fall of the Dannewerk, only Fredericia and especially Düppel remained as symbols of Denmark's determination to stand and fight the invader; both places had played a crucial role in the operations of 1849-50. The Düppel position itself was described by Dicey:

> A low plum-pudding shaped hill, surrounded by the sea on three fourths of its circumference and connected with the mainland on the fourth; the valley, which forms the base of the hill on the land side, being also the narrowest part of the isthmus, washed by the Alsen Sund on the north and the Wemmingbund on the south. On the western slope of this valley there runs an irregular range of hills or rather hillocks, lower, but not much lower, than Düppel Hill itself. This range, roughly speaking, starts at a little hill called Avn Bjerg, on the shore of the Wemmingbund, passes through Düppel churchyard, skirts the village of Rackebüll, and ends at Sand Bjerg on the Alsensund.[17]

There are, of course, no high hills in Jutland, and the gentle elevation of those at Düppel gave the lie to its public relations reputation as the Gibraltar of the North. There were ten forts, all, like those at Fredericia, earthworks, some with still incomplete bomb proof block houses, stretched across the peninsular covering the crossing point to Sonderburg.

In the centre was Düppel Hill, crowned by a windmill, which became the symbol of the position. The forts themselves had ramparts twelve to fifteen feet high and fifteen feet thick, their embrasures strengthened by gabions and sandbags. Around each fort ran a dry ditch, along which was planted a stockade of sharp pointed posts. Inside each fort the magazines were dug out beneath the rampart, roofed with timber beams. Visiting experts were unimpressed, noting that the works had been designed to withstand a bombardment only from smoothbore guns. Auberon Herbert, who arrived in March, and Captain Fritsch-Lang of the French engineers both observed that the works had been built without regard to any danger from Broagerland, from which smoothbore batteries would have been out of range. Captain Fritsch-Lang summed up his opinion of the works:

> The Düppel position was very advantageous, because, while less extended than the Dannewerk, it corresponded better to the means of command of the Danish Army; because it rested on the sea, where the Danes had the mastery; because it had a good view of the ground in its front; and finally, because the line of retreat, in case of defeat, was almost secure; it, however, lost much of its value from the employment of rifled cannon, by which it could be enfiladed from Gammelmark, which latter point the Danes should have foreseen.[18]

The forts stretched in an irregular line from the shore of the Wemmingbund to the Alsen Sund, along the crest of the modest slopes of Düppel Hill. In the centre, Forts No.4, 5 and 6 straddled the main road from Flensburg to the all important bridge head, from which crossed the main bridge and two pontoon bridges to Sonderburg. There was also a powerful barricade on the main road near Fort No.5. For the Danes, one essential problem was that the nature of the position, curving as it did across the end of the Sundewitt peninsula, meant that once an attacker brought up heavy artillery and completed siege works opposite the forts, artillery superiority was likely to be quickly gained by the enemy, even without the benefit of enfilade fire from Broagerland.

It had been clear by the end of February that an assault on the Düppel position could probably not be avoided. Although the siege guns had not yet arrived, and although Blumenthal had at that time still been continuing to work on his plan for a landing at the Alsen, it was evident that preparations must be put in hand for a formal siege and ultimate attack on the line of Danish works. Accordingly, after the bombardment had continued for two days, on the morning of March 17 a force under the command of Major General August von Goeben launched a brisk attack on the villages of Rackebüll and Düppel with a view to driving back the Danes from the advanced position they

This view of Düppel's Fort No. 4 after its capture gives some idea of the ditch, palisade and rampart arrangements erected by the Danes. (Rogers)

occupied in front of the line of forts. The attack was everywhere successful, the Prussians taking not only Düppel village but also the height of the Ruherberg southwest of the village. Gerlach, unwisely, launched an immediate counter-attack, briefly retaking the village; but he was, with the forces available to him, quite unable to hold the position and by nightfall had fallen back all along the line to the forts themselves. Gerlach's total losses amounted to 153 killed, 253 wounded and 267 captured; the bulk of these casualties were suffered during his fruitless counter-attack. The Prussian loss amounted to 33 killed and 105 wounded. The ground gained in the assault now permitted the establishment of powerful batteries directly in front of the forts. With the heavy siege guns now *en route* from Berlin, the way was clear for regular siege operations to be conducted against the Danish position.

On Easter Monday, March 28, a further reconnaissance in force was launched against the Danish positions. During Easter Sunday the bombardment had intensified before dying away, as a result of which an assault was not unexpected. The attack, when it came, was in part a feint, designed to distract attention from the planned descent upon Alsen, and in part a step towards the commencement of the long delayed siege operations.

Although speculations by observers on the Danish side that the Prussians had got involved in a more serious action than intended were entirely incorrect, the subsidiary objective of the operation had not been wholly achieved, since the position of the most advanced Prussian pickets had still not yet reached the point at which siege operations could begin with the opening of the first parallel. The engagement lasted in all about three hours; the Prussian advance was directed from Düppel village towards Forts No.6 and 7 and along the coast towards Forts No.1 and 2. Apart from distracting attention from Blumenthal's preparations, not a great deal had therefore been achieved; the Danish losses in the affair amounted to 60 killed, 101 wounded and 57 captured; interestingly, 18 of the latter were reported as having been deserters, an indication that Danish morale might be beginning to crumble. The Prussians lost 25 men killed, 132 wounded and 33 captured. Their losses on this occasion seem in part to have been caused by the over eagerness of their company commanders, who pressed on to the line of the forts instead of taking cover. One infantryman, replying to a question about the relatively heavy casualties, explained simply that 'when the lieutenant runs to the fort, we must run with him.'[19]

Prussian preparations for the siege continued at their own pace; and on the night of March 29/30 the first parallel was finally opened opposite the more southern forts, albeit at a distance of 1,000 yards from the Danish works. It was 750 yards long, and in rear of it, and at distances of up to 1350 yards from the forts, seven batteries, containing a total of 34 siege guns, were constructed. The bombardment commenced on April 2 with a purely token shelling, because much of the artillery had been moved north to Ballegaard to cover the Alsen crossing, and was intended only to distract the Danes' attention. It was not until April 7 that the artillery attack properly got under way, after the abandonment of the abortive Alsen crossing, and the return of the artillery to the siege lines.

Bismarck was becoming extremely concerned about the progress of the siege, since the approaching conference was reducing his room for manoeuvre. If there was to be an assault on Düppel it was vital that it should succeed before the conference convened in London and, since it had been provisionally fixed to begin on April 12, time was running out. The slow build up to the assault left Bismarck with no option but to delay the start of the conference; fortunately, a convenient excuse for this was provided by the protracted proceedings of the Diet at Frankfurt. This breathing space came as a relief to the Prussian headquarters since, the second parallel only being opened on April 10, the original date for the commencement of the conference represented an unachievable deadline. The Prussian military leaders were at least not as pessimistic as the official French observer at Headquarters, Clermont-Tonnerre, who 'repeatedly asserted that the Danish redoubts were so strong that it would take months to prepare properly for the storming of them.'[20]

The Prussians were inching forward; on the night of April 7/8 in preparation for the opening of the second parallel, an advanced post had been dug some 120 yards in front of the line it was to take. The parallel itself ran for 600 yards south of the main road and was dug by two battalions of infantry, covered by three battalions in the newly dug trenches. It had been the intention of Frederick Charles to launch the assault from the second parallel as soon as it was completed, but it seems that the King intervened at this point to require that a third parallel be dug to reduce the distance over which the storming columns must advance, and thus reduce their exposure to the enemy fire and also reduce the amount of time available to the Danes to bring up their reserves. Colonel Neimann, upon whose account of the siege operations Captain Fritsch-Lang drew for his paper, attributed William's intervention to advice which he had received many years before from the Duke of Wellington. In also insisting on the use of strong columns with large reserves the King remembered what the Duke had told him:

> In none of the assaults or entrenchments that he had directed had he ever succeeded, except where he had made use of strong storming parties; and that, on the contrary, he had always failed when he made the attempt with a restricted number of troops.[21]

With the failure of the crossing to Alsen, Moltke's concern was that the assault on Düppel should be properly prepared. He wrote to Blumenthal on April 6 with news of a crucially important strengthening of the high command there:

> It is necessary above all, for the assault on the Düppel position, that we have there a high ranking engineer officer with battle experience; but where can one find one there? But, as the attack is above all an artillery attack I believe that Lieutenant General von Hindersin, who leaves today for Gravenstein, will be able to support you. I have suggested that he be accompanied by Captain von der Burg who gained practical experience in Mexico and also took part, at Pueblo, in an attack principally carried out by artillery. If I see Hindersin again before he leaves, I will call his attention above all to the necessity of an absolute agreement with you for the success of this venture. As to that, I believe that it would be helpful to extend the attack substantially towards the left.[22]

Moltke added some works of encouragement about Blumenthal's Alsen plans.

Do not let your bold project be ended by this temporary set back. The outcome may be better, or it may be worse. Like Philip II and his Armada, you can despatch your barges against the enemy, but not against the elements.

Moltke had not lost sight of his proposal to invade Fünen in due course, writing to Roon on April 8 that he now had the impression that the Danes could, very soon, evacuate Düppel, in order to ensure the safety of their army. In that case, a landing on Alsen, or eventually on Fünen, would again have to be considered.[23] In his view the Danes would be much better advised to pull their army back to Alsen, where they would be less exposed to the constant possibility of a sudden assault. The Danes would, he thought, reinforce the northern end of the island at Meels, opposite Ballegaard. However, the drawback of a retreat to Alsen would be that, as he pointed out to Blumenthal on April 12, 'it is very dangerous to resist to the last in an island position, since a safe retreat cannot be assured.' Looking ahead to an eventual crossing, he suggested that the passage of the Sund depended in large part on the possibility of finding for the Prussian artillery, so much superior in terms of quality, a position from which it could render the Arnkiel peninsular untenable.[24] Meanwhile he had been examining a plan of Sonderburg in the light of the operations undertaken in 1849, and the report of these prepared by a Captain Wittge, which he forwarded to Blumenthal on April 15. He had now come to a conclusion as to the Danes' situation:

In the face of the reigning excitement at Copenhagen, General Gerlach could do nothing but await a serious assault; and the attempt made to present the skirmishes of March 28 in the following days as unsuccessful assaults is too ludicrous to deceive even the mob.[25]

Mindful of de Meza's fate, Gerlach was naturally reluctant to take any steps in the matter on his own account. Any decision was now a political rather than a military question. The Danish Government, however, was driven by considerations similar to those which led Bismarck to press for an early assault. With the London Conference now scheduled for April 20, it was vitally important to hang on to Düppel if at all possible; this after all had been, since the retreat of the Dannewerk, the central logic of their policy. Lundbye, the War Minister, told Gerlach firmly that the maintenance of the position was of supreme importance, in view of the impending conference, although he added a personal view that it was not the Government's intention to tie Gerlach's hands.

The effect of the prolonged build-up to the final assault was also continuing to take its toll on the morale of the Danish Army. Writing after the attack had taken place, Dicey recorded his awareness of this:

I have known for the last ten days that the army was becoming rapidly demoralised by the fearful trial to which it was exposed… that the troops were more and more unwilling to go to the front; that on more than one occasion regiments had refused to cross the bridges, and had only been induced to obey orders by the promise that they should speedily be led into action; their desertion had become common… and that, in the opinion of nine officers out of ten, the position was utterly untenable.[26]

The order to hold Düppel to the end was bitterly resented by the Danish army. Given no choice about this, Gerlach now contemplated making a surprise attack on the Prussians with the support of the *Rolf Krake* and all the warships that could be assembled. This would certainly be unexpected by the Prussians, and might gain some measure of success, although the disparity in the numbers of troops immediately available suggests that at best this would have been very short-lived. At all events, the plan was frustrated by the navy's refusal to take the risks involved in running into the Wemmingbund, where the now much more powerful Prussian artillery would have been presented with some particularly alluring targets.

Hindersin arrived to take overall command of the artillery operations on April 8, and made an immediate impact. Already one of the most distinguished artillery officers in the Prussian Army, he was renowned for his dour, humourless personality. In the next half dozen years he was to make one of the greatest individual contributions to the army's success, creating an artillery force which time and again would prove decisive on the battlefield. The operations in front of Düppel quickly convinced him of the enormous superiority that rifled guns possessed over smoothbore weapons, and thereafter he laboured ceaselessly to convert the whole of the Prussian artillery.

By April 16 the remorseless pounding of the fortifications was beginning to take effect and it was apparent to everyone that the assault would not be long delayed. The long period of preparation, intended to minimise casualties, enabled the artillery to achieve a complete domination of the battlefield, and it was very apparent to the Prussians that the Danish works had suffered severely, particularly as a result of the enfilading fire directed upon them from Broagerland. This was largely due to careful targeting. Colonel Neimann noted the effect:

> The artillery on our side was ordered to fire only for some well defined object, both to avoid waste of ammunition and injury to the guns. Each morning the repairs executed by the enemy during the previous night, as well as any new embrasures, were destroyed, especially if it was thought that any gun was concealed behind the latter. Woe to any of his guns which opened fire. They were immediately played upon by several rifled twelve pounders, and in all probability never opened fire again.[27]

Even Düppel Mill finally fell victim to the bombardment; used as an observation post by the Danes, it was destroyed by about thirty shots from the rifled twelve pounders, firing at ranges of 1,800 to 2,000 yards. There were now a total of twenty four batteries playing upon the Danish positions, for the most part at ranges that ensured that they were largely uninterrupted by the enemy. Some of the batteries were operating at a range of 3,500 yards, but the largest concentration of artillery was some 2,500 yards from the Danish works. The nearest batteries, however, were firing at a range of as little as 1,000 yards.[28] The Danish artillery was relatively inactive during the day time, but at night they were regularly in action especially from Alsen and from Forts No.3, 8 and 9, albeit to little effect.

Frederick Charles determined to launch his assault on April 18. He was still particularly anxious to do all in his power to limit the casualties to a minimum:

> The proper hour for making the final assault was a subject of much anxious consideration. It was decided, at any rate, not to make it towards dusk or during the night, daylight being considered an indispensable condition.[29]

At first it was intended to launch the attack at dawn, so that the troops could move to their jumping off positions under cover of darkness. The experience of dawn raids had, however, shown that the Danes were ready with grape shot; and in order to destroy their guns before they could be withdrawn, to smash down any repairs that the Danes had effected overnight, to enfilade the forts and finally to compel the Danes to keep their reserves well back, it was finally decided to wait until there had been some hours of artillery preparation on the day of the assault. Captain Fritsch-Lang thought this an excellent arrangement; although the Danes had expected an assault on April 18, when it failed to materialise at dawn they pulled back a large part of the garrisons of the forts to escape the force of the bombardment.

At this time the total of the Danish forces under Gerlach's command amounted to about 19,000 troops in all. Of these, about 10,000 were in and about the Düppel position with a further 2,000 in close support at Sonderburg. The rest were scattered around Alsen. The six southern forts had between them a total garrison of no more than 2,500 men, a number which was palpably inadequate to resist a really determined assault. The bridgehead was manned by three battalions of Brigade Kauffman. During the afternoon of Sunday April 17 the Prussian bombardment and the Danish counter-battery work had been stepped up. At times the shelling was so heavy that a large part of the garrison of the forts was pulled back to minimise casualties. For a while, during the night, the bombardment ceased, and the Prussian storming columns moved forward to their jumping off points, unobserved by the enemy as they assembled behind high parapets in the third parallel, some 400 yards from the enemy. It was a still fine night. Skinner described the scene:

> A bright moon shone upon Alsen Sund, which sparkled with the gentlest of ripples. The hillside lay calmly sleeping in a stream of silver light. Here and there could be faintly seen the Danish watch fires, and an occasional shell flew across Wemmingbund. On the bridges were many passengers, for most of the reliefs were sent out under cover of darkness.[30]

The assault force was under the command of Lieutenant General von Manstein. He had a total of eleven and a half battalions of infantry, in 46 companies, with five companies of pioneers and 150 artillerymen. They moved forward in six columns, each heading for one of the Forts No.1- 6. The columns attacking Forts No.2 and 4 were stronger than the others, comprising 10 and 12 companies of infantry respectively, with the rest of Manstein's force equally divided between the other four columns. Each column was preceded by a line of skirmishers, closely following which came the pioneers and some infantry heavily equipped with spades, axes, ladders and bags of blasting powder to enable them to surmount the expected obstacles. Behind these, at a distance of some 80 yards, came the main columns, with the reserves a further 120 yards to the rear. With possible booby traps in mind, the column commanders were ordered, in the event of a fort being taken without resistance, to withdraw their troops immediately while the blockhouses were inspected to see if there was any danger of explosion from them.[31]

The total strength of Manstein's force was 8,000 men of all arms; in addition to two brigades in central reserve, another brigade stood by at Rackebüll, ready to assault the four northern forts as soon as they could be taken in flank by the troops passing through the line of forts. Finally another brigade was posted on the shores of the Alsen Sund with orders to make a demonstration suggesting that a crossing to Alsen itself was about to begin.

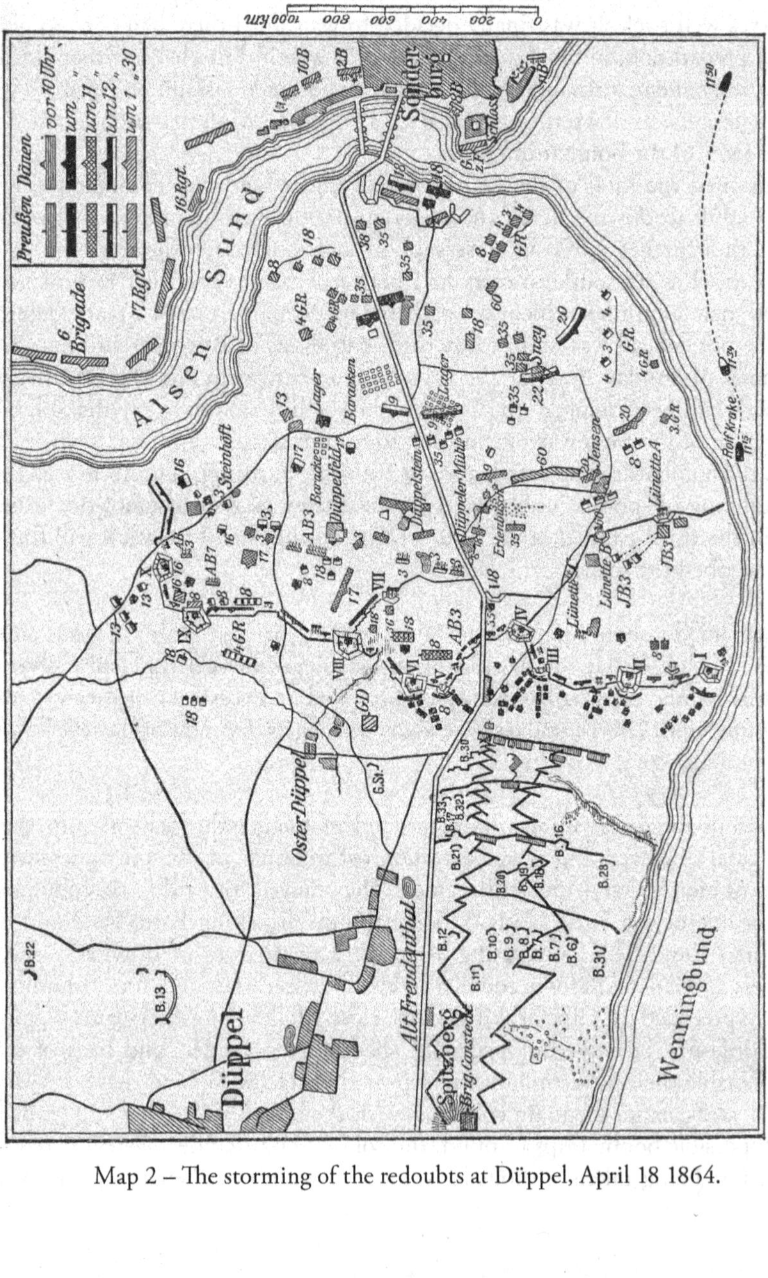

Map 2 – The storming of the redoubts at Düppel, April 18 1864.

As dawn broke on April 18, the Prussian bombardment resumed, more intensively than ever. By 9.00 am it had reached its latest height, especially along the front of the intended assault; but as it went on, and no assault materialised, the Danes began to withdraw a large part of the garrisons of the forts, sure now that the attack had been put off until another day. Suddenly, at 10.00 am the bombardment abruptly ceased; there was a moment's silence and then the storming columns poured forward from the third parallel across the narrow stretch of ground that separated them from the forts, whose defenders, dazed by the suddenness of the assault, were able to offer little resistance. 'The redoubts', wrote Skinner, 'were stormed with an ease that astonished the assailants, and the breast works or curtains between them were surmounted in an instant.'[32] So rapid was the advance that the forts were taken before the Danish troops that had been withdrawn to rearward positions could return to reinforce the weakened garrisons left there. In Fort No.6, as some of them were moving up to cross the bridge at its entrance, they were made prisoners before all had crossed. From some of the forts there was a short lived musketry fire and a few guns managed to open fire before the storming columns were upon them, but within twenty minutes it was all over; the last of the six forts to fall was No.4, but the Prussian flag was flying there by 10.22 am. Manstein, in accordance with instructions, now brought up the brigades waiting in reserve, passing them between the forts and, turning north, took Fort Nos. 7 – 10 in the rear. The Danes, hopelessly outnumbered, fought with a desperate courage; a counter-attack by Brigade Kauffmann from the bridgehead, moving forward by Düppel Mill, briefly retook the second line of fortifications. This success was, however, short lived, and was driven back with heavy casualties, among them General du Plat, killed leading a charge, and Major Rosen, his Chief of Staff. The northern forts, pressed in the front and in the rear held out for a while; but by 1.00 pm they were no longer tenable. The garrisons of Forts No.9

The Prussian 3rd Guard Grenadier Regiment storming the Danish redoubts at Düppel, April 18 1864. (Rogers)

and 10, the last to fall, were ordered to withdraw; but before the garrison of Fort No.9 could carry out this order it was again attacked and all were made prisoner. The whole of the position was now in Prussian hands, and Manstein turned his attention to the bridgehead, into which the remaining Danish troops on the mainland had withdrawn by about noon.

The defence works around the bridgehead had been left largely untouched by the bombardment; its interior was entirely commanded by the Danish batteries on the Alsen side of the Sund. A direct assault was therefore ruled out; for about an hour there were fierce artillery and rifle exchanges around the perimeter, by which time it was apparent to the Danes that unless they abandoned it voluntarily, they might not be able to leave the bridgehead at all. First the northern bridge and then the southern one were broken down and by 1.30 pm the Danes had made their retreat into Sonderburg.

Gerlach's force had been entirely broken, and there had never been any reasonable chance of holding the bridgehead. When his battered units began to regroup on Alsen, it was clear that the cost of the Danish Government's determination to hold on to Düppel as a bargaining chip had been desperately high. Total Danish casualties amounted to 4,789, of which 671 had been killed, 987 wounded and 3,131 taken prisoner. Many of the Danish casualties had been sustained during the abortive counter-attack, when the stopping power of the needle gun was demonstrated with deadly effect. Prussian losses had been much lower, at 257 killed, and about 950 wounded. One Prussian brigade commander, Major General Raven, had been fatally wounded. 118 Danish guns had been captured, and Gerlach's ability to defend Alsen had been seriously impaired. During the battle the *Rolf Krake* had been able to make very little contribution to the Danish defence; Dicey watched as she was shelled by the Prussian batteries:

The northern side of Fort No. 4 at Düppel after its capture, April 1864. (Rogers)

> Great water spouts sprang up on every side of her as the shot fell in showers about her; and every now and then there was a fearful crash heard above the roar of the cannon and the constant crack of musketry, and we could tell that a shot had hit her iron sides.[33]

Aboard the *Rolf Krake* one man had been killed and ten injured.

The relative lightness of the Prussian casualties, and the speed of their success, owed much to the completeness of the surprise achieved. News of the attack on the forts did not reach Gerlach's headquarters until the first six had already been taken, with the result that some of the Danish reserves were hardly able to get into action at all. The last line of defence had been intended to be provided by the Danish Guards; these did not even reach the bridge until too late to take any effective part in the action, and as a result they suffered only trifling losses.

As evening fell, even the occasional burst of rifle fire died down and the Prussians were able to enjoy their victory, and the Danes to ponder on their defeat. It had been an overwhelming success, and one of great omen, as the Crown Prince reflected thoughtfully in his diary:

> It is true that we have a wonderful army, but what will be the result of her victories under a Bismarck? This question has a crushing effect…I am sorry for my sister-in-law, the Princess of Wales.[34]

9

Alsen

Public opinion in Prussia, and indeed in Germany as a whole, was galvanised by news of the victory at Düppel. Although in truth hopelessly one-sided it was the battle's political rather than its military significance which completely changed the climate of opinion. German nationalism, avid for signs of national success, was generously stimulated at a particularly sensitive moment in its development. In Berlin the news was received with rapturous enthusiasm. The city was illuminated, and the streets decorated with flags and banners. In a state of great euphoria William read to some assembled regiments of the Guard the telegram he had received with the news. He telegraphed to Frederick Charles: 'Next to the Lord of Hosts, I thank my noble army and your leadership for this day's glorious victory. Express my highest acknowledgements to the troops and my thanks for their exertions.'[1] The press, predictably, had a field day; a wave of extravagantly patriotic sentiment spread outwards from Berlin across Germany in what Sybel described as 'a shout of patriotic exaltation in all hearts.' The popular emotions inspired by the victory at Düppel brought grave consequences to the liberals. As well as giving Germany a powerful shove in the direction of unity, it began the process of softening democratic resistance to autocratic government.

In Denmark, of course, the news of Düppel was greeted with the most profound gloom, but it had little or no effect on the attitude of the Danish government to the objectives it intended to pursue at the London Conference. Holding on to Düppel would, of course, have been a distinct plus; but Monrad was determined that its loss should not affect his intransigent policy. The Danish public received the loss of Düppel with 'consternation and profound dejection,' but without the bitterness occasioned by the retreat from the Dannewerk; at Düppel, at any rate, Danish honour had been preserved.

Moltke was naturally elated by the news of the victory, and had little doubt that Blumenthal, to whom he wrote on April 20, deserved much of the credit:

> I send you my sincere congratulations for the brilliant victory achieved on April 18 by our brave troops, and to which your tenacity, your intelligence and your forbearance has so effectively contributed. The significant losses which this great feat of arms has cost show clearly that the greatest sacrifices still will not guarantee success if the gun and the pick axe have not prepared it.[2]

Moltke went on to describe the celebrations in Berlin before turning to the next steps to be taken. Preparations must be made for a descent upon Alsen, but it was by no means sure that the Danish Army would wait there to be captured. He still favoured an invasion of Fünen; the right moment for this, he thought, would be when the Danes showed signs of retreating from Alsen. Much would depend on the timing. However, it was necessary to keep in mind that, for the moment, there would shortly no doubt be an armistice, although this would be delayed, the London Conference having again been put back until April 25.

Still buoyed up by the victory at Düppel, William made a snap decision to visit his troops at the front. Accompanied by Bismarck, he reviewed them as they marched past wearing the uniforms and carrying the equipment they had borne in the assault. Moltke, to his disappointment, was not included in the Royal party.

Meanwhile, in London, Lord John Russell was still trying to get the Conference underway, making a vain attempt to insist on its commencement on April 20. The news of Düppel had caused consternation, especially to Palmerston, who had not entirely abandoned hope of some kind of intervention. On April 18 he suggested to Russell that the news of the fall of Düppel might

> afford good grounds for sending our Fleet to the Baltic to protect the Retreat of the Danish Army....If the French and Russians and Swedes would agree with us, we might say to Austria at the meeting of the Conference on Wednesday that unless the German Powers agree to an immediate armistice on the basis of present occupation our Fleet is under orders and will go at once to the Baltic... Pubic opinion in this country would be most shocked if we were to stand by and see the Danish Army taken prisoner and Denmark thus laid prostrate at the feet of Germany.[3]

In Berlin it seemed to the British Ambassador that Bismarck's possible ultimate objective was beginning to emerge. Buchanan had an interesting conversation with his doctor, which he hastened to report privately to Russell on April 23. When he had remarked that peace would depend on Prussia's proposed conditions, his doctor was explicit in his response:

> 'Oh', he replied, 'a personal union is the only practicable arrangement, but here in Berlin we intend that it should not be with the Danish but with the Prussian Crown'. May not this be the objective of Bismarck's policy? Having first established the Union of the Duchies and got rid of the P. of Augustenburg by offering them to the King of Denmark, may he not calculate on Danish obstinacy and the progress of events for bringing things into such a position that in the interests of the Duchies and of Germany it may be expedient to adopt the views of the Berliners...It is painful to attribute *arrières pensées* to gentlemen who profess to be acting with disinterested motives, but the events of the last six months open up a wide field of speculation as to what the next six may bring forth.[4]

Moltke had meanwhile been very interested to receive a private report from Captain von der Burg, which he passed on to Manteuffel with his own comments, believing that it was an important insight into the working of Allied Headquarters:

> One can clearly see what a healthy influence Lieutenant General von Hindersin has had on the success of April 18. In particular we would have had a lot of trouble in seizing the bridgehead if we had not been able so quickly and effectively to deploy our field artillery. I am not familiar with the Cabinet Order which defines General von Hindersin's responsibilities, and I do not know if His Majesty wishes to employ

him in a supernumary capacity with the Army of Schleswig, with a specific task. Without this the presence of a general officer is always somewhat embarrassing.[5]

At Allied Headquarters, Wrangel had got the bit firmly between his teeth after the fall of Düppel and had got it into his head that the next step should be to storm the defences at Fredericia. Moltke was appalled, feeling very cut off from the policy making process, and wrote as a result a note to Manteuffel on the subject:

No doubt, in his Majesty's presence, the question of what should be done following the victory of April 18 was discussed and decided upon. But, as I was not summoned to this meeting, I am completely ignorant of the results of the discussion.[6]

With this note he enclosed his proposals, dated April 24, for the future conduct of operations. He was particularly opposed to the suggestion, which he had read only in the press, that Fredericia would be the next objective, giving as his opinion that all the available troops which could be withdrawn from Sundewitt should be used to occupy Fünen.

Following this up, Moltke felt able to write to Wrangel on the subject on April 25: 'I strongly advise against the siege of Fredericia, and I am instructed not to order your Excellency to make a landing in Fünen, but to authorise you to carry this out if circumstances appear to favour this operation.'[7] Moltke had, however, exceeded his instructions in endeavouring to put his favoured Fünen project on top of the agenda, and political considerations obliged him to write a further letter to Wrangel on the same day:

I have realised that, contrary to my expectation, the telegram sent today by His Majesty in reply to your report of yesterday, did not give you unfettered discretion. It is expected very soon that the Danes will propose an armistice on the basis of the *uti possidetis*, and it is desired in consequence to extend as far as possible the occupation of Jutland. The Fünen operation cannot be commenced at once, and the whole of the Army must be used to occupy Jutland as soon as possible.[8]

Moltke was, however, still determined to stamp on the Fredericia option as firmly as he could, and in a report to the King on April 26 he emphasised that there was now no possibility of the Danes lodging a counter offensive from the fortress. He recommended that the siege be lifted entirely, and that Gablenz should be sent north to join Münster, whose division was engaged in overrunning as much of Jutland as it could. He was persistent, however, in putting forward his primary scheme, ending his report with the proposal that Wrangel should be authorised from then on to carry out a landing on Fünen as soon as it seemed appropriate and the necessary transport had been assembled.[9]

His anxieties about Fredericia were, however, soon relieved; on April 28 the Danes unexpectedly evacuated the fortress, all their troops there retreating into Fünen. Moltke had not lost sight of the project for a seaborne assault on Alsen, writing to his nephew Henry on April 27:

> Under the circumstances, the crossing over to Alsen was, and still is, a matter of supreme importance. One may doubt the advisability of embarking on this expedition with the existing means of transport, but there can never be the slightest question as to its extreme importance... As to what remains to be done with regard to Alsen, now that the defeated army has recovered from the first shock, and that part of our forces at the Sundewitt have been withdrawn, can only be decided by one who is on the spot. The greater the difficulties there become, the more decisive must be the blow which is struck in another quarter, for the Danish resistance is as yet no way broken.[10]

Moltke ended his letter with another expression of his frustration, remarking that although it would be very interesting to look at the battlefield, he had no wish to be there as a mere spectator without any authority.

In London, the much-delayed Conference finally began to assemble. The leading delegates were the ambassadors of the Great Powers in London – Bernstorff, Apponyi, La Tour d'Auvergne and Brunnow. The Danish delegation was led by Quaade, the Foreign Minister. Palmerston continued to supply Russell with advice, suggesting that the German Powers should not be asked to state their demands, since it would then become difficult to talk them out of them. The first key problem, though, was to effect a ceasefire, and this immediately ran into difficulties, since the Danes refused to lift the blockade as one of its conditions, while the Prussians and Austrians regarded this as indispensable. So that Bernstorff and Apponyi could seek further instructions, the Conference adjourned until May 4.

In Berlin Moltke's feelings of frustration, especially the lack of reliable information, continued to trouble him. Writing to Blumenthal on April 28 to congratulate him on the award of the Pour le Merité, he commented:

> Since April 17 I have not received any letters from you, and for me this is a real hardship. If this is because, since the assault, nothing important has occurred in your front, it is nonetheless vitally important for me to be kept informed with intentions and plans. I am often asked, at short notice, my opinion on important questions, but at other times it is not felt necessary to tell me of what is proposed or what has occurred. It is thus necessary for me to seek, at least in a private correspondence, sufficient information to keep me up to date with what has transpired.[11]

It was the lack of direct involvement which was particularly upsetting; referring to the discussions as to future policy, which had taken place during the King's visit to the troops after Düppel, he added a regretful comment that he had not been designated to accompany William on this trip.

It was the King's visit to the front, however, which was soon to bring about a radical change in Moltke's position, ending his frustration for good. Manteuffel had been especially concerned by the apparent disorganisation at Headquarters, which he had no doubt was largely the fault of the erratic Vogel von Falckenstein; he had little difficulty in persuading the King and Roon that Moltke should take Falckenstein's place as Chief of Staff of the Allied forces in Schleswig and Jutland. Falckenstein himself was placed in command of an enlarged III Corps, operating in the north of Jutland. With undisguised relief, Moltke set off at once, scarcely leaving himself time to pack. He arrived at Headquarters at Veile on the morning of May 2, and that night he wrote to Mary:

> It was certainly very cold, and from Roten Krug onwards I had to go in an open peasant's wagon with relays of horses. I stayed during the night for several hours at Christiansfeld, and, having laid myself down on a bed there, slept very soundly. Early next morning I found everything frozen hard. The country is very pretty, and the vegetation generally not much behind that of Berlin. The beech trees have already quite beautiful foliage. I am here in a nice house, and have a splendid bed, but it must still be warmed up a bit.[12]

Moltke at once embarked on a tour of as many of the key areas as he could; visiting Fredericia with the Crown Prince, he found it 'a very respectable stronghold', and thought it lucky that it had not been necessary to take it by storm.

Although the British Government had been concerned that the Austrian Fleet commanded by Commodore Tegetthoff might enter the Baltic, this was not the intention. His objective was the Danish fleet, under Commodore Suensen, which was blockading the mouths of the Elbe and Weser and which was somewhat more powerful than Tegetthoff's force. On May 6 the latter sailed from Cuxhaven to seek out the Danish Fleet, which consisted of two frigates – *Niels Juel* of 42 guns and *Jylland* of 44 guns – and the corvette *Heimdal* of 16 guns. Tegetthoff had *Schwartzenburg* and *Radetzky* of 49 and 31 guns respectively together with the Prussian gunboats *Blitz*, *Basilisk* and *Adler* which were, however, of limited effectiveness. Tegetthoff encountered Suensen off Heligoland, and at once cleared for action and closed with the enemy. The engagement that followed was unique in naval history, being the only fleet action between wooden ships under steam and armed with heavy shell guns; it was not, however, particularly informative as to the effect of modern technology on naval tactics, since no particular use was made of steam power, and the damage caused by the shells was not much greater than solid shot. Tegetthoff opened fire at a range of 2,000 yards, closing after the initial broadsides to 1,000 yards, and steering east to prevent Suensen cutting off the gunboats, which had fallen behind. As *Schwartzenburg* turned she was hit by a raking broadside from *Niels Juel*, a shell exploding in the gun deck, while two others started small fires. The two squadrons now ran to the southwest, exchanging fire at a range of 500 yards. After two hours, at around 4.00pm *Schwartzenburg* sustained a hit which ignited the foresail, and the fire rapidly got out of control. To prevent it spreading, Tegetthoff was obliged to steer into the ESE wind, towards Heligoland; when he entered into British territorial waters Suensen did not attempt to follow, perhaps due to the presence there of the British frigate *Aurora*.

It had been a tactical victory for the Danes; but the blockade had been raised, and the Danish fleet thereafter exercised little direct influence in the war. Tegetthoff could certainly claim a moral victory and was deservedly promoted to Rear Admiral.

In the north of Jutland, Falckenstein was opposed by Moltke's old friend Hegermann, whose 4th Division was heavily outnumbered. Moltke was critical of Gablenz for having let Hegermann escape previously; now, the Danish commander retreated behind the safety of the Lijmfjord, leaving the Allies to take possession of the rest of Jutland undisturbed. Hegermann had at least succeeded in keeping his force in being; but he was not strong enough to mount any significant operations against his enemy. With the withdrawal from Fredericia, this left only Alsen and Fünen as potential military objectives. The latter operation was at first supported by Gablenz; but on further reflection he concluded that it might be a rather more ambitious project than Vienna would countenance and it was, for the moment, shelved.

When the Conference reconvened on May 4, the German Powers had put forward their proposal for an armistice based on the removal of the blockade in exchange for the withdrawal of their previous demand for financial contributions from the population of Jutland; they were also prepared to concede the restoration of the Danish civil power there. The Danes responded by demanding that, if the blockade was to be lifted, the Allies should withdraw entirely from Jutland. Bernstorff's counter proposal, which it was clear would not be acceptable, was that if a withdrawal was what the neutral Powers wanted, it could only be on the basis of a complete evacuation of the Schleswig islands still held by the Danes and the return of all captured shipping. The Danes, as expected, refused this; Russell, irritated by the length of time the armistice negotiations were taking, adjourned the Conference again, this time until May 9, for the belligerents to consider the latest proposals from the neutral Powers. This was for an armistice on terms that the blockade be lifted, and both Jutland and the Schleswig islands be evacuated by the Allies and Danes respectively.

Soon after he had settled in at Headquarters, Moltke wrote a long letter to Blumenthal, to review the position in the light of the protracted armistice negotiations. He believed that there was no likelihood of the Danes embarking on any significant operations while these went on. As usual he applied a remorseless military logic to the situation. His belief was that the Danes had given up any attempts to hold on to the mainland; instead he expected that they would continue to occupy the islands with the protection of their fleet, and hope for some foreign development to turn up:

> I do not believe, therefore, that they will give up any of their islands of their own accord or without another defeat. Will the Danes conclude a reasonable armistice, or continue their resistance? That question will no doubt be answered when the Conference resumes in London on May 9. After this date it does not seem to me that we can avoid undertaking something, even at the risk of heavy losses. If it appears that the Cabinet in Copenhagen sees some advantage in not agreeing to some reasonable proposal, it remains only to continue the war until the enemy is destroyed, and everything should be done to achieve that; we cannot, as a matter of fact, stay for years with 60,000 to 70,000 men in the Cimbrian peninsula and, on the other hand we cannot restrict our scope of action without danger, standing for such a long time on the strict defensive that we lose the initiative.[13]

He added that the most effective step would be to launch an assault on Alsen; a demonstration should be made opposite Sonderburg, where the Danes had been throwing up defences, but it would be at Ballegaard that the crossing would be most easily affected.

Returning to the Conference on May 9, Quaade announced his Government's objections to the proposal of the neutral Powers; and then surprised everyone by accepting instead the terms put forward by the German Powers. The Danes apparently believed that even in the presence of the occupying troops, both revenue and recruits could be raised in Jutland; the possession of the Schleswig islands could not be foregone, as these were militarily secure. They were, however, only prepared to agree to an armistice for one month, and in spite of strong pressure refused to extend this. The armistice was to run from May 12, from which date the blockade would be lifted. For their part the Allies agreed not to interfere with the regular commerce and the civil government of Jutland, nor to levy contributions from the population. Both sides remained in their present positions.

Bismarck found these terms perfectly acceptable, having in these exchanges succeeded in wrong footing the Danes, due to their foolish and persistent obstinacy. Moltke, on the other hand, was extremely discontented, and set out his views in a series of memoranda pointing out the practical difficulties. In the first of these, he wrote that on both sides of the line it was necessary that the belligerents acted in the same way – either in perfect freedom or on the basis of some specifically agreed limitations. There would, he thought, be no advantage in limiting the parties' freedom of action and in any case it was impractical to do so. As an example he cited the impossibility of controlling merchant shipping and fishing, on which the population's livelihood depended. 'Are the population not to go fishing? How do you prevent a fisherman from Veile from landing at Bogense?' In any case, he felt it crucially important that the inhabitants of Schleswig could go to Alsen and Fünen with the same freedom as the Danes in Jutland.[15] He was also concerned that it had been agreed that the occupying troops should pay for their provisions, while the Danes were free to levy taxes and collect supplies and men:

> The occupation of Jutland, under the terms agreed at London on May 9 gives us, in my opinion, neither political nor military advantage…The Danes can reinforce themselves with recruits, get from England rifled guns and other war materials, refresh their exhausted troops and re-establish their morale, while we, needing neither rest nor reinforcements have simply halted our operations.[15]

In Berlin, Roon was equally outspoken, insisting to Bismarck that the army's views should be taken into account; it was entitled to oppose a long armistice during which it was left in an exposed position in a foreign country. Roon added that 'when a Government depends – and this is our situation – particularly upon the armed part of the population…the army's views on what the Government does or does not do is surely not a matter of indifference.'[16]

Moltke was feeling a lot happier now that he was actively involved, writing as usual observant and informative letters to Mary about his activities and the country in which he found himself. On May 15 he remarked:

> The manner of life in this place suits me admirably. Our dinner hour has changed, and for the better, from 5pm to 3pm, so that one has time in the evening to ride out. By midday it is already quite warm. We have been having a continuous course of the nicest weather. In any case it is much pleasanter here than being at the spring parades on the Tempelhofer Feld.

He commented also on the political situation:

> In consequence of the very disadvantageous conditions of the armistice, and judging from the fact that no changes have been made as yet in the higher posts, I conclude that at Berlin they anticipate an early peace.[17]

He would have been glad to be quickly proved wrong about command changes; on May 18 Frederick Charles, with whom he enjoyed an excellent relationship, was appointed Commander in Chief in succession to Wrangel.

Moltke's speculation that an early end to the war might be contemplated had not distracted him from his task of planning the next operations should they become necessary, and on May 23 he placed in the hands of his new commander a detailed analysis of the situation, which Frederick Charles took with him next day to a meeting with the King. Moltke submitted that there were two alternative strategies – for the Allied army either to restrict itself to a permanent occupation of the territories it had conquered, or for it to proceed to make further conquests. As to the first:

> The essentially defensive occupation of the whole of the Danish mainland does not exclude entirely active operations against any enemy attack. Nothing would be better than a Danish offensive to recapture the lost territories. Our three Corps will be concentrated at Flensburg, Kolding, and Aarhus, the better to watch the coasts rather than defend them. Each of them is strong enough on its own to deal with what the Danes can dispose for an offensive, which would soon encounter two of our Corps with double effect. A victory in the open field, followed by a siege of several days, would drive them to the shore and lead them to a decisive catastrophe.

The second alternative meant that the Allies must seek out the enemy in his island position. The principal object was not to conquer fresh territory but rather to beat and destroy the troops that held it. The Danes were now roughly divided into three groups – on Alsen, on Fünen and in the north of Jutland – if they did not evacuate the latter, which would be the correct course for them to follow. An attack on Alsen or Fünen where he expected to find the bulk of the Danish troops at the expiry of the armistice raised the question of the support to be expected from the Austrian fleet. It would be for the King to decide which strategy to pursue but Moltke was in no doubt which was preferable. In the first case, the initiative would be left to the enemy:

> Our action will depend on his decisions. If on the other hand we should continue the offensive, we can only act against Alsen and Fünen and it would be for the Commander in Chief which of these islands to attack at once or better still to act against both simultaneously.[18]

Moltke's more ambitious hopes were to be disappointed, as a result of Austrian anxieties about the effect on Britain if a landing on Fünen should be attempted, and he later mournfully added a note to his paper: 'Political considerations prevent the operation against Fünen, as a result of which only that against Alsen is to be carried out.' Meanwhile Moltke balefully watched the tortuous proceedings of the Conference in London, to which he had despatched the reliable Lieutenant Colonel von Stiehle 'to watch over our military interests.'

On May 26 Moltke submitted to Bismarck a report on the army's situation in Jutland under the terms of the armistice. These, he said, were being rigorously applied by the Allied army and carried out to the letter. Danish commercial activities and civil administration were freely carried on. The demarcation line had been agreed with General Gerlach to ensure that there was no collision between the opposing forces. One of Moltke's previous anxieties had been overcome, firm steps having been taken to prevent the Danes collecting recruits: 'At Viborg and Moegeltondern, the raising of troops has begun during the armistice by Danish officials. On their refusing to desist the officials have been arrested, and the dozen recruits already raised put in prison.' Generally, Moltke was satisfied with the practical working out of the armistice arrangements although not, of course, changing his view as to the military considerations which led him to find its terms objectionable.[19]

Following his meeting with the King, Frederick Charles reported on the reception of Moltke's plan for future operations:

> The King, to whom I read your paper, decided for the offensive if the armistice is not extended. An extension is expected here; the Conference will decide the day after tomorrow. It seems that an extension, even under the existing circumstances, is more desired here than war.[20]

In reply, Moltke was able to report that all was quiet: he enclosed an outline of the measures to be taken if the armistice was not extended, as usual keeping alive the possibility of a simultaneous attack on Fünen and Alsen. Moltke also issued precautionary orders to the three corps and to the 5th Division (in Schleswig) as to the position to be taken up on June 11.

Bismarck had asked for a military opinion about the possibility, which it seemed that the Danes might put forward, of exchanging Jutland for Alsen; in a response which he drafted for signature by Frederick Charles, Moltke advised that, if offered, such an exchange would be beneficial. After a peace treaty, Jutland would have to be given back anyway but the German powers would want to hang on to Alsen. Holding it would tend to push any final demarcation line further north, while it would enable the better concentration of the Allied forces.[21] In the event, no such proposal arose; instead, it was agreed in London that the armistice should be extended by a further fourteen days; Moltke had telegraphed in the name of Frederick Charles that this was, militarily speaking, grossly inconvenient. Bismarck wrote a soothing note in reply explaining that the military aspects had been considered but it was felt necessary to agree to the extension in view of the unanimous wishes of all the other powers.

In spite of this Moltke continued to feel on the top of his form, telling Mary that: 'for me the stay here is as good as a mineral spring treatment.' He liked the Jutland countryside enormously:

> It is lovely here. From my window I overlook a splendour of lilacs, laburnums, and white and pink hawthorns. Jasmine and roses are beginning to bloom, the corn is

The Prussian 64th Line Infantry Regiment storms Alsen, painting by Becker. (Reimer)

> waving in full ears, and one does not see anywhere a trace of the war which but lately swept over this district.[22]

It was pretty clear, as the Conference ground on, that no results would be obtained, thanks to the senseless intransigence of the Danish Government, and also that no further extension of the armistice would be permitted, so Moltke continued to perfect his plan of operations. It was still not for the moment certain whether Falckenstein should take the offensive and go after Hegermann behind the Lijmfjord, or await a Danish offensive or perhaps be pulled back for an attack on Fünen. What was clear was that the operation against Alsen should be undertaken as soon as possible after the expiry of the armistice on June 26, and plans proceeded on this basis. On June 23, Franz Joseph expressly forbade the Fünen plan, following a conversation between Moltke and Gablenz on the subject which the latter had reported to Vienna; and William, no doubt at Bismarck's behest, sent a somewhat peremptory note requiring Moltke to outline what his intentions now were. In his reply, sent in the name of Frederick Charles, Moltke somewhat defensively pointed out that it had been on Wrangel's instructions, with the approval of the Crown Prince, that he had put in hand the planning process of an attack on Fünen, to be undertaken when the moment seemed right. He assured the King that, in the operational orders now being issued 'the attack on Fünen was seen as a last resort to put pressure on Denmark; but no order for its execution has been given.'[23]

The Alsen crossing was to be carried out by the I Corps, now commanded by General Herwarth von Bittenfeld; Blumenthal continued to serve as his Chief of Staff. The operation required careful planning. Herwarth had 25,000 troops at his disposal, and outnumbered Steinmann, who now commanded on Alsen, by about two to one. Nonetheless, there were considerable risks involved. The Danes had had plenty of time to prepare for the assault, which they had long foreseen, and they should have had little difficulty in collecting all the intelligence they needed. Along the whole of the western coast of Alsen redoubts had been erected, supported by numerous batteries and a complex trench system. Steinmann, however, faced the problem that he could not be strong everywhere; the paucity of his forces obliged him to scatter them thinly along his entire front, maintaining a mobile reserve of no more than 3,000 men. This was stationed at Wollerup, about five miles from the crossing point selected by the Prussians. Steinmann had in all twelve battalions of infantry, organised in four brigades. Four battalions were concentrated in the Sonderburg sector but only two battalions guarded

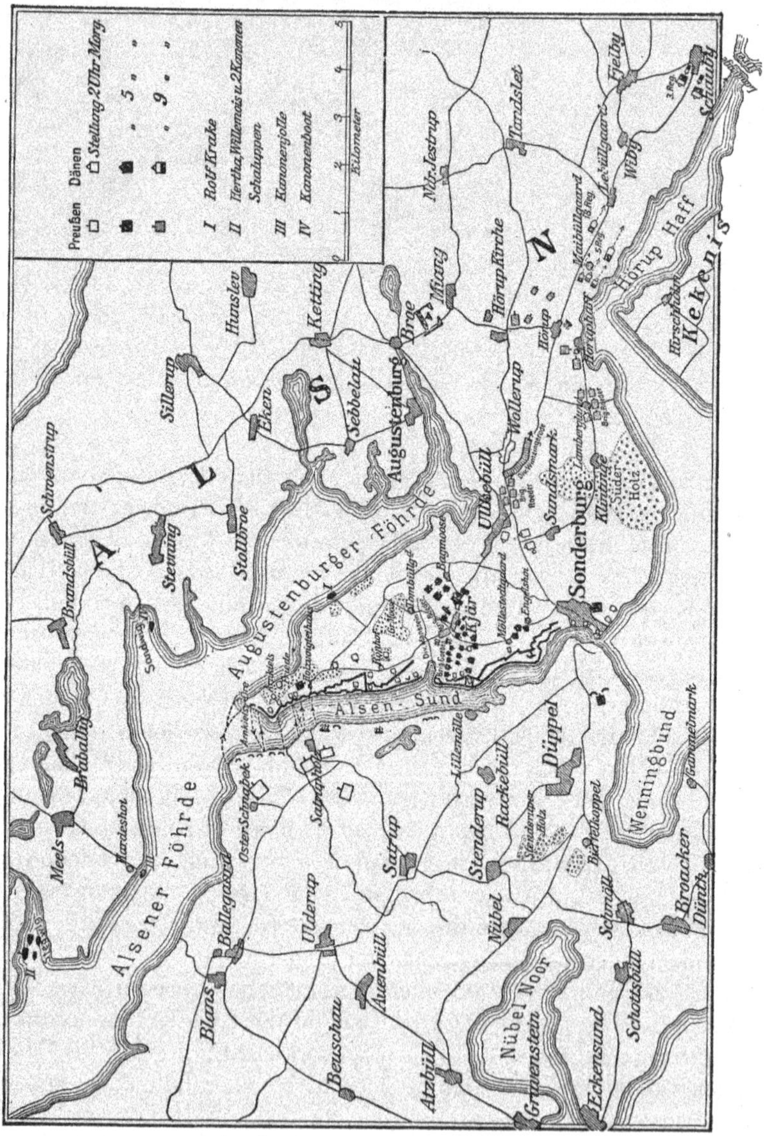

Map 3 – Alsen June 29 1864

the northern end of the Alsen Sund, covering what would be the actual point of attack. There, on the night of 28/29 June Herwarth concentrated his corps in and about the Satrup woods. To support the crossing, and to discourage the *Rolf Krake* from taking an effective hand, a series of heavy batteries had been established. Moltke, with Frederick Charles and the headquarters staff watched the operation from Fort No.10 at the Northern end of the Düppel line.

During the hours of darkness the boats and pontoons to be employed in the assault were assembled in four groups. There were a total of 163 boats capable of carrying 2,350 men. The troops began to embark at 1.00am. Within half an hour the first wave, consisting principally of the 24th Brandenburg Regiment from Roeder's 12th Brigade, pushed silently off from the shore. Half way across they were spotted by the Danish outposts, and a heavy fire was poured on the four columns of boats as they pulled across the Sund. Casualties were, however, light; only seven boats were sunk. Ten minutes later, at 2.00am, the first wave hit the beach, and at once stormed the Danish positions, which were held by men of the 4th Infantry Brigade under Colonel Fanborg. Meanwhile, behind them, the following waves of assault troops were crossing; Roeder's brigade, which comprised the 24th and 64th Regiments, was followed over by Goeben's 26th Brigade, consisting of the 15th and 55th Regiments. At this point the *Rolf Krake*, which had been lying at anchor in the Augustenburg Fjord, put in an appearance with four gunboats. Instead, however, of attacking the boats crossing the Sund, it commenced a futile engagement with the batteries established on the mainland. Once again the apparent command of the sea exercised by the Danes had failed in its effect. Soon becoming convinced that the Prussians were now securely established on Alsen, the captain of the *Rolf Krake* concluded that the best he could do was to cover the Danish retreat, and withdrew from the scene, proceeding to the eastern coast of Alsen to pick up a party of troops that had been cut off by the swift Prussian advance.

Manstein, who was in overall command of the Prussian troops on Alsen, having got two brigades safely ashore, at once deployed his troops to follow up his advantage. His leading units soon captured the Rönhoff Forest, and then fanned out. By 6.00 am Roeder had taken Kjär. By now it was becoming evident to Steinmann that his situation was already practically hopeless. He telegraphed Gerlach's headquarters in Fünen to call for all available transport vessels to concentrate at Horup Hav to take off the retreating troops.[24] The chosen point of attack had effectively split the defending forces in two; the Danes in the north of the island were powerless to intervene, as Goeben pushed along the Sund and approached Sonderburg. Here two battalions, in a brief show of defiance, launched a counter-attack from Baadsager, obliging Goeben to deploy six companies from his reserve. Attacked in both front and flank, the Danish advance soon fizzled out, when the troops were driven back to their start lines. There was a brief hand-to-hand struggle in the northern outskirts of Sonderburg, before the town fell to Goeben's advance. Behind him, Wintzingerode's division had now crossed to Alsen. This consisted of the 25th Brigade (Schmidt) and the 11th Brigade (von Canstein), and it deployed to attack Kauffmann's brigade, which was holding Ulkeböll. There was a short fierce struggle before Kauffmann was driven back. By 9.00 pm Steinmann's troops were everywhere in retreat, having sustained heavy causalities, and the battle for Alsen was as good as over. As Manstein consolidated the Prussian gains he was now in such strength that any further counter-attack was pointless.

Steinmann directed his retreat on Horup Hav and the Kekenis Peninsula, where he had some hope of putting up a stand for long enough to get the bulk of his troops away. The prepared defences there into which his exhausted troops retreated were strong enough to require a major assault to take them, and Moltke, the victory won, saw no point in sustaining heavy casualties to storm the position. Steinmann was left unmolested and, over the next two days, he embarked his troops. By July 1 the last of the Danish troops had left Alsen. It had been a brilliant victory and, as a French historian observed, by far the most important military event of the campaign.[25] It had cost the Prussians 81 killed and 285 wounded; total Danish casualties were approximately 3,200 men, of which 2,500 were prisoners. Moltke watched the battle throughout; he was on his feet for eighteen hours, from when he arrived at Fort No. 10 until 4.00 pm on the following afternoon. He wrote his own vivid and detailed account of the battle in a letter to Mary of July 3, a copy of which he placed in the official archives.[26]

Predictably, public opinion in Copenhagen was utterly dismayed by the fall of Alsen. Although thoughtful observers had warned of the island's vulnerability, it was the popular belief in the Danish command of the sea which had sustained the stubborn position taken by the Danish negotiators in London. The hope of practical support from any of the Great Powers swiftly waned, and it seemed that not only Fünen but also Zealand itself might no longer be secure. The Danish press now began to argue for the conclusion of an early peace, and King Christian himself also intervened, sending his brother John to Brussels to seek King Leopold's help in negotiations with the German Powers. He also made a final attempt to get help from Napoleon III; on July he got a negative response. By now Christian had had enough and sent for Monrad to dismiss him. With Monrad gone, and the stuffing knocked out of the Eider Danes, Christian was free to choose whom he wanted to bring the war to an end as quickly as possible. His choice fell on the experienced Bluhme, who at once made contact with Berlin and Vienna with a view to arranging an immediate armistice.

In Jutland the Allied forces had encountered little effective resistance. There was a foretaste of things to come in a skirmish at Lundby on July 3. A company of 190 Danish troops launched a charge at 184 Prussian infantrymen, who were armed with the needle gun and lying behind a hedge. In a few minutes the Danes lost two officers and 85 men. If the Austrians were paying attention they would have realised that here was a lesson to be learned for the future. On July 10 Gablenz crossed the Lijmfjord, behind which Hegermann had taken up a position for a final stand. He can have had little heart personally for the fight (Sybel reports him as having offered Christian the use of his troops for a *coup d'état* to remove Monrad from power) and by July 13 he had abandoned further resistance and embarked for Zealand. His opponents were close behind him; later that day Vogel von Falckenstein rode into Frederikshavn, where Hegermann had had his headquarters. Next day the Prussian commander, having ridden to Skagen, the northern most point of Jutland, enjoyed the symbolic gesture of raising the flags of the German Powers in sight of Danish vessels standing off the coast.

Although it did not seem likely that significant further operations would prove necessary, Moltke drafted on July 12 a paper outlining what might next be done, returning predictably to the possibility of a descent upon Fünen. For this, it would be necessary to bring up sufficient artillery to deny the use of the Little Belt to the Danish navy, using siege guns to sweep it along its length. He was sure that sufficient boats could be assembled for the crossing to Fünen where he reckoned that the Danes had about 25,000 men. With the superior forces at his disposal, he was satisfied that a successful crossing could be accomplished and, once ashore, the defeat of the Danes was very likely, even if it required the use of most of the army.[27] But it soon became increasingly academic for such plans to be prepared; that day Colonel Kauffmann arrived with a message from Steinmann announcing the change of government and requesting a suspension of hostilities. Stiehle was charged with the armistice negotiations; after a very brief delay it was agreed between Stiehle and Kauffmann that the armistice should come into force at midnight on July 19/20.

The last military engagement of the war had been in the four Frisian islands of Amrum, Sylt, Föhr and Pellworm, off the west coast of Schleswig, where the Danish forces were holding out under the skilful leadership of naval Captain Hammer. In the shallow waters around the islands, the larger Allied vessels under Rear Admiral Wullerstorff could not penetrate, and Hammer put up a tenacious defence. Finally, however, a squadron of small gun boats, the Austrian *Seehund* and *Wall*, and the Prussian *Basilisk* and *Blitz* succeeded in putting ashore an Austrian battalion on Fohr on July 14. Hammer held out for a further five days before capitulating to Captain McLean of the *Blitz*, and with this the fighting finally came to an end.

Even during the discussions leading to the new armistice, originally set to last a month, Moltke was still concerned to keep the attention of Berlin on the possibility of further military action becoming necessary, and he was still convinced that his Fünen project would be the most effective, writing another lengthy report on the subject that came on July 19. He went personally with Frederick Charles to reconnoitre the Little Belt, and telegraphed the King on his return to Headquarters to report that preparations for an assault were already far advanced if should it prove necessary.[28] There was, however, little need for Moltke to worry about these plans, although he was concerned to remain at headquarters until peace was finally concluded, even though he conceded to Manteuffel that Podbielski could perfectly well manage in his absence. His contribution to the final success of the campaign was very well understood as the King made plain in a letter of thanks dated August 14, which Moltke was delighted to receive:

> When I despatched you to the seat of war, I could not foresee with any degree of certainty that your position there would be of any long duration, or that you would find much opportunity of proving your military talent in any very brilliant manner. From the moment, however, that your present position became an established fact you have rewarded my confidence and my expectations in a way that demands my heartiest thanks and full recognition. Both these I now most joyfully beg to offer you. Alsen and the whole of Jutland have fallen into our hands through your ably conducted operations, and June 29 stands gloriously side by side with April 18. The Army has throughout behaved in the most praiseworthy and honourable manner, and has achieved a great 'résultat', which 'diplomatie' has on this occasion not spoiled, but brought to a most astonishing conclusion. As a token of my recognition of your services in this campaign, I decorate you with the Order of the Crown of the First Class with swords; Prince Frederick Charles, from whom you will receive this decoration, begs me to give you a high distinction, which is why I give him the pleasure of personally presenting it to you.[29]

It was generous and well-merited praise; and it marked a momentous advancement of Moltke's influence. Oddly, there appears to have been some suggestion that, on his return to Berlin, Moltke should be posted to the command of the VII Corps, a suggestion on which he modestly commented to Mary on August 25:

> I have been too long out of the regular army and have not sufficient talent to amass the detail to be able to take the chief command of a Corps. I cannot imagine any better settlement than to leave things as they are at the present, where I have had a fortunate campaign, and have the entire satisfaction of my King.[30]

Although the peace terms to be demanded had been entirely clear to Bismarck as early as July and were no longer a matter in which he need consult the wishes of the neutral Powers, the discussions were protracted. On July 11 he had written to Rechberg to lay out the minimum requirements on which the Allies should insist:

> In my opinion the conditions ought to involve Christian's renunciation, in favour of the Allied Powers, of all those rights which he has had, or claims to have, south of the Königsau, and Denmark's recognition and assent to whatever final disposition the two Allied Powers may make of the three Duchies, and the territory belonging to Jutland, lying in Schleswig. A proper share of the whole public debt, besides the costs of the war, would fall heavily upon the Duchies, unless the expenses of the war, as really belonging to Denmark, can be added to a part of the old state debt.[31]

Bismarck was not at all attracted by Christian's suggestion that the whole of Denmark should enter the German Confederation; apart from preserving a Danish connection with the Duchies, he had no wish to see the admission of a non-German State. In order to keep the pressure on the Danes, Bismarck entirely supported the active steps which Moltke was taking to prepare for an assault on Fünen, and was quite unmoved by Rechberg's timorous protests about the possible effects on the British Government.

In fact, once the armistice had been agreed, there did remain one potentially embarrassing task to perform. The Federal troops had throughout the campaign remained in occupation of the fortress of Rendsburg, and there had been continuing friction between them and the Prussian troops quartered there. There had already been one incident, which might have served as a flash point for more serious trouble, when a Hanoverian Colonel had ordered the taking down of Prussian and Austrian flags. Then, in mid-July, there was a brawl between the Saxon and Hanoverian troops on the one hand and the Prussians on the other, in the course of which stones were thrown at the Prussian military hospital. Indifferent to the sensibilities of the lesser German states, Bismarck decided that the time had come to act. Without further ado, Goeben was ordered, on July 21, with some 6,000 troops, to take possession of Rendsburg; Hake, the Federal commander, could see that the Prussians meant business, and immediately evacuated the town. Bismarck could not have more clearly demonstrated his intention that the Confederation should exert no further influence on the future history of the Duchies.

Moltke, meanwhile, had seen his wish to remain at Headquarters until peace was signed duly granted. That autumn was, of course, a relatively undemanding time for him, and he enjoyed himself, writing regularly to Mary with news of his activities. Looking ahead, he was mindful of the interests of the minority in the Duchies:

> I try as far as I can to bring it about that the Danish speaking folk of Schleswig don't lose any of their rights, and that we do not ourselves commit the same injustice which led to the campaign being undertaken.[32]

His final task was to oversee the evacuation of Jutland, which, following the peace treaty concluded on October 30 whereby the Danish King's rights over the Duchies passed to Prussia and Austria, began on November 16. It was December before Moltke himself was back in Berlin. In January he was off again, this time to Vienna for military talks with the Austrians and the beginning of the next stage of his career, which was to culminate on a battlefield in northern Bohemia.

10

Mounting Tension

The formal proprieties of bringing to an end the joint command structures that had led the Allies to victory in the war against Denmark were scarcely out of the way before Moltke was turning his attention to the possibility that he might find himself at war with his erstwhile colleagues. On March 4 1865 Roon, prompted by Bismarck, put a number of significant questions to Moltke. First, he enquired the present strength of the Austrian army and, crucially, how much time it would require to begin hostilities on a large scale. He still wanted to know whether, apart from money, it possessed 'an adequate supply of all the other objects of equipment necessary for the purpose.' Moltke responded with a detailed account of the Austrian forces available for operations in Italy, against Russia, against Prussia and against France. At this point still seeing France as Prussia's most likely opponent, he reckoned that Austria and Prussia acting together against France represented a very powerful force; but he was quick to emphasise his preference for an alliance defining specific action agreed in advance rather than a general alliance.[1] As the year wore on, however, the increasing complexity of the relationship between Austria and Prussia began to point not to cooperation but to the possibility of war between them, and he started to refine his plans for hostilities in Germany itself.

The likelihood that the Austro-Prussian alliance would long survive the attainment of its immediate objective was not substantial. The opposing interests of the two German powers inevitably pushed them towards conflict. The Prussian Crown Council meeting on May 29 1865, to which Moltke was as usual invited, confronted the issues starkly.

In February Bismarck had put forward the Prussian conditions for agreeing to the formation of a separate state of Schleswig-Holstein. He demanded the integration of the armed forces of the Duchies with those of Prussia and an oath of allegiance by them to the Prussian King; the entry of the Duchies to the Zollverein; Prussian control of the posts and telegraphs and the proposed North Sea Canal; and the cession of Friedrichsort and Sonderburg and the mouths of the canal. Not surprisingly, the Austrians had rejected these proposals as completely unacceptable; they had also, although less definitively, rejected the alternative bait of a financial settlement which Bismarck had dangled before them. As to this, Moltke had returned from his courtesy visit to Vienna with Frederick Charles with the conviction that if in addition to a cash settlement the cession of the principality of Hohenzollern was thrown into the scales, the Duchies might still be annexed without conflict.[2]

By May, however, the situation had deteriorated; and Bismarck was ready to play a new card by sending Manteuffel off on a mission to Vienna. His proposed instructions provided that he should

> leave no doubt that we do not fear a rupture; that we do not renounce our legitimate demands... and that to attain them we shall eventually seek and find elsewhere the support that Austria will not give us.[3]

It was this posture that was making William decidedly nervous, and was the immediate occasion for the calling of the Crown Council.

Moltke made a note of the discussion, which Bismarck opened by setting out three options: the creation of an independent state on the basis of the February demands while giving up the oath of allegiance, which would be seen by public opinion in Prussia as a retreat; a financial settlement with some territorial compensation for Austria thrown in, which William had ruled out; or outright annexation, which would probably lead to war against Austria. In that case, he expected France and Russia to observe a 'benevolent neutrality.' War with Austria was probably inevitable in any case. Bismarck concluded:

> One cannot proffer the advice to His Majesty to make a great war upon Austria. The decision thereto can only derive from His Majesty's free conviction. Then, (in that case) however, one would gladly follow him in it.

With the exception of the Crown Prince, who vigorously argued that annexation would lead to civil war in Germany, the ministers generally favoured it. Bismarck rejected the suggestion that a war with Austria would be a civil war; he contended that only by war with Austria could Prussia gain anything. The King turned to Moltke to ask him the opinion of the army. In his reply Moltke went well beyond the confines of the question:

> My personal conviction is that annexation is the only beneficial solution for the Duchies, as for Prussia. The gain is such a great one that very considerable sacrifices must be made, as well as the chances of a war be tolerated. I cannot speak for the opinion of the army, but what I know and have heard of, it is for annexation. I have had to ask myself whether Prussia can take on the struggle against Austria. It would lead us too far if I went into details here, but as the outcome of my investigations I can declare that, besides the excellence of our army, numerical supremacy can be attained at a decisive point.[4]

Since Bismarck did not yet feel that the time was right for an immediate military confrontation, he was content to let the meeting end with William reserving his decision. The discussion had, however, served to prod the reluctant King a few steps further down the road to war, while Moltke was left in no doubt that his immediate task was to ensure that the army was constantly prepared for the imminent outbreak of war, and that his plans for its execution should always be in a high state of readiness. Moltke saw the position with his usual clarity. As he explained in a letter to his brother Adolf on June 24:

> There are only two alternatives, to indemnify the part owner, or to make war on him, (or make him declare war against you). The first would involve a cession of Prussian territory and this has hitherto been absolutely rejected by the King; the other course, therefore, is not impossible and its consequences are incalculable.

King Victor Emanuel II of Italy. (*Album della Guerra del 1866*)

Moltke had not, however, entirely ruled out the possibility of a peaceful solution, cherishing the hope 'that an understanding may be come to which will lead the way to the reconciliation between the two German Powers.'[5]

While Bismarck continued to manoeuvre diplomatically to keep all his options open, he was very conscious that either by design, or more probably by accident, the Austrians might create conditions in which an immediate war could erupt, and he certainly did not intend to be caught napping. On July 7 he addressed to Roon, and to Hindersin as Inspector General of Artillery, enquiries about the army's state of readiness. The fact that his questions were addressed to them rather than to Moltke demonstrates that at that time Moltke's gradual move to the top of the military pyramid still had quite a long way to go. To Roon, Bismarck wrote that 'Austria is supposed to be able to place a hundred and eighty thousand men on our frontier within four weeks. Can we do the same?'[6] Within two days came Roon's reassuring response: 'I can furnish what you may require in case of need,' and he followed it up with confirmation that within the prescribed period of four weeks 250,000 men would be ready to move into Bohemia, while 46,000 would be available for operations in western Germany.

In August the immediate threat of war was lifted by the Convention of Gastein, whereby the crisis was for the moment averted by a *de facto* division of sovereignty in the Duchies. Austria was to administer Holstein and Prussia Schleswig; Franz Joseph sold his rights over Lauenburg to William for cash, and the Duchies were to join the Zollverein. Although the principal importance of the deal lay in the postponement of war, it was a not inconsiderable diplomatic achievement, and Bismarck was raised to the status of Count. At the same time Manteuffel was despatched to Schleswig as Governor, a move which served not only to put a politically experienced general into this highly sensitive post, but also to remove from the position of Chief of the Military Cabinet a man whose input Bismarck found highly disruptive. The Austrians sent Gablenz to fill the same position at Holstein.

Throughout the crisis Bismarck had kept a wary eye on the likely attitude of Italy in the event of an Austro-Prussian war breaking out. To the Prussian envoy in Florence, von Usedom, he wrote that it was 'of the highest importance to know that we can count upon decisive and immediate action on the part of Italy, or whether she will hesitate, postpone and depend upon foreign impulses.'[7]

Moltke had always emphasised the military necessity of a convincing Italian threat, which must pin down in Venetia a substantial section of the Austrian army, and this concern was ever present in the ensuing months. Bismarck spelt out his own programme for the winter with ironic relish, as reported by Thile:

> Tread on Austria's corns, present her with a categorical "either-or", close an alliance with Italy, castrate the Augustenburger, violate the chastity of the Diet, and other similar atrocities.[8]

He was greatly heartened in pursuing this programme of diplomatic misbehaviour by his visit to Napoleon III at Biarritz, from which he had returned confident that the French benevolent neutrality which he had predicted in May would indeed materialise in case of war. And after Gastein he was in no doubt that war would indeed come.

Moltke in the meanwhile was preparing his overall scheme for a campaign against Austria. From the outset he had assumed that a significant part of the paper strength of the Austrian Army would be required elsewhere. The most substantial detachment would, of course, be that made for the protection of Venetia. His careful calculation of the forces available on each side, and of the numbers that each must assign to other theatres led him to the conclusion that he could put into the field against Austria a force roughly equal to that which he expected to confront. In the winter of 1865-66 he wrote a lengthy paper reviewing the probable situation on the outbreak of war, setting out in detail his plans for the concentration of the Prussian Army. His assumption was that Bismarck would be able to deliver on his promise that France and Russia would remain neutral, and that it would not be necessary to place substantial forces on the Rhine; unless this was indeed the case he would not have sufficient strength to take the offensive against Austria. The Austrians, he thought, could count on Saxony and probably South Germany; Italy, on the other hand, he hoped would be an active ally. If that were the case, the Austrians could withdraw none of the 80,000 odd troops presently in Venetia, Tyrol and Dalmatia, and which when placed on a war footing would be augmented by a further 90,000 men. He reckoned that Austria would, including 25,000 Saxons, have 265,000 men available against Prussia.

Moltke's first imperative was to consider the situation of Berlin, only six days march from the Saxon border. He expected that 'Austria's goal will probably be not directly to conquer Silesia and afterwards to defend it, but to obtain the greatest possible advantages by the overthrow of the power of Prussia.' That meant an all-out offensive towards the Prussian capital, and an Austrian advance in this direction would encounter no fortresses nor any strong defensive position:

> Our whole theatre of war as far as the sea is only about 140 miles in depth. The loss of Berlin cuts the state in two, cuts all communications from the Rhine to the

> Vistula, and would politically be infinitely more important than the loss of Breslau or of all Silesia, for the reconquest of which all our forces could be assembled.

In choosing between Lusatia and Upper Silesia for the point of concentration of the principal Prussian forces, Moltke had in mind that Austria would be ready to advance from Bohemia at the same time as the Prussian Army could assemble in Lusatia, while an Austrian concentration in Moravia would be quicker and a Prussian concentration in Upper Silesia would be slower. That being so, Lusatia must be the place to concentrate, and the question was then whether to do so behind the Lusatian Mountains or the Riesengebirge. The former position would indirectly protect Silesia; and since in any case he intended an offensive strategy, and the Lusatian Mountains offered seven roads converging on Prague, while there were few practical roads through the Riesengebirge, it must be behind the Lusatian Mountains that the principal force should be assembled. Here he proposed to concentrate six corps, between Dresden and Görlitz, amounting to 193,000 men, leaving two corps with 54,000 men available for Silesia between Freiburg and Schweidnitz. Only one corps, and the garrison of Mainz, would be detached for operations in Western Germany. The strategy then to be followed must depend on prevailing circumstances, but essentially there were two options; either to take up positions between Görlitz and Zittau, which the Austrians could not bypass, or to advance into Bohemia and strike 'a deadly blow' against the Austrian left.

So far as Saxony was concerned, which could mobilise within fourteen days, Moltke wished to launch an attack without waiting to complete his mobilisation, since he feared that to delay would give the Saxons the chance to retreat and join the Austrian main body: 'The only way to prevent this is to surprise and disarm the Saxon troops in their quarters before they are on a war footing, and before they are concentrated.' For this operation he calculated that 16,000 men would be required.

Finally, he calculated that the troops earmarked for Western Germany, although potentially facing some 80,000 South German troops, would be sufficient to prevent the latter from cooperating effectively with the Austrian Army. Although on the face of it the disparity of forces there made it a risky strategy, it was a risk that Moltke was content to take; in the end, even if the Bavarians got their act together soon enough to enable them to invade the Rhine provinces, in reality everything turned upon the outcome in Bohemia.[9]

The deterioration in relations between Prussia and Austria, which Bismarck had cheerfully predicted, made it increasingly evident to Moltke that war was becoming inevitable. But he was not indifferent to the political desirability of avoiding the public impression that it was Prussia that was to blame for this. On February 22 1866 he wrote a memorandum which reflected this:

> Austrian measures have the appearance of aggression. It is politically important to give time for this to become clear to Germany and to Europe. The impression in our favour would be destroyed if we also were to arm. The question is how long we can wait without danger.

Austria, he reckoned, could immediately collect up to 100,000 men in twenty one days, a figure that could be increased to 150,000 in twenty eight days and 200,000 in thirty six days, and it would be a total of six weeks before such a force could reach the Prussian frontier. Given the need for the Austrian Army to collect 53,000 horses, he concluded that:

> As long as the purchase of horses on a large scale has not been ordered, and the regiments in Italy are not placed on a war footing, we need not believe that there is serious intention to attack us.[10]

Meanwhile the Italian Government, although still deeply suspicious of Bismarck, especially since the Convention of Gastein, in which they believed they had been let down, were letting it be known to Usedom that they were coming round to the idea of concluding a formal alliance. It was at this point that William convened a Crown Council meeting for February 28 to review the situation. Moltke attended, as did Manteuffel, and also Alvensleben, the Adjutant General. Goltz was also present, in order to give the latest situation report from Paris. The King opened the debate with a short summary of the situation in terms which made it clear that he was, in theory at any rate, now personally ready to assert Prussia's aims even at the risk of war. He was followed by Bismarck, who put matters rather more bluntly:

> A war with Austria must certainly come, sooner or later. It is wiser to undertake it now under these most favourable conditions than to leave it to Austria to choose the most auspicious moment for itself.

After Goltz had spoken to confirm that Napoleon would remain neutral in a war over Schleswig-Holstein, and would probably not oppose any wider Prussian war aims, Moltke was asked for an analysis of the military position.

He emphasised that for Prussia to be absolutely sure of victory, it was necessary that Italy take part in the war. It would limit Austria to not much more than 240,000 men for its army in Bohemia, which Prussia could match even after despatching 50,000 men to deal with Bavaria and the other South German states. Bismarck proposed that, in view of the importance of Italian participation, Moltke himself should go to Florence to negotiate the terms of the treaty, and this was readily agreed. As usual, the Crown Prince, who spoke last and opposed the war, was in the minority; the only other to share his views was Bodelschwingh, the Finance Minister. The King summed up by saying that the possession of the Duchies was worth the war, but that it should not be declared too hastily.[11] William, now ready to fight for the Duchies, had come a long way since his meeting at Schönbrunn with Franz Joseph some eighteen months earlier, when he had shrunk from asserting his claim to them.

On March 3 Moltke and Bismarck sat down to discuss the terms of his instructions for his mission, and two days later Moltke produced a draft. In a covering note, he expressed the view that Italy would probably stand out for a solemn pledge from Prussia to go to war, and to fix a date to do so. In a brief outline of the military terms, the details of which were to be left to his discretion, he suggested that Prussia should agree to put 300,000 men in the field, and Italy 220,000. The most sensitive point was that the parties should be required to put their armies on the frontier not later than four weeks after Prussia had taken the decision to declare war. Above all, however, he saw

General Giuseppe Govone, despatched by Italy to Berlin to broker an agreement with Prussia in 1866. (*Album della Guerra del 1866*)

no need to particularise the operations to be carried out; they would be conducted in separate theatres, entirely independently, and the advantage lay not in their being combined towards a particular objective but merely that they be simultaneous. In the draft instructions he defined Italy's war aim as the possession of Venetia, while that of Prussia was 'to gain certain rights in the north of Germany, and for Austria to be compelled to recognise them.'[12]

After Bismarck had revised the draft, and gone through it with William, the final text was settled on March 12; but just as he was preparing to set off on his mission, Moltke learned that his journey might for the moment not be necessary. News came from La Marmora, the Italian Prime Minister, that he was sending the politically experienced General Giuseppe Govone to Berlin for military and diplomatic discussions. This step did not mark a sudden urge on the part of the Italians to go to war; it was rather calculated to unsettle the Austrians to make them perhaps more amenable to the suggestion now being floated that, to avoid war, Austria should cede Venetia to Italy and get Romania in exchange.[13] This, however, was a non-starter; while Napoleon had been prepared to listen to the idea when Nigra, the Italian Ambassador, put it forward, it soon became clear that the British Government did not approve, while the Czar was even more explicit, commenting in a marginal note on the despatch: 'Inadmissible *jusqu'à la guerre*.'

Govone arrived in Berlin on March 14, armed with instructions that exactly reflected La Marmora's shifty disposition. His first objective was, he was told, to get a result which might induce Austria to hand over Venetia without a fight; in any case, there was, La Marmora later claimed, little confidence on the part of the Italian military in the solidity of the Prussian Army.[14] Bismarck, of course, knew perfectly well what La Marmora was up to, and approached the negotiations with Govone accordingly. In these, Govone was joined by Barral, the Italian Ambassador, who was particularly suspicious

Emperor Franz Joseph of Austria, a photograph taken in 1866. (Rogers)

of Prussian motives and intentions; and the first meeting ended without agreement, the principal sticking point being, as Moltke had foreseen, the Italian reluctance to leave the initiative as to the outbreak of hostilities entirely in Prussian hands. Bismarck suggested that in that case the parties should simply sign a treaty of friendship with no particular obligations to be agreed until the outbreak of war. Even this seemed unacceptable to Govone, although in reporting to La Marmora he suggested that he should hang on in Berlin for a while, and perhaps even sign such a treaty, remarking deviously: 'In this way we may gain the time and means for making other combinations, and the adder will have bitten the snake charmer.'[15]

So Govone remained, his presence in Berlin now well known across Europe; as Karolyi monitored the continued discussions, his reports to Vienna gave rise to mounting indignation, particularly on the part of Franz Joseph, who pointedly omitted his usual birthday letter to King William. Moltke prepared on March 20 an *aide mémoire* for Bismarck for use during the negotiations. He had been reviewing suggestions from Florence that the Italians might be able to assemble at least 250,000 troops for offensive operations; all told, he reckoned that the Italian army when mobilised would be 264,000 strong, but that after detachments for Naples, Bologna and Placentia, no more than 200,000 would be available to cross the frontier.[16]

Negotiations between the would-be allies continued, in spite of the sustained and mutual mistrust which characterised their relationship. But the significant developments which increasingly pointed to the probability of war did much to reassure the Italians, and it was the hitherto suspicious Barral who came up with a revised suggestion, which, after discussion with Govone, was put to La Marmora. This was that there should be concluded a treaty along the lines proposed by Bismarck but with a term limiting its duration to two months (a period which, at Bismarck's request, he lengthened to three months). Since this would tie Italy's hands for only a short time, La Marmora responded favourably, but before taking it further he instructed Nigra to see what Napoleon III had to say about it. He got an immediate, and encouraging, response; as a result La Marmora was able without difficulty to secure the approval of Victor Emanuel and instructions went back to Govone and Barral to proceed accordingly. La Marmora could now feel confident that, if he was let down by Prussia, he could look to Napoleon for support.

In the final text of the treaty, Italy abandoned her claims to the Tyrol, but on the other hand was no longer to be obliged to declare war against those states of the Confederation which took Austria's side. There was, however, one last hitch. Barral objected to the treaty being expressed to be 'a treaty of friendship and alliance.' It must, he insisted, be called 'an offensive and defensive alliance.' Bismarck shrugged his shoulders; if that was what the Italians wanted, then well and good. It was in this form that the treaty, which was to remain secret, was signed in Berlin on April 8 and ratified a week later.[17]

Bismarck had thus achieved the diplomatic success that Moltke regarded as indispensable. While the latter would have much to say about the best way for the Italians to conduct their campaign, it was the mere fact of their participation in the war that mattered. This was of decisive importance in giving Bismarck, and Moltke, the freedom to make plans which would ensure that Prussia's position, both diplomatic and military, could be maximised. Moltke could now look at the first steps towards mobilisation being taken by Austria secure in the knowledge that a significant part of his opponent's strength would be tied up in Italy. As for Bismarck, he graphically expressed his view of his newly acquired allies when he remarked on a later occasion that 'the Italians have large appetites but rotten teeth.'

Part II
PREPARATION

11

Mobilisation

For a long time, in spite of an increasing number of straws in the wind, Franz Joseph and most of his advisers had failed to address the urgent military issues that were central to any orderly preparation for war. As late as February 21 Franz Joseph had wound up a meeting of the ministers by going with the majority view, saying

> that he should leave warlike preparations for the time being aside and should continue to seek the maintenance of the honour and dignity, as well as of the interests, of the country by diplomatic means.

The necessary preparations could, he thought be made on paper.[1] Warnings that Prussia meant business continued, however, to arrive. Karolyi advised that, for Bismarck, annexation of the Duchies was 'a matter of life or death for his political existence', and in alliance with many military figures his influence for war upon the impressionable King was 'ceaselessly active' in this direction. Karolyi's reports were complemented by those from his Military Attaché, Colonel Pelikan, who quoted Roon as saying that 'the Prussians must confront their enemy before the latter has time to think about it.' Pelikan added that Prussia would, once action was decided on, strike quickly.[2] In the context of their awareness that their mobilisation would take far longer than that of Prussia, the Austrians were playing with fire in delaying. Bismarck's mischievous response to the wife of the Saxon ambassador in Berlin, when she asked him if it were true that he planned to fight Austria and conquer Saxony, seriously alarmed Beust, who conveyed at once to Vienna what the Minister-President was reported to have said in reply:

> Certainly it is true, my dear Countess. From the first day of my ministry I have entertained no other thought. Our cannon have been cast already and you shall soon see how much better they are compared to the Austrian artillery.

He went on to advise her not to go to her estate in Bohemia, 'for just there, if I am not mistaken, right in the neighbourhood of your estate we shall whip the Austrians.'[3]

In the face of all this the Austrians began to look at operations in earnest, and on March 7 Franz Joseph began a series of meetings with senior military figures. To these meetings he summoned from Verona Ludwig von Benedek, upon whom it was intended to confer command of the Army of the North in Bohemia. Benedek struggled to avoid the poisoned chalice; but eventually, after a final appeal that if the Archduke Albert were to command, and was defeated, Franz Joseph would have to abdicate, he accepted, saying later that 'after such an explanation I should have been a rotten fellow if I had not taken the command.'[4]

The first step taken in Vienna, on March 2, in response to news that the Berlin Landwehr had been called out, had been to mobilise six cavalry regiments and six batteries. On March 7 the key decision to move troops into Bohemia was taken – a turn of the ratchet that must bring war nearer. The number involved was not huge – it involved only ten battalions and thirty squadrons – but it was significant not only in that it helped Bismarck portray Austria as being of warlike intent, but also because it sharpened the anxiety of Moltke and his senior colleagues that Austria might start to erode Prussia's advantage. Bismarck continued to provoke such actions on Austria's part; on March 16, in a reply to a direct question from Karolyi as to whether Prussia harboured 'the object of tearing up the Gastein Convention with forcible hands,' he gave an unequivocal denial; but added 'but, my dear Count, you don't really think I should have answered any differently if I did intend war, do you?'[5] On March 24 Bismarck published a circular to the members of the Confederation in which he gave details of Austrian troop movements, and asked if Prussia could look to them for help.

The effect of all this was apparent at the next meeting of the Prussian Ministerial Council on March 28: those present had no difficulty in accepting the need to raise the military ante by calling up some 11,000 troops to strengthen the infantry divisions based in southern Silesia, putting the fortresses there on a war footing, and at the same time authorising the purchase of horses for the field artillery. Moltke, who had prepared a detailed paper for this meeting pointing out that Austria had gained the advantage of being able to assemble an army in Bohemia more quickly than Prussia could put down an opposing force of equal strength at any given point, was very disappointed by the outcome. In this paper he had argued that while Austria might presently have no immediate plan to attack, she could change her mind if she saw the chance of putting 100,000 men on the frontier before Prussia had made any preparations.[6]

Prussian troops leaving Berlin for the front, painting by Klein. (Voss)

In the days following the meeting he despatched a series of notes to Roon and to Bismarck reporting on the measures taken by Austria, and warning increasingly sharply of the risk of delay in responding. On April 3 he spelled out to Roon his position in the most emphatic terms. As a result of the start the Austrians had made, he calculated that, assuming general mobilisation began on both sides simultaneously, it would be eighteen days before Prussia caught up. From then until the forty second day the advantage would be with Prussia: 'every day gained by Austria in arming is a day lost to us after the incalculably important period for operations.'[7]

Moltke's anxiety was occasioned not only by the continuing delay in ordering Prussian mobilisation, but also by the possible consequences of Bavaria joining Austria. He analysed the position in a paper which he wrote for the King on April 2:

> The probability of a war with Austria, or the impossibility of avoiding it, are political questions outside my competence; but from my personal point of view I believe I should express the conviction that success or failure in this war essentially depends on the determination to undertake it being reached sooner than it is by Vienna and, if possible, at once.

The key advantage possessed by Prussia, he pointed out, was the ability to move the army over five railway lines, thereby to obtain a concentration on the frontier within twenty five days; Austria, on the other hand, had only one railway line into Bohemia, and would require forty five days to assemble 200,000 men there:

> If, however, Bavaria makes common cause with Austria, it is not so much that her army which threatens us as the utilisation by Austria of the railway line Regensburg-Pilsen-Prague, since this will reduce by about fifteen days the period calculated as absolutely necessary for the concentration of the Austrian Army.[8]

On reading this paper the King became decidedly jittery, noting on it:

> I am very painfully affected by the changed attitude of Bavaria. If only Württemberg does the same, this will equal another 100,000 men with Austria against us. As a result we will need more than the VII Corps available against the South; and thus our forces in Bohemia, which Moltke calculated as equal to the Austrians when including the VII and VIII Corps would be reduced by 60,000 men, and these 60,000 men are all that we have to oppose the South of 100,000.[9]

Roon, in an effort to allay William's fears, asked Moltke to write something to encourage him. In this, however, Moltke was not disposed to be helpful, preferring to keep up the pressure for mobilisation by spelling out the situation as bluntly as he could. He replied to Roon on April 5:

> That the Austrians – if we give them time – can assemble as many troops as we can, is not new, and I have said this at all the conferences that have taken place. The point is not the absolute number of troops available, it is the time required on each side to put these troops into a position to fight....No one can think of persuading

the King to begin a war like this, but one must make it easier to take a decision by an exact and clear exposition of the real state of things.[10]

Although for a few days there were some signs that in response to diplomatic developments Austria had briefly suspended her operations, the extent of the advantage his enemy had gained continued to trouble Moltke. On April 12 he pointed out to Bismarck that the Austrian units directly facing Silesia could very soon reach a total strength of 88,000 men, while even after mobilisation the Prussian forces opposing them would only amount to 45,000 men. This threatening disparity was, he said, due to the fact that since the steps taken at the end of March no further counter measures had been ordered.[11] And in the ensuing fortnight, as intelligence reports continued to arrive, Moltke sent a stream of notes to Roon to warn of the continuing progress of the Austrian preparations. On May 2 he told Roon that it was no longer possible to doubt that the Austrian mobilisation would soon be complete, and that Benedek's troops were ready to take the field; there were now indications that they had begun to move up to the frontier.

During this period, whilst Moltke was fretting over the progressive erosion of the advantage on which he had originally been able to count, Bismarck had continued to be active on the diplomatic front. Among other steps which he took, he unveiled his outline proposals for the reform of the Confederation, which prompted outrage throughout Europe. During this time his manoeuvres attracted the censure of most of the Great Powers, among whose leaders was shared a general belief that he was riding for a fall. This was an opinion also held by his ambassador in Paris, whose personal hostility to Bismarck was displayed in a number of thoroughly disloyal comments. To his British

Austrian troops depart Vienna for Bohemia, painting by Klein. (Voss)

colleague, Goltz predicted hopefully that 'Bismarck will be eventually driven from power', while to Bismarck himself he urged that the reform proposal be withdrawn.

Bismarck, however, knew perfectly well what he was doing. He was not ready to commit himself to war until the position of the Austrians was hopelessly compromised, and with each step that he took the Austrian response was to blunder further into the trap. In any case, there was another compelling reason to delay mobilisation; a prolonged period of active military preparation was ruinously expensive, and although he had amassed some financial reserves during the previous year at the time of the crisis which led to the Gastein negotiations, Bismarck was very conscious of the advice of Bodelschwingh, his Finance Minister, and of Bleichröder, his personal banker. It was essential that expense be kept to a minimum.

Meanwhile efforts by various members of Europe's royal families, orchestrated by Rechberg's successor Mensdorff and led by the Coburgs, had served to put pressure on William to suspend preparations. For a few days it seemed that both sides might be prepared to draw back from the brink, with a proposal that each side should disarm. But both William and Franz Joseph were also subject to sustained pressure from their respective military advisers, which was extremely hard to resist. Franz Joseph, indeed, would have been prepared to suspend preparations unilaterally;[12] but although he was supported by his foreign minister in his willingness to seek ways to halt the slide to war, Mensdorff's influence was declining. As luck would have it, Mensdorff was absent from a meeting of the Austrian Ministerial Council on April 21 due to an injured foot. At this time he was awaiting a response from Berlin to an offer he had made of disarmament; but the meeting was much more influenced by intelligence reports (later found to be inaccurate), which appeared to suggest an Italian concentration of some 40,000 men at Bologna and the purchase of additional horses. Confronted by this, the meeting was resolved on the mobilisation of the Army of the South. Although a cautiously favourable response from Bismarck to the disarmament proposal was before the Ministers at their meetings on the next two days, Mensdorff was conscious that he had begun to lose control of the situation, observing: 'It is really difficult to say what ought to be done now; the most skilful statesman would be at a loss for a clear, definite answer.'[13] By April 27, the assertion of Henikstein, the Austrian Chief of Staff, that 'when we arm we can speak a language which is bound to have an effect,' was a good deal more representative of feeling in Vienna than the flagging efforts of Mensdorff and Esterhazy to preserve peace. It was on that day that orders went out for the mobilisation of the rest of the Austrian Army.

Determined as he was that Austria should be seen as the aggressor, Bismarck could not conceal his satisfaction at this development, which finally created the conditions in which William's reluctance to take an irrevocable step could be overcome. On May 3 the first of a series of orders for the mobilisation of the Prussian Army was at last, to Moltke's great relief, issued. This was, however, confined to the five corps closest to the Austrian frontier; and although it meant that Moltke could now begin to plan his deployment in earnest, he did so in the knowledge that the long period of delay would cost him numerical superiority at the outset of the campaign. It was now almost certain that war would break out; the military machines picked up speed across Germany and it was apparent that, as a modern historian has noted, an era had ended – 'an era when gradual escalation was still possible, when armies could be partly mobilised and held in their garrisons as the last threat short of war.'[14] Moltke himself realised this; the Official History of the war produced under his guidance observed that 'of old it was possible to prepare the Prussian Army for war without actually calling it into action. This can hardly ever now be the case.'[15]

While Moltke worked on his plans for the deployment and revised his strategy in the light of the changing situation, and his staff laboured heroically to make good the lost time, international efforts to avert the war continued. With the issue of mobilisation orders it was evident that little time was left, and that any step to get effective negotiations going would require concentrated action on the part of the other Great Powers. This, however, was markedly lacking; on May 6 Napoleon exploded a bombshell in his speech at Auxerre in which he roundly denounced the treaties of 1815. French self-interest was an unpromising basis on which to bring about any united action, and the international efforts to achieve a peaceful solution were wholly ineffective. Next day another, very different, event made the headlines; an attempt was made on Bismarck's life by a student who succeeded in firing two shots before Bismarck, with great presence of mind, turned swiftly and seized his opponent and handed him over to two guardsmen who ran up. The news produced a popular demonstration in Bismarck's favour, although there were some who were less enthusiastic: 'How bad revolvers are in this country,' one prominent academic was said to have grumbled.

One rather more promising scheme to settle the Schleswig-Holstein dispute was produced by the Gablenz brothers. Anton von Gablenz, a Prussian citizen, and his brother Ludwig, the Austrian Governor of Holstein, had since 1865 been working on a plan which in a revised form Anton took to Vienna on April 20, where he met secretly with Esterhazy and Mensdorff. This provided for the independence of the Duchies under a Prussian prince, the division of the military command in Germany between Prussia and Austria, the reimbursement to Austria of her costs of the Danish war, and an alliance between the two Great Powers who would themselves settle the question of Federal reform. For the next five weeks Anton von Gablenz shuttled back and forth between Berlin and Vienna, receiving a sympathetic hearing both from Mensdorff and Bismarck. The latter instructed Werther, his Ambassador in Vienna, that the Prussian Government regarded the proposals as a basis for discussion; but as time went by, both Governments cooled in their response to the suggestion, Franz Joseph becoming especially sceptical about a scheme which had come too late. How sincere the two governments were in encouraging Anton von Gablenz is unclear; the Austrians were certainly interested in any scheme that would avert war, if the terms were right, but they were also looking to play for time. On the other hand Bismarck was always keen to keep his options open, and with some revision might have seen the plans as achieving his objective, while he was quite unable to reject absolutely a scheme in which William was certainly interested.

Meanwhile all the smaller German states had mobilised; at a conference of ministers at Bamberg it was evident that there was a pronounced hardening of their opposition to Prussia, which was the fruit of Mensdorff's energetic search for allies during the preceding weeks. The military discussions which were at once put in hand demonstrated the considerable difficulties which the allies, all driven by self interest, faced in welding together the various contingents that made up the Federal 8th Corps. Prince Alexander of Hesse was appointed to command this force; his orders were to cooperate with the Bavarian Army under Prince Charles, but first he had to negotiate individually with the smaller states to get his force together. The total number of troops available in Southern Germany was, on paper, impressive, and it had certainly worried William. Moltke, however, had a clear understanding of their true effectiveness and made his dispositions accordingly.

Still energetically pursuing French self interest, Napoleon proposed a Congress; Bismarck, outwardly cooperative, agreed to attend, but Austria's acceptance was on the condition that the outcome must in advance be agreed as not allowing the acquisition of any territory or increase of power of any state attending. This effectively scuppered the plan. Instead there were secret Austro-French discussions which led in due course to a treaty whereby France was to remain neutral and it was agreed that Venetia should be ceded to France at the end of the war; the hope was that Austria might be compensated by the acquisition of Silesia. But although the various diplomatic initiatives to avoid the outbreak of war appeared to have run into the sand, the identification of an appropriate *casus belli* still remained to be made as May drew to a close.

Moltke, who had an audience with the King on May 25, was in no doubt that any further delay should be avoided. In his notes of the meeting he set out two alternative scenarios which might arise. After reviewing the offensive options available to the Austrians he pointed out that the strategic deployment of the nine Prussian corps on the frontiers of Saxony and Bohemia would be complete by June 5:

> From a military point of view there is no doubt that from then on we must not wait a single day before acting. It is not at all likely that by that date the Austrians will have transported all the forces which they count on using against us in this

Prussian reservists leave Halle. (*Illustrirte Kriegs-Chronik*)

> campaign. But however strong they are, it is absolutely certain that each passing day will add to their strength, and that a new adversary may arise in Franconia within a few weeks. It is essential that before this happens we must strike down our principal enemy, the one that is ready, in which case the 7th and 8th Federal Corps will doubtless never do anything...From a purely military point of view it is very desirable that any diplomatic action should be brought to a close by June 5.[16]

The problem was that even now it was not a simple question of choosing the most convenient date on which to commence hostilities; William was still profoundly uneasy, and very reluctant to accept the responsibility for the actual outbreak of war. As late as June 10 Bismarck remarked to the Hungarian General Türr, whom he hoped would be able to stir up trouble for Austria behind their lines: 'I have not yet succeeded in convincing the King that war is immediately necessary. But what does it matter – I have put the horse at the ditch and ...he must jump.'[17]

By then, indeed, events in Holstein and the Diet had moved beyond the point of no return. On June 5 Gablenz had summoned the Holstein Estates for June 11 in accordance with instructions received from Vienna. To this Manteuffel, his opposite number in Schleswig, responded at once, complaining that the Austrian reference of the issues to the Confederation was a breach of the Convention of Gastein and that Prussia would accordingly exercise her right to joint occupation of both of the Duchies; and would, starting on the following day, establish garrisons in Holstein. Gablenz at once concentrated his troops, some 4,800 strong, and withdrew to Altona under protest, while Manteuffel proceeded to occupy the whole of Holstein. Manteuffel's forces were instructed to march on Altona, from which Gablenz adroitly extricated himself. Bismarck was discontented at Manteuffel's double success, which deprived him of an immediate excuse to commence hostilities, grumbling to Barral: 'If only there had been an exchange of shots.'[18] In Vienna, too, there was disappointment; it had at least been expected that events in the Duchies would compel Prussia to fire the first shot. Nonetheless, the events there were sufficient to justify Mensdorff in instructing Karolyi on June 12 to demand his passports.

Meanwhile, the proceedings of the Diet had moved towards the final breakdown. The last days of that normally somnolent body were characterised by vigorous activity. Austria's reference of the Schleswig-Holstein question was followed by a Prussian protest on June 3 at this breach of the Convention of Gastein; and the collapse of Napoleon's Congress plan cleared the way for Bismarck to publish a circular dispatch denouncing Austria's determination to provoke a war come what may. On June 9 Prussia responded to Austria's motion before the Diet by denying that Schleswig was any of the Confederation's business, while the position in Holstein was unclear. Next day Bismarck published his details of Confederation reform, the key elements of which were the exclusion of Austria and a call for a national parliament elected by universal suffrage.

On June 12 Bismarck had outlined to a meeting of the Prussian Ministerial Council two alternative scenarios. If, after all, the Middle States remained neutral, all the troops scattered through Western Germany could be moved to the decisive theatre in Silesia and Bohemia; if not, their current deployment must be well placed to take immediate action against the Middle States, starting with Hanover. Immediately after the vote was taken in the Diet, Nassau, Hesse-Cassel, Hanover and Saxony would be called upon to declare their neutrality and their acceptance of the scheme for Confederation reform. In the event of a negative response, war was to be declared at once.[19] There was no doubt at the meeting that it was the latter scenario which would actually develop.

In fact up to the last it was not entirely certain which way the vote would go in the Diet. When the vote was taken, however, nine of the votes supported the Austrian motion (as amended by Bavaria) calling for mobilisation of the Federal forces excluding those of Prussia and Austria, with five against. All Austria's allies supported them; Baden abstained, at the instigation of its pro-Prussian Grand Duke. After the announcement of the outcome, Savigny, the Prussian delegate, rose to declare that the Confederation had been effectively dissolved by reason of Austria's proceedings, and that Prussia would accordingly withdraw; then, alone, he left the Chamber. The long period of intricate and ineffectual diplomatic activity was at last over; Bismarck had his war.

William had in the meantime taken an extremely important step towards ensuring that the war would be won. Until June 2, although Moltke was Chief of the General Staff, which was responsible for preparing the Army's operations orders, these were edited and distributed by the War Ministry. On that day, however, William issued an instruction that marked the recognition of the place that Moltke now occupied, and which effectively conferred upon him supreme authority over the Prussian Army. He wrote to Moltke:

> I send you herewith a copy of the order which I have today addressed to the Ministry of War by virtue of which from this date my orders for the operations and the movements of the main army and its isolated detachments will be communicated to subordinate commanders by the Chief of the Great General Staff of the Army. You will, for your part, at the same time keep the Ministry of War informed of developments.[20]

The significance of this step can hardly be overstated, and it has of course been the subject of careful scrutiny by historians. As Professor Craig has noted, the official historians of the General Staff seem to have found in the apparent supersession of Roon, Bismarck's close colleague, an explanation of some of the conflicts that marred the subsequent relationship between Bismarck and Moltke during the Wars of Unification: 'When Moltke on June 2 finally stepped into Roon's place as the first military adviser of the King, he must have appeared to Bismarck to a certain extent as an intruder.' Professor Craig finds this unconvincing, not least because Bismarck made no objection. On the other hand, as he points out, Roon was much more politically aware than Moltke, who was to take a much more rigid line in objecting to civilian interference to military questions.[21]

12

Deployment

In considering the strategy to be adopted against Austria, Moltke had always insisted that Prussia must seize and maintain the initiative. This was essential even if the enemy attempted to pursue an offensive strategy. He reckoned that his opponent had two options for this; either to advance with the bulk of their forces directly on Berlin, which lay only 94 miles from the frontier, or to embark on the conquest of Silesia. As has been seen, the first substantial paper which Moltke had written outlining the strategic choices to be made had been produced in the spring of 1860, at a time when the political and military circumstances were rather different from those obtaining in 1866. In a detailed analysis of the options available to them, he had little doubt as to which the Austrians ought to choose, pointing out that an advance on Breslau would give time for the Prussian army to concentrate on the Oder, and that the Austrians would 'do better at once to seek that army in the direction of Berlin and to conquer Silesia in Brandenburg. This is the shortest way to the most complete and rapid decision.'[1] But in practice a properly conducted defence would, he thought, compel the Austrians to extend their right wing into Silesia. 'The most advantageous, and therefore most probable plan is for Austria to direct the principal operation against the Marks, and at the same time a minor operation against Silesia.'[2] This meant that the first concentration of the Austrian army must be on the line Prague – Pardubitz, from which they would advance on the right bank of the Elbe through the Lusatian mountains. For this, seven good roads were available. At the same time a smaller force could move through Trautenau in the direction of Breslau.

If one single point of concentration could suffice to resist such an offensive, Görlitz would, Moltke considered, be the place for it, being far enough to the east to enable operations to be conducted against an enemy advance into Silesia, as well as being served by good railway connections with Breslau, Posen and Berlin. But in reality, the opportunity to strike at the flank of an Austrian army moving into Silesia was illusory, since it would expose the direct line towards Berlin. It would not immediately be possible to divine the real intention of the enemy:

> Neither the concentration of the Austrian army in Northern Bohemia, the establishment of magazines there, nor even the partial crossing of the frontier, will give us any definite indication of the direction in which the enemy is arranging his principal blow.[3]

In consequence, the Prussian deployment must be arranged to cover the line of advance on Berlin, since this was the more dangerous enemy option. The larger part of the Prussian army should therefore concentrate nearer the Elbe, in a position from which it could flank an Austrian advance northwards to Berlin, while a separate force defended Silesia. But a passive defence was not at all what Moltke had in mind:

We do not believe that a flank position behind the Elbe will hold the enemy spellbound, or hinder him from advancing past it towards Berlin, but we expect this result from an offensive based upon the Elbe.... If the offensive stroke delivered from the Elbe succeeds, it drives the enemy away from Bohemia, and back upon the, as yet, unconquered Silesia. If it fails, we shall find behind the river a more complete and nearer protection than by retreating northwards, and the strong places secure to us the possibility of again advancing across the river after the shortest respite.[4]

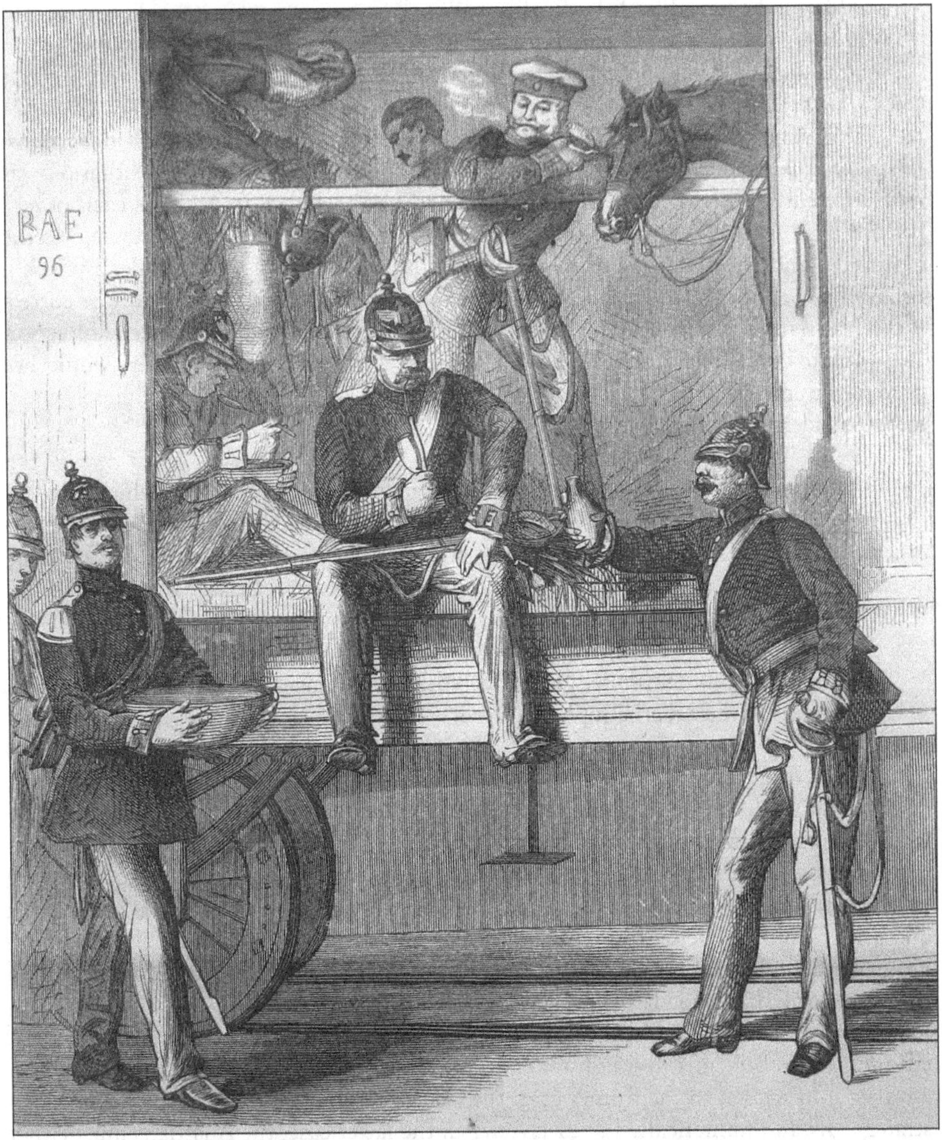

Prussian artillerymen during railway transport to the front pause for food. (*Illustrirte Kriegs-Chronik*)

In any event, it was also Moltke's intention to seize Dresden, thus compelling the Saxon army either to retreat into the fortified position of Pirna, or into Bohemia to join the Austrians, and the possession of Dresden would threaten the Austrian left flank much further to the south. What Moltke was seeking was a quick result:

> That in the active defence based upon the Elbe, decisive battles must take place immediately, is in no way to be regarded as a disadvantage. It would be a complete mistake to wish to save up our army. Once we have our corps together there is nothing to be hoped for from further waiting;… on the contrary it would be very difficult to supply them long in that close concentration which is necessary for battle, and we cannot quickly enough bring about the decisive actions.[5]

The general plan on which Moltke was to base his strategy for the operations against Austria was produced during the winter of 1865-66. By now the political situation was very different, while the contending armies had had a chance to evaluate each other's performance during the Schleswig Holstein War of 1864. In this scheme Moltke examined, and rejected, the possibility of locating his principal force in Silesia where it could be poised for an advance on Vienna. In his view this strategy would only be correct if the Prussians could appear very early and in great strength upon the scene of action. This Moltke considered unlikely. And in any case a defensive position there would not prevent the enemy from advancing along the Elbe. Reckoning upon approximately equal forces, he identified the key issue:

> The only question is whether we are to assemble our principal force behind the Lusatian Mountains or behind the Giant Mountains. The latter position protects most of Silesia directly and indirectly protects the Marks against an Austrian advance on the right bank of the Elbe… But the position behind the Lusatian Mountains also indirectly protects Silesia; in both cases, however, this protection depends not upon the defensive but upon an advance to attack, for which purpose the Lusatian Mountains offer greater facilities of movement than either the Giant Mountains or their southern prolongation.[6]

As was invariably the case in Moltke's strategic analyses, this paper breathed the offensive spirit throughout, and his proposals for the deployment of the Prussian army were designed to ensure that the initiative was seized from the outset. His plan was to concentrate three corps (IV, VII and Guard) at Dresden and to the east of the city, three corps (I, II and III) at Görlitz and to the west, and two corps (V and VI) at Freiburg and Schweidnitz in Silesia. If the Austrians did choose Silesia as their objective, the latter group would not be strong enough to defend Breslau, but must retreat on Lauban, while the main army had the choice either of concentrating on the line Görlitz – Zittau to meet an advance on Berlin, and compelling the Austrians to launch an attack there, or of advancing into Bohemia to smash that part of the Austrian army left there to support an advance into Silesia. In the former case, the Austrians must fight a battle 'in conditions strategically and numerically in our favour;' in the latter case, the Austrians must either turn back or face an assault from their left rear. All would depend on the Austrian decision as to the selected objective, and the size of the Austrian force in Bohemia.

Moltke added one note of caution: 'It remains to consider whether the Austrians, using their best possible means of preparation, can disturb our concentration if it is fixed at points so far to the front.'[7]

This last anxiety, that notwithstanding their normally sluggish mobilisation and deployment the Austrians might in some way get first run on him, never left Moltke, and he was of course especially haunted by it during the spring of 1866, as political considerations and royal indecision seemed to combine to create his nightmare scenario. During the first months of 1866 Moltke was hamstrung by the continuing uncertainty as to the circumstances that would prevail once war actually broke out; as the situation developed, he produced a stream of memoranda intended to fine tune the strategic plan in the light of the changing circumstances. Between the Ministerial Council meetings of March 28 and May 3 he wrote no less than twelve detailed papers reviewing the strategical situation and revising his plans to deal with it. Some of these were prompted by the need to carry the King and the ministers with him; others were analyses written down as much for his own benefit as anything else. They were all written before the order for mobilisation of the Prussian army, and they reflected not only his ongoing anxiety about the erosion of his advantage by the delay in issuing the necessary orders but also his minute attention to the incoming intelligence about Austrian movements.

He still regarded an Austrian offensive as a live possibility, but by April 3 his calculations showed that even with an immediate Austrian mobilisation the most vigorous advance on Berlin could reach the area of the capital no earlier than April 30, and even assuming that Prussia did not mobilise until April 15 the invaders would have at once to retrace their steps to escape a probably fatal attack in front and rear. This advance, therefore, he dismissed as impracticable. Applying the same timetable to an Austrian advance into Silesia, he reckoned that the V and VI Corps would not be in a state to meet the enemy on April 22, which he thought the earliest date the Austrians could reach Breslau; they would have to retreat behind the Oder. Even if they fought and lost a battle there, the Austrian advance would by April 30 come to a standstill about Glogau. Assuming a simultaneous mobilisation, the various offensive operations available to Benedek would each in their turn expose the Austrian army to the risk of a major defeat. Looking therefore at the growing possibility that the Austrians would remain on the defensive, he examined the alternative situations of an enemy advance into Saxony, from which they would soon have to withdraw, or a concentration in Northern Bohemia, where they would await the Saxons. In that case he intended to move fast:

> Our effort will be to force a battle before the 31st day. For that purpose we must bring up the army from Torgau to Dresden as quickly as possible, and seize the railway by pushing on the division or brigade first ready. From Dresden and Görlitz concentric advance of 225,000 men towards Jungbunzlau. If the principal Austrian army is at Prague, a battle facing west is possible; 50,000 men through Trautenau on Pardubitz. If the whole is at Pardubitz, simultaneous attack by all three armies.

Finally he considered the possibility that the Austrians might retire in front of a Prussian advance into Northern Bohemia to Olmütz. If they did, it would be the forty fifth day before they could be attacked, but it would mean their abandonment of the whole of Northern Bohemia and this he thought improbable.[8]

Based on an assumption of simultaneous mobilisation, Moltke concluded in a paper he wrote on April 9 and 10 that an immediate Austrian advance on Berlin could in theory arrive at the capital with 45,000 men by the 21st day; but in practice, with three Prussian corps concentrating at Görlitz, it would be out of the question. To avoid being cut off the Austrians would have to retreat by the 18th day, and taking into account the four additional Prussian corps that would become available, any sustained move on Berlin would be fatal. A more prudent move would be an Austrian advance pushed only far enough to disrupt the Prussian concentration, by moving forward on the left bank of the Elbe. Another possibility was an Austrian advance in the direction of Leipzig and Torgau, but on the whole Moltke thought it 'probable that there will be no battle in Saxony, and that on the approach of our three corps the enemy will withdraw into Bohemia.' The most threatening move which the Austrians could make would be an advance into Silesia, where they could arrive before Breslau as early as the 15th day. Here, he concluded, was 'the point where we must make up our minds in time to get a few days' start of the Austrians in armament.'[9]

In his next paper, written on April 12, Moltke repeated his concern that Silesia was the most directly threatened sector. He had little doubt that an attack on Breslau would be the most effective step that Austria could take, and he wanted to move up troops to the frontier there to cover the Prussian mobilisation in Silesia.[10] In a very detailed note to William two days later he set out the proposed points of concentration of the various corps, explaining that these were determined by the need to move the troops as quickly as possible into the war zone by every available railway, 'and to be as strong as possible in Silesia upon the shortest road for attacking the enemy.'[11] In reviewing the various alternative scenarios that might arise, he was confident in each case of being superior at every point. Moltke ended his exposition on a familiar note; once the army was mobilised it must strike at once, for delay would make its position decidedly worse.

The town and fortress of Olmütz. (*Illustrirte Kriegs-Chronik*)

Moltke was beginning to reach the conclusion that it would be necessary to reduce the strength of the right wing in order to have sufficient forces available in Silesia. On the right, he reckoned he needed only two corps in Lusatia to provide a force strong enough to protect Berlin, whereas he now believed he would require five corps in Silesia. He reasoned in a memorandum of April 20 that while an advance from Lusatia would merely push the Austrians back towards Olmütz and upon their newly arriving reinforcements, an advance from Silesia could bring a decisive victory by driving them back across the Elbe and cutting their communications. In any case, an Austrian advance in the west would serve only to hasten their doom; it was in Silesia that there lay their best hope to gain some military advantage. Above all, though, he repeated his insistent belief that the key to victory was the promptness with which the Prussian army acted to take advantage of its numerical advantage over the enemy:

> It follows that we must not lose this precious time by waiting, must not shun the reproach of aggression, must not delay in our operations once our forces are assembled, and, therefore, that the order to mobilise and the determination to have war must come together.[12]

At a meeting with the King on April 27 Moltke produced a table to demonstrate that the crucial period was the three weeks beginning with the 25th day of mobilization, when the Prussian preparations would be complete. On the 45th day, 'after we have weakened ourselves by occupying Saxony and observing Leitmeritz and Josephstadt we shall lose

Austrian hussars and cuirassiers arrange quarters on the Bohemian-Silesian border. (*Illustrirte Kriegs-Chronik*)

our superiority.'[13] Next day, reflecting on the current intentions for the concentration of the army, he reiterated his belief that the right wing was disproportionately strong:

> We ought to make our left stronger if the railways would permit of it without too much loss of time. But even as it is, the Second Army must immediately take the offensive and concentrate about Nachod by the 30th day.[14]

As the days went by without the order for Prussian mobilization, Moltke's anxiety increased. By May 2, the day before the order was finally given, he was calculating that the Austrians could, if they had already completed their own mobilisation, by now have 162,000 in Saxony, Northern Bohemia and at Josephstadt, a total which could be increased by a further 63,000 by June 5. Another week of delay on the part of the Prussian government could result in the army having to face the whole of this Austrian force at the outset of the campaign. This would, in effect, allow the Austrians to seize the initiative. An army of 100,000 to 120,000 men could move forward from Dresden in the direction of Berlin on May 25; or, more probably, an Austrian army 50,000 strong could advance on Breslau as early as May 19, compelling the Prussian forces in Silesia to fall back either beyond Breslau or between Liegnitz and Glogau. Immediate mobilisation of the whole of the V and VI Corps at Schweidnitz and Neisse was, he reckoned, 'absolutely necessary.'[15] Next day, at last, his advice prevailed, with the decision to mobilise five corps in the first instance.

Even now, however, his anxieties were not at an end. He presented the King on May 4 with a proposal to concentrate the VI Corps at Neisse by the 17th day, the V Corps at Schweidnitz by the 20th day, and the III, IV and Guard Corps at Cottbus, Torgau and Berlin respectively by the 22nd day. Given his conviction that the truly critical period would begin after the 25th day, he was concerned that the necessary movement orders should be issued at once, pointing out that

> the corps cannot be at the points named on the dates given unless Your Majesty now authorises the Central Railway Commission immediately to carry out the necessary preparations on the lines concerned with their transport.[16]

To Moltke's great relief William, after a discussion with Roon, approved the proposals without more ado. During the following week a succession of further instructions completed the order for the general mobilisation of the whole of the Prussian army, and Moltke, the days of speculative reflection at an end, got on with the task of supervising its concentration.

This was, however, a process over which he was still obliged to exercise strict control. Steinmetz had written to Roon to tell him that he proposed to assemble his V Corps between Schweidnitz and Liegnitz, a decision to which Moltke did not object; but he was at pains to point out to Roon that, once the mobilisation process was under way, individual corps commanders must not interfere with railway administration. After the boundaries separating the cantonments of the three easternmost corps had been defined, they must be respected:

> Within the regions thus bounded the commanding generals may do as they please, but the moment there is a prospect of hostilities must close up their corps, so that each corps can be concentrated in one day and all three in two more days.[17]

There was naturally a continuing requirement that Moltke take account of political anxiety about the potential threat to Berlin. Notwithstanding his confidence in military terms that the Austrians could not mount any effective offensive against the capital, he took care to draw up plans against that eventuality. On May 7 he drafted a memorandum recognising that an advance from Dresden might be along the lines Herzberg-Luckenwalte or Cottbus-Lübben or between the two. The most likely was the first of these, and he intended to meet it in a position at Elsterwerda. An advance through Cottbus and to the east of the Spreewald he judged unlikely, since it would be a very roundabout route; while the third option, which would invoke an advance through Senftenberg could be dealt with by taking up a position at Dobrilugk.[18] Although he alluded to the possibility of an Austrian advance on the capital from time to time thereafter when making a presentation to the King, it was always to dismiss the threat out of hand, his mind turning more and more to his own plans for the offensive.

For that, he foresaw the need for the maximum flexibility and it led him to consider the possibility of dispensing with the corps commands and allowing the army commanders to give orders direct to divisions. The immediate cause of a letter he wrote to Tresckow, the Chief of the Military Cabinet, on the subject on May 9 was a request from General von Schack, at that time commanding the IV Corps, that Albrecht von Stosch, his Chief of Staff, should not be moved from that post. Moltke pointed out to Tresckow that the distribution of General Staff officers, and especially the Chiefs of Staff, could not take place until the constitution of the armies had been decided. For the moment, he thought that each of the army commanders should be assigned a Chief of Staff, while the final composition of the armies remained to be settled; and that army commanders should take under their command the divisions as and when the necessary strategic decisions had been taken as to their deployment. In the meantime the appointment of General Staff officers to divisions could go ahead.[19] With the benefit of hindsight, it is doubtful if the flexibility which Moltke gained by this system really made up for such a major, last minute change in the mode of operation.

Meanwhile, as the elements of the Prussian general mobilisation fell into place, Moltke was continually assessing the intelligence reports coming in about Benedek's progress in assembling his army. By May 9 he was warning Roon that the Austrian mobilisation was now almost complete, and that the rail transport of units was about to begin. Next day he passed on the news of Austrian troops arriving at Königgrätz and Josephstadt, while on May 14 he reported that as expected the Austrian rail movement had begun three days earlier. He also noted that Benedek had arrived at Vienna on May 12.[20] All of these gave the clearest possible indications that the Austrian preparations were now well advanced; it was also evident that their state of readiness was far ahead of that of their German allies. It was at a point that he emphasised to William at their meeting of May 14:

> The 8th Federal Corps, nominally of 40,000 men, is said to be assembling in Württemberg. It is difficult to believe that it intends to operate against us

> independently; but it might be able to effect a juncture, nearer Bamberg, with a Bavarian army of 40,000 men. The preparations for action and the concentration of this combined army of 80,000 men will take a long time. On the other hand, an incomparably stronger army will very soon be concentrated in Northern Bohemia and Saxony, ready to act against us … In our present position it seems much wiser to concentrate all our forces against our principal enemy, especially since a first victory over him will probably result in our other adversaries being put completely out of action.[21]

He went on to propose that a strengthened 13th Division should be assembled at Minden, which with the troops from Holstein should be sufficient to deal with Hanover, while the remaining units in Western Germany should be concentrated at Zeitz and Halle to operate against the Saxons and the Austrians. As he confirmed to the King later that day, this would mean that he would have by June 45,000 men available against Saxony, 130,000 in Lusatia, 34,000 at Görlitz and 60,000 in Silesia, and three days later a further 24,000 in reserve. William duly accepted his advice; but the decision was not an easy one, as Moltke subsequently acknowledged in the Official Staff History.[22] Nonetheless, provided that he was allowed to employ these troops with the minimum of delay, Moltke could feel that the worst danger was past.

13

The Prussian Army

The outcome of Scharnhorst's reforms after the humiliation of 1806 led in due course to creation of a national army, in which every citizen was liable to military service from his seventeenth to his forty fifth year of age. Every man physically fit to do so was required to serve two years in the regular army, while for the remainder of the period he was liable to serve in various reserves, culminating in a term in the Landwehr. The total period of service in the line and in the reserves, originally fixed at twenty years, had by 1860 been reduced to twelve years. The yearly intake was set at 40,000 men, representing 0.5% of the population in 1807; but by 1869 the population of Prussia had doubled.

It was in part to take account of this that William had been so committed to his programme of army reform, and had insisted on increasing the period of service with the colours to three years, even though Roon had not thought the benefit worth the bitter hostility which the proposal aroused. Even more importantly, the annual contingent of recruits was raised to 63,000. These reforms enabled some enlargement of the peacetime army and, of course, a major increase in the size of the army once fully mobilised.

In 1866 the army was organised in eight territorial army corps, each recruited from one province, plus the Guard Corps which was based in Berlin. Six of the corps were from the eastern part of the monarchy: I Corps (East Prussia), II Corps (Pomerania), III Corps (Brandenburg), IV (Prussian Saxony), V Corps (Posen), and VI Corps (Silesia). From the western monarchy came the VII Corps (Westphalia) and VIII Corps (Rhineland). Apart from the Guard Corps, which was somewhat larger, each corps consisted of two infantry divisions together with additional corps troops. Each division consisted of two brigades of two regiments each. The regiments were divided into three battalions of four companies. Each division had in addition a regiment of cavalry and one Abteilung of field artillery, four batteries each of six guns. The corps troops consisted of one Abteilung of horse artillery of three batteries and one of field artillery of four batteries. All told, therefore, each corps disposed a total of ninety guns. In addition, each corps had a battalion of Jägers, a battalion of pioneers, an army service train battalion, and a cavalry brigade of three regiments. Finally, each corps was provided with nine ammunition columns, a pontoon column and three or four field hospitals. Apart from Landwehr units, there were ten cavalry brigades in all, of which four were incorporated in two cavalry divisions, the rest operating under army or corps command.[1]

The peacetime strength of a battalion was about 600 men, increased on mobilisation to just over 1,000 by the addition of the first class of reserves. The older classes of reserves were formed into reserve battalions, the cadres of which were maintained in the Landwehr districts, to which all reservists including officers had to report annually. A cavalry regiment fully mobilized was 682 strong. The field army amounted to a total of 342,000 men, of which in peacetime some 217,000 were with the colours. With the reserves (excluding the Landsturm), the total available when fully mobilised would amount to 660,000 men, with 1,000 guns. Mobilisation required that some 88,000 additional horses be procured; if sufficient could not be purchased on the open market, there was legislation giving the authorities the power of compulsory acquisition.

The inherent standard of the troops was extremely high, enhanced by the quality of the non commissioned officers, which was outstanding. The field officers were also a good deal better than some uninformed external observers supposed. Among those who believed that the Prussian army would not be a match for its Austrian opponent was Friedrich Engels, who wrote a series of articles on the war for the *Manchester Guardian*.

He set out his assessment of the officers and men in the first of these, published on June 20, 1866:

> The Prussian soldiers, especially the men of the reserve and such Landwehr men as had to be taken to fill up vacancies in the line (and there are many) go to war against their will; the Austrians, on the contrary, have long wished for a war with Prussia, and await with impatience the order to move. They have, therefore, also the advantage in the morale of the troops. Prussia has had no great war for fifty years; her army is, on the whole, a peace army, with the pedantry and martinetism inherent to all peace armies. No doubt a great deal has been done latterly, especially since 1859, to get rid of this; but the habits of forty years are not easily eradicated, and a great number of incapable and pedantic men must still be found, particularly in the most important places – those of the field officers.[2]

Writing after the war had ended, with the benefit of hindsight but also of consistent open-mindedness Colonel Stoffel, the French military attaché in Berlin observed:

> The superiority of the Prussian army is displayed in every grade. The body of officers is superior, especially the higher officers and company commanders. The non commissioned officers are superior. The soldiers are superior.[3]
>
> He readily found a reason for this, in the great power that the army derived
>
> from the presence in its ranks of persons well educated and well brought up, belonging to the better classes, who, as officers, non commissioned officers, and soldiers, devote to the defence of their country their intellects and lives.[4]

The army reforms, coupled with the way in which each corps drew its recruits locally, enabled the Prussian system of mobilisation to be far more efficient than that of its opponents. Lessons, too, had been learned from the partial mobilisation against Denmark in 1864; and in 1866 most corps succeeded in mobilizing their reserves within a fortnight.

The most striking innovations, however, had come in the new equipment available. The adoption of the needle gun had given the Prussian infantry an outstanding advantage over their opponents. By 1866 all the regular infantry regiments had been equipped with the breech loading rifle, and the re-equipment programme was being rolled out to Landwehr units; the light cavalry were also being reequipped with Dreyse carbines.[5]

The evidence provided by the Danish War of 1864 of the effectiveness of the needle gun was there for all to see, and Moltke was quick to draw the necessary conclusions. It confirmed the views which he had already propounded as to the effect of the new weapon on infantry tactics. He restated his beliefs in 1865 in an essay, published anonymously, entitled 'Remarks on the Influence of the Improved Firearms upon Battle.' Analysing this document, Spenser Wilkinson considered it an example of historical study that good staff work should produce for the development of military doctrine. In this essay Moltke addressed a number of the prejudices that were only with difficulty being eradicated from Prussian military thought. While acknowledging that to use the rifle effectively soldiers must be taught to shoot, he considered that sharpshooting must be the exception. To be effective on a large scale, rifle fire should be at a range short enough for errors in estimating the distance to be immaterial. Care must be taken to prevent the waste of ammunition. Firing would be in a formation two deep, while manoeuvring within range of enemy artillery should be in small columns, rapidly deployed and easily handled.

Moltke summarised the effect of the new weapon:

> Generally speaking, the consequence of the peculiarities of the improved firearms will be to strengthen the defence as against the attack. The defender can choose his position in such a way that the enemy must advance over an open plain. He will usually have time to measure accurately the distances of certain features of the ground, or of individual objects, in order to obtain the best effect from his fire.

The attacker of course retained the initiative; and ultimately the defender would himself have to go over to the offensive to obtain a decisive result. But it raised another question:

> Ought we not first to seize and make the most of the evident material advantages of the stationary fire-fight before we begin our attack? To attack is not merely a matter of tactics. A skilful commander will very often be able to choose defensive positions of a strategical nature so offensive as to compel the opponent to attack us in them.

Moltke went on to examine the larger consequences of these tactical considerations:

> The less the chance of success for a frontal attack, the more surely will the enemy turn against our flanks, and the more important it becomes to secure them … The smaller the force and the shorter its front the easier it is to turn its defensive positions … As the extent of the front increases, for example, in the case of an army corps operating alone, the difficulty of turning it becomes greater.

And where the defensive position of an army was concerned, it had become impossible for it to be turned tactically. With a front of four or five miles, or even longer, 'the turning movement becomes a march, after the completion of which there is no time left to fight on the same day.'[6]

The Prussian army had also learned some lessons as far as the artillery was concerned, largely as a result of Hindersin's appointment as Inspector General of Artillery in 1864.

Prussian Line Infantryman 1866, painting by Herbert Knötel. (Lezius)

Prussian Guard Jäger 1866, painting by Herbert Knötel. (Lezius)

Prussian Dragoon 1866, painting by Herbert Knötel. (Lezius)

Prussian Hussar officer 1866, painting by Herbert Knötel. (Lezius)

Prussian Uhlan officer 1866, painting by Herbert Knötel. (Lezius)

Prussian Line Artillery officer 1866, painting by Herbert Knötel. (Lezius)

Hindersin brought a far more open mind to equipment issues, as well as a harsh efficiency in raising performance standards. But the two years that had elapsed since the Danish War had not been long enough to reequip the Prussian artillery, which went into war in 1866 with more than a third of its batteries still equipped with smoothbore twelve pounders with a maximum range of one thousand five hundred metres. The rest were breechloading rifled four pounders and six pounders, with a range of over four thousand metres, and of these about one hundred and sixty were Krupp cast steel guns.[7] Unlike the infantry, who had become thoroughly versed in the use of the needle gun as their basic weapon, the delay in reequipping the artillery meant that units were inadequately trained in the new weapons. The considerable disadvantage to which this put the Prussian artillery became apparent during the campaign; practically all the Austrian batteries had been equipped since 1864 with rifled guns, although all of these were muzzle loaders, and their gunners had accordingly been fully trained in their use. Regrettably, Prussian artillery doctrine had not been brought up to date, either, and was so cautious that Hohenlohe feared that artillery was coming to be regarded as a kind of ballast.[8] Reviewing the disparity in rifled guns, he pointed out that if each side had been equally skilful in the use of its artillery, the Prussians should have made good their numerical inferiority by the effectiveness of their breech loaders, but this proved not to be the case due to faulty doctrine, particularly in the delayed deployment of the Prussian batteries.[9]

The development of artillery technology, and the internationalism of arms manufacturers, prompted Roon to write a precautionary letter to Alfred Krupp on April 9:

Prince Frederick Charles, commander of the Prussian First Army. (Rogers)

> I venture to ask if you are willing out of patriotic regard to present political considerations, to undertake not to supply any guns to Austria without the consent of the King's government.[10]

The assurance which he sought was promptly and emphatically given, Krupp responding on April 13.

The wide arc over which his troops would be deployed against Austria, whatever might be the final strategic balance, made it clear to Moltke that it would be desirable to organise them in three rather than two armies. This was not least because of the particular need to operate against Saxony at the outset of the campaign. In part, this task was to be assigned to the Army of the Elbe, which would consist of three divisions, with twenty six squadrons of cavalry and 144 guns. Command of this army was given to the seventy year old General Karl Herwarth von Bittenfeld, who had done well in the campaign of 1864, when he led the corps that landed on Alsen, but who was to prove a cautious and unimaginative army commander. As his Chief of Staff there was assigned the very capable Colonel Karl von Schlotheim. Now aged fifty, his baptism of fire had come in the campaign of 1849 against the insurgents in Baden, in which he took part as adjutant to the reserve cavalry of the II Corps.

Herwarth's three divisional commanders were Lieutenant General Count Münster-Meinhövel (14th Division) who had also been a successful divisional commander in Denmark; Lieutenant General Philipp von Canstein (15th Division); and Lieutenant General Franz von Etzel (16th Division). The two cavalry brigade commanders were Major Generals Count von der Goltz and von Kotze. Moltke's intention was that the

The Crown Prince of Prussia, commander of the Prussian Second Army. (Rogers)

Army of the Elbe should invade Saxony from the north, with its left wing in touch with the units of the First Army which were to enter Saxony from the east.

The First Army, comprising the forces to be concentrated in Lusatia, was to be under the command of Prince Frederick Charles. Following his successful campaign in Denmark, and as the most prominent member of the Royal family to have a full time career in the army, there was never any doubt that he would take a prominent role in the forthcoming campaign. As his Chief of Staff, he had the fifty seven year old Lieutenant General Konstantin von Voigts-Rhetz, a very capable soldier who did not, however, enjoy the best of relations with Moltke, apparently out of professional jealousy. He had been head of the General War Department in the War Ministry in 1859, and had become a strong advocate of the new guns produced by Alfred Krupp, with whom he enjoyed a warm friendship. His Quarter Master General was Major General Wolf von Stülpnagel, aged fifty three, who was one of Moltke's most trusted officers. Stülpnagel served in Berlin during the March Days of 1848, and took an active part in the street fighting there.

The units initially assigned to the First Army were the III and IV Corps, together with Prince Albrecht's Cavalry Corps. The four divisions making up the two army corps were, as previously suggested, to operate independently, without a corps staff structure, under the direct command of the First Army. Apart from a possible increase in flexibility, no very clear explanation has ever been put forward for this experiment, which was not repeated during the Franco-Prussian War. The divisional commanders of the III Corps were Lieutenant Generals Wilhelm von Tümpling (5th Division) aged fifty seven, and the sixty one year old Albrecht von Manstein (6th Division); both had experience from the Danish war and both were determined and reliable commanders. The divisional commanders of the IV Corps were the outstanding Lieutenant General Eduard von Fransecky (7th Division), who had first attracted attention when serving on Wrangel's staff in Denmark in 1848 and who was now aged fifty nine, and Lieutenant General Heinrich von Horn (8th Division).

Crown Prince Frederick William was designated as the commander of the Second Army, based in Silesia. Now aged thirty five, he had found his experiences on Wrangel's staff in Denmark extremely frustrating, but his influence there had steadily increased and he had displayed considerable common sense and sound military ability. This was, however, his first experience of high command. He had the benefit of having as his Chief of Staff the fifty six year old Major General Karl von Blumenthal, who had added greatly to his reputation with his performance in Denmark. Blumenthal had wondered if he might be appointed to the staff of Frederick Charles, having served as the latter's Chief of Staff in Denmark, but was delighted with his appointment to the Second Army, noting in his diary on May 19:

> The position is exactly the one I should have most desired. The youthful buoyancy of the Crown Prince's nature suits me much more than the severe earnestness of Prince Frederick Charles. Lightheartedness is the spirit in which to go to battle.[11]

Another key member of the Second Army staff was its Quartermaster General, Major General Albrecht von Stosch, a close friend of the Crown Prince.

Initially assigned to the Second Army were the V Corps and the VI Corps. The V Corps was commanded by the aggressive, choleric and eccentric General Karl von Steinmetz.

Born in 1796, he had fought in the Wars of Liberation. Slow progress upwards found him in 1848 a lieutenant colonel, commanding two battalions of infantry during the street fighting of the March days before going with his regiment to take part in the Schleswig Holstein campaign. Thereafter he was successively promoted before reaching the rank of General of Infantry. His Chief of Staff was the capable Colonel Friedrich von Wittich. The two divisional commanders were Major Generals Julius von Löwenfeld (9th Division) and Hugo von Kirchbach (10th Division). The commander of the VI Corps was the seventy year old General Louis von Mutius, who had enjoyed a steady but unspectacular career. His Chief of Staff was Colonel Ernst von Sperling. Lieutenant General Alexander von Zastrow commanded the 11th Division and Lieutenant General Conrad von Prondzinsky the 12th Division. Commanding the Second Army's reserve cavalry was Major General von Hartmann.

This left three other corps, whose disposition depended on the strategic choices yet to be made. The I Corps was commanded by General Adolf von Bonin, who was to prove an unimaginative and timid leader. His Chief of Staff was Colonel August von Borries; his two divisional commanders were Lieutenant General Georg von Grossman (1st Division) and Lieutenant General Karl von Clausewitz (2nd Division). The II Corps, provisionally assigned to the First Army, was led by Lieutenant General Stefan von Schmidt, aged sixty seven, whose Chief of Staff was Major General Georg von Kameke. The divisional commanders were Lieutenant General August von Werder (3rd Division) and Lieutenant General Friedrich Herwarth von Bittenfeld, the brother of the commander of the Army of the Elbe, who led the 4th Division. Finally, there was the Guard Corps, commanded by the obstinate and not particularly able Prince August of Württemberg; his Chief of Staff was Colonel Ferdinand von Dannenberg. The commander of the 1st Guard Division was the fire-eating Lieutenant General Hiller von Gärtringen, aged fifty nine, who had been an active collaborator with Edwin von Manteuffel in the latter's planning for a possible *coup d'etat*.[12] Hiller had served as a major on William's staff during the 1849 campaign in Baden. Much of his regimental service had been with the Guard, and he was one of the officers particularly close to the King. The 2nd Guard Division was led by Lieutenant General Heinrich von Plonski.

These were the forces that would confront the Austrian and Saxon armies in Bohemia. Moltke had deliberately strengthened them as much as he could at the expense of the forces remaining to him for operations against Austria's other allies in Western Germany, which he had reduced to the equivalent of three divisions. Placed in command of these was Vogel von Falckenstein, last seen being replaced by Moltke as Chief of Staff of the Allied army in 1864 after a thoroughly indifferent performance. The three divisions available to him were the 13th Division, (Goeben), a Combined Division, commanded by Major General Friedrich von Beyer; and another Combined Division, consisting of the forces in Holstein, which took the field under Manteuffel's command.

Events were to prove that many of the senior officers, although not in the first flush of youth, were of outstanding quality; but in 1866, although some of them had had battle experience in Schleswig Holstein in 1848, or Baden in the following year, or in the Danish campaign of 1864, most had not. The coming war would be the first time that they had occupied senior positions on the battlefield. For all of them, there was the added test of making the most of the new weapons available to the troops. The promotion and appointment of these officers did not lie directly in Moltke's hands, but was the responsibility of the Chief of the Military Cabinet. During the period that Manteuffel had held this post, its authority had been steadily increased; Manteuffel had achieved a great improvement in the overall quality of the Prussian officer corps, although some of those with strong liberal opinions had found their careers had not progressed and, no doubt, those of Manteuffel's way of thinking had been advanced. His successor was Major General von Tresckow, who had a much lower profile, and was much less politically ambitious. Although he wielded a good deal less influence than Manteuffel, he still retained, on the King's behalf, the administrative authority that he inherited, even after an attempt by Roon to recapture it.

14

The Austrian Army

From the moment he came to the throne, the interests of his army were of central importance to Franz Joseph. Throughout his reign, he 'would remember his debt to the military, cherish his position as supreme warlord, and regard the army as his chief support and main concern.'[1] It was the army which had brought the monarchy through the trials of 1848, had ultimately defeated Piedmont's attempt on Milan and had recovered Northern Italy, and had then overcome Hungary's attempt to gain its independence. Thereafter, although the preservation of the monarchy and of the integrity of the empire had for the moment been secured, it was still necessary to maintain and even increase the size of the army to cope with continuing threats, both internal and external.

During the first decade of his reign, up to his unhappy experiences in Italy in 1859, Franz Joseph to a great extent exercised in fact as in name the effective command of his armed forces; sadly, however, it amounted to ten years of marked deterioration. The blame for this has chiefly been laid at the door of Count Grünne, the First Adjutant General, who was by far the most influential of the Emperor's military advisers. Neither he nor Franz Joseph was disposed to consider the development of the army in intellectual or technological terms; Franz Joseph was quoted as saying the 'the quality of my army does not depend on learned officers, but on brave and chivalrous men.'[2] And Grünne was more concerned to maintain the *status quo* than to promote innovation; in pursuit of this aim, he prevailed on the Emperor to remodel the command structure with the result that all effective power rested in the hands of the First Adjutant General. The struggle for power between the progressives and the reactionaries which ensued, and which in Austria resulted in such a decisive defeat for the progressives was, as has been pointed out, mirrored by a similar contest at the same time in Prussia.[3] But there, however, the outcome was very different. In each case, the result was largely determined by the influence of the monarch; the ultimate consequences were to make themselves felt with decisive effect in 1866.

Others who contributed to the reorganization of the Austrian army were the aged Radetzky, whose influence was still considerable, and Hess, his Chief of Staff. In September 1849 the latter assumed the offices of Quarter Master General and personal Chief of Staff to Franz Joseph. For a while Hess, an able man, was able to maintain both the authority of his position and a reasonable working relationship with Grünne, but by 1853 he had been effectively sidelined, and his influence almost completely eliminated. As a result, his personal relationship with Grünne broke down altogether.

On the other hand, although undergoing these internal political stresses, the army could not complain of undue financial restraint. In spite of the chaotic state of the Empire's economy, annual spending on the army doubled after 1848, and during the years of the Crimean War it effectively quadrupled, but the money was not on the whole wisely spent. Apart from the introduction of the Lorenz muzzle loading rifle, a

The commander of the Austrian Army of the North, Ludwig von Benedek, c 1866. (Rogers)

considerable advance on the previous infantry weapons, there was little technological advance in the army's equipment. In particular the artillery still had to do the best it could with obsolete smoothbore muzzle loaders.

During this decade, the army was organised in fifteen army corps. Internal security was always the first consideration in the mind of Austrian military leaders; as to external threats, Italy, where six corps were usually stationed, was seen as the principal area to be covered. The first serious test of the army's ability to respond to an international crisis came in 1850, with the confrontation with Prussia over the question of German national unity. The flashpoint came in Hesse Cassel, where the Elector was temporarily driven from his throne by a popular uprising. Austria backed the Elector, but Prussia, pursuing an opportunist policy, moved troops into Hesse to secure her east-west lines of communication. Austria and her allies mobilised; it was planned to push five corps under the command of Radetzky from Bohemia towards Berlin, in conjunction with the Saxon army, cooperating with the South German forces on the western flank. Austria mobilised a quarter of a million troops in Bohemia and was still able to leave eighty thousand in Italy, with ninety thousand in Hungary and Galicia; in addition, Bavaria, Saxony and Württemberg mobilized a further ninety thousand men. It was an impressive demonstration of Austrian military power, but its effectiveness was not to be tested on the battlefield, because Prussia backed down at Olmütz.

In 1853 began the long diplomatic struggle with Russia, which led to progressive mobilization, first of an army of observation of 130,000 troops in Hungary and Transylvania and then in April 1854 a larger scale mobilization, involving the Third and Fourth Armies, in Hungary and Galicia. Finally, that autumn, with the further escalation of the diplomatic crisis, Franz Joseph ordered the full mobilization of fifteen corps, eleven of which were to be deployed against Russia. Hess, who drew up the war plans, was pessimistic, fearing that to match the size of Russia's army unacceptable risks would have to be taken. Fortunately for Austria, the Allied successes in the Crimean War ensured that peace negotiations could be brought to a successful conclusion.

In 1859 came the conflict with France and the Kingdom of Sardinia. It was a crisis forced on Austria by Napoleon III's pact with Cavour and which found the army unprepared. Austria's political leaders were well aware of this; Grünne and Hess separately warned Buol, the Foreign Minister, of the danger facing the army. When the campaign began, the Austrian problems were magnified by the timidity and incompetence of Gyulai, the supreme commander in Italy, and the persistent interference of Grünne. After the battle of Magenta, Gyulai was dismissed, and Franz Joseph, with Hess as his Chief of Staff, took personal command. This did not, however materially improve matters; Hess was given little real authority and was in any case obliged to function with an assistant, Ramming, who was Grünne's nominee. Unsurprisingly, this led to a defeat for the Austrians at Solferino after which both Napoleon and Franz Joseph, for different reasons, were keen to make haste to reach a deal to prevent further hostilities.

In the campaign, the Austrian troops had acquitted themselves far better than their leaders; poorly equipped by comparison with the French, they had sustained heavy casualties, but had fought bravely and effectively. Among the generals, Ludwig von Benedek emerged with an enhanced reputation. But the defeat was not, as Gunther Rothenberg has pointed out, the result of a sudden catastrophic series of mistakes by field commanders, but rather a product of the way in which the army had been managed over a long period. [4]

If the army was to be able to cope with the still more serious dangers that would lie ahead, a lot would have to be done.

The defeat in Italy led Franz Joseph to take one pace back from the supreme command, although he retained a close personal interest in all major decisions. And Grünne went, his successor as Adjutant General being de Crenneville, a close associate of the Archduke Albrecht and an orthodox officer whose approach mirrored the conservative attitudes of most of the Austrian generals. In spite of military defeat, these men were anxious above all not to experiment with innovation, preferring at a time of political uncertainty to preserve the army's traditional stance of loyalty to the dynasty at all costs. Given the increased influence of the Reichsrat over the military budget, there was a lot less available money to spend on new technology (with the exception of the artillery). Nor was there much reform in the command structure of the army, although no less than one hundred and thirty five generals were removed after 1859.[5] The Adjutant General now exercised less formal influence; but there was no corresponding increase in the authority of the post of Chief of the General Staff, to which Benedek was appointed upon the dismissal of Hess in 1860, in response to public opinion which blamed the latter for the defeat of 1859. It was regarded as a sufficiently unimportant appointment for it to be a part-time position, since Benedek held the post simultaneously with first his governorship of Hungary and later with his command in Italy. Benedek was quite content with this view of the General Staff and brought to all the tasks required of him the essential simplicities of a front line officer, believing that success came from courage and enthusiasm, and not from an intellectual approach to military problems. [6]

Under him, and his successor von Henikstein, a good friend of his, the role of the General Staff stood no chance of growing in importance to match its opposite number

General Alfred Henikstein, Chief of Austria's General Staff during 1866. (Rogers)

in Berlin. Henikstein seems also have been infected by the general uncertainty at the top of the Austrian army, commenting on his appointment: 'I am not the man for this important position. I lack the ability, the knowledge, and therefore the necessary self confidence.'[7]

The restrictions on the military budget had a major effect on the actual size of the army, which fell far short of the eight hundred and fifty thousand men which the size of the annual intake should theoretically have produced. The intake in fact varied from year to year, while the term of eight years service was reduced in practice to three for the infantry and six for the cavalry and artillery. There was no proper organisation of the reserve, in which conscripts were supposed to serve two years, and there was no Landwehr. Conscription could be avoided by the wealthy by hiring substitutes, with a resultant reduction in the average educational standard of the army as a whole. And large numbers of the troops were from districts of the Empire whose loyalty was doubtful, so these units were usually posted away from their place of origin. Only just over a quarter of the troops were of German origin; a fifth were Czechs and Slovaks, while over 10% were Italians. In 1866 only 528,000 men were actually mobilised, and it has been calculated that, in all, this produced two combat armies totalling 320,000.[8]

The experience of 1859 led to a number of practical changes. The army was reorganised into ten army corps, but these now were normally to consist of four brigades, the divisional command level having been chopped out. In the mounted arm there was an increased emphasis on light cavalry, regarded as more suitable for reconnaissance and independent action. Although the technical problems associated with breech loaders had not been overcome, the artillery benefited from the introduction of greatly improved bronze muzzle loading four pounder and eight pounder guns, with a range of 4,000 yards.

Austrian Infantryman, painting by Herbert Knötel. (Lezius)

Austrian Jäger, painting by Herbert Knötel. (Lezius)

Austrian Dragoon officer, painting by Herbert Knötel. (Lezius)

Austrian Pioneer, painting by Herbert Knötel. (Lezius)

Attention was also paid to the tactical experiences in Italy. In 1862 new infantry regulations were issued, largely based on what was seen as the highly successful use by the French of bayonet attacks, by which they overcame the advantage in range possessed by the Austrian Lorenz rifle over the French infantry weapons of that time. Friedrich Engels, in a survey of infantry weapons written in 1861, noted that it had 'stood its trial in the Italian campaign of 1859, and the great number of French soldiers, and especially officers, who succumbed to it, testify to its excellence.'[9] The French use of the massed bayonet assault on a battalion front of 100 men, six deep, was flattered by the fact that the curved trajectory of the Lorenz was ineffective in covering the whole of the ground of the assault. Nevertheless, the rule now prescribed for the Austrian army was for battalions to be kept concentrated for an attack over a front even narrower than that adopted by the French, since the infantry's primary function was 'to deliver the mass assault with the bayonet.'[10]

The performance of the Austrian and Prussian armies in the Danish campaign of 1864 offered the high command on both sides an excellent opportunity to compare them, and not least to judge how far the application of the lessons of 1859 had gone. The Austrian contingent under Gablenz, comprising four infantry brigades and one cavalry brigade, was somewhat smaller than the Prussian contingent. Against a brave and tenacious enemy that was, however, almost always outnumbered, the Austrians fought well; the high casualties incurred as a result of the adherence to the assault with the bayonet failed to disturb the conviction that this was the way ahead. And most foreign observers took the view that the overall balance of the comparison was all in favour of the Austrians.

A typical reaction was that of the French military attaché in Berlin, Clermont-Tonnerre, who told Friedrich von Holstein how pleased he was with the reckless attacks of the Austrians adding:

> Your troops are good and obedient; they do as they are told. But the Austrians, ah, they have one of the best armies in the world! It took us all our time to beat them… Since then, as I can see more clearly every day, the Austrians have learnt a lot from us.[11]

Holstein thought that Clermont-Tonnerre's reports profoundly influenced Napoleon's political and military assessments of the relative position of Prussia and Austria in the period leading up to the war of 1866 (although the military attaché was to alter his opinion before the war broke out). Even the performance of Prussia's new infantry weapon, the Dreyse needle gun, was not seen as making up for the difference in performance between the armies. And although Austrian observers had plenty of opportunity to note the disparity in the casualty lists, it did not overcome the prejudice in favour of the bayonet or indeed the unwillingness of the Austrian high command to contemplate the enormous financial implications of the adoption of a breech loader.

The views of Colonel Ferenc Vlasits, a staff officer responsible for planning Austrian operations in Denmark, were not untypical of senior military opinion in Vienna. In 1865 he described the Prussian operations as being:

General Gideon Krismanic, Director of Operations with Benedek's Army of the North during the 1866 Campaign. (Rogers)

> too turbulent ... Although Prussian strategists appreciate the value of initiative, the rash deed and an exploited victory, they do not understand the critical, nay, decisive importance of lines of communication. They are incorrigible optimists, and have failed to organise life-sustaining arteries to the rear in the course of their tumultuous forward operations.[12]

Benedek's reluctance to accept the command in Bohemia and his consciousness of his unsuitability might have led him to insist that he should be allowed to take with him his extremely competent chief of staff in Italy, von John. Instead however, he left him there so that use could be made of his knowledge of that theatre to complement the leadership of the Archduke Albrecht. On the latter's advice, he accepted the self-assured, pedantic but inexperienced Major General Gideon von Krismanic to head his staff with the title of Director of Operations.

Krismanic came from Croatia; born in 1817, he had fought under Radetzky in Italy, after which he embarked on a detailed survey of Bohemia and its military history. In 1859 he became Professor of Strategy at the Military School in Vienna and in the following year came to the attention of the Archduke Albrecht, who was greatly impressed by his evident depth of intellect. Friedjung commented that he had 'a great receptivity of mind, combined with strong self assurance and the emphatic utterance which may conceal from an observer the lack of true originality or balanced judgment.'[13] His was an entirely historical and extremely cautious approach based on an out of date belief in the importance of defensive positions and secure lines of communication. In addition, however, Benedek compounded this error of selection by agreeing that the cynical and sarcastic Henikstein should also accompany the Northern Army; the latter was wholly pessimistic about the likely outcome of the campaign and apt to be very much a negative thinker in reviewing other men's ideas. One Austrian general, Karl

Möring, later observed of the performance of this duo of chiefs of staff in 1866 that 'my overlearned but lazy friend Krismanic and my unlearned friend Henikstein, who is as fit for his place as I am for composing an opera, appear to have bungled!'[14]

It was not the strongest of teams with which to confront the Prussian army, but in June 1866 its shortcomings were not generally apparent; after a review of what he regarded as the Prussian 'system for ensuring defeat at the very headquarters of an army,' Friedrich Engels looked with favour on Benedek who, he said, was 'an experienced officer and who, at least, knows his mind. The superiority of supreme command is decidedly on the side of the Austrians.'[15]

Benedek's corps commanders were of variable quality. The 1st Corps was led by the wealthy, aristocratic and incompetent Clam Gallas, who had performed without distinction in Italy in 1859 but whose survival of the later purge has been described as 'a commentary on the nepotism and privilege which weakened the Austrian army in the years between Solferino and Königgrätz.'[16] The 2nd Corps was commanded by Karl Thun-Hohenstadt, an unexceptional general whose performance hitherto had been at least competent. The 3rd Corps and the 8th corps had Archducal commanders in Ernst and Leopold; the 4th Corps was in the hands of the inept Tassilo Festetics while Wilhelm Ramming, who had made an equivocal contribution in 1859 as assistant chief of staff to Hess, with whom he had not got on well, led the 6th Corps. The line up was completed by the reliable Gablenz, freshly returned from Holstein, in command of the 10th Corps. Among the commanders of the cavalry divisions the most notable was the dashing Edelsheim, who had gained a considerable reputation in Italy, and who led the 1st Light Division. Finally the Archduke William was appointed as Director of Artillery.

In addition to his own troops, Benedek would have the Saxon army, of corps strength, commanded by the extremely able Crown Prince of Saxony. In all, Benedek's army comprised 247,000 men, together with 24,000 Saxons; this figure was extremely close to that projected by Moltke and his staff and on which much of Prussian planning had been based.

15

Final Plans

Carefully though he had analysed the strategic issues before war began, Moltke had by no means settled on the final plan to be adopted, as his constant musings on the various possibilities during April and May demonstrated. He was determined that there should be an entirely flexible approach to the planning process, in order that his options would remain open. The basic principles of the strategy which he applied were set out later in an essay written in 1871:

> The first task of strategy is the final assembly of the fighting forces, the first deployment of the army. Here, multifarious political, geographic, and national considerations come into question. A mistake in the original assembly of the army can scarcely be rectified in the course of the campaign. But these arrangements can be considered long in advance and – assuming the war readiness of the units and the availability of the means of transport – must unfailingly lead to the intended result. Also included in the broader tasks of strategy are the combat employment of the assembled units, thus operations. Here one will soon encounter the independent will of the enemy. We can limit this only if we are prepared and decisive in taking the initiative ... No plan of operations extends with certainty beyond the first encounter with the enemy's main strength. Only the layman sees in the course of a campaign a consistent execution of a preconceived and highly detailed original concept pursued consistently to the end.

Certainly the commander in chief will keep his great objective continuously in mind, undisturbed by the vicissitudes of events. But the path on which he hopes to reach it can never be firmly established in advance. Throughout the campaign he must make a series of decisions on the basis of situations that cannot be foreseen.[1]

These were the precepts which Moltke followed during the anxious spring of 1866, a time when it was already beginning to be evident that his clarity of purpose was neither shared nor understood by a number of those others involved in the preparations for the campaign. Although he was scrupulously careful not to interfere in the making of political decisions, Moltke was nonetheless very mindful of the effect of the political situation on the development of his strategy. It was quite clear to him, for instance, that he must aim to achieve a quick victory, for both economic and political reasons. Popular opinion in Prussia and in Germany as a whole was by no means sympathetic to the prospect of war; a paper produced by his staff and put before him on May 18 emphasised the importance of speedy action: 'The public opinion of the country must not be overlooked. At the moment it is increasingly hostile to the idea of war. Unless the army is set in motion its morale will be seriously affected.'[2] And although, largely due to the efforts of Bismarck's banker, Gerson Bleichröder, Prussia had the financial muscle to go to war, it could not afford to fight a long campaign without serious damage

General Konstantin von Voigts-Rhetz, Chief of Staff of the Prussian First Army, 1866. (Rogers)

to Prussia's treasury and the national economy. Finally, there was the constant prospect of external interference, a threat that was never far from Bismarck's mind. The longer it took to achieve a result, the more vulnerable would Prussia be to concerted action by the other Great Powers.

On May 25 Moltke wrote an *aide mémoire* for a crucial meeting at the Royal Palace in Berlin. In it, he addressed a particular fear of the King when he dismissed the possibility that there was any serious threat to Berlin from an attempted Austrian advance on the capital; as to an enemy push in Silesia, this could go no further than six or eight marches before the pressure of the Prussian corps assembling at Bautzen – Bischofswerda and Dresden was felt. Once these forces moved into Bohemia, the Austrians must retreat. An Austrian advance on Görlitz was, he considered, pointless and as such improbable. What was crucial was for Prussia to move at once to the offensive:

> From the military point of view we certainly ought not to postpone action for a single day after June 5. By that day the Austrians can hardly have transported all their forces to be used against us. But with every succeeding day they will become stronger, and in a few weeks there may be another enemy in Franconia. The vital thing is to strike down the principal enemy, the one that is ready, before this happens … Military considerations then make it desirable that our diplomatic action should come to a conclusion by June 5.[3]

Blumenthal attended this meeting, and noted in his diary part of the debate which followed. He thought that the King was still clinging to the hope of peace but remained fearful that the Austrians would march on Berlin. The Chief of Staff of the First Amy was openly critical of Moltke's proposed deployment:

> Voigts-Rhetz blamed the disposition of the forces, as being too greatly extended for the first forward movement, stretching as they do from Zeitz to Upper Silesia – a matter of sixty miles. General von Moltke justified it by reason of the improved means of transport, namely, the railroads, which alone make such an extension possible.
>
> In the successive marches onwards the columns can always be brought into closer touch. The general opinion was that, instead of placing ourselves so close on the Elbe, we ought to have the main force at Görlitz, as an irruption was to be expected at that point.[4]

The meeting broke up without any firm conclusion being reached, but it left Blumenthal expecting that the role of the Second Army would be to conduct a fighting retreat while awaiting the arrival of the First Army. This was not, however, Moltke's view; in an exchange of notes with Frederick Charles after the conference, he agreed that the Austrians were unlikely to divide their forces, and an advance against the First Army was more likely.[5]

With the political situation still unclear Moltke drafted orders on May 29 to shift his centre of gravity eastward by moving the II, III and IV Corps nearer to the Second Army. He also directed Herwarth to take up command of the Army of the Elbe, while the Guard Corps was directed to concentrate at Cottbus. These movements were to start on June 5. The extent to which Moltke's strategy was not understood by some of his colleagues was further demonstrated by a long and querulous letter, dated May 29, which he received from Steinmetz complaining that the effect of Moltke's dispositions amounted to an invitation to the Austrians to invade Silesia, and that the Rhine provinces were inadequately protected. In a reply on June 1 Moltke patiently explained his strategy:

> We have only one really dangerous enemy, the mainspring of all the other armaments in Germany. This enemy stands there fully armed; it would be a mistake to leave a whole army corps on the Rhine facing an opponent who does not yet exist.

As to the concerns which Steinmetz raised about Silesia, Moltke wrote:

> The I Army Corps is in the right place. If we meet the main Austrian force in Saxony or in Northern Bohemia it would join the First Army. If the enemy's main operation is directed at Silesia it is at hand to reinforce the Second Army … That all military reasons speak for the initiative is plain. But other considerations relating to the question are outside my competence.[6]

But Moltke was already coming to the conclusion that in any event the I Corps ought to be assigned to the Second Army. As he evolved his plans, however, he was still seen by some, such as Blumenthal, as being irresolute. On June 1, when he learned from

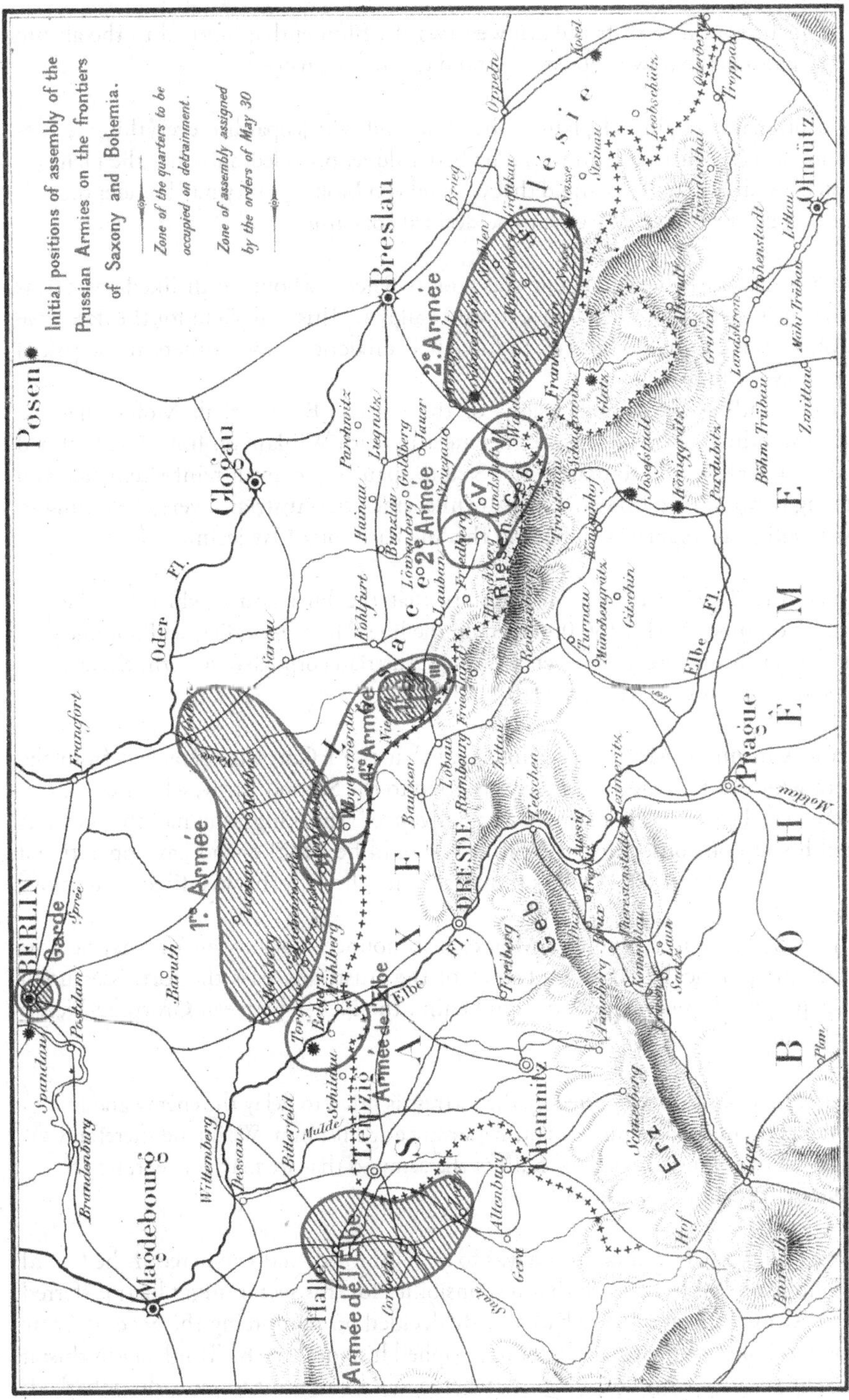

Map 4 – Initial positions of assembly of the Prussian armies on the frontiers of Saxony and Bohemia.

Moltke of his intention to shift the army eastwards, Blumenthal jumped to the absurd conclusion that Moltke now proposed to stand on the defensive:

> This continual changing of plans is dreadful, and will jeopardise everything. It does not signify whether a thing can be better done, provided only that the plan adopted be adhered to. I am afraid that General von Moltke is very much under the influence of others, and can come to no decided conclusion.

Blumenthal also believed that it was Voigts-Rhetz, whom he disliked, who was behind the decision to shift the balance towards Silesia: 'This is all right for the defensive, but I cannot admire a man who tries to force his convictions upon others at the risk of jeopardising everything.'[7]

Notwithstanding the apprehensions of the volatile Blumenthal, Moltke had no intention of standing on the defensive. In a meeting with William on June 3 he outlined his proposals for Herwarth to march into Saxony, pausing to await reinforcements, and then moving forward into Bohemia. Meanwhile, since the Austrians were, according to the latest intelligence reports, still behind the line Pardubitz-Oswiecim:

> We may therefore calculate with certainty that the First Army, which can be deployed on June 15 with 130,000 men on the line Bautzen-Görlitz, will not find a superior enemy before it, not even if the first Austrian corps abandons the Saxons in Prague and moves off to its right.

With this in mind, Moltke recommended that the I Corps be detached from the First Army, which did not need it, and transferred to the Second Army, which was much more likely to feel the weight of any Austrian advance.[8] The King, who had the previous day issued his famous order that thereafter it should be Moltke who gave operational orders to the army, approved Moltke's proposals, and the I Corps was directed to move to Hirschberg.

On June 8 Blumenthal wrote to Moltke to announce that in view of what he now regarded as the practically certain advance of the Austrians past the fortresses upon Breslau, he proposed to take up a position behind the Neisse between Grottkau-Neisse and Patschkau:

> This defensive position supported by the fortress is fitted to delay the enemy and in favourable circumstances for an offensive advance against him. We intend therefore to leave here on June 11 with the bulk of the army so that we may concentrate on the Neisse no later than June 16.[9]

He went on to say how anxious he was to be reinforced, and wondered if the Guard Corps might be moved to Brieg so that responsibility for this sector might be transferred to the First Army. In fact, Moltke had already decided on reinforcing the Second Army, and before receiving Blumenthal's letter telegraphed him on June 8: 'Think about this: if you were sent another army corps by rail, where would you want to see it disembarked? Greiffenberg, Liegnitz, Breslau or where? Reply tomorrow morning.'[10] Blumenthal was quick to respond, suggesting Brieg as the right destination, for the reasons set out in his letter. However, Moltke had by now received that letter; while he certainly intended to give his army commanders a wide discretion, he did not want his strategic plans compromised by their taking independent decisions in this way, and he very promptly dispatched a telegram to Blumenthal to make it plain that no major movement should be undertaken without approval. Blumenthal was suitably chastened by this, recording that Moltke had forbidden his proposed advance: 'Such a movement, he says, must not take place without the sanction of the King. I dare say he may be right; but one thing I see, and that is, that we are not to be given a very free hand!'[11]

Rightly guessing that Blumenthal would be put out by his instruction, Moltke followed up his telegram with a firm but tactful letter to reiterate the way he intended to conduct the campaign:

> Do not conclude from my telegram of today that it is the intention here to restrain by strict instructions the freedom of operation of the army once it is in contact with the enemy. I will do all I can to ensure that this does not happen. But general instructions, those which determine whether an army is to operate offensively or defensively, which decide if it is to advance or retreat, can only come from His Majesty, for the movements of this army must necessarily be in close relation with those of the other armies.[12]

In itself, Moltke said, the proposed move to the Neisse seemed to him to be entirely correct, but such a move must coincide with the advance of the First Army, and he wondered whether the move might in the first instance be made by the VI Corps alone. However, having reviewed the position further, he authorized the proposed advance, and confirmed the transfer of the Guard Corps to the Second Army.

Moltke was, however, not going to permit the forward movement of the armies to get out of step, and on June 11 issued instructions to the First Army to continue its move towards Görlitz. Writing to Blumenthal that evening, he reflected that if the Army of the Elbe had, as he wished, been allowed to advance into Saxony, it would have been able to reduce its front to the position Dresden-Görlitz, and would probably have compelled the Austrians to divert two or three corps, thus relieving the pressure on the Second Army.

> But it is with known quantities that we must reckon, and not with our desires and hopes. Powerful reasons, albeit not military, will prevent this entry of our troops into Saxony for the next eight days, and we should not waste this time while we are waiting. The First Army will be in cantonments from Niesky to Greiffenberg and Hirschberg by June 18, by which date you will be on the Neisse.

Moltke was, however, still wary of a possible Austrian offensive against Breslau:

> An energetic leader like Benedek will not let himself be put off by this from his operations in Silesia. There he has Hungary and the Galician railway at his back, and will direct all his forces straight at the objective in front of him.[13]

At the same time Moltke, perhaps mindful of Blumenthal's impetuous temperament, offered some sage advice:

> You are better placed to judge these things than I am from here: I wish only that you should resist the temptation to give battle in every circumstance. It is obviously easier to advise resistance at all costs, rather than to retreat, however necessary.[14]

Moltke also wrote that day to Stülpnagel, reviewing the political situation, which remained uncertain. It might be, he said, that the First Army would be ordered to move into Lusatia, while being given discretion as to how much of its forces it should commit. That would depend on the strength of the Austrian forces in Northern Bohemia. It was becoming apparent, however, that hostilities were now imminent, and Moltke was working on the basis that Herwarth would at last be able to move into Saxony on June 16. For the next few days, his principal preoccupation was with the preparations for swift action in Western Germany, but on June 14, in the light of the very latest intelligence reports as to enemy movements in Bohemia, he prepared a brief outline of his intentions for the advance against the Austrians. In this, he had already identified Gitschin as the point to which the movements of both the First and Second Armies should be directed.[15]

Moltke's forces were, however, moving forward on an arc some 300 miles in length. Noting this, the Official History observed:

> This was palpably not the real strategical march of the army for concentration, but only the first step thereto. Whether the further marches of the still separate parts of the force should be made towards different points of this periphery, or towards the centre, depended whether it was decided to assume the offensive or the defensive.[16]

The French commentator General Bonnal detected some economy with the truth here; the decision to take the offensive had already been effectively taken by the end of May, and he saw these words as intended to obscure the fact that, in allowing the Second Army to move to the Neisse, and in ordering the First Army to move still further eastwards, Moltke allowed a serious strategical error to be made. Indeed, for Bonnal, for whom the unwavering application of Napoleonic strategic principles was the only acceptable test of the correctness of any decision, it was 'a strategic blunder so enormous that Prussia would infallibly have been ruined had her opponents been inbred with the Napoleonic spirit of vigour and of manoeuvre.'[17]

On the other hand General von Caemmerer, a German commentator, brushed aside the criticism of Moltke; it was 'unmistakably clear that it is just such an early offensive on the part of the enemy which he is the least afraid of,' not least because he could depend upon 'harmonious cooperation between the widely separated armies.'[18] This view, rather than that of Bonnal, has justly been the verdict of history; Moltke was well aware of the offensive options available to Benedek, and, as his extensive correspondence shows, was calmly prepared to meet them. Justification for his wide deployment came as early as June 11, when his intelligence reports revealed that five of the seven Austrian Corps were still in Moravia.

But at the time the wide dispersal of the Prussian army was certainly seen by some independent observers as a serious mistake. Friedrich Engels, writing in the *Manchester*

Friedrich Engels, amongst other things military critic of *The Manchester Guardian* in 1866. (Wikipedia)

Guardian, had pronounced at the outset that 'the superiority of supreme command is decidedly on the side of the Austrians.' Once the deployment of the Prussian army became known, he was delighted to note the 'signal strategic blunder' which he perceived to be the inevitable consequence of royal participation in the campaign. He expressed his view trenchantly:

> An officer proposing such a plan of campaign was not fit to hold even a lieutenant's commission … nobody could possibly expect that the fatal consequences of kings and princes taking high command would come out so soon and so strong.[19]

Closer to home, the retired General von Willisen observed that the move to the Neisse was 'the worst fault that could have been committed – dissemination of forces in two widely separated groups.'[20]

Throughout the weeks leading up to the campaign Moltke had also been keeping his eye on what was happening in Italy. At the beginning of June Theodore von Bernhardi was sent to Florence with Major von Lucadou to act in a liaison capacity with the Italians. Bernhardi, a military historian and indefatigable diarist, had for many years been close to the centres of power in Prussia, and was trusted by Bismarck and Moltke as a reliable emissary. He kept Moltke closely informed on the stormy debates among Italian leaders as to the correct strategy to adopt. Moltke was to find this an intensely frustrating experience since, as will be seen, his efforts to influence Italian strategy were entirely unsuccessful.

It had, however, always been the fact of Italian participation rather than its effectiveness which mattered to Moltke. There would be no redistribution of the Austrian army in the next few weeks, and it was with Benedek's Northern army with which he had to deal. None of the possible offensives which Moltke had expected the Austrians to consider seemed to be materialising. This was not only because Krismanic intended in any case to adopt a defensive strategy; the decision to concentrate at Olmütz was also due to the need to concentrate well back from the frontier because of the slowness of the Austrian mobilisation process. This, it was agreed at Benedek's headquarters, ruled out completely any question of an advance on Berlin; and there is no evidence that the alternative, a spoiling attack towards Breslau, was ever seriously entertained by Krismanic.

In spite of this the orders issued by Benedek's staff for public consumption were based on the proposition of an Austrian advance. Rules were announced regulating the behaviour of the troops while on enemy territory, and Benedek's reputation for boldness was quite enough to buoy up the Austrian press in its belief in an attacking strategy. But the reality was very different. Benedek, who only arrived in Bohemia in the middle of May, had left Verona with undisguised regret, murmuring 'Here, I know every tree on the road to Milan: up there I shall be a stranger,' and he readily accepted Krismanic's prescription of a cautious and defensive strategy. The latter could not rid himself of the notion that it was the experiences of a century earlier, in the wars against Frederick the Great, that should provide the inspiration for his planning. He had no doubt that Olmütz must be the focal point of Austrian concentration, rather than further to the west or the north, even though this had political as well as military consequences. At Olmütz, Benedek would be too far to the east to offer effective direct support to Saxony, which suggested that Krismanic had written off any hope of cooperation with the Bavarians as well.

This caused mounting concern in Vienna; Beck was sent up to Olmütz on June 6 to press for a movement westward into Bohemia, but met with a blank refusal. Benedek accepted the firm advice of all his staff that such a movement was for the present out of the question; it was too far, and in any case the Austrian concentration was still far from complete. Cooperation with the Saxon forces would, for the moment, have to be confined to the 1st Corps of Clam Gallas, which was at that time the only substantial Austrian force in Northern Bohemia. Quite apart from Franz Joseph's not unreasonable concerns for his army, the decision was militarily foolish in the extreme, for the Saxon army represented an important accession of strength to the Austrians. As Spencer Wilkinson put it:

> The way to protect the Saxon army was, at the proper time, to beat the Prussians. The Saxon army was there to be used and not saved, and the way to use it was to put it in such a position that it would help to defeat the Prussians and so guarantee the independence of Saxony.[21]

Beck had been told to make it plain that he brought only advice rather than instructions; this altogether too diffident approach was quite ineffective against the defensive convictions of Krismanic and the others, whose thinking was determined by an absolute assumption that they could not possibly be ready in time.

Certainly Krismanic felt that he could depend on the Prussians to advance and appears to have expected this to happen sooner than it did; but he was entirely content to wait in Olmütz to see the line the Prussians took, in the hope that an opportunity would then arise of which he could take advantage. And in one other particular his defensive thinking was unshakable; he did not intend to let the army become divided and face defeat in detail. Instead, he would wait until all the missing troops and their supplies and ammunitions had arrived and only then move forward if that was what was called for. If it did become necessary to move into Bohemia, then the point of concentration there would be the fortress of Josephstadt, on which position Clam Gallas and the Saxons could fall back if they were heavily attacked.

This defensive, and purely opportunist, approach played into Moltke's hands. As the Prussian mobilisation proceeded, and the ground that had been lost by the delays in commencing it was rapidly made up, it became less and less likely that Moltke's plans for his concentration would be disturbed. The *Österreichische Militärische Zeitschrift* offered another reason for the decision to concentrate at Olmütz, suggesting that it had kept 'Prussia in doubt, and had compelled her to divide her force.' In fact, as the Prussian Official History points out, it had the opposite effect:

> As soon as the position near Olmütz was known, every doubt vanished. An invasion of Prussian territory could only be directed against Silesia; corresponding measures were taken, and no care was hereafter requisite for the security of Berlin.[22]

Thus, as the opening of the campaign approached, Moltke refined his strategy in the light of the changing circumstances. Including the Reserve Corps in course of formation under von der Mülbe, which consisted of Landwehr troops and was intended for the reinforcement of the Army of the Elbe, he would have available nearly 279,000 men. In fact, von der Mülbe's troops were to see no action, so Moltke took into the first stage of the campaign 255,000 men, of which 93,000 comprised the First Army, 115,000 the Second Army and 46,000 the Army of the Elbe. To oppose him, Benedek had 247,000 men in the Northern Army and the 24,000 men of the Saxon Army, so he enjoyed a narrow margin of numerical superiority. For an army on the defensive that was a potentially significant advantage and so, according to the military theorists, was his opportunity to operate on interior lines. Benedek was the antithesis of Moltke, impulsive and positively anti-intellectual, but Moltke nonetheless entertained some respect for his aggressive instincts. The Prussian General Staff, however, which assessed all its potential opponents, noted simply of Benedek: 'No commander in chief nor strategist; will want a deal of assistance in running an army.'[23]

16

Countdown to War

European opinion was divided as to the likely outcome of the war. In general the press, which provides a possible indication of the state of public opinion, took the view that Prussia would get the beating which the conduct of its Minister President had brought on it. That, at any rate, was the stance taken by most of the British press, for whom Bismarck was practically the devil incarnate. *The Times*, in a series of violent editorials, reflected the general belief that Austria was much the stronger power; contemplating the discussions between Prussia and Italy, it observed with considerable satisfaction: 'A more suicidal alliance has never been formed in Europe since Prussia and Italy lay together at the feet of the first Napoleon.'[1]

In France the press was more anxious that Napoleon III might be drawn into the war than concerned to take sides in any very marked manner. Typical of French papers was *Le Siècle*, a democratic opposition paper that had some connection with the government; it argued 'for watchful neutrality and for intervention only if Austria endangered Italian unity or if the German conflict harmed France's position by a shift in the balance of power.'[2] The semi-official press reassuringly confirmed that France would remain neutral. A slightly different, but more prescient view came from Adolphe Thiers, who denounced the threat of Prussian expansion, as well as the government's help in achieving Italian unification. Although he agreed with a policy of neutrality 'because no one here is foolish enough to insisting on plunging into a war to avoid a war,' the risk of a decisive victory for Prussia was that a weak German Confederation might be replaced by a strong Federation:

> Go, go anywhere in France, go into the smallest towns and villages, and you will see whether this policy, which would tend to reestablish the ancient German empire by placing the power of Charles V in the north instead of in the south of Germany, whether that power [Prussia], supported by Italy, would be popular in France. No, there is too much common sense in France ever to welcome such a policy.[3]

As to the evil consequences which would flow from the war, *The Times* was perfectly indifferent; these were likely to be no more than it had expected: 'The present disunity of Germany is only the natural penalty for her flagrant disregard of all moral obligations towards Denmark and Europe.'[4] And as for Bismarck: 'No Minister ever conceived a more audacious scheme of territorial plunder, or prosecuted it with more insolent effrontery.'[5] Eager to see his comeuppance, it relished the prospect that the Prussian army would be unwilling to fight, commenting on May 22: 'The Prussian government … should have known the reed on which they leant when they supposed that [the] army was to be relied on for the purpose of foreign war.' And on the following day it engaged in a further bout of wishful thinking:

> The Prussian army which … contains a large proportion of educated men, has no spirit … for a war which can give no real glory, and the ultimate consequences of which are likely to be a great national misfortune.[6]

Thunder of this kind was also to be heard from other newspapers; the *Manchester Guardian* expected that the Austrian cause would be supported by the 'sympathies and approval of Europe, which Count Bismarck does not care much about now, but may learn to value more highly hereafter,' while the *Morning Post* confessed that it would be 'delighted' if Austria beat Prussia.[7]

The opinions of individuals perhaps less fond of the sound of their own voice were more cautious. Lord Clarendon, the outgoing Foreign Secretary, expressed his concern for Austria to Lord Bloomfield in Vienna: 'The anxiety here is great, for everybody wishes her well, and fears that she is not ready to meet her very active enemy.'[8] And Robert Morier, who was at the time based in Darmstadt, and who was profoundly convinced that it would be much better if Austria was to be excluded from a united Germany, and better for Austria too, saw things more clearly, predicting that 'the Italians will get a most tremendous licking,' but that Benedek would 'either get the worst of it or fight a fearfully bloody and indecisive battle.'[9] One other individual view as to the probable outcome of the conflict that should be recorded is that of Napoleon III. In his complex manoeuverings among all the parties, he had been informed by a personal conviction that either Austria would win, or that there would be a long drawn out and inconclusive war. Either outturn would, he calculated, provide France with the most favourable opportunity to gain something out of it. Interestingly, though, Napoleon's military attaché in Berlin was now among the few who thought Prussia would prevail.[10] The Emperor's speech at Auxerre on May 15 set the diplomatic dovecotes fluttering when he put down a marker for the future with an outspoken attack on the treaties of 1815. Napoleon may not have held the best informed opinion; but outside the protagonists he had the most to gain. And even if his opinion proved wrong, and Prussia was successful, he might hope that Bismarck would at least feel disposed to reward him for his neutrality.

Ultimately the outcome would be determined by the quality of the troops and the abilities of their leaders, but behind these factors there were a number of indications that suggested that the two nations were, in terms of making war, more evenly matched than might appear, leaving aside for the moment the numbers of troops that each could mobilise and then deploy on the decisive battlefield. True, the population of the Habsburg Empire was 37.5 million, nearly double that of Prussia, with 19.3 million, but the homogeneous and well educated population of Prussia might well (other than by *The Times*) be expected to yield a higher quality of better trained troops than the many races that made up the Austrian armies. And a glance at a few basic economic indicators discloses a striking variation. By 1866 70% of the Austrian labour force was still engaged in agriculture, compared with 45% in Prussia; nonetheless, the latter's annual grain production was 800,000 tons, compared with 700,000 tons produced in Austria. Coal production in Prussia was of the order of 12 million tons, while in Austria it was 5.7 million tons. Even more significantly, Austria's annual production of pig iron was only 460,000 tons while Prussia's was nearly double, at 850,000 tons.[11]

The development of the respective railway systems had seen much more rapid progress in Prussia than in Austria. As early as 1847 the number of kilometres in operation in Prussia was over double that in Austria; as the building of new railways continued, Prussia went on adding twice as many kilometres to its network. This was one further instance of the upward spiral effect of industrial progress, as John Breuilly observed:

> A more complex and advanced economy, with higher levels of urban and manufacturing populations, favours a greater development of new forms of transportation such as railways and has more capital as well as know-how to use for technically advanced forms of production.[12]

A comparison of the respective treasuries also demonstrated that Prussia was potentially less vulnerable to the economic consequences of a war. The development of the Prussian economy had been immeasurably enhanced by its membership of the Zollverein, which was reflected in the progress of its industries and the taxation which their wealth produced. The successful struggle by Prussia to resist Austrian entry into the Zollverein was by no means the least of the factors that affected their relative national strength. While Austria collected annual revenue of 292 million thalers, and Prussia 240 million thalers, Austrian state borrowing was as high as 1670 million thalers, and that of Prussian only 290 million thalers. And, reflecting the size of the respective armies, the Austrian military budget was 51 million thalers and that of Prussia 45 million thalers; it would be the shock of battle itself that would soon demonstrate which budget had been better spent.

In fact, although it may have appeared to some observers who thought themselves well informed that Austria would prove the stronger, not least for the reasons relied on by Friedrich Engels for reaching that conclusion, the strictly military indicators pointed the other way. As has been seen in the comparison of their respective military development over the preceding decade and a half, Prussia had benefited to a remarkable extent from a comprehensive modernisation in strategical and tactical thought, in technology and in military practice in all fields. John Breuilly summed it up as follows:

> Military historians may still debate whether, by the time battle was joined in both 1866 and 1870, there were still chances for the war to go another way, but there is no question that by being the first to exploit so systematically the "beginning of the modern" in warfare, Prussia created the necessary conditions for victory in those wars.[13]

But if the military conditions for victory had thus been created – and to a not inconsiderable extent by Moltke – the decision to go to war remained a high risk strategy. One aspect of the risk was that the war might be long drawn out, a possibility to which Morier referred, which might put severe strains on the Prussian nation, with incalculable political consequences. As a number of historians have pointed out, Bismarck himself later encouraged many others in the view that his policy had throughout been carefully calculated. Lothar Gall noted:

> The impression given is altogether that of a man who was in complete and virtually risk free control of every stage of the game, since he always made sure he had a way out. In reality what he did in 1866 particularly, for all his shrewd calculation of

> details and for all his indubitable skill and his ability to bide his time, was to stake absolutely everything on a single card in a game in which, besides skill and mastery of the rules, chance and luck tipped the scales at the crucial moment; it was no accident that even on the Berlin stock exchange most people reckoned right up until the war that Vienna would emerge as the victor.[14]

It is not even clear that Bismarck fully appreciated the strength of the weapon that Moltke had placed into his hands. The rapid developments that were to prove of central importance in the conduct of the war were of such recent origin that their probable effect may well not have been entirely apparent even to those at the centre of Prussia's leadership – Moltke perhaps excepted. Thus there was an element of recklessness in Bismarck's decision to have 'another go at the aforesaid lottery' of power politics in which his whole stake was put on the table, as he had put it in a letter to Otto von Manteuffel in November 1851.

That he was conscious of the extent of the risk which he ran for himself as well as his country was apparent in his famous conversation with the British Ambassador, Lord Augustus Loftus, when he walked with him in the gardens behind the Wilhelmstrasse on the night of June 15. As the clocks struck midnight, Bismarck remarked: 'If we are beaten, I shall not return here. I shall fall in the last charge. One can but die once; and if beaten, it is better to die.'[15]

Part III
WAR

17

Confronting the Middle States

As soon as the news from Frankfurt of Prussia's withdrawal from the Diet was received in Berlin, confirmatory instructions went out at once to the various Prussian ambassadors in accordance with the decision of the Ministerial council on June 12. In Dresden on June 15 Count Schulenburg went at once to Beust, presenting an ultimatum that Saxony enter forthwith into alliance with Prussia, reducing her army to its peacetime level and agreeing to the Prussian proposals for the reform of the Confederation, or face war. Beust, as expected, refused; and that evening Schulenburg handed to him the formal declaration of war. As he did so, Herwarth's advanced units crossed the Saxon frontier. They met no resistance; as arranged, the Saxon Army Corps had prepared to retreat into Bohemia, and King John and his ministers accompanied it.

In Hesse–Cassel, typically, things were not so well organized. The government had immediately on June 14 decreed mobilization; next day Parliament passed a resolution to revoke the decree and seek neutrality. This was, of course, largely academic. On the morning of June 15 General Roeder, the Prussian ambassador, arrived to present the ultimatum to the chief minister, Abée, who argued, pointlessly, about the constitutional effect of the Diet's decision and only grudgingly agreed that Roeder should see the Elector. At two, Roeder was summoned; the Elector made a number of ungracious observations about Bismarck and truculently refused to contemplate an alliance, pompously declaring that 'he had never forsaken the path of rectitude' and ultimately dismissing Roeder as a 'disturber of the peace.'[1] During the afternoon, orders went out to the Hesse-Cassel troops to retreat via Fulda to Hanau, and at ten o'clock Roeder received the formal rejection of the ultimatum; he forthwith declared war. Early next morning the leading units of Beyer's division set out from Wetzlar to invade the Electorate, occupying Cassel on June 19. The Elector, to his disgust, was taken into custody and removed first to Minden and then to Stettin, while his country, without any evident dislocation of government, managed very well without him.

It was in Hanover, however, that most complications ensued. The blind King George had also immediately ordered mobilization, although the poor state of readiness of the army meant that it would be weeks rather than days before it could be completed. After a ministerial council meeting, the Prussian ambassador Prince Ysenburg was told that the ultimatum was rejected; but it was not until late in the evening that the formal response was finally drafted. Meanwhile Platen, the Chief Minister went to see Ysenburg to ask for time, a request that was denied; and in the event Ysenburg was obliged to present the declaration of war to Platen on the steps of his own house. Later that night a deputation from the city of Hanover went to the royal palace to get the King to change his mind about a Prussian alliance, but also got a blunt refusal, and at 4 am on June 16 King George, with a number of ministers and senior officers, set off to Göttingen where, the previous day, the army had been ordered to concentrate.

King George V of Hanover. (Voss)

The whereabouts and immediate movements of the Hanoverian forces for the moment occupied the principal consideration of the Prussian high command. If the military power of Hanover could be taken out in the first weeks of the campaign in Western Germany, before any junction with other Federal units could be effected, the great disparity of numbers faced by the Prussians could be significantly reduced. But the problem was not only numerical inferiority; the key Prussian units were widely dispersed,

Hanoverian troops in 1866, painting by Richard Knötel. (Voss)

and it would take prompt decision and rapid and well coordinated movement if this disadvantage was also to be overcome. From the start of his planning for the campaign Moltke had proceeded on the bold premise that he could take care of Austria's German allies by employing no more than one corps, with support from Landwehr and garrison troops; and in his final memorandum for the Prussian deployment against Austria, written in the winter of 1865-6, he had again planned on the basis that he need not divert any substantial part of Prussia's military effort against Austria.[2]

Moltke's plans were accordingly based on taking swift action. As early as June 14 preparatory orders had gone out on the basis that hostilities would begin on June 17. Beyer was told: 'On Sunday 17th at noon you are in any case to invade Hesse, unless you previously receive an order to stop you.'[3] On the following day, as the diplomatic situation became clear, Beyer, Falckenstein and Manteuffel were all ordered to launch the invasion on June 16, subject in the cases of Beyer and Falckenstein to any contrary instructions they might receive from the ambassadors at Cassel and Hanover respectively.[4] And with an eye to the future and to the public relations aspects of the action being taken, they were all ordered at 10.30 pm on June 15 that they should 'on invading issue soothing proclamation to inhabitants that we are not coming as enemies. Private property to be strictly spared. State property to be treated as our own.'[5] Moltke continued to coordinate the movements of the three divisions of Beyer, Goeben and Manteuffel from headquarters in Berlin, notifying all three on June 16 of the news that the Hanoverian Army was moving to Göttingen; Beyer was additionally told to destroy the Frankfurt railway at Nauheim. This distant exercise of command was not without its difficulties; a telegram on June 16 to each of the commanders sharply reminded them of the need to acknowledge receipt of telegrams. It was an injunction that subsequent events were to demonstrate was all too necessary in the case of Falckenstein.

The military situation faced by the Prussians in Western and Southern Germany had been created in part as a result of Mensdorff's emphatic success in the struggle to find allies among the Middle States. What Prussia lost in this way would have now to be won on the battlefield. But although Mensdorff's limited diplomatic objectives in the weeks before the outbreak of war had been almost completely achieved, the military advantages which they were intended to confer had not been realised. Whole hearted strategic cooperation, which meant submerging particularist interests completely in the Austrian cause, was not so easily come by.

In his notes for an audience of the King in May, Moltke had clinically analysed the strength of the Middle States, and their possible effect on the campaign in Bohemia:

> 8th Federal Corps, nominally 40,000, said to be collecting in Württemberg. It can hardly operate independently against us but might join Bavarian 40,000 about Bamberg. These 80,000 will take a long time to get ready and be concentrated. Meanwhile a much stronger army will soon be actually ready in Northern Bohemia and Saxony. Saxons apparently intend to concentrate at Annaberg…so … probably mean to join Bavarians in Franconia. Accordingly we have to dispose our forces to meet an enemy distributed on the line Bamberg – Prague. In our rear we have to watch the Hanoverians, who with the Brigade Kalik will make about 23,000 men. If we tried to meet with an equal force these 100,000 Federal troops not yet ready

King John of Saxony. (Voss)

> we should have to face with inferior forces the Austrian Army which will be quite ready.

Moltke reasoned that all his forces should be assembled against the principal enemy

> the more so as a first victory over him will probably prevent our other opponents from acting at all. But in that case we must immediately employ a reinforced division to act against Hanover, and for this purpose it must be kept ready at Minden.

If this strategy seemed too bold to the King, Moltke was prepared to leave the 16th Division at Coblenz.[6] At a later audience on May 25, Moltke reiterated the importance of swift action against the Austrians to preempt the Federal forces getting into the action at all:

> In a few weeks there may be another enemy in Franconia. The vital thing is to strike down the principal enemy, the one that is ready, before this happens, in which case the Federal Corps will probably never do anything, and if they do, we shall have the means of acting against their flank from Plauen or Eger.[7]

Moltke noted on this paper that Bismarck supported him in his view that troops were no longer needed to watch South Germany on the left bank of the Elbe.

As the political situation developed, Moltke kept his eye on Western and Southern Germany. On May 30 he forwarded to Bismarck his proposal, which was approved, to concentrate 16,000 men in Holstein. He kept Blumenthal, in whom he had the

Prince Charles, commander of the Bavarian Army in 1866. (Voss)

greatest confidence, well informed of his thinking on the subsidiary campaign, since the developments there might give some indication as to the Austrian plans. On June 11 he noted to him that the Brigade Kalik might move off from Altona 'at any moment, and the next day we shall have an ultimatum.'[8] By now, Moltke was irretrievably committed to his strategy of concentrating on the Austrians and leaving his commanders in Western and Southern Germany to take care of the situation with very modest forces, whatever William might say.

On paper, Moltke was adopting a high risk strategy in his plans to deal with the Middle States. The Hanoverian Army, organized in four brigades under von dem Knesebeck, de Vaux, von Bülow and von Bothmer, was a not inconsiderable opponent. Command of the army was finally given to the very capable von Arentschildt; his Chief of Staff was Colonel Cordemann. Serving as Adjutant General was Colonel Dammers, described by Sybel as 'a well informed man of lively, easily excited temperament and restlessly busy', who was to play a considerable part in the events that were shortly to unfold.[9] At full strength Hanover could put into the field 20 battalions, 24 squadrons and 52 guns. The Electoral Hessian Army, under von Lossberg, comprised two divisions under von Buttlar and von Osterhausen and the cavalry brigade of von Bardeleben; the total strength of this force was 10 battalions, 8 squadrons and 16 guns. The largest force faced by the Prussians was of course the Bavarian Army, commanded by Prince Charles, which comprised 45 battalions, 44 squadrons and 144 guns, being organized in four divisions – 1st Division (von Stephan), 2nd Division (von Feder), 3rd Division (von Zoller) and 4th Division (von Hartmann). The Reserve Cavalry Corps was commanded by Prince Taxis. Chief of the Staff was the capable Ludwig von der Tann. Finally, there was the 8th Federal Corps, made up of contingents from Württemberg, Baden, Hesse-

Darmstadt and Nassau, with an Austrian brigade to stiffen it. Its total strength amounted to 46½ battalions, 36 squadrons and 134 guns. The 1st Division, from Württemberg, was commanded by von Hardegg. The 2nd Division, from Baden, was commanded by Prince William; the 3rd from Hesse Darmstadt, was under von Perglas and the 4th, including the Austrian brigade of von Hahn and troops from Nassau and Electoral Hesse was commanded by Count Neipperg. The combined total of the Allied armies amounted to 121½ battalions, 112 squadrons, and 346 guns.

It would be wrong, however, to conclude from the apparent boldness of Moltke's plans that the military power of the Middle States was ineffectual, or that no account was taken there of military developments. After the war of 1859, military reform was not confined to the Great Powers. In Germany the lesser states recognized that developments in technology, as well as an increasingly volatile political situation, rendered military cooperation an urgent necessity. And if practical cooperation in war time was important, it was just as important in preparing for war, particularly in the choice of weapons that had to be made. The advent of the Dreyse needle gun in the hands of the Prussian Army, and its recent evident success in the Danish war, concentrated the minds of soldiers in the lesser states upon the importance of introducing breech loaders. The difficulty was in getting agreement. Württemberg, Baden, Hesse and Bavaria had, after a lot of argument, agreed on a common carbine (the Austrian) for the different varieties of muzzle loading Minié rifles being introduced; and there was a good deal of reluctance to go through it all again over the needle gun. Württemberg meanwhile began to tinker with the possibility of adopting American breech loaders that had been perfected during the Civil War, although the problems of production and supply that this would entail inclined official opinion towards the needle gun.[10]

As it happened, final agreement on the equipment of the Federal troops had not been reached by the time the events of 1866 overtook the confused debates, and the South German States opposed to Prussia in the coming war had to fight with weapons which many now believed were significantly inferior to those of the enemy. Hanover meanwhile had insisted in going its own way; its Minié rifles used a unique calibre, while other North German States followed the Prussian pattern in both organisation and equipment. Saxony, for its part, had adopted Austrian systems.

The total Allied strength was much greater than that of the forces that Moltke allocated to the campaign. In Prussia before the war, of the nine Army Corps areas, seven were in the eastern part of the country and two (VII and VIII Army Corps) in the western; in addition there were the troops under Manteuffel in Schleswig. Moltke broke up both of the western corps, sending the 15th Division from Cologne to Halle to join the forces massing against Austria, together with the 31st Brigade from Coblenz; the 32nd Brigade, under Beyer formed the core of a Combined Division. The commitment of three-quarters of the VIII Corps to the campaign in Bohemia had, however, deeply worried Bismarck who, concerned about the possibility of French intervention, induced the King to cancel these orders; fortunately Moltke, when he learned of it, was successful in restoring the original plan. From the VII Corps, the 14th Division under Count Münster was also sent off to the Army of the Elbe, while Goeben's 13th Division, concentrating at Minden and Bielefeld, was assigned to the campaign in Western Germany. The third component of the Prussian force was the Combined Division from Holstein. Collectively, this force was ultimately to be named the Army of the Main.

General Eduard Ernst Vogel von Falckenstein, commander of the Army of the Main. (Rogers)

When all its elements were in the field the army comprised 53 battalions, 29 squadrons and 12 guns.

With their German allies, who could not contribute very much, the Prussians disposed of rather less than half as much infantry as their opponents, and about a third each of their cavalry and artillery. In addition, their forces were widely dispersed and their initial concentration areas were inconveniently located. And they enjoyed one other disadvantage; the command of these forces was in the first instance given to General Ernest Vogel von Falckenstein. Aged 69, he was appointed in spite of his performance as Chief of Staff of the allied forces in Denmark in 1864, where he had aided and abetted the misdeeds of the aged Wrangel until he was removed and replaced (at the behest of Edwin von Manteuffel) by Moltke himself. The latter would have been deeply perplexed by the description of Falckenstein, in the hagiographical *Men who have made the New German Empire*:

> Next to Moltke … unquestionably the greatest strategist and the most accomplished staff officer of the Prussian and German armies, also the most consummate tactical leader in the field, and altogether the first of the great military captains of the age.[11]

In the course of Falckenstein's military career, which stretched back to the Wars of Liberation, he had taken part also in the Danish War of 1848-50. He also enjoyed a considerable, and perhaps better deserved reputation as a painter of glass and porcelain. He established on the orders of King Frederick William IV the Royal Institute for Painting on Glass, of which he became the head. He was, though, an obstinate man with a one-track mind, and this unfortunate trait was to manifest itself more than once during the coming campaign.

Field Marshal Prince Alexander of Hesse, commander of the Federal 8th Army Corps. (Voss)

Among his subordinates was Edwin von Manteuffel, later to succeed him in the overall command, who brought with him the forces that had been occupying Schleswig and which had overrun Holstein. His energetic involvement in political decision making had continued to bring him into conflict with Bismarck, whose efforts to reach some accommodation with the opposition he had frequently frustrated, most notably in May 1865. After this Bismarck had finally removed this serious obstacle to his policy by getting Manteuffel appointed, following the Convention of Gastein, as governor of Schleswig.

Much the ablest of the Prussian field commanders in Western Germany was Lieutenant General August von Goeben. Born in Hanover in 1816, he now commanded the 13th Division, after a decidedly colourful career. Bored by peacetime soldiering, he joined in 1836 the army of Don Carlos in Spain, reaching the rank of Lieutenant Colonel by the age of twenty four, and being wounded five times. With the collapse of the Carlist cause, he made his way home through France, largely on foot as he was completely broke. Starting again at the bottom in the Prussian Army, he quickly climbed the ladder, leading the 26th Infantry Brigade at Düppel and Alsen. In appearance he was a decidedly untypical Prussian general, notoriously sloppily dressed, with thick pebble glasses. But he was highly intelligent and possessed a great sense of humour, entirely deserving Sybel's description of his leadership qualities:

> He considered the advantages and the obstacles, and held with an iron calmness a firm rein upon his inward impulses, until the right moment came and the ardour of his own enthusiasm led on the troops to an irresistible attack.[12]

Prussia, of course, enjoyed the priceless benefit of a unified command, even if advantage was not always to be taken of it. The Federal forces were in a less satisfactory position. The Bavarian Army was commanded by Prince Charles of Bavaria, succinctly dismissed in his diary by Prince Chlodwig von Hohenlohe as 'too old to be Commander in Chief.'[13] The Federal 8th Corps was to be commanded by the competent Prince Alexander of Hesse, the brother of the Czarina. He had served for a time in the Prussian Army before joining the Austrian Army, in which he achieved distinction as a divisional commander in the Italian War of 1859. Closely connected by marriage to many of Europe's royal families, he was the father of the future Prince Louis of Battenberg, British First Sea Lord in 1914. Alexander was extremely hostile to Prussia in general and Bismarck in particular and could certainly be counted on to do his best. He was under no illusions as to the difficulty of his task, writing to his sister on June 25:

> I am standing at the most important crossroads of my life. All those parts of Germany which have remained true to the Federation are relying on me. Six sovereigns have entrusted me with their troops. The Federation is acting solely upon my instructions. Shall I be able to justify their confidence? Shall I succeed in defeating the Prussians with this hotchpotch of troops, and in reinstating the exiled Princes of Cassel and Hanover?[14]

The lack of any concerted Federal strategy was soon to make itself apparent. Even more importantly, the practical preparations for a campaign had been largely neglected in the Middle States, and the outbreak of war, therefore, caught them entirely unready. Prince Alexander's wife wrote to the Czarina:

> They have nothing, neither munitions nor horses nor transport. When they went off, it was just as if they were going to a parade, and there was nothing to be done but to send them to the garrison in Mainz until they had been provided with the barest necessities.[15]

18

Langensalza

Most of the political leaders of the Middle States were thoroughly second rate, and quite unfitted to cope with the pressure of great events. For the most part their titular rulers were even less able to respond sensibly or effectively to what some of them could see was a potentially terminal crisis for their dynasties. Nowhere was this air of unreality more evident than in Hanover. When confronted by Ysenburg with the Prussian ultimatum King George had boasted of the strength of his army of 50,000 men. Whether he really believed in this estimate of military power or was merely whistling to keep up his spirits is unclear; Ysenburg pointed out to him that his effective strength was, at that moment, a third of that claimed. Mobilisation would take weeks to bring the army to its full strength and it was evident even to King George that he could not wait that long.

When he went off to join his army at Göttingen King George was accompanied by the Crown Prince, Count Platen, von Brandis the Minister of War, the Austrian ambassador, and a number of senior officers. When they reached the army they found that the reserves had already begun to arrive, and by nightfall on June 17 the total strength had reached 19,000 men and forty two guns. Morale among the army's leaders was not high; they were in a state of considerable agitation over the command structure proposed. The original plan that the blind King should be nominally in command, thus effectively giving control of the operations to Lieutenant General von Tchirschnitz, his First Adjutant General, had not been well received. Nor were the ranking officers, Generals Gebser and von Sichart, the Chief of Staff, regarded as acceptable; and the senior officers put pressure on the King, through the Crown Prince, to appoint von Arentschild. The latter took over the command with the deepest reluctance, having no illusions about the situation in which he, and his army, had been placed. The immediate question that had to be settled without delay was the proposed move of the army southwards to link up with either the Bavarians or the Federal 8th Corps. The King was determined that such a move should start at once; but his senior officers were adamantly opposed to any movement before the troops had been properly organized. The provision of horses for the artillery, and for the ammunition and provision trains, was incomplete; equipment was lacking; and stocks of ammunition were low. Reluctantly, the King gave way, allowing time for these wants of preparation to be, to some extent, made good. Large quantities of supplies and ammunition had been stockpiled at Hanover, and these fell into the hands of the Prussians when Goeben's division reached the capital on June 17. The Prussians were moving quickly in their bid to deal with the Hanoverians, and Manteuffel, on the same day, advanced towards Lüneburg and Celle with the intention of advancing on Hanover; on June 19, Falckenstein ordered Goeben to push on towards Göttingen in pursuit of the enemy.

There the operations of the Prussians, insofar as they were known to the Hanoverians, were viewed with mounting concern. Two staff officers, Lieutenant Colonel Rudorff and

Major Jacobi, went to the King to advise him that although the army could march, it could not fight and that, in consequence, there should be immediate negotiations with the Prussians. To this suggestion King George was prepared to pay no attention at all, and the debate continued as to the course now to be adopted. Staff opinion was split between standing at Göttingen, where an early attack from Falckenstein was certain; or retreating southwards into the Harz mountains with a view to establishing contact with the Bavarian and Federal troops. To remain at Göttingen was clearly extremely hazardous, and the decision was taken to move south. The first plan was to head south and west towards Frankfurt through Hesse-Cassel, across the Werra at Bebra and through Fulda. But a reconnaissance in force on June 19 by Bothmer into the outskirts of Cassel showed that Beyer's division had begun to arrive there in strength, and other indications that the Prussians were now fanning out across the whole of the Electorate made any direct march on Frankfurt much too dangerous. No reply had been received from the messages sent to the Bavarians and to the Federal 8th Corps; but it was obvious that if the Hanoverians did not get away quickly to the south any prospect of a junction with

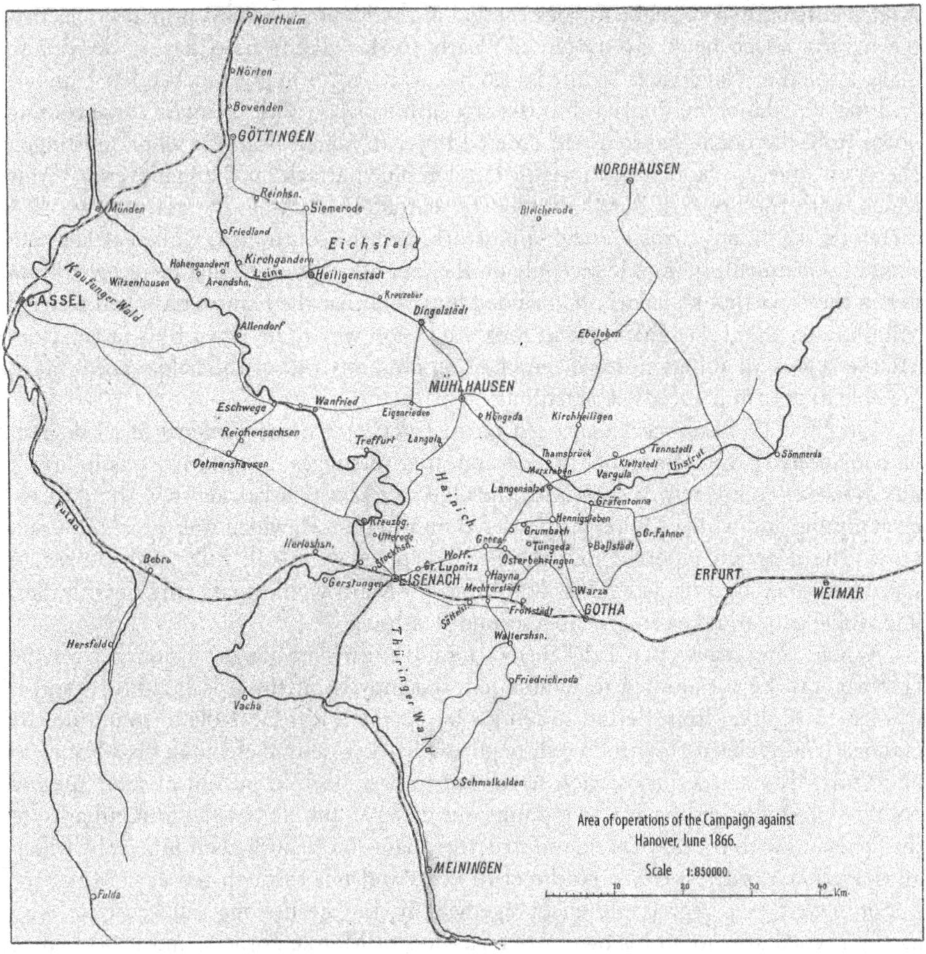

Map 5 – Area of operations of the Campaign against Hanover, June 1866.

their South German allies would be entirely lost. Accordingly it was decided instead to march on June 21 to Heiligenstadt and from there to Eisenach in two columns through Mühlhausen and Wanfried. It was estimated that the bulk of the army might be in its new position around Eisenach by nightfall on June 23.

By comparison with the disarray in which the Hanoverian army had first assembled, its condition as it marched off was greatly improved; the short breathing space had enabled much to be done to prepare the army for the campaign.[1]

It was a blazing June that year, and as the month moved on the temperature rose still higher. As the Hanoverians marched south on June 21 they experienced great discomfort; and, next day, it was hotter still, and the inexperienced troops suffered intensely in the windless air. Firm intelligence as to the Prussian movements was not to be had, and there was real anxiety that, at any moment, units of Beyer's division might catch them in flank from the west.

In fact, however, the danger was much less than Arentschild feared, as a result of a number of events quite unknown to him and his colleagues. Falckenstein had been given explicit instructions to make the destruction of the Hanoverians his primary objective; the reports which he received pointed clearly to the Hanoverians having decided to make a stand at Göttingen, and he issued his orders accordingly. Goeben left Hanover on June 19; Manteuffel moved into the city in his place. With his main force coming down from the north, Falckenstein ordered Beyer to march from Cassel on Göttingen. There, on June 23, he planned to launch a combined attack on the Hanoverian Army which, with the Prussian forces entirely concentrated, could hardly fail. For two days, therefore, the Hanoverians marched undisturbed to the southwards while Falckenstein closed in on an empty trap. It was only on the evening of June 21 that he received from Berlin the news that his quarry had eluded him, and that the Hanoverians had reached Mühlhausen. Next day Falckenstein took a decision which, in view of his orders from Moltke 'above all things to force the Hanoverian Army out of the field, and as far as possible to disarm it', needs explanation.[2]

On June 19 Bismarck had passed on to Falckenstein the contents of a telegram he had received from Karlsruhe which appeared to suggest an alluring possibility; it was, however completely at odds with the objective at which Falckenstein should have been aiming and which Moltke had ordered him to pursue, which was the Hanoverian army. The telegram reported that the Federal forces were 'still fully disorganised. A speedy advance by Prussia against Frankfurt-am-Main would make any organization impossible and would easily lead to a second Rossbach'.[3]

When, three days later, Falckenstein found himself no longer in touch with the Hanoverians, he succumbed to temptation and moved off towards Frankfurt, and it was left to Moltke, from Berlin, to reorganize all the forces available to round up the Hanoverians. A sharp order followed, requiring Falckenstein to abandon his advance to Frankfurt. Bismarck's intervention seems not to have been in pursuit of some specific political objective; rather, as Craig points out, it was a product of the unfamiliarity of the Prussians with the new command structure that was established on June 2, by which all operational orders were to go direct to units and not through the War Ministry.[4] But it served as a regrettable encouragement to the headstrong Falckenstein, who hardly needed any, to go his own way regardless of Moltke's orders, and it planted in his mind the notion that Frankfurt was an objective of greater importance than any of the presently widely separated forces opposed to him – the Hanoverians, the Bavarians and the Federal 8th Corps. Accordingly, he 'gave himself up wholly to the prospect … of gaining brilliant laurels in Frankfurt;'[5] he sent a message to the King that he 'could say nothing about his further operations: from Göttingen he should turn in whatever direction he might hope to fall in with any considerable hostile force.'[6] The Official History passes over this incident in tactful silence, but it was a matter of urgent concern to take steps to head off the Hanoverian retreat with whatever troops were available.

For this Moltke had few resources to play with. As early as June 19 he had pointed out to Falckenstein that it would be desirable to send one of his divisions via Magdeburg to Eisenach; had this been done, of course, there was no way that the Hanoverians could have hoped to escape to the south. As it was, the only troops immediately available to bar their way were some Landwehr and garrison troops which Moltke sent to Gotha to join Colonel von Fabeck's two battalions there and two Guards battalions under Colonel von Osten-Sacken which were dispatched to Eisenach. The importance of the latter place, in view of the direction taken by the Hanoverians, was obvious; Moltke continued to bombard Falckenstein with instructions to move troops south by rail to Gotha via Magdeburg. To the latest such order of June 21 Falckenstein, his mind firmly set on Frankfurt, turned a deaf ear, claiming that it was doubted whether the detachment could arrive in time at its destination.[7]

The most that Falckenstein was prepared to do was on the morning of June 22 to order Beyer to concentrate at Ottmannshausen on the Werra and to reconnoitre towards Eisenach, while Goeben and Manteuffel paused at Göttingen preparatory to marching via Cassel towards Frankfurt. Fabeck, meanwhile, having moved to Eisenach and taken command there, was still the only obstacle to the Hanoverians.

By June 22, therefore, the latter were in a better position than they could possibly have hoped; all that was needed was that the movement south be pushed on as vigorously as possible and that any resistance be resolutely brushed aside. Beyer was two or three days march away, and Goeben and Manteuffel even further off. The situation was a lot clearer to Moltke in Berlin that it seemed to be to Falckenstein, on the ground; and he telegraphed the latter once more to tell him to use the railways to recover the ground lost. This time, Falckenstein was ordered to send troops from Göttingen by Cassel to try to intercept Arentschild; his excuse for ignoring this was the fact that a tunnel on the Göttingen-Cassel line had been blocked by the retreating Hanoverians, who had also blown up a railway bridge at Münden. In fact, the problem could have been overcome by using the railway as far as the tunnel and then making a short march to the bridge over the Werra, there to pick up other trains; but Falckenstein announced that his intention to cut off the Hanoverians had been frustrated; he grandly outlined his plans as follows: 'It is my intention to annihilate the 8th Confederate Corps at Frankfurt, and then cover the Rhine Province, disengage Baden, and draw away the Bavarians from Saxony and Bohemia.'[8] Evidently Bismarck's previous telegram with its historical allusions was still in the forefront of his mind.

On June 23, Fabeck, moving back and forward between Gotha and Eisenach like a goalkeeper watching several opponents bearing down on him at once, again returned to the former place on the basis that the latest indications pointed to this being the objective of the Hanoverians; but he would be outnumbered four or five to one, and the best that could be hoped for was to delay Arentschild long enough to let his pursuers catch him. Even this was hardly likely unless Falckenstein could be induced to do as he was told; but in an effort to slow down the Hanoverians' southern movement, Moltke instructed Fabeck to summon them to surrender on the basis that they were, effectively, surrounded. This was, of course, literally true; but any force that is surrounded may be able to fight its way out, and Fabeck's prospects of resisting the Hanoverians were, self evidently, not good.

At Hanoverian headquarters in Langensalza Fabeck's demand, brought by Captain von Zielberg, kindled again the fears of the doubters. The view that the army could march, but could not fight, was still largely held; and if the army was to gain southern Germany, some negotiated deal would be essential, even though surrender was out of the question. The possibility of making a deal was, therefore, extremely tempting; and since Zielberg had no powers to negotiate, Major Jacobi was sent forward to Gotha, there to negotiate by telegraph with Moltke in Berlin. He was also, as far as he was able, to ascertain the strength of the enemy's position.

That evening Jacobi reached Gotha, where he was at once put in touch with Moltke, who proposed that the Hanoverian Army should return to Göttingen and then be sent on leave, while the King returned to his residence outside Hanover. For his part Jacobi proposed that the Hanoverians be allowed to proceed to southern Germany against an undertaking that they would not, for say six or eight weeks, take part in any hostile action. He added that there could be no question of surrender unless he was convinced that the army was surrounded by an overwhelmingly superior force.

Meanwhile Arentschild had been collecting intelligence directly from the local inhabitants and from some Landwehr prisoners taken that day; and he had reached the firm conclusion that there stood before him in Gotha no more than five battalions. In this view he was, of course, almost precisely right and given the strength of his force, it is not surprising that he issued for the next day orders to advance on Gotha. After these orders had gone out, news came in that Eisenach was no longer occupied by the enemy, and Bülow's brigade was told off to occupy it, Colonel Rudorff being sent to supervise the movement. The rest of the army, meanwhile, assembled just south of Langensalza ready for the next day's advance.

When Jacobi got back to headquarters a long Council of War took place, in the course of which he reported his belief that a large body of enemy troops had been collected around Gotha, and that Goeben's division had itself gone there by rail. Jacobi told his colleagues, most of whom were looking for any excuse not to fight if it could be avoided, that although he had received no reply to his proposal, he expected that when it came it would be favourable. All of this was quite enough to encourage those who wanted to talk rather than fight, and the upshot was that Colonel Dammers was ordered to accompany Jacobi next day, June 24, to Gotha, to see what could be done, while the advance on Gotha and Eisenach was for the moment put on hold.

When Dammers and Jacobi arrived next morning in Gotha they found that the only Prussian general in the city was Duke Ernest of Saxe Coburg Gotha, who held no official military position. He was, however, willing in his capacity as Duke to see what he could do to try to broker an armistice, and he sat down with Dammers to agree the text of a despatch to Berlin proposing that the Hanoverian Army be allowed free passage to southern Germany in exchange for which it would not take part in any hostilities for one year.

This was, however, proving to be one of those negotiations in which each side had a particular object in mind but no intention of giving away anything of value to obtain it. And Dammers' immediate purpose was even simpler than it appeared; unpersuaded by Jacobi's view of the Prussian strength at Gotha, he formed his own, and more accurate opinion, and dispatched to headquarters in Langensalza another officer, Captain Krause, with a secret message to the effect that all negotiations should be broken off and that an advance should commence at once to Eisenach. With a degree of mild duplicity, however, Colonel Dammers remained for the time being in Gotha; in fact, for other reasons, the Hanoverians had already decided to break off negotiations and Captain von der Wense was sent at 11.00 am to Gotha to recall Dammers. Von der Wense met the latter, however, already on his way back to headquarters, which he reached at 3.00 pm.

These events would not, of themselves, be important had it not been the case that Jacobi remained behind, in Gotha, to await the arrival of Lieutenant General von Alvensleben, at a time when events were moving fast elsewhere. Von der Wense went on to Gotha to tell Jacobi what had occurred (including, privately, the decision to advance on Eisenach). When, during the previous day, it had become increasingly clear at Langensalza that, whatever may have been the position at Gotha, Eisenach was only weakly held, Bülow had prepared to attack the place and had first sent a summons to evacuate the town to Colonel Osten-Sacken, who with his two Guards battalions had returned to defend it. The summons reached the Prussians at 9.00 am, and Osten-Sacken predictably rejected it. Rudorff, however had seen enough to convince him that the move on Eisenach, suspended as a result of Jacobi's report the previous day, should certainly proceed, and he hastened back to Langensalza himself to report, arriving at 10.30 am. It was this, rather than Dammers' emissary, that persuaded King George that the attack should proceed, the blind king receiving Rudorff's report with characteristic excitement. 'No strong garrison in Gotha! No one in Eisenach! Then it was a piece of unfounded swaggering on the part of Moltke to announce that we were completely surrounded'.[9] And it was in this mood of sudden optimism that the order to advance on Eisenach was given.

The advanced guard of Bülow's brigade soon took Meckerstädt and had broken up the railway and telegraphs lines, and was driving in the weak line of Prussian skirmishers, when a telegram from Jacobi in Gotha reached its commander, Lieutenant Colonel Knipping. 'Hostilities are to be avoided, as the conditions laid down by Hanover have found acceptance on the part of Prussia.'[10] In the face of this Knipping felt he had no choice but to seek a cease fire, sending an officer at once to Osten-Sacken for the purpose at about 7.00 pm. It was agreed between Bülow and Osten-Sacken that there should be a temporary truce till 8.00 am next day, the truce to end on three hours' notice. The preponderance of force that Bülow enjoyed at this point made it quite possible that he would have been able to take Eisenach; what is a good deal less likely is that the rest of the Hanoverian Army could have moved with sufficient celerity to get over the river and down the roads to the south before Falckenstein's belated moves to intercept them took effect. But Hanoverian apologists were quick to blame the unfortunate Jacobi for thus interfering with the course of events.

In fact, the message he sent was based on the facts. The Duke of Coburg's reaction to the hardening attitude of the Hanoverians was one of amazement. 'This looks like felony', he said. Later in the day the Duke received from Bismarck a message responding to the proposal for a year's parole for the Hanoverian Army:

> Count Bismarck accepts the Gotha proposals, but demands that Hanover should give guarantees that she will carry out the conditions which have been agreed on. Lieutenant General von Alvensleben has therefore been dispatched to arrange the guarantees with the King of Hanover.[11]

The Duke sent this at once to Hanoverian headquarters in the hands of Captain von der Wense; and, not long after, wishing to avoid needless bloodshed, induced Jacobi to send the telegram which halted Knipping at the gates of Eisenach, since it seemed to both of them that the Hanoverians' decision to advance must have been taken in ignorance of the progress which the armistice talks seemed to be making.

King George's response to the Duke was to make plain that the one year condition of no hostilities was unacceptable to him; he asked that Jacobi be sent back, but confirmed that he would be 'most happy to receive Adjutant General von Alvensleben … and shall also be glad to enter into negotiations with him for the purpose of sparing my subjects the miseries of war.'[12] None of these proceedings suggest that anyone at Hanoverian headquarters was especially keen to fight if some sort of satisfactory way out could be found; and in the overall situation in Germany at that moment, it is to their credit that they sought to avoid useless bloodshed. In this humane objective, however, they were to be disappointed; while the talking was going on at Gotha and over the telegraph wires, the Prussian forces were briskly on the move.

After he had received and rejected Rudorff's demand for the surrender of Eisenach, Osten-Sacken sent urgent messages calling for support. Beyer had previously told Falckenstein that at most he could get two battalions up in support of Osten-Sacken that day. But on receiving the latter's further appeal for help, five battalions marched through the night to Kreuzburg to be ready to fight at Eisenach next day. Goeben, who had got to Münden on the morning of June 24, likewise prepared to assist, notifying Falckenstein that he would go on to Cassel and from there send reinforcements by rail to Eisenach, which five of his battalions reached before dawn on June 25. There was no further prospect of the Hanoverians breaking through to the south at this point.

Moltke was, however, less content with Falckenstein's response to the situation, and was concerned also to slam the door at Gotha. Twice his orders to reinforce Gotha had been disregarded; at 8.00 am on June 24 a peremptory instruction went to Falckenstein to use the Magdeburg railway for this purpose, but even this did not produce compliance. At 6.00 pm Moltke telegraphed Falckenstein again, his irritation showing very clearly:

> Orders from His Majesty this morning early to send troops via Magdeburg to Gotha and Eisenach. Reinforcements of the small detachments there most imperative. Negotiations with the Hanoverian Army continue. Presumably they will not end today and be broken off tomorrow. What measures have you taken?[13]

In fact, albeit sluggishly, Falckenstein had at last taken action, reporting at 5.00 pm that half of Goeben's division was to go to Eisenach while Manteuffel was sending five battalions under von Flies to Gotha. Falckenstein's slow response meant, though,

General Eduard von Flies, Prussian commander at the Battle of Langensalza. (Rogers)

that the latter, experiencing difficulties with rail transport, did not get to Gotha until late on June 25. Meanwhile Alvensleben had arrived at Langensalza to try and make a deal with the Hanoverians. He found King George in a haughty and obstinate mood. As to the neutralisation of the Hanoverian Army, the King was only prepared to agree to eight weeks, rather than the year which had been suggested; and for this he would give no guarantees, asserting that his royal word should be enough. Alvensleben was unimpressed by this; but it was finally agreed that there should be a twenty four hour truce. At least, that was what the Prussians intended; the document signed by Alvensleben and Dammers suggested that the truce should continue 'until further notice;' and on the Hanoverian side it was perceived as of indefinite length until brought to an end.[14] Reporting this by telegraph to Berlin, Alvensleben asked that Falckenstein be told of it from Berlin; a message was also sent to Goeben, but with the pressure of other events in Bohemia it did not reach him at Eisenach until 9.00 pm.

Falckenstein had by now himself reached Eisenach. He was in a thoroughly bad temper as a result of the postponement of his planned advance on Frankfurt. The commitment of Flies' detachment to oppose the Hanoverians particularly annoyed him, and he was in no mood to be receptive to approaches from the Hanoverians. When Rudorff turned up at Eisenach and asked for a train to take him to Berlin to discuss the armistice arrangements he rudely told him that he could ask Alvensleben for a train. Rudorff was allowed to send a telegram to Berlin to report Falckenstein's refusal before he returned to report to King George. This abrupt dismissal of his envoy caused violent rage on the part of that monarch, who saw in it a breach of the armistice arrangements; and he ordered that Bülow's troops be pulled back from Eisenach. By now both Falckenstein and King George were each convinced that the other was trying to pull a fast one.

For his part, Falckenstein, on the basis of a false report that the Bavarians had reached Vacha, only eighteen miles from Eisenach, telegraphed Moltke that he must attack next day, June 26, lest he otherwise be caught between the Hanoverians and the

Bavarians. Next morning, at 4.00 am, he received Moltke's reply to the effect that the truce would expire at 10.00 am on that day, unless Colonel von Döring, who was being sent to negotiate with the Hanoverian King at Langensalza, should extend it. Greatly annoyed by this, Falckenstein grumpily sent a message to King George that he would respect the truce; the latter now contemplated again sending off Rudorff to Berlin to repeat the offer of an eight weeks' neutralisation.

During the night however, the arrival of a Hanoverian foraging party at Mühlhausen led to a false report reaching Bismarck that the Hanoverian Army had reached that place. The only explanation of this could be that they were now trying to escape encirclement by retreating northwards, and on receipt of this news Bismarck telegraphed to Duke Ernest that Döring's mission would be to no purpose, while Moltke sent orders to Falckenstein and Flies to commence operations against the apparently retreating Hanoverians. When Döring arrived at headquarters it was to find that it was well understood there that the orders from Berlin were based on false information, so he proceeded after all on his mission to Langensalza. At the same time Rudorff set off to Gotha on his way to Berlin, only to encounter the troops of Flies who had already moved out in response to Moltke's overnight instructions. Flies refused to let him pass, on the basis that the armistice had expired; but in the face of Rudorff's protests, agreed to stand fast for two hours, and allowed Rudorff to send off yet another telegram to Berlin, asserting that the armistice was still in force.[15]

At Langensalza, King George was angrier than ever, and at first refused even to talk to Döring; when finally granted an audience the latter had a hard time with the infuriated King. When Döring said that he had orders to try and bring about a suspension of hostilities the King interrupted him:

> "Who gave you the orders?" To Döring's reply that they were from His Majesty, the King of Prussia, the question followed: "From the King himself"? Döring answered: "Through the President of the Ministry, Count Bismarck;" to which the King cried: "What is that creature after?" The Colonel begged the King most respectfully to consider that he was speaking of a Prussian Minister. "Well, then!" said the King, "We are all creatures for that matter! Tell me your mission."[16]

Döring's explanation that he had come to reoffer the alliance proposed before the outbreak of hostilities elicited a snort of rage: 'Oh, pshaw! An alliance!' followed by a furious tirade against the Prussians' conduct. When Döring pointed out that the armistice had expired, the King angrily claimed it was for an unlimited time. In that case, Döring told him, he was authorised to give notice of its expiry; and the meeting finished with negotiations at an end. When news of this reached Falckenstein he issued orders for the further operation of his troops; but instead of concentrating all his forces to deal with Arentschild he divided them, having again become convinced of the threat posed by the Bavarians. Flies and Manteuffel (from Göttingen) would operate against the Hanoverians, while Beyer and Goeben faced south. Since Manteuffel was still so far away, Flies was told not to move unless the Hanoverians themselves tried to move off. In Berlin there was mounting disappointment. Unaware of the comings and goings of the envoys, Moltke and King William had been expecting news of the intended assault; when none came a messenger in the King's name spelt out the instructions again:

> I repeat the order sent through General Moltke, that you are to concentrate everything at your disposal per march and per railway, and force a capitulation, *coûte que coûte*. Bavarians are said to be in Meiningen.[17]

Falckenstein sent a bland reply assuring the king that his commands would be executed; but in fact did nothing about it and prepared next day to set off to Cassel to attend, in his capacity as Provisional Governor, to administrative matters arising out of the occupation of the Electorate. He left at 3.00 pm in spite of being told at that time that Flies was in action on the Unstrut; and he casually put in his pocket a further imperative order from Moltke to do as he was told:

> All Bavarians and Imperial troops now secondary. Unqualified will of His Majesty that the Hanoverians be at once attacked and disarmed. What arrangements has General Falckenstein made for today? Answer immediately.[18]

Moltke could hardly have been blunter; but even his marble calm must have been shaken when Falckenstein's reply that night from Cassel disclosed his disobedience. At midnight, another order, again in the King's name, repeated in still harsher terms his instructions to move everything against Arentschild, pointing out that Flies had been driven back 'for want of sufficient support.' Even Falckenstein's conviction of his own infallibility could hardly withstand such an instruction.

The message about Flies was all too accurate. That grizzled veteran was always likely to interpret his instructions energetically, and the King's message that the Hanoverians should be overcome '*coûte que coûte*' had been copied to him, so he set off northwards in pursuit of what he took to be a retreating enemy. In fact the Hanoverians, also in

A panoramic lithograph of the Battle of Langensalza, June 27 1866, indicating the principal positions of the battlefield. (Rogers)

receipt of the inaccurate information that the Bavarians had reached Vacha, had taken up a good defensive position along the Unstrut to await the arrival of their allies. The position had been materially strengthened by throwing up earthworks along the heights of the northern bank of the Unstrut, and a number of batteries had been established

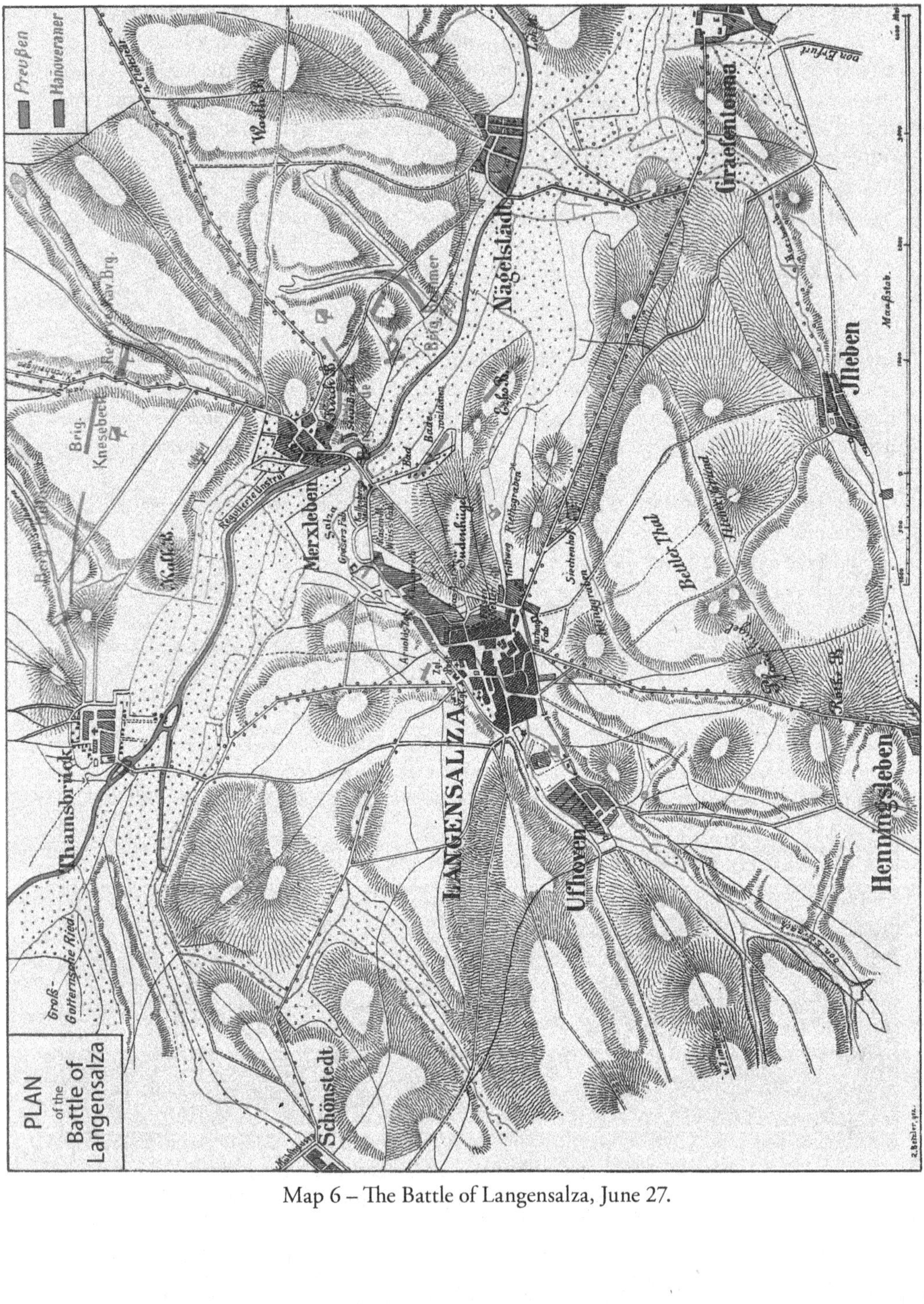

Map 6 – The Battle of Langensalza, June 27.

commanding the river crossings. The key to the position was the village of Merxleben; the height of the Kirchberg commanded the bridges over the river, which were the only practicable means for an attacker to get cavalry and artillery forward.

Arentschild had posted Bülow on the right at Thamsbrück to cover any advance from Mühlhausen. Vaux was in the centre, occupying Merxleben, with Bothmer on the left near Nagelstadt. Knesebeck was in reserve behind Merxleben. With 9,000 men Flies was outnumbered two to one. To have managed in this way to expose a portion of his force to such a numerical disadvantage is sufficient testimony to Falckenstein's incompetence, but this disparity did not daunt Flies. Weak Hanoverian advanced detachments were soon driven out of Langensalza south of the river and the Jüdenhugel, a height which commanded the main Hanoverian position, was taken. But it was soon clear to Flies that he faced more than a rear guard, as Knesebeck's brigade came forward to reinforce the main defensive line. At this moment Flies was overcome by heat stroke, and for a crucial hour was unconscious. His staff did not feel able to order a retreat on their own initiative and it was not long before Arentschild, who had arrived on the Kirchberg, perceived the weakness of his opponent, and began to feel more confident about his position. Although Prussian guns had taken post on the Jüdenhugel and from this height were inflicting considerable damage to the Hanoverian artillery, their effectiveness was soon reduced when Arentschild was able to bring forward two mounted batteries to open fire from the flank of the Prussian position, while Bothmer's infantry moved forward to a position from which he believed they could counter-attack across the Unstrut.

Major Jacobi, having abandoned diplomacy for his military duties, reported to Arentschild the position on the left of the line, and the Hanoverian commander saw

The Hanoverians storm Kallenberg's Mill during the Battle of Langensalza. (Rogers)

that his chance had come. His artillery had by now got the upper hand, and at 1.00 pm Bülow and Knesebeck were ordered forward to cross the river. Although the banks and river bed of the Unstrut meant that the officers had to lead their units dismounted, they soon drove back the Prussians opposite them, and had Bothmer, on the left, been as successful a major defeat for Flies would have been unavoidable. Bothmer, however, ran into difficulties, the river crossing in his front soon necessitating that he give up the attempt as impracticable in the face of sustained Prussian artillery fire. In spite of attempts by Colonel Rudorff to persuade him to try again, Bothmer refused, remaining on the north back of the river. It was now left to Vaux's brigade, in the centre, to try to cross the river which, reinforced by two battalions from Knesebeck's brigade, they succeeded in doing, pushing forward to take Kallenberg's Mill, a position which the Prussians had been stoutly defending, and taking one hundred prisoners.

Flies, who had by now recovered, could see that he had no choice but to withdraw. The Prussian Official History notes laconically that

> considering the serious superiority of the adversary, a further prosecution of the fight did not appear advisable to General Flies; besides, the object of the action – the detention of the Hanoverian Army – had been fully accomplished, and indeed too much had already been done for the purpose.[19]

General von Flies at Langensalza. (Rogers)

After extricating his infantry, not without some difficulty, from the attentions of the Hanoverian cavalry, Flies fell back first to Henningsleben and then, having assembled all his retreating units, to Warza. The Hanoverians concentrated at Langensalza. Fought in blazing heat, it had been a fierce and exhausting encounter which, in the context of the overall strategic position, was wholly unnecessary. Many Prussian soldiers were taken prisoner as they fell, utterly exhausted, by the roadside; Hanoverian estimates put the number of prisoners taken by them at 907. The Prussians had sustained, in addition, losses of 170 killed, 643 wounded and 33 missing. On their side too, the Hanoverians had sustained heavy losses, a total of 1,429 being killed and wounded. As night fell, Rudorff was sent to make another offer of a truce to Flies, on the basis of a two month parole and free passage to the south for the Hanoverian Army. On instructions from Berlin Flies naturally declined; by now Moltke had finally succeeded in getting control of the wayward Falckenstein, and the combined movement of Manteuffel, Beyer and Goeben, intended to bring the campaign to an immediate close, was already under way.

King George joined Arentschild and issued a vainglorious order of the day to his troops congratulating them on winning 'a glorious victory' for which he offered his everlasting thanks, commending their cause 'which, as rightful, is God's own.'[20]

In the evening, he convened a council of war, at which Platen urged an immediate advance on Gotha in the hope of escaping south to the Thuringian Forest. Senior officers were a lot more realistic and a lot less enthusiastic about the position. Rather than endorse their king's sententious observations they sat down next morning to compose a memorandum recording their views of the impossible position in which the army found itself. It pointed out the need for rest, the shortage of ammunition, the lack of provisions, the fact that the army was now surrounded and the fact that no improvement in their position was to be hoped for:

> Under these circumstances we can but regard any further combat or resistance as useless and a vain shedding of blood, and can only recommend His Majesty the

The charge of the Hanoverian Cambridge Dragoons led by *Rittmeister* von Einem at Langensalza. (Rogers)

> King, according to our dutiful conviction, to renounce resistance, and accept a capitulation.[21]

It was signed by Arentschild and all his senior officers. In the face of this, the King's belligerence must needs give way at last to common sense, and a message seeking terms went off to Flies. He, in turn reported to Falckenstein, who drew up a document which was sent to Arentschild, and accepted by the latter. When in the meantime it was learned that Moltke had, in a deliberate snub to Falckenstein, designated Manteuffel to settle the terms of capitulation, it was agreed that if these should be more favourable, the arrangement made by Falckenstein should not be valid. When Manteuffel arrived on June 29 this was indeed found to be the case. Bismarck was already looking ahead; the conditions stipulated by Manteuffel in the name of his king were decidedly less onerous than those put forward by Falckenstein, and later that day at Langensalza, Manteuffel and Arentschild duly signed the capitulation. It was a mercifully quick end to a campaign which could only have been justified by some mediaeval sense of a need to satisfy the honour of the House of Guelph. It was, soon, to mark the end of the independent existence of the Kingdom of Hanover. For the moment it disposed of one of the minor, if pressing, military concerns which Moltke faced; but there remained the Bavarians and the 8th Federal Corps to deal with, and although their movements had so far been sluggish, their potential strength was still considerable.

Schlieffen succinctly analysed the lessons to be learned from this short campaign:

> The success, obtained by the Prussians on June 28, after overcoming numberless difficulties, committing mistakes and misunderstandings, after numerous marches and countermarches and after the loss of a bloody battle, could have been attained on June 24 smoothly, unhesitatingly, and without bloodshed, if Moltke's simple plans had been adopted. But the Prussian generals, notwithstanding their prominence and excellence, could not enter into the cycle of ideas of the gray-haired theorist who had never commanded even a company... Moltke endeavoured calmly and indefatigably to rebuild the broken cycle. In the beginning he limited himself to kindly persuasion. He was forced in the end to resort to royal commands of the most peremptory character. It is not the least of his achievements that he carried out his will, and brought everything to a fortunate conclusion.[22]

19

The Advance into Bohemia

At 6.00 am on June 16 the leading troops of the Army of the Elbe crossed the border into Saxony. Captain Hozier, reporting the invasion for *The Times*, described the last few hours before the war began:

> The main bodies were collected together about midnight, and the soldiers piled arms to rest and wait for dawn. Few slept; a dull and heavy murmur continually rose from the crowded columns, and told the subdued but deep excitement which pervaded the hearts of the men; and this excitement was not without a cause, for the soldiers thought the Austrian was in Dresden, and that there would be a battle on the morrow. At last the first faint streaks of dawn appeared; the troops eagerly fell into their ranks, and before the sun had risen the advanced guards were pushing briskly over Saxon ground.[1]

However the Austrian was not in Dresden, but a long way off, and the concern of the Saxon army was to retreat, not to bring on a battle. Steps were taken to wreck the railway lines, in order to delay the invaders; but in the time available these were ineffectual. And the attempt to burn the large railway bridge over the Elbe near Riesa, which had been expected by the Prussians, was also unsuccessful; only two of its piers were damaged, and the Prussian engineers quickly effected repairs.[2] The leading Prussian troops soon established that the Saxons had evacuated Dresden and were retreating along the Elbe to Pirna. During the next few days the Prussians took possession of the whole of Saxony without firing a shot, with the exception of the fortress of Königstein, the reputation of which for impregnability was not tested, since its garrison of 1,200 men was not seen as offering any significant threat and could be safely left alone. By June 20 the occupation was otherwise complete. The Reserve Corps of von der Mülbe, who was appointed as Military Governor of Saxony, now came up from Berlin to take over the garrison role, thus releasing the Army of the Elbe to push forward to the Bohemian border. The Prussian troops were under strict orders to respect the inhabitants, as Hozier noted:

> The excellent discipline of the Prussian soldiery showed itself conspicuously in Saxony. The fears and prejudices of the inhabitants subsided more and more every hour, and the Prussians within a few days regarded themselves and were regarded as if in a friendly country.[3]

Simultaneously with Herwarth's advance to their right the leading troops of the First Army crossed the border, Horn's 8th Division reaching Lobau on the first day and Bautzen on June 17. On June 18 von Etzel's 16th Division occupied Dresden and pushed on; communications were evidently not of the best, for just after midnight Moltke was still in ignorance of the true situation, telegraphing von Schlotheim: 'No report come.

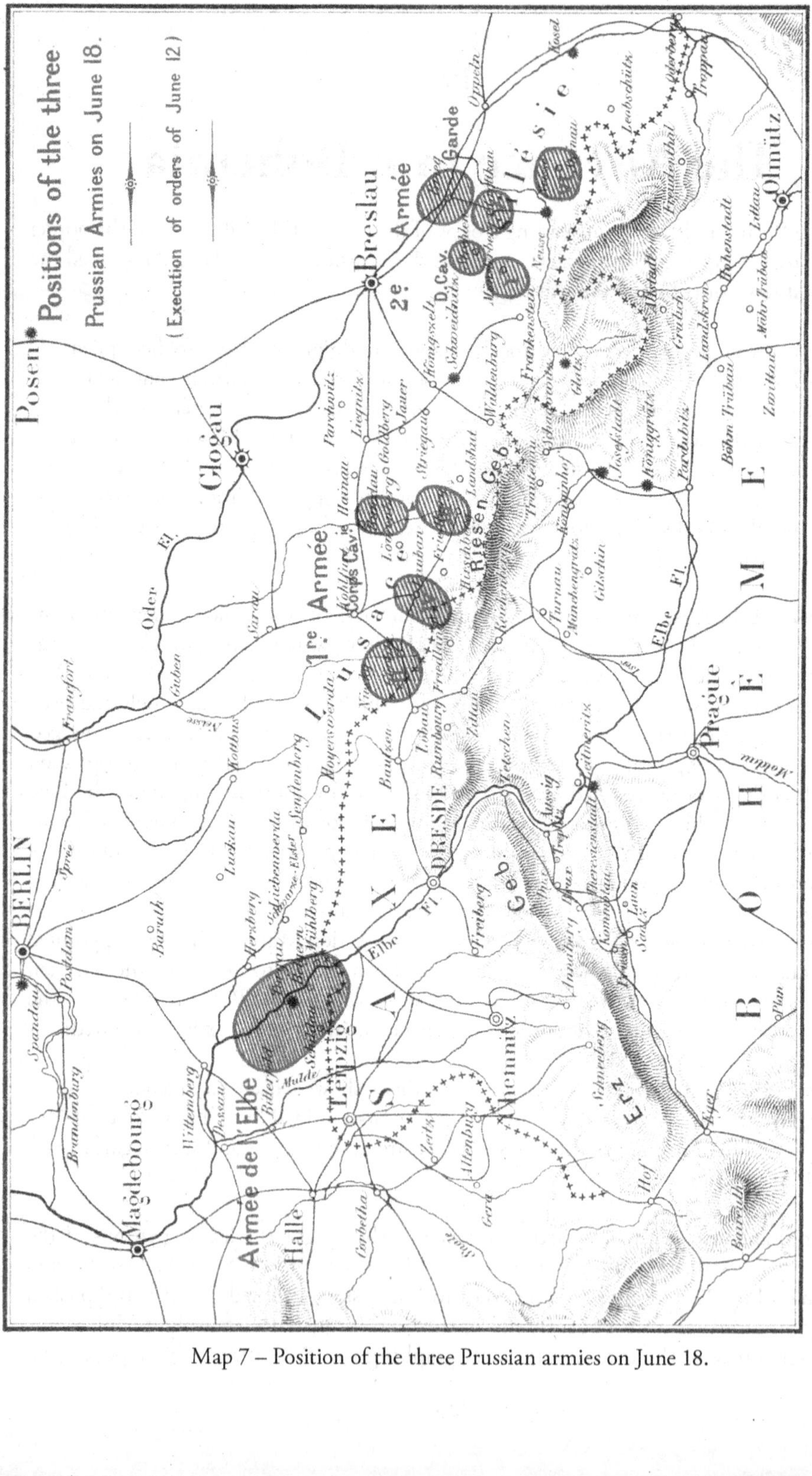

Map 7 – Position of the three Prussian armies on June 18.

Prussian troops enter Leipzig on June 19. (*Illustrirte Kriegs-Chronik*)

Has General Herwarth entered Dresden? Where are the Saxons? Have any Austrians joined them?'[4] Schlotheim reported on June 19 that Etzel had indeed entered Dresden and that no opposition, Saxon or Austrian, had been encountered; but the tardy report illustrates the extent to which Moltke now and later in the campaign was frequently very much in the dark as to his adversary's position. The Official History emphasizes the point, noting:

> The intelligence of the position of the Austrian Army was various and partly false. It all tended to say that the 1st Corps which had been nearest the frontier on both banks of the Elbe had been reinforced by the 2nd Corps, and that even the Saxon Corps had been added.[5]

The suggestion by General Bonnal that on June 19 the Prussian staff got 'positive information that the six Austrian Corps grouped round Olmütz were beginning to move towards Bohemia' was demonstrated by Colonel Whitton to be inherently unlikely, having regard to the fact that on June 11 the Prussian General Staff had obtained a copy of the Austrian Order of Battle.[6]

Moltke's immediate concern with the Saxon Corps had been prompted by a fear that it might retreat not into Bohemia, where it could be dealt with at the same time as the Army of the North by the three invading armies, but towards a junction with the

General Eberhard Herwarth von Bittenfeld, commander of the Prussian Army of the Elbe. (Rogers)

Bavarian Army in Franconia. This, he wrote to Stülpnagel on June 18, would be 'very unwelcome', since it would draw off Herwarth from the Elbe.[7] Herwarth's role, and it was crucial to Moltke's plan, was to operate as the right wing of the invasion force. 'As soon as ever General Herwarth becomes available, that moment I think we will in God's name march into Bohemia.' To facilitate the command structure, the Army of the Elbe was on June 19 placed under Frederick Charles. Moltke was already formulating his plans for the junction of Frederick Charles with the Crown Prince; as early as June 19 in a draft memorandum he noted that 'the reports coming in point to a concentration of the main Austrian forces towards Northern Bohemia'; and he identified Gitschin as the point to which Frederick Charles should be heading. In an order to the Crown Prince that day he gave instructions that 'a movement of the Second Army is necessary to hasten the union… only one army corps must for the present remain upon the Neisse.'[8]

The balance between the two forces was still occasioning some anxiety at the headquarters of the First Army; oddly, since the position had been made clear on June 4, Stülpnagel still felt obliged to ask Moltke hopefully on June 21 whether the I Corps belonged to the First or Second Army. It was an enquiry that was born of the concern of Frederick Charles that he might find himself confronted on his own by the whole or a very large part of Benedek's army. This was not something that worried Moltke; he did, though, feel that there was a possibility that Herwarth might be attacked in his flank as

General Leonhard von Blumenthal, Chief of Staff of the Prussian Second Army in 1866. (Rogers)

he advanced into Bohemia, and wrote to Stülpnagel privately on June 22: 'Would it not be advisable to support him with at least the 8th Division by letting it halt at St Pankraz until he comes up?' In the same letter he gave a clear warning to Stülpnagel as to his overall plans:

> Though the direction of Gitschin must determine your movement as a whole, yet you may go out of your way for a tangible success if you get it. Only the departure from the general direction must not be a blow in the air.[9]

It was on the afternoon of June 22 that formal instructions were telegraphed for the invasion of Bohemia and for both armies 'to seek their union in the direction of Gitschin.' In the written orders which followed, Moltke noted that the only reason Gitschin was chosen was 'because the distances, the communications by road and the railways made it seem suitable. Of course this does not mean that Gitschin must be reached in any circumstance; that depends on the course of events.'[10] And to Frederick Charles he added an important rider:

> As the weaker Second Army has the more difficult task of issuing from the mountains, it is the more incumbent on the First Army, as soon as ever its junction

> with the force of General von Herwarth has been effected, to shorten the crisis by its swift advance.[11]

The next few days were clearly going to be an anxious time for Moltke, and regulating the forward movements of his two armies to ensure that neither was exposed to defeat in detail was going to be the most difficult task of the whole campaign.

In this, he was not aided by any reliable intelligence. On June 23 he was writing to Stülpnagel that 'the Austrians are in full march towards the north. The point is to reach the Iser before them,' while at the same time expressing anxiety that the Second Army, advancing towards Arnau, would 'draw upon itself a considerable part, I am afraid even too great a part, of the enemy's forces.' But he sought to emphasise, once again, the need for a speedy advance, and to prod the cautious commander of the First Army to action: '100,000 men with Prince Frederick Charles at their head and a reserve of 50,000 men a march behind them, have the greatest chance of victory.'[12] His assumption that the Austrian march was directed much further west than was in fact the case was repeated next day to Blumenthal, albeit with a complaint about the quality of his information:

> The intelligence is in a bad way in spite of all our trouble. If it proves true that the Austrians are concentrating at Jungbunzlau the union of our Army would be assured if only the advance from both sides is quick.

And some indication of the mounting stress Moltke was feeling came in his added comments that 'a great decision is coming. God will not desert us. I am hardly able to get to bed at all.'[13]

As a matter of fact, the risk was much greater than Moltke may at this time have realised. If he supposed that Jungbunzlau, rather than Josephstadt as was in fact the case, was Benedek's objective, then he might reasonably have counted on uniting his armies before meeting Benedek's main force. As it was, Benedek could certainly interpose between the Prussian armies. This lack of reliable intelligence was explained by von Caprivi, at the time a captain in the Intelligence Department:

> Everything had to be created in 1866. Although two years earlier we might have had to contend with the Austrians, we had very little information as to the dislocation (sic) of their various Corps when war broke out.[14]

And this problem was compounded, as Colonel Whitton points out, by the indifferent use by the Prussians of their cavalry for reconnaissance purposes. Neither as they crossed the frontier nor until the eve of the decisive battle of the campaign is there any evidence of effective scouting by the cavalry of either Frederick Charles, or the Crown Prince, so that 'the invariable result was a game of blind man's buff with the enemy.'[15]

When the Prussian armies crossed the frontier on June 23, no formal declaration of war had been issued. Since the result of the Diet vote effectively created a state of war, the Prussians confined themselves to notifying the Austria outposts that 'the state of war had practically broken out and that the Prussian troops had instructions to act accordingly.'[16]

This evidently disappointed Blumenthal, who on June 22 wrote in his diary: 'So we are to have no declaration of war after all!' More importantly, however, he reflected on the dangers that lay ahead. 'I cannot conceal from myself the fact that our march over the mountains is a most critical operation and open to failure. It is, however, necessary if we do not wish to lose time.'[17]

In their advance, Frederick Charles and the Crown Prince were crossing respectively the Erzgebirge and the Riesengebirge, which form the sides of a flattened triangle of which the base runs through Prague. Frederick Charles had somewhat further to come but he could expect to cross his mountains and reach the plains of Northern Bohemia without encountering much in the way of opposition; for the Crown Prince the distance from his starting points to Gitschin was only about thirty five miles as the crow flies, but the passes were narrower and there was a far greater chance that his emergence from the mountains would be challenged, as Blumenthal was all too well aware. The other natural obstacles that would determine the strategy of the initial movements were the rivers. The Elbe flows south from the Riesengebirge past the fortresses of Josephstadt and Königgrätz as far as Pardubitz before it swings westward towards Prague and then northwards to Tetschen and through the Erzgebirge. In this section of the Elbe its two most important tributaries are the Moldau, which flows northward through Prague to join the Elbe some twenty miles north of that city, and the Iser, which joins the Elbe some fifty miles west of Pardubitz. It was this latter river on which the eyes of both commanders were, for the moment, firmly fixed.

Benedek had been waiting to see on what line Moltke proposed to advance, although he continued to believe that it was more likely to be from Silesia. In response to a telegram from Franz Joseph of June 16, not unreasonably calling for an immediate commencement of operations, he displayed considerable uncertainty as to the course to be followed. He had been enduring a difficult time with Henikstein and Krismanic who had an entirely different, and much more defensive view of the way the campaign should be conducted. In response to the Emperor, his concentration around Olmütz would, he said, be completed by June 20; thereafter, he added:

> the army will then be ready to fight at Josephstadt in eleven days if the enemy's main forces remain in their present positions around Görlitz and Landshut, or in four days if they are in Upper Silesia as seems probable.[18]

Next day he learned that his assumption was wrong, and accordingly at last gave orders for the army to move from Olmütz to Josephstadt. The members of the Viennese press called him 'the crouching lion' and were gratified at this move towards the enemy; but as he himself left Olmütz for Böhmisch Trubau on June 20, he wrote a mournful letter to his wife:

> If I come home to you as a beaten leader, then be forbearing towards me and let me carry my ill fortune in silence as beseems a man. I go tranquilly and with determination towards my fate.[19]

While his opponent's forces were scattered as they prepared to negotiate the passes of the Erzgebirge and the Riesengebirge, Benedek at least still had his forces more or less concentrated. And his position at Josephstadt would leave him well placed to turn against one or other of the Prussian armies; in that position he was, of course a good deal closer to the points at which the Crown Prince would debouch from the mountains,

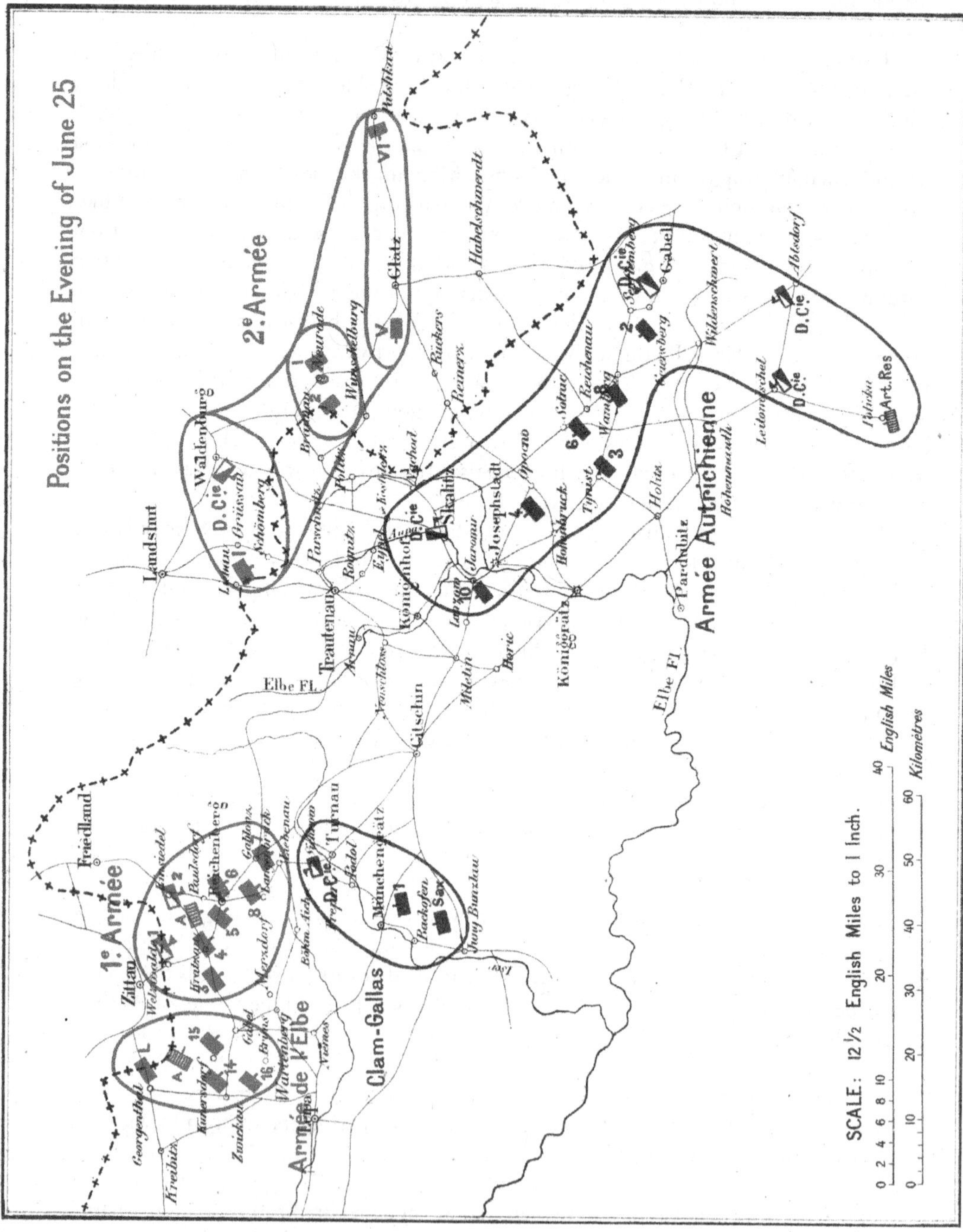

Map 8 – Positions on the evening of June 25.

Crown Prince Albert of Saxony. (Fontane)

and this certainly underlined the tricky nature of the operation which Blumenthal, on the other side of the hill, was pondering. Benedek's spirits began to rise. On June 21, after riding out to reconnoitre the ground over which he would have to deploy against a Prussian thrust from Silesia, he is reported to have remarked: 'Yes, I believe after all that I shall beat them.'[20] However, the uncertainty shown by his earlier telegram to the Emperor was still apparent in the orders he sent to Clam Gallas and the Crown Prince of Saxony. Originally the intention had been that the Saxons take up a position on the Elbe on the left flank of the main army; but on June 20 orders went out that they were to concentrate instead on the Iser and join Clam Gallas to detain the advancing Prussians. The order reached Clam Gallas on June 21 but the Saxon Corps did not receive this order until midnight on June 22, necessitating its recall from the direction it had in the meanwhile taken in pursuance of the original plan towards Pardubitz.

Benedek was still following Krismanic's overall intention not to divide his main force, and the move to Josephstadt maintained the potential advantage of his central position. If he was, though, to operate on interior lines and to realize that advantage, it would be necessary to act swiftly and decisively. He could leave a sufficient force to delay the Crown Prince's exit from the mountains, and move at once to join Clam Gallas and the Saxons on the Iser; or he could leave them to hold up the progress of Frederick Charles and Herwarth, and launch his concentrated army against the Crown Prince. What was essential was that he made up his mind one way or the other; once the Prussian armies advanced to a point at which they could support each other, the benefit of his central position was gone, and the initiative passed conclusively to his adversary. As the Prussian Official History put it, 'to reap the advantages of an inner line of operations it is necessary that one enemy should be attacked while several marches distant from the other.'[21] For the moment, Benedek seemed to have decided to choose the Crown Prince as his first target. The Official History goes on to point out, though,

General Eduard Clam-Gallas, commander of the Austrian I Corps. (Rogers)

that however obvious that move might appear with hindsight, Benedek was justified in keeping his options open for as long as possible:

> Now that all is over, any one may say that the best plan would have been to have fallen with all force on the Second Army debouching from the mountains. But the march of the Crown Prince behind the county of Glatz was not even known, and could hardly have been known except at the moment that his Army was already issuing from the defiles.[22]

The Riesengebirge are not in themselves a particularly forbidding range of mountains; the peaks are not especially high above the passes. But they are high enough to preclude the passage of large bodies of troops other than through those well defined passes that gave the Austrians only a limited number of questions to answer. The most northerly exits from the mountains debouched from Liebau to the north and from Schomberg to the east of Trautenau; next came the road from Braunau through Pickau to Nachod; and then the road from Glatz through Reinerz to Nachod or alternatively southwards towards Senftenberg. At Josephstadt, Benedek's army was admirably placed to cover all of these. The most difficult assignment for the advancing Prussian columns was that which Steinmetz was set. He was to take the road from Glatz and Reichenstern to Nachod. Moltke stressed the point to Blumenthal on June 24. 'The V Corps has there a difficult task; to cover the flank of the whole army. It may easily be that General Steinmetz must retire northward upon Braunau.'[23] He should look to the Guard Corps for support, while Moltke went on to endorse the possibility of an offensive stroke by the VI Corps southwards from Glatz or Neisse to relieve the pressure. For the Second Army the situation was now extremely tense. Although the Crown Prince's headquarters were at Kamenz, about seven miles northeast of Glatz, they were by no means out of the danger zone, as Blumenthal recorded in his diary on June 25:

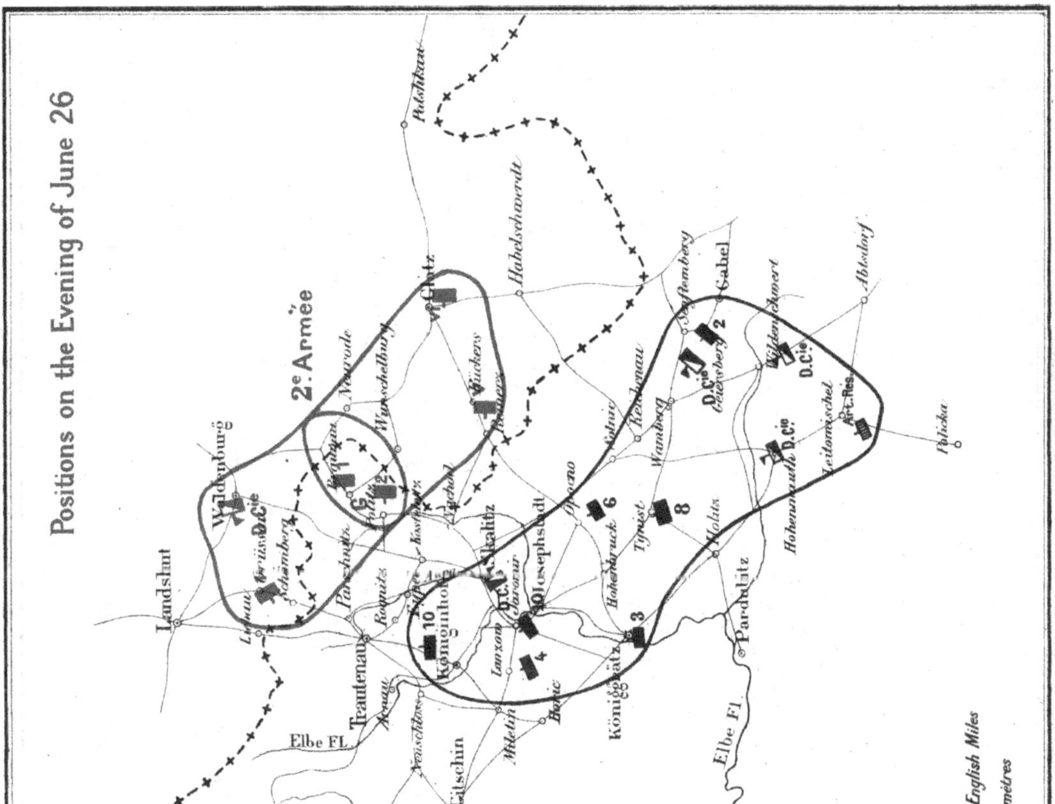

Map 9 – Positions on the evening of June 26.

I discovered yesterday, after dinner, that when Steinmetz moves forward we shall be so exposed that we shall have no escort. If the Austrians know it, all they will

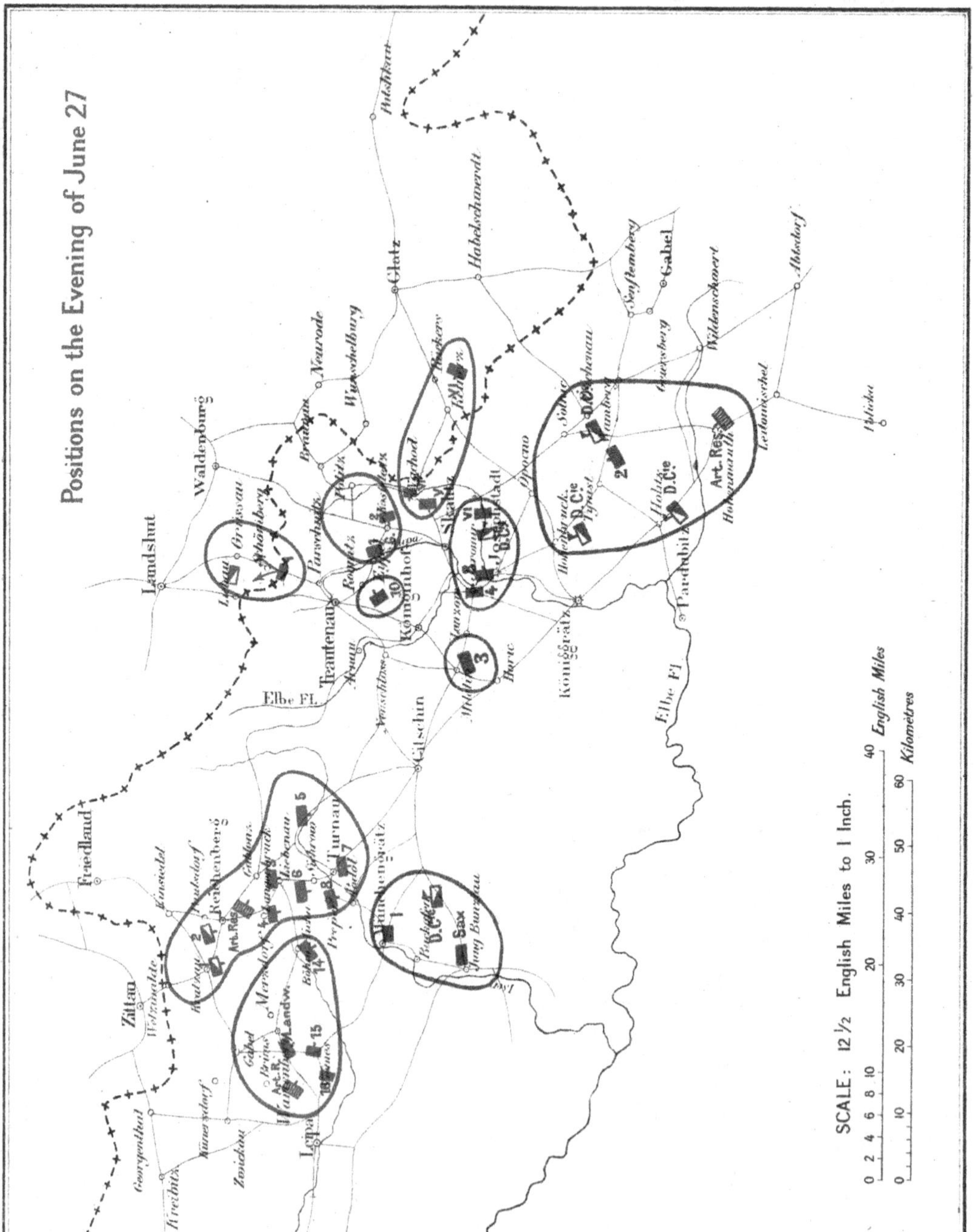

Map 10 - Positions on the evening of June 27.

> have to do is to reach out and grab us. It is through my carelessness that my Prince has been brought into danger.[24]

The weather was now threatening to take a hand, heavy storms having broken out in the mountains. Apart from this, all was now ready for a simultaneous advance through the passes on June 26. The northern route was to be taken by von Bonin's I Corps; the Guard Corps was to move through Braunau, towards Eypel, while Steinmetz was to act as the flank guard in his advance towards Nachod. The VI Corps, having made a demonstration towards Freywaldau in the east, was to follow as a reserve. The decision to pull it back from its position on the Neisse to support directly the advance of the Second Army was potentially of great importance, particularly if Benedek pursued his intention of concentrating against the Crown Prince rather than against Frederick Charles.

In the meanwhile the First Army and the Army of the Elbe had been advancing into Northern Bohemia. Frederick Charles delayed the move of his army through the Erzgebirge until it could coincide with Herwarth's advance. By June 24 the First Army, which had crossed the frontier on a wide arc from Zittau to Marklissa, had succeeded in concentrating around Reichenberg. The Army of the Elbe had reached Gross Mergenthal, and was echeloned back through Rumburg, so it was still well to the west of Frederick Charles at this stage of the advance. Ahead of the principal units, cavalry skirmishes indicated that more serious encounters with Austrian forces were shortly to be expected, but the passage through the Lusatian mountains had been completed without opposition.

Clam Gallas had originally been ordered to take up a position between Jungbunzlau and Münchengrätz, his objective being defined as 'to facilitate the approach of the Saxons to the main body of the Austrians and to keep in view his own approach thereto.'[25] Clam, who lacked imagination, carried out these instructions literally, as he did the revised orders he got on June 21 to concentrate with the Saxons at Jungbunzlau, without any clear idea of why he was doing so. It was still uncertain whether Benedek intended to march his main body to the Iser, to oppose Frederick Charles, or whether Clam and the Saxons were merely to fight a delaying action while Benedek launched six corps towards the Crown Prince. For their part, the Prussians were also uncertain how strong was the Austrian force on the Iser; at this stage they believed that there were two Austrian Corps there.

By the evening of June 25 the leading units of the Army of the Elbe had reached Gabel, while the head of Frederick Charles' foremost unit, the 7th Division, was south east of Gablonz, about fifteen miles from the Iser. The rest of the First Army was well closed up behind, around Reichenberg and Eischicht. The most advanced Austrian unit was Edelsheim's 1st Light Cavalry Division, west of the Iser at Turnau. Clam's 1st Corps was on the Iser, just short of Münchengrätz, while the Saxon Corps was moving to join it, and was just southwest of Backofen, to the north of Jungbunzlau.

For June 26 Herwarth was ordered to reach Niemes and Oschitz, a position which would put him south and southwest of Gabel on an arc of some ten miles. His leading troops pushed on through Niemes and by mid morning encountered Austrian cavalry in front of Hühnerwasser, which fell back upon infantry patrols posted in the woods there.

After some confused skirmishing a strong Austrian infantry force was identified, in an adjoining wood – it was in fact Leiningen's Brigade – and at 11.00 am Schöler launched an attack which drove it back. He then consolidated his position and occupied

Hühnerwasser. Later, at 6.00 pm the Austrians launched a counter-attack which was, however, driven off with heavy losses. During the course of the day the Prussians lost 7 killed and 43 wounded; the Austrian loss was estimated at 270. It was an early reminder of the superiority of the needle gun.

Further to the north, the First Army was also having its first serious taste of combat. The intention had been to slow its advance to enable the Army of the Elbe to come up on the right, but in the meanwhile, uneasy about the strength of the forces directly opposed to him, Frederick Charles ordered Horn's 8th Division to push forward its advanced guard through Liebenau as a reconnaissance. This force comprised two battalions of the 72nd Regiment, a four pounder battery and a squadron of Uhlans, and was supported by the 2nd Cavalry Division (Hann von Weyhern). Just south of Liebenau it encountered at Sichrow advanced units of Edelsheim's 1st Light Cavalry Division, which put up an energetic and skilful defence that was sufficiently effective to lead Frederick Charles, who had come on the scene in person, to order the rest of his army to move forward, particularly Fransecky's 7th Division on Horn's right. Edelsheim, with only cavalry and horse artillery at his disposal, was ultimately obliged to retreat through Turnau. While Horn's division paused at Sichrow, Fransecky pushed on towards Turnau. When he arrived in the course of the afternoon he was pleasantly surprised to find it unoccupied, although the bridge over the Iser had been partly destroyed; he also learned that Edelsheim had fallen back on Clam's main body at Münchengrätz. He at once ordered a pontoon bridge to be constructed, and moved over the river in strength to hold the town, since this bridgehead over the Iser would enable Frederick Charles to turn the Austrian position further south along the river line.

The abandonment of Turnau arose from a difference of opinion between Clam Gallas and the Crown Prince of Saxony. On June 24 the latter had been placed in overall command of the Allied forces on the Iser, and the order to this effect also brought the news that Benedek was now proposing to make Frederick Charles the object of his first assault. Prince Albert closed his own corps up towards Clam Gallas at Münchengrätz, and put to his Austrian colleague the suggestion that he should extend his line northwards to cover Turnau. Clam, however, talked him out of this, with the unfortunate result that Fransecky was able to take Turnau unopposed. News of this arrived at the Saxon Crown Prince's headquarters during the course of the afternoon at much the same time as an order came from Benedek ordering him to hold the line of the Iser, with Turnau and Münchengrätz, at all costs, thus presenting him with the difficult problem of how he was to restore the position.

The plan decided on was to launch an attack that evening to retake Turnau and to occupy the hills beyond Podol on the west bank of the Iser, an operation which, even if successful, would as a result of the advance of the Prussians have placed the Austrians in a decidedly hazardous position.[26] As it was, the advance from Podol ran at once into the forward units of Horn's 8th Division, which had been ordered to seize the village to secure the river crossings there. In that, they had been successful, and by the time the first wave of the Austrian assault was launched at 8.30pm it had first to drive back the enemy and to clear the village of the Prussian troops which had now occupied the place, before pressing on over the river, crossing all four bridges.

The Austrian advance was led by Poschacher's brigade; two battalions were sent over the river on the left towards Lankow, while the main body, led by Colonel von

Bergon, pushed forward towards the stone bridge. In the face of what was evidently a powerful assault Major Flotow, the senior Prussian officer, who had only five companies at his disposal, at 11.00 pm resolved to fall back. Meanwhile, however, von Bose, the commander of the 15th Brigade, at Preper, had heard the sound of heavy firing around Podol, and collecting up the only two battalions immediately available, about 1300 strong, advanced to meet the enemy. As he marched forward he encountered some of Flotow's men beginning to fall back, and learned of the strength of the Austrian assault. However, reasoning that the crossing was important enough to take the risk, he pushed on in the bright moonlight to recapture the bridge. An Austrian column, advancing in close formation, sustained heavy losses from the massed fire of the needle guns of Bose's leading battalion; further attacks also broke down with heavy loss and the village was gradually cleared. Finally, as reinforcements arrived, the Prussians marched forward to storm the bridges with Bose and Colonel Drygalski at their head. The attack faltered under heavy Austrian rifle fire; Drygalski was killed, but Bose, snatching up a rifle, led the column forward and after savage hand to hand fighting, retook the stone bridge and pressed on to secure it.

By now Clam Gallas had himself come to the scene, and launched a further series of uncoordinated attacks by units of the brigades of Piret and Abele, which were however unsuccessful. By 1.00 am, when the fighting finally ceased, there had been a further heavy imbalance of casualties. The total Prussian loss was 130, of which 32 were killed, 81 injured and 17 missing, while the Austrians lost 111 men killed, 432 wounded and 509 prisoners.[27] Coupled with Fransecky's seizure of Turnau, the defeat at Podol was of critical importance, since it meant that the Crown Prince of Saxony could no longer hope to hold the line of the Iser; the approach of the Army of the Elbe and the rest of the

The night battle at Podol, June 26-27. *(Illustrirte Kriegs-Chronik)*

First Army meant that to remain where he was, let alone to launch any further attacks, would without substantial additions to his strength be extremely risky. When, next day, he received a telegram from Benedek that the main army was still located around Josephstadt, it was clear that no immediate reinforcement was to be expected; Benedek's stated intention to be in position at Gitschin by June 30 was of no help in this respect. Accordingly, Prince Albert had no choice but to prepare to abandon the line of the Iser, and march to Gitschin, an operation which he scheduled for June 28.

The uncomfortable situation of the enemy opposed to him did not, however, entitle Frederick Charles to look on his performance with any satisfaction. His orders had been to shorten the crisis by a rapid march towards the Second Army and his progress so far was disappointing. Nor did the plans he now prepared for the following day improve matters significantly; instead of a flat-out advance towards and through Gitschin, he spent the whole of June 27 preparing an elaborate attack on Münchengrätz, with the object of destroying Prince Albert and Clam Gallas, or at any rate eliminating any threat they might pose to his right flank. As a result of this there was little effective forward movement on June 27. The advanced guard of the Army of the Elbe halted at Hühnerwasser, its three divisions closed up, the 14th at Böhmisch Aicha, the 15th at Plauschnitz and the 16th at Barzdorf. Nor did the First Army make much progress. Horn and Fransecky remained on the Iser near Turnau, and were now followed closely by the 6th Division at Luzan. The leading troops of the II Corps (the only corps operating with a corps command structure) were at Liebenau, while on the left, the 8th Division moved up to Eisenbrod. It was symptomatic that the Cavalry Corps remained well back, at Reichenberg. As his biographer noted, it was an anxious time for Moltke: 'During the evening of the 27th he must have spent the most anxious hours of his sixty six years of life.'[28] Frederick Charles was again displaying his obstinate reluctance to accept firm direction. It was a characteristic that Moltke had noted in peacetime staff rides, remarking that 'the Prince offended his officers by his rude manners and overbearing disposition.'[29]

It was evidently going to take all Moltke's patience and determination to keep the First Army moving forward fast enough to ease the pressure on the Crown Prince.

20

The Second Army in the Mountains

The movement of the Second Army towards the passes of the Riesengebirge was well in hand by June 24. Bonin's I Corps was at Landshut, the Guard Corps at Silberberg and the V Corps was already on the Glatz-Reinerz road. During that day there had been patrol skirmishes as Benedek's cavalry felt out the Second Army's movement, not without success. By June 26 Bonin was in position to cross the frontier, at Liebau and Schomberg; the Guard Corps was already across, its 1st Division at Dittersbach and the 2nd Division at Pickau, while Steinmetz was at Nachod. Behind them, the Second Army's cavalry division stood at Waldenburg, and the VI Corps was closing up on Glatz. The disposition of the three leading corps was such that the Guard Corps was placed to come to the support of either Bonin or Steinmetz, standing roughly equidistant between them.

The firm intelligence which Benedek was receiving of the Crown Prince's movements did not, however, prevent his acceptance of the new plan presented to him on June 26 by Krismanic. This provided for an advance by the main body of the Austrian Army to join Crown Prince Albert and Clam Gallas on the Iser, there to attack Frederick Charles, leaving two corps to contain the advance of the Second Army. Krismanic's military logic was very persuasive, as Benedek subsequently explained in a rueful comment a couple of weeks later to the Archduke Joseph:

> You know, your Highness, one should never think oneself stupider than those about one. At Josephstadt I thought the best plan for me was to attack the Crown Prince with my whole strength; but then came Krismanie and said something

The town and castle of Nachod. (Regensberg/*Nachod-Wysokow*)

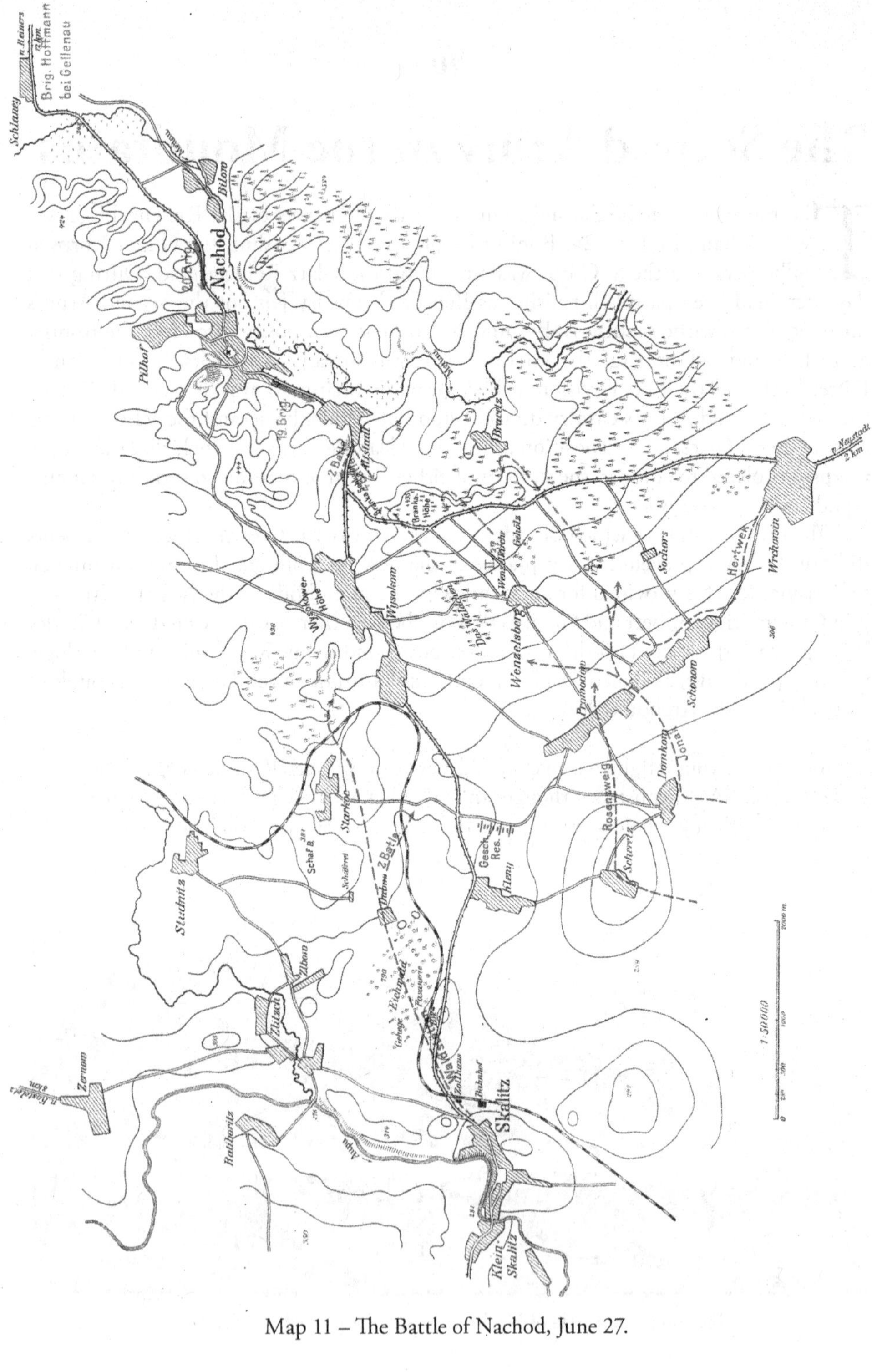

Map 11 – The Battle of Nachod, June 27.

> about primary and secondary force. A success over the primary force must needs bring about success over the secondary, but not the other way about. The primary force (he said) was to be sought beyond Gitschin.[1]

This plan, the so called 'secret plan', was the occasion for Benedek's instruction that the line of the Iser was to be held at all costs; and it was rendered almost at once obsolete by Fransecky's unopposed occupation of Turnau. By midnight on June 26, as the news of the Crown Prince's advance indicated that he was moving more quickly than expected, headquarters began to temporize. To Prince Albert went a message that after all the line of the Iser was not crucial, and to Vienna Benedek reported that what had occurred was

> only a temporary postponement of the offensive and I shall take the offensive as soon as the army is fully concentrated and I have ascertained the position of my opponent, which I hope will be the case in a few days.[2]

But he could not afford to take that amount of time; unlike Frederick Charles, the Crown Prince was moving fast, and the next day brought immediate confrontation between the Second Army and the leading Austrian corps. Additionally, the advantage which Benedek had possessed, that his army was at least concentrated while the Prussians were divided, was also disappearing. The Prussian armies were still about 50 miles apart, but were now moving towards each other in tighter groups; while on the other hand the Austrians were getting spread out. Even apart from the two corps on the Iser there was still a considerable distance of ground between the leading troops of Gablenz's 10th Corps north of Königinhof and that part of the army that was still making its way from Olmütz.

During the afternoon of June 26, the advanced guard of the I Corps had reached the bridge over the Mettau at Nachod, which marked the border. Hearing that Nachod itself was still held by the enemy, Major General von Löwenfeld, the commander of the 9th Division, rode forward to investigate. Although he had few troops with him, the Austrians made no serious attempt to hold the town and, after a perfunctory artillery exchange with part of a Prussian four pounder battery, withdrew, leaving the Prussians to repair the bridge over the Mettau, which had been broken, and to hold the town against any possible counter-attack. The Austrians also abandoned the castle, about three quarters of a mile from the river, that would have been a tough nut for the Prussians to crack if it had been held with any determination at all. No counter-attack came; the bridge was repaired and two other crossings built by 3.00 am the next morning.

The battle of Nachod, together with the other battles fought in the high hills of the Riesengebirge, illustrates perfectly the confused, incompetent and wasteful strategy and tactics followed by the Austrians. Whatever might be the overall plan, there was no point at all in abandoning the exits to the passes through which the Prussians must come. Steinmetz, who did not break camp until 5.00 am on June 27, was obliged to move his whole corps on a narrow road through a defile five miles long on the road from Reinerz; it was there at the bridge over the Mettau and in the town of Nachod that he could be held up with minimal forces and it was there that the Austrians had their best chance of inflicting a sharp defeat on him before he could properly deploy.

General Wilhelm Ramming, commander of the Austrian 6th Corps in 1866. (Rogers)

As it was, Ramming, whose 6th Corps was moving forward from Skalitz to intercept Steinmetz, had not even beeen told that the Prussians had occupied Nachod. He himself reached Skalitz about 8.15 am, at much the same time as Steinmetz got to Nachod. By the time that Ramming's leading troops arrived on the scene, Löwenfeld had pushed his advanced guard through the town to take up a position on a plateau southwest of Nachod above the village of Wysokow.

The first Austrian assault came in from the south. Hertweck's Brigade had formed up at Prowodow, and advanced through Wenzelsberg towards Löwenfeld's position on the plateau and in the woods above that village. The Austrian Jägers soon occupied the church at Wenzelsberg and from there engaged in brisk musketry exchanges with the Prussian Jägers lining the edge of the woods. As Hertweck brought his advanced guard forward, it was taken in flank by the two half battalions of the 2nd Battalion of the Prussian 37th Regiment which had moved southward down the Neustadt road, and was forced to retreat on the main body of the brigade south of Wenzelsberg. On

Map 12 – Panoramic sketch showing the battlefield of Nachod, looking east from Prowodov at the Prussian positions on the Wenzelsberg ridge.

General Karl Friedrich von Steinmetz, combative commander of the Prussian 5th Corps, and dubbed 'the lion of Skalitz' in the wake of his successes in 1866. (Rogers)

the left, small units of Prussian cavalry drove back Austrian hussars advancing towards Wysokow.

Hertweck's main attack was now launched through Wenzelsberg towards the woods, but in spite of considerable numerical superiority was thrown back with heavy loss by the

The church at Wenzelsberg, scene of fierce fighting during the Battle of Nachod, June 27 1866. (Rogers)

58th Regiment; Major General von Ollech, the commander of the Prussian 17th Brigade, was injured in the fierce fighting here. Reinforcement for Hertweck was, however, close at hand. By 9.00 am Jonak's Brigade was forming up at Domkow in support and as it pushed forward behind Hertweck was followed by Rosenzweig's Brigade which stood between Prowodow and Schonow. To the left, Ramming pushed a cavalry brigade under Prince Solms through Kleny, followed by Waldstatten's Brigade and his reserve artillery, and then another cavalry brigade, so that by 11.00 am he had his whole corps on the field. A concerted assault would not only put Löwenfeld in a very dangerous position but might still, if launched soon enough, jeopardise the deployment of the rest of Steinmetz's corps. So far, only von Wnuck's Combined Cavalry Brigade had arrived, having trotted seven thousand yards over broken and hilly roads to take up a position on the main road east of Wysokow, from where its artillery joined in the action.

Ramming's assault was led by Rosenzweig to the east of Wenzelsberg, followed by Jonak's Brigade to its right; the heavy Austrian numerical superiority soon forced the Prussian Jägers to abandon the wood and fall back on the Neustadt road. As Jonak's advance made itself felt, the 58th Regiment also had to retreat. Ramming was close to success:

> General Löwenfeld was now in a very critical position. Pressed back to the utmost edge of the plateau and to the wooded hillside at Brazetz, his troops stood in one single line 3,000 paces long and without reserves.[3]

But Rosenzweig, in the centre, was able to make no further headway in the face of the stopping power of the needle gun; and meanwhile on the Austrian left there was developing the most spectacular phase of the battle.

Prince Solms' Cavalry Brigade consisted of two cuirassier regiments, the 'Kaiser Ferdinand' and the 'Hessen.' As the Austrian infantry pushed forward in the centre and out on their right, Solms' brigade came down the Wysokow road and occupied that village. The threat to the Prussian right and to the defile out of Nachod was obvious, and Wnuck's brigade, consisting of the 8th Dragoons and the 1st Uhlan Regiments, was called up to meet it. The uhlans charged the main body of Austrian cavalry; the dragoons advanced on their left. The uhlans' charge took them straight through the Austrian lines. Soon there was a fierce melée, as fresh Austrian squadrons came up to join the fight:

> It was an exciting moment. The Prussians, nerved by the importance of the issue of their charge, and with the eyes of the infantry upon them, sprang forward readily; the Austrians, however, proud of their high renown, and eager to wipe out the memory of the former skirmish, also bounded forward as soon as they saw the Prussians approaching. The two lines met about half way, for one moment formed a tangled struggling crowd, and then the Prussian uhlans, with their lance-points low and heads bent down, were seen pursuing. The most famous cavalry in Europe had been overthrown.[4]

Seizing the opportunity, Prussian infantry of the 37th Regiment advanced to retake Wysokow; unfortunately, their speedy success led Wnuck to take them for Austrian reinforcements, and he broke off the pursuit by his brigade of the retreating cuirassiers. While he was regrouping near Wysokow, he came under heavy Austrian artillery fire; but just at this moment a fresh target offered itself in the shape of the Austrian infantry falling back towards Wenzelsberg after having failed in its assault on Löwenfeld's attenuated line. Although the Austrian troops hurriedly formed defensive knots or *Klumpen*, they were unable to resist the charge of the Prussian dragoons, and were driven back, effectively out of the battle.

Meanwhile Löwenfeld's long stand against the odds had achieved its objective, as the main body of the V Corps arrived on the battlefield. By noon the leading elements of Kirchbach's 10th Division, which had marched thirteen and a half miles to get there, were coming into position.[5] The Crown Prince himself, riding down from Braunau, also now arrived to witness Steinmetz reap the rewards of his soldiers' long struggle. But victory was still not to be easily won. The Austrian artillery still dominated the battlefield, and the Prussian reinforcements had to deploy under heavy gunfire. Ramming also had some fresh troops at hand, as Waldstätten's Brigade came into line, and as soon as he could do so, at about 1.00 pm, he launched a two battalion attack on the wood between Wysokow and Wenzelsberg which had been occupied by the advancing Prussian infantry. The attack broke down with heavy loss; and so, after his leading troops had got into that part of Wysokow not occupied by the Prussians, did Waldstätten's attack on that village from the direction of Starkoc. And while this was going on, another Austrian assault on the northern end of Wysokow was also repulsed, again with heavy loss.

On the north side of the village, an Austrian cuirassier regiment and some artillery had taken up a position which, with the failure of the infantry assaults, was somewhat exposed, as Captain Haenisch, Kirchbach's ADC, noticed. At the time he was on his way with orders to Wnuck to advance with his cavalry brigade; quick thinking, he led two squadrons of uhlans through a farmyard in a dash on the Austrian guns. Neither

The cavalry fight at Nachod, drawing by Anton Hoffmann. (Regensberg/*Nachod-Wysokow*)

The site of the cavalry battle at Nachod today. (Rogers)

The splendid memorial to the two Austrian cuirassier regiments – the 4th and the 6th – at Nachod. (Rogers)

Prussian dragoons ride down Austrian infantry during the Battle of Nachod, drawing by Anton Hoffmann. (Regensberg/*Nachod-Wysokow*)

cuirassiers nor gunners stayed to receive his charge, and two guns were captured. It was only now, as the afternoon wore on, and the Prussian lines pushed forward across the plateau, that Steinmetz was able to bring up sufficient guns to suppress the Austrian artillery which had enjoyed superiority throughout the battle. Nonetheless, in spite of the advantage which his artillery had given him Ramming had completely failed in his attempt to prevent the V Corps deploying out of Nachod, and as his beaten units limped back to Skalitz, it was only the intense heat in which the battle had been fought, and the consequent utter fatigue of the Prussians, that saved them from close pursuit. As it was, the Austrians had sustained heavy casualties – a total of 7,510, of which about 2,500 were taken prisoner. On their side the Prussian losses were far lighter, amounting to 283 killed, 825 wounded and 14 missing.[6]

This important victory meant that Steinmetz had successfully fought his way through the mountains and was poised to exploit his advantage on the following day by pushing on to Skalitz. Ramming, on the other hand, conscious of just how vulnerable he was in the position in which he now found himself, reported gloomily to headquarters on the outcome of the battle, requesting immediate reinforcement. This, indeed, he might have had during June 27, but for Krismanic's confident belief that the Crown Prince could not bring any very substantial force through the mountain passes. So convinced of this was he that, when the news came through about midday that Ramming was in action at Nachod, he refused to ride to the front to see what was going on. 'I know of something better to do; I am going to sleep,' he said, and retired forthwith to bed.[7] What Benedek would have made of this can only be guessed; but he himself was in bed all day, suffering

The haunting monument to the Austrian 6th Jäger Battalion at Nachod. The figure is gazing in the direction of the Battalion's mass grave a short distance away. (Rogers)

from a severe gastric illness, so there was very little central direction coming out of the Austrian headquarters.

This was all the more unfortunate because at the northern end of the Crown Prince's advance matters had gone a great deal better for the Austrians. Bonin's I Corps moved out of its bivouacs at Liebau and Schomberg at 4.00 am with orders to advance through Trautenau and Pilnikau. The plan was to move in two columns, the right column providing the advanced guard. Unfortunately this column had been held up, so that the planned occupation of Trautenau was not executed until 10.00 am, when Prussian cavalry entered the town and had some brisk skirmishes with some Austrian dragoons who soon withdrew. The delay in Bonin's forward movement had, however, given his

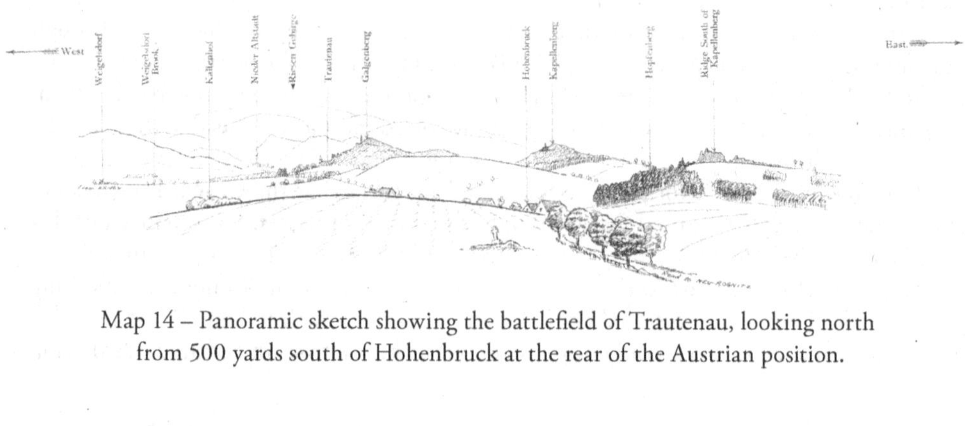

Map 14 – Panoramic sketch showing the battlefield of Trautenau, looking north from 500 yards south of Hohenbruck at the rear of the Austrian position.

immediate adversary an opportunity to bring up sufficient troops to contest his advance. Trautenau lies south of the river Aupa; on its southern side, the town is commanded by three steep hills, being, from east to west, the Galgenberg, Kapellenberg and Hopfenberg. Bonin made no immediate move to secure these key positions, a failure which had serious consequences, since unknown to him Gablenz and the 10th Corps were hurrying north to bar his further progress. The leading Austrian unit was Mondl's Brigade coming north up the road through Hohenbruck, and it was soon in action against the leading Prussian troops in the western side of Trautenau with all the advantages of the high ground. As a result, Bonin found it necessary to launch an attack on these commanding heights before he could hope to push on down the road to Pilnikau. Two regiments were detailed for this attack, aimed to hit the left flank of the Austrian advance by storming the Galgenberg, a task that was easier set than done, since it led into extremely difficult terrain:

> The steep banks could only be climbed in open order, the wooded ridges could only be passed in single file ...it not only taxed the strength of the men to a high degree, but also caused much loss of time.[8]

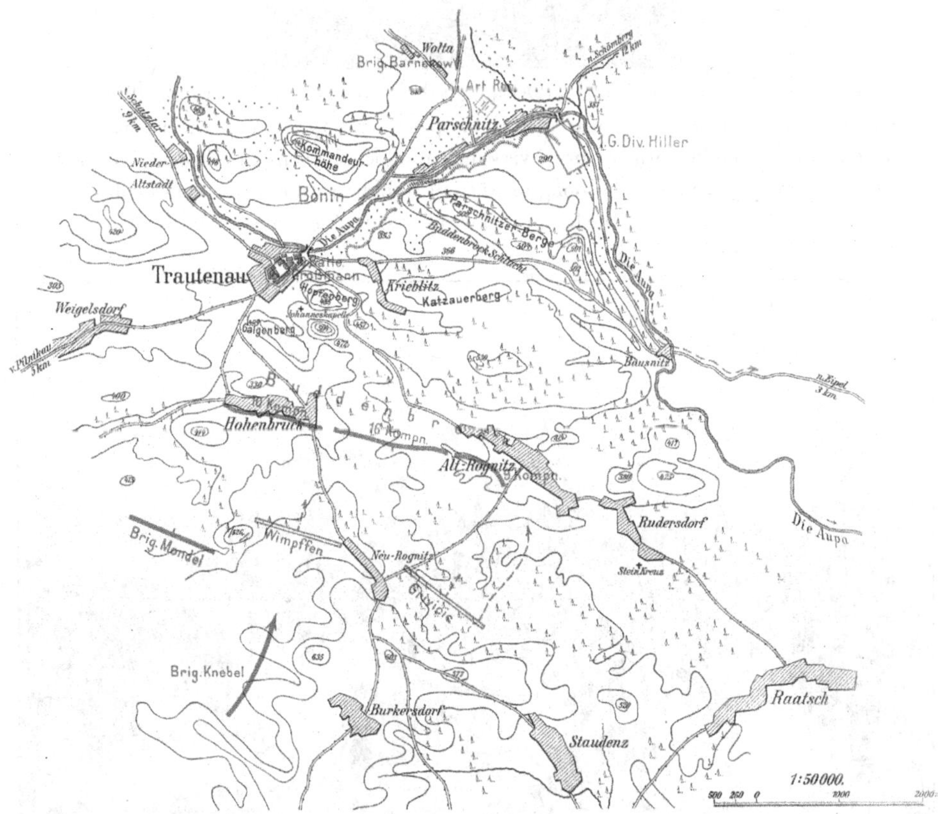

Map 13 – The Battle of Trautenau, June 27.

The Gablenz memorial at Trautenau. Although this is an image taken around 1900, the monument – actually to the Austrian 10th Corps rather than its commander – has been recently restored to its former glory. Every inch a soldier, Gablenz gave instructions that his final resting place was to be alongside the fallen soldiers who fought so magnificently for him on June 27, and he lies buried within yards of this memorial. (Rogers)

Knebel's brigade successfully assaults the Hopfenberg at Trautenau. (Rogers)

General Adolf von Bonin, commander of the Prussian 1st Corps. (Rogers)

Nonetheless, the attack was gradually successful, and Mondl was pushed back off the three hills through Hohenbruck and from the eastern end of the position to the outskirts of Alt Rognitz.

The retreating Austrians were not however, followed up, an omission which was explained by the exhaustion of the Prussian troops who had been on the move since 3.00 am. By about 3.00 pm firing ceased, and Bonin was able to turn his attention to his advance westwards to Pilnikau, pulling back some of the troops that had been employed in the attack on the heights. Half an hour later he had cause to regret this failure to consolidate his position on the heights, as Gablenz put in a fresh attack, with Mondl's Brigade advancing again from Hohenbruck and Grivicic's Brigade on its right which fell upon the small force standing at Alt Rognitz. In spite of taking heavy casualties, the Austrian infantry came forward in a determined attack which soon put them in possession again of the Galgenberg and the Kapellenberg; and after fierce fighting the arrival of Gablenz's reserve on the right of his line, Knebel's Brigade, led to the retaking of the Hopfenberg as well. The possession of these hills made any attempt by Bonin to remain in Trautenau quite impracticable; under cover of a rearguard consisting of the 3rd Regiment, the I Corps fell back through Parschnitz, and although Bonin intended to halt there and to the north of Trautenau, the momentum of the retreat meant that the corps continued its retirement all the way back to its starting off points of the night before. Limp and ineffectual leadership on the part of Bonin had led to a reverse which was certainly unnecessary, as the Official History points out:

> The I Corps was during the whole day, thus held in a disadvantageous position, because, at the commencement, Trautenau and the heights commanding it had not been immediately occupied, and the *debouché* of the main body thus secured. Its early superiority thus remained without influence. While the main body remained on the near side of the Aupa only detachments were engaged on the further side…

The chapel atop the Kapellenberg at Trautenau. (Rogers)

The rolling countryside around Alt-Rognitz, and the scene of bloody fighting for Grivicic's Austrian brigade during the Battle of Trautenau on June 27. The brigade disintegrated the following day at Rudersdorf under attack from the Prussian Guard. (Rogers)

> The Infantry fought almost alone; it had little support from the Cavalry, and the greatest part of the Artillery remained in positions whence it could have little effect on the important field of action.[9]

Even this victory, however, which showed that aggressively and skilfully handled the Austrian troops had had an excellent chance of preventing or at any rate significantly delaying the Crown Prince's advance through the Riesengebirge, carried a grim warning for the future. Against Bonin's losses of 244 killed, 1,008 wounded and 86 missing, Gablenz suffered total casualties of 5,782. The Austrians could not afford many victories like that. Not surprisingly, Gablenz made no move to follow up the retreating Prussians; the Austrian Official History records that 'owing to the fatigue of the troops and to the darkness of the night there was no pursuit.'[10] The Prussian Official History, on the other hand, is more critical of Gablenz and his failure to follow up his victory, remarking:

> He was unwilling to run the risk of compromising, by a fresh undertaking, the success he had already obtained. This determination had a decisive influence on the subsequent operations, although in other points the fortune of war had been in favour of the Austrians.[11]

But in truth a pursuit of Bonin would have seriously exposed Gablenz to a flank attack from the Guard Corps, and it would have been folly to push too far forward.

There was one other aspect of Bonin's defeat that required explanation. The Guard Corps, advancing from Dittersbach and Pickau towards Eypel, had been well placed to offer assistance to whichever of Bonin and Steinmetz might require it. At 1.00 pm Bonin received a visit from an officer of the Guard Corps with the news that its leading units were only four and a half miles east of Trautenau and hence in a position to help. Bonin refused. As the Official History noted:

> The proximity of the 1st Division of the Guard, at 2 o'clock in the afternoon, which could have, by a close advance on the enemy's right flank, decided the issue, was not taken advantage of. The division marched away at the very moment when the enemy had concentrated his force, and advanced to the renewed attack.[12]

Blumenthal, on the other hand, seemed almost disposed to blame the Guard Corps rather than Bonin, remarking that 'the Guards gave no assistance, either to the right or to the left, but remained inactive in the middle', a comment which reads oddly in conjunction with his entry for the previous day, to the effect that he had ordered the Guard Corps to support Steinmetz.[13]

As it was, the activity of the Guard Corps on June 27 was not very eventful. After a long march, the 1st Guard Division reached Eypel, and the 2nd Guard Division Kosteletz, from which positions it sent forward cavalry patrols to the west and southwest. One of these patrol missions led to a sharp skirmish between three and a half squadrons of uhlans and two squadrons of Austrian lancers near Czerwenahora.[14] It was the Crown Prince's intention, after the successful outcome of the battle of Nachod, to use at least the 2nd Guards Division to support Steinmetz in his advance on Skalitz; but when at 1.00 am on June 28 he got the first news of the fighting at Trautenau, he cancelled this, and ordered the Guard Corps to continue its march towards Keile; 'if the action at Trautenau be still going on, it will then march on the latter place and engage the enemy immediately. The Corps will set off as early as possible.'[15] At this time news had not reached the Second Army headquarters that Bonin had retreated all the way back through the mountains.

Meanwhile, to the south, orders were issued by Austrian headquarters in response to the news of Ramming's mauling at Nachod. At 6.00 pm the Archduke Leopold was earmarked to hold Skalitz against any further advance by Steinmetz. Ramming's battered corps was to stand in reserve; its commander had, at much the same time as the order was issued, reported to the Archduke, saying that 'after the long and serious action in which my troops were engaged today, they are exhausted, and not in a condition successfully to repulse an attack, which may be expected early tomorrow.'[16] It was only towards morning however that the Archduke Leopold's troops were finally able to relieve Ramming's Corps and take up a position on the heights above Skalitz.

Benedek had recovered by June 28, and was up early, anxious to resume control of operations. Whether in fact, before being taken ill, he had ordered 3rd, 4th and 8th Corps to support Gablenz and Ramming, only for this to be countermanded by Krismanic, is unclear.[17] But there is no doubt that the atmosphere at headquarters was not good, and it is certainly understandable that, if this had indeed been his instruction, Benedek would have been extremely angry with Krismanic. At all events, that morning Benedek rode off to Skalitz to get a first hand view of the situation. His appearance was well received by his men:

> When Benedek rode through the waiting troops on the bright June morning he was greeted everywhere with the greatest enthusiasm. The doubt and pessimism … gave way before the appearance of the beloved commander in person, and a storm of cheering followed the familiar figure as it passed on horseback, spare and upright, with the salient features and the piercing dark eyes under the plumed hat.[18]

When Benedek arrived Leopold's troops were already in position on the heights, with Ramming's corps behind. The 4th Corps (Festetics) was also close by, at Dolan, so that with about 70,000 men in hand there were plenty of troops available with which to resist any further advance by Steinmetz.

It was one of the decisive moments of the campaign. There was no conclusive evidence on which to base his judgment, but Benedek, having firmly in his mind that the principal concentration should be in the west to oppose Frederick Charles, concluded that Steinmetz would not advance on Skalitz and that there was no occasion to order an assault on the V Corps. It was not a point of view that commended itself to those around him. The enthusiasm of the troops for their commander's arrival was matched by that of the officers, who felt that there was now the chance for a decisive victory, which might be expected from the central position of the Austrian Army. Benedek was unmoved. 'Raising his voice so that all the officers standing by could hear, he declared there must be no serious fighting here, as he was determined to abide by the decisions he had already made.'[19]

Instead, he instructed the Archduke that, if there was no sign of an advance by Steinmetz by 2.00 pm he was to retire with the 8th and 6th Corps towards Josephstadt

General Ludwig Karl Wilhelm von Gablenz, commander of the Austrian 10th Corps in 1866, and victor of Trautenau. He had already won many plaudits for his performance in Schleswig-Holstein in 1864. Disastrous financial losses caused him to commit suicide in Zürich in 1874. (Rogers)

with a view to marching towards the Iser, as part of the concentration against Frederick Charles. Festetics was to cover the withdrawal. With this order a substantial opportunity had been thrown away. Steinmetz was advancing into what, properly handled, could well have been an ambush, in which he would be heavily outnumbered. Although he did not yet know it, the 2nd Division of the Guard Corps, which he was expecting to support his advance towards Gradlitz, had been switched to the north. And the only reason for failing to take the chance thus offered seems to have been Benedek's conviction that he must adhere to Krismanic's plan, come what may. There, at any rate, he left the situation as he rode away from Skalitz at about 11.00 am down the road back to Josephstadt. On the way he met Ramming, to whom he confirmed his intentions for the retirement; the latter had already heard gunfire from the direction of the mountains, and protested, but Benedek comfortably assured him that it could be only a rearguard action as Steinmetz moved northwards.[20]

In fact things were very different on the other side of the hill. Steinmetz had been given Gradlitz as his objective for the day, and since he had been promised the support of the 2nd Guards Division, he sent off at 7.00 am a detachment under Löwenfeld, to his right, to Studnitz, to make contact with these reinforcements. Meanwhile, in the centre, his advanced guard under Colonel von Voigts-Rhetz moved towards Starkoc. The main body, Kirchbach's 10th Division, moved out at 8.00 am, so the Austrians had plenty of time to gather intelligence as to the real intentions of the V Corps, although presumably Löwenfeld's move towards Studnitz may have created or contributed to the impression that Steinmetz was going north towards Trautenau. Certainly it was only in the Studnitz area that, at the time of Benedek's visit to the front, there was any contact

Archduke Leopold, commander of the Austrian 8th Corps. (Voss)

between the opposing forces, when there were some artillery exchanges prompted by the movement of Schindlöcker's Heavy Cavalry Brigade to take up a position on the left of the Austrian line at Zlitsch. There it connected with Fragnern's Brigade, on the heights north of Skalitz while Schulz's Brigade covered the south west of Skalitz, in position between the railway station and Spitta. Kreyssern's Brigade was in reserve in the centre, on the main road that ran through Skalitz.

At 10.45 am Steinmetz received the news that he was not, after all, to get any assistance from the Guard Corps, so he resolved to push on with his movement directly towards Gradlitz. The defensive position taken up by the Archduke Leopold was now clear to him, and it was obvious that he must first occupy the Dubno wood, lying north east of Skalitz to the north of the main road. He directed Löwenfeld to attack the wood from the north, moving down from the Schafberg, which overlooked it, while Voigts-Rhetz was ordered to move up to the left of the main road, and break into the wood from the south side. It was not apparent at that time how heavily defended the wood actually was; and in fact at the outset there were only Austrian skirmishers to bar the way of the Prussian advance. But Leopold, in direct defiance of the order to fall back on Josephstadt, had remained in position on the hills east of the Aupa when Festetics and Ramming began to retreat, and the spectacle of the advancing Prussian columns was too much for him. He was not a particularly able man, but touchy and conceited, and may well have been put out by Benedek giving Gablenz what seemed an independent command.[21] At all events, apparently underestimating the strength of the force which Steinmetz could bring against him and perhaps, as Friedjung suggests, feeling it dishonourable to retreat at the first sight of the enemy, he permitted his brigade commanders to launch a series of assaults.[22] In consequence, instead of remaining in the strong defensible position they

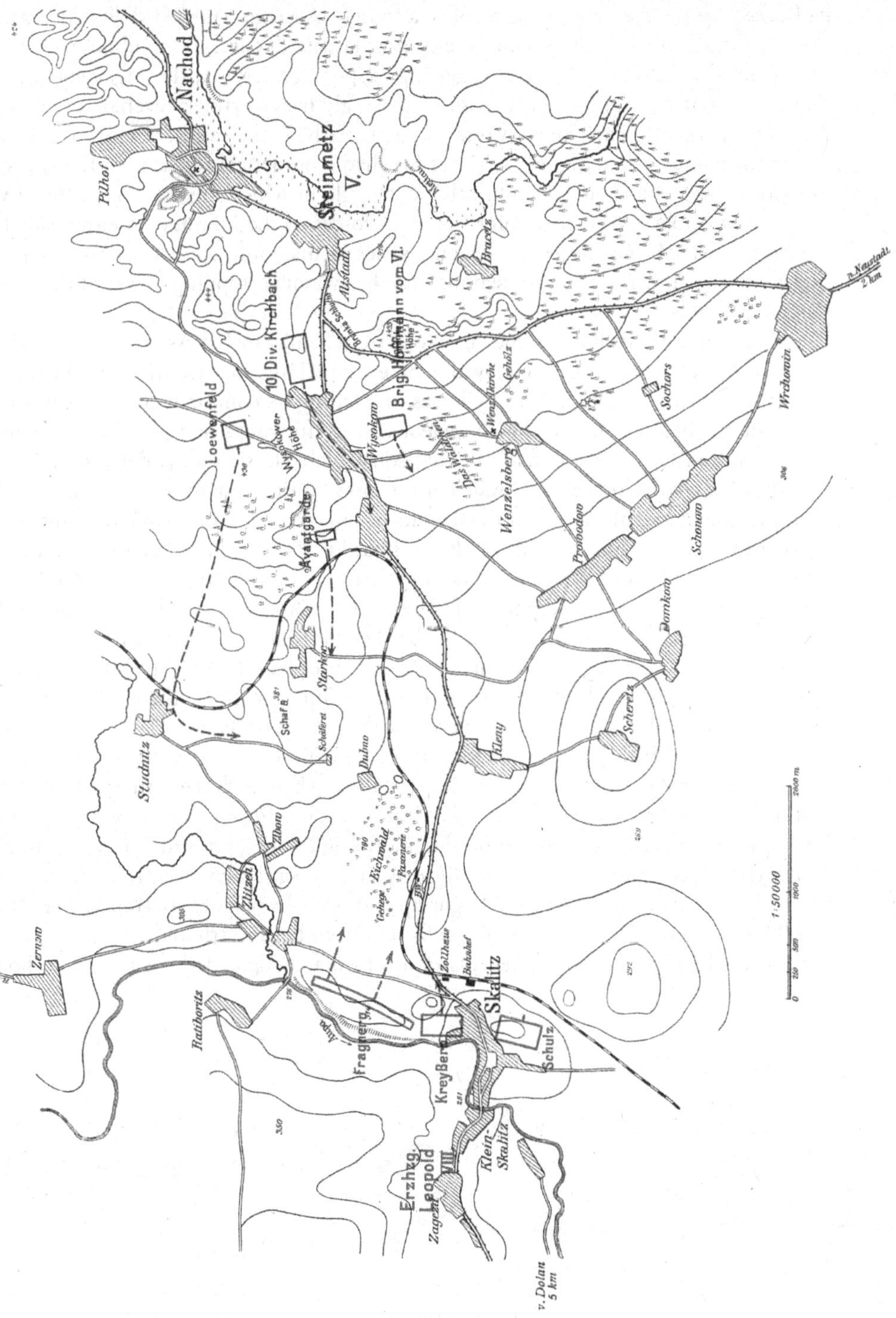

Map 15 – The Battle of Skalitz, June 28.

had taken up on the heights north of Skalitz, the Austrians moved down the eastern slopes to attack the Prussians who were by now largely in control of Dubno wood.

By noon the infantry battle was getting properly under way, the engagement up to that time having taken the form of an increasingly heavy artillery exchange, in which the Austrians had gained the advantage, particularly at the southern end of the front. But in the woods, where the Prussians at first had a numerical superiority, the Austrian units there were soon put to flight after a struggle in which any effective control was all but impossible. Up to this point the main forces of the infantry on either side had not been engaged; but there now began a series of uncoordinated Austrian attacks, in brigade strength, which were to demonstrate the awesome stopping power of the needle gun.

First came an assault down the main road from Skalitz by Kreyssern's Brigade, which was met by six half battalions deployed in an extended line southwards from the railway line; it was thrown back with heavy losses, (including its commander, who was killed) although not before some of the courageous Austrian troops had got close enough to deliver a bayonet charge, and had inflicted considerable losses on the defenders. Behind the advanced guard, however, Kirchbach was now coming up; on the right he sent his 20th Brigade in a flank attack on the heights occupied by the Austrian left, while in the centre he was able to reinforce Voigts-Rhetz's hard pressed advanced guard. And behind him, to the left of the Prussian line, the corps artillery came into position around Kleny, from which it was able to respond effectively to the Austrian gun line on the heights. By now the Prussians were present on the battlefield in such strength that all chances of an Austrian success was gone. When Schulz sent three battalions of his brigade forward from a position just south of the station, it was cut up so badly by the Prussian artillery that the attack collapsed before it could get within range of the Prussian infantry.

The moment had clearly come for a Prussian counterstroke; with its band playing, the 47th Regiment led the advance into Skalitz, where a fierce struggle took place, especially around the very substantial railway station built on three storeys, in which further heavy losses were inflicted on the intermingled Austrian units. In the course of this bitter fighting another Austrian brigade commander, Fragnern, was killed.

As the advance on the Prussian right up and over the heights continued, Steinmetz at 3.00 pm ordered an all out assault on Skalitz from both north and east; after further fierce street fighting, in which the Austrians obstinately defended their position house

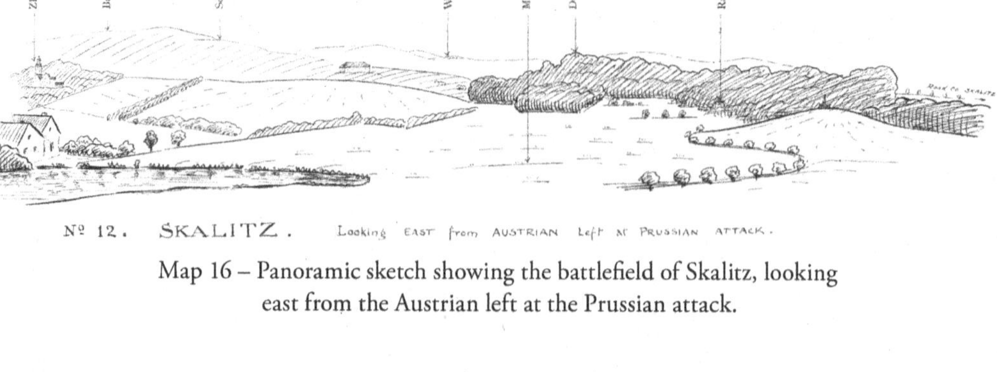

Map 16 – Panoramic sketch showing the battlefield of Skalitz, looking east from the Austrian left at the Prussian attack.

by house, the Prussians gained the upper hand, and followed up their retreating enemy as far as Zagezd. The total Prussian losses were 1,365 men, of whom 296 were killed; the Austrians, on the other hand, sustained over 5,570 casualties, and Leopold's troops were streaming back down the road towards Josephstadt, crossing the Elbe to bivouac at Salney. Ramming's corps, meanwhile, had retreated to Lanzow while Festetics remained at Dolan to cover the withdrawal.[23]

Steinmetz had enjoyed himself; Colonel Walker, the British military attaché who accompanied the Crown Prince's headquarters, reported him as saying to one aide de camp who had been sent to get an update on his progress: 'I don't know the name of the next village, but I know that I have carried two positions and I mean to take a third.'[24]

It had been a strange day for both the opposing commanders. Convinced all too readily by his brief reconnaissance that no Prussian advance was intended, Benedek on his ride southwards was prevented by a heavy thunderstorm from hearing the roar of gunfire from the battlefield of Skalitz that was entirely audible in Josephstadt; and on arrival there he was apparently untroubled by a message from Leopold's headquarters that 'the enemy are pressing strongly on Skalitz' because of what he supposed to be the reassuring proximity of both Ramming and Festetics.[25]

The same electrical storm brought considerable anxiety to the headquarters of the Second Army. The Crown Prince had taken up his position at Kosteletz, roughly midway between the areas in which the Guard Corps and the V Corps were to operate on June 20, so that he would be well placed to go to either battlefield if the situation demanded

Skalitz - A view looking towards Dubno wood from the Austrian positions. Kreyssern's Brigade passed immediately from behind the camera through these fields towards the woods. (Rogers)

The final Prussian assault on Skalitz, drawing by Anton Hoffmann. (Regensberg/*Von Skalitz bis Königgrätz*)

The Austrian memorial to their dead at Skalitz, on the fringes of the Dubno wood. (Rogers)

it. The storm so distorted the sound of the gunfire from the south as to suggest that Steinmetz might be in action with as many as three Austrian corps, a prospect which caused considerable alarm to the staff. But not to the Crown Prince, as von Verdy du Vernois recorded. Calmly smoking his pipe, he enquired if anyone had any suggestions to made as to what needed to be done; no one had, and he remarked: 'Well then, we've done our duty and taken care of everything that goodwill and our limited understanding make possible. Now it's up to God.'[26]

His confidence was entirely justified, for in the centre the Guard Corps was successfully redeeming Bonin's setback at Trautenau the previous day. In fact, as the day began, there was still no idea at the Second Army headquarters that Bonin's precipitate retreat across the frontier had taken his corps completely off the board, and it was assumed that the advance of the Guard Corps would mean that Gablenz would be attacked from two sides; the orders issued at 2.00 am on June 28, which had required the Guard Corps to continue its march towards Keile, had contemplated this. The headquarters staff of the Guard Corps wasted little time; by 4.30 am the troops were on the road, and by 7.45 am the 2nd Guard Division (von Plonski) had followed the 1st Brigade of Hiller's 1st Guard Division through Eypel. Hiller's other brigade was in the lead, and marching on Ober Raatsch, well through the defile and *en route* for Praussnitz-Keile.

This objective was of considerable significance. Although successful in his battle at Trautenau, Gablenz was painfully aware of how badly mauled his 10th Corps had been at the hands of the Prussian infantry. At 9.30 pm on the evening of June 27, reporting to headquarters, he asked that reinforcements be sent to Praussnitz-Keile to cover his

Skalitz railway station, scene of fierce fighting on June 28 and virtually unchanged since 1866. Bullet holes from the battle can still be seen today. (Rogers)

right flank against any Prussian advance through Eypel. Reassuringly, he learned at 6.00 am on June 28 that four battalions of the 5th Corps had been told off to occupy this position, and Eypel as well, thus bolting the door against any advance across the Aupa at this point. Unfortunately the detachment in question went not to Praussnitz-Keile, but to Ober-Praussnitz, ten miles away; and what was worse, no one told Gablenz, who determined his plans for the day on the basis there was no threat to his flank and hence to his line of retreat on the main body at Josephstadt.[27]

At 7.00 am, with reports coming into Krismanic of strong Prussian columns marching west from the Eypel defile, he ordered Gablenz to take up a position at Praussnitz en route to Josephstadt. Gablenz obeyed; the bulk of his corps moved south down the road through Neu Rognitz, but the brigade of Grivicic was detached to advance through Alt Rognitz and occupy Rudersdorf, in order to cover the march of the rest of the corps. Given the lack of the expected reinforcement at Praussnitz-Keile, Gablenz was in a hazardous position. It might have got much worse much sooner had not the advance of the 1st Prussian Guard Division been halted and then reversed as a result of an incorrect report that heavy Austrian reinforcements were moving on both Trautenau

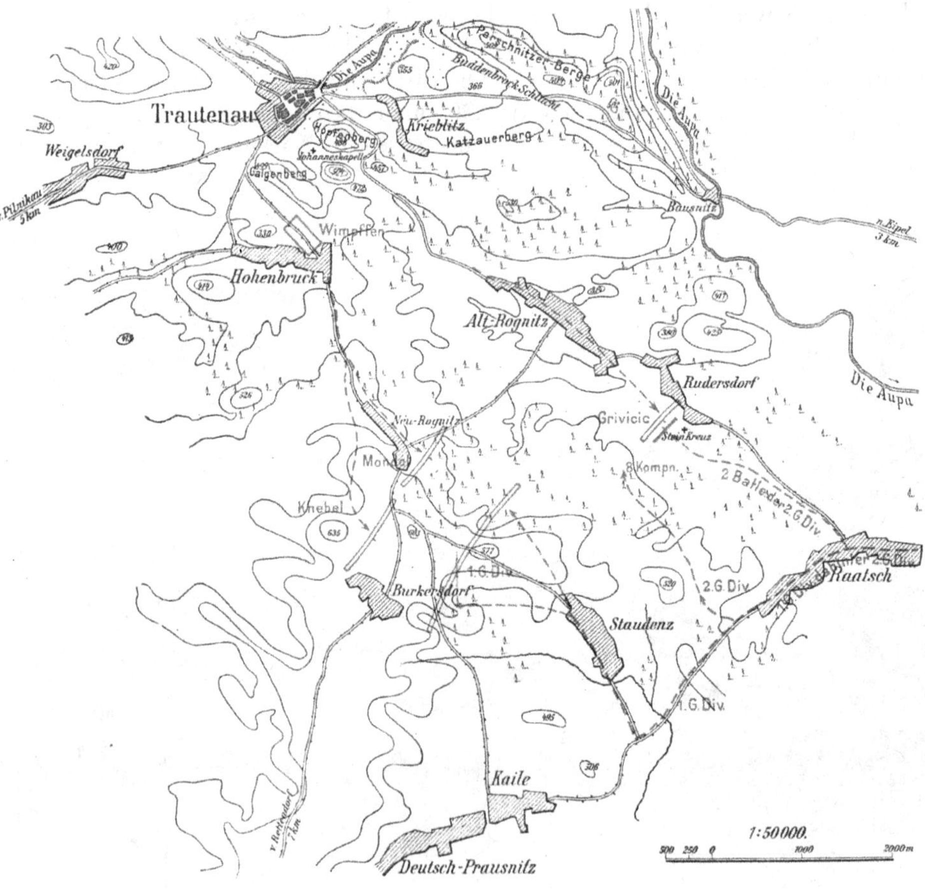

Map 17 – The Battle of Soor/Burkersdorf, June 28.

Prince August von Würtemberg, commander of the Prussian Guard Corps in 1866. (Rogers)

and Eypel; the only suitable defensive position being behind the Aupa, it was in this direction that Hiller retired. By 9.00 am, however, this report had been proved false, and Prince August got the Guard Corps back into position to go forward again. Hiller's advanced guard, followed by the rest of his division, was to advance through Staudenz in the direction of Burkersdorf, and they moved fast enough to encounter the brigade of Knebel, as it led the main body of the 10th Corps southward, in the woods west of Staudenz. Launching an immediate attack over the undulating cornfields south of the wood, the infantry of the advanced guard under Colonel Kessel soon drove Knebel's troops back through the woods and into Burkersdorf.

Burkersdorf in 1866. (Regensberg/*Von Skalitz bis Königgrätz*)

By 11.00 am the main body of Hiller's division was through Staudenz and in a position to follow up the attack on Knebel, who was now supported by Mondl who had reached Neu Rognitz. Gablenz had ordered his other brigade to march west towards Pilnikau, following the corps' baggage trains. The main thrust of the attack fell on Knebel, who was soon forced out of Burkersdorf, retreating in some disorder in the direction of Soor; the far right wing of Hiller's attack, the 2nd Battalion of the Guard Fusiliers, got separated from the rest, and found itself entangled with Mondl's brigade in the woods south of Neu Rognitz. Undaunted, the fusiliers under Lieutenant Colonel von Knesebeck stormed through the wood and one company got into the village, before being driven back by heavy columns of Austrian troops. With the increasing disintegration of the main body of the 10th Corps, now in full retreat to Soor, there was no point in leaving this small unit exposed, and the fusiliers were for the moment pulled back, not least because to the east of their position Grivicic, blithely unaware of what was going on, was in accordance with instructions taking up his position at Rudersdorf.

Gablenz had sent an orderly to warn him of his danger, but the message did not get through, and Grivicic faced virtually the whole strength of Plonski's 2nd Guard Division

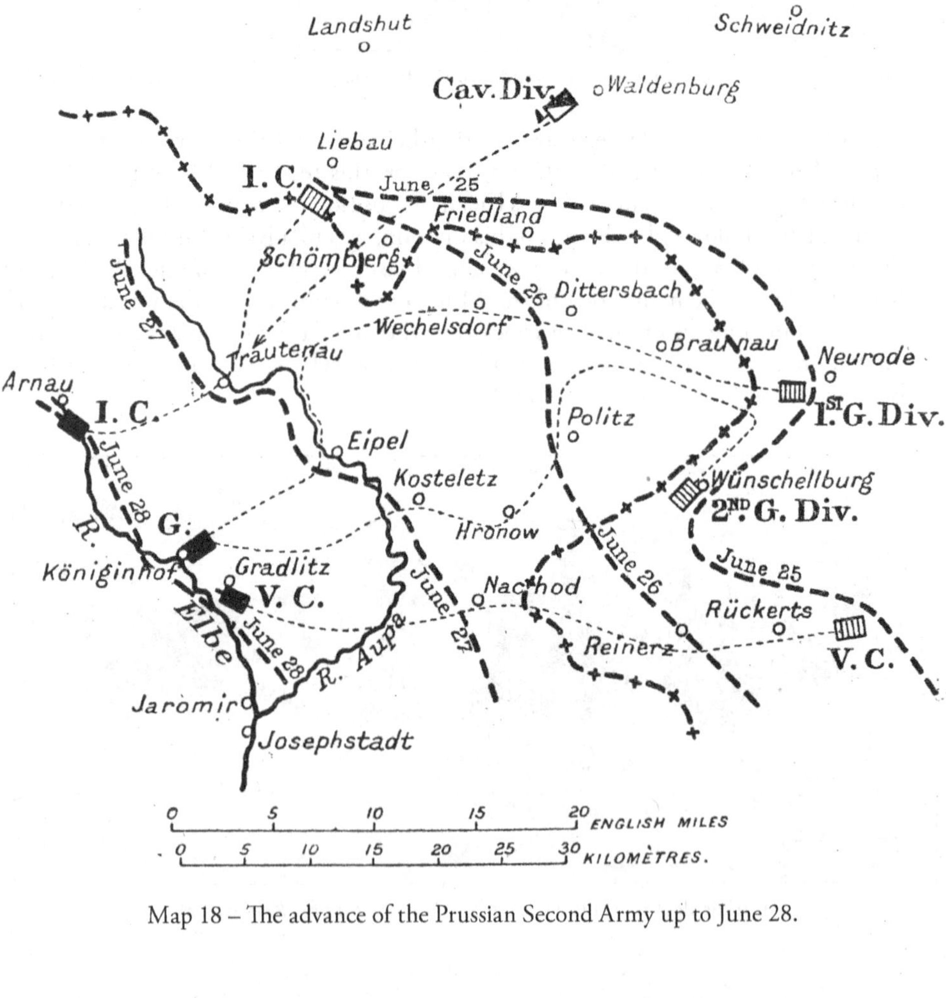

Map 18 – The advance of the Prussian Second Army up to June 28.

Grivicic's Austrian brigade at Alt-Rognitz, June 28, a drawing by Anton Hoffmann. (Regensberg/*Von Skalitz bis Königgrätz*)

at just the moment when his communications with the rest of the 10th Corps had been effectively severed. For a while he was able to hold his position against a lone battalion of the 2nd Guard Grenadiers, whose commander fell in an unsuccessful attack on the village. But by 12.30 pm Prussian reinforcements began to arrive; at 3.00 pm an assault was launched on Grivicic's position which soon drove him back out of Rudersdorf and into Alt Rognitz. Attempts to make a stand there, and in the cemetery on a hill beside it, were in vain; Grivicic's brigade lost all cohesion and as it fell back, large numbers of prisoners fell into Prussian hands, including the unfortunate Grivicic himself.[28]

Plonski pressed the pursuit hard; by 5.30 pm Trautenau and the surrounding villages were in Prussian hands, and although part of Grivicic's Brigade escaped for the moment, it was surrounded and taken prisoner next day when it tried to cut its way out through the woods east of Burkersdorf. The victory of the Guard Corps had however largely been gained by its infantry; the artillery had managed to play only a small part. The reserve artillery, under Prince Kraft zu Hohenlohe, had been held back when it reached Kosteletz, until it should become clear whether it would be more use at Skalitz or Soor. It was not until 5.00 pm that Hohenlohe got orders to rejoin his corps; after marching through the Eypel defile, he bivouacked between Ober-Raatsch and Staudenz. Next day, after a series of delays occasioned by encounters with disorganized groups of Austrian infantry, he made his way to Burkersdorf. Here, to his chagrin, he met with friends in the infantry who accosted him, saying: 'Here you are at last! Where in the world have you been? We had to allow innumerable guns of the enemy to overwhelm us with a hail of projectiles. We kept on looking to see if you were coming, but you did not come!' Hohenlohe wrote afterwards that at the time he was driven to despair by what he felt was unjust criticism; but his later research demonstrated conclusively how much more successful the Austrians had been in getting their artillery into action. This was to be by no means the last time the Prussian artillery came from too far back to realize its full effect.[29]

Total Prussian losses during this battle were 713 men, of whom 155 were killed; Gablenz had suffered losses of 207 dead, 311 wounded and 2,908 captured or missing.[30] The engagement had been fought over Frederick the Great's 1745 battlefield of Soor, from which the Prussians gave it its name. It had completely reversed the effect of the previous day's battle at Trautenau, had seriously damaged the effectiveness of Gablenz's corps, and coupled with the events at Skalitz to the south, had disrupted the plan to which Benedek and Krismanic were still clinging.

21

Gitschin

Still uncertain of the true strength of the opposition in his front, Frederick Charles had set about the task of preparing his attack on Münchengrätz with characteristic thoroughness. In the orders he issued on June 27 to the units directly under his command – and there were twelve of these, which certainly did not make for rapidity of action – he announced that 'it seems probable that the enemy will accept battle near Münchengrätz' and that he intended to dislodge him from this position on the next day.[1] His concerns as to the size of the forces facing him, and the reports of entrenching that had reached him, led him to carry out an operation involving practically all his forces; on June 28 Herwarth was to attack across the Iser at 9.00 am while the First Army, coming down from the north on what was supposed to be enemy's flank and rear, would stand by from 7.30 am ready to advance as soon as the sound of Herwarth's guns reached them.

In fact, however, the bird had flown, or had at any rate commenced to do so in sufficient time to avoid the fate which Frederick Charles had prepared for it. The Crown Prince of Saxony had little choice, in view of Benedek's instruction that he should 'retire upon the main body should the enemy appear in superior strength,' and he had ordered all his forces to begin a retreat towards Gitschin early on June 28; this manoeuvre was well advanced by the time Herwarth launched his attack on the position still held by Leiningen's brigade, which was to act as a rearguard. There were still some Austrian troops west of the Iser, and they were well supported by artillery; this necessitated a complex operation to take the village of Kloster, which appeared strongly held. Once outflanked, however, it was found that there was little resistance, and the leading troops of Herwarth's advanced guard soon reached the Iser, where the bridge was found in flames. Crossing at a ford a little down river, they entered Münchengrätz at 11.30 am, only to find that units of the 14th Division had beaten them to it, crossing the Iser somewhat to the north of the town, in spite of the attentions of the Austrian artillery on the Muskey Berg.

This was a commanding height to the east of Münchengrätz, on which had been posted a number of batteries that were within range of the Iser crossings. It was towards the Muskey Berg that the divisions of Horn and Fransecky directed their southward advance as soon as the sound of the firing west of the Iser reached them. Their march through Brezina and Zdian soon brought them within range of the Austrian guns, whose superiority could not easily be overcome by the Prussian artillery still well to the rear. Fransecky, up with the advance of his leading troops, soon drove back the Austrian infantry supporting the batteries on the Muskey Berg; by 1.00 pm the Austrian rearguard, men and guns, was in precipitate retreat and the action was at an end. Although the main body of the Austrians and Saxons had in this way been enabled to get away, it was not without substantial cost; casualties of the order of 2,000 had been sustained, of which 1,390 prisoners fell into Prussian hands. Prussians losses were 341, of which 46 were killed.[2] The Iser had thus been successfully passed at all points; but as

Prussian troops successfully capture the Muskey Berg at Münchengrätz, June 28, a drawing by Georg Lebrecht. (Regensberg/*Von Dresden bis Münchengrätz*)

has been pointed out, the easy success of the operation at Münchengrätz brought with it a serious logistical problem for Frederick Charles as a result of the advancing troops all reaching their objective:

> He discovered now that he had so many troops concentrated in so small a space – 100,000 men within one square mile – that it was impossible either to move them or to feed them.[3]

In fact they were not quite as densely concentrated as that; but even the Official History mournfully records that 'the troops were but scantily fed, more especially as only a part of the provision trains reached the bivouacs.'[4]

Moltke's anxiety, not surprisingly, continued to mount. At 1.00 pm on June 28 he sent off to the First Army a brief report of the first news of Nachod and Trautenau, adding pointedly that 'the complete débouchement of the Second Army will be greatly facilitated by the advance of the First Army.'[5] Next morning, at 6.35 am, he sent a more detailed telegram to Stülpnagel recording the progress made by the Second Army. He went on to add an emphatic comment on the need for haste to assist the Crown Prince:

> It seems to me absolutely necessary that he should be disengaged by the First Army, which, five corps strong, has against it only the 1st and 3rd Austrian and the Saxon Corps. The opportunity of making the most of so great a superiority will perhaps not recur.[6]

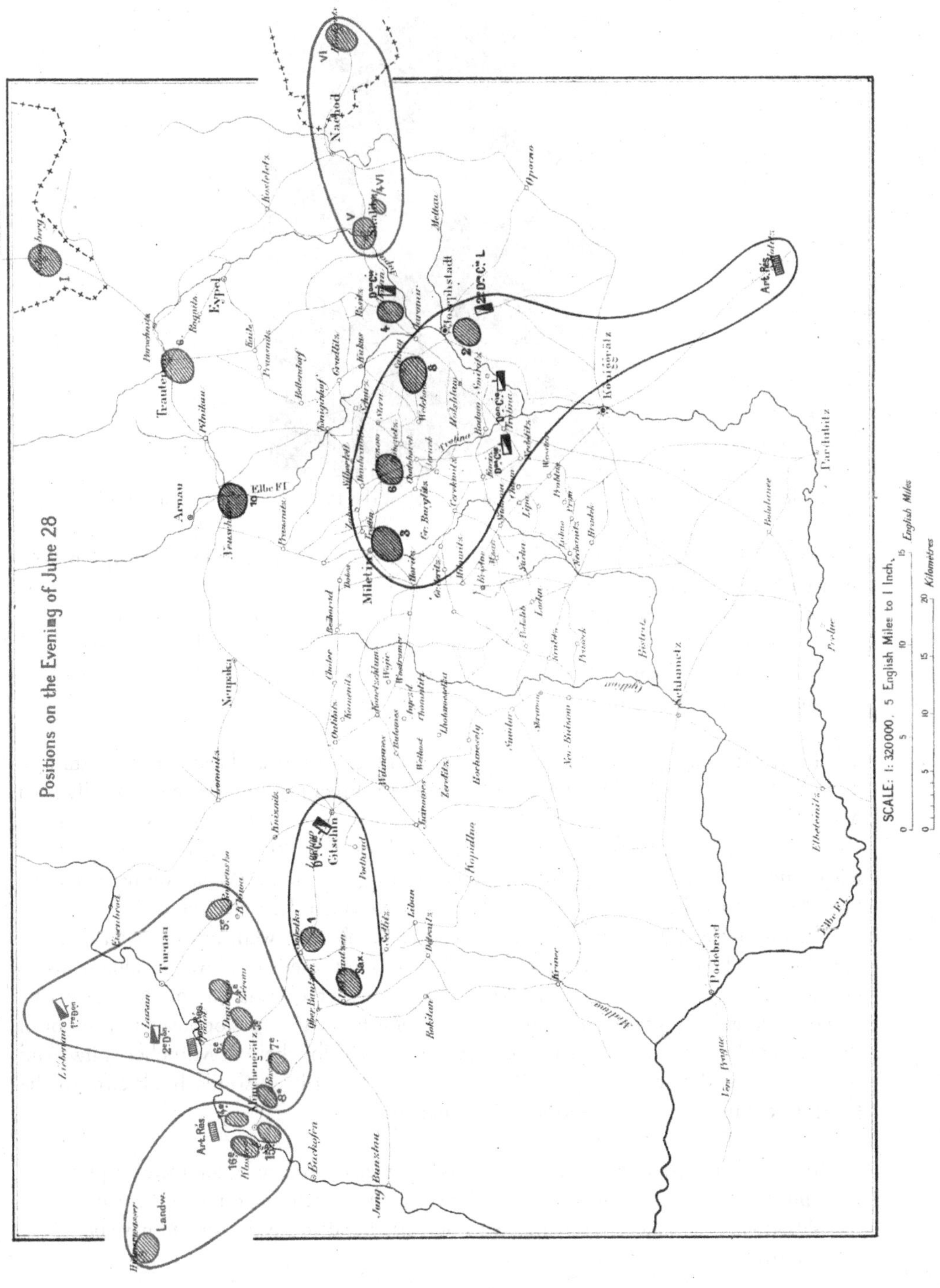

Map 19 – Positions on the evening of June 28.

General Ludwig Karl Tümpling, commander of the Prussian 5th Division. (Rogers)

Evidently feeling that even this prod would not suffice, he followed it up an hour later with a telegram to Frederick Charles himself:

> His Majesty expects that the First Army by a quickened advance will disengage the Second Army which, in spite of a series of victorious actions, is still for the moment in a difficult situation.[7]

Fortunately it was almost time for Moltke, and the King, and the rest of the staff, to leave Berlin and travel to the front, and there exert direct pressure on the laggardly First Army. The telegraph did not, so far, seem to have done the trick in getting its obstinate commander to move forward quickly enough. A hint of Moltke's impatience crept into a telegram from Moltke to Blumenthal on the evening of June 29. 'Whatever happens, the First Army must come towards you. It has received this order twice today.'[8]

In one important respect neither side had done very well, and that was in the handling of their cavalry. Frederick Charles had continued to allow his squadrons to follow, rather than precede, his advancing infantry, which was one of the reasons he remained largely in ignorance of the precise strength of the forces opposed to him, or of their escape from the trap he had ponderously evolved for them at Münchengrätz. And the strength and direction of the Prussian advance had been similarly obscure to the Austrian commanders, with serious consequences:

> The sudden appearance of the Prussians at Turnau came as a complete surprise, and the plan for retaking that place shows an entire misconception of the general situation; a misconception which with properly handled cavalry should have been impossible.[9]

This quite unnecessary uncertainty about the position, and movement, of the enemy was to recur from time to time on both sides until the end of the war.

While Frederick Charles prepared to sort out his excessively concentrated troops on the evening of June 28, his enemy was well away. Apart from an outpost in a strong position at Podkost, which held up the leading Prussian detachments during the night and for an hour or two next day, the bulk of Clam Gallas' corps was at Sobotka, while the Saxon Corps had reached Brezno and Unter Bautzen; the cavalry, which was leading the march eastward, had reached Gitschin, where it was joined at nightfall by a brigade of infantry.

The main body of the First Army did not set off in pursuit until noon on June 29, but Frederick Charles does not seem to have expected a great deal of opposition. Tümpling was to leave Rowensko and advance on Gitschin from the north, through Kuiznitz. Starting from Sobotka and Podkost, Werder's 3rd Division was to march on

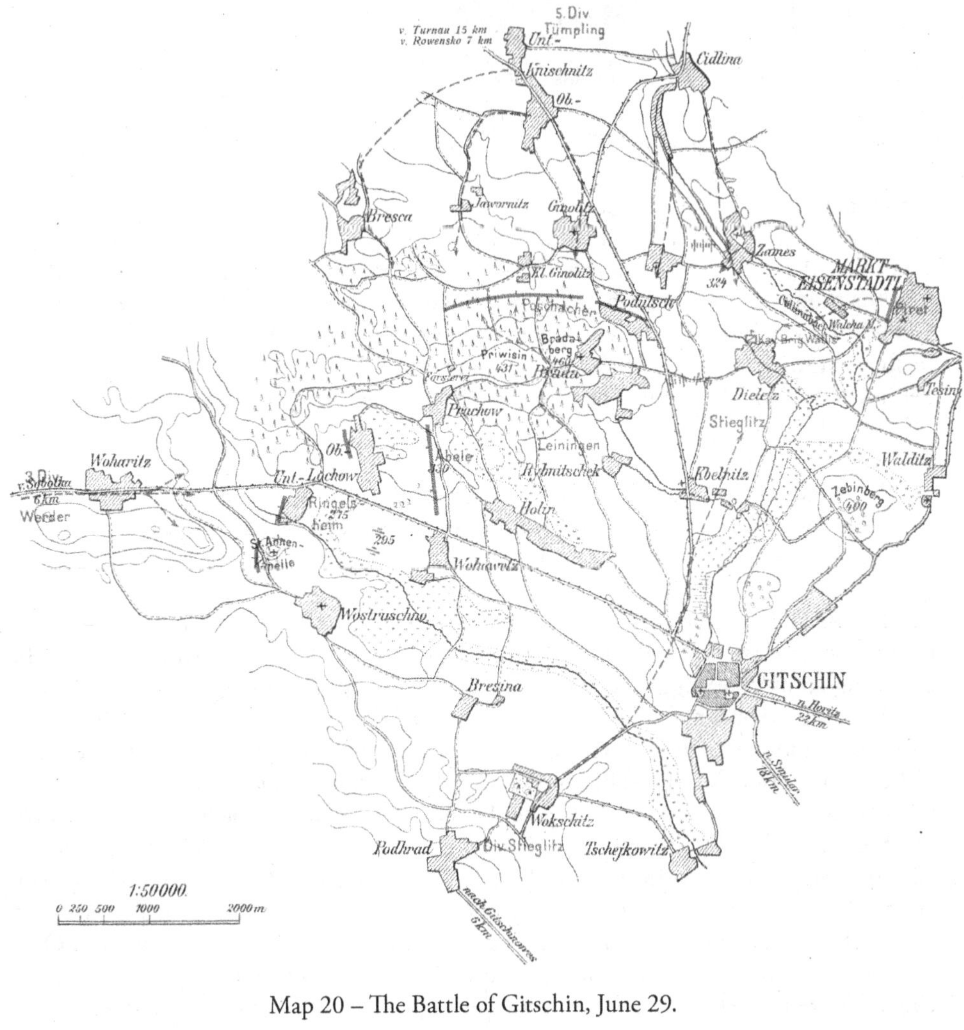

Map 20 – The Battle of Gitschin, June 29.

General August Leopold von Werder, commander of the Prussian 3rd Division. (Rogers)

Gitschin from the west, through Lochow. Behind these leading units came the rest of the First Army together with the Army of the Elbe which was intended to follow Tümpling through Libun towards Gitschin. The orders suggested that Werder would find that Gitschin would 'probably be already in the hands of Tümpling's Division.' In any event 'Gitschin must be occupied today without fail.'[10] As usual, the cavalry was to follow the infantry, Alvensleben's division behind Herwarth, and Hann's division behind Manstein. Reflecting on the First Army's problems in sorting itself out, the Official History observed:

> On this day it became evident with what great difficulty the moving of large masses of troops is attended when they are once assembled. It is obvious how important it is to keep an army in separate columns as long as possible.[11]

It is possible to read into this comment some element of censure upon the conduct thus far of the First Army, whose slow advance was now to be delayed still further by the bunching up of its leading troops after the taking of Münchengrätz.

The position on which the First Army was now advancing was, as it was to discover, a strong one; and the battle that was now to be fought was another of the 'might have beens' of Benedek's campaign. Gitschin was obviously a critically important road junction if this part of Bohemia was to see a clash of the main armies; major roads run from it north, north-east, east, south and west. The Crown Prince of Saxony and Clam Gallas met in Gitschin during the morning of June 29 to discuss what to do. Clam Gallas had by 9.00 am got his corps into position to defend the town, with three brigades deployed along the heights to the north with a fourth, that of Ringelsheim, covering Unter and Ober Lochow and a fifth, that of Leiningen, in reserve. The Saxon Corps had set off from Unter Bautzen at 3.00 am after only a brief night's rest and arrived exhausted during

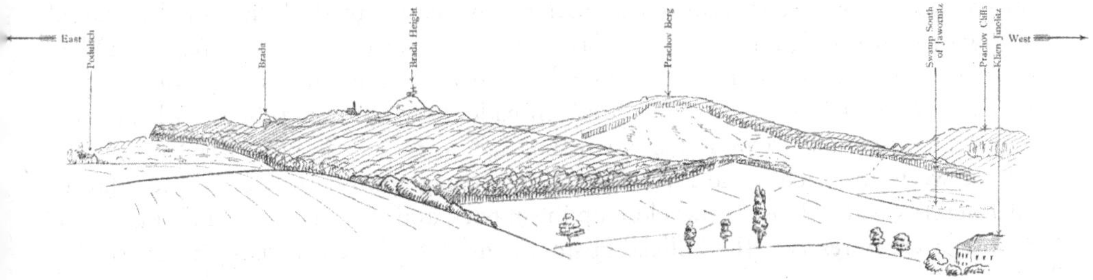

Map 21 – Panoramic sketch showing the battlefield of Gitschin, looking south from Jinolitz at the left section of the Austrian position.

the course of the morning. The Crown Prince was expecting Benedek to arrive in the area of Gitschin the following day, so on the face of it the right thing to do would be to stand and fight. However, to make sure, he sent off at noon a telegram to Benedek's headquarters to seek instructions. He got no reply. Two hours later, however, a courier rode in from Josephstadt with a dispatch from Benedek to the effect that the 3rd Corps would reach Gitschin that day, and that the main body was following close behind in pursuance of Benedek's plan for an advance towards the Iser. This movement had, however already been abandoned; but the receipt of the dispatch confirmed the Crown Prince and Clam Gallas in their view that they should hold Gitschin. Accordingly, the position to the north of the town was reinforced by the Saxon 1st Brigade (von Hausen) while the Saxon 4th (Life) Brigade (von Boxberg) was brought up in close reserve.

The Crown Prince and Clam Gallas made in many ways an odd couple. The Crown Prince was a most competent soldier, as he showed throughout the 1866 campaign and was again to do so during the Franco-Prussian war. Clam Gallas, however, was described in the confidential Prussian General staff appreciation in unflattering terms: 'Dines more willingly than he fights. Has the bad habit when it comes to a fight, of taking the wrong course. Needs a very strong *adlatus* which he has in the person of General Gondrecourt.'[12]

Tümpling was thus advancing towards a position of considerable natural strength, held by a force which substantially outnumbered him. The far left of the Austrian position, held by Abele's Brigade, was located on steep, rocky slopes on which grew spruce and silver firs and was almost inaccessible. In the centre Poschacher's Brigade was also strongly positioned on the heights of Prywicin and Brada, which had been

Map 22 – Panoramic sketch showing the battlefield of Gitschin, looking south-east from Nieder Podulsch at the right (eastern) section of the Austrian position.

entrenched and were strengthened by batteries which swept the whole of the ground over which Tümpling must advance. East of Poschacher's position the village of Diletz was held by the Saxon 1st Brigade, while finally on the right flank in front of the town and ironworks of Eisenstadt stood Piret's Brigade. Diletz lies in a dip, and hence was somewhat vulnerable to an attack down the slope to the north; but it was an essential link between Poschacher and Piret. Behind it a strong gun line supported the infantry. Edelsheim's cavalry division was close up in support, and the brigades of Leiningen and Boxberg were in reserve. The Official History commended the Prussian plan of attack:

> With a correct *coup d'oeil*, General Tümpling determined to attack the enemy's right wing – a movement which at the same time most effectually threatened the communications of the Austrian 1st Corps with its main army.[13]

Directing all his units to push forward with the church steeple of Gitschin as their objective, he brought up his artillery at about 4.30 pm to support the attack. In the early stages of the action, however, the Austrian artillery dominated the battlefield and it was clear to Tümpling that until he took the village of Podulsch he could not hope to get his guns far enough forward to compete. The village was, ironically, garrisoned in part by a company of the Austrian 34th Regiment (King of Prussia) as well as a rifle company. An assault from the village of Zames by a battalion of the 48th Regiment carried Podulsch itself but failed to take a group of buildings to the south west of the village.[14] On the

The village of Diletz today, changed little since it was fiercely contested between the Saxons and Prussians during the Battle of Gitschin. (Rogers)

other hand an Austrian assault on Zames from the direction of Eisenstadt was beaten off with heavy loss. To the right, von Kamienski's 10th Brigade launched a series of attacks through Ginolitz and Bresca, and beyond the latter place to Prachow; as the fighting went on, Kamienski was obliged to commit his reserves and a stalemate seemed to be developing. Eastwards, nine Prussian fusilier companies under Lieutenant Colonel von Gaudy entered Diletz at about 6.30 pm; at the same time the Saxons of the 1st Brigade launched a counter-attack which drove the widely scattered Prussians out of the village, and reoccupied it with three battalions. Seeing this, Tümpling brought up three batteries to support Gaudy's attack which ultimately succeeded after a fierce hand-to-hand fight in the village. Meanwhile Colonel von Berger had led a battalion of the 8th Regiment around Diletz to drive back the Saxon reserves, only in his turn to face a charge from six squadrons of Edelsheim's cavalry which was beaten off with heavy loss. By 7.30 pm Diletz was firmly held, and the Saxons fell back behind the Cydlina, leaving Boxberg, their commander, a prisoner in Prussian hands.[15]

All the same, Tümpling's efforts had not yet been completely successful, taking the battlefield as a whole. Abele and Poschacher had not yet committed all their forces, while Piret had been largely left undisturbed. Tümpling accordingly broke off the fighting around Ginolitz, and prepared for an assault on Brada, which he saw as the key to the Austrian position. While he was engaged in this task, Clam Gallas and Crown Prince Albert had received some bad news. First, Ringelsheim's position at Lochow, crucial to the line of retreat, was under threat, which was bad enough. Then the expected support from the 3rd Corps had completely failed to materialise; and at 7.30 pm Count

A mass grave of Saxon soldiers killed during the Prussian assault on Diletz, at Gitschin. (Rogers)

Sternberg arrived from Josephstadt bringing with him instructions which, as usual, bore little relation to the actual situation of those to whom they were addressed. Ludicrously, Sternberg, uncertain of Albert's location, but hearing that he was to spend the night at Schloss Milicowes, just outside Gitschin, decided to stay there and wait for him. It was only after he heard the sound of gunfire that he thought he had better go and look for the addressee of the important orders he bore.[16] These orders were 'to avoid any encounter with superior forces of the enemy, and to effect a junction with the main army by Horitz and Miletin, the four other corps having in the meanwhile been otherwise disposed of.'[17]

In the face of these orders, there was no choice but to retreat; but the situation on the ground made this extremely difficult, with Tümpling's troops pressing on through Diletz and preparing to attack Brada and Werder pushing forward behind the hills to threaten the line of retreat through Gitschin itself.

Werder, as he marched with his division down the road from Sobotka, was entirely cut off from Tümpling and had no idea what was happening on the other side of the range of hills that Tümpling was attacking. At about 4.00 pm he heard artillery fire from that general direction but it stopped soon after, and he continued his march toward Gitschin without any clear expectation of seeing action that day. At 5.30 pm, however, as his leading troops approached the two Lochow villages either side of the main road, they came under fire from the artillery posted at Ober Lochow by Ringelsheim, who also had some detachments of Abele's Brigade in position there. Werder's advanced guard pushed on down the road, while to the right von Januschowsky's 5th Brigade deployed to the south of the road. By 7.15 pm a battalion of the 2nd Regiment took Unter Lochow, but was there pinned down. Ringelsheim, whose position was along the rim of a plateau that

The men of the 2nd Battalion, 2nd Grenadier Regiment take Unter-Lochow during the closing stages of the Battle of Gitschin. (Rogers)

The monument to the Austrian 42nd Infantry on the battlefield of Gitschin. It formed part of Ringelsheim's Brigade, and conducted a stoic defence during the Battle of Gitschin. The Regiment was, however, decimated, over 500 men being killed. (Rogers)

The night battle at Gitschin, between Saxons and Prussians, 29-30 June. The buildings shown in the illustration are all easily recognisable today. (*Illustrirte Kriegs-Chronik*)

ran along the edge of the road, above Unter Lochow, was well placed to resist the Prussian efforts to get a footing on the slopes firm enough to make further ground against him. In the woods Ringelsheim had posted marksmen behind the trunks of the trees and they soon began to take a heavy toll of Werder's infantry.[18] It was soon clear to Werder that although the Austrians were being steadily pushed back, continued frontal assaults on this position could only cause heavy loss to the attackers. The responsibility for pushing back the defenders was now transferred to Januschowsky's turning movement through Wostruschno, which he reached by 8.00 pm. Almost at once, Ringelsheim, by now in receipt of orders to fall back on Gitschin, launched an assault on Unter Lochow by his 73rd Regiment which was repulsed with heavy loss; it had, however, achieved enough to give him time to get the rest of his battered brigade along the road to Gitschin and by 9.00 pm the Austrians were in full retreat. They were not closely pursued; it was getting dark, and Werder's troops were exhausted after the fierce struggle.

Just at this point, Schmidt, the commander of the II Corps, came up to join the leading units, and since there was no water available to refresh his tired troops he resolved to lead them forward into Gitschin itself. As they marched down the road they

The struggle for the Brada heights at Gitschin. (Fontane)

encountered a body of Austrian troops of the 33rd Regiment falling back from Holin on their left; after a brief exchange of fire these surrendered. But it was 10.30 pm by the time Schmidt entered the town, where he encountered the Saxon Life Brigade which had been given the task of acting as a rear guard to cover the retreat of the main body.

Meanwhile, north of the town, Crown Prince Albert had been endeavouring to extricate those units facing Tümpling, some of whom were still closely engaged. Accordingly, Piret's Brigade launched a powerful assault across the Cydlina towards Diletz and Zames intended to enable the Saxon 1st Brigade to disengage; although by 8.00 pm it was driven off with heavy loss by counterstrokes by the Prussian 48th and 8th Regiments, Piret's attack succeeded in its objective, enabling the Saxons to fall back through Gitschin. On the other hand, the position at Brada was still obstinately defended by nine companies of the Austrian 34th Regiment; and it was not until an assault led

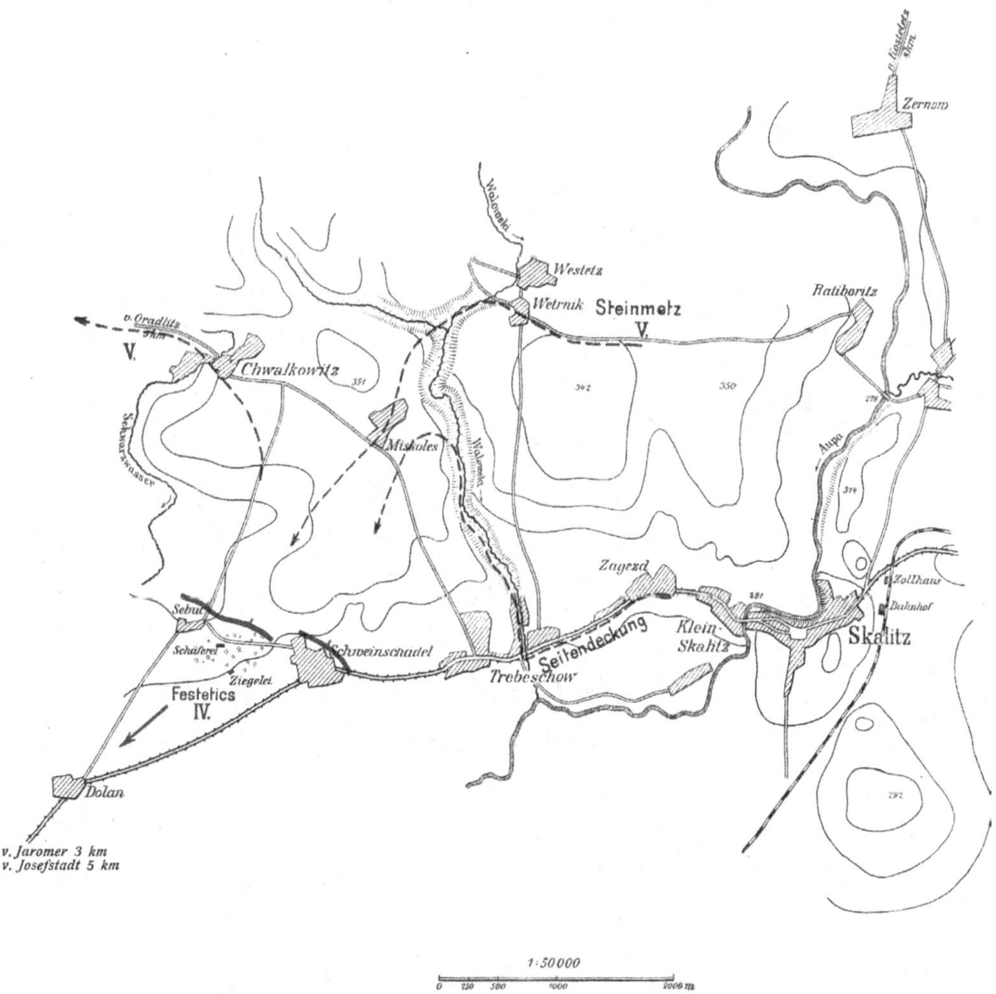

Map 23 – The Battle of Schweinschädel, June 29.

by Tümpling himself, in which he was himself hit in the arm, that the Prussians were able to take the summit of the Brada hill. Kamienski, who took over the command of the division, sent Gaudy over the Cydlina round to the east of the town, to outflank the Saxon rearguard that still held its northern entrance. Inside Gitschin, there was a chaotic situation, as the retreating Austrian units became hopelessly intermingled; by 11.00 pm the confusion was at its height when word spread that the Prussians had

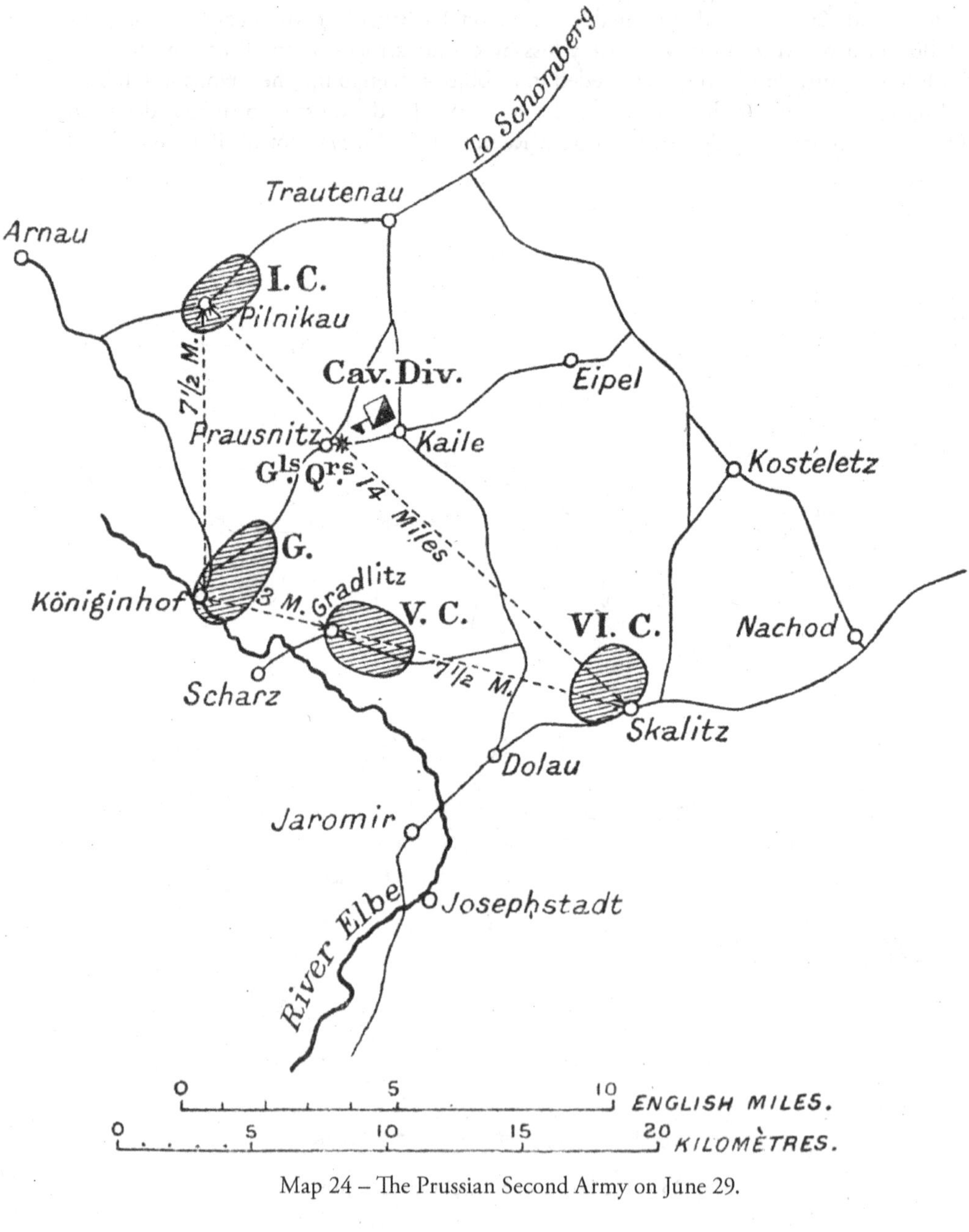

Map 24 – The Prussian Second Army on June 29.

penetrated almost to the town centre. At this Clam Gallas, who with his staff was giving instructions to unit commanders as to the lines of retreat, lost his head completely and abruptly withdrew, leaving his troops to fend for themselves. In spite of the courageous rearguard actions fought in the market square and elsewhere by the Saxon Life Brigade, Clam Gallas' corps completely disintegrated in the course of its retreat during the night and on the following day. The Saxon Corps, on the other hand, retreated in good order in the direction of Smidar. That night, the victorious Prussian troops bivouacked in the colonnaded arcades around Wallenstein's famous market square, having won a considerable victory. The total Prussian casualties amounted to 1,553, of whom 329 were killed and 1,212 were wounded. The Austro-Saxon losses were much greater; a total of 5,511, of whom over 3,300 were taken prisoner.[19]

Although in the end it was the shattering news from Josephstadt that played a major part in the Austro-Saxon retreat from the position at Gitschin, Werder and Tümpling had won a well-deserved victory against heavy odds. With no more than 26,000 men, they had faced an opponent who could have deployed a total of 66,000 men, even though in practice probably no more than 42,000 were actually engaged. Clam Gallas, moreover, also had the advantage of an extremely strong position; and it is tempting to speculate just how much of an opportunity Benedek had wasted when he had hesitated, instead of quickly pushing forward with the minimum force needed to hold off the Second Army force while sending his main body more swiftly against Frederick Charles. Gitschin was certainly the sort of position which should have commended itself to the defensively-minded Krismanic.

As it was, Benedek had had another very bad day, for while in accordance with his orders the Saxon Crown Prince was fighting and losing an entirely unnecessary battle at Gitschin, there had been further engagements on the eastern front, as the Second Army pushed forward towards a junction with Frederick Charles. The first of these came at Königinhof, to which Hiller was ordered to march his 1st Guard Division. Some detachments of Gablenz's 10th Corps remained in the place, although only ten companies strong. After some sporadic house-to-house fighting in the outskirts of the town, they received some reinforcement from the Brigade Mondl, at that time some way down the road toward Josephstadt. More significantly, four batteries from the 10th Corps, and one from the 3rd Reserve Artillery Division, came into action on the right bank of the Aupa. There ensued a prolonged artillery exchange with the two batteries of Hiller's advanced guard, while in the town itself the Prussians under Lieutenant Colonel von Waldersee pressed on to drive the Austrians over the Elbe. Total Prussian losses were only 70, compared to the Austrian casualty list of 597, of which over 400 were taken prisoner.[20]

Further east, Festetics with his 4th Corps blocked the exits from Skalitz, which was occupied by the exhausted troops of Steinmetz's V Corps. On the morning of June 29, Steinmetz allowed his troops to rest before resuming their march to Gradlitz in the afternoon. Behind them the VI Corps was moving towards Skalitz. The Prussians were now somewhat uncertain as to the precise location of the Austrian corps in their front, for some papers had been found indicating that there had been three corps in the area on the day before. However, the Chief of Staff of the V Corps, Colonel von Wittich, had personally reconnoitred the Austrian positions at Trzebeschow, and concluded that he could reach Gradlitz by going around the Austrian left through Ratiboritz, Wetrnik and

Chwalkowitz. A flank detachment of the 20th Infantry Brigade, commanded by Major General Theodor von Wittich, and Wnuck's cavalry brigade was to cover this march by moving through Zagezd and Miskoles. The main body set off at 2.00 pm, followed half an hour later by the flank detachment. This, however, soon became entangled with the advanced units of Festetics' corps; while the main body, as it marched through Langwasser towards Chwalkowitz was fired on at long range by four Austrian batteries north of Schweinschädel. In fact Festetics had two brigades in position; the Archduke Joseph held a line from the Aupa to Schweinschädel, while Poeckh's Brigade prolonged the line as far as Sebuc. Another battery, south of Schweinschädel, opened fire on the 20th Brigade at 3.30 pm, and Kirchbach resolved to assist the flank detachment by dispatching Tiedemann with the 19th Brigade to its assistance. Wittich succeeded in outflanking the Austrian artillery and forcing its retreat; when Tiedemann came up there was a sharp struggle with Poeckh's Brigade, whose retreat was hampered by the fact that the Archduke Joseph's Brigade was by now occupying the road to Jaromir. The local commanders were keen to follow up their success, but with an eye to rejoining the rest of the Second Army as soon as possible, Steinmetz forbade this, and Festetics was able to fall back without further fighting on Salney. He had lost 1,484 men in all, together, according to the Official History, with some 3,400 unwounded prisoners; the V Corps had sustained total losses of 394 men.[21]

Moltke could now for the first time for some days breathe more freely, with the Second Army having reached the line of the Elbe and being largely concentrated, while Frederick Charles now seemed well enough placed to push forward and join hands when the right moment for this was judged to have arrived. There was now no practical danger that Benedek could safely concentrate all his forces against one of his antagonists.

A Saxon and Austrian camp near Stösser following the Battle of Gitschin. (*Illustrirte Kriegs-Chronik*)

For the Austrians, on the other hand, the sense of crisis had materially deepened. Early on the morning of June 29, following the grim news of the battles of Skalitz and Soor,

A present-day view looking down at the village of Schweinschädel from the Prussian lines. The village, even its individual buildings, is remarkably unchanged since June 1866. (Rogers)

The Prussian advance on Schweinschädel, June 29. (Fontane)

came Gablenz himself, haggard and spent, all his gallant small vanities shattered, his hair unkempt, his clothes disordered, his eyes bloodshot with smoke and lack of sleep, to tell the tale of his disaster and to speak his bitter reproach.[22]

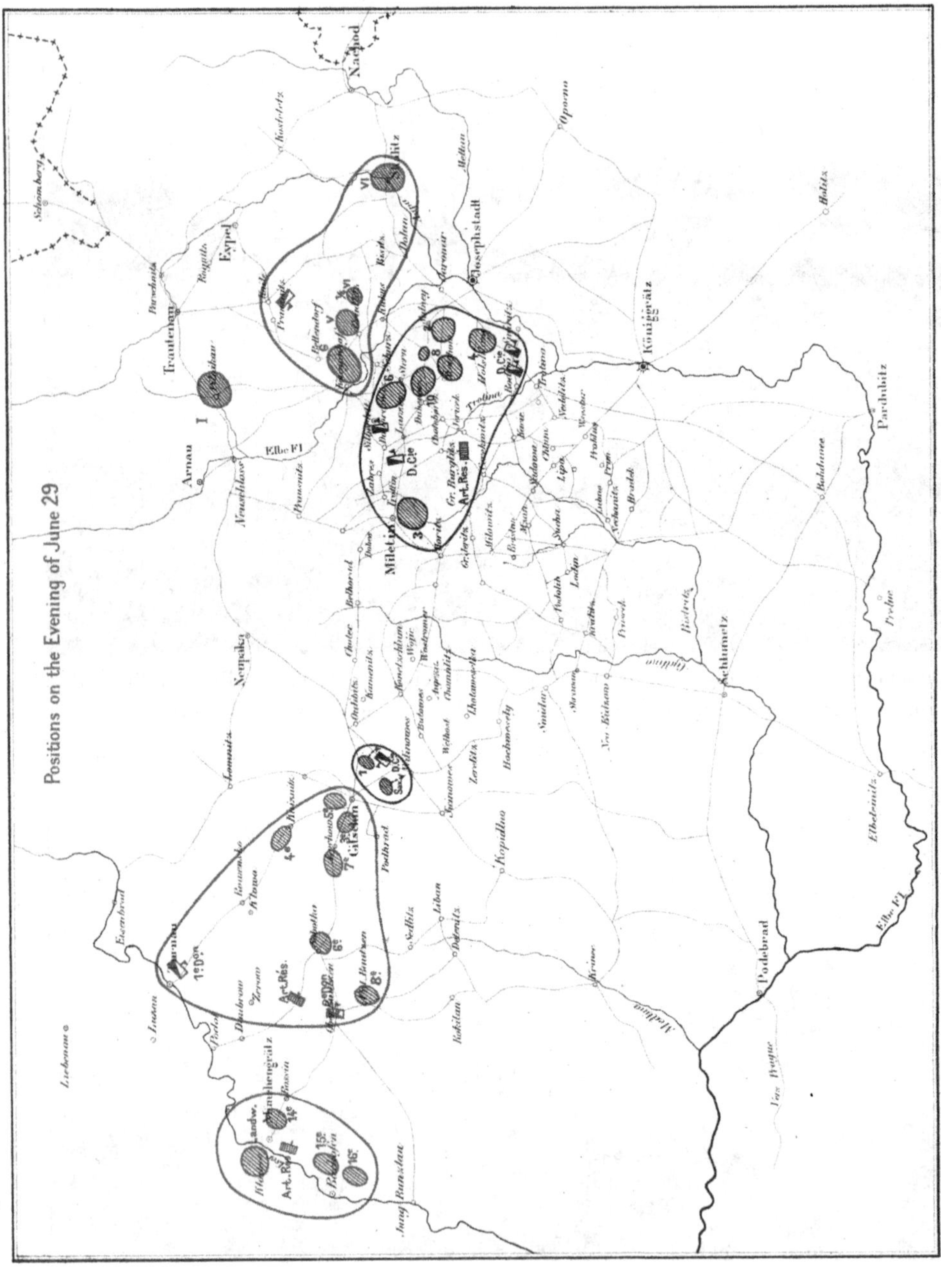

Map 25 – Positions on the evening of June 29.

It was a gloomy morning at Austrian headquarters, where it was becoming clear that a march in the direction of Gitschin was now of very doubtful wisdom. All the same, there was pronounced disappointment when, after Benedek's staff conference that morning, it was announced that the new plan was to be a retreat on Dubenetz, to a

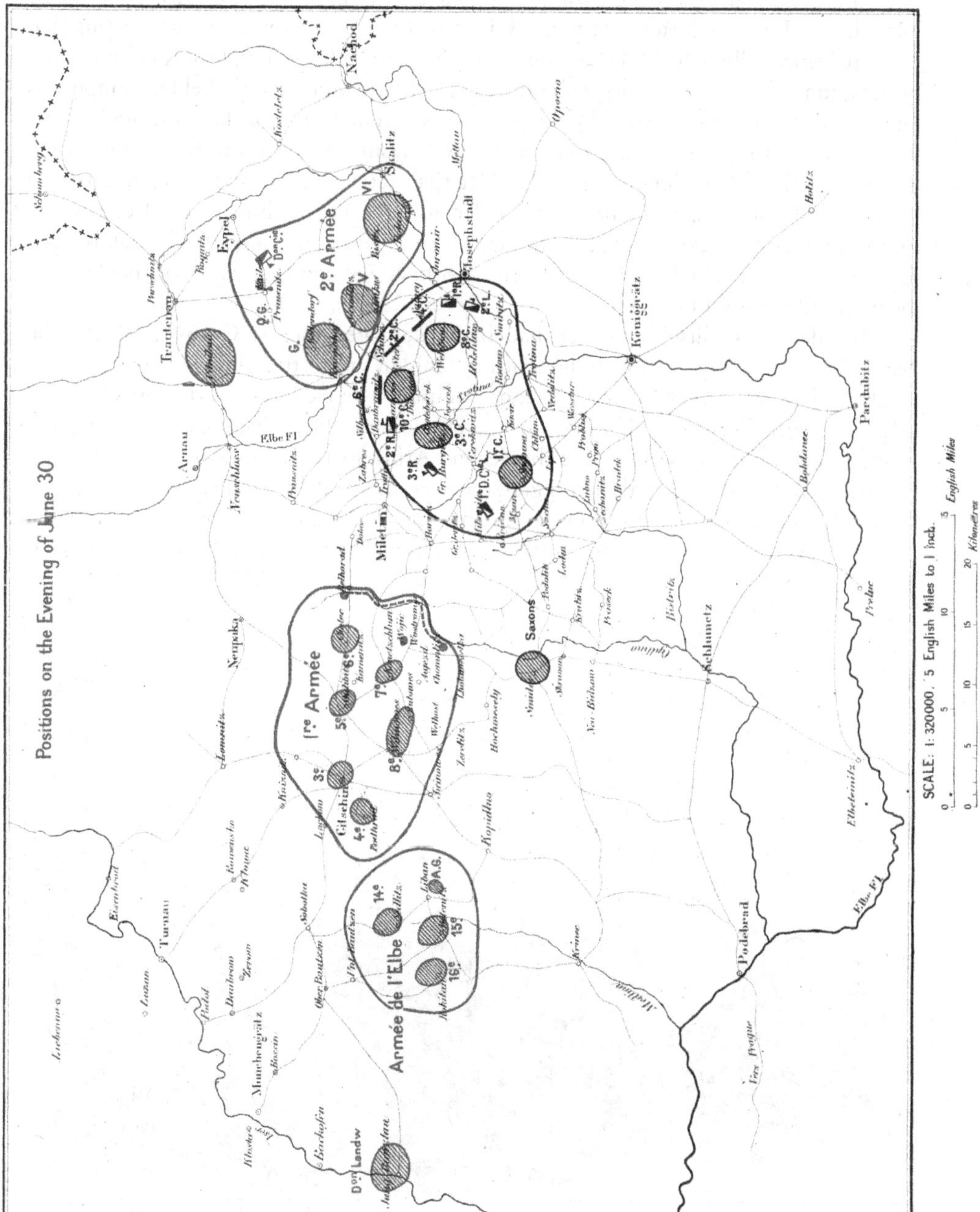

Map 26 – Positions on the evening of June 30.

position that had been occupied by the Emperor Joseph II a century before against Frederick the Great during the War of the Bavarian Succession, and which no doubt appeared to Krismanic for that reason to be particularly suitable. All the same, the latter was clearly now becoming very rattled by events; it was noted that in preparing the new march orders he at first entirely overlooked one cavalry division.[23] So it was that on the morning of June 29, headquarters moved off to Dubenetz. It was because of this that Crown Prince Albert had received no response to his telegram from Gitschin seeking instructions; there was no telegraph office at Dubenetz and the only field telegraph was out of order. The letter carried by Sternberg was dictated early in the morning but was not sent off until after the move to Dubenetz; as a result, Benedek and Krismanic passed the rest of the day in ignorance of the fact that acting on their previous orders, the Crown Prince and Clam Gallas had decided to fight at Gitschin. And, of course the support which they expected from the Archduke Ernest's 3rd Corps never materialised because he had received the message, sent to him at 7.45 am that day, that there was to be no stand at Gitschin.[24]

The defeat at Gitschin, which had badly damaged the 1st Corps, and sent the Saxon Corps in a long retreat to the south to Smidar, meant that the Dubenetz position could no longer be regarded as a safe concentration area; clearly, with the units hitherto opposing him effectively off the board for the moment, Frederick Charles could easily come in behind the position while the Second Army struck it from the north and east. A retreat southwards, towards Königgrätz, seemed unavoidable; and early next morning Benedek reported this to the Emperor: 'The débâcle of the 1st Army Corps and the Saxon Army obliges me to retire in the direction of Königgrätz.'[25] This message caused

Wounded from the Austrian, Saxon and Prussian armies at Melnik, following the battles along the Iser. (*Illustrirte Kriegs-Chronik*)

bewilderment at Vienna: discarding an idea that he should go himself to the front, Franz Joseph sent the trustworthy Colonel Beck north to find out what was going on. He left Vienna at noon on June 30; when he got as far as Böhmisch Trubau he found that the line had been destroyed, and he continued his journey on foot. When he was past the break in the line he hitched a lift on a locomotive to Pardubitz, and then took the road to Königgrätz, encountering the chaotic remnants of some of the units of the 1st Corps that had got thus far in their flight from Gitschin. It was a depressing spectacle, and it was in a suburb of Königgrätz, surrounded by this evidence of catastrophic defeat, that early next morning he encountered Benedek and his staff. Not surprisingly their morale was extremely low; not only had all confidence in Krismanic been lost, but the events of the last few days had seriously damaged their faith that Benedek could somehow redeem the situation. And for the moment Benedek's nerve had gone too. Before leaving Dubenetz to ride down to Königgrätz he wrote a letter to his wife that showed clearly the extent to which the last few days had told on him:

> My dear kind Julie, perhaps today I speak to you for the last time. I told the Emperor honestly, both in conference and *tête á tête*, that, if he so wished it, I would sacrifice for him even my military and civilian honour – and that has now happened... It is possible that I shall yet see you again. Better for me if a bullet found me, yet for my own part, I would like to see disgrace if I could do a last service for the Emperor and the army.[26]

In this grim frame of mind, Benedek and his staff sat down with Beck on July 1 to review the situation. Benedek and his officers were entirely pessimistic; only an immediate end to the war could save the army, Benedek even remarking to Beck that 'today, if a Prussian brigade attacked me, I could not stand against it.' In the face of this, there was not much that Beck could do but agree, and at 11.30 am a telegram went off to Franz Joseph over Benedek's signature: 'Beg your Majesty most urgently to make peace at any price. Catastrophe for the army unavoidable. Lieutenant Colonel Beck returns immediately.'[27] After the staff conference, Beck saw Benedek alone, and gave him a personal letter from Franz Joseph seeking his choice of successor if he should be struck down. Benedek emphatically selected the Archduke William, the Chief of Artillery, calling him 'the only man with a head on his shoulders.' In the same conversation he gloomily foresaw the war's outcome as it concerned him; there must be a court martial, he said, for he alone was answerable. After this, Beck set off for Vienna, profoundly impressed with all that he had seen and heard. When he got as far as Pardubitz, he sent a telegram to Crenneville reiterating the seriousness of the Austrian position: 'Armistice or peace unavoidable, as telegraphed from Königgrätz, since a retreat hardly practicable. It breaks my heart, but I must speak the truth.'[28]

At Vienna, the original telegram was not surprisingly received with dismay, and a prompt reply was personally drafted by the Emperor, and sent at 2.30 pm. 'Impossible to make peace. I command you to begin a retreat, if unavoidable, in the greatest possible order. Has a battle taken place?'[29] The final sentence was added by Crenneville, albeit with the Emperor's approval, and has been interpreted as conveying a message so clear that it was of decisive influence on Benedek's mind when he was pondering his next course of action. At all events, for the moment Benedek and his staff busied themselves with sorting out the mess into which the army had got itself, and by the end of the day had to some limited extent began to recover their morale. At 11.00 pm another telegram from Benedek went to Vienna reporting on the position. During the discussions with Beck, consideration had been given to the best line of retreat; perhaps behind the Elbe at Pardubitz or even as far as Olmütz, the course of action preferred by Krismanic. This had by now evidently been agreed on, because the telegram indicates the intention to do so, adding a more encouraging comment to the effect that the situation was better than at first had seemed during Beck's visit; units were reforming and, given a little time, the situation might be improved.

And, in fact, just this breathing space was now being given to the Austrian army, since there had been no close pursuit by the First Army after the battle of Gitschin, while the Second Army had also paused for a rest day in the Königinhof area. The Prussian Royal Headquarters had, on June 30, set off from Berlin for the front; it was accompanied by an enormous party of followers and occupied no less than six trains, causing considerable logistical problems.[30] During its journey southwards, Moltke kept in touch; when he reached Kohlfurt news came in from the Second Army that it now held the line of the Elbe, although the outcome of the battle of Gitschin was still unknown; accordingly Moltke sent off at 12.45 pm the following instructions:

> The Second Army will hold its ground on the Upper Elbe; its right wing will be prepared to effect a junction with the left wing of the First Army, by way of Königinhof, as the latter advances. The First Army will press on towards Königgrätz without delay.[31]

Herwarth was to cover the right flank. Even without any clear knowledge of Benedek's situation, or any hint of his intentions, Moltke was determined to retain the initiative and keep open his options to get around one or other of Benedek's flanks. His thinking was not, however, firstly appreciated by all his subordinates, as Professor Craig points out:

> They were not thinking in terms of pursuit and encirclement, because, despite their victories, they regarded everything that had happened so far as a mere testing of strength, an introduction to the real fighting that was to come, and for that they wanted the whole army to be massed.[32]

At midnight, Royal Headquarters reached Reichenberg, where it ensconced itself in the castle of the luckless Clam Gallas, and it was here that Moltke first got news of the victory at Gitschin. Bismarck distracted him briefly from his strategic consideration by raising a security problem. Noticing that only a few hundred artillerymen were available to guard the headquarters, he asked if, given the apparent proximity of enemy cavalry, this might be dangerous. Moltke was unmoved; 'Yes', he said, 'in war everything is dangerous,' consciously or unconsciously quoting Clausewitz.[33] Bismarck was thoroughly unimpressed with this response, and arranged for the artillery to be moved discreetly to the castle where the King had his quarters. He grumbled about it next day in a letter to his wife and, apparently still brooding on it, on the following day he asked her to send him 'a revolver of large calibre, a saddle pistol.'[34]

Bismarck's own account of the incident written many years later suggested that his interference in so patently a military matter as the King's security

> was the germ of a bad feeling towards me on the part of the military authorities on account of my personal position towards the King, which proceeded from departmental jealousy, and was destined to develop still further in the course of this campaign and of the French war.[35]

It was not the first time Bismarck had interfered in exclusively military questions, and it was not to be the last; it is interesting that he assigned particular significance to this incident.

Part IV
KÖNIGGRÄTZ

22

Contact Regained

Moltke woke at Reichenberg on July 1 to find that, once again, he was needlessly deprived of crucial information as to his enemy's location. On both fronts, touch had been almost completely lost with the Austrian Army, thanks again to the misuse of the Prussian cavalry, and he was obliged to base his planning for what ought obviously to be the decisive battle on a number of alternative scenarios. He was entirely unaware of the Austrian move to the position at Dubenetz, or its subsequent retreat. During the morning Royal Headquarters moved southwards, to Castle Sichrow. Here Moltke received a report from Second Army headquarters which thoroughly perplexed him, since it announced that Bonin's I Corps was to cross the Elbe and move to Miletin, and that the rest of the army was to follow. Since this was directly contrary to his previous instruction, he sent off an irritable enquiry at 1.45 pm:

> According to yesterday's cipher telegram Second Army had to maintain itself on the left bank of the Upper Elbe. Had that telegram not been received or what reasons led to the decision to go with the whole army on to the right bank?[1]

Getting no reply, and feeling the need to clear up any misunderstanding of his intentions, he sent off a further telegram at 4.20 pm: 'I am going this evening to Gitschin. First Army rests tomorrow, perhaps also next day. A talk with one of your officers desirable.'[2] Such a talk most certainly was desirable, because even in his journal in an entry written some days after the battle Blumenthal was still recording that it was, on July 1, the intention of the Second Army to cross the Elbe, Moltke's instruction of June 30 having evidently had no effect. The Official History suggests, however, that this intention was formed before the receipt of his Kohlfurt telegram.[3]

During June 30 the First Army and the Army of the Elbe had been marching through and beyond Gitschin, with the object of moving towards a junction with the Second Army, and had dispatched a cavalry regiment to try to make contact. Similarly, the Crown Prince, like Moltke in ignorance of the battle of Gitschin, also sent out cavalry patrols westwards from the I Corps to establish communications. Apart from some artillery exchanges over the Elbe between the V Corps of Steinmetz and the Austrian 8th Corps, (now commanded by Weber in succession to the Archduke Leopold) there was no activity, and little movement on the front of the Second Army. Moltke might not know the whereabouts of his enemy, but he was perfectly satisfied with the present position of his two main armies, relative to each other, as he recorded in the Official History:

> The Prussian armies were now at liberty to unite immediately, if such a measure should be deemed expedient; but it was considered preferable to remain divided, as this caused no strategic change, and might produce considerable tactical advantage;

> should the enemy be found in a position too strong to be overcome by a mere frontal attack, one would only have concentrated all forces to separate them again for the necessary flank attack.[4]

The present position of the armies, he thought, offered no risk.

The marching orders for the First Army on July 1 would bring the front of that army on to a line curving round from Miletin through Gross Jeritz and Milowitz, while the Army of the Elbe was echeloned some way back, with its advanced guard at Hochwesely, northwest of Smidar. The Second Army did not make any very substantial movement, apart from the move of the I Corps over the Elbe from Arnau to Ober – Praussnitz, which had so annoyed Moltke. This movement, due west, was to leave Bonin's corps some way behind the rest of the army when the time came to march south towards the enemy.

These Prussian movements thus had no effect on the Austrian army's retreat from the position at Dubenetz, which began at 1.00 am on July 1. With their march undisturbed, and indeed quite unknown to the Prussian high command, the Austrians headed south towards the position that Benedek had earmarked for them between the Bistritz and the Elbe, going into camp during the course of the afternoon.

Moltke's plan for July 3 was necessarily somewhat tentative. Orders issued from Gitschin during the morning of July 2 stressed the desirability of reestablishing contact with the enemy:

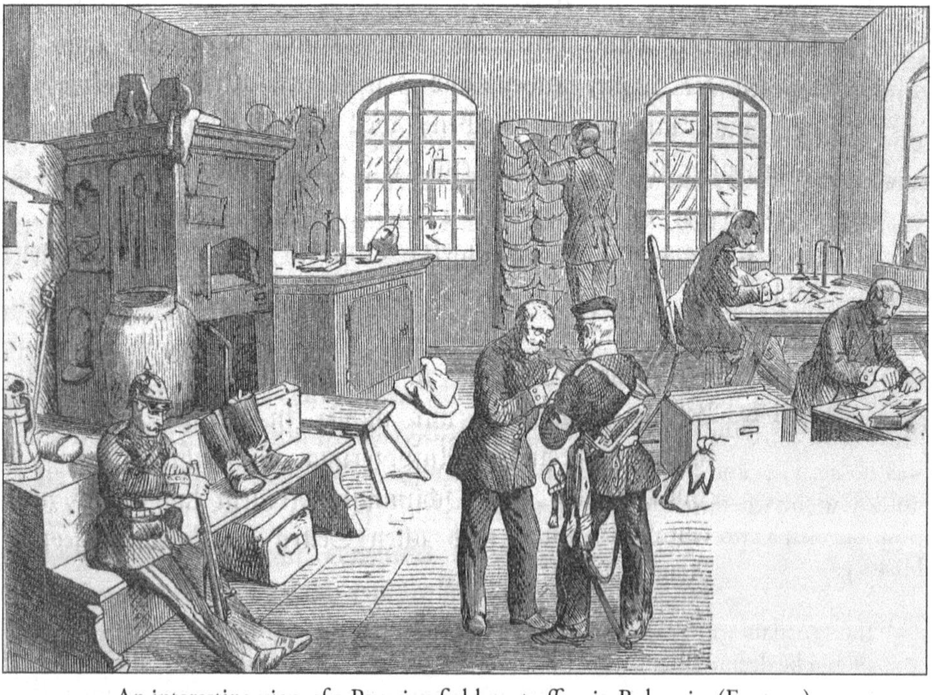

An interesting view of a Prussian field post office in Bohemia. (Fontane)

The all-important point for the next operations is to get to know the position at this moment of the enemy's main force, as in spite of a series of fortunate actions

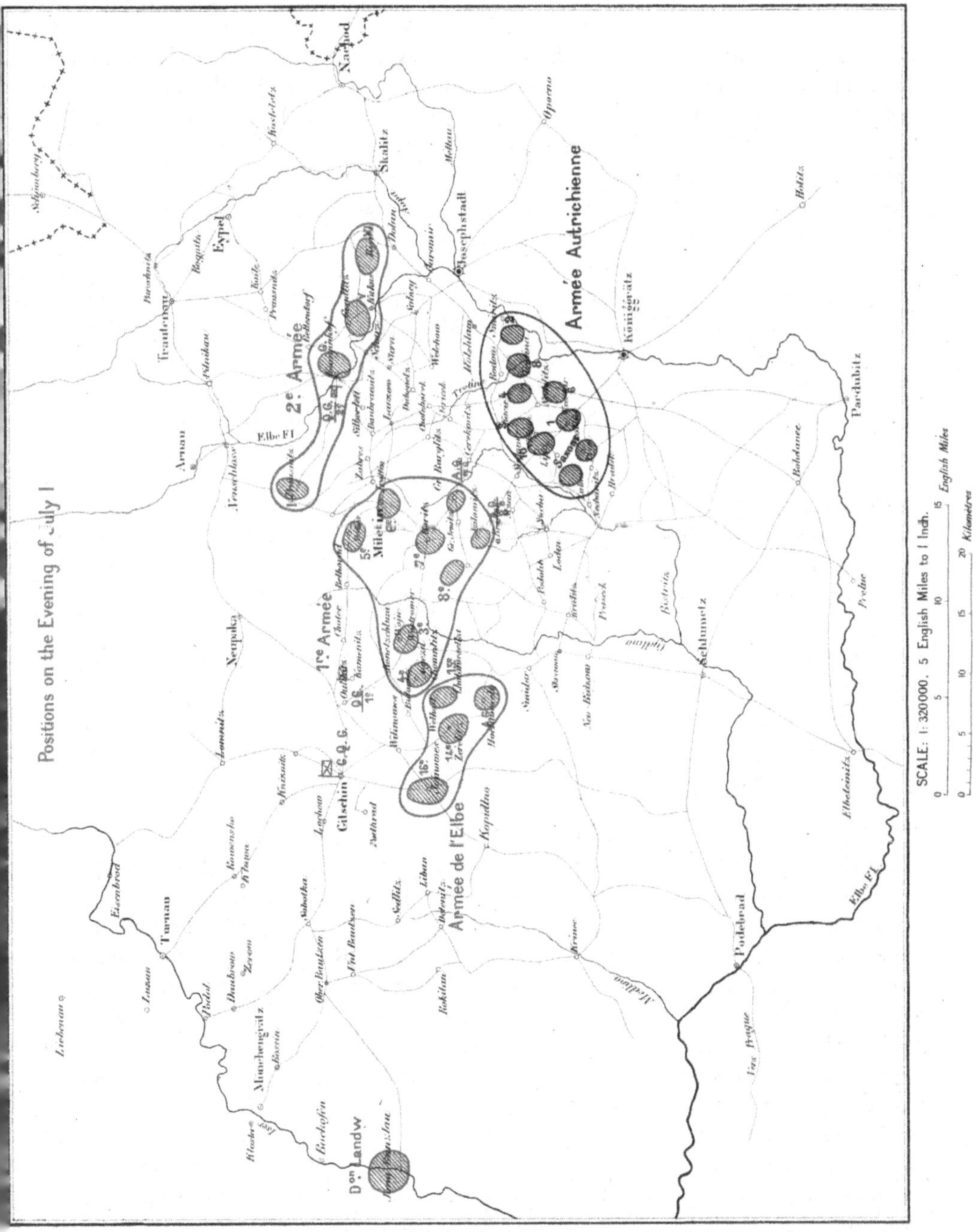

Map 27 – Positions on the evening of July 1.

> touch with the enemy has been lost. It is further necessary to know the conditions in which an attack on him can be made.[5]

Accordingly, the Army of the Elbe was to 'observe towards Prague and to secure the crossings of the Elbe from Pardubitz downwards,' while apart from a detachment to reconnoitre the line of the Elbe between Josephstadt and Königgrätz, the First Army was to move forward only to the line Neu Bidschow-Horitz. Apart from Bonin's I Corps, which was to go to Burglitz and Cerekwitz , the Second Army was to stay put, and reconnoitre the left bank of the Elbe towards the Aupa and the Mettau. Clearly, Moltke believed that Benedek was not going to stand in front of the Elbe, a belief based on his view that a position behind it between the two fortresses would be much the strongest:

> In the Royal headquarters at Gitschin nothing certain was known. It was supposed that the main body of the hostile army was still advancing and that it would take up a position with the Elbe in its front and its flanks resting on the fortresses of Josephstadt and Königgrätz. There were, then, these alternatives – either to turn this extremely strong position or to attack it in front.
>
> For such an attack, the Second Army must be kept on the left bank.[6]

These initial instructions for July 3 were of course intended by Moltke to keep the two armies apart; but, among others, Blumenthal was much annoyed by what he called 'orders for an extraordinary disposition of the troops… with a matter of 250,000 men in hand, reconnaissances of this sort are sure to lead to our being beaten in detail.' His description of what followed is characteristically egocentric:

> At ten o'clock I jumped into my carriage, and in company with Verdy drove the twenty eight miles through Miletin to Gitschin, to have a talk with the King and Moltke about it. I think I persuaded the latter both of the futility of reconnaissances in force and of the expediency of marching straight on Vienna after the first battle won, without looking to the right or to the left.

In fact neither Moltke, nor the King, (who 'laughed in his kindly way, and doubtless thought I was not in earnest') were likely to have been so easily persuaded of a proposition that was directly at odds with Moltke's determination to win a decisive battle of encirclement. After a heated debate attended also by the Adjutant General Gustav von Alvensleben, and by Frederick Charles and Voigts-Rhetz from their headquarters at Schloss Kamenetz, no change was made in the plans for July 3. Blumenthal did not enjoy his visit to Gitschin, and the failure to get his own way clearly made him extremely cross: 'Headquarters was to me not an impressive experience. A crowd of long-faced loafers is always an odious sight, especially when they greet one in a sort of condescending manner.'[7]

It is curious that Blumenthal's fury should have focused on the suggested reconnaissance of what was suspected to be the Austrian position along the Elbe between Josephstadt and Königgrätz, rather than the possible development of Moltke's strategy that was sketched out in the order; if the reconaissances suggested that a concentric attack would be too risky, 'then the whole army will continue its march in the direction of Pardubitz.'[8] Since this would mean asking the Second Army to march right across Benedek's front, it might have been expected that its choleric Chief of Staff would have something to say on the matter. Certainly later critics have done so, General Bonnal criticising both the suggested flank attack down the left bank of the Elbe as being insufficiently strong, and the march off to the south as 'an astounding project.'[9] But Moltke was always prepared for a bold step if the situation warranted it, and would not allow himself to be hidebound by excessive orthodoxy. Experience had already shown him that the Austrian Army was not being handled well; and his flank march would no doubt have been protected by sufficient troops in positions strong enough to ensure that, with the aid of the needle gun, any attempt to interfere would be swiftly repelled. And, of course, if Benedek did come out of what Moltke regarded as his strong positions along the Elbe, it would provide an opportunity for a counterstroke that could encircle and destroy the Austrian army completely.

In the circumstances, until more was known of Benedek's intentions, a rest day for most of the army was the only sensible course. A similar pause for recuperation after its exertions of the past week was also afforded to the Austrian army, now placed to defend the position along the Bistritz, if Benedek, contrary to his announced intention, decided after all to stand and fight. His morale, which had already begun to rise somewhat following the conference with Beck on July 1, continued to improve as he spent July 2 in the saddle, riding from unit to unit to see for himself how his army was recovering from the experiences which had so seriously sapped its confidence. By the end of that day he was able to feel that he had an army which 'once more went into bivouac on the night of July 2, a disciplined and orderly, if a weary and discouraged, fighting force'. This was a considerable achievement, for which, as his biographer noted, 'not enough credit has been given, either to Benedek or to his officers of all ranks, for the courage and ability shown by this piece of reorganisation.'[10]

It may have been because his spirits had been lifted by this contact with his men, or because a defensive battle seemed less dangerous than a retreat under mounting pressure, that Benedek had decided to stand in the position his army had now taken up. But there is also the possibility that he reached this conclusion in response to the Emperor's command, either indirectly in the form of Crenneville's addition to the telegram of July 2, or directly in the form of a definite instruction. The evidence for the latter is sketchy, and is based on research by his biographer which produced evidence from the niece of Benedek's closest friend, Eugen Müller. After the latter's death his brother was instructed to destroy his papers; before doing so he showed his wife and daughter a telegram which he had found among them from the Emperor to Benedek of July 2: 'A battle must be fought. Franz Joseph.' No other evidence of such a telegram exists. Presland concluded that the circumstantial evidence was strong enough to support the theory that there was such a command, pointing to a number of factors:

> Benedek's striking change of mind between July 1 and July 2; the anxiety of the Emperor and those in his confidence to bind Benedek to secrecy concerning all that passed between them; the Emperor's demand that all documents should be destroyed and no material supplied by Benedek for memoirs or a biography; Benedek's own deep conviction that he had been wronged.[11]

The absence of any copy of such a telegram in the official records in Vienna might be explained by the fact that a small packet of papers is missing from the folder, apparently having been taken out for the proposed court martial in November 1866; and certainly Presland makes out a persuasive case. But the apparent lack of any awareness of such a telegram on the part of any member of Benedek's staff points strongly the other way; the arrival of such a telegram must almost certainly have been known to others beside Benedek himself, and no one ever appears to have suggested the existence of any such direct order. Benedek's change of heart seems, outwardly at any rate, to have come gradually during July 2, as his morale improved.

A meeting with his senior generals at 1.00 pm that day had a surreal quality. According to Gondrecourt, the decision to remain in the Bistritz position was decided by Benedek 'without any discussion of strategic or tactical questions;' Thun claimed that there was 'nothing about operations.'[12] Those attending the conference later dismissed Benedek's description of the meeting as a council of war, pointing to the lack of information as to the intentions of the enemy.

Whatever may have been the actual process of decision making, Benedek had by nightfall on July 2 made up his mind to stand and if necessary to fight, and in doing so was certainly acting in a manner consistent with the curious Habsburg sense of what was fitting. Apart from this change of policy, however, there were also to be changes of personnel. During the day instructions came through from Vienna that he should dismiss Clam Gallas (whom he replaced in command of the 1st Corps by Gondrecourt) and also both Krismanic and Henikstein. He was left to select a new Chief of Staff, and his choice fell on the capable Major General Alois von Baumgarten, but he appears to have deferred making this change until the morning of July 3. Since Henikstein also remained at headquarters the result was, as Professor Craig put it, that Benedek 'was served on this fateful morning by three Chiefs of Staff, one inexperienced, one resentful, and the third – Henikstein – as sarcastic and unhelpful as usual.'[13]

Although Moltke, working on the assumption that his enemy would follow the wisest course, was firmly convinced that this meant a retreat behind the Elbe, the position in which Benedek was prepared to offer battle was nonetheless potentially a strong one. Although the Bistritz is only a small stream, it had been swollen by the recent heavy rain. Behind it, the chain of hills on which the Austrian army was to stand effectively commanded the route to Königgrätz from the west which Frederick Charles must take. The key to the position was the range of hills on which stood the villages of Lipa and Chlum, along the base of which runs the road from Horitz which crosses the Bistritz at Sadowa. North of these hills is a large wood called the Swiepwald, behind which rises the height on which Maslowed stands and, further north, the hill of Horenowes. Benedek planned that his right flank, facing northwards towards the direction from which the Crown Prince must come, should run along the ridge eastwards from Chlum to Nedelist, so the heights of Maslowed and Horenowes were outside his intended position. South of Lipa and Chlum the chain of hills consisted of those on which stood the villages of Tresowitz and Popowitz and then, running south-east away from the Bistritz, Problus and Prim. Another wood, the Holawald, lay to the west of Lipa, south of the main road, while all along the Bistritz there were small villages offering useful defensive points which had been barricaded and prepared with abattis.

Archduke William, Inspector General of Artillery in the Army of the North, and one of the men principally responsible for the excellent positions adopted by the Austrian artillery for the Battle of Königgrätz. (Fontane)

Notwithstanding these advantages, the opinion of some in Benedek's headquarters was not favourably disposed to the position which the army had taken up, one officer apparently considering it 'abominable.' Geoffrey Wawro suggests that it was 'an antique eighteenth century position' based on eighteenth century gun ranges and army strengths. It is, however, incorrect to conclude, as he does, that it was 'hardly defensible.'[14] As Professor Craig points out, not all Benedek's officers had neglected their duty:

> For the past two days, his Inspector General of Artillery, Archduke William of Austria, had been painstakingly reconnoitring the area, making note of all positions with a clear field of fire and measuring and marking ranges; and on the heights of Lipa and Chlum he had positioned batteries in tiers so that they commanded the bridge at Sadowa and the rim of the Dub valley beyond. During the same period the Chief of Engineers, Colonel Franz Karl Freiherr von Pidoll zu Quintenbach, had laid out an elaborate system of trenches and field works and had ordered the trees on the wood above Sadowa to be cut down and their tops and branches set towards the direction from which the enemy would come, so as to form an abattis.[15]

In this way the time that had been allowed to the Austrians on July 1 and July 2 had been turned to good effect by their engineers and artillerymen. Thus their artillery was well placed to dominate the battlefield that Benedek had selected, and clearly indicated that the Austrians had learnt some of the lessons of the earlier battles of the war. In a strong defensive position, with no hopeless bayonet charges doomed to destruction at the hands of the Prussian infantry and the needle gun, the Austrian army could give a good account of itself. Its assailant had not the numerical advantage which, in these circumstances, an attacker would need in order to be confident of overcoming the advantages of such a defensive position. It is not therefore surprising that, as he watched his troops preparing for the coming struggle, Benedek should have felt more confident than he had during his mournful ride from Dubenetz the previous morning. What however he did not know was the position of his enemy, or when the battle would take place, and he seems to have made little effort to find out.

This ignorance had of course hitherto been shared by his adversary. The conference at Gitschin had broken up, and the intemperate Blumenthal was on his way back to Königinhof, when events took a dramatic turn. Colonel von Zychlinski, with the advance guard of the 7th Division, had reached the castle at Cerekwitz. From here about five miles north of the river crossing at Sadowa, he had during the night of July 1/2 seen many camp fires on the heights to the east and south east, and on the following day he probed the Austrian position. One of his cavalry patrols picked up a prisoner from which he learned that the 3rd Corps was in position in the Lipa – Chlum area. This intelligence, which he sent off at once, at about noon, to Schloss Kamenetz, reinforced his previous reports which had already led to action being taken by the First Army to investigate the position further, and a number of cavalry patrols rode off towards the east to reconnoitre.

One of these, led by Major von Unger from the First Army's staff, trotted down the road from Milowitz towards Dub. *En route*, in a skirmish with some Austrian cavalry, he picked up two prisoners from whom he learned that there were four corps on the Bistritz. Pushing on through the village of Dub he gained the hill beyond it, from which he could see enough of the Austrian position to confirm the intelligence which he had already gathered. Thus far he had generally encountered no opposition, his troops apparently being taken for Saxon cavalry; but then he was spotted and was vigorously pursued by

Major von Unger on his daring and crucial reconnaissance ride prior to the Battle of Königgrätz. (Fontane)

a squadron of Galician uhlans and although getting away in the end, he only escaped narrowly with his vital information. This he brought into First Army headquarters at Schloss Kamenetz before 7.00 pm. Meanwhile another patrol, led by Lieutenant von Heister, also came in with crucial intelligence; he had been exploring the Bistritz valley further north, towards Benatek; he too had seen extensive Austrian bivouacs there, making it clear that the enemy was in force along the heights beyond the river.[16]

For Frederick Charles and Voigts-Rhetz the news was electrifying, and seemed to indicate that the Austrian concentration was the precursor to an assault, rather than a pause in the retreat. Either way, it was clear to them that immediate action to bring up the whole of the First Army was called for. By 9.00 pm the staff were ready to issue the marching orders for all of its units, most of which were required to move off by 2.00 am, the object being that 'at day break tomorrow the First Army will be formed on the Horitz-Königgrätz road ready for action against the position on the Bistritz at Sadowa.'[17] Separate instructions went to Herwarth, but these were confined to a requirement that he should 'move forward with all available troops to Nechanitz, where he will arrive as early as possible.' Since Frederick Charles had no information as to how far south the enemy position extended, this brief order suggests that Herwarth's role was intended principally as a protection for the army's right flank, especially since he had much further to march than the leading divisions of the First Army. Herwarth got these instructions by 12.30 pm and issued his own orders for a march commencing at 3.00 am.

Of more immediate concern to Frederick Charles and Voigts-Rhetz was the security of their left flank, and at 9.45 pm Lieutenant Normand went off with an urgent letter to the Crown Prince. On the basis that Austrian troops had crossed the Elbe near Josephstadt (it is not entirely clear where he got this intelligence from), Frederick Charles wrote:

> I can only look upon it as their intention to operate against my left flank in case I push on towards Königgrätz. Such a diversion would compel me to divide my forces, and I should then not be able wholly to obtain the desired result, the destruction of the enemy's corps.

Accordingly, he asked that at least the Guard Corps should cross the Elbe and move by way of Königinhof towards Josephstadt, since Bonin was likely to be too far off to help.[18]

Once these orders had gone out, Voigts-Rhetz rode back to Royal Headquarters at Gitschin to report developments. It seems extraordinary that it was only now that news of the location of the Austrian army was conveyed to the high command. Many years later, apparently nettled by suggestions that a council of war had been held before the battle of Königgrätz, Moltke wrote an account of what followed:

> General von Voigts-Rhetz brought the news at eleven o'clock in the evening to the King at Gitschin, and His Majesty sent him over to me. This information dispelled all doubts and lifted a weight from my heart. With a "Thank God!" I sprang out of bed, and hastened across to the King, who was lodged on the other side of the Market Place. His Majesty also had gone to rest in his little camp-bed. After a brief explanation on my part, he said he fully understood the situation, decided

> on giving battle next day with all three armies in cooperation, and desired me to transmit the necessary orders to the Crown Prince, who was at once to cross the Elbe. The whole interview with His Majesty lasted barely ten minutes. No one else was present. This was the 'Council of War' before Königgrätz. General von Podbielski and Major Count Wartensleben shared my quarters. The orders to the Second Army were drawn up forthwith and dispatched in duplicate by two different routes by midnight. One, carried by General von Voigts-Rhetz, informed Prince Frederick Charles of all the dispositions; the other was sent direct to Königinhof.[19]

The orders were brief and to the point. After outlining the situation of the First Army, the Crown Prince was instructed immediately to 'make the necessary arrangements to advance with your whole force to the support of the First Army against the right flank of the expected advance of the enemy, and will attack as early as possible.'[20] Lieutenant Colonel Count von Finckenstein, the King's ADC, was entrusted with the order to the Crown Prince, and he set off at once on the twenty-eight mile ride to the headquarters of the Second Army, passing through the forward units of the I Corps *en route*, and handing over an order to Bonin that he should concentrate his corps at once, 'in order to be perfectly in readiness when the orders of His Royal Highness the Crown Prince arrive'; the order went on to instruct him, if necessary, to act independently, as circumstances might demand.[21] Finckenstein rode on to Königinhof arriving at 4.00 am.

There, Blumenthal had himself returned at 2.00 am and reported to the Crown Prince on his visit to headquarters before going to bed, only to be woken by the message from the First Army which he somewhat inaccurately if characteristically summarised in his journal as telling him that Frederick Charles 'in carrying out his reconnaissance in force ... had fallen into imminent danger, and prayed me to come to his aid.'[22] Still very surly about his reception at Royal Headquarters, Blumenthal's response was unhelpful; Frederick Charles could have only the I Corps and the cavalry, since the Second Army would need all the rest of its force to support its own reconnaissance on the left bank of the Elbe. Notably, Blumenthal did not regard this exchange of correspondence as sufficient to justify disturbing the Crown Prince. With Finckenstein's arrival, however, everything was dramatically changed: 'I immediately woke up the Crown Prince, and then dictated aloud to my staff the orders for moving the whole of our army across the Elbe to the support of Prince Frederick Charles.'[23] The orders went out at 5.00 am and by 7.00 am the leading troops of the Second Army were on the road. Blumenthal himself set off at 7.30 am. The prospect of battle had restored his spirits entirely:

> It was very cold, but bracing. I had no feeling now of weariness, although the previous day I had driven fifty six miles, had eaten hardly anything, and had only had a short hour's sleep from 5.30 to 6.30.[24]

The exploits of Major von Unger and Count von Finckenstein were of crucial importance to the Prussians as they prepared for next day's battle. Without the intelligence gathered by the former, or the safe delivery of the orders borne by the latter, the events of July 3 might have turned out somewhat differently. The curious thing is, though, that despite all the technological advance which so heavily conditioned Moltke's strategy, neither of them performed their duties in a way fundamentally different from the way

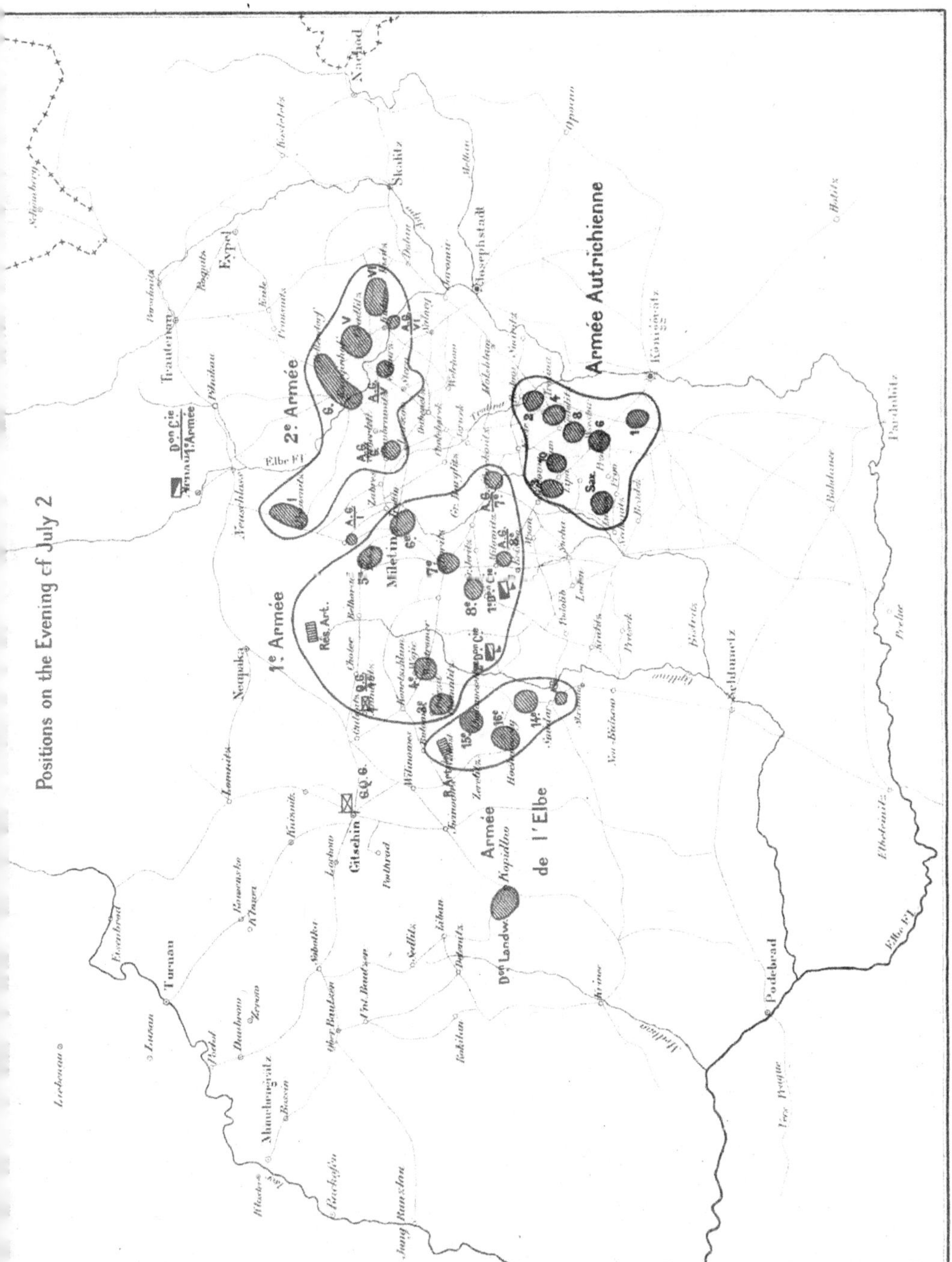

Map 28 – Positions on the evening of July 2.

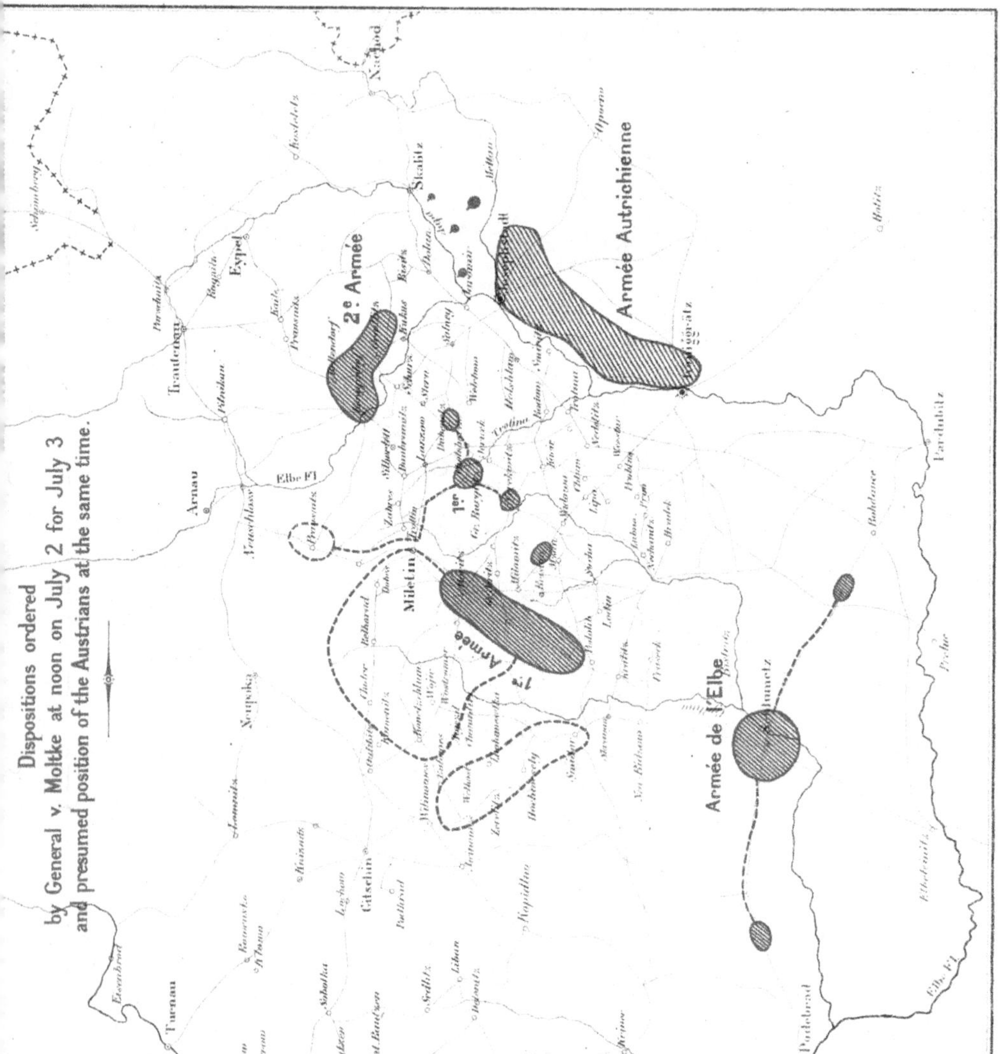

Map 29 – Dispositions ordered by von Moltke at noon on July 2 for July 3, and presumed position of the Austrians at the same time.

in which they would have done so two thousand years earlier. When it came down to it, it was still a man on a horse who was capable of making such a substantial contribution to the success of his army. The vulnerability of such means of communication was ironically demonstrated in the early hours of July 3 when an Austrian patrol led by a Captain Barja captured a Prussian soldier of the Second Army from whom he learned that the Crown Prince was already on the march southwards. A telegram conveying this intelligence failed to get through to Benedek, while two mounted messengers carrying this important news were themselves captured.[25]

Although relieved to know at last the position of the Austrian Army, and willing to take immediately the necessary decisions for an attack, Moltke was obliged to take into account a number of issues that could exert a considerable influence on the outcome of the battle. He could see very clearly that if he left matters as they stood, Frederick Charles would be advancing into a conflict with the whole of Benedek's army with, quite possibly, inadequate support from the Second Army. This, as noted above, was in fact the case; not appreciating the true situation, Blumenthal was demonstrating marked unwillingness to commit himself to a direct advance against Benedek's flank.

Even an immediate reaction would give the Second Army scarcely adequate time to reach the enemy's right flank. It would be 4.00 am before Finckenstein could reach Königinhof, and much later than this before the various units of the Second Army could be set in motion. And even then they would have a long march over the rain-sodden terrain before they could come into action. There were clearly risks to be run in leaving Frederick Charles to hold, on his own, what might be the sustained assault of the whole Austrian Army.

Another option available to Moltke was to postpone any assault by Frederick Charles until the following day, by which time both the full cooperation of the Second Army could be counted on, and a clearer picture obtained of the Austrian deployment. Against this, he would almost certainly lose the priceless advantage of surprise, and give Benedek another day to sort himself out. If Benedek chose to retreat, rather than make a stand on the Bistritz, it could only be to the still stronger position on the Elbe; if he fought in his present position, the envelopment of the Austrians at which Moltke had always aimed became a real possibility. In his immediate decision to grasp the opportunity that presented itself, Moltke showed that he had all the boldness of the truly great commanders, as a biographer observed:

> It merits even higher praise when it is remembered that it was the decision made by a man nearing his seventieth year, who had done practically no field service for forty years, who had never commanded a brigade or battalion or even a company in action, and who had only just arrived in the theatre of war.[26]

Even the usually critical General Bonnal acknowledged that Moltke's swift response to the news from Voigts-Rhetz proved that he 'possessed an exalted conception of the war of masses,' and that his 'greatness is shown in the order to the Second Army to assist the First with all its forces.'[27]

The final consideration in Moltke's mind was wholly political. The news on July 1 that the French ambassador, Benedetti, was on his way to the Royal headquarters, was a sharp reminder of Napoleon's propensity to interfere. If the Prussians were to win a victory from which they could draw the maximum advantage, it would be as well to win it quickly.

Benedek had of course been no better served by his reconnaissances than Moltke, but in one sense this mattered rather less. He knew the general direction from which each of the Prussian armies must come, and his immediate concern was to put his own army into the best possible order for the battle. At midday on July 2 he held a conference at his headquarters in the Prague suburb, on the west side of Königgrätz, with his corps commanders and their chiefs of staff. His morale had noticeably improved; whatever might be his understanding of the Emperor's requirements, he spoke calmly and firmly of his plans, and by all accounts was inclined to instruct rather than consult them about the next day's battle.[28] Although the Austrian Official History was later to condemn him for fighting on the Bistritz rather than behind the Elbe, the position he had chosen had sufficient tactical strength to lift the confidence of the Austrian commanders. And given the repeated failures of Austrian assaults upon Prussian positions in the face of the needle gun, they should have found no difficulty in accepting the sense of his decision to stand on the defensive.

The Austrian staff work had not however improved. Although Benedek had clearly settled the outline of his plans earlier in the day, the orders did not go out from his headquarters until the evening of July 2, in many cases not reaching their destination until after 4.00 am on the following day.[29] The orders prescribed the positions to be held by the various corps. On the extreme left stood the Saxon Corps at Popowitz, with Weber's 8th Corps in support. Next came Gablenz, with the 10th Corps, whose forward positions extended to Dohalitz and Mokrowous. In the centre, in the Lipa – Chlum position that was the key to the whole defensive system, stood Archduke Ernest's 3rd Corps. Next, Festetics with the 4th Corps and Thun with the 2nd Corps were to occupy the positions prepared by Pidoll covering the flank of the army along the ridge from Chlum to Nedelist. The reserve consisted of Gondrecourt with the 1st Corps (Clam Gallas having now departed), Ramming's 6th Corps and the artillery reserve, together with the five cavalry divisions. Sensibly, Benedek also gave orders for the construction of bridges over the Elbe and the Adler, to facilitate a retreat should this be necessary.

It was a cold, wet night. On both sides the troops had bivouacked in the open. Many hours before dawn the Prussians, tired and hungry, got into extended columns and set off down the roads towards the Bistritz. By 1.30 am Frederick Charles and his staff rode out from Schloss Kamenetz. *The Times* correspondent described the scene:

> The moon occasionally shone out brightly, but was generally hidden behind clouds, and then could be distinctly seen the decaying bivouac fires in the places which had been occupied by the troops along the road. These fires looked like large will-o'-the-wisps as their flares flickered about in the wind... Day gradually began to break, but with the first symptoms of dawn a drizzling rain came on, which lasted until late in the afternoon. The wind increased and blew coldly upon the soldiers, for they were short of both sleep and food, while frequent gusts bore down to the ground the water-laden corn in the wide fields alongside the way.[30]

At 4.00 am Moltke, in company with Podbielski and Wartensleben, drove out of Gitschin in his hunting carriage to Horitz. There, they picked up their horses, and rode off to Milowitz, passing as they went the long columns of marching infantry, heading for an encounter which would decide the fate of Prussia and, as it turned out, of Europe.

23

The Swiepwald

Frederick Charles and Voigts-Rhetz had drawn up their orders for the concentration of the First Army and the Army of the Elbe on the assumption that it would be they who fought the decisive battle, while the Second Army's role would be confined to providing support for their right flank. When he was told the news that Benedek was in position along the Bistritz, it would of course have been open to Moltke to make substantial changes to the deployment of Frederick Charles' forces for July 3; but, recognising the possibility of confusion if late changes were made after some of the various units were already on the move, he chose to leave the orders as they were, and to take a view about the early operations once the two armies were more or less in position.

With one striking exception, the orders for the First Army were perfectly suited to the role Moltke had in mind. Keeping the two divisions of the III Corps (Tümpling and Manstein) back in reserve south of Horitz either side of the main road to Königgrätz, Frederick Charles intended to use his other four divisions for any initial assault. Schmidt's II Corps, comprising the 3rd Division (Werder) and 4th Division (Herwarth) was to concentrate south of Milowitz, at Psarek and Bristan respectively. The 7th Division (Fransecky) was ordered to concentrate at Cerekwitz, on the far side of the Bistritz. It was this latter decision that was in all the circumstances surprising and, in the light of the First Army's objectives, potentially dangerous. It cannot have been supposed that Cerekwitz would be an appropriate point to place a flank guard; in any case, when drafting the orders, the First Army staff were counting on the Second Army to protect the left flank. And if it were proposed to fight an offensive battle, Fransecky was not strong enough single-handed to execute a decisive attack on Benedek's right flank, the position and extent of which was in any case not known. It might have been more useful for the cavalry to take post on the Prussian left flank but, for the moment, it was ordered to remain in its bivouacs.

By 5.45 am all the units of the First Army were in position; and it was at this time that Frederick Charles received a report from the Army of the Elbe to the effect that it would reach Nechanitz between 7.00 and 9.00 am with 36 battalions.[1] There was no further news of the Austrians; their outposts had fallen back, and the extremely poor visibility meant that the Prussian concentration had taken place behind the outpost line without the Austrians having any idea of the weight of the blow that was about to fall. The news from the Army of the Elbe meant that Frederick Charles could now move forward, and at 6.00 am he gave orders for an advance to the Bistritz. His troops had no time for more than a cup of coffee before the advance began. Horn was ordered to move down the main road, on Sadowa; to his right, the line was prolonged by the divisions of Herwarth and Werder, advancing across country over the sodden cornfields. The divisions of Manstein and Tümpling followed them, either side of the main road; the Cavalry Corps now also moved out, on Petrowitz, with orders to remain behind the II Corps and keep in touch with the left of the Army of the Elbe. No attack was contemplated for the

General Eduard von Fransecky, commander of the Prussian 7th Division whose epic defence of the Swiepwald contributed greatly to the eventual victory at Königgrätz. (Rogers)

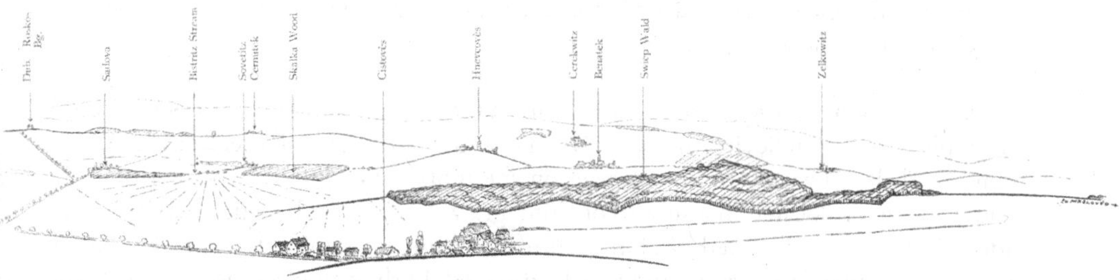

Map 30 – Panoramic sketch of the battlefield of Königgrätz, looking north-west from the main Austrian position at Lipa-Chlum.

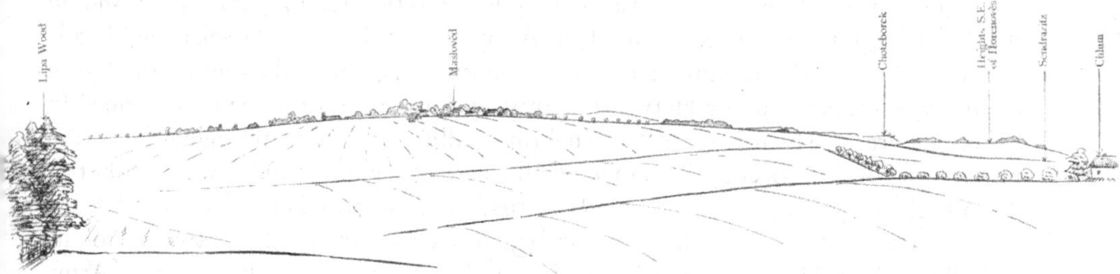

Map 31 – Panoramic sketch of the battlefield of Königgrätz, looking north-east from the main Austrian position at Lipa-Chlum.

moment; but the orders to Fransecky were 'to advance from Cerekwitz as soon as the action commenced at Sadowa, and to join in it as circumstances might demand.'[2] These instructions could hardly have been vaguer; but in Fransecky Frederick Charles had a divisional commander on whose judgment he could with absolute confidence depend.

Until the advance began at 6.00 am, Frederick Charles could not be certain that the enemy had remained in position along the Bistritz; but as he trotted forward up the slope of the hill above Dub that particular anxiety was dispelled by the sight of the activity in the valley and on the slopes began:

> The air was thick and hazy, the rain came down steadily, and the wind blew bitterly cold… At seven o'clock Prince Frederick Charles pushed forward some of his cavalry and horse artillery. They moved down the slope towards the Bistritz at a gentle trot, slipping about on the greasy ground, but keeping the most beautiful lines; the lance flags of the uhlans, wet with rain, flapping heavily against the staves… Then the Austrian guns opened upon them from a battery placed in a field near the village at which the main road crosses the Bistritz, and the battle of Königgrätz began.[3]

Although the actual movements of the Prussians were concealed from him, Benedek was in no doubt that in his chosen position he was about to fight the decisive battle of the war. Early that morning he dashed off a philosophical note to his wife:

> Today, or at latest tomorrow, I expect a big decisive battle. If my old luck does not quite desert me, it may end well, but if it happens otherwise then I say humbly: "God's will be done."[4]

The situation at headquarters was of course far from ideal following Franz Joseph's telegraphed orders relieving both Krismanic and Henikstein of their posts. As has been noted, Baumgarten only took over on the morning of July 3, at which time the headquarters was located in a suburb of Königgrätz. From there Benedek had issued his orders, in which he observed: 'Judging from the enemy's position, it is possible that an attack may be made tomorrow, and may be directed, in the first place, against the Royal Saxon Corps d'Armée.' After giving instructions in relation to such a limited assault, in particular he directed that the 4th Corps should move up on the right of the 3rd Corps, with the 2nd Corps on the extreme right flank. If there was to be a general action, his headquarters would be on the heights of Chlum.[5] While on the other side of the Bistritz the main body of the First Army was moving into position for a general assault should that be ordered, the advanced guard of the Army of the Elbe under Schöler was already in action at the vital Nechanitz crossing. The position actually taken up by the Saxon Corps, which was to oppose Herwarth's advance, was not that originally prescribed in Benedek's orders which reached Crown Prince Albert at about midnight. These had provided for him to occupy the range of hills east of Popowitz and Tresowitz; but as dawn broke on July 3 it soon became clear that the position was not ideal for defence and that a better position could be found further south on the heights between Problus and Nieder Prim. Here it would be much better placed to resist the advance of the Army of the Elbe, which must come over Nechanitz. Benedek had no difficulty in approving the change. Moving eastwards from Kobilitz, at 6.30 am Schöler ran into the 6th Saxon

Battalion in Alt Nechanitz; the latter, outnumbered more than three to one, fell back to Nechanitz itself and joined the 7th Battalion there, removing the planks from the bridge over the Bistritz and then setting fire to it as it went.

Fritz Hoenig, later a distinguished military commentator, was a junior officer in the Army of the Elbe and described what followed:

> F./28th unbuckled the cooking vessels, and adopted a country method formerly used for putting out fires in the home of this regiment. They formed two ranks of men, to whom the remainder continuously carried water drawn from the Bistritz in the cooking kettles… the energy of the leaders and the determination of F./28th succeeded in mastering the fire, saving the bridge, and stopping the holes in the roadway by using boards and planks, which the same battalion dragged to the spot. Thus the smart Rhinelanders of F./28th did here a piece of work that would redound to the honour of trained Pioneers.[6]

Without the presence of mind of this battalion, the progress of the Army of the Elbe would have been much delayed. It was the only crossing; to the left, the Fusiliers of the 17th Regiment waded up to their shoulders across the swampy meadows of the Bistritz; across the bridge now clattered the Reserve artillery of the Army of the Elbe, leaving the commander of the 57th Regiment, most of whose troops had crossed before the guns, chafing on the western bank waiting to bring over the rest of his men. Schöler now prepared to move forward through Nechanitz. When he did so, the 8th Saxon Battalion that had formed its garrison soon withdrew towards Lubno under the cover of artillery fire.

Behind the Army of the Elbe, the Cavalry Corps moved up to Sucha, where it was roughly equidistant from the Nechanitz crossings and the area along the Bistritz between Mokrowous and Dohalitz, on which the divisions of the II Corps were directed. These, with the corps artillery, were making their way not without considerable difficulty over the heavy ground; by 8.00 am Werder's 3rd Division had reached Zawadilka, and the heads of Herwarth's 4th Division were in Mzan. Horn, with the 8th Division, had pushed on down the main road from Klenitz past Dub; its advanced guard was deploying to attack the brickfield in front of Sadowa, which was still held by the Austrians.

To the north Fransecky had been impatiently waiting for the signal to move out of Cerekwitz. He had been ready since 3.00 am, at which time he sent off the first of a series of messengers to the Second Army to give notice of his position and to request support. The order that he join in the action of the 8th Division, advancing on Sadowa, according to circumstances, reached him at 7.00 am and his immediate decison was that he would advance on Benatek just as soon as he heard the first shot fired in Horn's action against Sadowa. This was at 7.30 am, and his advanced guard under Zychlinski set off at once. As soon as the latter reached the village he was fired on by Austrian artillery on the heights of Horenowes and Maslowed, and also from the Skalka wood; these guns were under fire from Horn's artillery west of the Bistritz on the Roskosberg, and as soon as Fransecky brought some of his own artillery into action they fell back towards Lipa. Benatek itself was quickly taken, and Zychlinski fanned out south and south west of the village, coming under 'a severe but ineffectual fire' from the Swiepwald, which appeared strongly held. He paused, momentarily, to await reinforcements.[7]

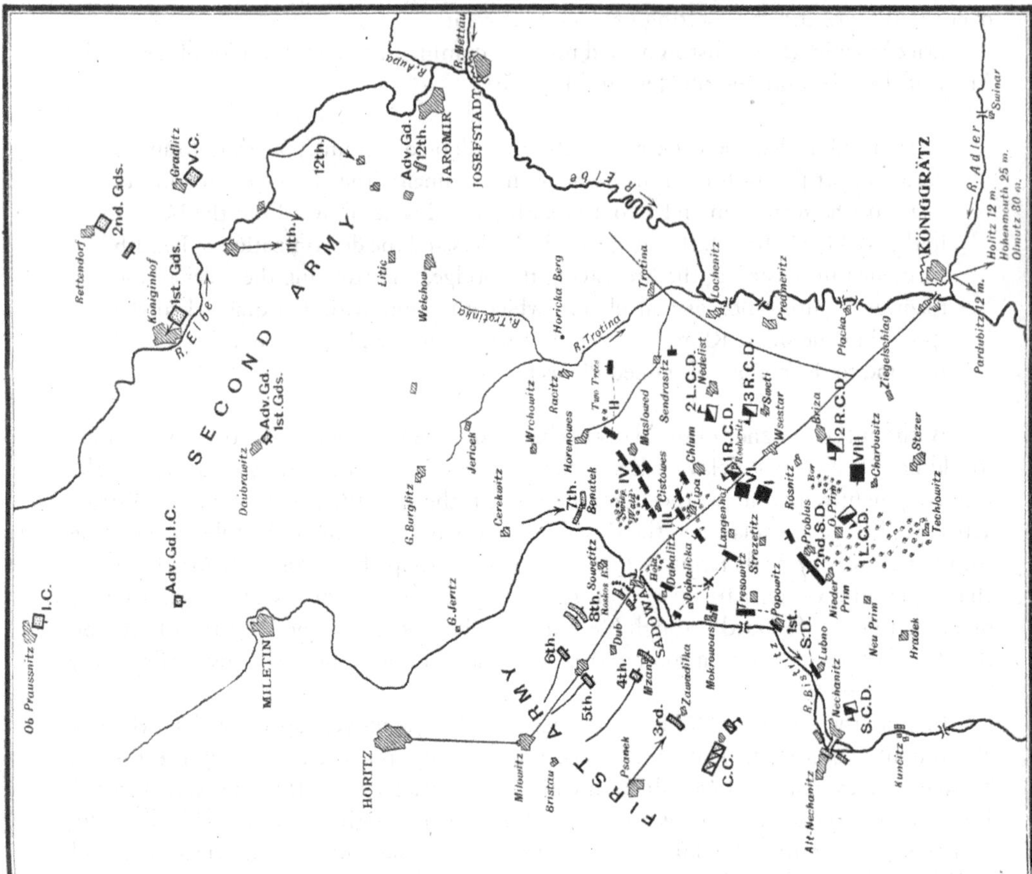

Map 32 – The Battle of Königgrätz, July 3, 8.00 am.

During these preliminaries Frederick Charles had been much frustrated by the poor visibility, and in an effort to try to see for himself the strength of the enemy deployed in his front, he rode off to the right wing of the First Army, ahead of the 3rd Division as it moved towards the Bistritz. From here, however, he could see little more, and it was only the extent of the heavy artillery fire from the Austrian position directed at the leading Prussian units that led him to conclude that he was faced by a substantial portion at least of the Austrian Army. For the moment he ordered all his divisions to respond to the Austrian artillery with slow deliberate fire until the position was clarified; while the infantry was to close up to the Bistritz it was not, for the moment, to seek to cross it.

The Austrian artillery had come immediately into action all along the front, in response to the Prussian cannonade, as Hozier described:

> As soon as the Prussian fire actively commenced Austrian guns seemed to appear, as if by magic, in every point of the position; from every road, from every village, from the orchard of Mokrowous, on the Prussian right, to the orchard of Benatek, on their left, came flashes of fire and whizzing rifle shells, which, bursting with a sharp crack, sent their splinters rattling among the guns, gunners, carriages and horses, often killing a man or horse, sometimes dismounting a gun, but always ploughing up the earth, and scattering the mud in the men's faces.[8]

King William had set off from Gitschin at about 5.00 am, driving in an open carriage until he reached Klenitz, where horses were waiting for him and his immediate suite. Accompanied by Bismarck and Moltke he rode forward to the Roskosberg, arriving at 7.45 am amid the cheers of the infantry moving forward along the main road. The Roskosberg rises gently back from the Bistritz south west of Sowetitz, just north of the main road, and gave a reasonably good view of what was to be the crucial angle of the Austrian position. Soon he was under fire, several Austrian shells bursting close by. The Minister President felt uneasy. 'Do you know how long this towel is whose corner we have grabbed here?' he asked Moltke. Moltke's reply was characteristically cautious: 'No, we don't know exactly; only that it is at least three corps and that it is perhaps the whole Austrian army.'[9] For the moment Bismarck had to be content with that; whatever the strength of the enemy, the Austrians were clearly holding the line of the Bistritz in considerable force. Moltke's concern was not however that the force in front of Frederick Charles might be too strong, but the reverse. The one thing he did not want was for Benedek to pull back from the trap which might, before the day was out, close on him.

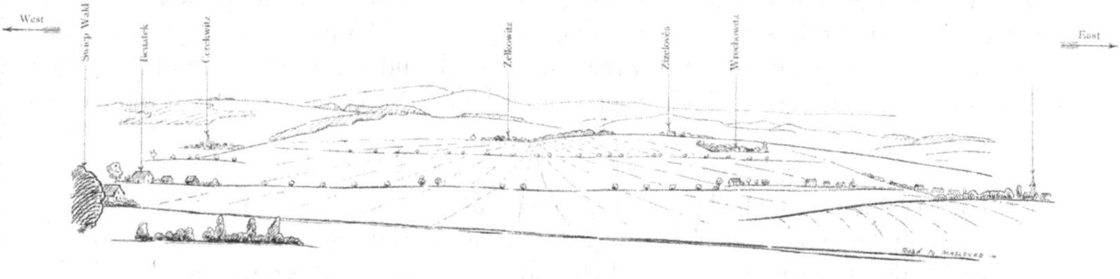

Map 33 – Panoramic sketch of the battlefield of Königgrätz, looking north from the Austrian forward positions between the Swiepwald and Maslowed.

Count Festetics, commander of the Austrian 4th Corps. (Voss)

Accordingly, having considered such information as was so far available, the First Army was ordered to move forward and cross the Bistritz along the whole of its front; only in this way, Moltke reasoned, could he be sure of holding on tight to the Austrian Army and preventing its escape. It had from the beginning of the campaign been his intention that, when the battle came, it should be decisive; neither militarily, nor financially, nor above all politically could Prussia afford a long drawn out war, and today he had the chance to end it at one blow. It was an opportunity that Moltke had no intention of letting slip; later in the day, when the casualties of the First Army mounted and no apparent progress was being made, he told Bismarck that 'the important thing was to hold the enemy for a battle of the whole.'[10] Whatever might be the temporary anxieties of those around him, Moltke knew what he was doing.

Behind the front of the Austrian position which the First Army was to attack, a number of Austrian units were still on the move, partly in order to take up the positions prescribed in Benedek's general orders and in one case to disregard those orders. Festetics, commanding the 4th Corps, and Görz his Chief of Staff, were extremely discontented with the position assigned to the corps guarding the right flank along the ridge from Chlum to Nedelist. It was here that Pidoll zu Quintenbach's pioneers had prepared the trenches which it was intended that the 4th Corps should occupy; the staff of the corps had apparently not been told of this previously, and they were not impressed when they saw them:

> Their position in the hollow of the ground only excited a feeling of surprise, and led to the supposition that they were merely intended, in the event of a retreat, to enable the troops to make some slight stand on this slope, which was overlooked from all sides.[11]

Three memorials to July 3 stand in the foreground of the Swiepwald. (Rogers)

The same Austrian journal from which these words were taken also recounted the reasons, which seemed so convincing to Festetics and Görz, for concluding that instead of taking up the position assigned to the 4th Corps, it would be justified in moving its right wing forward to the heights of Maslowed, 'under the impression that this would only be acting in accordance with the tenor of the Commander in Chief's orders' since the advantages of the Maslowed position were 'so striking that one is convinced at the first glance that the possession of these heights must have a considerable influence on the issue of the battle.'[12] This attempt to justify the disobedience of Festetics goes on to conclude that 'since the 2nd Corps was to take post on the right of the 4th Corps, it must certainly move to the heights south of Horenowes and Racitz, and that to resist an advance from the north east, the line Chlum – Maslowed – Racitz was a far more suitable position for the right wing of the Army than the line Chlum – Sendrasitz.'[13] The Prussian Official History prints an extensive quotation from this apologia without comment; and, indeed, none is called for.

Festetics accordingly moved his troops forward to the line Chlum – Maslowed, in which position, inevitably, he got drawn into the conflict in the Swiepwald. The troops which Fransecky's advanced guard had originally encountered there were two battalions of Brandenstein's Brigade, which formed part of the 4th Corps. It had, the previous day, been engaged on outpost duty on an arc from the river through Benatek to Horenowes, extending its front to Racitz during the early morning of July 3 when the bulk of the 8th Corps was moved away southwards from this position to support the Saxons on the extreme left of the Austrian front. The Swiepwald measured about 2,000 yards from east

The distinctive memorial to the Austrian 8th Jäger Battalion seems to stand guard at the entrance to the present-day Swiepwald. (Rogers)

to west and 1,200 yards from north to south. Behind it lay the village of Cistowes, which was held by two battalions of Appiano's brigade from the 3rd Corps. The Swiepwald covered a ridge, of which much the steeper slope faced north; it consisted in part of thick oak scrub and in part of taller trees, with patches of dense undergrowth. Along the centre of the Swiepwald, on the ridge, ran a track later to be known as the 'Avenue of the Dead'.

Zychlinski had two fusilier battalions available for the assault on the wood; these were reinforced by the 1st and 2nd Battalions of the 27th Regiment, and overall command of the attack was taken over by Major General von Gordon, the commander of the 14th Brigade. He was supported by the division's artillery, although the gunners were hampered by the fact that the 7th Division's flank was effectively open to the east towards Horenowes. After suffering considerably casualties from Austrian skirmishers around that place, the two batteries firing on the wood from the height east of Benatek limbered up and withdrew before joining other batteries close to the village.[14]

The attack went in at about 8.30 am, and Brandenstein soon found himself unable to resist its impetus, falling back through the wood towards Cistowes. Gordon spread out, following up the retreating Austrians with the 27th Regiment and occupying the northern part of the wood with one Fusilier battalion. Soon, however, he came under heavy artillery fire as Festetics moved up into the position he had selected for himself between Chlum and Maslowed. 'The enemy's guns, which were firing in this direction, gradually increased their fire until it attained an uncommon degree of vehemence.'[15] Inevitably, in the course of their advance, through the thick woods and up the steep slopes, the Prussian units became heavily intermingled; but, although not without loss, they succeeded in pushing forward towards the southern edge of the Swiepwald. Here Zychlinski, who had led forward the 2nd Battalion of the 27th Regiment, found that

The memorial to the Austrian 13th Jäger Battalion stands silently on the fringes of the Swiepwald. This battalion formed part of Fleischhacker's Brigade, 4th Corps. (Rogers)

two companies of the 1st Battalion had got into open country, one in position behind a bank fronting Cistowes and one on the edge of the wood.

The Austrian response was not long in coming. The first somewhat disjointed counter-attacks came at the northern end of the wood, as Brandenstein threw two infantry battalions from the direction of Maslowed into the wood which were however unable to retake the positions already occupied by the Prussians. Gradually, they too were forced back, and Gordon was soon in possession of most of the Swiepwald, although the confused and broken line of battle meant that within the wood fierce fighting continued. The first fresh unit of the 4th Corps to arrive was Fleischhacker's Brigade. As the Austrian artillery increased their fire in preparation for the counter-attack, the Prussian guns around Benatek responded; at 9.30 am a shell burst close to Festetics' headquarters, wounding him and killing Görz. Command of the 4th Corps now passed to Mollinary, who at once committed the corps to a series of persistent attempts to retake the Swiepwald. Although he had been deputy to Festetics, he claimed later not to have known the latter's intentions, or those of Benedek.[16] The assault of Fleischhacker's six battalions came up the Cistowes road; at that village Zychlinski had been making good progress, occupying the buildings on its west side and then launching an attack from the north, which was practically successful in driving out the two battalions of Appiano's Brigade that had been its garrison.

It was just at this moment, however, that Fleischhacker launched his assault; by weight of numbers he retook Cistowes, and drove back Zychlinski's scattered companies

Count Karl Thun von Hohenstein, commander of the Austrian 2nd Corps. (Voss)

into the Swiepwald, and in the case of two of them westwards towards the Sadowa wood. In this phase of the action the Prussians sustained heavy casualties as they fell back, fighting, into the wood, followed up by Fleischhacker's Brigade. The odds facing the Prussians lengthened, as the remaining brigades of the 4th Corps (those of Poeckh and the Archduke Joseph) arrived at about 9.30 am. The Prussian Official History calculated that at this stage there were immediately opposed to Fransecky's six battalions some twenty eight battalions actually in the Swiepwald, plus two more of the 8th Corps and, closing up, fourteen more of the 4th Corps. Eighteen Prussian guns were duelling with ninety six Austrian guns. Even more serious for Fransecky was the arrival on Mollinary's right of the leading units of Thun's 2nd Corps. Their commander was also soon injured, although not seriously; the danger to which the commanders were freely exposing themselves on both sides was further illustrated by Fransecky's experiences. Both he and his ADC had their horses shot under them in the north-east corner of the wood. As he went forward on foot to inspect his leading units, Fransecky then found himself surrounded by Austrian rifleman; but for the timely assistance of a score of Prussian soldiers who had got cut off from their own unit, he might well have been taken prisoner.

It was at just about this time that he received a visit from Stülpnagel, who arrived from the headquarters of the First Army to bring Fransecky a warning that he should not extend his position too far to the left. Having regard to the odds already confronting the 7th Division, this was obviously a wise precaution; Thun's leading brigades were already taking up positions around Horenowes and to the south of that village towards Maslowed, and a rifle battalion from Württemberg's Brigade had been sent to the help of Brandenstein's right, which was falling back from the Swiepwald. Both sides were getting reinforcements on this part of the front; Fransecky had brought up the rest of Schwarzhoff's 13th Brigade, and was threatening to debouch from the wood, so at Mollinary's request Württemberg detached two further battalions to occupy Maslowed. This Austrian pressure in turn forced Schwarzhoff to commit his last reserves into the Swiepwald. A fusilier battalion that he sent to reinforce Gordon, who was pinned down in front of Cistowes, was unable to fight its way through. Another battalion forced its way almost to the southern edge of the Swiepwald; pushing forward, it ran into heavy fire from Austrian reinforcements; then, itself reinforced, it wheeled to the left and took up a position on the edge of the wood opposite Maslowed. On its left a battalion of the 66th Regiment tried to push forward towards Maslowed, but was driven back in its turn.

On the right, too, the battle swayed to and fro. Gordon, like Schwarzhoff, had been obliged to commit the last reserves of the 13th Brigade, which he sent forward under Colonel von Bothmer, arriving on the edge of the wood opposite Cistowes just in time to stabilise the position there. So confused had the fighting become that two of Bothmer's companies had got drawn into the fighting opposite Maslowed, while behind the most advanced of the Prussian units heavy fighting continued deep in the wood:

> The Prussian companies in this part were fighting singly, and without any connection with each other, and the powerful detachments of the enemy even succeeded in regaining the western skirts of the wood, and actually crossed the tract over which Colonel Bothmer had marched shortly before them.[17]

This present-day image conveys something of the nature of the interior of the Swiepwald, which would have looked virtually identical on July 3 1866. (Rogers)

Fortunately for the Prussians, Gordon had sent to Horn's 8th Division for assistance; marching up to the Swiepwald from the Skalka wood, they drove the Austrians back, and established contact with the thoroughly intermingled units of Gordon's brigade within the wood.

On the other side of the Swiepwald, Mollinary now launched an attack by Poeckh's Brigade, supported by the Archduke Joseph and part of the 4th Corps artillery. He also asked Thun to support the attack, by carrying out 'an offensive movement against the Prussian left flank in order to disengage the troops fighting in the wood as much as possible, to obtain possession of the latter, and to force the enemy to retreat.'[18] Thun readily agreed, ordering Saffran to attack the north eastern edge of the Swiepwald with the bulk of his brigade, supported by a reserve column consisting of the rest of his brigade and part of Württemberg's. Poeckh's attack, which went in first, was directed at the south-eastern edge; held up at first, and sustaining heavy casualties, particularly among the officers, the charge of its second line succeeded in driving back the Prussians in various directions. On the left, Poeckh ran into Bothmer, and in spite of fierce fighting failed to dislodge him from his position in front of Cistowes, even though the leading Austrian troops pressed on through the Swiepwald as far as the crest of the hill. To the west of Cistowes Gordon and Zychlinski also maintained their position.

Saffran's first assault on the north-eastern edge of the Swiepwald, and that of its supporting column, completely broke down with heavy losses; however, the effect of Poeckh's advance on their flank and rear was now felt by the Prussians in his part of the wood, and under continual pressure they too fell back into the wood. By 11.00 am, albeit at terrible cost, the assaults of Mollinary and Thun had regained the largest part of the Swiepwald and their continued advance was putting Fransecky at serious risk. Even this sacrifice however, would be worthwhile, as the Official History, reflecting Moltke's views, made clear:

The 9th Company of the Prussian 27th Line Infantry Regiment pours fire into Austrian troops near Cistowes, on the edges of the Swiepwald, painting by Carl Röchling. (Voss)

> So great a numerical superiority might prove very dangerous to the 7th Division – might even lead to its destruction, but even in the latter case, the issue of the battle would have been considerably influenced by the firmness with which this single division had held two corps d'armeé of the enemy at bay, and had, by engaging their forces itself, drawn them away from their proper destination.[19]

Reporting to the King, Lieutenant Colonel von Loe, one of his adjutants, suggested that Fransecky should be reinforced; with a clear sight of the real position, and the purpose for which his reserves might be needed, Moltke firmly scotched the idea:

> I must seriously advise your Majesty to send General von Fransecky not a single man of infantry support. Until the Crown Prince has begun his attack, which is the only thing that can bring help to the general, we must be on the look out for an Austrian offensive. We will beat it off as long as we have III Army Corps at our disposal… In any case, I know General von Fransecky, and I know that he will stand firm.[20]

Many hours were to pass before the three separate advances for which Frederick Charles was responsible began directly to affect one another and before the influence of the Crown Prince's advance could be felt. All morning, Fransecky on the left, Horn, Herwarth and Werder in the centre, and the Army of the Elbe on the right, fought entirely

The same fringes of the Swiepwald now stare at a more peaceful scene in the autumn of 2008. (Rogers)

The 'avenue of the dead' in the Swiepwald. Today the sound of gunfire has fallen silent, but the area remains eerily atmospheric, with no birdsong audible. (Rogers)

Prussian infantry repel an assault by Austrian Jäger in the Swiepwald. (Fontane)

separate battles against the Austrian corps so strongly posted on the slopes against them. Other than in the Swiepwald, there was no very great disparity of numbers immediately engaged, although Benedek could still call upon a somewhat larger number of troops standing ready in reserve.

Horn's advance with the 8th Division had begun at 8.00 am, when he led his main body to its left, behind Sadowa where his advanced guard was engaged, and behind the Roskosberg, to Sowetitz. Posting his guns on the higher ground north and west of that village, he soon gained artillery superiority over the Austrian batteries on the other side of the Bistritz. Once news reached him that Fransecky was through Benatek, Horn launched von Bose's 15th Brigade over the river, with orders to establish communication with the 7th Division and then wheel to the right, advancing towards the main road to Königgrätz. Bose's advance immediately threatened the flank and rear of Prohaska's Brigade, which was still holding the forward Austrian positions in Sadowa. Prohaska's appeal for help to the Archduke Ernest was met by the response that 'the brigade was not to expect any reinforcements, but could retreat, if absolutely necessary, of which, however, it was previously to apprise the neighbouring 10th Corps.'[21]

Prohaska needed no urging, and at once fell back down the main road on Lipa, where the rest of the 3rd Corps was concentrated.

This meant that Horn's crossing of the Bistritz could proceed largely unopposed. Bose was now ordered to take the Holawald, just south of the main road. About one thousand yards square, it contained a good deal of high timber, oak, beech and fir but there was also a lot of very dense undergrowth.[27] The cohesion of the advancing Prussians was soon broken up by the thick woods; although encountering little opposition in its advance, Bose's brigade arrived at the other side of the wood in very confused order, to be met 'with a perfect hailstorm of shells' from the 'powerful line of Austrian artillery, which the 3rd and 10th Corps had planted on the brow of the heights sloping from Lipa towards Stresetitz.'[23] It was clear to Bose that any attempt to debouch from the woods would meet with disaster and he recalled his leading units with orders simply to hold the edge of the wood. Apart from the two battalions of the 72nd Regiment that had been detached to support Gordon in the Swiepwald, the rest of the 8th Division, comprising eight battalions, was by 10.00 am concentrated in support of Bose, behind the Holawald.

To Horn's left, the 4th Division had begun its advance on the Bistritz from Mzan at 8.00 am. As it moved up to the river it came under heavy fire from the massed Austrian artillery along the slopes, which soon began to inflict considerable casualties, not least among the gunners endeavouring to engage the enemy in spite of their substantial numerical inferiority. Seeing this, Schmidt, the commander of the II Corps, ordered Werder to advance with the 3rd Division as rapidly as possibly, and to bring his artillery to the front to support the 4th Division. In the ensuing artillery duel, in spite of having to withdraw the smoothbore batteries out of range, the Prussians did well enough to oblige Gablenz to seek reinforcements for his artillery, a request which was however refused. Benedek certainly did not want to be drawn into an engagement at close quarters on the Bistritz itself; his intention remained to take advantage of his position on the heights. The advance of a battalion of the 49th Regiment from von Schlabrendorff's 7th Brigade secured the sugar factory, on the river itself; the advance guard of the 4th Division made for Dohalitz while the main body moved through Sadowa at 9.45 am. These movements made it impossible for Gablenz to maintain his forward positions in any case, so by

One of the most distinctive battlefield monuments amongst the dozens at Königgrätz is this, commemorating the Austrian 8th Jäger Battalion of Poeckh's Brigade, 4th Corps. (Rogers)

degrees he fell back towards the main position on the slopes west of Langenhof and Stresetitz. On the Prussian side, the main body of the 4th Division took up a position behind the Holawald; on its right, a fusilier battalion probed towards Dohalicka, but found that the 3rd Division had already taken possession of the village.

Werder had completed his deployment at Zawadilka by 9.00 am and pushed forward to the river through Kopanina. On his right, von der Goltz's 3rd Cavalry Brigade, on loan to the II Corps from the Cavalry Corps, moved forward to exchange artillery fire at maximum range with a Saxon battery to the east of Tresowitz, but then fell back again behind Sucha. An attempt to drive back the offending battery with a smoothbore battery from the Cavalry Corps was ineffective.

These rather pointless exchanges ended, however, when as a result of the advances of the 8th and 4th Divisions, Werder found the opposition in his front falling back, enabling him to push forward to the river. At this point, the Bistritz runs through high banks; but the leading troops of the 54th Regiment advancing on Mokrowous unhesitatingly jumped into the river, waded across, and within minutes had taken the village along with nearly seventy prisoners. An attempt to push on up to the avenue of trees leading towards Langenhof was however checked by the Austrian artillery. The bulk of the 3rd Division now took up a position across the Bistritz and on the road to

Dohalitz. Because of the lack of bridges here, the artillery remained on the west bank; the reserve artillery of the II Corps moved up river to Dohalitz, and crossed there.

While the infantry had been advancing, the Cavalry Corps had remained behind Sucha. At 10.30 am Prince Albrecht, fretting at the sight of the battle evidently moving away from him, applied for permission to cross the river. While waiting for a response from army headquarters he received an erroneous message to the effect that the Army of the Elbe needed cavalry support; as a result, Frederick Charles ordered Albrecht to detach Alvensleben's 1st Cavalry Division for this purpose, and to move with Hann von Weyhern's 2nd Cavalry Division to Sadowa. It was a decision that infuriated Moltke – 'by no means in accordance with the intentions of the Commander-in-Chief,' records the Official History grimly; 'it thus happened that the Cavalry Corps, which during the whole advance of the army had been held together at the cost of many a sacrifice, was now on the decisive day separated in two halves.'[24] The suggestion of the need for cavalry support for the Army of the Elbe appears to have resulted from Herwarth's reluctance to respond at once to a request to advance on a broader front than that dictated by his use only of the crossing at Nechanitz.[25]

Finally, on the far right, the Army of the Elbe was slowly feeding its main strength into a battle line behind Lubno and Hradek, preparing to resuming its assault on the Saxon Corps, which had withdrawn in good order to its main position on the heights of Problus and Prim. By 11.00 am the third of Herwarth's divisions, Münster's 14th Division, had still not begun to cross the bridge at Nechanitz. For the moment, Schöler's advance guard of seven battalions was the only part of the Army of the Elbe in actual contact with the enemy, and at this time on this front it was the artillery that alone was in action.

It was at the northern end of the struggle along the Bistritz that the fighting continued to be fiercest. Standing in the Swiepwald, surrounded by the sights and sounds of battle all around him, Fransecky, the one time military historian, drew on his academic past. Speaking to a staff officer from the Second Army, who had brought news of the Crown Prince's advance, he said: 'In school we learned the saying: "I wish the night would come, or Blücher." We are no Wellingtons here, but that's exactly how we feel!'[26]

24

Anxiety on the Roskosberg

From the moment Count Finckenstein arrived with Moltke's orders for the Second Army, the atmosphere at its headquarters was electric. Blumenthal's orders, which went out at 5.00 am, were a model of clarity, intended to get the whole army moving south as quickly as possible. There would be time enough to determine the precise arrangements for an assault on Benedek's flank when the actual position of the Austrians became apparent. For the moment, Blumenthal was prepared to find Benedek pushing forward across the Bistritz; his orders reflected this:

> According to information received here, an attack of the enemy on the First Army at Horitz, Milowitz and Cerekwitz may be expected; the Second Army will advance to the support of the latter as follows:
>
> 1. The I Corps will march in two columns by Zabres and Gross Tuhn to Gross Burglitz.
> 2. The Cavalry Division will follow the I Corps to the same place.
> 3. The Guard Corps will move from Königinhof on Jericek and Lhota.
> 4. The VI Corps to Welchow; on arriving there it will post a detachment to watch the fortress of Josephstadt. The demonstration originally ordered for today will not be made.
> 5. Two hours after the departure of the VI Corps it will be followed by the V Corps, which will advance as far as Choteborek.
>
> The troops will start as early as possible and will leave trains and baggage behind, neither of which will be brought forward unless specially ordered by the Commander-in-Chief.[1]

These orders had, by 6.00 am, reached only the Guard Corps and the V Corps. The I Corps had, however, received Moltke's order delivered by Finckenstein to his outposts as early as 5.15 am; but characteristically Bonin did no more than issue an order putting his corps on alert; no effort was made to get the troops in motion. Mutius, whose VI Corps had been scheduled to lead the reconnaissance towards Josephstadt, was still preparing for that operation, the new orders for the day not being yet to hand. Prondzynski, with the 12th Division, was to move out of Gradlitz at 6.00 am, crossing the Elbe by a pontoon bridge near Kukus. Zastrow, with the 11th Division, was to move out with the 21st Brigade at 7.00 am and the 22nd Brigade an hour later, crossing at Stangendorf and Schurz. Mutius got the new orders at 6.30 am and, to speed up his advance, ordered Zastrow to pull out at once, sending on to Prondzynski who had by now reached Salney a pencilled note ordering him to march on Westetz and Ertina, covering the left flank.

Plonski, with the 2nd Guard Division, was to the rear of Königinhof at Rettendorf; at 7.00 am he received orders to push south at once through Königinhof, where the bulk of Hiller von Gärtringen's 1st Division was billeted. The orders from the Corps headquarters were to move on Jericek, and the division was on the road by 8.00 am. To the rear, the V Corps was leaving its bivouacs at Gradlitz at much the same time. The whole of the Second Army was thus moving off in accordance with the urgent spirit of Blumenthal's orders – with one exception. In spite of Moltke's order Bonin declined to move until expressly told to do so. The Second Army orders arrived at 7.15 am, and it took him an hour to issue marching orders to his corps, with the result that it was 9.30 before it was on the road towards its outpost positions at Zabres. Another victim of Bonin's tardy start was Hartmann's Cavalry Division; getting Blumenthal's orders at 8.15 am, it set off at 9.00 am. It had first to clear the road of baggage wagons but then ran into the back of Bonin's reserve artillery, which would not let it through, so it had no choice but to follow.[2] Blumenthal was seething:

> Of the Cavalry Division nothing on earth was to be seen – it might almost have disappeared into the earth; and when severe strictures began to be passed on its leaders, I comforted myself with the reflection that it would turn up somewhere unexpectedly. However, nothing was ever seen of it.[3]

The Crown Prince and Blumenthal rode out after their leading troops in heavy rain at about 7.30 am, reaching the Guard Corps an hour or so later as it was with difficulty crossing the river, and moving south. The Crown Prince at least was not thus far expecting to fight that day:

> At this hour I joined the Guard Corps, and with them made the excessively heavy march, in pouring rain, over the steep bank of the Elbe and the mountains lying to the back of it. The paths were obliterated, which terribly hindered the advance of all the regiments, and made the march difficult to a degree. I did not believe in the possibility of a big engagement, because I was of the opinion that the Austrians would not attempt to give battle, with their backs to the Elbe.[4]

The advanced guard of the Guard Corps, under Konstantin von Alvensleben, was at Dombrowitz, where the distant rumble of artillery from the Bistritz valley could be plainly heard. Alvensleben resolved not to wait for the main body, but to push on south at once, sending a message to Fransecky that he would be at Jericek by 11.30 am, and leaving a report for corps headquarters of where he had gone.[5] In fact, his fast-marching infantry got there by 11.00 am. Behind him, the main body of the 1st Guard Division marched up the steep slopes to Dombrowitz and then turned off to the east towards Dubenetz, marching straight across country. Behind it came the advanced guard of the 2nd Guard Division and then, interposed at the last minute to the profound relief of Hohenlohe, its commander, came the reserve artillery of the Guard Corps, which had originally been intended to follow behind the last of the infantry. Hohenlohe reached the Elbe and began to cross at 10.00 am; once he had got to Dombrowitz he was ordered to move still further to the front, at the head of the main body of the 1st Guard Division:

Map 34 – The Battle of Königgrätz, July 3, movements until midday.

The guns trotted past the columns, straight across country and through the high standing corn, but the long straw, mixed with the clayey soil, wound itself in thick wreaths round the wheels, and rendered such extreme exertion necessary that by the time they reached Jericek several horses had fallen dead before the guns from sheer fatigue.[6]

Further east, the VI Corps was making the best of its way towards the battle. Ground conditions were just as bad there, but Mutius' cavalry, scouting in advance of the 12th Division, ran into some Austrian cavalry retreating from Josephstadt, and followed it to Smiritz. A quick pass over the Elbe there showed that there were no significant Austrian movements on the east bank, and the cavalry reformed at St Wenzel and Habrina to await the infantry.

Prondzynski had a brief artillery exchange with the fortress guns of Josephstadt on his way past; Mutius ordered him to keep in touch with the 11th Division which he could see on his right, moving towards Welchow, and he himself pressed on southwards over bad roads, reaching the foot of the Horicka Berg, to the north east of Racitz, by 11.00 am. Zastrow, meanwhile, having got across the Elbe, was moving flat out towards the sound of the guns to the south. Everything possible was done to try to keep the individual battalions closed up but inevitably, moving down narrow muddy roads, the division began to get strung out. Reaching the Trotina the leading battalions of the 21st Brigade waded chest high across the stream. By 11.00 am, attaining the heights between Luzan and Racitz, the division ran into opposition for the first time, as the distant Austrian artillery opened fire from the Horenowes ridge.

Behind Mutius, and to the north, Steinmetz was also pressing forward with the V Corps. He was moving with his cavalry to the front, followed by the 9th and 10th Divisions, and his reserve artillery to the rear. At 11.00 am he was approaching Choteborek. By this time, therefore, the leading units of the Second Army had made sufficient progress to ensure that they would reach the Austrian right, wherever it was to be found, in time to bring support to the First Army.

But in the Bistritz valley, on the Roskosberg, nothing was known of the advance of the Second Army; to King William and his retinue this was by no means apparent and they were to endure several anxious hours. Moltke might calmly calculate, in the words of the Official History, that 'the Prussian centre was in no danger'[7] but there were others who were not so sure. The Prussian infantry in the Holawald as well as in the Swiepwald were taking a fearful pounding from the Austrian artillery, and the Prussian guns were not making a very effective reply. There were some two hundred and fifty well-sited Austrian guns firing on the centre of the First Army, in many cases using the measured ranges prepared the day before. By 11.00 am there were only twelve Prussian batteries on the left bank, and only seven of these had been able to come into action, which meant that only forty two guns were engaging the enemy.[8] Moltke maintained his *sang froid*, while the nerves of those around him became more and more strung up. There was no one to minute these conversations that took place during the anxious hours of the late morning, and as Professor Craig points out, it is possible only to guess at which stage of the battle Moltke made the various observations that later passed into legend. In an

A view from atop the Roskosberg looking approximately eastwards; rising slightly on the far horizon is the dark mass of the Swiepwald. (Rogers)

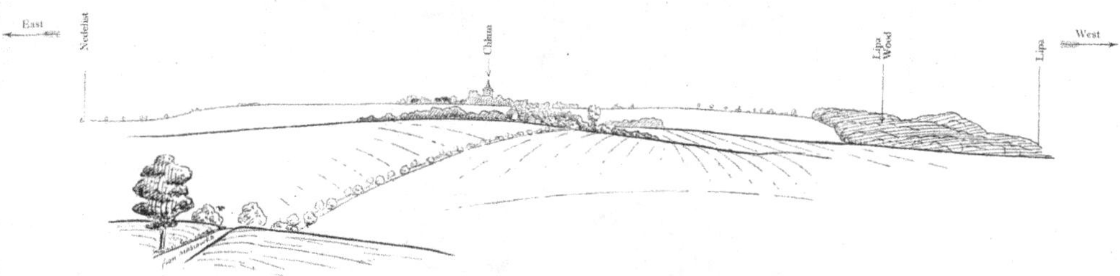

Map 35 – Panoramic sketch of the battlefield of Königgrätz, looking south from Maslowed at the main Austrian position.

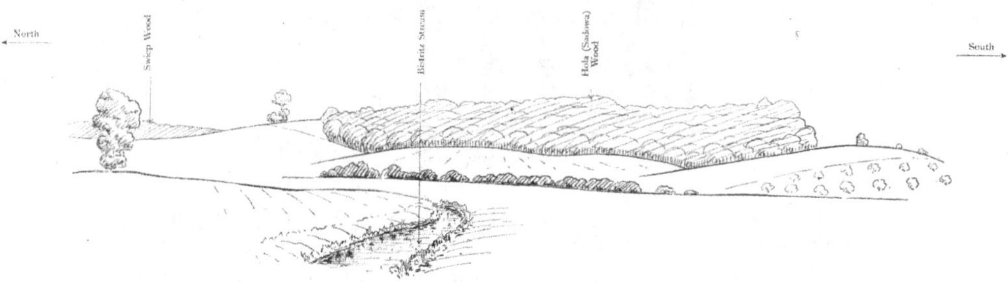

Map 36 – Panoramic sketch of the battlefield of Königgrätz, looking east from Sadowa at the Austrian forward positions.

account which he wrote many years later he described an exchange with the King, who seems to have been the edgiest of the lot. The King exclaimed: 'Moltke, Moltke, we are losing the battle.' To this Moltke laconically replied: 'Your Majesty will today win not only the battle but the campaign.'[9] A little later Bismarck, who was also, understandably, getting very tense, proffered Moltke his cigar case, and drew some comfort from the care with which Moltke made his choice of cigar.[10]

Benedek and his staff, at Lipa, were just as ignorant as those on the Roskosberg of the progress southwards of the Crown Prince's Army. Their attention was fixed on the struggle in their immediate front, in the Swiepwald and the Holawald, and so far as they could tell the battle was going by no means badly for them – so much so, in fact, that Benedek began to entertain hopes of being able before long to make a counterstroke over the Bistritz. There was, however the problem caused by the forward movements of first the 4th Corps and then the 2nd Corps, resulting in the abandonment of the trench lines prepared by Pidoll for their occupation. Benedek had known about this since 9.00 am, when Baumgarten had ridden over to Chlum and found the trenches empty; and both Pidoll himself and Colonel Neuber had confirmed this a little later. Benedek, however, did not immediately order the 4th and 2nd Corps to move back, apparently accepting for the moment the desirability of keeping up the pressure on Fransecky in the Swiepwald. Instead, he ordered up Ramming's 6th Corps to occupy a position on the Chlum – Nedelist line, only to change his mind soon after, perhaps because he wanted to keep his reserve in hand for the counter-attack. But the position on his right flank could not be left as it was, and at 11.00 am he sent an order to Mollinary delivered orally by Count Falkenhayn; 'The 4th Corps must retire on the Chlum – Nedelist line, and keep touch

Major General Anton Mollinary, who succeeded to the command of the Austrian 4th Corps on the wounding of its commander, Count Festetics. (Mollinary)

with the 3rd Corps and the 2nd Corps.[11] Mollinary did not comply, returning a message to the effect that he was in a good position and that to withdraw would be detrimental to the offensive of the 3rd Corps. This presumably referred to a counterstroke being contemplated by the Archduke Ernest, although Benedek had not ordered it.

At 11.30 am came a telegram from the commandant of the fortress of Josephstadt reporting on the march southwards of the Second Army; in the face of this obvious threat, the open right flank of the Austrian Army clearly must be made good, and another staff officer was sent to Mollinary and Thun with orders to pull back. Again Mollinary disobeyed, this time riding back to Lipa to discuss the position with Benedek himself. He had a strong and optimistic view of the situation that he wanted to convey to Benedek; the battle for the Swiepwald was, he believed, almost won, and nowhere else were the Prussians making significant progress. This, therefore, was the moment for the counterstroke.

Such a message was never going to be well received by a staff confronted by the hugely ominous threat presented by the advance of the Second Army and it provoked a fierce argument. When Mollinary arrived, and began to explain his assessment, Baumgarten interrupted:

> Putting an admonitory hand on his arm, [he] read the telegram from Josephstadt and began to explain the position caused by the advance of the Crown Prince's Army. Mollinary, not knowing that Baumgarten was now Chief of Staff and resenting the interruption, asked angrily whether they had not a large number of reserves in hand with which to meet the Crown Prince. "That is just what I have been saying!" cried Krismanic from the outermost edge of the sacred circle round Benedek.

Benedek did not comment, but asked the Archduke William, whose opinion he had come to value above all, if the time had come to counter-attack. Evidently the latter's advice was in the negative, for after a private talk, Benedek returned to the group and replied to Mollinary's request for further orders by saying: 'I cannot help it, you must retire.'[12] It was a dramatic and revealing moment, which illustrated all the different facets of the confused and divided leadership of the Austrian Army; but, in truth, the moment had already passed when what Presland calls 'the penetrating insight, the flash of imaginative power of the great general' could have saved the Austrians from defeat.

Mollinary's view of the situation had, at least as far as the Swiepwald was concerned, some reasonable basis, since by 11.00 am Fransecky's position was becoming desperate. Heavily outnumbered, the troops on his right had been steadily forced back to the northern edge of the wood suffering, as well as inflicting, heavy losses. To his left, where the western corner of the wood projects towards Maslowed, a few companies of infantry under Major von Wiedner were clinging on to a position near the Maslowed – Cistowes road; to their right, and indeed behind them, Austrian troops were pushing forward to the northern edge and preparing to advance on Benatek.

The advance of Thun's corps was directed towards clearing out the last of the Prussian defenders of the Swiepwald. The leadership of the officers was crucial in a battle of this kind:

> The companies had all become mingled together as the fight swayed backwards and forwards in the dense wood; no unity of guidance was possible on ground where hills and wood shut out all view of the surrounding country, and all that the commanders of the different detachments could do, was to lead their men by their own personal example.[13]

As the five fresh battalions of Thun's corps moved up to attack the Swiepwald, the defenders were heartened by the rumour that quickly spread that the Crown Prince was coming; but this hope was the only reinforcement they would get for some time to come.

The advancing Austrians were themselves were confused and unsure of their direction; one entire battalion, having pushed through the wood to emerge on its north-western side was charged by a squadron of Prussian hussars under Captain von Humbert, and promptly surrendered, the total haul being 16 officers and 665 men. They were followed by another detachment of riflemen and, seeing them, Fransecky dispatched two companies under Captain von Ploetz to round them up. 3 officers and 200 men were surrounded and taken prisoner. But the pressure was unceasing and the advance out of the wood of a fresh column forced Ploetz back to a position east of Benatek.

Much the same position continued to obtain on the right, at the north-eastern edge of the wood, where Bothmer was in command. Again and again the Austrians advanced, on two occasions driving the defenders from their positions, only to recoil in the face of fierce counter-attacks. But the pressure was beginning to tell, and towards the end of the morning it became necessary to pull back Wiedner's troops from the north-western corner of the Swiepwald, in order to give Fransecky some reserves with which to meet any concentrated assault in the direction of Benatek that the Austrians might be able to mount.

But the long ordeal of the 7th Division was nearing its end. Although the Austrians had almost succeeded in recapturing the Swiepwald, the indirect effect of the advance of the Second Army now began to be felt. Although not all units of the 4th and the 2nd Corps received at once the orders issued by Mollinary and Thun pursuant to Benedek's instructions, and were to continue the struggle for more than an hour, by soon after 1.00 pm there was a perceptible slackening of the pressure.

Moltke's calm resolve to wait, and to hold on, in the centre with the First Army until the advances of the Second Army and the Army of the Elbe should enable him to achieve a decisive victory, was unaffected by the fearful hammering which Fransecky was absorbing in the Swiepwald, as well as by the steadily mounting casualties in the Holawald. By noon, however, Frederick Charles found his patience giving way, and brought the whole of the III Corps, which was standing in reserve, over the Bistritz, a move which was flagrantly at odds with Moltke's intentions. Noting that they were now ready to advance 'as soon as the flank armies came up,' the Official History notes with careful lack of emphasis that 'the moment for this had not arrived yet, and the patience and endurance of the First Army had still to undergo a long trial.'[14] The problem for the Prussians was that in the centre the battle had

> assumed essentially the character of a combat of artillery, to be sure of a most unequal one, in which the Prussian Infantry was for a long time condemned to the trial of passive endurance under a most severe fire of artillery.[15]

The Austrians were able to bring some two hundred guns into action along the Bistritz; they had the advantage of occupying prepared positions largely concealed from the Prussians on the higher ground. Much of the Prussian artillery, on the other hand, could not even be brought over the Bistritz because there was no way it could be effectively used. Behind the Holawald, and on both sides of the main road, and again in

Prussian artillery at Mokrowous. (Fontane)

front of the Skalka wood, individual batteries did most distinguished service. In every location, however, they were heavily outmatched in weight of metal and were firing from most unfavourable positions.

All this time the infantry of the 8th Division still occupied the Holawald, enduring a heavy artillery fire that caused significant casualties. The need to hold the wood was seen as essential; certainly, if it had been necessary to cross the Bistritz at all, the Holawald could not be allowed to fall into Austrian hands, so not only was it necessary to hold the edge of the wood in strong force, but large reserves, also exposed to the incessant artillery fire, were obliged to stand in readiness behind it.

Further south the 3rd Division was somewhat less exposed to the fire of the Austrian artillery, and had succeeded in establishing itself rather more securely in the villages of Dohalitz and Mokrowous that it had succeeded in occupying. In Dohalitz, for instance, the church and the school house were quickly made into strong points to resist any Austrian counter-attack. However, there was difficulty in bringing forward all the artillery on Werder's front, due to the lack of practicable bridges over the Bistritz, and it was not until later in the day that a number of batteries were able to take up positions east of the river.

Beyond Werder, the Army of the Elbe, upon which so much of Moltke's plan for the battle depended, was moving slowly into a position from which it could make a contribution to the working out of that plan. For some considerable time, though, for the main body of the Army of the Elbe, not a lot seemed to be happening, and a sense of unreality prevailed, due to the very slow process of getting the army over the bridge at Nechanitz. Fritz Hoenig observed the scene at Alt-Nechanitz:

> The long rest there, from half-past 10 in the morning till 1 o'clock, gave quite the appearance of some assembly of troops for peaceful objects. The officers of the different regiments went to see each other, talked together, and shared among them what little they had to eat, but seemed to have no foreboding that the 3rd of July was to become a marked day in German history. Certainly the attention of the groups in conversation was often arrested, as was natural, by the battlefield, which spread itself in comparable grandeur up to the extreme left, and was covered with gigantic masses of fire and very dark, slow-moving, heavy clouds of smoke.[16]

Once over the bridge, however, the scene changed, with traces of the earlier engagement of the advanced guard, and beyond this the leading units of the Army of the Elbe were finally getting into position.

The enemy, meanwhile, had been doing the same. The front line was held by the Saxon 1st Division (Schimpff) from Stresetitz to Nieder Prim; the key to the position was the village of Problus. Behind it stood the 2nd Division (von Stieglitz) and to its right the Saxon Cavalry Division, maintaining contact with Gablenz's 10th Corps. Crown Prince Albert posted his reserve artillery behind the 1st Division, near the Bor wood. Finally, the 8th Corps had also come up in support, and was held in reserve in the Bor wood, although it soon became necessary to advance part of its infantry into the Stezirek Wood south of Ober Prim, while two of its 8-pounder batteries joined the Saxon gun line at Nieder Prim.

Fighting at Problus. (Fontane)

Herwarth had been up with the advanced guard to examine the enemy positions. The Saxons barred the way between him and a direct junction with the First Army. He could achieve this objective either by marching up the left bank of the Bistritz, with a view to coming into action directly on Werder's left, or by attacking the position at Problus. The former course would have been entirely at odds with Moltke's intentions, as well as being pointlessly risky, and Herwarth resolved, ('very rightly' as the Official History points out), upon an assault on Problus, even though a large part of his army had yet to get over the Nechanitz bridge.

At 11.30 am he ordered Canstein to move through Hradek to Ober Prim, while Münster, with his troops still only part way across the river, was ordered to move through Lubno and Popowitz before swinging eastwards on Problus itself. This latter movement was preceded by the advanced guard, which soon reached the wood east of Popowitz, finding it unoccupied. 'The possession of this wooded hill gave an *appui* for the advance of the 14th Division, which at this time was only just beginning to debouch from Nechanitz.'[17]

On the right flank, Canstein's advance was led by elements of Schöler's advanced guard, which marched through Jelitz into the pheasantry which lay between it and Neu Prim. Crown Prince Albert quickly observed that this advance was not substantial, and decided on a counterstroke to be made by the Leib Brigade, which he brought up from its position behind Problus and launched at Schöler's leading units in Neu Prim and the pheasantry, reinforcing it with part of Schimpff's Division from Nieder Prim. Some of the Prussian troops on whom the assault fell ceased firing, having taken the Saxon uniforms for Prussian, and very soon the two Prussian battalions in the pheasantry were being bundled back towards Jelitz and Hradek with considerable losses. Indeed, the advance of the Leib Brigade would have caused Canstein very considerable problems had it not been checked at this moment by a sudden and unexpected threat to its left flank from the Stezirek wood. There, a battalion of the Prussian 56th Regiment had driven back the Austrian infantry that had moved into the wood and then turned northwards out of the wood towards Ober Prim, causing the Leib Brigade to halt and face south to meet its advance. It was now 12.45 pm; if the Army of the Elbe was to operate effectively as the southern arm of Moltke's pincer movement, Herwarth would have to get a move on. Certainly the ill effect of confining the crossing of the Bistritz solely to the one bridge at Nechanitz was being seriously felt. Practically all critics accept that it should have been possible to construct two or three bridges, and if this had been done Herwarth would have been able to get his troops forward into an attacking position very much earlier.

By this time the atmosphere on the Roskosberg was one of deepening gloom. As the day wore on, the King's anxiety led him to ask Moltke what steps he had taken to cover a withdrawal if that should prove necessary. Moltke's firm response at this time was characteristic: 'Here there will be no retreat. Here we are fighting for the very existence of Prussia.'[18] Certainly his confidence had not wavered for a moment and he was shortly afterwards able to demonstrate it in a way that was entirely uncharacteristic in its extravagance – albeit quite understandable, given the tension around him that he had endured all day.

Soon after 1.00 pm an anxious Bismarck was staring through his telescope to the west, beyond the Austrian lines. There seemed to be movement along the ridge at Horenowes; and Austrian artillery now seemed to be trained towards it. Moltke looked also, and was able to see for the first time the leading units of the Second Army coming into action. Riding over to the King, he announced: 'The campaign is decided and in accordance with Your Majesty's desires.' The King, bewildered and anxious, retorted that he did not understand, and that they must concentrate on the present battle. Moltke, in a rare moment of grandiose pomposity, insisted on his point. 'No, the success is complete. Vienna lies at your Majesty's feet.'[19] He was, of course, quite right; but the battle had a long way to go before the point was proved.

On the other side of the valley, Benedek was again harbouring thoughts of a counterstroke. Riding over to his right, he found evidence that Mollinary and Thun were at last beginning to obey the order to retire. The heavy clouds of smoke that hung low over the battlefield obscured from him any sight of the advancing Second Army, and he seems to have been able to put it out of his mind for the present. No doubt he supposed that, dug in and facing the oncoming enemy, Mollinary and Thun would be able to hold the Chlum-Nedelist position; at any rate, considerably heartened, he returned to Lipa. There, he wondered out loud if now might be the time to launch the counterstroke. When members of his staff objected that it would be better to wait until the smoke cleared, he shrugged his shoulders and did not press the point.[20] Figuratively, if not literally, the smoke was to clear for Benedek very soon.

25

The Taking of Chlum

As the Crown Prince and Blumenthal trotted southwards past the long lines of marching infantry, it was becoming increasingly clear to them that their initial view as to the improbability of a significant engagement that day was wide of the mark. Ever since they had passed through Dobrowitz, at about 9.00 am, the sound of the guns had been growing louder, and in spite of the poor visibility clouds of smoke were apparent in the distance. By the time they reached Choteborek, at about 11.00 am, it had become obvious that a major battle was in progress, and that the line of advance being taken by the Second Army was going to bring it down on to Benedek's right flank. To Blumenthal, the need for haste was clear:

> We could plainly see and judge, by the lines of smoke, the whole extent of the battlefield. The right wing of the Austrians seemed to be resting on Horenowes. At first the Austrians seemed to be falling back, then again to be gaining ground. It was quite plain that the army of Prince Frederick Charles was engaged in a pitched battle with the whole of the Austrian forces. It was of the greatest importance for us now to engage them as quickly as possible, and by threatening their right flank and rear to make them relinquish their position.[1]

Looking south from Choteborek, one landmark stood out, as the Crown Prince noted in his diary: 'Half an hour straight in front of us, at the height of the village of Horenowes, stood an enormous and solitary tree. This I gave to the different corps as their main *pointe de vue*.'[2] It was in fact two tall lindens, either side of a crucifix, and it was to pass into German military legend as one of the most memorable images of the war. From Choteborek they could also see Austrian artillery in action against the First Army to the west. 'The firing indeed seemed to stop at times, only to begin again with renewed activity; and it seemed to be gaining ground in that direction.'[3] Although from Choteborek an extensive view opened out, the rising ground hampered a clear view of the battlefront, as the Official History noted:

> The view in front was limited by the ridge which extends from Horenowes to the Trotina. On its highest point two trees formed an object which was visible from very far off, and which had long since attracted the attention of both armies. From a distance of about 2½ miles, and in the dull atmosphere, these heights resembled a mighty rampart which seemed to bar all further progress.[4]

What was by no means clear at this time was the extent to which Benedek might have anticipated the advance of the Second Army, and posted strong units on his right flank to meet it. It was assumed that these lay out of sight beyond the Horenowes ridge, on which at present only one Austrian battery could be seen, close to the trees;

A photograph of the famous 'two lindens' near Horenowes, close to the memorial of the Austrian 57th Infantry Regiment. (Rogers)

Blumenthal's concern was the exposure of the infantry battalions of the Guard Corps as they descended the opposite slopes and marched towards the ridge. At least, however, most of the Crown Prince's units were closing up fast; news soon reached him of Mutius' arrival at Welchow, while in the centre Wnuck's cavalry brigade preceded the rest of the V Corps in its march towards Choteborek.

The Crown Prince and Blumenthal with their staff, and with Colonel Walker in attendance, stood on the heights at Choteborek, urging on the columns of infantry of the Guard Corps as it marched past them towards the Horenowes ridge, where the linden trees stood out as their clear objective. The men were in great spirits, waving their caps as they passed the Crown Prince. Walker was greatly impressed by their demeanour, and said so.[5] Then, looking southwards at the undefended heights and the valleys empty of Austrian troops, he turned to the Crown Prince and said with a flourish: 'Your Highness, God has given your enemy into your hand!'[6]

By 11.15 am the advanced guard, on the right of the Second Army's advance, had passed through Zizelowes and pushed on towards Wrchownitz and Zelkowitz. The strength of the Austrian artillery positions on the Horenowes ridge, and south of

Horenowes on the road to Maslowed, firing westwards towards Benatek and the Prussian troops on the northern skirts of the Swiepwald, was very obvious, and the batteries of the advanced guard were soon in action. It was evident, however, that the sooner the reserve artillery of the Guard Corps could take a hand, the better; the decision to bring Hohenlohe forward in advance of most of the 2nd Division was now to be amply vindicated.

Further east, an urgent message had gone to Mutius to bring his artillery into action as soon as possible. By 11.30 am four batteries from Zastrow's 11th Division, which had crossed the Trotinka stream by the bridge south east of Luzan, were in action on the heights north of Racitz, firing on the Horenowes ridge. Racitz itself was still held by the Austrians, and an infantry assault was necessary to clear the village. This was undertaken by Hanenfeldt's brigade from its position to the north; in fact its commander simultaneously received somewhat conflicting instructions from his corps commander and divisional commander to attack the wood on the Horicka Berg, and Racitz, respectively. Although he chose the latter objective it was of no great moment; the Horicka Berg was taken soon after by Prondzynski with the 12th Division. The latter had reached the heights of Habrina and St Wenzel with his leading troops by 11.00 am; seeing Austrian infantry in the woods on the Horicka Berg, he ordered the 23rd Regiment to attack at once, without waiting for the rest of the division to come up. The extended line held by Henriquez' Brigade, which reached all the way east and south east to the Lochenitz bridge over the Elbe, was naturally only weakly held; in the face of Prondzynski's attack Henriquez was obliged to pull back behind the Trotina. The

The Crown Prince points to the 'two lindens' whilst the Guard Corps file past him. (Voss)

advance of the 12th Division had however taken it too far to the right, and it threatened to impede that of the 11th Division, whose commander, Zastrow, asked Prondzynski to shift his line more to the east.

By noon the Second Army was, all along its line, coming up to what might have been a really effective defensive position for Benedek's right flank had he chosen to occupy it ; but, except at Horenowes and along the ridge immediately east of the village, it was barely held at all. By noon, the Prussians had forty eight guns in action against Horenowes. For once, they had the advantage of numbers, since they were opposed by only five Austrian batteries posted on the Horenowes ridge to cover the withdrawal of the corps of Mollinary and Thun to the Chlum-Nedelist line. The Prussian artillery superiority was substantially increased by 12.30 pm, when Hohenlohe was finally able to bring the Guard reserve artillery into action south of Jericek, and two of Prondzynski's batteries also joined in. The unequal contest did not last long, and the Austrian artillery soon fell back; Hohenlohe and his colleagues believed that it was because they had had for once the better of the exchange, but in fact it was by way of completion of the withdrawal of the 2nd and 4th Corps.[7] The last of the Austrian guns to disappear over the ridge was the battery that had first come into action by the two linden trees.

Meanwhile more and more of the infantry units of the Second Army were coming into action. On the extreme right, four companies were sent towards Benatek, in support of the hard pressed 7th Division, while to their left Alvensleben launched five companies in an assault on Horenowes. By 1.00 pm the village was in his hands. Beyond it, the last of the units of Thun's corps were hurriedly pulling back; they offered a tempting target to those Prussian cavalry units that were close up to the front of the advance, although the speed with which the Austrian infantry formed defensive formations, and the broken nature of the terrain, made it difficult for the Prussian horsemen to make much impact. Further east, Zastrow pushed on over the plateau north of Sendrasitz, meeting little opposition except at very long range. Similarly, to his left, Prondzynski's advance was held up only by artillery fire from Henriquez' brigade well beyond the Trotina. Once across the stream, his leading troops pushed on to Sendrasitz, easily dislodging the weak Austrian force found there, which retreated in part to Nedelist but principally to Lochenitz. On the far left of the advance of the 12th Division a handful of companies crossed the Trotina at the mill, and at the railway embankment; taking a considerable number of prisoners, who seem to have put up very little resistance, the Prussians moved south towards Lochenitz. Henriquez still held the bridge there; but his communication with the rest of the 2nd Corps was now seriously endangered by Prondzynski's advance to Sendrasitz and beyond.

The bulk of Thun's corps was still retreating, being echeloned back down the Maslowed-Nedelist road. Meanwhile the 4th Corps was also belatedly complying with Benedek's orders to occupy the Chlum-Nedelist position, in which it was supported by sixty four guns of Benedek's reserve artillery under the command of Lieutenant Colonel Hofbauer. Although therefore the adventurous morning of the 4th Corps and the 2nd Corps meant that the Austrian right was completely disarranged, there remained nevertheless a lot of troops and, more importantly, a lot of guns, for the Second Army to overcome. And, from north of the Horenowes ridge, the position and strength of their enemy was still unknown.

Map 37 – The Battle of Königgrätz, July 3, situation during the afternoon.

The key to the position was of course Chlum itself. It was held by the 46th Regiment, commanded by Colonel von Slawetzki, who had posted one battalion in the village, with another just to the east. His regiment, which belonged to Appiano's Brigade of the 3rd Corps, had been in Chlum since 9.00 am. There were also, however, a substantial number of units of the 4th Corps in position around the village, many having now occupied the prepared positions around Chlum that had previously been intended for them. In the first line were five batteries, together with the brigade of the Archduke Joseph, which was as yet entirely fresh, as well as the remains of three rifle battalions the had been severely hammered in the Swiepwald. In the second line, there stood part of Brandenstein's Brigade, with two more batteries and the remnants of two other regiments which had also been through the cauldron of the Swiepwald. Further east, Saffran had got his brigade into line, and along the ridge to Nedelist were Hofbauer's eight batteries. Properly handled, the forces immediately available for the defence of Chlum could yet give the advancing Prussians a lot of trouble.

The assault was to be undertaken by Hiller's division with the support of Hohenlohe's artillery. The latter was by now well to the front, and better placed to take part in the advance than Hiller's own divisional artillery. Having opened fire from his first position just south of Jericek, too far out of range to do much harm, Hohenlohe had moved forward to a point near Horenowes, where he engaged the enemy at a range of 1,900 yards. An Austrian battery trotted across his line of sight; all his batteries at once opened fire on such an inviting target but, to his dismay, with little effect:

> The shells fell in front or in rear, but not one hit the enemy. The battery escaped without losing a single man or horse, and disappeared behind the hill. I felt as angry as a hunter who has missed a royal stag.[8]

A little later he obtained some consolation when his guns broke up an infantry battalion coming out

The memorial to the unfortunate Austrian 46th Infantry Regiment, which was destroyed at Chlum. (Rogers)

of Horenowes. Encouraged by this, Hohenlohe rode on ahead of his batteries to find a suitable position for them to support the attack on Chlum. Passing through the site on which the Austrian batteries had stood, he was extremely surprised and disappointed to find little trace of any serious damage having been done by his gunfire to his Austrian opponents:

> Not one gun with broken wheels, not an atom of any limber box torn to pieces by its explosion, not a horse with shattered limbs, absolutely nothing marked the place where the enemy's artillery had stood.[9]

As the infantry pressed forward towards Chlum, Hohenlohe's batteries, which had been about 1,000 yards north east of Horenowes, came under fire at extreme range from the Austrian artillery concentrated either side of Chlum. Moving forward to a position close to the two linden trees, his guns returned fire, while he galloped ahead to Maslowed to find another position closer to the enemy gun line. On his way he encountered Major General von Colomier, the commander of the Guard artillery, who was up with the leading infantry, and who agreed that Hohenlohe should come forward. He found a position half way between Maslowed and Nedelist, and sent for his guns to come there. While waiting for them, as he stood watching them carefully descend the Horenowes ridge, he was bracketed by shells which burst first 100 yards short, and then 100 yards over his position. A third landed close by, and he guessed that his opposite number, recognising that Hohenlohe was marking the position for the advancing

Prince Kraft zu Hohenlohe-Ingelfingen in a photograph taken long after the war. Commander of the Guard Artillery in 1866, he was a talented gunner whose legacy has been a number of intelligent and important writings connected with warfare in the later 19th Century. (Hohenlohe-Ingelfingen)

Prussian artillery, was fixing the range accordingly. Hohenlohe ordered his guns up; as soon as they approached the selected position the whole Austrian gun line opened fire; at once he led his own guns 300 yards closer to the enemy under the hail of shell fire, through which they passed unscathed and evidently without the enemy realizing their advance, for the Austrian shells continued to land in the first position selected.[10] Hohenlohe replied, at a range of about 1,350 yards.

Preceded by skirmishers, the whole of the main body of Hiller's division was now advancing towards Chlum, taking as its objective the church steeple. Pushing forward under a rain of shells on either side of the village, the leading troops in places soon reached the first line of entrenchments. Their advance was largely obscured not only by the poor visibility, and the folds of the ground, but also by the fact that it was mostly through fields of corn standing five foot high. The Austrian gunners had remained in position in the earthworks right up to the last, and now paid the penalty; many of the batteries had left it too late to get their guns away before the Prussian infantry was upon them. One battery, cut off from the rest, tried to get away to the north but coming under close range infantry fire, lost six guns and then a seventh to the commander of the Guard Hussars, Lieutenant Colonel von Krosigk.

The defenders of Chlum had remained silent during the earlier part of the advance, partly because the forward movement had not been detected and partly apparently because the appearance of the Guards in their immediate front had been taken by the defenders, improbably, for Saxon infantry. It seems hardly likely that they were unaware that they might now be in the front line; the heavy artillery exchanges alone must have alerted them to the fact that sooner or later they must face an assault. And this they soon did; the troops on the right of the Prussian advance, the 1st Battalion of the 1st Foot Guards Regiment, wheeled to their right and, fanning out, enveloped the south and south eastern end of the village, while a company of riflemen swept into the northern end. Apart from a brisk fight in the centre of the village, in the course of which Slawetzki was killed, resistance was soon overcome, and the victorious Prussians pushed on to the western outskirts. There, they came under heavy fire from the 8th Horse Artillery Battery of the 3rd Corps under Captain von der Gröben at a range of 200 yards; but almost immediately, the Fusilier Battalion of the 1st Foot Guards Regiment, swinging around the south end of Chlum, bought a heavy fire to bear on the Austrian gunners. Within five minutes von der Gröben and another officer were killed and 52 men and 58 horses were killed or wounded, and only one gun escaped. The Austrian gunners had fought to the last; and to this day there stands at the scene a monument to what became known as the 'Battery of the Dead.' By 2.45 pm mopping up in the village was complete, and Hiller was in possession of the key to the whole Austrian position. It was, perhaps, the defining moment of the battle, although much fighting remained to be done.

While the victors of Chlum moved forward to positions to consolidate their hold on it, the left wing of Hiller's advance had reached the Austrian gun line between Chlum and Nedelist, and halted there by the captured guns; two companies pushed on alone towards Sweti. The advance on the left had been opposed only feebly by the demoralised infantry of Brandenstein's Brigade, which soon fell back, taking with them the wreckage of Poeckh's Brigade and the still-unblooded troops of the Archduke Joseph. As Hiller's men began to take up a position south of Chlum, the Austrian Reserve Cavalry Division

The Prussians assault Chlum. (Fontane)

under Prince Schleswig-Holstein deployed at the southern foot of the hill on which Chlum stands, with Schindlöcker's Brigade on the right and that of Prince Solms on the left. Schindlöcker launched a charge directed at the Prussian infantry that was in the act of debouching from the village in the direction of Rosberitz. The first line of cavalry comprised both lancers and cuirassiers; another cuirassier regiment followed. The Prussian infantry held their fire until the range was less than 200 yards; when they opened fire, the needle gun did such dreadful execution that some of the first line of cuirassiers turned away into the lancers while others wheeled round completely and plunged straight back into the advancing second line. In a few moments the brigade suffered some 200 casualties, and the survivors, in great disorder, fell back on the brigade of Prince Solms which had moved off to Langenhof.[11] Colonel von Kessel, who commanded the Guards battalions that had done the damage, now led his troops down the slope and into Rosberitz.

Schindlöcker's charge was not the only counter-attack launched by the Austrians; both from the direction of Lipa, and from Langenhof, uncoordinated assaults were made with the object of recovering the guns captured in the Prussian advance. Although initially successful in gaining ground, and in one case entering Chlum itself, these attacks broke down with heavy loss.

On the left of Hiller's main thrust into and through Chlum, a column led by Major von Erckert came down the hill to the east of Rosberitz, and caught part of the Austrian reserve artillery retreating on Wsestar. Erckert and his ADC rushed forward

The view of Chlum and its church from the position of the Austrian 'battery of the dead' commanded by Captain von der Groeben. (Rogers)

and personally captured two guns; all along the front, the advancing Guards seized guns on the point of driving off, and the impetus of their charge secured Rosberitz.

As soon as Chlum had fallen, Hohenlohe began to bring forward the reserve artillery again, in order to support Hiller's 1st Division, riding himself on ahead to a position on the hill south of the village, overlooking the main road to Königgrätz. There, he found in front of him an irresistible opportunity:

> I certainly had before me there a target which it would have been impossible to miss, whether my guns had been rifled or not. Two Austrian corps were drawn up on the plain, at the very foot of the hill; their lines were admirably dressed, and their white uniforms showed up plainly against the green of the cornfields waving in the wind. They were massed with their front towards Sadowa, and consequently showed me their right flank. These battalions, squadrons, and masses of artillery, concentrated in good order in their formation on parade, looked from above like the squares on a chess board.[12]

Hohenlohe paused for a moment to admire the spectacle; Colomier, however, who had joined him there, was more business-like. 'This is no time for admiring pretty things. Get your batteries up here!' he snapped.[13]

To Hiller's right, Alvensleben had fallen in behind the advance of the main body. At about 2.30 pm, having by now reached a position to the south of Maslowed, he came upon the remains of Fleischhacker's Brigade. This had been left, by mistake, in Cistowes, when the rest of Mollinary's corps began to pull back. The brigade's retreat now brought it directly towards Hiller's rear as he struggled to take Chlum. Led by a hussar regiment, it first encountered two companies of pioneers under Captain von Adler, marching on Chlum, and then some of Hohenlohe's batteries as they moved forward to their new positions there. The latter swiftly wheeled to their right, opening fire at short range and causing heavy casualties among the hussars, who at first tried unsuccessfully to retreat through Chlum and failing in this, next turned north towards Maslowed, followed by a battery and some infantry. The rest of Fleischhacker's Brigade meanwhile engaged Alvensleben's advanced guard. Coming under heavy rifle fire, the Austrian cavalry then abandoned two guns and wheeled off towards Sendrasitz, a course which brought them full tilt upon the Crown Prince and his staff, who were themselves obliged to wheel round and fall back on the 2nd Guard Division as it made its way forward. The Austrian hussars were soon however dispersed by a squadron of the Prussian Guard Hussar Regiment, and most of them taken prisoner, a fate which soon overtook the accompanying infantry and the remains of the battery. Alvensleben soon put the rest of Fleischhacker's troops to flight and would have followed up their retreat to the west of Chlum when Hiller rode up at 2.45 pm and ordered Alvensleben to break off the pursuit; his troops were needed in Chlum itself.

East of the Guard Corps, Mutius had also been making swift progress. After the 11th Division had taken Sendrasitz, his leading units pressed on towards Nedelist, more or less in line with Hiller's advance. In spite of coming under fire from the Austrian reserve artillery, the 2nd Battalion of the 50th Regiment, under Major von Berken, stormed Nedelist, evidently taking its occupiers entirely by surprise; many fled, and the remainder were taken prisoner. To the west of Nedelist, two companies of the battalion, advancing unobserved through the high corn, fell on and captured a battery of Austrian artillery.

The capture of Nedelist put paid to any further chance the Austrians might have had to hold any part of the line originally earmarked for the right flank, and intended to cover Benedek against the advance of the Crown Prince. The advance of the leading units of the VI Corps had been so rapid, however, that Berken now had to wait for the rest of Hanenfeldt's brigade to catch up. Meanwhile, Henriquez' Brigade, south of Trotina had, in addition to the galling fire of the advancing Prussians, to endure a fresh and unexpected danger. A Prussian shell 'had fallen amongst a number of beehives, and the insects fell upon the troops, who could scarcely protect themselves from their fierce attack.'[14] By 3.00 pm Hanenfeldt's 21st Brigade had come up, followed closely by Hoffmann's 22nd Brigade and the divisional artillery, putting Zastrow in a position to resume his advance deep into the flank of the Austrian army. Meanwhile, on Zastrow's left, Prondzynski had also been pushing forward, although his troops had also been advancing so quickly that they had become very strung out. By 3.00 pm his leading companies had reached Lochenitz, and made a first, though unsuccessful, attack on that village. It was time for the Second Army to draw breath after its headlong advance; thus far it had been successful all along the line, but there was still a lot of fighting to do before the day was over.

26

The Advance of the Army of the Elbe

In the First Army's front the long drawn out, and very unequal artillery duel continued and the lack of progress, and the mounting losses had done nothing to calm the increasingly frayed nerves on the Roskosberg. In spite of the indications of the advance of the Second Army, Frederick Charles was particularly frustrated by his inability to take any effective action against the dominant Austrian artillery:

> The batteries which had been brought over the Bistritz, with both trouble and loss, found their range very much limited by patches of wood. Just those positions from which the Austrian artillery did the most harm, were the most difficult to get at, so for instance, that of the powerful battery in front of Lipa, which poured an incessant shower of shrapnel and shells, not only in the Sadowa wood, but also on the reserves which stood behind it.[1]

Finally, Frederick Charles could bear it no longer, and ordered Manstein to launch an assault to clear the Austrian artillery from the slope. This was, however, precisely the kind of intemperate response that Moltke was determined to avoid; to commit Manstein at this stage would not only be to use up the First Army's reserve, but to replicate the kind of mistake the Austrians had made in the Swiepwald. He understood that the

The gun lines of the Prussian 2nd Corps near the Bistritz. (*Illustrirte Kriegs-Chronik*)

longer the struggle in the centre continued, the more certain it was that the Austrian defeat would be decisive. In the Official History, Frederick Charles' order to Manstein is explained by his 'supposing that the heads of the Second Army to be now sufficiently near'; in his letter next day to his wife Moltke commented on the impatience at the headquarters of the First Army to take action against the Austrian guns at Lipa:

> It was not in our interest to break through here at any cost, and I countermanded the orders which had already been issued to General Manstein to take the battery in question by storm. The advance of the two wings must inevitably force the evacuation.[2]

The problems caused by the Lipa batteries had continued throughout the morning; attempts to build up sufficient artillery strength north of the main road had resulted in substantial losses among the Prussian guns posted there, and one battery had been withdrawn. The location of some of the batteries was also far from ideal: 'The position of the batteries in front of Cistowes was very much cramped by the low meadows on their right flank, into which they could not descend without losing all view of the surrounding country.'[3] And they were sufficiently close to the infantry engagements in and around the Swiepwald to be threatened by any Austrian advance. Major General Schwartz, the commander of the First Army's reserve artillery, was obliged to collect up whatever troops he could find to provide an infantry screen for his batteries, including those separated from their regiment, and a detachment of pioneers. He also pressed into service as a support for his gunners a couple of squadrons of uhlans that happened to be close by.

South of the Holawald, the Prussian artillery had also been reinforced to a total of sixty guns, although this was still less than half the number of Austrian guns opposed to them. The efforts to strengthen the gun line here had produced a chaotic command situation:

> A want of unity in the direction of the artillery was painfully evident on this part of the field ... the eleven batteries there present belonged to five different artillery divisions, some of them to the divisional artillery and some to the reserve.[4]

Two batteries were pulled back because a report circulated that the infantry were pulling out of Unter-Dohalitz; others retired because they had exhausted their ammunition or were too exposed to the fire of the Austrian batteries from the slopes above them. The problem was compounded by the scarcity of crossings over the Bistritz, most of which were in any case blocked by infantry as a result of the ill-judged decision of Frederick Charles to bring the divisions of Manstein and Werder over the river.

The infantry in and around the Holawald were no better off. As a result of the increasing casualties in the wood, reinforcements were brought in to replace some units which were pulled out to regroup. Four battalions from the 4th Division were moved into the wood. One, in a move which was repeated several times during the struggle here, tried to move forward beyond the edge of the wood on its own initiative, but was driven back again, after beating off two charges of Austrian cavalry. Along the side of the main road a company of the 61st Regiment pushed forward to occupy an Austrian camp of

The distinctive monument to Knebel's Austrian brigade at Dohalitz. (Rogers)

huts, from which position their rifle fire caused casualties to the nearest Austrian battery. A charge by two squadrons of Austrian lancers in an attempt to dislodge them was beaten off with heavy loss; but efforts to consolidate the advance failed, and although they hung on to the camp, all the other Prussian infantry units that had come up in support were pushed back to the Holawald.

However, the most serious threat to Prussian occupation of the Holawald developed out of an Austrian attack that was not intended. Archduke Ernest had, at about 1.00 pm, come to the conclusion that the time had arrived for a counterstroke, and he sent off a courier to Benedek to ask permission to launch an assault. This was refused; but Kirschberg's Brigade had already been put in motion, and one regiment attacked Ober Dohalitz, while about two and a half battalions moved on the corner of the wood at the main road. The attack broke down with heavy loss, albeit on both sides; the Prussian defenders of the wood at this point comprised five different regiments all hopelessly mingled together. By a curious irony, in the fierce fighting along the edge of the wood, the commanders of both the Austrian 49th Regiment and the Prussian 49th Regiment were killed within a few yards of each other.

Not one Austrian soldier had penetrated the wood, but Schmidt, the commander of the II Corps, was sufficiently unnerved by these events to take action on his own initiative for which he was later severely criticized:

> The 4th Division had lost so many men in the wood that General von Schmidt thought it necessary to extricate it from its position. Without further orders he drew the five battalions nearest at hand out of the wood towards the high road … As soon as the leading battalions came into the open country they suffered severely from the fire of the Austrian batteries, and General Schmidt ordered them to fall back behind the 9th Regiment – a command that was most unwillingly executed by both officers and men.[5]

Beyond the Holawald, Werder had been able to minimize casualties in the 3rd Division by forbidding any advance of any kind. Somewhat more safely ensconced in the buildings which they had occupied than the troops in the Holawald, his units were ordered to take the maximum advantage of the shelter they had. They stayed put, strengthening the defences of the villages in their position, and awaited further orders. As a result, Werder's division suffered far fewer casualties than those on his left.[6] It was further to the south, in the front of the Army of the Elbe, that events were beginning to take a decisive shape. This was, of course, what Moltke had been waiting for, with barely concealed impatience. Indeed, the only written order he dispatched during the course of the day was addressed to Herwarth in an effort to get things moving on the right flank. Issued at 1.45 pm, it read:

> Crown Prince at Zizelowes; retreat of the Austrians to Josephstadt cut off. It is of the utmost importance that General von Herwarth should advance on the opposite wing, whilst the centre of the Austrians still holds out.[7]

There is no record of the time this message actually reached Herwarth; as it was, as the Official History points out, the advance of the Army of the Elbe was already well under way at the time of its issue, and the situation was about to undergo a rapid change.

The Saxon Crown Prince's counter-attack had pushed the Prussians almost back to the Lubno-Hradek ridge, and he now determined to capitalise on this success by a major offensive. His intention was to launch the Saxon Life Brigade, supported by the 2nd Saxon Brigade, in a frontal attack, using the Austrian 8th Corps to cover his left. After the attack had begun he planned to use his cavalry to swing around the Prussian right, thereby rolling it up. His advance began shortly before 2.00 pm, and the 2nd Brigade was soon able to come up on the left of the Life Brigade, pushing forward to Neu Prim

Map 38 – Panoramic sketch of the battlefield of Königgrätz, looking south from between Tresowitz and Stresetitz at the Austrian left, and the Saxon positions.

and the Hradek wood. On their left, the brigades of Schulz and Wöber from the 8th Corps had begun to deploy.

Unluckily for Crown Prince Albert, Herwarth's own plans for an offensive matured simultaneously. Canstein's advance had been held up by the delayed arrival of the 29th Brigade (von Stuckradt). The 30th Brigade (Glasenapp) was already in place west of a hill in the middle of Stezirek Wood, in a position on the flank of the Austrian advance. Stuckradt finally arrived with his leading troops at Neu Prim at about 1.30 pm with the rest of his force strung out in line of march from Hradek. Canstein waited no longer, and ordered the advance to begin. The advance of Schulz's Brigade on the Austrian left had been led by the 74th Regiment (Nobili) and this was at first successful in pushing back one battalion of the Prussian 56th Regiment, which was skirmishing in its front at Ober Prim, into Stezirek Wood. Unknown to the Austrians, however, Colonel von Gayl's 68th Regiment had moved up through Stezirek Wood; as the Austrians crossed an open space in the wood, they came within sight of Gayl's troops who, after a brief exchange of fire, charged them and drove them out of the wood: 'The centre of the Austrian line, which extended through Ober-Prim to Neu-Prim, was broken through. This vigorous charge produced indescribable confusion in the ranks of the enemy.'[8] The brigades of both Schulz and Wöber disintegrated; those troops to the east of Gayl's attack retreated rapidly to Ober-Prim, while those to the west, trying to retreat northwards, were taken in flank by Stuckradt's advance on Neu Prim.

The mob of fugitives swept into the flank of the unfortunate Saxon 2nd Brigade which was engaged in its advance to Hradek:

A view towards Stezirek Wood, from which the Prussian infantry erupted and threw the Austrian and Saxon troops into disorder. The memorial is to the Austrian 74th Infantry Regiment which lost heavily on this spot. (Rogers)

> The fleeing troops hit the Saxons like a thunderbolt, and the struggling mass rolled westwards, right into the guns of the Prussian 29th Brigade. This completed the collapse of Austrian morale, and a rout might well have followed had it not been for the behaviour of the Saxons.[9]

The Saxon 2nd Brigade's attempt to cover its flank by deploying its 6th Battalion was wrecked by the onslaught which swept away both that unit and the 8th Battalion; it was only the steadiness of the 5th Battalion and the 2nd Rifle Battalion, which had been in the second line of the 2nd Brigade's advance, that enabled it to retreat towards Nieder Prim. The advance of the Life Brigade was also aborted in the face of this débacle, and both brigades continued their retirement to a position behind the Problus hill.

The unexpectedly successful outcome of Canstein's assault had been achieved by the infantry alone. The cavalry was well back, and although by 1.00 pm Herwarth's artillery commander, Colonel von Rozynski, had built up a total of 66 guns on Lubno hill, the range was too great for the artillery to take any part in the fighting at close quarters in front of Nieder Prim. Canstein, thus unsupported, had only got seven battalions in hand, but it was obvious to him that he should follow up the advantage he had gained without delay. Glasenapp was ordered to attack Ober Prim at once; Stuckradt was to advance on Nieder Prim with whatever troops he could collect of his brigade, which was still well strung out.

In the broken and wooded terrain, the units of the 30th Brigade had become to some extent intermingled, but Glasenapp set off at once to attack Ober Prim from the west with the 68th Regiment and some detachments of the 40th and 65th Regiments

Disorder strikes the Crown Prince of Saxony's efforts to launch a counter-attack at Prim. (*Illustrirte Kriegs-Chronik*)

under Colonel Zimmerman, and from the woods to the south with two battalions of the 28th Regiment. The Austrians, and particularly the regiment of Colonel von Gerstner, put up a brave struggle and even after Glasenapp had taken the village attempted a counter-attack; but they were driven back with heavy loss, and the remaining defenders retreated, some to Problus and some to the Briza Wood. Casualties on both sides had been high, and included General Schulz, the commander of the Austrian brigade upon whom Canstein's original advance had fallen, who was killed as his troops retreated under heavy Prussian fire.

The loss of Ober Prim posed a severe threat to Crown Prince Albert's position at Problus, and he took swift action to shore up his flank. His 1st Saxon Brigade was dispatched to hold the southern edge of the wood between Problus and Charbusitz, while two smoothbore batteries and some horse artillery took up a post on the southern slope of the hill to the east of Nieder Prim. Later reinforced by two more batteries, the Saxon artillery checked Canstein's advance for long enough to enable the Saxon infantry to escape. For the moment the Prussians were unable effectively to respond to the Saxon bombardment, and Ober Prim was soon in flames, forcing Glasenapp's infantry to abandon the village for a while.

Stuckradt had not yet been able to develop greater strength with the 20th Brigade, but pressing forward with the troops immediately under his control, he harried the retreating Saxon infantry back to Nieder Prim, and was soon in touch with Zimmerman's troops west of Ober Prim. As the Prussian infantry surged forward, Rozynski now brought forward his guns to a position about two thousand yards from Nieder Prim, and for the first time in this part of the battle the Prussian artillery began to shoot with great effect; and under the cover of their heavy fire, the 65th Regiment and Zimmerman's troops stormed into the village. The Saxons fell back on Problus.

In front of that village Münster's 14th Division was now preparing to advance. It was only able to complete its deployment behind Lubno hill by 1.30 pm, as a result of the delays at the Nechanitz bridge. When it finally moved off soon after this, the advance was led by Schwarzkoppen's 27th Brigade to the left; on the right Hiller's 28th Brigade followed about half a mile in rear. By 2.30 pm the division was in position to assault Problus, which was still held by the Saxons, and which was their last remaining strong point. To Crown Prince Albert, however, it was evident that it was not a position he dare hold on to for very much longer. From his headquarters position on the hill close to Problus he could see all too clearly that events at Chlum, on the Austrian right, made a retreat of the whole army unavoidable. Immediately to the north of his position Gablenz was obviously making preparations to fall back, while at the far end of the battle line, Canstein's advance threatened his own line of retreat. The Saxons had fought bravely and well, but it was obviously time to go.

Münster's troops had had little combat experience so far, except briefly at Münchengrätz. They were now coming into action in conditions which were far from ideal:

> The troops of the division had marched 13½ miles the preceding night, over very heavy roads and through standing corn; they had been for 12 hours under arms and, like the rest of the army, had been without any provisions whatever.[10]

Nevertheless they moved forward in fine style, with the regimental bands playing under a hail of fire within about two hundred and fifty yards of the enemy positions. It was an impressive spectacle. Fritz Hoenig, with the 28th Brigade, recorded the view that greeted the advancing Prussians as they came over the Popowitz ridge:

> Just as if the curtain had gone up in a theatre, now a stage lay suddenly before our eyes. And what a stage! The whole of the enemy's front was, in the true sense of the word, veiled in flames and smoke, from Prim over Problus, Stresetitz to Lipa and Chlum. Between Prim and Problus one perceived a connected array of artillery, and on this side, as far as the view ranged, there were skirmishers and columns advancing, colours flying, music playing ... I have never since seen anything which approached this battle-piece in effect on the imagination.[11]

Schwarzkoppen's brigade enjoyed the cover of the woods east of Popowitz for a while, but as they emerged they were hit in front by the batteries at Problus and in their flank by a battery posted east of Tresowitz. Undaunted by the gaps torn in their ranks by the enemy artillery fire, the infantry pushed on and soon their skirmishers were within rifle range of the Saxon batteries, which fell back over the ridge, leaving the defence of the Problus position to the Saxon infantry, as the Official History recorded: 'A new and obstinate struggle ensued in each farm-yard, each step in advance cost heavy sacrifices, and the enemy had to be driven from position to position until the further side of the village was reached.'[12]

Problus had been taken by the 27th Brigade by 3.00 pm, and the line of advance of Hiller's 28th Brigade was changed, switching to the right to pass between Problus and Nieder Prim. The Saxon artillery having fallen back by the time it reached the steepest part of the height, the brigade suffered much fewer casualties than Schwarzkoppen's men. A brief counter-charge by two Saxon battalions was beaten back, and the brigade pressed forward, urged on by its divisional commander. It was, in effect, the only unit of the Army of the Elbe sufficiently fresh, and far enough forward, to exploit the victory gained. Canstein's division was strung out and disorganised by its success, while Etzel's 16th Division and the cavalry, which would have been of crucial value at this stage of affairs, did not even start to cross at Nechanitz until 2.00 pm.

Although, therefore, Herwarth had decisively won his battle, the Army of the Elbe was not in a position to deliver the *coup de grâce* to the Austrian army. The main road to Königgrätz was temptingly close; but, although defeated, the Saxon Crown Prince had put up enough of a fight to ensure that Herwarth was not in a position to cut off Benedek's only effective line of retreat.

27

Rosberitz

On the heights of Lipa, Benedek remained in ignorance of the extent to which his army was threatened by the taking of Chlum. Soon after 2.30 pm, Colonel Neuber of his staff, who had been dispatched on a mission to Edelsheim on the extreme left of the Austrian position, rode to Chlum to pick up a fresh horse. Horrified by the discovery that it was in Prussian hands, he rode back to headquarters, and asked Benedek, who was dictating an order, if he might speak to him in private. 'We have no secrets here,' was Benedek's airy reply. 'Then I have to inform you that the Prussians are in Chlum.' 'Don't talk such nonsense!' snapped Benedek, repeating emphatically 'Plauschen's nicht!' But Neuber insisted; Benedek sent him off on his original assignment to Edelsheim and, still doubting that it could be true, he at first asked Baumgarten to check Neuber's report and then decided himself to go and assess the situation at first hand.[1]

He rode off at once with his staff towards Chlum, passing in front of the Austrian troops that had retreated from the village. He was soon left in no doubt as to just how bad things were. *The Times* correspondent accompanying Austrian headquarters recorded next day the reception that Benedek encountered:

> More quickly than I can fairly tell Prince Esterhazy was down, his horse shot under him; Count Grünne was wounded, it is said, mortally; Baron Henikstein's English

Austrian troops assemble for the efforts to retake Chlum and Rosberitz. (Fontane)

Archduke Ernst, commander of the Austrian 3rd Corps. (Voss)

> mare was severely wounded, and there were many casualties among the men ... The key of the position was in the hands of the enemy, and consternation was on every face. No one was cooler than Benedek himself as, attended by all who caught sight of him, he rode off to bring up some of the reserves and to retake the position.[2]

It was the kind of situation to bring out the best in Benedek, and he immediately rode forward and placed himself at the head of the 52nd Regiment and led it in an assault on Chlum, reaching the edge of the village. This was as far as it could get, however, and having suffered heavy casualties, the 52nd fell back again. Benedek could see clearly the threat to the Sadowa-Königgrätz road; Chlum must be retaken, or the whole army faced disaster. There was no choice now but to commit his reserves, carefully husbanded for what he had hoped would be the winning counterstroke, in an effort to restore the situation. Accordingly, he directed Ramming, conveniently at hand as Hohenlohe had seen when looking down from the heights of Chlum, to recapture the village with his 6th Corps.

The taking of Chlum was in particular a serious threat to the rear of the 3rd Corps. Its situation had been further threatened by the capture, at about 3.15 pm, of the Lipa Wood by a concentric assault of various units of the Guard Corps. In the course of this fighting the Austrians sustained heavy losses, and retreated towards Lipa and Langenhof, leaving some 1,600 prisoners in Prussian hands. Colonel Benedek (who was no relation to the commander in chief), whose brigade was principally involved, was wounded; the Prussian loss on the other hand was by no means great. The 3rd Corps did however, have some unused infantry still available; Kirschberg's Brigade had of course been involved in the abortive attack on the Holawald, while Appiano's battered troops were endeavoring to regroup on the southern slopes of the Chlum heights. But the brigades of Abele and

Prohaska were still fresh, and the latter was now launched in an immediate offensive to retake Lipa wood and in particular the hill to the west of Chlum. Led by Colonel von Catty, the brigade advanced across the main road and up the hill in close columns. It was met by a concentrated hail of fire at close range from the needle guns in its front and also from its flank at Rosberitz. The Prussians held their fire until the last moment with dramatic effect on the tightly bunched infantry:

> When the Austrian masses were within 100 paces, they first delivered two volleys and then commenced a file-fire of most extraordinary effect. The enemy halted for a moment and then fell back behind the high road, suffering enormous losses from the Prussian fire during his retreat.[3]

For Benedek the key, not to victory but to survival, was Rosberitz. Unless he could retake this village, he could not get under way any proper counter-offensive to recapture Chlum, and this was essential to him. Rosberitz was now held by troops from several units, totalling the equivalent of only three battalions; if the Austrians moved quickly enough, before the village was reinforced and before the advance of the VI Corps came down through Sweti, there was every chance of a successful counter-attack. From the moment it had fallen to the Prussians Rosberitz had come under heavy artillery fire, while the front line of Austrian riflemen was only the other side of the main road which separated them from the south end of the village.

By 3.30 pm dense masses of Austrian infantry could be seen concentrating for an assault on Rosberitz; and it was at this time that Hohenlohe's artillery came up to him on the heights of Chlum. Colomier ordered him to post his batteries in the ravine immediately to the south of Chlum, and it was from this position that Hohenlohe was able to open fire on the troops of the 6th Corps massing from the assault. 'The densely

The Prussian 2nd Foot Guards at Rosberitz. (Fontane)

crowded columns of the Austrian infantry afforded a mark for the aim of the rifled cannon which could not be missed, and the losses at this spot increased to an enormous extent.[4] Hohenlohe was told later by a friend of his, Major Erckert, who commanded the three companies that held the south end of Rosberitz, and who lay wounded and taken for dead in front of Rosberitz, of the effect of the Prussian artillery fire:

> The Austrian battalions, who were passing over his body as they advanced to the attack of Rosberitz, stopped short in their rush at the first shot fired from the hill of Chlum; they were seized with fear, and seemed held fast to the spot by a magic force.[5]

But the success of the Prussian artillery was not without cost; the Prussian gunners suffered themselves from the ferocious counter battery fire of over 100 Austrian guns.

The first Austrian assaults on Rosberitz, each about two or three battalions strong, had been directed at the western side of the village, and all had been beaten off by the concentric fire of the needle guns in the outskirts. Ramming now changed his tactics, switching his attack to the southern end of Rosberitz, putting in an assault in three columns from the brigades of Jonak and Rosenzweig there, and simultaneously launching a compact mass of six battalions against the western side of the village. It was during this assault that Erckert fell; in spite of the dreadful losses inflicted on the advancing Austrians, the huge disparity of numbers forced the Prussians back, and a savage house-to-house combat ensued. Paul von Hindenburg was a second lieutenant

The view from Rosberitz up the slopes to Chlum that faced the Austrian infantry as they prepared to try to retake the key to Benedek's positions. Chlum and its church spire can be seen at the top right of the photograph. (Rogers)

Austrian infantry from 1st Corps ascend 'the path of the dead' during their efforts to retake Chlum. (Fontane)

in the 3rd Regiment of Foot Guards; his half battalion arrived in Rosberitz in time to reinforce its hard pressed defenders:

> Fearful as was the effect of fire from our needle guns, as each wave collapsed a fresh one came to take its place. Murderous hand-to-hand fighting took place in the streets between the thatched cottages on fire. All idea of fighting in regular units was lost. Everyone shot and stabbed at random to the best of his ability.[6]

The Austrian pressure was irresistible, however, and gradually the Prussians were forced back out of the village, Hindenburg and his men escaping at the last minute under cover of a barrier of flame and thick smoke from a burning roof which collapsed into the street. The retreating Prussians fell back up the slope towards the eastern side of Chlum. At the entrance to the ravine in which Hohenlohe's batteries stood, Lieutenant Colonel von Waldersee checked the retreat 'by planting the flag of his battalion in the ground, and inspiring his men with the unanimous determination not to give way another step.'[7] He collected around a nucleus of his own men and those of other units as they came back up the hill, exhausted and smoke begrimed, and there formed a defence line to await the next assault.

The Austrians halted at the northern end of Rosberitz to regroup. Then, with horns blaring and the regimental bands playing, they came forward in dense columns. They were received by heavy artillery fire both in front and on their flank, and sustained heavy casualties both from the grapeshot of the Prussian guns and from the needle guns of the skirmishers lying in the ravine at a range of no more than one hundred yards. The way up to Chlum became known as the 'Path of the Dead.' The Austrian advance was

General Friedrich Wilhelm Hiller von Gärtringen, commander of the 1st Prussian Guard Division, killed at the height of the fighting for Chlum on July 3. (Rogers)

halted; they tried to return the fire of the Prussians but when three companies of the Guards sprang forward and charged them, the Austrian infantry broke and fled. For the moment they remained in position at the north end of Rosberitz, and no further attempt was made to advance from there.

On the left of Ramming's advance, however, repeated efforts were made to reach the south end of Chlum. Although the Prussian infantry had been able to bring up fresh supplies of ammunition, Hohenlohe's gunners had expended nearly all theirs and, because of the risk of becoming immobilized by the high rate of casualties among the artillery horses, the order was given at 4.30 pm for the reserve artillery to withdraw. Hohenlohe fell back to the height running from the northern end of Chlum toward Nedelist. But the loss of his support for the defenders of Chlum was to be made good by the arrival, at last, of the leading troops of Bonin's I Corps. It was just as well; although a messenger from Mutius had arrived with the news that VI Corps was regrouping at Nedelist and a request to know where they could be of most help, it was clear that it would be some time before an advance on Rosberitz, for which Hiller asked, could have an impact.

Hiller was at the south-western end of Chlum, watching anxiously as wave after wave of Austrian infantry came up the hill only to be driven back by the intensity of the fire of the needle guns which greeted them. He was accordingly delighted when Major von Sommerfeld, commanding the leading battalion of the I Corps, rode up to him with the news that the rest of the advanced guard of the corps was close behind. 'Now everything will be all right,' cried Hiller; but at that moment he was hit by a shell splinter and slipped from his saddle, and died while be was being carried to the rear. At Waterloo, his father had commanded a Prussian brigade which stormed Plancenoit at the critical

General Leopold Count Gondrecourt, commander of the Austrian 1st Corps at Königgrätz. (Lukeš)

moment of the Prussian advance; by his own success in taking and holding Chlum he had played an even more decisive role in ensuring Prussian victory at Königgrätz.[8]

Sommerfeld wasted no time in throwing forward his rifle companies as they came up in reinforcement of the widely extended positions of Hiller's division along the brow of the Chlum hill:

> The ten fresh companies that the I Corps had brought into action, and the detachments of the Guards which remained in their position, now swept the whole face of the hill towards Rosberitz with so effective a fire that the Austrian columns westward of this village were also obliged to desist from all further attempts to advance.[9]

Before this, one final assault up the hill was made, only to be repulsed with further heavy loss; and it appeared to Lieutenant General von Grossmann, the commander of the 1st Division who had now appeared at Chlum and taken over command there, that it was now opportune to make an attempt to clear the Austrians out of Rosberitz. This task he gave to von Pape, commanding the 1st Brigade, supported by such detachments of the Guards as were immediately available.

At the same time Hoffmann with the 22nd Brigade from the VI Corps was moving up in response to Hiller's earlier request for support, and his right wing was approaching Rosberitz from the north east, while the rest of his brigade moved on Wsestar. As Pape led the advanced guard down the slope towards Rosberitz, 'they saw beyond the high-road a considerable body of cavalry, coming up at a rapid pace from the direction of Sadowa.'[10] It was Count von der Groeben with the 12th Hussars, leading the cavalry of

'The path of the dead' snakes up the slope to Chlum. This area witnessed unimaginable slaughter on July 3, one Prussian officer commenting about the desperate Austrian efforts to retake Chlum, "Crazy formations, crazier courage". (Rogers)

the First Army in pursuit of the retreating Austrians. The battle was beginning to enter its final phase.

To the east of Pape and the troops massing for the assault on Rosberitz, Mutius had been pushing forward on the Austrian right flank. Sooner rather than later this advance, if it was not checked, must begin to threaten the Austrian line of retreat, and the leading units of the 11th Division found themselves harassed by a regiment of Austrian hussars. The cavalry were however, soon beaten off, and Mutius brought up the combined Cavalry Brigade under Lieutenant Colonel von Wickmann to follow them up. The brigade was led by the 2nd Silesian Hussars followed by the 2nd Silesian Dragoons:

> In their eagerness to meet the enemy as soon as possible, the hussars omitted to throw out *éclaireurs* in their front, and when they were already in a gallop they unexpectedly came upon a deep gully, which had been hidden from view in the high corn.[11]

The result was total chaos. Some of the hussars pulled up in time but many went down into the gully, and only a few were able to scramble up the other side. Seeing their opportunity the Austrian Palffy Hussars charged, and caused considerable casualties before falling back to the bridges of the Elbe, taking the same direction as the main body of Thun's 2nd Corps, which was now in headlong retreat to Lochenitz and Predmeritz

General Louis von Mutius, commander of the Prussian 6th Corps during 1866. Mutius died of cholera in Moravia in August 1866. (Rogers)

Chlum looms into view at the top of 'the path of the dead'. Remarkably, some Austrian troops managed to penetrate into the outskirts. Meanwhile thousands of their comrades lay dead or wounded in this area, whilst others cowered for cover in the shelter the ravine offered. (Rogers)

in order to get to the other side of the Elbe, having made no significant effort to hold Nedelist or later to retake it from Zastrow's 11th Division.

Henriquez, whose brigade had alone been in a position to put up effective resistance to the advance of the VI Corps, was now engaged in an attempt to hold Lochenitz long enough to keep the Elbe bridges open. A sharp struggle ensued in the streets of the village as Prondzynski attacked it with units of the 22nd and 23rd Regiments, which soon overcame the Austrian defenders and drove them out. This enabled Prondzynski to shut off the escape route over the Lochenitz bridge, and removed any danger to the left flank of Mutius' southward advance.

Mutius, with no immediate opposition in his front, now decided to wheel to his right to support the hard-pressed defenders of Chlum, and ordered Zastrow to move on Rosberitz, Wsestar and Sweti. Prondzynski was to close up on Zastrow, to cover the left flank, and he accordingly pulled back the troops which had taken Lochenitz to enable him to shift to his left. One company of infantry remained to hold the Lochenitz bridge; another pushed on to take and hold the bridge at Predmeritz. Zastrow deployed Hoffmann's brigade in front of Rosberitz, facing south-west, while Hanenfeldt moved south on Wsestar and Sweti. By 3.45 pm he was in a position to advance, coming under heavy fire from the Austrian reserve artillery in front of Sweti, which was reinforced by some of Ramming's artillery. Try as they might, the Prussian gunners were unable to gain fire superiority, and Zastrow's men took heavy casualties as they pressed forward undaunted towards Sweti. As they came forward the Austrian gunners, and their supporting infantry, hurriedly pulled back, and Hanenfeldt's brigade surged forward to take the village which fell soon after 4.15 pm. Hoffmann meanwhile moved forward to Rosberitz, in time to support Pape's attack on the village from the direction of Chlum.

At the same time, on the far side of the battlefield, the Army of the Elbe, having taken the Problus heights, still faced stiff opposition from the Saxons, whose 1st Brigade held the Briza wood to the east of Problus, and from the cover of which they poured a heavy fire on Hiller's 28th Brigade. Without cover, Hiller could see that his troops were dangerously exposed, and he resolved to take the wood at once. He ordered the second and third lines of his brigade to close up; just as they were ready to attack, a false alarm of cavalry caused the Prussian infantry to form square, bringing the advance for the moment to a halt.[12] Once the situation had been resolved, Hiller rode to the front of his brigade:

> As he reached the line of skirmishers, he dashed forward, holding up his sword .... The whole line rose and rushed resolutely on, while the drums beat. There was no end to the shouting of 'Hurrah', and the assault ensued almost simultaneously at all points.[13]

Notwithstanding their heavy field equipment, the infantry covered the two hundred metres to the abattis at the edge of the wood without a pause, and were soon over it and into the dense wood itself. For some reason which no one could understand there was all along the Saxon front 'a beckoning with handkerchiefs which gave a general impression that the adversary desired to yield,' which was very far from the case.[14] The Saxons fought resolutely and, with the benefit of the thick undergrowth to retard their attackers, gave ground only slowly. Finally, however, the wood was cleared, and Hiller's leading troops paused at the north-eastern edge of the wood beyond Bor. The success had been dearly bought; the brigade had suffered 200 casualties in killed and wounded, although the Saxons probably suffered as much, leaving in addition over 200 prisoners in Hiller's hands.

While Hiller had been breaking into the western edge of the wood, units of the 15th Division had attacked it from the south. The 28th Regiment, which had been posted on the eastern side of Ober Prim, had come under fire from an Austrian battery near Charbusitz and had moved out of the burning village to seek cover in a copse of fir trees to the east. Having taken the copse, the leading battalion pursued its defenders into the Briza wood while another battalion went into the south-western edge of the wood. The 28th Regiment met with little resistance and soon reached the north-eastern edge to link up with Hiller's troops there.

By now, Crown Prince Albert's preparations for a retreat were well advanced. He held a temporary line on the heights between Rosnitz and the Briza wood for long enough to pick up the last of his retreating battalions, and then began to fall back, in the absence of any clear orders, in the direction of the bridge at Placka. Soon after this, however, an order came from Benedek that he was to head further south, to the crossings at Opatowitz and Pardubitz. Weber's 8th Corps was scattered between Rosnitz and Charbusitz, but it also now began to retreat.

Further north Gablenz, too, had begun to pull out, in company with the 3rd Reserve Cavalry Division. The movement was, as usual, covered by the admirable Austrian gunners. Those in position at Stresetitz had also remained at their post, subjecting Schwarzkoppen's 27th Brigade, which was in the open near Problus, to a heavy fire. While the 27th Brigade was engaged in redeploying it was hit by a sudden attack from Piret's Brigade, from the 1st Corps, which Benedek had brought forward from his reserve to try to stabilise the southern end of the front. Piret made some progress at first, driving the 27th Brigade skirmishers back into Problus; but a brisk counter-attack on both flanks of Piret's advance soon sent him tumbling back with heavy loss. By 4.00 pm, the Army of the Elbe had driven back its immediate opponents all along its front; the Briza wood was clear of the enemy; and Herwarth was in a position to reform the 14th and 15th Divisions. The 16th Division was, however, still a long way back. By this time only the 31st Brigade now under Colonel Schuler von Senden, was over the Nechanitz bridge. The rest of the division had been held up by Major General Hermann von Alvensleben, who had pushed his 1st Cavalry Division forward, getting it somewhat disorganized in the process. He headed, with those units which he could assemble, in the direction of Stresetitz.

Moltke was disappointed. Although Herwarth had broken the Austrian left flank, he had not had sufficient force to achieve the whole of the Chief of Staff's objectives. The Official History makes a telling comment on the absence of the 16th Division without directly apportioning blame:

> Great results might have been attained by General von Herwarth's Army if he had had fresh reserves at hand to push straight on towards the Elbe … The Army of the Elbe was thus deprived of part of the fruits of this victory, which the men of the Rhineland and Westphalia had so materially assisted in gaining.[15]

28

Victory

Soon after 3.00 pm the gradual slackening of the Austrian artillery fire had become unmistakable, and clear signs could be seen of the beginning of the Austrian withdrawal. The moment had clearly arrived in which Moltke, alone of those on the Roskosberg, had always had perfect confidence. Both Schmidt and Manstein asked that cavalry should be brought to the front, and Hann von Weyhern was ordered to move forward with his division. Orders for a general advance of the First Army immediately followed. Prince Frederick Charles, keen to be in the forefront of the advance, rode forward at the head of von der Groeben's 3rd Light Brigade, which crossed the Bistritz at Sadowa; Duke William of Mecklenburg's brigade crossed at Sowetitz, followed by King William and his suite. The advance of the cavalry was severely impeded by the other traffic on the road, and by the masses of infantry and artillery that were moving out in pursuit of the retiring Austrians.

Moltke rode with the King, noting with particular interest the Austrian artillery in front of Langenhof,

> which had proved such an obstacle to our getting out of the forest of Sadowa, and which had up to the last moment resisted our fire. Only a part of the guns mounted here had been carried off; ten 8-pounders had been left behind, and the men and horses lay dead or wounded about the place.[1]

In fact many of the infantry units in the front line did not wait for the order to advance. As soon as it was clear that the troops appearing on the heights near Lipa were Prussian, Colonel von Sandrart, at the north eastern edge of the Holawald, advanced with six companies to make contact with the leading troops of the Guard Corps. South of the Holawald, three batteries of the 4th Division galloped up to take a position from which to open fire on the Austrian artillery covering the retreat. And all along the line, as the leading infantry units began to probe forward to try to maintain contact with the disappearing Austrians, the main body of the First Army began to advance.

By about 4.00 pm, the cavalry had more or less succeeded in threading its way through the masses of marching infantry and had reached the line Langenhof-Stresetitz, led by von der Groeben's brigade along the high road. Its commander rode on ahead looking for the kind of objective for which his troops had been trained. As he neared Rosberitz he saw the perfect target, as columns of retreating Austrian infantry and artillery were moving eastwards towards Königgrätz. He had two regiments, the 12th Hussars (von Barnekow) and the 3rd Dragoons (von Willisen) although only two squadrons of the latter had followed him down the main road; Willisen had led the other three squadrons towards the original objective of Stresetitz. Von der Groeben wasted no time, ordering Barnekow at once to charge the retreating infantry. Soon breaking up the infantry battalion, the hussars were fired on by artillery, whereupon von der Groeben led one squadron full tilt at the battery, sabreing the gunners and capturing four guns before he was himself seriously wounded.

While the hussars, flushed with success, were regrouping, they suddenly saw a large mass of Austrian cavalry bearing down on them. The nearest Prussian unit was the 5th squadron of the 3rd Dragoons, which had been on the right of von der Groeben's advance, and this at once wheeled to attack the advancing Austrian horsemen, who consisted of Schindlöcker's Brigade, supported by the rest of Holstein's Reserve Cavalry Division. Holstein had himself begun to fall back on Königgrätz when he saw the situation of the retreating infantry and artillery, and he wheeled around to come to their support. The Prussian dragoons were, of course, hopelessly outnumbered, but their charge broke through the first line of the Austrian 9th Cuirassier Regiment before they fell back on their own 4th Squadron. Schindlöcker's men followed them up, driving the dragoons, as

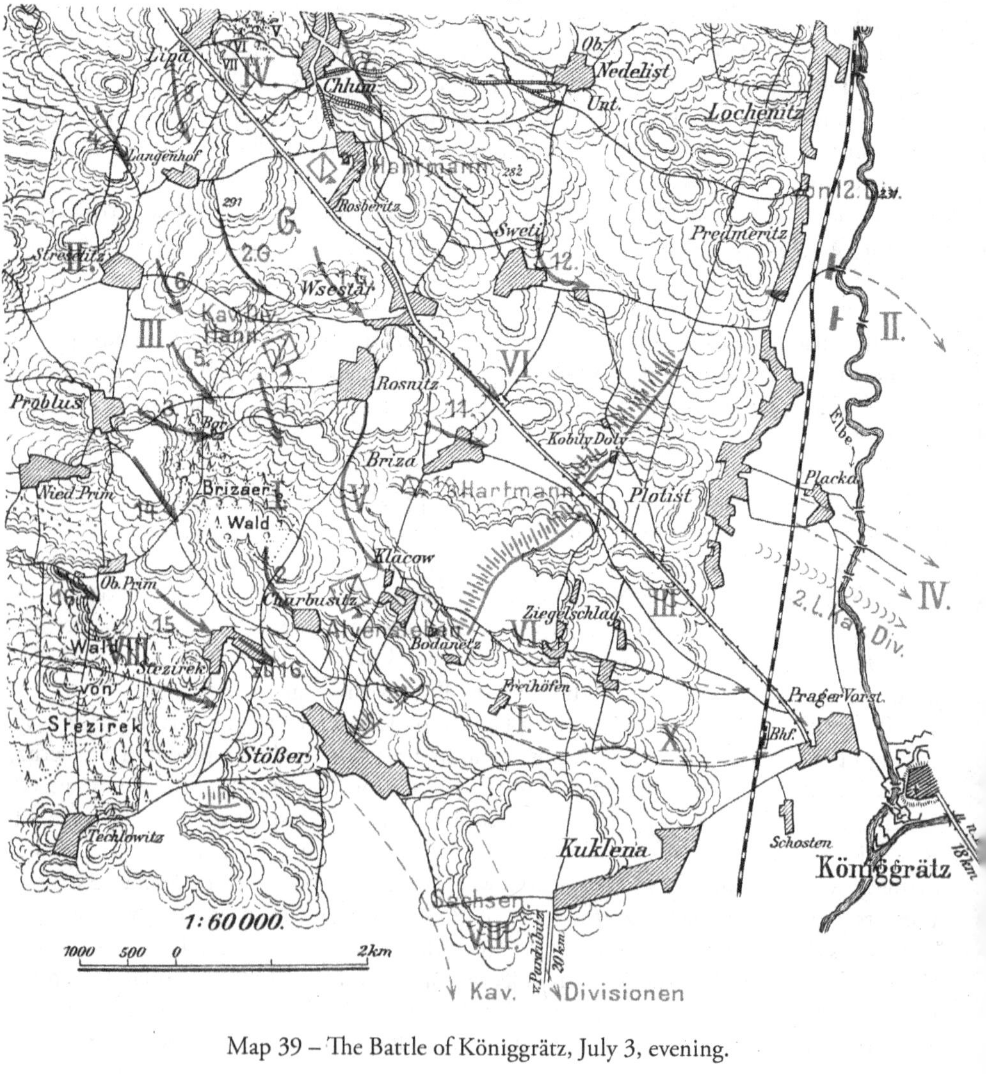

Map 39 – The Battle of Königgrätz, July 3, evening.

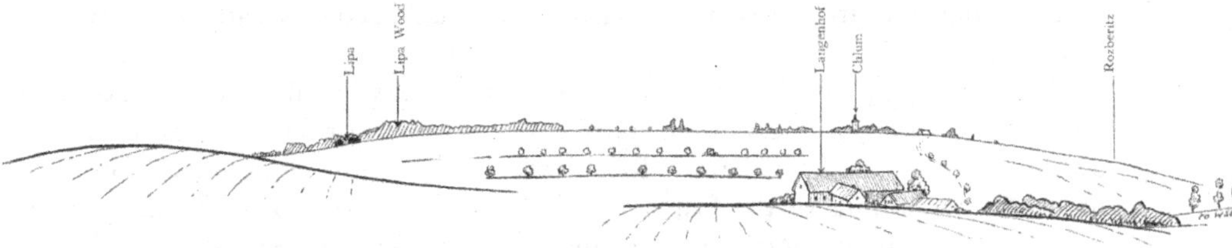

Map 40 – Panoramic sketch of the battlefield of Königgrätz, looking north-east from between Tresowitz and Stresetitz at the Austrian centre.

well as those of the hussars close enough to join in the melée, back in the direction from which they had come. As the Austrians advanced, however, they came under heavy fire from the Prussian infantry advancing down the high road, and from those in the farm buildings to the west of Rosberitz, which slowed them up.[2]

At this point the 4th Uhlan Regiment came on the scene. Commanded by Colonel von Kleist, it had trotted up the dell to the north of the high road in support of the rest of the II Corps, when it suddenly came upon Schindlöcker's Brigade pursuing the remains of von der Groeben's brigade. Hastily forming into line only sixty yards from the enemy, two squadrons of lancers slammed into their front, while the rest of the regiment galloped around the Austrian right, then wheeled to their right and struck the enemy's flank. This quite unexpected assault forced the Austrian cuirassiers to fall back

The site of the cavalry actions at Langenhof, facing the Austrian lines. (Rogers)

towards Langenhof; the Prussian lancers however, had become greatly disorganised in the course of the action.

As the struggle rolled southwards, fresh participants in this complex and rapidly moving series of engagements were appearing. From the east Solm's Brigade advanced towards the scene, led by the 4th Regiment of Cuirassiers, while on the other side the leading squadrons of the Prussian 3rd Hussars, part of Duke William's brigade, had reached the brook north of Langenhof. This village had been taken by the most advanced units of the Guard Corps, coming down from Lipa, and had been reinforced by five companies from the 4th Division and two from the 5th Division. The Guards had moved on to occupy the buildings of a sheep farm (Schäferei) some two hundred and fifty yards south of Langenhof, and it was towards the Schäferei that the Austrian cuirassiers first directed their advance:

> Riding past it on both sides, the cuirassiers broke into a gallop and advanced towards the south end of Langenhof. They had already received infantry fire from the Schäferei, and from the enclosure of the village, and had swerved somewhat to the south in consequence. When the 3rd Hussars arrived at the village, Lieutenant Colonel von Kalkreuth and Captain von Thile crossed the brook close to the village with 1½ squadrons, and General von Hann led them against the right wing of the cuirassiers. The distance was so short that there was no time to form line, but their shock nevertheless sufficed to overthrow the cuirassiers, who were already much shaken, and who now retreated towards Bor, a running fight continuing for some time between them and the hussars.[3]

The Prussian 11th Uhlans in the great cavalry battle at Königgrätz, painting by Freyberg. (Voss)

Once again however the tables were to be turned, as yet another line of Austrian cuirassiers advanced towards the left flank of the 3rd Hussars. Hurriedly reassembling, the hussars prepared to receive this new enemy, which was the 6th Cuirassier Regiment. As it trotted in close order towards Langenhof, one and a half squadrons of Kleist's lancers, which had ridden down to the east of the Schäferei, charged the cuirassiers in the flank, while Duke William charged them in front, for the moment completely surrounding the right of Solms' advance. During the ensuing melée the Austrians came off the worst, and retreated southwest towards Stresetitz.

During this part of the cavalry action, following von der Groeben's initial charge, the Prussian squadrons sustained heavy losses, particularly the 3rd Dragoon Regiment which alone suffered 103 casualties; the other regiments lost a further 100. The Austrian losses were greater, however; some 317 cuirassiers fell in these exchanges.

While all this had been going on, Willisen had also found action with the remaining three squadrons of the 3rd Dragoons. Riding south, he reached Stresetitz under heavy artillery fire, and took shelter in a hollow while he pondered his next move. He was just about to attack some retreating Austrian infantry when he saw, coming up over the heights of Rosnitz, some advancing cavalry, and trotted forward to meet it. It was in fact the first line of Coudenhove's 3rd Reserve Cavalry Division, led by Windischgrätz's Brigade, headed by the 8th Cuirassiers. Coudenhove, like Holstein, had turned back on hearing of the advance of the Prussian cavalry, and was now advancing on Stresetitz. Willisen was, of course, hopelessly outnumbered; but knowing that there was now a substantial force of Prussian infantry at Stresetitz, supported by one battery and a regiment of uhlans, he thought he might perhaps lure the Austrian cavalry within range of their guns. He fell back towards Stresetitz, followed by Windischgrätz at a distance of about half a mile, whose squadrons came under fire as they advanced from the Prussian infantry in the Schäferei.

Willisen now turned, and trotted back towards the advancing cuirassiers. At a distance of 150 yards his small force charged, hitting the cuirassier line obliquely:

> The Austrian cuirassiers had already received infantry fire from the Langenhof Schäferei. They met the charge of the dragoons with a firm, compact line, but did not increase their pace beyond a trot. The shock was very vehement, and the foremost lines of both parties broke through their opponent's line.[4]

Each line overlapped its adversary's right and there was soon an intense melée into which the infantry and artillery at Stresetitz had to cease firing. Inevitably the dragoons were on the point of being overpowered when they were rescued by the timely arrival of the 11th Uhlan Regiment (Prince Hohenlohe), which had became separated from the rest of Duke William's brigade by the advance of the Guard infantry arrived near Stresetitz. Seeing Willisen's plight, Hohenlohe deployed and charged, three squadrons riding into the left wing of the cuirassiers, and another into the part of the right wing which was pursuing a small group of Willisen's dragoons in the direction of Langenhof. Overwhelmed by Hohenlohe's assault, the left wing of the cuirassiers ran into the fire of the 31st Infantry Regiment which had taken post to the south of Stresetitz, and were dispersed, while the rest of the first line disappeared in the direction of Rosnitz. In the course of this action the Austrian cavalry suffered severely; Windischgrätz himself was severely wounded and his brigade sustained a total of 276 casualties, while their opponents lost 146.

To the south of this engagement another cavalry action was fought, this time with King William and his immediate staff as onlookers. The King had pressed forward to be as near to the front of his advancing army as he could get. By the time he reached Lipa, the enemy fire caused Bismarck deep anxiety for his sovereign's safety, an anxiety which appeared not to be shared by the royal staff who did nothing to get him to safety. Bismarck was angry and rode up to the King. 'As a major I have no advice to give to Your Majesty in time of battle,' he said, 'but as Minister President it is my duty to beg Your Majesty not to expose yourself to danger in this way.'[5] With this advice this King grumpily complied. A little later he had made his way south from the high road to a point about 400 yards north west of Stresetitz and here he witnessed the third of the clashes in which the Austrian cavalry sacrificed itself to bring relief to the retreating army.

Alvensleben's 1st Cavalry Division had got considerably disorganized in getting across the bridge and then passing through the infantry detachments of the Army of the Elbe. He was riding with the 1st Guard Dragoons (von Barner) some way ahead of his next unit when this fresh advance of Prussian cavalry was spotted by Major General von Mengen, whose brigade was part of Coudenhove's Reserve Cavalry Division. Mengen had been prevented by the Prussian infantry and artillery fire from intervening in Windischgrätz's battle and was at this moment retreating. He wheeled round and advanced with his 11th Lancer (Emperor Alexander) Regiment to his left and the 10th Cuirassier Regiment on his right. Barner, who was supported at this moment by the 5th Hussars who had ridden down from Unter Dohalitz, deployed and charged and the two forces clashed at full speed, each left wing overlapping the enemy's right. The Austrian right was driven back towards Stresetitz; on the left, the Austrian lancers drove back part of the Guard Dragoons and galloped on towards Problus, where they were met at short range by the grapeshot of Captain Caspari's battery. Unable to check, the survivors rode between the guns before wheeling around to rejoin the rest of the regiment which was being chased towards Stresetitz.[6]

Meanwhile the 5th Hussars, catching the Austrian 10th Cuirassier Regiment before it could deploy, broke it up and drove it back in confusion. The 12th Cuirassier Regiment, which was Mengen's reserve, took no part in the action. The Austrian lancers that had been driven north to Stresetitz got into further difficulty there, however, meeting fierce infantry fire before being charged in flank by Major General von Rheinbaben, who arrived at this moment with three squadrons of the 1st Guard Uhlans. Part of the Austrian force wheeled away in retreat, but about a hundred raced north, heading straight for King William and his staff. Count Finckenstein, fearing for their safety, was about to lead half a squadron of the King's personal escort in a charge on them when they ran into the concentrated fire of three battalions of infantry, and the few survivors turned back to the south to make their escape.[7]

Another interested spectator of this engagement was Fritz Hoenig, who with the men of his company watched fascinated from their position north and west of the Briza wood:

> I do not think one man of the company delivered his fire, and in fact the view of these noble lines of horsemen was so overpowering that the men quite forgot their weapons in their wonder and close attention, although, the distance being about 700 paces, we might have been expected to fire with effect. I their leader was no better![8]

The total losses of the Austrians here were 295; the Prussians lost 83. The Austrian cavalry, whose courage and determination matched that of the artillery in their support of the battered infantry, had been thoroughly broken up in these three engagements. They had, crucially, bought time for the infantry to retreat, but in the face of Prussian artillery fire, now mounting in intensity, they were unable to reform, and could only ride back towards the Elbe and out of the line of fire.[9] It might, however, have been better for them to operate on the right flank, as the Prussian Official History points out. In country well suited to the operation of cavalry the Austrian right had been largely uncovered by the retreat of the 2nd Light Cavalry Division over the Elbe, and the dispatch of the 2nd Reserve Cavalry Division to a position far out on the left flank with Edelsheim and the Saxon cavalry.

Although the retreat of the hard-pressed infantry had been greatly assisted by the initiative of Prince Holstein and Coudenhove, they were not yet out of danger. Pape's assault on Rosberitz, and the continued advance of the VI Corps, had posed a serious threat to the Austrian retirement.

With fifteen companies of infantry of the I Corps Pape attached Rosberitz on three sides, supported by some detachments of Guards. The Austrians defended the village obstinately, retreating from house to house, until the attackers broke into the village and 3,000 Austrians, now surrounded, gave themselves up. Pape's skirmishers pushed on from the south end of the village to the high road, taking six guns in the process. The fall of Rosberitz coincided with the fierce but brief cavalry encounters which occupied the centre of the battlefield.

To the left Hoffmann was advancing on the line Rosberitz – Wsestar. He encountered little resistance, beating off some half-hearted cavalry attacks, until his own right wing under Major von Ostrowski ran into a large force of Austrian infantry retreating from Rosberitz. At the same time on his left, a company led by Captain von Wunster broke into the outskirts of Wsestar, capturing three guns and two ammunition wagons before wheeling to take Ostrowski's opponents in flank. After another abortive cavalry attack, Ostrowski gave the order to charge, and the Austrian force was broken up; 700 were taken prisoner.

Advancing on Wsestar from the north-east, the rest of Hoffmann's brigade met fierce resistance until a battery in the churchyard, which had poured grapeshot on the attackers, was taken, at which the village's defenders fell back across the high road towards Rosnitz. Zastrow's advance was now irresistible. Hanenfeldt's 21st Brigade was also moving forward, towards Sweti, where it faced a powerful gun line formed by the Austrian Reserve Artillery, which again attempted to slow the Prussian advance, this time with less success than before:

> During this advance, already, the 5th and 8th Companies had come upon the right wing of the Artillery, and had forced it to fall back with the loss of one gun. Two

> cavalry attacks were repulsed, and the companies pressed on past the west side of Sweti, where they again reached a position of the enemy's Artillery, upon which the skirmishers and their supports rushed with such vehemence, that nine guns had no time to drive off, and were captured. Five others fell into the hands of the 10th and 11th Companies, which advanced further to the right.[10]

The batteries that escaped fell back, some to Briza and some down the high road to Königgrätz.

It was now the turn of the Prussian gunners. Mutius concentrated fifty four guns on the slopes above Wsestar and Sweti and opened fire:

> The enemy's columns that were hurrying back to Briza and Königgrätz afforded an aim which the Prussian guns could not miss. In vain the Austrian batteries with the greatest self-devotion, took up even now fresh positions, and attempted to draw the Prussian fire upon themselves.[11]

But there was now little they could do; the Prussian fire superiority was complete as forty two guns of the I Corps, in position on the heights of Chlum, came into action against the tempting targets presented by the retreating Austrians.

It was now that the Prussian cavalry might have had the chance to catch up and destroy the Austrian units as they made their way towards Königgrätz and the safety of the Elbe crossings; but Holstein and Coudenhove had, in the course of the three cavalry actions, succeeded at least in disorganising the Prussian cavalry to the point that their pursuit was hopelessly delayed. Even Alvensleben, who had brought only a small part of his division into action, was unable to disentangle it soon enough to overtake the enemy infantry. As it was, it was left to the artillery to inflict what damage it could, and to silence the Austrian batteries that had, for the moment, formed a powerful gun line at Rosnitz to hinder the pursuit.

Benedek had by now become separated from his staff, and his contribution to the closing stages of the battle was entirely personal:

> There are momentary glimpses of him appearing at different parts of the field, exhorting the hard pressed troops who were fighting rearguard actions trying to organise resistance here, to arrest a panic there. In one instance he galloped forward in person through the thick of a cavalry engagement to inspire by his presence and example the Austrian cavalry, which was being forced back by the charging Prussians.

But although it might appear that he was in this way seeking death in the moment of defeat, in order, as Hozier put it, 'with his blood to wash out the memory of his misfortune,' he specifically denied it, writing to his wife: 'I never thought of suicide, I only rode into the thick of the fire because I had to help.'[12] He stayed during these last desperate hours until he thought that the last of his infantry had escaped the closing jaws of Moltke's pincers, and then, finding again part of his staff, he rode off towards Hohenmauth. By now the devastating events of the day had begun to take their toll of him; a captain on his staff recorded that he seemed 'morally and physically crushed.'[13]

And, indeed, the Austrians had only just succeeded in pulling back in time, thanks to their heroic artillery, and the self-sacrifice of the cavalry, as well as to the inevitable delays caused by the intermingling of the advancing units of the First and Second Armies:

> Although the point of junction of the three Prussian Armies lay four miles and a half behind the front of the original Austrian position, still the enemy was already driven back beyond it, when the concentric advance of the armies brought them to the spot.[14]

Etzel had the only fresh troops in the Army of the Elbe, but only Senden's brigade was in a position to move forward, Herwarth having held back the rest of the 16th Division even after it had got over the Nechanritz bridge. Until the reserve artillery came up, Etzel was not strong enough to move forward against the Austrian artillery that was still in his front. As the Official History notes, 'far more disastrous for the enemy was the continued advance of Lieutenant General von Zastrow's Division, whose two brigades were pressing irresistibly onwards against Rosnitz and Briza.'[15] Stiff resistance was still encountered, but the impetus of the Prussians soon resulted in the fall of both villages, and the taking of many prisoners and guns. Indeed, by the time Hanenfeldt was obliged to halt his advance beyond Briza to sort out his intermingled regiments, Zastrow, whose division had been for eight hours continuously in action, had taken during the last two hours nearly 5,000 prisoners and 52 guns. Not surprisingly his troops by now badly needed rest.

There were, in any case, some fresh Prussian troops still coming up to whom the pursuit could safely be left. There were still problems to be faced from the Austrian artillery which, posted among the farm buildings that were dotted over the countryside on the way to the Elbe, had a clear field of fire at the Prussians as they advanced down the slopes from Rosnitz and Charbusitz towards the Elbe. Still greater problems were caused by the concentration of so many troops in such a small area at the point of junction of the armies: 'at midday the front line of the Prussian Army had still been above 16 miles long; now that Briza was taken, it was reduced to little more than two miles, the distance from this village to Bor.'[16]

On the heights of Chlum, from which he had been watching his artillery shell the retreating Austrians, the Crown Prince had an emotional meeting with his cousin Frederick Charles:

> We waved our caps to each other from afar, and then, amid the hurrahs of the troops of my extreme right, and his extreme left wing, with whom I raised an enthusiastic cheer for our King, we fell into each other's arms.

On the other side of the battlefield Etzel, in position between the Briza and Stezirek woods, found himself pinned down by the still potent Austrian artillery, some of which had taken up a position to the west of Stössen. Rather than expose the infantry to needless casualties in advancing against the Austrian guns, Prussian artillery from a number of corps arrived to form a gun line from Briza to the north of Charbusitz and later on the heights of Stezirek, and there followed a fierce artillery duel. Meanwhile the forward movement of the armies continued to the point where the advances of the

The Austrian retreat turns to panic at Königgrätz. (Regensberg/*Königgrätz*)

Second Army and of the Army of the Elbe crossed in front of the First Army. It was clear to Moltke that the time had come to call a halt, and at 6.30 pm he issued what was only his second written order of the day:

> Tomorrow will be in general a day of rest; only such marches will be made as are necessary for the comfort and the re-formation of the troops. Outposts will be thrown out towards Josephstadt by the Second Army, towards Königgrätz by the First Army, and the troops of General of Infantry von Herwarth will, as far as is possible, carry out the pursuit of the enemy, the greater part of whom has retreated in the direction of Pardubitz. The division of Guard Landwehr will be sent forward in the direction of Chlumetz.[18]

Other Prussian troops were still pressing forward when this order was issued. Steinmetz, with his V Corps, had taken no part in the battle, but had been on the march for twelve hours when he finally received Moltke's order to stop, by which time he had reached Klacow, adding further to the overcrowding in the forward areas.

Riding forward from the Bistritz, Moltke and the staff had observed that the first signs on the battlefield were of an orderly retreat; but as they came further forward the increasing quantity of knapsacks, Czakos, and even uniform coats which the enemy had thrown away, as well as numerous side-arms and muskets lying about in all directions, bore evidence to a serious degree of disorder among the ranks of the Austrian infantry.[19]

Clearly, though, the enemy cavalry and artillery still possessed considerable power of resistance, as their conduct during the closing stages of the battle had demonstrated. But their courage did not prevent disaster behind them, as the disorganised infantry reached the Elbe crossings, where the commandant of the fortress of Königgrätz had closed the gates:

Hundreds of wagons, either overturned or thrust off from the high road, riderless horses and confused crowds of men trying to escape across the inundated envious of the fortress and the river, many of them up to their necks in water; this spectacle of wildest flight and utter rout immediately before the gates of Königgrätz, was naturally hidden from the view of the pursuing enemy.[20]

Moltke, therefore, although well aware that he had won a decisive victory, was not aware of just how comprehensive that victory had been, and his rather tentative orders for the pursuit bear witness to this; and having been in the saddle for over twelve hours himself, at the age of sixty six, it is not surprising that exhaustion should have overcome him. He had to go back with his staff to Gitschin, meeting on the road 'endless trains of ammunition columns, which were going to replace the large expenditure of the day, so it was midnight before we reached our quarters.'[21] On the way he got his first food of the day, begging some sausage from a passing uhlan; when he got to Gitschin all he could find was a cup of tea; then, 'feverish with exhaustion I threw myself on my bed in my clothes as I had early in the morning to obtain from His Majesty at Horitz

King William of Prussia amongst his victorious troops at Königgrätz. (Fontane)

permission for the arrangements which were now rendered necessary.'[22] But he could feel an absolute satisfaction: 'the daring of his plan had been completely justified, and he lay down to rest, wearied and exhausted, but the victor in the greatest battle that had been fought since Leipzig.'[23]

The King, meanwhile, accompanied by Bismarck, had been riding among his victorious troops and, as the sun set in the west, met the Crown Prince, who had been looking for him. For the Crown Prince it was an encounter that was both emotional and formal:

> I informed him of the presence of my army on the field, and kissed his hand, and then he embraced me. Neither of us could speak for some time; then he was the first to find words, and told me he rejoiced that I had so far achieved successful results, and had shown capacity for command.

The King had already awarded his son the *Pour le Merité*, but the telegram had not arrived 'and thus it was on the battlefield, where I had with him decided the victory, that my King and father presented me with our highest military order.'[24] The King rode back to Horitz where he slept on a makeshift bed put together from a sofa, two chairs, and a table. His Minister President was less fortunate; looking for his quarters, Bismarck slipped and fell into a manure pit before composing himself for sleep on a carriage cushion under the colonnade in the town square of Horitz.

Bismarck asleep in Horitz after the battle. (Hofmann & Rohling)

Voigts-Rhetz, contemplating the day's events, paid tribute where it was due in a letter which he wrote to his friend Alfred Krupp a few days later:

> When the battle was over, I could only shout the word "Victory!" to you, and that was enough, too, at that time. You knew that we had overthrown the proud Austria, and you were particularly concerned, apart from patriotism – for you have helped us in the most effective way, with your guns. These children of yours conversed for long hot hours with their Austrian cousins; it was an artillery duel with rifled guns, highly memorable and interesting, but also very destructive.[25]

Benedek, riding silently southward with his staff, paused at an inn at Neu Königgrätz. The wine was left untouched until he 'lifted his glass and said "Let us think of the many brave comrades who have fallen today in vain." And as he spoke, they say, the tears ran down his face and splashed on the rough wooden table.'[26] Moltke later reflected upon what must have been the intensity of Benedek's grief and bewilderment, when he subsequently wrote:

> A defeated *Feldherr*! Oh, if civilians had even the remotest idea of what that means! The evening of Königgrätz in Austrian headquarters! Oh, when I try to imagine it to myself! And such a meritorious, brave and prudent general as Benedek![27]

Although it was ending for the leaders on both sides on a note of anti-climax, the day had been one of the most remarkable in European history. The statistics spoke for themselves. On the Prussian side the First Army had suffered most, recording 1,065 officers and men killed, and 4,075 wounded, with 120 missing. The Second Army had lost 514 killed and 1,650 wounded, with 101 missing, while the Army of the Elbe's losses amounted to 356 killed, 1,234 wounded and 57 missing. The total amounted to 9,172. The Austrians and Saxons had suffered losses almost five times as great; total casualties were about 44,200 officers and men, of whom 19,800 had been taken prisoners.[28]

Moltke's victory had been stunning; it now remained to be seen what could be made of it.

Part V
AFTERMATH

29

Custozza

Moltke was under no illusion as to the military effectiveness of his Italian allies. His view of their capabilities was summed up in a telling passage in the Prussian Official History of the war:

> The Italians could hardly be suspected capable of difficult or lengthy sieges. They could less reckon on directly acquiring Venetia by the power of their own arms than on gaining possession thereof, if the general operations of the war compelled Austria to resign it.[1]

Nonetheless he was anxious to exert what influence he could over the strategy to be followed by the Italians, but he was to find this to be an extremely frustrating experience.

The Italians would begin the campaign with a pronounced numerical superiority. Apart from Garibaldi's volunteer forces, intended to operate in the Trentino, the Italians could put a total of 200,000 men with 370 guns into the field. They were organised in twenty infantry divisions and one cavalry division. Formally, Victor Emmanuel took overall command during the campaign, although the army was effectively commanded

Italian infantry in 1866. (*Album della Guerra del 1866*)

General Alfonso La Marmora, commander of the Italian army at Custozza. (*Album della Guerra del 1866*)

by General Alfonso La Marmora, who served as Chief of Staff; however, his political responsibilities as Prime Minister continued until June 18. Moltke depended for his understanding of what was going on at Italian headquarters on the reports which he received from Theodore von Bernhardi, the military historian and indefatigable diarist, who had been sent to Italy at the beginning of June; his particular responsibility was to put forward Moltke's suggestions for the coming campaign. Bernhardi was a shrewd observer of the political scene, who was close to the government, and who was regarded as a reliable envoy.

Bernhardi's reports were not encouraging; they described a military organisation that seemed far from ready to embark on a campaign. He was especially unimpressed by the habit of Italian officers of wearing civilian dress rather than uniform. More importantly, it was soon apparent to Bernhardi that no coherent strategy had been developed for the conduct of the war. Fundamentally there was a choice of two options; to concentrate the principal army on the Mincio and move east on Verona, or to strike northwards from Mantua. The geography of the Po valley determined the front of attack from the south, as Geoffrey Wawro points out:

> A Po crossing could not be attempted anywhere near Mantua because a crossing west of Bologna would have landed the Italian army in the willow swamps between Mantua and Legnago. Farther east, the Po delta was too marshy and pestilential to attempt crossings or marine landings from the Adriatic.[2]

Moltke strongly preferred the option of attacking from the Po valley, and Bernhardi strenuously advocated this course of action. In this he was not surprisingly supported by General Cialdini, whose 4th Corps, consisting of eight divisions, was assigned to this sector.

However, La Marmora favoured an attack across the Mincio, as Bernhardi reported on June 9. La Marmora, somewhat reluctantly, disclosed that his intention was to gain possession of the Quadrilateral by siege, for which, as Moltke knew, the Italian army was certainly not well prepared. La Marmora planned to attack the Austrian army in its front, while Cialdini, with a much smaller force, advanced from the Po valley. Bernhardi's urging of the alternative course, with only a demonstration over the Mincio while the main army moved north from the Po, was dismissed as being too daring. According to General della Rocca, the commander of the Italian 3rd Corps, La Marmora's reaction to Moltke's suggestion was a good deal stronger than this; the plan was seen as being 'almost entirely to the benefit of Prussia;' and La Marmora 'deemed it offensive and unacceptable.'[3] It was Bernhardi's gloomy conclusion that 'an energetic and effective

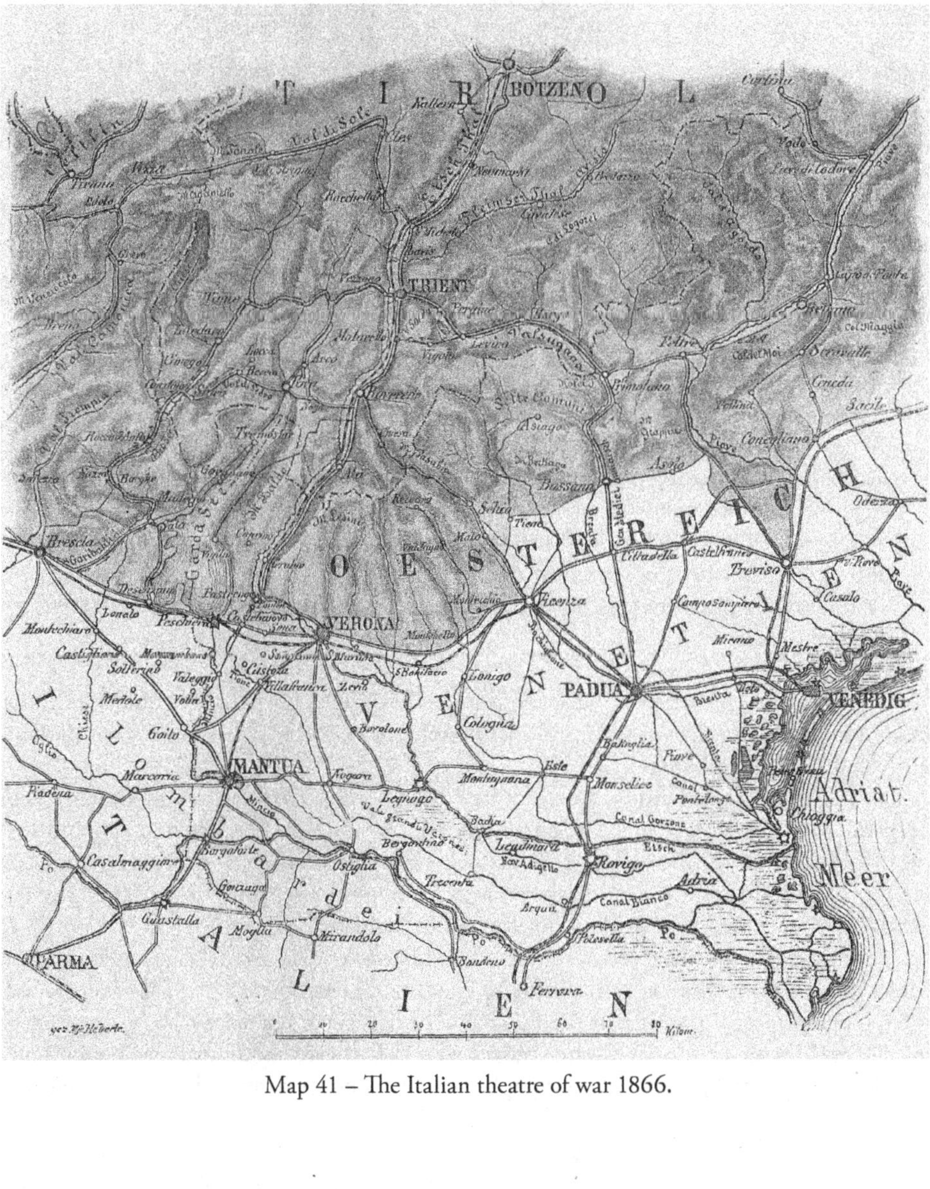

Map 41 – The Italian theatre of war 1866.

General Enrico Cialdini, commander of the Italian 4th Corps. (*Album della Guerra del 1866*)

action of the Italian army, such as would draw off considerable Austrian forces from the northern theatre of war, was not to be expected and could not be counted on.'[4]

Moltke, in his reply of June 15 was dismayed, if not very surprised:

> It is remarkable that they should fail to see at Florence that the Quadrilateral is easier to gain by beating the Austrians in the open field than by besieging the fortresses. This latter undertaking may last for months, nay, for years, without leading to the goal. An advance upon Padua cuts the enemy's arteries. It compels him to move out, because he would have nothing to eat. But to do that Cialdini's force is much too weak... Do they not see on the Arno that nothing but a substantial weakening of the Empire gives any guarantee of being able to maintain a conquest even if it has been made?[5]

Moltke ended his letter with the pious hope that Victor Emmanuel would see things in another light and that 'at the last decisive moment he will lead his fine and numerous army through the Polesina.'

It was not merely because in the wars of 1848 and 1859 the Italian strategy had been to cross the Mincio that La Marmora preferred that option. As long ago as 1862 the King's Military Cabinet had ruled out anything more than a diversion across the Po, on the grounds that it would take an attacking force three days to get across the Po, exposing it to an Austrian stroke from Rovigo or Legnago.[6]

John Pocock, in his recent account of the battle of Custozza, has suggested that Moltke, in arguing for an advance into the Polesina, did so because he 'had never visited the region and knew nothing of the fiendishly difficult marshy terrain to be negotiated once across the great river.'[7] With great respect, this is a very questionable conclusion; Moltke above all was a master of topography as well as being enormously careful to ensure that he formed a view only after acquiring all the relevant information. And it certainly does not explain Cialdini's advocacy of the plan or the willingness of the Italian high command to consider seriously the option of an advance across the Po. Quite apart from the enormous advantage of bypassing the Quadrilateral, the difficulties of the terrain would hamper the Austrian counter-measures as much as the Italian advance, once it had got across the Po. Of course, to do so, the Italians would have had to have prepared very carefully for the crossing in order to minimise the time taken and hence the risk; and this they clearly had failed to do. As it turned out, a concentration on the Po would have been a mistake; a period of heavy rain, coupled with the melting of the mountain snow, raised the level of the Adige and the Po to such an extent that it was feared that the dams would break, and the whole area flooded. In these circumstances, if the bulk of the Italian army had been deployed with the intention of striking northward from the Po, there would have been very serious difficulties in getting the troops across the river.[8] As it was, Cialdini was obliged to retire from the first line of advance he had taken, to move down river to find a better position at which to cross the swollen river.

La Marmora, therefore, was assigned three corps to carry out his plan; these were the 1st Corps (General Durando), with the 1st, 2nd 3rd and 5th Divisions, the 2nd Corps (General Cucciari), with the 4th, 6th, 10th and 19th Divisions, and the 3rd Corps (General della Rocca) with the 7th, 8th, 9th and 16th Divisions. The Reserve Cavalry Division was commanded by General de Sonnaz. Della Rocca, after taking command of his corps, called on General Pettiti, the chairman of Victor Emmanuel's Permanent Commission for Defence, to protest at the strategy to be adopted of dividing the army into two widely separated forces. He recorded the discussion in his Autobiography:

> "You are right in theory", replied Pettiti; "but our case is an exception. The Austrians, engaged in Bohemia, cannot throw a large army into Italy, so either of our two armies will be equal to the enemy wherever he may attack us – on the Mincio or on the Po." "Very well, said I; "but remember the old proverb, Union is Strength. It seems to me the best tactics would be to keep together, await an attack, and repel it with our whole force."[9]

Pettiti had negotiated some sort of compromise between La Marmora and Cialdini, the result of which was to give the latter a larger force than originally intended, apparently with the objective of crossing the Po and aiming at rejoining La Marmora's army on the middle Adige. This was agreed at a meeting between the two generals on June 17, after which Cialdini seems to have convinced himself that it would be his corps that would strike the decisive blow.[10]

The interaction of the two principal Italian leaders was, in the view of Victor Emmanuel's biographer, always likely to lead to disaster:

> It would have been as well to have employed any two other men instead, for La Marmora and Cialdini were bitter political enemies, and had each the utmost contempt for the other's capacity. Cialdini ...hung back and let La Marmora dash himself against the Quadrilateral unsupported.[11]

Archduke Albrecht, commander of the Austrian Army of the South in 1866. (Rogers)

General Franz von John, Chief of Staff of the Austrian Army of the South. (Rogers)

On the Austrian side there was a rather clearer appreciation of what needed to be done. The overall commander of the Army of the South was the Archduke Albrecht. His appointment, announced in mid-April, was something of a surprise to many. He had had very little combat experience, becoming a corps commander after the war of 1859, in which he had taken no part, holding this post until 1863, when he became Army Inspector, which was a rather empty title. He was the eldest son of the Archduke Charles, who had been one of Napoleon's most effective adversaries. The Austrians had some 130,000 men in Italy, including the garrison of the Quadrilateral fortresses and the troops in the Tyrol assigned to confront Garibaldi. The field army with which Albrecht would face the Italian attack consisted of three corps, each of three brigades, with two brigades of cavalry and a Reserve Infantry Division, of three brigades. The corps commanders were Major General Gabriel von Rodich, who took over the 5th Corps shortly before hostilities commenced, as a result of the illness of Prince Liechenstein; Lieutenant Field Marshal Joseph Maroicic, commanding the 7th Corps; and Lieutenant General Ernst Hartung, commanding the 9th Corps. The Reserve Infantry Division was led by Major General Heinrich Rupprecht von Virtsolog. Albrecht's Chief of Staff was the extremely capable Major General Franz von John. The total strength of the Army of the South was 71,284 men, with 3,536 cavalry and 168 guns.[12]

Albrecht began the campaign with his three corps strung out across Venetia, with the 5th Corps at Verona, the 9th Corps at Vicenza and the 7th Corps at Padua. In June, he concentrated all three within the Quadrilateral on the left bank of the Adige, from where he could move either west or south in response to the first moves made by the Italians. He reported to Franz Joseph on June 3:

> In this position I can hold both enemy armies in check, for I would require only one forced march in either direction to meet the closer of the two with a reasonable chance of success.[13]

Well aware that La Marmora would, or should, be able to move forward more quickly than Cialdini, he pushed a light cavalry brigade towards the Mincio to keep an eye on any movement by the Italians to cross the river. Albrecht intended to use his central position to retain the initiative. Maroicic, nearest to Cialdini, well understood this, having instructed his brigade commanders in May:

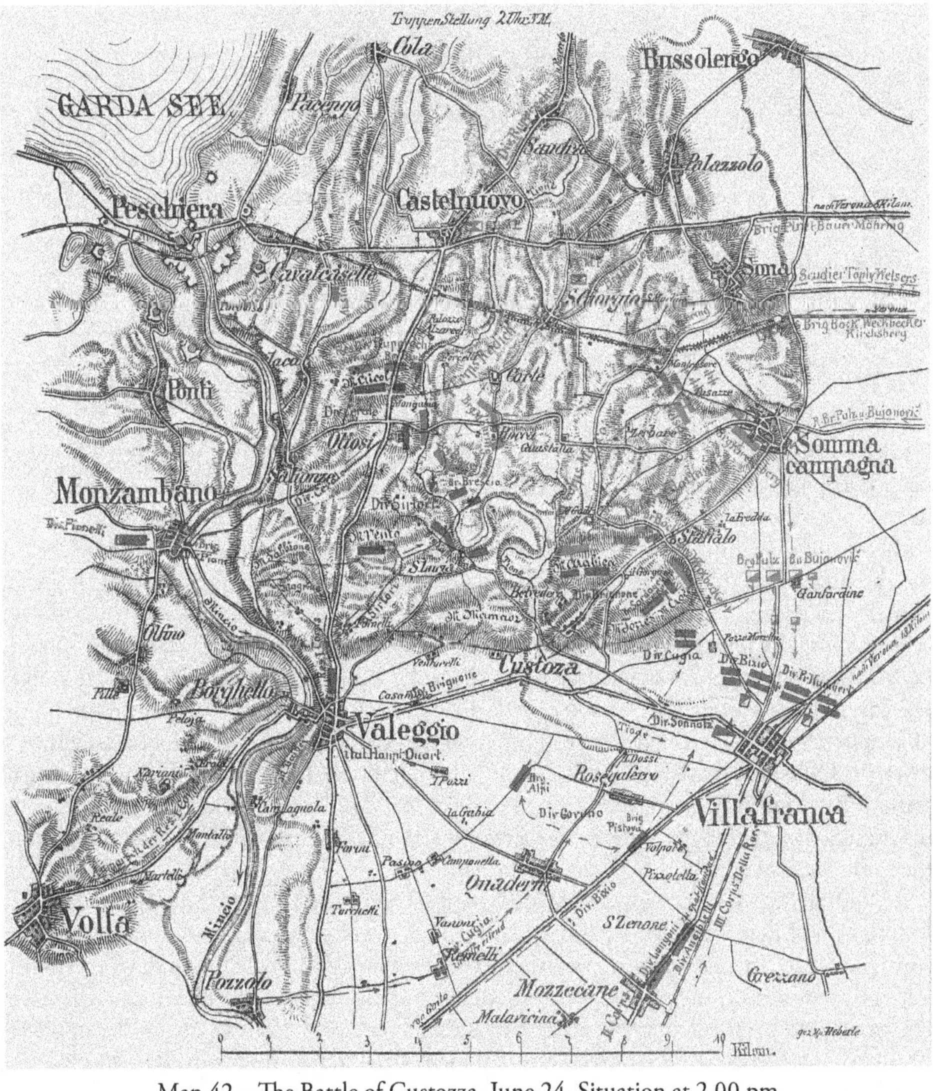

Map 42 – The Battle of Custozza, June 24. Situation at 2.00 pm.

General Joseph Freiherr Maroičic di Madonna del Monte, commander of the Austrian 7th Corps. (Lukeš)

> The Italians will be unable to develop their numerical strength in this broken, irrigated terrain. Remember: march always to the sound of the guns. If the enemy advances in several columns, we will fall on the first one with superior force and throw it back into the Po, then turn on the next, hit it in the rear, and destroy it.[14]

La Marmora finally sent the Italian declaration of war to the fortress of Mantua on June 20, four days later than called for by the terms of the alliance with Prussia. Next day his army edged forward towards the Mincio; the watching Austrian cavalry reported to headquarters that a crossing was imminent. It was clear that, comparing this advance with that of Cialdini, it would be in the Mincio sector that the first battle would be fought; and Albrecht and John resolved to take advantage of the heights above Custozza, Sommacampagna, and Santa Lucia by occupying them before the Italians could do so. Once having occupied these hills, the Army of the South would be well placed to strike La Marmora's flank as his army, having got over the Mincio, marched towards the Adige. Having moved westwards from Verona late on June 23, the Austrian right, consisting of Rupprecht's division, led the way on June 24, turning south through Castelnuova towards Oliosi. Next came Rodich, moving north of Sona before swinging south westwards. Maroicic, alongside him, marched through Sona, with Hartung, moving through Sommacampagna, the pivot of the Austrian left wheel, on the left. Beyond him, the flank was covered by Pulz's cavalry brigade.

The Italians were crossing the Mincio by the bridges at Valeggio and Goito that the Austrians had helpfully left undamaged for them, and by two further pontoon bridges constructed by their engineers. But the process was a good deal slower than had been hoped; by nightfall on June 23 only about half of the Italian army had crossed, with the rest closed up to the bridges and ready to cross next day. A report from de Sonnaz's cavalry division that no Austrian troops remained west of the Adige must have comforted La Marmora, with his army so dangerously exposed in this way.

General Giovanni Durando, commander of the Italian 1st Corps. (*Album della Guerra del 1866*)

This incorrect reconnaissance report may well also have contributed to La Marmora's decision to send more than a flank guard into the hills, into which, unknown to him, the whole Austrian Army was now moving. For June 24, Durando's 1st Corps was ordered to wheel north, pivoting on Valeggio, and to occupy the heights of Custozza and Sommacampagna. During the night of June 23/24 a violent thunderstorm broke over the troops of both armies. When each army broke camp early on the morning of June 24, it was with the intention of getting as far as possible into position before the blistering heat of the day, which had caused both sides extreme discomfort on the previous day, a number of men dying of heat exhaustion. The Austrians were on the move by 2.30 am, while the Italians set out an hour later. Although both commanders had chosen to advance into the hills, there was one essential difference; Albrecht did so in the reasonable confidence that there would be a battle on June 24, while La Marmora had no idea of such a thing.

Pianelli's 2nd Division from Durando's 1st Corps had been left behind to watch the Peschiera forts; the remaining three divisions of the corps advancing into the hills were, from left to right, Cerale's 1st Division, advancing on Oliosi, Sirtori's 5th Division, directed at St Lucia, and Brignone's 3rd Division, moving towards Custozza. Della Rocc's 3rd Corps was moving on Villafranca; since no Austrian opposition was to be expected in Durando's front, Della Rocca was to remain in the plain.

As the Austrians moved into the hills, first reports from their leading units were reassuring, no opposition having been met. It was not until 6.30 am that firing broke out to the north of Villafranca, where Pulz's cavalry brigade was in contact with the advanced guard of Della Rocca's 3rd Corps. Meanwhile, at the western end of the Austrian movement, Rupprecht had encountered the leading brigade of Cerale's division near Oliosi. The meeting might have occurred further to the north but for Cerale having been seriously delayed by his columns having got mixed up with those of Sirtori's division after crossing the Mincio at Valeggio. La Marmora, hearing the gunfire from

General Enrico Della Rocca, commander of the Italian 3rd Corps. (*Album della Guerra del 1866*)

Oliosi, put it down to a cannonade from the Austrian forts at Peschiera. Riding on to Villafranca, he was still confident a little later, telling the units of the 3rd Corps which he met there that there were no Austrian troops west of Verona and that they could stand down and cook breakfast.[15]

His sense of security was abruptly shattered shortly afterwards; having taken a few of his staff to ride to the summit of Monte Croce, a hill some 115 metres high immediately south of Staffalo, he was shocked to see columns of Hartung's 9th Corps heading towards him only a few kilometres away. With only Brignone's division at Custozza, he sent at once to Durando and Della Rocca for reinforcements, as he hastily began to arrange a defensive line around Custozza.

Della Rocca, however already had his hands full. Two of his divisions, the 7th (Nino Bixio) and 16th (Crown Prince Umberto) were deployed in and around Villafranca, awaiting the order to advance on Verona. The 8th Division (Cugia) was on the Valeggio – Villafranca road, with the 9th Division (Govone) just to the south. The cavalry division of de Sonnaz was located in the fields to the south of Villafraca. Until about 7.00 am not a lot was happening, or expected to happen, in this sector. The tranquillity ended abruptly when an Austrian cavalry regiment led by Colonel von Rodakowski, which was intended merely to conduct a reconnaissance, launched a full-blooded charge which emerged from cover to strike a point between the divisions of Bixio and the Crown Prince. Pulz, Rodakowski's brigade commander, felt obliged to support his headstrong subordinate, and sent forward the rest of his brigade. For a while, the Italian infantry was thrown into intense confusion, and the Crown Prince narrowly escaped capture; but after a while, after suffering heavy losses (Rodakowski lost two-thirds of his 600 men), the Austrian cavalry retreated, Pulz having been joined in the later stages of the action by Bujanovic's cavalry brigade. Although suffering greater casualties than it had inflicted, the Austrian cavalry had seriously unnerved Della Rocca, Bixio and the Crown Prince,

Colonel von Rodakowski leads his Austrian Uhlans on a death or glory ride at Custozza, painting by Koch. (Rogers)

who met and agreed that they should stand fast where they were, in order to meet the infantry assault which they were sure would follow.[16]

And La Marmora's confidence, shaken by the appearance of Hartung's corps as well as by the attack of the Austrian cavalry on his right, would not have been improved had he witnessed the events on his extreme left. There, Cerale's 1st Division had been marching north on the road to Oliosi, while Sirtori's 5th Division had been heading for St Lucia. Unfortunately Sirtori's advanced guard, of two battalions and six guns under General Villahermosa, took a wrong turning and fetched up on the Oliosi road in front of Cerale's advanced guard, where it came under fire from the leading troops of Rupprecht's division as well as from artillery of the 5th Corps on the other side of the Tione valley. Villahermosa launched an attack on Benko's Brigade on Monte Cricoli; although initially successful, he was heavily outnumbered and fell back in disorder. At this point Cerale's advanced guard (Villarey) arrived on the scene, followed shortly afterwards by the rest of the division. Cerale's assault on Monte Cricoli, which was delivered with a substantial advantage in numbers, was successful, and Benko's Brigade was driven back off the hill.

The advantage that the Italians had thus gained was, however, nullified by an extraordinary charge by three troops of Austrian lancers under Captain Bechtoldsheim. At 8.00 am, coming up beside Benko's brigade, they were launched at the advancing Italian infantry; breaking through, they smashed into a roadside conference of Cerale, Dho, one of his brigade commanders, and several other officers, killing one and wounding

General Ernst Hartung, commander of the Austrian 9th Corps. (Lukeš)

Cerale and Dho before galloping on down the road. Next they hit an artillery unit, which panicked and fled through the following infantry, breaking several battalions into fragments of dazed and panic-stricken soldiers. Bechtoldsheim finally managed to recall his lancers, although as they returned to the Austrian lines they suffered fearful casualties, only 17 out of 101 making it back. But their success had been extraordinary, and the damage done to Cerale's division had been immense, causing it to retreat to take up a position on Monte Vento, south of Oliosi and due west of St Lucia.[17]

On the road to the latter place Sirtori had been advancing with his main body, though no longer preceded by his advanced guard. Climbing the slopes out of the Tione valley, the Italian infantry collided with Bauer's Brigade. In an effort to drive the

The Austrian 65th Infantry at Custozza, painting by Fritz Neumann. (Rogers)

Austrians from their position along a ridge just south of Pernisa, Sirtori launched a series of bayonet charges, all of which failed; an Austrian counter-charge suffered even heavier casualties, but succeeded in driving the Italians back across the Tione, where they took up a strong defensive position at St Lucia.

Further east, on the Austrian left, La Marmora's hasty call for reinforcements to secure the heights towards which he had observed Hartung's 9th Corps advancing had come just in time, and the Italians now held the Belvedere and Custozza heights with Brignone's division as well as Monte Torre and Monte Croce. Cugia's division was coming up from the plain in support, followed by Govone. North of the Belvedere the Italians also held Monte Molimenti. In this sector of the battlefield, Hartung's advance was supported by Scudier's Brigade from the 7th Corps of Maroicic; his other two brigades were in reserve behind Hartung's corps. Hartung directed two brigades, those of Weckbecker and Böck, on Monte Croce, and Scudier on Monte Molimenti. The Austrians suffered fearfully as they struggled uphill towards the Italian positions, but in spite of this Scudier was able to push forward to take the summit of the Belvedere, and reach the outskirts of Custozza.

Meanwhile on the left Weckbecker and Böck had taken Monte Croce, and threatened Monte Torre. An Italian counter-attack by Cugia's division, supported by artillery, came just in time to drive back first Weckbecker and then Böck, enabling Govone, whose troops arrived on the scene at 10.45 am, to turn his attention to Scudier's Brigade. Under heavy pressure, and badly outnumbered, Scudier fell back to the Belvedere, and held on there until reinforcements reached him; when they did, he pulled his own troops back to Sona. This enabled Govone to push forward and ultimately retake the Belvedere at about 3.00 pm.

By now the respective commanders in chief had more or less lost control of their armies, whose units were fighting a series of independent battles for the heights. Visibility was limited; information was scarce. The difference was in their response to what seemed to each to be a poor situation; La Marmora had no clear plan on which to proceed, and was at best engaged in ineffectual crisis management, while the Archduke Albrecht resolved to launch a fresh offensive. La Marmora was not greatly helped by some of his subordinates; Della Rocca, for instance, had seen Victor Emmanuel during the first part of the morning and had been highly critical of La Marmora:

> I know that I could not restrain my indignation at the ignorance of the staff concerning the positions of the enemy. Trusting to false information that the Austrians were on the other side of the Adige, when they were in the Quadrilateral, they had thrown our army into the clutches of the enemy. I also alluded to the inexpedience of the long line extending from Peschiera to Villafranca, and to the lack of an army headquarters.[18]

The Austrian offensive was to begin on the right flank, where Rodich and Rupprecht were to open the assault with a heavy bombardment of the Italian positions on Monte Vento and around St Lucia. At 2.00 pm Piret's Brigade, supported by those of Weimar and Benko, moved forward against Monte Vento under heavy rifle fire from the defenders; by 3.00 pm the hill was in Austrian hands. Immediately to the east, Möring's Brigade was

General Gabriel Freiherr von Rodich, commander of the Austrian 5th Corps. (Lukeš)

launched in an assault on St Lucia. With Piret's advance on Monte Vento clearly gaining ground Sirtori, fearing for his left flank, felt obliged to fall back.

But it was in the Custozza position that the Archduke believed that the battle would be decided, and he resolved to commit all his reserves in an effort to take it. Govone, having taken the summit of the Belvedere, was resting on his laurels when at 4.00 pm a heavy bombardment of his positions began; it lasted an hour, in the course of which the Italian artillery was effectively silenced. Meanwhile Welsersheimb's Brigade prepared to storm Custozza; it was supported by Möring's Brigade, which advanced from St Lucia

Italian prisoners after Custozza, in the Roman amphitheatre at Verona. (*Album della Guerra del 1866*)

across the Tione, and entered the village from the west at the same as Welsersheimb entered on the north and east. The defenders of Custozza fell back in disarray, many of them being taken prisoner by the troops that Möring had pushed forward into the plain.[19]

By now there was no hope on the Italian side that defeat could be avoided, and all along the front, in varying degrees of disorder, Italian units were streaming down from the hills into the plain, making for the crossings of the Mincio. Of Della Rocca's 3rd Corps, the divisions of the Crown Prince and Bixio had been anchored around Villafranca all day by the fear of an Austrian advance on the town; now, the Crown Prince was ordered to retreat to the river, leaving Bixio and a cavalry brigade to cover the army's withdrawal. It was harassed by Pulz's cavalry, which was in action against the retreating Italians until 9.00 pm. Soon after this Bixio fell back to the Mincio; thereafter there were only the troops covering the bridgeheads on the left bank of the river. The victorious Austrians remained in their final positions on the battlefield during the night.[20]

At Victor Emmanuel's headquarters there were painful scenes. La Marmora, grief stricken, insisted on resigning; the King sent Della Rocca to him to try to talk him out of it, but unsuccessfully. The commander of the 3rd Corps declined the post of Chief of Staff for himself, but suggested Bixio, whom the King thought too young; otherwise he proposed that it should be Cialdini.[21] In the event, La Marmora remained for the moment in charge, and notwithstanding further negotiations continued as Chief of Staff until the end of the war.

Austrian infantry on the march after Custozza. (*Illustrirte Kriegs-Chronik*)

Albrecht's failure to pursue the broken Italian Army attracted criticism, both at the time and since. Geoffrey Wawro considers that he 'had a golden opportunity that evening to destroy half the Italian Army with little risk... 'Destroying' the Mincio Army would really have been a matter of pursuing it and accepting its surrender.'[22] But such an operation would not have been straightforward; and there was still Cialdini's undefeated army to take account of. On the other hand, it is surely right to say, as Wawro does, that Albrecht could have been more active in relation to the latter, as it marched westwards to join the rest of the Italian army behind the Oglio. By the time that the news of Königgrätz arrived, Albrecht had tentatively probed across the Mincio; but he was by now apprehensive of the threat posed by Cialdini's junction with La Marmora's army, and he soon pulled back to Custozza. Thereafter there could be no question of further operations against the Italians, since the South Army must at once be recalled to the north to help defend Vienna. Cialdini, therefore, faced no opposition as he marched northwards into Venetia.

Custozza had been a striking victory, against heavy odds – theoretically; but Wawro points out that La Marmora's incompetence had meant that instead of facing odds of two to one on the battlefield on June 24, Albrecht actually enjoyed a marginal advantage in numbers, fighting with 75,000 men against 65,000.[23]

Total casualties in the battle showed an interesting pattern; the Austrians had 78 officers and about 2,000 men killed, with 219 officers and about 4,700 men wounded and 10 officers and about 1,600 men taken prisoner. The Italian losses were 61 officers and about 1,000 men killed, with 226 officers and about 3,000 men wounded, and 70 officers and about 4,000 men prisoners. The heaviest Austrian losses were sustained by Hartung's 9th Corps and Rupprecht's Division; Brignone had the heaviest casualties on the Italian side.[24]

Moltke, his hands full with his own operations in both Bohemia and Western Germany, made no comment on the outcome of Custozza, although he cannot have been greatly surprised. The withdrawal of the South Army from Venetia for the defence of Vienna was of course something he had to take account of; but the Italian Army had done all that he really required by taking the field at all, and the result of the battle made little difference to Moltke's calculations both before and after Königgrätz.

30

Advance to the Danube

The task awaiting Moltke when he woke on 4 July was extremely complex. The first problem was to sort out the intermingled units of the victorious Prussian armies and send them on their way in pursuit of the Austrians; and, of course, to ascertain the direction of Benedek's retreat. Thereafter it would be a matter of hitting him hard again as soon as possible, for although badly beaten at Königgrätz, the professional resilience of the Austrian army would soon bring about a recovery of sorts if the pressure was not maintained. And then there was the considerable possibility of reinforcements reaching the Army of the North from Italy, where the defeat at Custozza had for the moment at any rate put paid to any serious threat from the Italian army. Finally, and this was by no means the least of the problems, there were the diplomatic complications that were bound to ensue from the moment the guns fell silent over the battlefield of Königgrätz. Although soon to disagree about matters of high policy, Bismarck and Moltke were united in realizing the need for prompt and decisive action to exploit the victory.

It would of course immediately be necessary to reestablish contact with the retreating Austrians. Basically Benedek had two options. He might retreat due south directly on Vienna, taking the roads through Iglau and Brünn to bring himself to the Danube; or he might retreat east and south east to Olmütz to take up a position on the flank of any Prussian advance. In reality Benedek really had little choice:

> In its present state the army could not pursue its march in the former direction; it would have become totally disorganised on this march of 135 miles. It was imperative first to rally the troops somewhere or other, in which case the start which they had gained upon the Prussian Army would be lost, and the latter would be again at their heels.

There was no river line on which they could stand north of the Danube. On the other hand:

> The entrenched camp at Olmütz was only half as far off, and afforded a safe place of refuge, which could be reached without danger of the army being totally dispersed, and where the latter could be rallied and could be restored to a fit state for again taking the field.[1]

It was to Olmütz therefore that Benedek directed the retreat of all his forces, save the 1st Light Cavalry Division and the three Reserve Cavalry Divisions which, operating under the command of Prince Holstein, were to fall back towards the Danube in front of the advancing Prussians, delaying them as much as possible; and the 10th Corps, which was directed to Brusau and Lettowitz, there to be transported by rail direct to

Vienna. The rest of the army made its way over two roads, through Hohenmauth and Wilderschwerdt, to Olmütz.

On the day after the battle, Hohenlohe lay in an exhausted sleep. Lieutenant von Schell, his ADC, tried for half an hour to wake him:

> At last I woke, shaken in desperation by my good Schell. "For God's sake wake up, won't you? His Majesty the King is inspecting the troops. The batteries have already lined up. Make sure you are on the right wing. The King is already on his way." Schell had already tried to wake me anxiously. Lame and half asleep as I was, I stumbled to my place. The King arrived immediately afterwards... we shouted hurrah! I was graciously asked some questions, but I noticed that the King was not overjoyed to see the artillery. The Crown Prince was extremely friendly to me and was full of praise for the batteries and the support I had given to the 1st Guards Division.[2]

Hohenlohe at first put the King's demeanour down to the death of Hiller, whose loss he greatly mourned; later, however, he learned that the King had been very dissatisfied with the performance of the artillery fighting in his vicinity, and had extended his disapproval to the whole artillery.

Hohenlohe, whose batteries had suffered in an incident of friendly fire, had another potentially embarrassing encounter that morning, when 'a senior gentleman whose name is not important' asked him if he was happy with his people. Hohenlohe assured him that the conduct of all had been exemplary, except for the moment when he had been fired on by Prussian batteries from the rear, when all his authority had been needed to maintain the troops' composure. 'Yes, yes,' said the senior personage, 'I can well imagine that happening yesterday,' and he rode on. One of his staff, however, told Hohenlohe that he had said the wrong thing – it was the gentleman in question who had given the order to fire at Hohenlohe's batteries.[3]

Hohenlohe felt deeply the unjust criticism of the artillery by public opinion:

> Wrongly deployed in the order of marching and shackled at the rear by the ban on advancing, the artillery was able to engage the enemy only late and sporadically, and had to fight against an enemy with a three to five fold numerical superiority. And then the word was: "The artillery weren't there, they were useless," and the blame was apportioned to them everywhere.[4]

Meanwhile, in what was to be the first of several attempts by the Austrians to buy some time Gablenz, who was supposed to be *persona grata* at the Prussian Royal Headquarters, was sent on July 4 to seek an armistice. After passing through the Prussian lines, his eyes bandaged, he encountered the King on the high road near Sadowa. He was sent on his way to see Moltke, who was unmoved by his appeal; while Prussia would be ready to negotiate a definitive peace, 'a standstill in the military operations was too much to expect of the Prussian Army.' On the other hand a three day truce might, Moltke suggested, be possible on condition that the three fortresses of Theresienstadt, Josephstadt and Königgrätz were surrendered.[5] Since Gablenz had no authority of any kind to negotiate, he was then politely escorted back to Königgrätz.

Moltke now removed the Army of the Elbe from the command of the First Army, and directed it on Chlumetz, from which it was to move due south to cross the Elbe, taking the Iglau road. In the centre, the First Army was to take the direction of Prelouc, while the Second Army was to move on Pardubitz and, crossing the river there, move on towards Chrudim. In the country immediately to the south of the battlefield, most of the villages were deserted, the inhabitants having hurriedly packed up and fled with the retreating Austrian Army. Hozier described the scene, as the Prussians moved forward:

> For the most part the country in front of the army was still and silent. No church clocks sounded, for their guardians had fled. There was no one to wind them up, and the hands stood motionless on the dials. No horses neighed, for they had all been taken to carry away the flying inhabitants, or perhaps to aid in dragging off the retreating Austrian guns ... The cattle had been driven away, and the pastures were vacant. Broad belts of corn, trodden flat to the ground, showed the lines along which the Austrian battalions had hurried, and here and there lay a knapsack or ammunition pouch.[6]

The armies reached the Elbe on the evening of July 5; it had been unclear whether any resistance would be encountered, but the reconnaissance patrols were soon able to report that there would be no opposition at the river crossings. Hartmann was the first to cross with the Second Army's cavalry reserve at a ford near Pardubitz. A few stragglers were picked up, but the only Austrian cavalry he saw avoided battle, and he was able to turn at once to the task of repairing the bridges over the Elbe at Pardubitz.

Prussian troops march into Prague, July 8. (*Illustrirte Kriegs-Chronik*)

The Army of the Elbe was also up to the line of the Elbe, its leading units crossing at Kladrub and Recan, so that by nightfall on July 5 the Prussians stood along the line of the river from Pardubitz to Kladrub. The columns of marching troops had closed up, compressing the whole army into a space of about twenty five square miles, causing considerable logistical problems in supplying the troops, as well as for the security of the lines of communication. The Second Army, therefore, was to leave behind the VI Corps to watch the fortresses, and to clear up the battlefield. A brief bombardment of Königgrätz by the artillery of the 11th Division provoked a sharp response, and since there was no cover close to the fortress, the bombardment was halted, and the Prussians remained content with a rather distant observation. Meanwhile, in order to aid the reestablishment of the rail network, Herwarth was ordered to send Rosenberg, with the Guard Landwehr Division, to occupy Prague. This task it carried out unopposed, since the Austrian army and authorities had abandoned the city. By July 8 the Prussian flag was flying from the Hradschin. The municipal authorities were cooperative in the matter of billeting and provisioning the troops. The railway from Turnau to Pardubitz could now be reopened and the effectiveness of the line was vastly increased by the seizure of thirty engines and about a thousand railway carriages. As a bonus, several million cigars at the Sedletzer tobacco factory fell into Prussian hands.[7] Logistics were in the forefront of Moltke's mind at this time; even more important than regaining contact with his beaten enemy, the proper supply of the army was essential if the rest of the campaign was to be concluded swiftly, and the stream of orders he issued on the subject reflect his concern.

Moltke finally moved from Horitz to Pardubitz on July 6, crossing the battlefield as he did so. It was a depressing experience. Mass graves were still being dug; buildings in the burnt-out villages were still smouldering, and makeshift hospitals were still full of wounded.

> Long trains of wagons brought the more slightly wounded back. Further on the corpses became less numerous, but the signs of a headlong flight increased. Thousands of knapsacks, caps, belts and sabres covered entire fields.[8]

Moltke finally arrived in Pardubitz on foot, after his carriage was badly damaged in a traffic accident, but his spirits were high; for a change he was in very good quarters, with a hostess who was an excellent cook. More importantly, the information brought in by his patrols confirmed that the bulk of Benedek's army was heading for Olmütz, allowing him to take some firm decisions as to his immediate strategy.

Next day he issued orders that demonstrated his awareness of the state of the Austrian army, and the extent to which any offensive intentions on its part could be discounted. Only the Second Army need follow Benedek, and would do so as flank guard for the advance of the other two directly on Vienna. For logistical reasons it was necessary to broaden the front of the advance, and he set out his intentions:

> The two wing armies must always spread their billets towards the outer flank in order to compress as little as possible the district in which the centre army can be billeted.

At the same time, he stressed the need for mutual cooperation:

> With a view to the support, which may possibly become necessary in the improbable case of the enemy's attack from the direction of Olmütz, the Second Army must keep up a constant communication with the left wing column of the First Army.9

On July 8 Gablenz turned up again. He brought with him some specific proposals, including the suggestion of an armistice for at least eight weeks, on the basis of which the armies were to halt on their present line; Josephstadt and Königgrätz were to be handed over but without their garrisons and matériel. He arrived first at the Crown Prince's headquarters. Blumenthal, sending him on to Royal Headquarters, hurried off himself to make sure that his views on the undesirability of an armistice were made known. He need not have worried. Moltke swiftly sent Gablenz packing, as he observed laconically to his wife: 'He did not see the King, as I dismissed him at once. Tomorrow we make a further advance.'[10] Moltke had no intention of letting the Austrians gain time to bring up the Army of the South for the defence of Vienna. As the armies moved south there were a series of minor cavalry engagements. On July 7 a specially formed cavalry detachment 700 strong under Barnekow was sent forward to Zwittau in the hope of catching part of the Austrian rearguard at a disadvantage. Arriving at nightfall, Barnekow surprised the 8th Corps, and two battalions and four batteries of the Saxon Corps, which had thrown out no outposts for their protection. There was a brief exchange of fire, which threw the Austrians into great confusion; but the strength of the opposition he had encountered led Barnekow to withdraw, taking with him four officers and 112 men as prisoners. Incidents such as this contributed further to the high morale of the Prussian troops, as Hozier noticed:

> The troops on the road pushed along as steadily and perseveringly as on the first day they entered Saxony. The infantry, with their trousers turned up and boots often drawn on outside them, trudged along merrily, and seemed little to feel the heavy yellow cow skin knapsacks and mess tins for cooking which they carried on their backs. Their helmets had suffered in the campaign more than any other part of their equipment; many had lost the spike on the top, carried away by a bullet or the splinter of a shell at the battle of Königgrätz.[11]

On July 10 there was a sharp skirmish in the small town of Saar, on the road to Brünn, when the 9th Uhlan Regiment arrived to find Austrian hussars of the Hesse Cassel and Radetzky Regiments getting ready to parade in the market place. The Austrians were taken entirely by surprise, but while the leading uhlans waited for the rest of their force to come up they managed to form a line. It was a colourful spectacle, as Hozier described:

> As soon as their supports came up the lancers formed a line across the street, advanced a few yards at a walk, then trotted for a short distance, their horses' feet pattering on the stones, the men's swords jingling, their accoutrements rattling, and their lances borne upright, with the black and white flags streaming over their heads.

Then, as they reached the market place, they charged, just as the Austrians did the same:

> Their blue pelisses, trimmed with fur and embroidered with yellow, flowing freely from their left shoulders, leaving their sword-arms disencumbered. Their heads, well up, carried the single eagle's feather in every cap straight in the air.[12]

After the first shock of the collision, the uhlans' formation was unbroken, but the Austrian hussars were largely dispersed. A few were killed; 33 were taken prisoner. The uhlans lost one man killed and seventeen injured. Hozier thought the prisoners were

> smart, soldier like-looking fellows of a wiry build; they looked the very perfection of light horsemen, but were no match in a mêlée for the tall, strong cavalry soldiers of Prussia, who seemed with one hand to be able to wring them from their saddles, and hurl them to the ground.[13]

By July 11 Benedek had assembled all his troops at Olmütz. The forced retreat had not enhanced their morale, but it now seemed clear that they would not have the opportunity for the rest and refitting that they so badly needed. The camp at Olmütz was decidedly overcrowded; more importantly, the southward march of the Prussians had taken them to within a day's march of Brünn, with a consequent threat to Benedek's communication with Vienna. There was no time to lose; orders went out that the whole of the Army of the North, save one corps that was to garrison Olmütz, was at once to proceed to Vienna. For the moment, the railway was still open, and the leading troops could take the train; but the line could not shift the whole army, and the rest would have to march on foot. The 3rd Corps, followed by the Saxons, began to move out that evening. On the same day Benedek was informed that, although he was for the time being to remain in command of the Army of the North, he was thereafter to be under the orders of the Archduke Albrecht, who was placed in supreme command of all the Imperial armies. Virulent criticism of Benedek had been expressed in the Vienna press but neither this nor his supersession moved him from his devoted loyalty. He wrote to his wife to tell her that his morale was unshaken:

> The stupid gossip of the newspapers, the judgment of the world – to all, to all of this I am indifferent. Only my whole attitude is determined by a feeling of duty and of unconditional devotion to my Emperor and my country.[14]

Moltke, meanwhile, was not far from his adversary that day. On his way from Zwittau to Czernahora, he paid the Second Army headquarters an unexpected visit. Blumenthal took the opportunity to urge on him his own ideas for the disposition of the Second Army, which he believed should take up a position south of Olmütz, at Prossnitz, the better to be able to support Frederick Charles if the need arose. To Blumenthal's annoyance, Moltke 'turned a deaf ear. Instead of discussing the point with me, he began to find fault, saying that we had marched too slowly.' Blumenthal was mollified, however, when next day his proposal was accepted and the Second Army ordered to move forward.[15]

On July 12, after another sharp cavalry skirmish at Tischnowitz, Duke William of Mecklenburg, leading the advance guard of the First Army, was approaching Brünn, the capital of Moravia. In spite of the lack of resistance thus far, Moltke was cautious, issuing from Zwittau orders that Frederick Charles should judge for himself what opposition was likely to be encountered there, but adding:

> According to the information received through the Second Army, and yesterday evening communicated from here to the First and Elbe Armies, the enemy is likely to have at Brünn nothing more than the 10th Austrian Army Corps, which retired in that direction, a part of the cavalry and whatever reinforcements it had been practicable to bring up from Vienna.[16]

Four miles from the city the advanced guard halted, and staff officers went forward to reconnoitre. The situation was soon apparent:

> The sun shone brightly on the spires of the churches and on the roofs of the houses, but no swords or spearheads glittered in its light; and on the fort of the Spielberg, on the western side of the town, no guns could be seen, and no sentinels stood upon the ramparts. White flags of truce were flying from every steeple and from every tower, and, instead of the Austrian colours, a white sheet waved from the flagstaff of the fort.[17]

Later that day Frederick Charles arrived at Brünn at the head of Manstein's division, where he found complete cooperation from the Burgomaster, Dr Giskra.

Back in Vicenza, meanwhile, the Archduke was packing up to leave, taking with him John, his Chief of Staff. He had been taking the necessary steps to get as much of his army up to Vienna as quickly as possible:

> The Infantry Reserve Corps of the army was broken up, and the 5th and 9th Corps increased to four brigades each. The former of these corps was then to march through Tirol, the latter through Styria to the Danube, whereas one corps on the Isonzo, and one division in Istria were all the troops which were deemed necessary to check the advance of the Italian Army.[18]

In Olmütz, Benedek prepared for the southward march of the Army of the North which, it was intended, should be down the valley of the March via Kremsier and Göding to Pressburg, and thence to Vienna. On July 13 the King with Moltke and the Royal Headquarters staff arrived at Brünn. The rapid progress southwards of the First Army had taken its toll, and Moltke granted Frederick Charles' request for a two day halt there to rest and recuperate. His attention was now concentrated on the Second Army, with the progress of which he was still not altogether satisfied. It was still well to the north, but it was nonetheless on the Second Army that must now devolve the principal responsibility both for harrying the Army of the North in its present position and disrupting any attempt on its part to move south:

> The second of these tasks can be best fulfilled by the nearer approach of the Second Army to the fortress of Olmütz, and by the interruption of the railway line at some suitable point attainable by the army between Prerau and Lundenburg.[19]

This of course was in effect the proposal that Blumenthal had put forward two days before, and it was shortly to lead to the first substantial engagement since Königgrätz.

At the same time Herwarth was ordered to proceed directly to Znaim, on the River Thaya, since it was obvious that the First Army had little opposition in its front, and would need no help from the Army of the Elbe.

Hozier sent a report for the readers of *The Times* from Brünn with a pen picture of Moltke:

> A quick light blue eye, a high forehead, and a well set figure, mark him as an intellectual and energetic man, but though quick in action he is so prudent in discourse and so guarded in his speech that from this quality and his wide knowledge of European languages he is known in the army as the man who is silent in seven tongues. Careful and laborious, he has worked out with his own hand and himself calculated almost every detail of the operations in which he has taken Europe by surprise from the lighting rapidity of his strokes and the tremendous consequences of his dispositions, before which the Austrian army has withered away almost before it was gathered together, and which have won for him from his countrymen the title of the first strategist in Europe.

At the same time, however, William Howard Russell, *The Times* correspondent with the Austrian army was suggesting that all was not over:

> The arrival of the troops from Italy has given new life to the army. They are full of confidence and are not at all afraid of the needle gun. The bearing and look of the men I have seen inspire one with confidence in their power to fight, and their Generals are men of experience and skill.[20]

Reflecting next day on the movements to be undertaken when the First Army was once again in motion, Moltke issued more detailed instructions for the march on Vienna. The main bodies of the First Army and the Army of the Elbe were to cross the Thaya, at Muschau and Znaim respectively, not later than July 17. By way of reserve, the Army of the Elbe was to bring up the divisions of Rosenberg and Bentheim, using the railway from Prague to Brünn as soon as it was in full working order. Later in the day, pondering the fact that both armies ought to be on the Thaya by July 15, he amended the instruction, to the effect that there was no objection to the crossing of the Thaya before July 17.

That night, important news came in from the Second Army to the effect that the bulk of Benedek's army was pulling out of Olmütz in the direction of Prerau. It was based on a report from Hartmann, whose leading patrols, pushing down the road from Konitz towards Kosteletz, had during the early morning seen to the eastwards long clouds of dust, which appeared to indicate the march of considerable forces. Hartmann himself rode to the front, at 11.30 am, but could see nothing. Reporting back to Steinmetz, he received orders to push on to Prossnitz, and to send forward patrols to Prerau. He had, however, already put this in hand, and later that afternoon sent back a further report:

> The result of all observation is that the enemy is retreating southward. I request permission to throw myself by way of Dụb on his line of ṛetreat near Krzmann or Kokor, or else by way of Tobitschau on Prerau.[21]

For this he asked for infantry support which Steinmetz, whose corps was not close enough, was unable to provide. Accordingly Steinmetz, in his turn, applied to the Second Army headquarters, confirming Hartmann's opinion of the Austrian movement and suggesting that the I Corps could provide the necessary support. For his part, he authorised Hartmann to go ahead.

On hearing all of this Moltke, at 8.00 am on July 15, revised his plans extensively. For the moment, Herwarth and Frederick Charles must give up the direct march on Vienna, and instead be prepared to attack the enemy if the opportunity should arise. The Army of the Elbe was to reconnoitre towards Vienna, to detect any sign of an advance from the Austrian forces around the capital. The First Army was to move on Lundenburg and from there to attack Benedek as he marched south towards a junction with the forces at Vienna. The task for the Second Army was emphasized as still being 'to watch Olmütz and to delay, as long as possible, the further departure of the enemy.' The Guard and VI Corps were to be brought up to Olmütz; the I and V Corps were directed upon Kremsier and Napagedl. And there was also a change of railway policy; the line from Oderberg, on the Silesian border, joined the southbound line from Olmütz to Lundenburg at Prerau, and Moltke might need to use it, as he pointed out:

> It is now important to observe that the railway line Oderberg–Weisskischen–Lundenburg may become of great importance for our own use, and that it is, therefore, not to be destroyed, but to be protected as well as possible from enterprises from Olmütz, especially at Prerau.[22]

It may have been the outline of these orders, repeated by Captain Mischke when he returned to the Second Army headquarters, that caused Blumenthal the considerable annoyance which he recorded in his diary:

> The dispositions which Moltke communicated to Mischke were absolutely incomprehensible in several points, and when I heard from Mischke that Moltke had several times broken out into reproaches about our slow rate of marching, I could contain myself no longer. Considering our almost superhuman exertions, this was most undeserved.[23]

Having got himself into an impressive rage, Blumenthal succeeded also in winding up the Crown Prince, to the point at which, according to Blumenthal, he contemplated resignation. They compromised by sending Stosch, 'compasses in hand, to point out to Moltke his mistake.' Like many of the tempests, real or imagined, that raged around Blumenthal, this proved a storm in a teacup, and Stosch returned in due course to report that Moltke approved all that had been done.

During the late afternoon of July 14 there had been a sharp exchange near Kralitz between the Prussian 1st Hussar Regiment and some Saxon cavalry; after the Saxons had been driven back, the hussars suffered a number of casualties from artillery and infantry fire, indicating the presence of more substantial forces. The Crown Prince heard of this while on the road to Neustift, and he at once ordered Bonin to send a brigade of infantry, with a battery, to Tobitschau, to support the move which Hartmann proposed to make the following day. Bonin did not, however, get the order until 10.30 pm, so it was agreed that his troops should not move until early the next day.

However, the main body of the cavalry had already moved off at 4.00 pm. Colonel von Barby, with the 1st Cuirassiers, led the advance, reaching Kralitz as night was falling. In the half-light he saw what appeared to be enemy cavalry, and gave orders for the charge. As he approached, though, he found that it was an infantry battalion which had formed square. The charge broke the square into two, but inflicted no further damage and, when Austrian artillery and additional infantry moved up, Barby fell back to Prossnitz. The infantry battalion that he had encountered was from the 2nd Corps

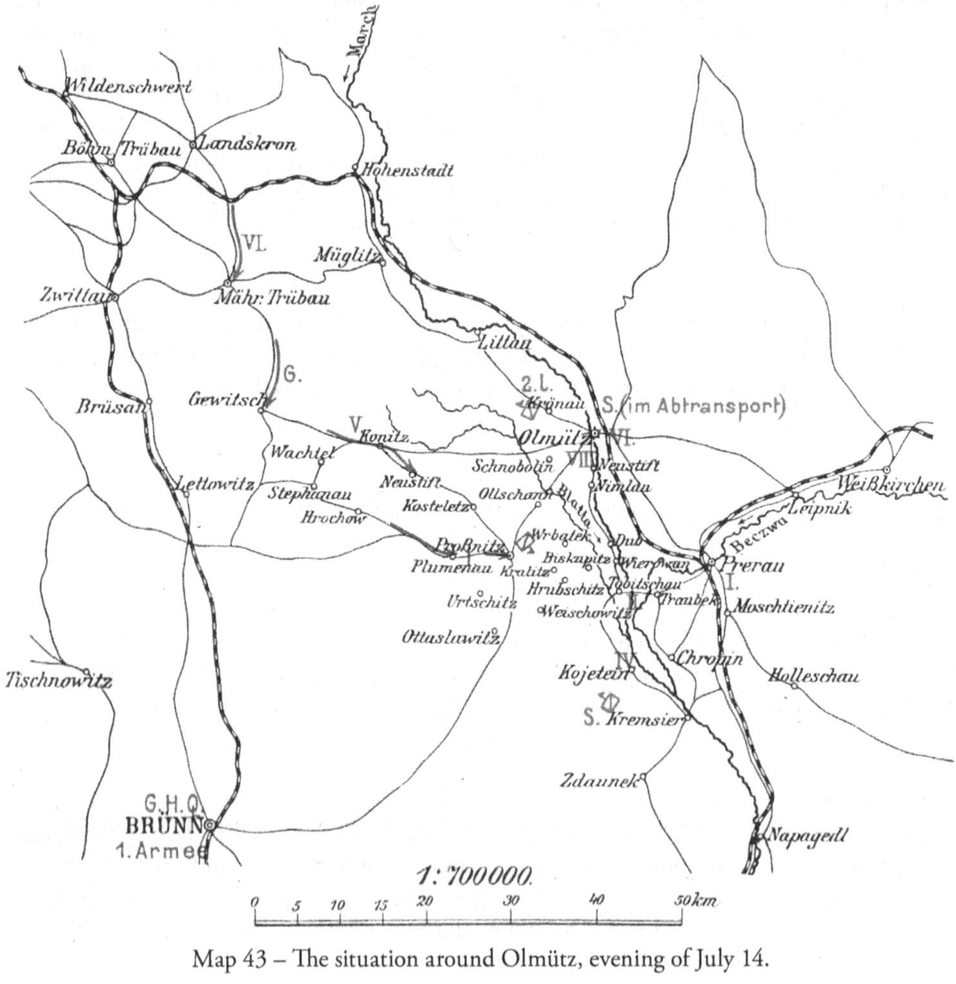

Map 43 – The situation around Olmütz, evening of July 14.

which was heading south from Olmütz in the wake of the 4th Corps. These represented only the first echelon of Benedek's army as it moved south and not, as the first reports reaching Moltke had suggested, the rearguard.[24]

The brigade assigned by Bonin to the task set by the Crown Prince was von Malotki's 3rd Brigade, which broke camp near Stichowitz at 4.00 am on July 15 and set off through

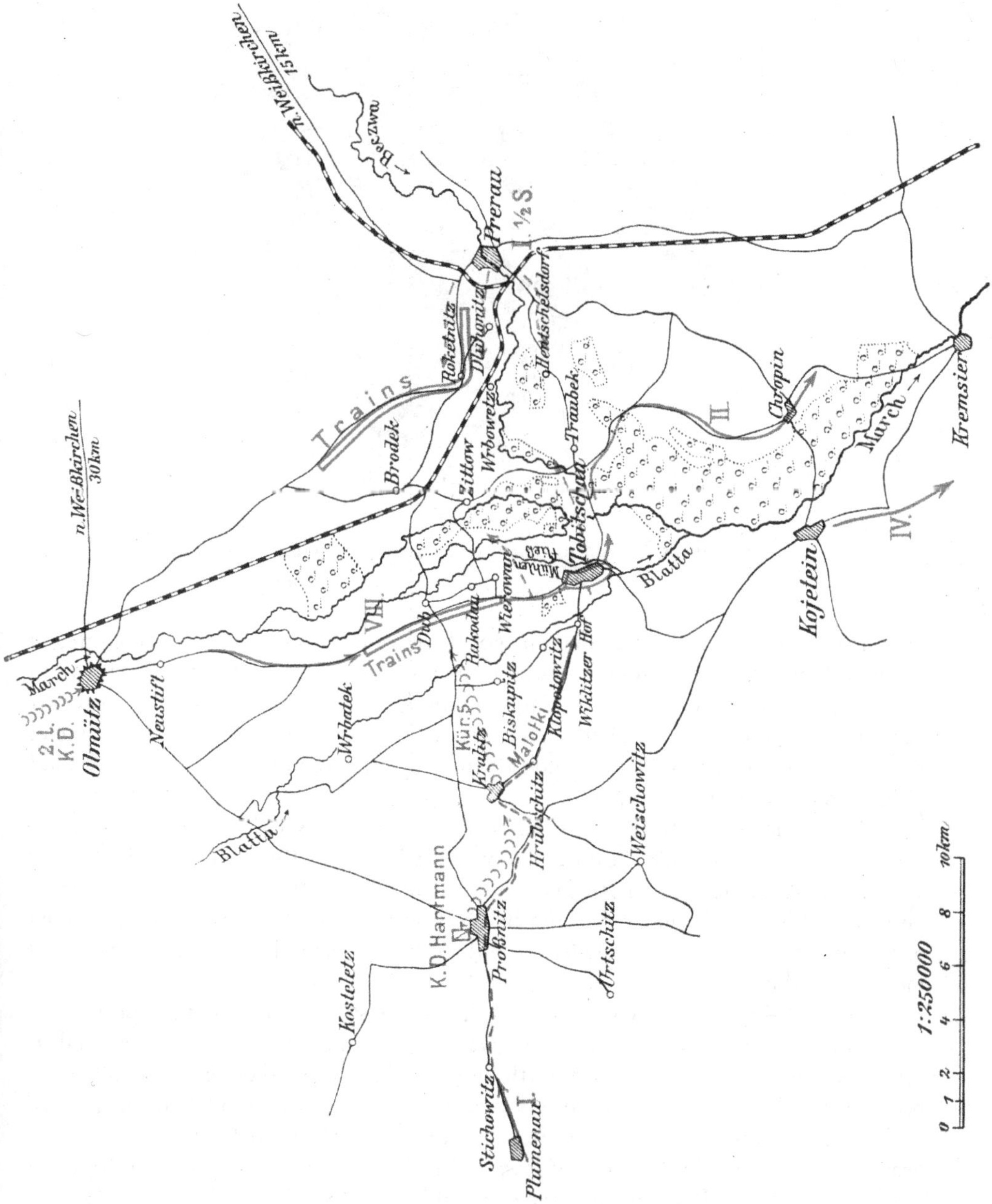

Map 44 – The Battle of Tobitschau, July 15.

Prussian cuirassiers capturing Austrian guns at Rokeinitz/Tobitschau, July 15. (Regensberg/*Letzte Kämpfe und Friedenschluss*)

Prossnitz towards Hrubschitz. When he got there Malotki could see heavy columns of enemy infantry at Dub marching south on the high road towards Tobitschau. It was in fact Rothkirch's Brigade of the 8th Corps, a unit that had not previously been in action. Malotki decided on an immediate attack with the object of cutting the enemy's line of march at Tobitschau. Bonin, who had ridden forward, gave orders that the rest of the I Corps should come up in support.

Malotki advanced from a position between the farms of Klopotowitz and the Wiklitzerhof, coming under heavy artillery fire as he did so. One four pounder battery and two horse artillery batteries came up in support, but could not silence the Austrian guns. The 44th Regiment crossed the Blatta river and occupied a pheasantry, driving out a party of Austrian skirmishers, while the 4th Regiment also crossed the river and moved on Tobitschau.[25]

For some time the foggy weather and the smoke of battle obscured the position of the enemy, but when the smoke cleared it was seen that the Austrian infantry had taken up a position along the main road north of Tobitschau, while their artillery had fallen back towards Dub. Malotki wasted no time; the 44th Regiment at once stormed out of the pheasantry, attacking the Austrians in front and on their left flank and in spite of heavy firing drove them back on Wirowan. The Austrian gunners kept up a brisk fire until the advancing Prussian infantry got within rifle range, and then fell back to a position to the west of Wirowan.

Meanwhile Hartmann's sharp-eyed ADC, Lieutenant von Rosenberg, had found a bridge further up river, opposite the flank of the Austrian batteries, which he could see was unprotected by infantry. He reported his find to Lieutenant Colonel von Bredow who at once grasped the opportunity and rode forward with three squadrons of cuirassiers and clattered over the shaky bridge. Seeing this, Hartmann moved his two horse artillery batteries up to the Blatta to occupy the enemy's attention while Bredow, as soon as he was over the bridge, charged straight at the Austrian guns. As luck would have it, Benedek and his staff had been riding south with the 8th Corps, and were on the road close to the Austrian batteries when they saw Bredow's cuirassiers approaching:

> In the mist of the morning and the smoke of the Austrian guns it was not easy to tell whether they were Austrian or enemy cavalry. While Benedek hung in perplexity … the Prussians charged and captured eighteen guns of the battery under his eyes. The handful of dragoons who formed his escort threw the themselves against the cuirassiers, but it was a useless sacrifice, and Benedek and the whole of his staff stood in danger of being captured till he turned his horse and followed by a few of his officers rode from the field.[26]

It was, says his biographer, the nadir of his career. It had been a brilliant stroke by Bredow and the Prussian cuirassiers, seizing the kind of opportunity for which cavalrymen longed but which rarely came their way. At a cost of only ten men, the cuirassiers took eighteen guns, with limbers and artillery wagons, and 170 prisoners.[27]

This image conveys the suitability of the terrain for Bredow's cavalry attack at Rokeinitz/Tobitschau on July 15. Bredow's men assaulted from the right of the photograph. (Rogers)

They now assembled on the left bank of the Blatta to support Malotki's further advance on Wirowan, which he soon took, driving the Austrian infantry out of this place and the neighbouring villages of Rakodau and Nenakowitz, pushing them back to the north towards Dub.

During these engagements Hartmann had taken most of the rest of his cavalry in the direction of Tobitschau, supported by five companies of the 4th Regiment. After stiff resistance from three companies of the Austrian 71st Regiment, the town had been taken by Pannwitz; the enemy were pushed back to Traubeck, which was soon occupied by the infantry. Hartmann was now in a position to launch his thrust at Prerau; the cavalry were accompanied in their advance by one company of infantry in carts commandeered for the purpose. It was just as well that Hartmann wasted very little time; with a large part of Benedek's army still pressing south down the road from Olmütz, it was to be expected that there would soon be further opposition to face.

This was not long in coming; by 1.30 pm fresh Austrian batteries, which had taken up a position at Dub, opened fire on Malotki's brigade, while 'dense clouds of dust on the Olmutz road now announced the approach of fresh forces.'[28] Bonin's decision to bring up the rest of the I Corps to a position in which it could if necessary lend a hand now proved to be a sound one. The artillery of the advanced guard arrived on the scene at 2.00 pm, and took up a position near Biskupitz, from which it could open fire at long range at the advancing Austrian infantry.

The road outside Tobitschau, scene of a sharp engagement on July 15, where the Austrian 71st Infantry suffered severe casualties. (Rogers)

The attack of the latter, however, soon broke down in the outskirts of Rakodau and Nenakowitz, and as they scrambled back hurriedly to the position taken up by the Austrian artillery they left behind a considerable number of prisoners. Malotki chased them up the Olmütz road as far as Dub, and then left it at that; enough had been done to make it clear that there could be no further direct movement from Olmütz towards Lundenburg.

In the meantime Hartmann's troopers, crossing the Beczwa close to Prerau at about 3.00 pm, making for Dluhonitz and Rokeinitz, came upon 'a numerous suite' which appeared to be Benedek's staff; the Austrian confusion was further increased by the fact that at this time part of the 1st Corps was moving on the road to Prerau, but its principal commanders were not with the troops, having gone off for a conference with Gondrecourt, the corps commander.

The threat to Benedek and his staff brought five squadrons of Austrian hussars hurrying to the scene. Hartmann's hussars and uhlans enjoyed themselves, breaking up the marching columns, wrecking the wagon trains, and taking a considerable number of prisoners before, in the face of the rapidly-strengthening opposition, the recall was sounded. Even then Colonel von Glasenapp, retreating with three squadrons of Landwehr hussars, could not resist charging the very much stronger force of Austrian hussars who had arrived to protect Benedek; these trotted up to within ten paces of his troops as they made their way back. With about 130 riders, he charged into the mass of Austrian cavalry; the latter were, understandably, taken by surprise and halted, convinced that so rash an assault must indicate the presence of stronger Prussian forces close by. In fact, there were none; the Landwehr hussars disengaged and fell back, leaving their commander seriously wounded in the enemy's hands. In the course of their retreat they broke up the railway, and telegraph, before recrossing the Beczwa. Hartmann finally pulled back to the west of Tobitschau at 5.00 pm; Malotki remained in position until after dark. The Austrians did not pursue. During the course of these two actions the total Prussian loss amounted to 247; the Austrians sustained casualties of just over 2,000.[29]

That night Benedek slept at Prerau, where both the 1st and the 8th Corps remained after the clashes at Tobitschau and Rokeinitz; and it was there that he received the disturbing news that Göding, forty five miles to the south of Olmütz, was already in Prussian hands.

This meant that the route he intended to take to the Danube, down the valley of the March, was no longer practicable, and he was obliged to issue orders to those corps whose retreat southward had been interrupted to retire over the passes of the Lower Carpathians into the valley of the Waag, and thence to make their way to Pressburg.

Göding itself, fifteen miles north-east of Lundenburg, had not in fact been taken on July 15; but the news of heavy Austrian troop movements by rail through the town led Horn, whose 8th Division now had this as its immediate objective, to send a party of 150 uhlans, with some engineers, to wreck the railway:

> When the leading horsemen came in sight of the railway they could distinguish two trains, one close behind the other, with engines pulling and snorting violently, as if drawing a heavy load, steaming slowly in the direction of Lundenburg.[30]

It was clearly urgently necessary to act, and within a few minutes the line was effectively wrecked, just north of Göding, causing a train-load of Saxon troops hurriedly to reverse. Although the uhlans were soon driven off, the damage had been done; and

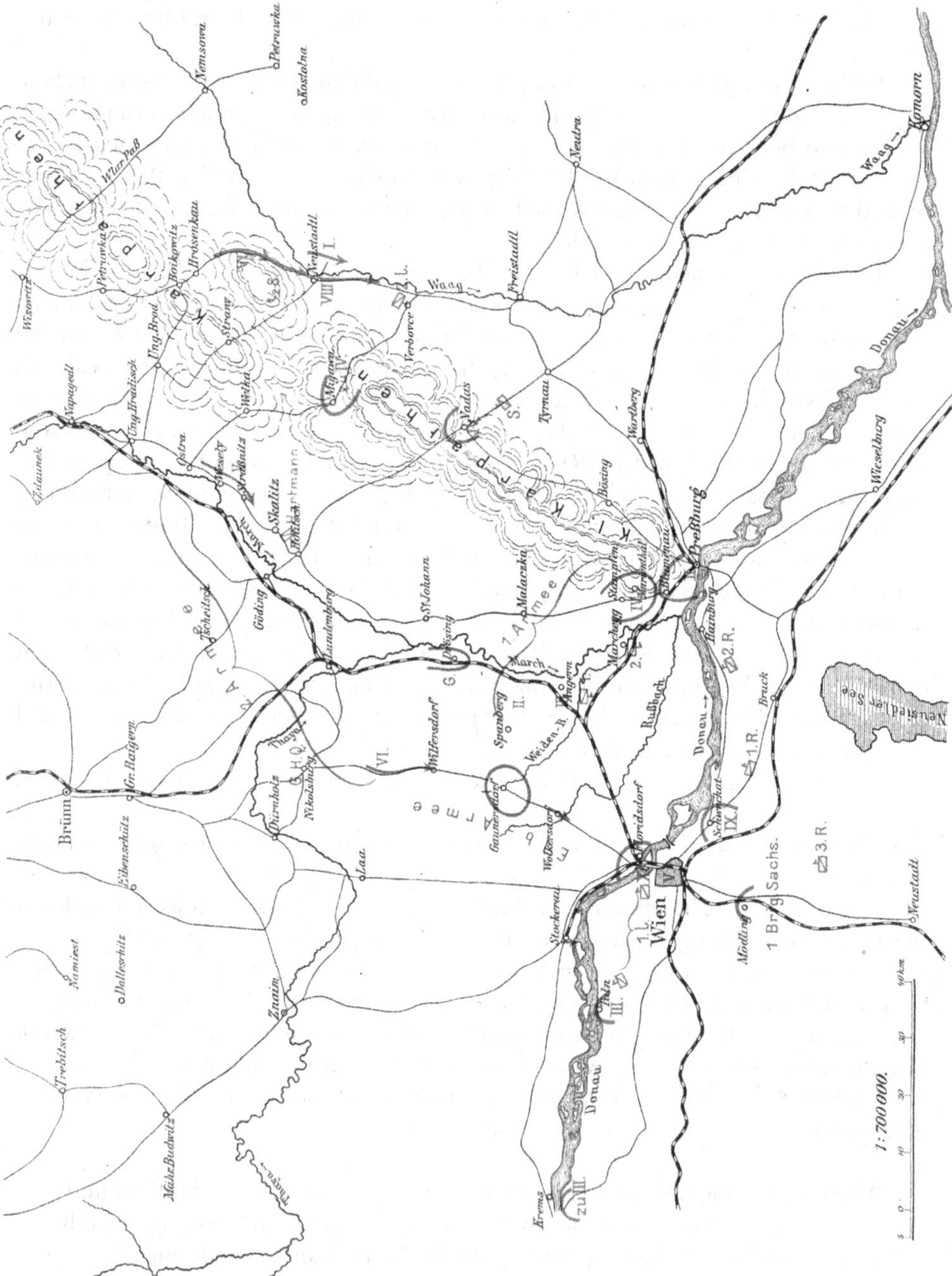

Map 45 – Situation on the evening of July 21.

in any case by 4.00 pm next day the leading troops of Horn's Division entered Göding from which the small remaining garrison soon retreated.

Fransecky had meanwhile marched with the 7th Division on Lundenburg, which had been designated as the First Army's immediate objective in the light of the news of Benedek's southward movement from Olmütz. Fransecky occupied Lundenburg on July 16, encountering little opposition. Behind these leading divisions, the rest of Frederick Charles' army also resumed its march southward. The Army of the Elbe, which did not receive the revised orders issued early on July 15, continued its march that day on Znaim but on the following day changed direction to move on Laa.

Benedek and his corps commanders displayed commendable energy in the retreat across the mountains into the Waag valley, moving so quickly that contact was entirely broken off, leaving Moltke entirely at a loss to know the direction the Austrians had taken. From Brünn on July 17 he issued a general instruction 'for an advance towards the Danube, but whether the direction is to be that of Vienna or of Pressburg cannot yet be determined.' But he went on to make it clear that he would retain tight control over the armies:

> The circumstances of the moment render it necessary to regulate from here the movements of the First, Second and Elbe Armies, and the directive instructions for them can be given for only a short time in advance.[31]

The First Army's task would be to prevent a movement by the troops at Vienna from moving to Pressburg, with the Army of the Elbe marching on its right on Vienna. The Second Army was to come up in support. Moltke was uneasy at this time about the possibility that the Austrian forces concentrating in the capital might launch an attack from the direction of Florisdorf, and over the next couple of days he worked out contingency plans to meet it, bringing up all his available reserves for the purpose. Only Bonin's I Corps would remain behind to watch Olmütz.[32] On July 19 the long columns continued southwards, advancing across a plain dotted with clumps of willow trees. The countryside appeared wild and strange to the Prussians:

> This plain was covered with droves of horses, pigs and large white cattle, with broad outstretched horns about as large as those of buffaloes. These droves were tended by boys clad, some in proper Hungarian costume, but more frequently in a white flannel cloak which, hanging from their shoulders down to their ankles, formed their only covering.[33]

That day Moltke spelt out to his army commanders his intentions for the battle which might have to be fought very soon, and which might either be a defensive battle to meet the possible Austrian attack from Florisdorf, or might provide the opportunity for an attack on that place followed by a brisk movement on Pressburg. Such a battle would be fought over historic ground: 'It is the intention of His Majesty the King to concentrate the army in a position behind the Russbach, with the Army of the Elbe at Wolkersdorf, the First Army behind Deutsch-Wagram, and the second as reserve at Schönkirchen.'[34] Not only the troops in reserve at Prague and Pardubitz were to be brought up, but arrangements were also made for heavy artillery to be brought down from Dresden to

Lundenburg 'at a moments' notice.' Moltke was taking very seriously the possibility that there was still a lot of fight left in the Austrians; and although with the diplomatic negotiations going on, the possibility of another major battle was evidently receding, he still hoped for more action; to his wife he wrote, after hearing of the successes of the Army of the Main: 'the Lord is evidently on the side of Prussia's standards. May He only continue to favour us here also; for we are on the road to most decisive events if only diplomacy does not intervene to prevent us.'[35]

Beyond the Carpathians, Benedek was also hurrying southwards. By July 20, the leading units of his army had reached Tyrnau, about twenty five miles north-east of

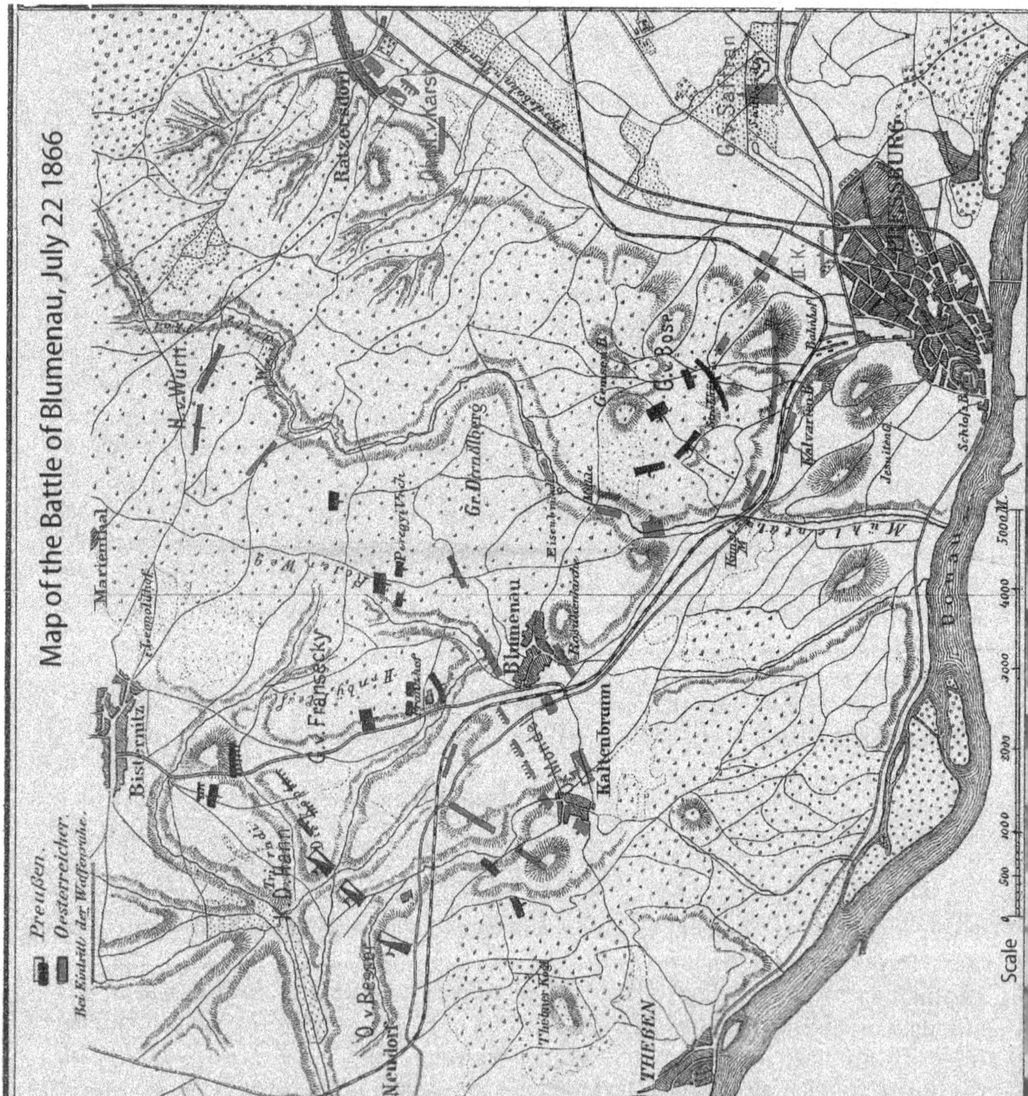

Map 46 – The Battle of Blumenau, July 22.

Pressburg; but although the leading brigade, that of Henriquez, was at once loaded on to carts and rushed to a position supporting Mondl's Brigade, which was the only effective cover for Pressburg, the rest of the Army of the North was well strung-out, and it would be some days before it could operate effectively as a cohesive unit. When and if it did so, it would not be under Benedek's command; as he rode down the valley of the Waag, a journey which he remembered making in 1849 at a time when his star was rising, he received news which he must have been expecting. A letter from Count Crenneville informed him that he was to appear before a Commission of Inquiry to answer for all that had occurred to the Northern Army, from the day he took over the command to the day when he was to relinquish it.[36] The Imperial selection of a scapegoat to bear most of the blame for the débacle had evidently been already made. At Vienna, the troops of the 5th and 9th Corps from the Army of the South were already arriving, and by July 20 some fifty thousand men were taking up positions in defence of the capital.

In concentrating his army in front of and to the north-east of Vienna, Moltke had in mind one immediate operation, which was to be a surprise assault on Pressburg before the Army of the North could arrive in sufficient force. During July 20 the advanced guard of the Army of the Elbe reached Wolkersdorf, while that of the First Army arrived on the Weiderbach and took up a position between Weikendorf and Schönkirchen. On the following day both armies remained in those positions, save for the forces to be employed in the thrust at Pressburg. Horn, the commander of the 8th Division, had evidently not given satisfaction, being posted to the command of a new Reserve Division being formed at Leipzig, to which he was at once dispatched; Bose took over for the time being, and was placed under Fransecky's command for the operation. Another reshuffle saw Schöler replaced by Goltz as commander of the Army of the Elbe's advanced guard; Moltke evidently intended to make it clear to all that only the highest level of performance was acceptable.[37]

Stülpnagel accompanied Fransecky and Bose on a reconnaissance towards Blumenau and Kaltenbrunn, finding only a battalion, a few squadrons and some guns in an advanced position between the two villages. He recommended, therefore, that the operation against Pressburg should take place the next day. For this Fransecky had eighteen battalions, twenty four squadrons and 78 guns. During the night of July 21/22 he took up a position with the 8th Division south of Bisternitz, the advanced guard having pushed on down the road to Blumenau, while the 7th Division was at Masst and Strampffen, and Hann's 2nd Cavalry Division at Marchegg. Permission to undertake the operation came with the arrival of Count Häseler from the First Army headquarters; he left there at 3.00 am on July 22, news not yet having reached Frederick Charles of the armistice which had finally been agreed at Nikolsburg to come into force at noon on July 22. He arrived at Fransecky's headquarters at dawn, after a rough ride through a moonless night; Fransecky, therefore, went ahead with his advance.

The principal Austrian forces had been located at Blumenau; on the right of the position rose the most westerly spurs of the Carpathians:

> The ground on the mountain sides is everywhere rough and broken, large stones are scattered over it, and in many places jagged lumps of rock start out of the soil and form natural fortresses to oppose the passage of troops up the hills. A dense forest of oak and pine trees, which, from being untended, have grown close together, and

> intertwined their branches… grows upon the sides of the ravines and the less steep spurs of the mountains.[38]

On the left flank of the Austrian position:

> Opposite to Blumenau, and about three-quarters of a mile to the right, lies the little village of Kaltenbrunn, situated on rough, broken hills called the Theben-Berger, which are thickly clothed with fir woods, and fill up the whole triangle enclosed between the railway, the March and the Danube.[39]

It was a dauntingly strong position and Fransecky decided to outflank it, sending Bose with the 15th Brigade, comprising six battalions of the 31st and 71st Regiments, about 5,000 men, over the mountain paths from Bisternitz to strike the enemy's rear near the Gämsenberg, seizing the Prohaska and Jäger mills and thereby cutting off the whole Austrian force from Pressburg, while the 7th Division attacked in front.

Mondl, whose brigade held Blumenau, had the close support of Henriquez' Brigade (now commanded by Colonel von Schutte) which was based around the Kunst Mill. Mondl's front line was along the railway embankment north-west of the town. In front of this position, two squadrons of lancers clashed with a squadron of Prussian hussars, which drove them back. Other troops were arriving in Pressburg, some still on the road through Bosing and St Georgen; Württemberg's Brigade was in Ratzersdorff and Saffran's Brigade on the road to Pressburg from Wartburg. Within easy reach of the battlefield the Austrians had 24 battalions, 11 squadrons and 24 guns, although how effective they were remained to be seen:

The Battle of Blumenau, July 22. (Fontane)

The railway embankment at Blumenau-Pressburg. (Rogers)

> The state of fatigue, in which those troops must have been, may be well imagined, if one considers what exertions had been demanded of them during the whole of the retreat from Olmütz, most especially on the 21st and the following night.[40]

Bose did not move off until 6.30 am, by which time the 7th Division had already begun its advance, led by a squadron of hussars. They encountered two squadrons of Austrian lancers, and at first retreated but then turned on their pursuers and chased them back behind the railway embankment. The artillery now opened fire at long range; Fransecky, concerned that Bose's late start meant that it would be some time before the effect of the flanking movement could be felt, sent forward two battalions against Kaltenbrunn and a larger force under the redoubtable Gordon against the enemy right. Mondl reinforced both flanks and sent a message to Thun, who had arrived in Pressburg, asking for help to hold the position.

At about this time Fransecky got news of the armistice that was to come into force, although not until midday. This gave him a serious problem. He was heavily engaged and it would be difficult to recall his troops:

> Great results might be expected from the measures that had been taken. Being perfectly justified in making full use of his freedom of action until midday, the General saw no reason for breaking off the action which he had commenced until this hour.[41]

Accordingly, he moved up his artillery to a closer range, and brought forward further infantry battalions in support of those attacking the Austrian flanks. Hann's cavalry was deployed on the right flank.

By 9.00 am Fransecky's right had reached the railway embankment, and pushed on through the woods towards Kaltenbrunn. On the opposite flank, Gordon was experiencing considerable difficulty in advancing under heavy fire over the broken ground in front of Franzhof. Bose, meanwhile, advancing in two columns over the mountains, aimed to unite them in Mondl's rear at the Gämsenberg by 10.00 am:

> The troops marched without knapsacks and in foraging caps, but this march over the heights and ravines of these wooded mountains was excessively fatiguing; the heads of the column were often obliged to halt for the files to close up.[42]

The 12th Company of the 31st Regiment had been left behind to act as rearguard; when it set off it took the wrong road, encountered two Austrian detachments, took 42 prisoners, and was then split into two parts but nevertheless got back to Marienthal with the prisoners, at a cost of 3 casualties.

Fransecky had no idea of Bose's progress; the uhlans appointed as message bearers had got involved in the adventures of the 12th Company. By 10.00 am, with two hours left to him, Fransecky decided on a frontal attack, supported by a prolonged artillery barrage. The advance was immediately successful, Gordon taking the Franzhof with the advanced guard, while still further to the left a battalion of the 67th Regiment drove back the Austrians for some way before encountering a regiment from Württemburg's Brigade that had come up from Ratzersdorf.

A memorial to the Battle of Blumenau-Pressburg atop the Gämsenberg. (Rogers)

Just as Fransecky began his advance, Bose's leading battalion arrived at the foot of the Gämsenberg and stormed the hill, driving back the Austrians with heavy loss. The Prussians now deployed on the hill, and the battle continued, with the Austrians being driven back step by step, until finally Bose seized the water mills and pushed his brigade across the road and railway to Pressburg.[43] Thun brought up reserves to take the 15th Brigade in flank; but Bose had detached one fusilier battalion to cover himself against an advance from Pressburg and the rest of his force wheeled to the right to attack Blumenau in rear. Two further battalions, however, missed his signal and followed the fusiliers towards Pressburg. Bose's advance was hampered by the rough and broken terrain, but after some brisk skirmishing the Austrians were seen to be retreating all along the front of the 15th Brigade. Bose had, when he reached the Gämsenberg, heard of the armistice; and at noon Austrian flags of truce began to appear all along the line. For a while firing continued, as news of the armistice only gradually spread, and then the order to cease fire was given:

> The sudden silence was curious and abrupt; there were none of the dropping shots or single occasional reports in which a cannonade generally dies away; in a moment the roar of artillery and the patter of small arms ceased, and a curious hum of conversation rose from the astonished soldiers.[44]

Not surprisingly the Austrians found it hard at first to believe that a large part of their force was effectively surrounded, although in the subsequent discussions to agree the armistice line they soon realised the extent of their predicament. Stülpnagel rode forward to Pressburg to negotiate a new armistice line with Thun; the positions agreed during the morning at Eibesbrunn between John, as the Archduke's Chief of Staff, and Podbielski, now bore little relation to the situation on the ground. In the light of this, Thun accepted the justice of Stülpnagel's claim that Bose's force should be permitted to remain on the line it had occupied until noon of next day, in this way demonstrating its success and the position it had gained.[45] Hozier described what followed:

> Then occurred a curious scene. The men of Bose's Prussian Brigade ... were surrounded by groups of those very Austrian soldiers whom they had been waiting to destroy. The men of the two nations mingled together, exchanged tobacco, drank out of each other's flasks, talked and laughed over the war in groups equally composed of blue and white uniforms, cooked their rations at the same fires, and that night Austrian and Prussian battalions lay down bivouacked close together, without fear and in perfect security.[46]

Whatever the diplomats still had to settle, these soldiers knew that the war was over.

In the action at Blumenau, the Prussians lost 27 killed, 169 wounded and 11 missing; the Austrian casualties amounted to 61 killed, 245 wounded and 184 missing. By the standards of earlier battles the losses were, as the Official History points out, 'trifling.'[47] It had been a well-planned and brilliantly conducted affair, and illustrated clearly the gap in military effectiveness that separated the two sides. But it had been perfectly unnecessary, and those that died on the field of Blumenau died for nothing more than an obscure and unsustainable concept of military honour.

31

Kissingen

In spite of mounting criticism in Berlin of his performance in the campaign so far, it was still Falckenstein's responsibility to deal with the Bavarian Army and the Federal 8th Corps, whose half hearted advances northward towards the beleaguered Hanoverians had brought them within easy striking distance of the Prussian troops now designated as the Army of the Main.

The first direct news of the Hanoverian intention to head southwards had reached the Bavarians as early as June 18, when a Hanoverian staff officer arrived at Schweinfurt and asked von Hartmann, commanding the Bavarian division there, for approval for the move; readily giving it, the Bavarians asked to know the intended route, and on June 21 were told that Fulda was to be the objective. It was here, therefore, that Prince Charles determined to concentrate his army, but progress was slow, and news came on June 25 that the Hanoverians had turned away from Eisenach, where large numbers of Prussian troops seemed to be concentrating.

Clearly something must be done urgently to coordinate the future movements of the allied forces, and on June 26 Charles met with Prince Alexander to discuss their future strategy. It was not a simple problem; and the instructions given to Alexander by Kübeck, the Austrian President of the Confederation, on June 23 were hardly conducive to close cooperation:

> In drawing up the Bavarian Commander-in-Chief's plan of operations, care must be taken that operations shall always be in harmony with the local interests of the various states in the allied armies and that consideration is given to the protection of the commanders' own countries as much as to the achievement of the main purpose of the war by the greatest possible concentration of the forces.[1]

Information about the Hanoverian movements was scanty; the most advanced Bavarian troops, Hartmann's division, stood echeloned from Neustadt northwards to Fladungen, while the Light Cavalry Brigade had been pushed forward to Meiningen, less than 35 miles from Gotha; and the 8th Corps was still concentrated around Frankfurt, the protection of which was Alexander's principal concern. His strong preference was for a movement north on Cassel, since this appeared to him the most effective means of covering Frankfurt while going over to the offensive which he hoped would force a Prussian retreat. Charles, on the other hand, preferred to make Eisenach the objective, and to move northwards while covering both Würzburg and Bamberg. It was finally decided to advance both parts of the Federal army to a concentration around Hersfeld, the intention being that this union should be achieved by July 7.

There was evidently no serious consideration given to hastening the Bavarians northward in the meantime to try to assist the Hanoverians; both the lack of information about the latter's fate, and the unreadiness of the Bavarians for immediate combat, would have made such a course extremely hazardous. On the other hand the two princes had set themselves a pretty optimistic target in aiming at Hersfeld, since although it would be a good position in which to bar a Prussian advance either to Frankfurt or into Bavaria, it was not very likely that the Prussians would let them get there; they were a lot closer to that point than the Federal Army.[2] June 26 was also the day that the young King Ludwig II reluctantly tore himself away from his beloved Hohenschwangau to visit his armies in the field at Bamberg. Although Ludwig much disliked all things military, 'the whole tour was a triumphant success,' as his favourite aide de camp, Prince Paul Thurn und Taxis reported to Richard Wagner, the King having spent twenty hours in the saddle.[3]

Hopes that the Hersfeld position could be reached in time depended on the Hanoverians holding up the Prussians for long enough or, better still, breaking through to join the allies. For the moment, though, whatever happened at Langensalza, speed was of the essence; but unfortunately Alexander in particular was quite unready to move immediately, and it was agreed to commence the manoeuvre on June 30. Charles, meanwhile, almost at once altered his own line of march, deciding to move to his right and to cross the Thuringian Forest towards Gotha in an effort to be of some assistance to the Hanoverians, while his cavalry took a position on his left to maintain contact with Alexander, moving on Vacha. In the first instance it was to concentrate at Kissingen. Charles accordingly shifted his headquarters to Meiningen; there, however, he learned of the Hanoverian capitulation, which rendered any move towards Eisenach pointless. For the moment he resolved to concentrate at Meiningen.

It was at once obvious, or should have been, that the whole of Falckenstein's army was now in a position to move south towards the allies. Unfortunately Alexander had, with one eye on the interests of the states from which his troops were drawn, decided to march first northwards, and then north-east, to the rendezvous, taking the road through Grunberg. On June 30 the bulk of his force was still at Friedberg, some eighty miles from Charles at Meiningen. Had he marched eastwards in the first instance by the Gelnhausen road, he would have been better placed to link up with the Bavarians further south, out of Falckenstein's reach. As it was, the Hanoverian collapse found the allies in a position in which the Prussians, if they moved fast enough, could get between the two halves of the Federal army.

On June 30 Charles wrote to Alexander to call for a return to their original scheme:

> I ... earnestly request your Highness to waive all secondary considerations and to join me with all your available forces, partly by the line Hanau-Fulda-Hünfeld; partly, and in particular, by the line Frankfurt-Gemünden per railway, and from there over Hammelburg to Kissingen.[4]

But Alexander's line of march made such a movement impracticable, quite apart from the political implications of taking a step that would uncover Frankfurt and the west if Falckenstein chose to take that direction. The best Alexander could do was to march on Fulda, rather than Alsfeld as originally intended, moving by Ulrichstein and Lauterbach. These extended marches did his troops no favours; the weather had broken, and it rained heavily as the 8th Corps trudged eastwards, without adequate food or tents, through a countryside devoid of supplies. Alexander's own morale was not improved, either by the course of his own campaign or by the news from Bohemia. He wrote gloomily in his diary on July 2:

> This shocking news came like a bolt from the blue... so all the newspaper reports about successes won by Ramming, Gablenz and Edelsheim were all lies. Our situation begins to be very critical. I am trying to link up with the Bavarians, but do not know where they are. Fifty thousand Prussians under Manteuffel and Beyer are encamped at Hersfeld. The line of the Main and Mainz are threatened, and Austria is evacuating Bohemia.[5]

Alexander was still apprehensive about his left, detaching the Baden brigade to clear the Wetzlar-Giessen area of suspected enemy activity, and leaving the combined Austrian-Nassau division in Frankfurt for the moment in case of any enemy movement from Coblenz. While he was trying to establish contact with Charles, the latter was by now in an exposed situation. Hartmann was at Wasungen and Wernshausen, covering the hasty manoeuvres by which Charles endeavoured to get the rest of his army over the Hohe-Rhön mountains in a westward shuffle towards Fulda. The passes over the mountains were not good, and this movement was not going to be easy. It was as well that Hartmann was in position around Wasungen, since it was soon apparent that the Prussians were moving south from Eisenach, as skirmishes on the evening of July 2 demonstrated.

That day, Falckenstein had moved off in two columns, Beyer on the right heading for Hünfeld and Goeben on the left towards Marksuhl and Lengsfeld, with Manteuffel in reserve behind them. It was Moltke's wish that the Army of the Main should aim for Schweinfurt, since only by such a move was it to be expected that both the Bavarians and the 8th Corps could be brought to battle. Falckenstein's continuing fascination with the idea of a thrust at Frankfurt suggested to him that Fulda was the point at which to aim; and for the moment, having regard to the position of his adversaries, that was probably his best target. It was entirely possible that he could reach Fulda before either Charles or Alexander. Recognising this, Moltke telegraphed Colonel von Kraatz-Koschlau, Falckenstein's Chief of Staff, directing the Army of the Main to Fulda; by confronting the Bavarians on their own territory, all the other enemy detachments would be compelled to retreat.[6]

The direction of Falckenstein's advance was such that it was all too possible that he would reach Fulda in force before either Charles or Alexander. The best of the roads for the Bavarians ran around the north of the Hohe-Rhön from Wasungen via Dermbach and Geisa to Hünfeld, and on July 3 Hartmann took this road, while the other three divisions crossed the mountains to the south. It soon became plain that the Prussians had indeed got further than expected, since patrols from Zoller's division found the enemy in possession of the crossroads at Dermbach, while Hartmann encountered a detachment at Wiesenthal, although this at once retreated.[7]

Falckenstein's intelligence reports gave him a pretty accurate view of the movements of the Bavarians, and he determined to continue his push towards Fulda, ordering Beyer to march on Hünfeld, while Goeben was to brush aside any opposition from the left and then fall in behind Beyer, with Manteuffel bringing up the rear. It was not therefore

General von Goeben, commander of the Prussian 13th Division in the Army of the Main. (Rogers)

expected that Beyer would encounter much opposition, but in the event it was in his front that the first clash occurred on July 4.

Prince Taxis, who was in command of the Bavarian Reserve Cavalry, had been moving north through Fulda in obedience to his orders to march on Vacha and act as a link between the two parts of the Federal Army. He had reached Fulda on July 3 and from there sent a message to Alexander asking for support, since he believed that the 8th

The panic-stricken flight of the Bavarian cavalry at Hünfeld, July 4. (Fontane)

Corps now to be not far off and he himself had no infantry at all. Alexander, though, had granted a rest day for July 4 and declined the request, so Taxis set off northwards from Fulda on his own, sending two cuirassier regiments on ahead to reconnoitre. Having got beyond Hünfeld, at 7.00 am these ran into the head of Beyer's division; when the Prussians brought two four pounder guns into action the Bavarians panicked and fled at once back to Hünfeld, leaving one gun and 28 prisoners. Their flight did not stop

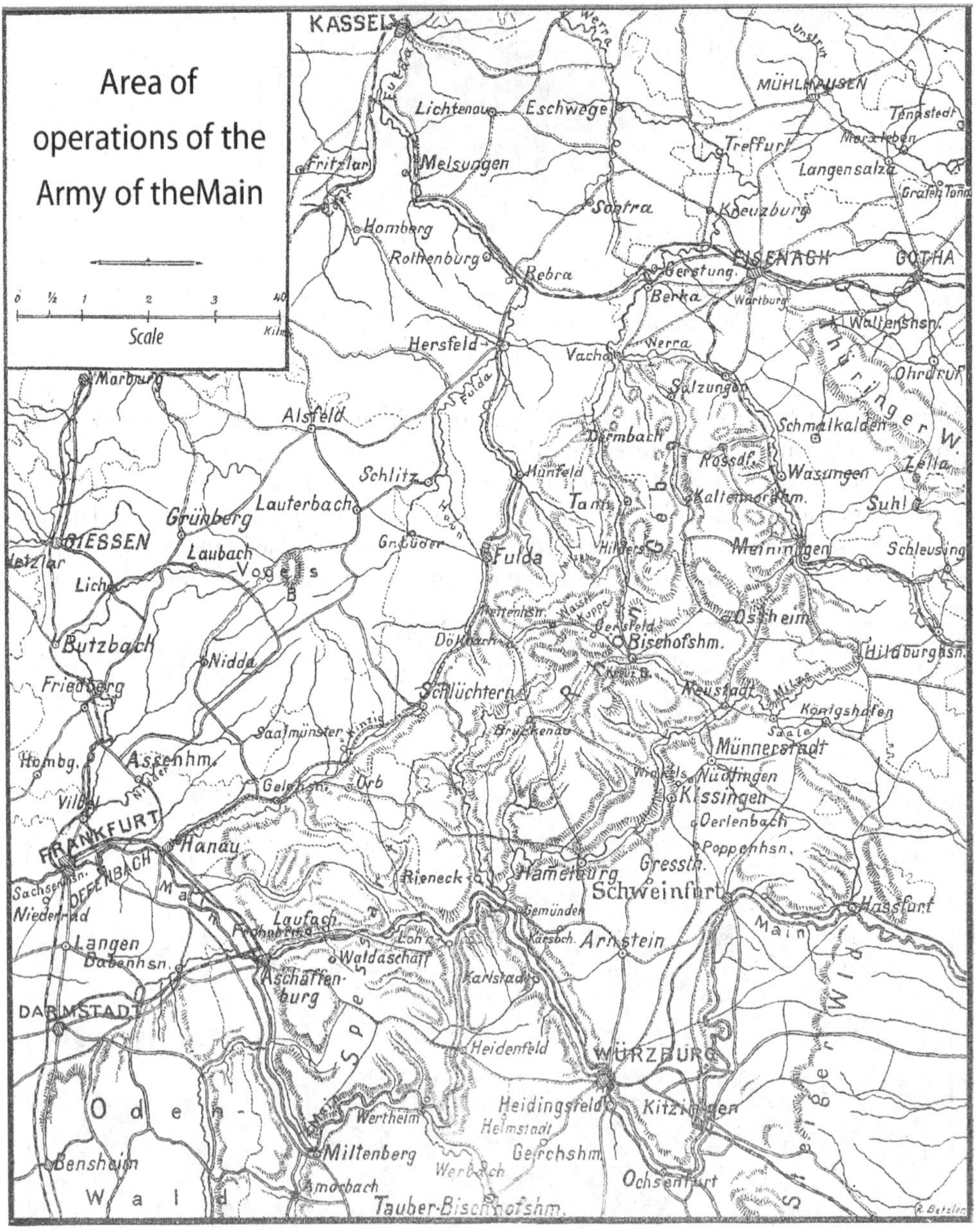

Map 47 – Area of operations of the Army of the Main.

there; soon, as they streamed southwards, they met the main body of Prince Taxis' force, which itself turned about and retreated precipitately, at first to Fulda and then beyond, not finally stopping until it reached Brückenau. Taxis himself rallied one regiment and

Map 48 – The Battle of Dermbach, July 4.

a battery of horse artillery, and took up a position at Döllbach, but it took several days before the rest of his force could be collected up and restored as a combat unit.[8]

Meanwhile Goeben had been in action as planned, sending Kummer at 8.00 am to attack the enemy in their position at Zella-Neidhartshausen, while Wrangel moved on Wiesenthal. The Zella position was naturally a strong one, the village standing on a height with steep slopes and protected in its front by marshy meadows. In the centre of Zella a convent with stout walls provided a strongly fortified redoubt. In spite of this, Kummer's leading troops forced their way into the village simultaneously from the north and the west. Soon after this Neidhartshausen fell to an attack by a fusilier battalion, while another battalion cleared the woods east of the road. Given the strength of the position and of the defending forces it was a brilliant little victory. The Bavarians fell back on Zoller's main body at Diedorf; from there throughout the day until 3.00 pm the Bavarians launched a series of unsuccessful counter-attacks.[9]

At Wiesenthal Wrangel had enjoyed similar success, his leading troops storming the barricaded village and driving out its defenders, who occupied a wooded hill, the Nebelberg, in front of Rossdorf. Fresh troops under Cella came up in support and took up a position on the steep slopes of the hill. Attacked by two battalions with a third in support, the Bavarians were, after a brisk artillery exchange, driven back and obliged to retreat to Rossdorf. Hartmann came forward with reinforcements and counter-attacked, almost regaining possession of the hill until Wrangel, in his turn, fed in further troops which drove the Bavarians back to Rossdorf again.

By mid-afternoon, in accordance with Falckenstein's orders, Goeben gave instructions to both Kummer and Wrangel to pull back and this, unmolested by the enemy, they proceeded to do.[10] Falckenstein, believing himself to be in the presence of the whole Bavarian Army, now decided to seize the opportunity of inflicting a decisive defeat on it, and recalled Beyer from his advance on Fulda and brought up Manteuffel as well. Unknown to him, however, the bird had flown; the strong Bavarian outposts that could be seen along the hills masked a complete retreat. It had been apparent to Charles

The Prussians assault the Bavarian positions at Zella. (Fontane)

that, with the Prussians across the Werra, it would be impossible to unite with the 8th Corps north of the Rhön; he must do so to the south, and this necessitated an immediate disengagement. The Prussian reconnaissances at daylight on July 5 showed that the Bavarians had got away, and Falckenstein returned to his original intention to move on Fulda. Charles made a fresh plan, telling Alexander on July 5 that he was retreating to the line Neustadt-Bischofsheim, aiming to be at Neustadt by July 7, and requesting that Alexander conform to that movement. This sounded straightforward enough, but, for the 8th Corps, it was not:

> The Bavarian Army might possibly reach Neustadt from Kallen-Nordheim in two days. It had at least one good road for its march, and was separated from the enemy by the Rhön mountains. The 8th Corps, on the other hand, was itself not yet concentrated, had double the distance to march, and to traverse those mountains by cross-roads and in the presence of the enemy.[11]

Given the lack of urgency so far displayed by Alexander, it was decidedly optimistic to expect him to keep this rendezvous, even without the intervention of the Prussians. But only in the immediate unity of the two forces lay, for all practical purposes, any prospect of victory.

It all looked even more difficult to Alexander than it did to Charles; before getting the latter's order of July 5 he had already heard from his liaison officer at Bavarian headquarters of the outcome of the fighting on July 4, and of the ensuing Prussian advance. As a result of this he selected Schlüchtern as his point of concentration, and next day the scattered units of the 8th Corps began to come together, while the Bavarians retreated more slowly than wisely, only reaching Ostheim and Fladungen by nightfall on July 6.

Towards the end of the day, however, both Charles and Alexander received the catastrophic news of Königgrätz, which put their immediate problems in a very different light. Clearly, nothing that they could do could reverse the outcome of a war that was palpably lost. On the other hand, the result of the campaign in western Germany might have a considerable bearing on the course of the peace negotiations. Unfortunately, this concentrated the minds of the various Federal governments and their military commanders on their own particular interests, which led to a further deterioration in the cooperation between the Bavarian Army and the 8th Corps. The various contingents of the latter felt that their duty was to cover their own homelands directly rather than by abandoning them and marching off to join the Bavarians. Accordingly the Confederation's Military Committee gave instructions directly to Alexander that he must defend the line of the Main rather than march eastward to seek a junction with the Bavarian Army.

The news of Königgrätz had of course 'made a tremendous sensation' in Munich as in all the other capitals of the Minor States; Hohenlohe recorded the general gloom and pessimism in his diary on July 5:

> The news from Bohemia is producing a very dispiriting effect here. Moreover, the Bavarian Army, owing to the sheer incompetence of its leaders, has not come to the rescue of the Hanoverians. The *Bayerische Zeitung* excuses this by saying that

> at headquarters "they did not know where the Hanoverians were." Is anything more ridiculous conceivable? In our War Ministry things are proceeding on the old bureaucratic red-tape lines. Self-satisfaction and dilatoriness everywhere. Von Lutz, the Minister for War… is a man of very small intellectual ability… Prince Charles is a nervous old gentleman; the officers on the General Staff are some of them no better than the Minister. I am watching the progress of the war with alarm.[12]

For the moment the 8th Corps continued its retreat as planned; but in the face of his latest instructions Alexander was obliged to conclude that 'the most pressing necessity was to regain the line of the Main.'[13] Without further ado he set off in that direction, sending a message to Charles to propose that they unite between Hanau and Aschaffenburg, instead of in Franconia. The retreat of the 8th Corps, by Ortenberg and Birstein, was well under way on July 7, no contact whatever having been made with the Prussians. With its left flank now exposed, the Bavarian Army was now extremely vulnerable, and Charles had sent off a request to Alexander that he turn once again and move back towards Schlüchtern; not surprisingly, Alexander felt unable to comply. He was not the only commander acting in conflict with a superior's wishes; Prince William of Baden had been engaged in some dubious manoeuvres of his own. Stationed on the left of the original advance of the 8th Corps, the Baden Division and the Reserve Cavalry had been charged with covering Frankfurt, and had taken up a position at Giessen. From there it had been established without difficulty that the direction of the Prussian advance was on Fulda, rather than further west; but in spite of this reassurance, Prince William remained decidedly apprehensive of Prussian movements in the Rhine valley that might threaten Frankfurt. Accordingly he retreated first to Butzbach and then, on July 6, behind the Nidda at Vilbel. Alexander disapproved; in accordance with the now well-established dance routine of the 8th Corps Prince William was ordered to advance again to Friedberg. As with the rest of the movements of the corps, however, this elegant quadrille was conducted without contact with the enemy. In the meantime Prince William had caused much bewilderment in Frankfurt when he and his staff arrived back in the city on July 7 and took up residence in the Hotel d'Angleterre.[14]

Meanwhile the Bavarian Army had been retreating, still very slowly, the troops by now thoroughly exhausted in the savage heat of that sweltering July. Charles seems to have got it fixed in his head that he had sufficient time in hand to move by short marches and to take up a defensive position at Poppenhausen, covering Schweinfurt, before Falckenstein caught up with him.[15] By July 8 the main body had reached Neustadt; detachments on a defensive arc north west of that town covered the movement. The Prussians were, however, a lot closer than Charles might have hoped, and a lot more concentrated than their adversary; while the Bavarians were strung out over twenty two miles, Falckenstein's troops were echeloned in a formation less than half as long. To the west, Beyer had marched down the Frankfurt road as far as Schlüchtern, which he reached on July 8; no trace of the 8th Corps being found, Beyer swung southeast towards Brückenau. At the same time Goeben had got to Döllbach, with Manteuffel behind him at Fulda. On the following day both divisions pushed on south towards Brückenau.

The joyful news from Bohemia had brought with it some anxiety to the Prussian leaders as they moved south. Goeben wrote to his wife on July 8:

> On Wednesday we are all marching to the Main… I hope that an armistice won't get in our way by then. We are very much afraid of that following the news according to which the Emperor Napoleon is offering his mediation to Prussia.[15]

On July 8 the spa town of Kissingen was peaceful. Three days earlier, when some eighty of Prince Taxis' troopers had gone clattering through the town, in their flight from Hünfeld, there had been a considerable panic among the visitors to the baths as well as

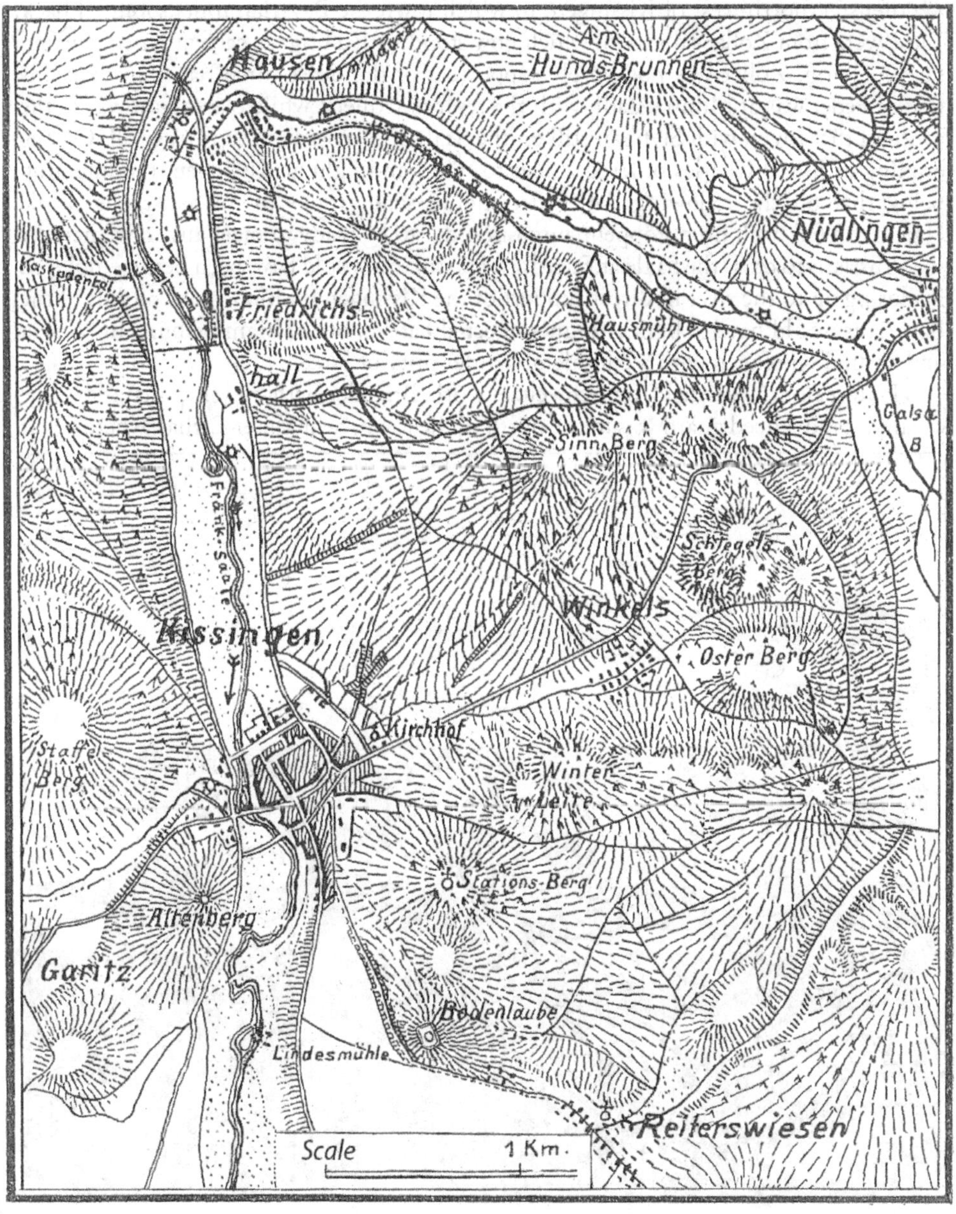

Map 49 – The Battle of Kissingen, July 10.

the inhabitants; but the Burgomaster had restored their peace of mind with an assurance that he would give twenty four hours' notice of any Prussian attack. Meanwhile, as Hozier noted, 'Bavarian staff officers sauntered about the Kurgarten as if in a time of the most profound peace.'[16]

While his enemy was relaxing in this way, Goeben had realised that conflict was imminent, as his advanced patrols reported frequent contact with the Bavarian cavalry; and this was confirmed when his advanced guard encountered resistance at Platz and Waldfenster, north-west of Kissingen, to which town the Bavarian units soon fell back. These were from Zoller's division, which now stood with a brigade each at Kissingen and Hammelburg. Zoller was not closely supported; of the other three Bavarian divisions, that of Feder was at Münnerstadt, with the reserve artillery, while Hartmann was to the south of that town, with Stephan still on the Saale at Neustadt, even further off. On the evening of July 9 Charles ordered Zoller to stand and fight at Kissingen, the intention being that on the following day Feder should send troops to his assistance, while Hartmann fell back from Poppenhausen in order to be ready to meet any movement by the Prussians to cross the Saale at Euerdorf. Hartmann would have been better employed in closing up to the river in direct support of the Kissingen position, since on July10 the Bavarians would have to fight two unconnected battles, one at Hammelburg and one at and around Kissingen with a considerable inferiority of force.

Hammelburg was held by Schweitzer's 6th Brigade, with eleven guns and some cavalry. Its advanced guard was to the north of the town, near Unter-Erthal, where it was

The spa town of Kissingen. (Voss)

encountered on the morning of July 10 by the advanced guard of Beyer's division; after a brisk cannonade the Bavarians were chased over the River Thulba into Hammelburg. Beyer, who had come to the front accompanied by Falckenstein, was uncertain as to the enemy strength owing to the nature of the country, and apart from a long range exchange of artillery fire held off taking any further action until his main body came up. Falckenstein was sufficiently concerned about the possible strength of the enemy to send word to Goeben that if he was not himself engaged with the enemy, he should move on the Bavarian right at Hammelburg; by this time, however, Goeben was indeed heavily engaged.[17]

After a further prolonged artillery exchange, which achieved little, Beyer moved forward, turning the enemy right by taking a hill called the Offenthaler Berg, which was held by one Bavarian battalion, and then following up these troops as they retreated into Hammelburg so closely that the outskirts of the town were soon carried. At this the Bavarians abandoned Hammelburg, which was in Beyer's hands by 3.00 pm. Losses on either side had been very light, the Prussians losing 10 killed and 72 wounded and the Bavarians about the same.[18]

Goeben was facing much stronger opposition at Kissingen. Initially the defence of the town was entrusted to Zoller's other brigade, the 5th led by Ribeaupierre; but although not immediately reinforced, it had some prospect of support from Hartmann's division, between Euerdorf and Poppenhausen, and also from Feder and Stephan to the north and east. The unfortunate tourists who had remained in Kissingen now found themselves obliged to witness events at very close quarters; none were allowed to leave the town for fear of their disclosing the Bavarian dispositions, although the occupants of the Hotel Sauner, on the right bank of the river, were allowed to move to less exposed parts of the town.[19] After the battle, Durig, Zoller's aide de camp, reported to Prince Hohenlohe that 'the visitors were walking about the streets on the very morning of the battle, until the first shell fell in the streets, and then they crept into the cellars, where many a one doubtless perished.'[20]

Bavarian infantry defend Kissingen. (Fontane)

Goeben's advance was led by Kummer's brigade, which was sent around the front of the town to attack it from the south-west, occupying Garitz at about 10.00 am. Under cover of an artillery duel between his own batteries on the heights opposite Kissingen and two Bavarian batteries northeast of the town, Kummer formed up his troops for an immediate assault on the forward Bavarian positions in the suburbs of Kissingen lying to the west of the river. These were soon taken, and their defenders retreated to the left bank.

Of the three bridges that spanned the Saale at Kissingen only one, the stone bridge carrying the main road, was immediately in a passable state; a wooden bridge higher up the river had been almost completely destroyed and the planking had been removed from an iron footbridge that, in happier days, carried visitors over the river to the baths. The stone bridge was heavily defended by a barricade and two guns. At this point the Saale cannot be forded, so for the moment Kummer's advance came to a standstill. In planning the next stage of the assault many of the Prussian staff officers had the advantages of being very familiar with the town of Kissingen, having frequently visited the fashionable spa.

Behind Kummer came Goeben's main body, headed by Wrangel's brigade, which came up on the right with the object of turning Zoller's left flank. If Hartmann had been brought up to the river, this would have been an extremely hazardous manoeuvre. As it was, Wrangel was able to seize the badly damaged wooden bridge; in spite of heavy rifle fire from the Bavarian infantry on the opposite bank, his engineers got to work to repair it with tables, benches and baulks of wood seized from nearby houses. They succeeded in rendering it passable in single file. The troops which got across formed up under cover of the thickets behind the rising ground to the south of Kissingen, and launched an immediate assault. Other troops coming over the bridge joined in the attack, which became a vicious house-to-house struggle in the southern part of the town:

Prussian infantry at Nüdlingen. (Fontane)

> The Bavarians fought with desperate courage. For every house and street corner, for the possession of the avenues in the gardens of the famous watering place, and about the graves in the cemetery, a fierce and bloody struggle ensued.[21]

As the Prussians inched forward, a company of the Lippe Fusiliers succeeded in clambering over the remains of the iron footbridge and establishing a bridgehead in the gardens of the baths. Soon after this, an attack on the stone bridge was successful, the fusilier battalion of the 53rd Regiment climbing over the barricade and penetrating to the centre of the town, followed by the rest of Kummer's brigade.[22] With this, the defence of the town crumbled; in spite of a vigorous rearguard action in and around the churchyard, the Bavarians fell back towards the village of Winkels, on the heights to the east of the town.

Goeben was never one to miss an opportunity. While Kummer's troops were regrouping in and to the east of Kissingen, Goeben passed through them the fresh troops of the 19th Regiment. Advancing to the attack against the Winkels heights, and supported by Wrangel's brigade, they quickly dislodged the Bavarians from the strong position that they had taken up. The Prussians drove forward towards Nüdlingen, where they were briefly held up before taking the village at about 4.00 pm, its defenders retreating further north-east. In the closing stages of the battle Zoller had been reinforced, much too late, by troops from Feder's division. Earlier support might have made all the difference. As it was, Goeben had won what appeared to be a decisive victory and, as the battle ended, Zoller was killed by a shell fragment.

But the Bavarians were not finished with. Prince Charles, who had himself come to Kissingen, had been sending off messages all day to Hartmann and Stephan to hasten to Zoller's support. The former seems to have received a variety of confusing instructions, and finally believed that he was to fall back again towards Schweinfurt, but Stephan had at last come up. Following Feder towards Kissingen, he began to deploy his division. Hidden in an area of dead ground and hence unnoticed by the Prussian outposts, his troops were able to form up for an attack from Nüdlingen towards Winkels, striking the Prussian left at about 6.30 pm. The Prussians took heavy losses from the Bavarian artillery at close range as they fell back. To Wrangel, the position seemed desperate, and he sent off messages to Goeben seeking support. Before any reply could reach him, his horse was shot under him and rolled on him, rendering him unconscious. Colonel Stoltz took command, and conducted a skilful phased withdrawal which held up the Bavarian advance. When Wrangel came to, he assumed command again, in time to get Goeben's response to his appeal – to the effect that with eight battalions he could hold the position against the world. 'Good heavens,' he cried, 'the position is already lost.'[23] Since retreat was thus denied him, and so was reinforcement, he determined to attack, and with drums beating the whole Prussian line advanced. In spite of heavy casualties the lost heights were regained, and as night fell the Bavarians retreated to Poppenhausen with the Prussian hold on Kissingen secure.

To the north, Colonel von der Goltz had been directed on Friedrichshall; arriving opposite that place he was fired on from two saltworks occupied by the Bavarians. For the moment, all he could do was to mask this force. At 11.30 am Manteuffel arrived on the scene with a squadron of dragoons and a four pounder battery. Ordered to support Goeben, he had ridden ahead to explain the position of his division, following a report that von der Goltz's two battalions were engaged with a superior force. The rest of his division was still some way behind, and it was immediately apparent that not much more could be done until infantry reinforcements came up. These arrived at 1.45 pm under von Freyhold; Manteuffel ordered him to employ the 59th Regiment at once in an attack on Hausen, where the ground was favourable. When the attack went in, the Bavarians did not wait to receive it, pulling back immediately. On the right, von der Goltz attacked the saltworks, driving their defenders back over the river. Pursuit was impossible, the Bavarians having broken down the bridge; by the time it was again usable, thanks to two soldiers who swam across to bring back a boat to ferry over some pioneers to repair it, the enemy had vanished.[24]

The last of the actions fought on July 10 was at Waldaschach, some four and a half miles north of Kissingen. While Manteuffel's division was moving south to Goeben's support, a patrol of dragoons reported that the place was occupied. Colonel von Canstein, commanding the main body, sent a rifle battalion to cover Waldaschach to prevent its defenders from interfering with the division's march. In a neat little action the riflemen effectively surrounded the place, causing its garrison to retreat precipitately across the Saale towards Münnerstadt.[25]

Thus the day ended with the Bavarians in full retreat from the river line they had sought to defend. Casualties on both sides had been high, partly due to the effectiveness of the needle gun, and partly as a result of the Bavarian artillery's success at Winkels in the evening. In all, the fighting around Kissingen had cost the Prussians 143 killed, 698 wounded and 58 missing; the Bavarians had lost 93 killed, 573 wounded and 555 missing, the bulk of the latter being unwounded prisoners.[26] Among the dead was of course General Zoller, whose body Durig had been able to bring out through the Prussian lines to Munich. He told Hohenlohe that the troops had fought very well everywhere, but that 'the head administration of the General Staff and of the Commissariat Department leaves much to be desired.'[27] To general disgust, King Ludwig declined to receive Durig; his lack of interest in the war prompted Prince Charles to write angrily to his brother: 'You'll see what will happen; it will end in his being deposed.'[28]

The defeat of Prince Charles was due, as the Prussian Official History points out, not only to his being taken by surprise as a result of his conviction that the Prussians could not attack before July 11, but also to the distribution of his forces. If the troops along the Saale were merely there to cover the Bavarian retreat on Poppenhausen and perhaps Schweinfurt, they were there in too much strength:

> but they were insufficient, if the passage of the river was to be disputed. As soon as the line of the Saale was once attacked at Hammelburg and Kissingen, reinforcements from Münnerstadt and Neustadt must necessarily arrive too late.[29]

In fact, the Bavarians were astonishingly unprepared; the only map the staff had was one that von der Tann borrowed from an inhabitant of a small town near Kissingen.[30]

The Bavarian retreat from the Saale was somewhat confused, not so much on the part of the troops involved but on the part of their leaders. The line of retreat was determined largely by fear of being attacked on the march from Kissingen. Feder, with part of Stephan's division and the reserve artillery, marched eastward directly away from the Prussians, making for Hassfurth, well to the east of Schweinfurt. Hartmann remained at Poppenhausen as a rearguard before himself going to Schweinfurt, while the rest of Stephan's division and the cavalry made for Würzburg. Reinforcements, in the form of the Reserve Brigade, had come up as far as Schweinfurt, and Charles took up a position there with about two and half divisions; but the Official History is putting it a little on the high side when it observes: 'He was determined, and indeed had no other alternative, to fight to the last man on this spot.'[31] What the Bavarians had succeeded in doing, by their divergent lines of retreat, was thoroughly to confuse the Prussians as to where they had got to. It was necessary for Falckenstein to push Manteuffel towards Schweinfurt to reconnoitre. In support, Beyer moved over the Saale by Euerdorf and Ramsthal, while Goeben remained at Kissingen. By midday on July 11, after a clash with Hartmann's rearguard had produced 34 prisoners, Manteuffel was reasonably certain that the Bavarians were making for Schweinfurt; but before he could get far in pursuit of them, political considerations supervened.

In Bohemia, Bismarck was becoming anxious about the campaign in Western Germany. Prolonging it might, he thought, expose Prussia to the risk of defeats there, while victories would not materially strengthen his hand. In any case, there could not be much time left for military operations, and to Falckenstein went a direct message:

> It is now of political importance to be in actual possession of the district north of the Main, for the sake of negotiations which will probably take place on the *status quo* basis.[32]

Wounded in the pleasure gardens at Kissingen following the battle. (Voss)

The General Staff was of course notoriously sensitive to political interference; but the Official History grudgingly concedes that on this occasion it might be justified, observing grimly:

> Without doubt the correct military step was to advance on Schweinfurt, but in the beginning and at the end of campaigns military considerations must give way to political ones.[33]

This instruction reached Falckenstein at 1.00 pm on July 11, and he at once issued orders for the whole army to swing to its right towards Gemünden to carry the new policy into effect, although Manteuffel did not learn of this until late afternoon. By then he was at Maibach, where he was contemplating an attack. Since his new instructions required him to march off to the west at once unless actually engaged with the enemy, he had to give up his plan. Next day the whole army was moving westwards, with Goeben leading the advance towards the main road through the Spessart to Aschaffenburg. By nightfall on July 12 he was at Lohr, with Laufach as his objective for the next day. Goeben's march through the mountains of the Spessart on July 13 was a tough assignment:

> The ascent was made in two columns, separated from each other by the distance of an hour's march, with a vigorous gait, that they might as soon as possible cover the fourteen miles to the watershed and the routes down the other side of the mountain. But it was a cruel march in the glowing heat, with no breeze stirring, in suffocating dust, up-hill and downhill, without shade and without water. In silence, slowly and more slowly, the companies dragged along.[34]

Goeben described the ordeal of his troops in a letter to his wife:

> We had to cross the Spessart, a high wooded mountain range, which was splendid to look at, but in the baking heat that we have now, it was hard going for the heavily burdened infantry.[35]

Behind Goeben came Manteuffel, who reached Gemünden on July 13, while Beyer took the road to Hanau through the valleys of the Sinn and Kinzig, reaching Rieneck on the same day. Their immediate adversaries, meanwhile, breathed a sigh of relief at the disappearance of the Prussians from their front. It gave Prince Charles a few days to reorganise his army and to give some thought to his strategic objectives. With the loss of the Hanoverians, and the disappearance to the west of the 8th Corps, it was not before time. The problem now was that Falckenstein had got firmly between the two halves of the Federal Army; much would depend on what Prince Alexander could or would do about it.

32

The Fall of Frankfurt

The various manoeuvres of Prince Alexander's corps, which may have assisted its disparate elements to get to know each other, had not otherwise helped it achieve a state of battle readiness. It was just as well that it had not so far succeeded in making any contact with the enemy. Hozier graphically described its condition:

> At this time the 8th Federal Corps was not practically fit to take the field… No firm union existed between the different divisions of the 8th Corps. The corps had not been concentrated for twenty four years, and the divisions were totally different in uniform, administration and organisation. The hussars of Hesse–Cassel were dressed and accoutred so similarly to Prussian cavalry, that the Austrians fired on them at Aschaffenburg. The small arms were of different calibres. The four field batteries of the 3rd Division were equipped on four different systems.[1]

The total strength of the corps was, however, by no means negligible, having by now reached a total of 49,147 men.[2] On paper, therefore, it might have been rash for Falckenstein to move westwards in widely scattered columns. Goeben was particularly exposed to the risk of attack from the whole of Alexander's forces, being some two days' march ahead of Manteuffel and entirely out of touch with Beyer. Attacking the advancing Prussians was not, though, uppermost in Alexander's mind just now. The 8th Corps headquarters was feeling particularly jittery as a result of Roeder's activities; with a mixed force of garrison and Reserve troops operating out of Coblenz from July 7 he had occupied Ems and Nassau and caused great dismay to the local rulers. Roeder's object had been merely to serve as a distraction and in this he was entirely successful. By the time he retreated again to Coblenz on July 13 he had fixed Alexander's attention still more firmly on what he saw as the exposed nature of his position. Having received confirmation on July 12 that the Prussians had abandoned their pursuit of the Bavarians and were now bearing down on him, he saw with sudden if belated clarity the advantages of an immediate union with Charles, and began to make dispositions accordingly. And he hastily revoked the assurances that he had given to the remaining members of the Diet as recently as July 9 that Frankfurt was in no danger, advising their immediate removal to Augsburg, whither they went, establishing themselves at the 'Inn of the Three Moors.'[3]

Meanwhile, as he crossed the Spessart on July 13, Goeben was riding with a squadron of the 8th Hussars at the head of Wrangel's brigade. At 2.00 pm they bumped into the leading troops of Frey's Hessian Brigade, which had been ordered to reconnoitre the Prussian advance but on no account to be drawn into serious combat. They fired on the hussars as they emerged on the high road out of Laufach, causing the latter to take cover behind a railway embankment until reinforced by infantry units that were following. Coming up at the double through the railway tunnel east of Hayn, these drove the

Hessians back through Laufach and then Frohnhofen as far as Weiberhöfe, three miles to the west. By now the leading troops of Kummer's brigade had come up on the left, and Goeben reckoned that his exhausted troops had done enough for the day, ordering them into bivouac for the night at Laufach, and leaving a fusilier battalion to keep an eye on the Hessians. It was with considerable surprise that Lieutenant Colonel von Rex, commanding this battalion, later noticed movement on the part of the Hessians suggestive of an imminent assault; he at once deployed north and south of Frohnhofen to meet it, and reported back to Wrangel, who pushed his tired troops forward.

The Hessian attack was launched after a brisk bombardment from artillery on the Geissen Berg, a hill overlooking Frohnhofen, and came up either side of the main road. For a while, Wrangel's men were hard pressed; but soon the Hessian attacks broke down in the face of the cruelly destructive power of the needle gun. First one brigade, and then another advanced only to fall back in broken ruin, leaving a swathe of casualties in front of the Prussian positions. As the Prussian artillery came up in support, the Hessians fell back in disorder to Aschaffenburg. They had lost a total of 777 men, of whom 79 were killed and 384 wounded. The total Prussian loss was 66.[4]

Frey's reconnaissance was part of Alexander's plan to re-establish direct contact with the Bavarian Army. Why Perglas, the commander of the Hesse-Darmstadt Division, thought he should launch the ruinous counter-attack is unclear. The courage of his troops was amply proved, but the decision to send in an assault over open ground against the needle gun in the hands of experienced troops was profoundly irresponsible. Alexander's belief that he could unite with Charles by advancing down this road is also unexplained; even the inadequate intelligence available to him had already identified Prussian troops moving westwards along this axis, and a march south-east from Aschaffenburg would have exposed the 8th Corps to the serious risk of a flank attack. As it happened, he was not long able to contemplate this course, since on the evening of July 13 Colonel

The Hesse-Darmstadt infantry assault at Frohnhofen, July 13. (Fontane)

Prussian infantry assault the Herstaller Gate at Aschaffenburg, July 14, painting by Burger. (Voss)

Schönfeld arrived with orders from Charles to move south, through the Odenwald and by Miltenberg and Tauberbischofsheim towards Uffenheim, to the southeast of Würzburg. This was a much more realistic point of union at which to aim; but even so the 8th Corps would have to move more quickly than it had so far done, and it would have to bear the principal burden of the marches to the rendezvous, while constantly at risk of intervention by the Prussians.

First, however, Goeben's advance must be contained at Aschaffenburg. Hahn's Austrian brigade had arrived there to relieve the shaken Hessians at Goldbach, two miles east of Aschaffenburg. Neipperg, the commander of the Combined Division, had been deprived of his other brigade by Roeder's activities, so the only support he had was Perglas' battered division.

As usual Goeben was on the move early. Wrangel moved out down the high road at 8.00 am, while Kummer took the line of the railway; Tresckow's cavalry brigade was in close support. Wrangel sent von der Goltz through the woods to the north with a force of about two battalions; as the Prussians advanced, the Federal troops abandoned first Hösbach and then Goldbach. Goeben now deployed the cavalry on the right of Wrangel's advance, and pushed on towards Aschaffenburg. The advance was seriously delayed by artillery fire from Austrian batteries skilfully posted on the Aumuhle, north of Aschaffenburg; the Prussian artillery could not get into a good position from which to respond, and the Austrian gunners had much the best of it until the 15th Regiment stormed the village of Damm and occupied a nearby hill crowned by a tower inside a high wall. From here, it was able by rifle fire to compel the Austrian artillery to pull back.[5]

To the south Kummer attacked and took the pheasantry with the 13th Regiment, and in following up the retreating Austrians inflicted heavy casualties. Then, with the 53rd Regiment, he pushed forward into the outskirts of Aschaffenburg; his objective was the bridge over the Main. Some Austrian units managed to get over the bridge before it fell to two companies of the 53rd Regiment under Captain von Bastineller; he also captured 200 Austrian troops who tried to cross the river in boats.[6]

North of the town Neipperg's left flank had effectively melted away when Perglas pulled out with virtually the whole of his division and marched off to Seiligenstadt, failing to notify his colleague of his retreat or the reason for it. As a result Neipperg had no choice but to fall back himself. The seizure of the bridge left many of his troops trapped in the town; these, for the most part Italians from the Wernhardt Regiment, gave themselves up without much resistance. The Federals had suffered badly during the battle, losing 2,469 men, of whom 707 were killed or wounded; the Prussian loss was 180.[7]

The intense heat, and the fatigue of his troops, meant that Goeben could make no effective pursuit of the beaten enemy. On the other hand it is surprising that Alexander did not take advantage of the massive numerical superiority which he had to concentrate in front of Goeben and attack him before Manteuffel, some thirty miles east, could have

Prussian troops from Goeben's division enter Frankfurt on the evening of July 16. (*Illustrirte Kriegs-Chronik*)

General Edwin Freiherr von Manteuffel, commander of a combined division in the Army of the Main. (Rogers)

come up in support. Even on July 14 he failed to make the best use of his resources; the 1st Württemberg Brigade had been marching from Gelnhausen to Aschaffenburg, but on hearing of the outcome of the battle turned back and crossed to the left back of the Main at Steinheim. As the Official History notes, 'had it appeared on the field during the action it might have had a very unfavourable influence on the Prussian attack.'[8] Effectively Alexander was using Neipperg to cover his flank while he got away to the south to the Odenwald, sending the rest of the Württemberg Division and the Baden Division by rail through Darmstadt to Dieburg and Babenhausen. The rest of the 8th Corps joined them there, and they set off on their march through the Odenwald, abandoning Frankfurt to Falckenstein's untender mercies.

The city had always been particularly hostile to Prussian interests, and could hardly therefore have been expecting especially gentle treatment. With both the Federal Diet and the 8th Corps having gone, the Senate on July 15 declared it to be an open city, and all further defensive measures were abandoned. By 10.00 pm on July 16 the city was occupied; next day Falckenstein announced his assumption of the government of Nassau, Frankfurt and those parts of Bavaria occupied by his troops, levied a contribution of six million florins, suppressed some anti-Prussian newspapers and abolished the eleven armed unions (*Vereine*) that existed. He then grandly telegraphed the King to announce that 'all the territory north of the Main lies at the feet of Your Majesty.'[9]

Ironically, these were to be his last actions as commander of the victorious Army of the Main; on July 11 the decision had been taken at the Royal Headquarters to replace him by Manteuffel and to post him to an 'important and difficult task' that had arisen as a result of the successful Königgrätz campaign. The Official History was careful to explain this: 'It was of primary importance to re-establish a well regulated state of administration in Bohemia and to re-organise this country which all previous authorities had forsaken.'[10] The abrupt removal of a successful and popular leader not

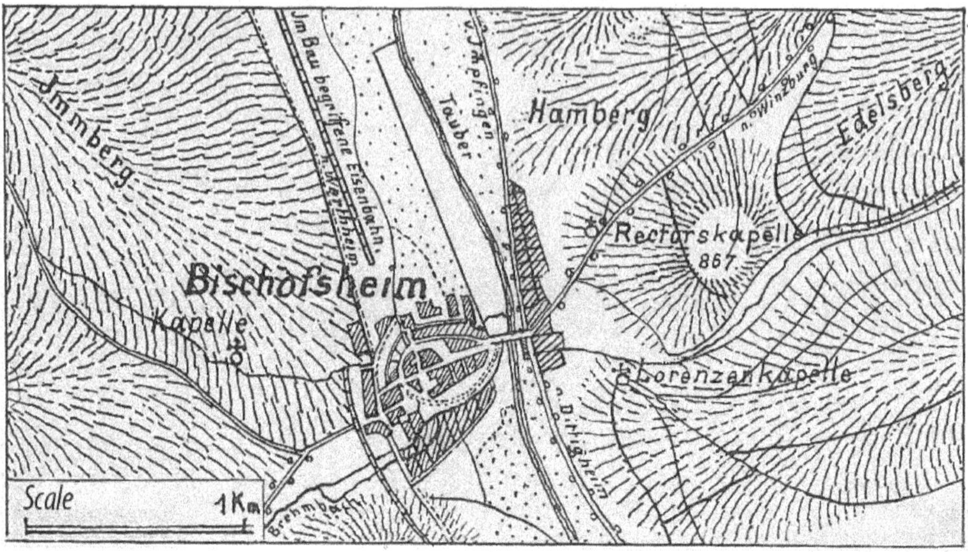

Map 50 – The Battle of Tauberbischofsheim, July 24.

surprisingly caused a storm of public protest mainly based on a belief that Manteuffel, a court favourite who had made plenty of enemies among the Prussian officer corps, had intrigued against Falckenstein. In fact, of course, this had nothing to do with it. Moltke had had quite enough of Falckenstein's disobedience and resolved to make the change before the next, and final, phase of the war in western Germany. There was no public hint of dissatisfaction with Falckenstein; Moltke was content to have got rid of his disruptive influence and to leave it at that.

Manteuffel, whose division had reached Aschaffenburg, set off at once to Frankfurt to take command. Arriving at noon on July 20, he paused only to add another twenty million florins to Frankfurt's war contribution before giving orders for the pursuit of the 8th Corps to be resumed. Flies took command of his division. Goeben moved south by Darmstadt and Dieburg, while the other two divisions moved along the left bank of the Main. By July 22 Goeben was at König, Flies at Laudenbach and Beyer at Wallstadt. Manteuffel kept in mind the possibility of active operations on the part of the Bavarians; reconnaissance across the Spessart found strong enemy forces at Marktheidenfeld although these did not, for the moment, seem to be making any move westward.

Alexander had no idea where his enemy had got to, and it was not until the Baden Division reported contacts with Flies on July 22 in and around Miltenberg that he realised that, as usual, the Prussians were moving a lot faster than he was, and had nearly caught him up. By now the Federal plans had undergone another change. At a meeting between Charles and Alexander on July 19 they had concluded that since the Federal army was now on the point of union the Prussians would stay put rather than attack a much superior force. This being so, the Federals should themselves advance to the attack. So far so good; but they were quite unable to agree as to how to do this. Charles wanted to move along the left bank of the Main, through Miltenberg and the Odenwald; Alexander's Chief of Staff, Baur, preferred to advance through the Spessart, since for the 8th Corps to retrace its steps would be demoralising. This conference broke up without agreement, and was reconvened on July 21 at Würzburg. The Official History was in no doubt that Charles was right:

> The best way of ensuring its success would have been for the 7th Corps, which was assembled at Wurzburg by the 17th, to have advanced to meet the 8th as far as Miltenberg by the 20th; for this there was ample time.[11]

At Würzburg, in order to achieve something – anything – Charles reluctantly agreed to the Spessart plan, with his corps aiming for Lohr while Alexander marched around the loop of the Main to Marktheidenfeld, preparatory to an advance on Aschaffenburg. Prince William of Baden took up a position at Hundheim with his division, with outposts at Freudenberg and Eichenbühl; a detachment was posted four miles north at Wertheim, on the Main, to maintain contact with the Bavarians. On July 23, the Prussians having covered in three days the same ground that had taken the 8th Corps twice as long, Flies advanced on Nassig, two miles south-west of Wertheim. Fabeck, with the Coburg-Gotha Regiment, two guns and some cavalry, drove back one battalion of Laroche's brigade and threatened the retreat of the rest; but, heavily outnumbered, then contented himself with occupying the ground he had taken. A rather half-hearted counter-attack by the Badeners was driven back; total Prussian casualties were 20, while the Baden losses were 92.[12]

Far to the south, Goeben's advanced guard had reached Walldürn, about twelve miles west of Tauberbischofsheim, where there was a vigorous clash in the streets between Prussian hussars and a squadron of Baden dragoons. The hussars had much the better of it, and the dragoons retreated on the Hessian Division at Königheim. Alexander's forces were getting dangerously strung out in front of and along the Tauber, from Wertheim in the north where the river joins the Main to a point south of Tauberbischofsheim. During the night of July 23/24 the Baden Division pulled out of Wertheim and Hundheim, retreating on Kulsheim.

These skirmishes caused a good deal of perplexity at the various Federal headquarters. The plan to advance into the Spessart had assumed that there was no possibility of the bulk of the Prussian troops having come down the left bank of the Main. Charles still supposed this to be so; in that case, too decided a move to his left would uncover the roads from Aschaffenburg towards Würzburg, if that was the direction the Prussians were taking. So the Bavarians stuck to the agreed plan, and began the move to Lohr, Gemünden and Karlstadt; by nightfall on July 23 the barely achieved union of the Federal army was again ruptured, and it was additionally spread out over a front of thirty six miles.[13]

Since he could not look to the Bavarians for support on July 24, Alexander decided to fall back behind the line of the Tauber, his enthusiasm for an offensive having rapidly waned. He did, though, in his order to the 8th Corps, explain the reason for the withdrawal to be 'for the purpose either of opposing the enemy, who was advancing between Walldürn and Miltenberg, or of operating against his flank.'[14] The position he took up was seven miles long; the Baden Division was between Werbach and Werbachhausen, the Württemberg Division at Impfingen and Tauberbischofsheim and the Combined Division between Paimar and Grünsfeld. The Hessians were in reserve at Gross Rinderfeld. The position was effectively nine miles in depth, with the reserve artillery at Schönfeld and Ilmspan, and the cavalry at Ober and Unter Altertheim.

As the Tauber winds northward to its junction with the Main, it passes through a narrow valley mostly not more than four hundred yards wide. Steep hills on either side rise to about three hundred feet. The river itself, no more than fifty feet wide, is usually fordable in most places, but the steep river bank sides and hillsides would make an opposed crossing difficult, even for infantry. In 1866 the little town of Tauberbischofsheim had about 3,000 inhabitants; it lay on the west bank of the Tauber in a hollow surrounded by commanding heights on both sides of the river. The Heidelberg-Würzburg railway ran past the town on a thirty foot high embankment, crossing the river by a wooden bridge built on stone piles about seventy yards long. If the town itself was strongly held, and the garrison was well supported by artillery from the other side of the river, it would not be an easy position to take. Further north, the Werbach position also allowed the Federals to hold a bridgehead on the west bank, at Hochhausen; there, the railway bridge had been destroyed but a small bridge for foot traffic had been erected. At Werbach the bridge was barricaded. This position, too, potentially offered a considerable challenge.

However, the disposition of the Federal troops suggested that the purpose of holding the river line was purely temporary, and rather more intended to cover a fighting retreat to positions around Würzburg on the Main than to inflict a serious check on the advance of the Prussians. This came as a surprise to Manteuffel and his divisional generals, who had expected to encounter strong resistance west of the Tauber which would require them to close up before they could think of attacking on July 24. But on the evening of July 23 intelligence reports suggested not only that the whole of the 8th Corps might have crossed the river, but also that the crossings might not be strongly held. Goeben, in particular, needed no urging. Although Kummer and Tresckow were too far back to take part, he still had available at Wolferstetten the brigades of Wrangel and Weltzien, the latter brigade being composed of Oldenburg and Hanseatic troops and which had reinforced his division for the march south from Frankfurt.

Wrangel covered his right flank with a detachment under von der Goltz of two battalions, two guns and one squadron. With the rest of his brigade he made straight for Tauberbischofsheim, which he found to be occupied by part of the 2nd Württemberg Brigade. One regiment was posted in the town in a position resting on the churchyard

Württemberg infantry counter-attack during the Battle of Tauberbischofsheim, July 24. (Voss)

to the north and the railway embankment to the south. One company held the bridge, with two others in reserve. There were two guns on the Dittigheim road; the rest of the brigade, under Fischer, was at Impfingen. The remainder of the Württemberg Division was out of sight about three quarters of a mile behind the town. Wrangel began his attack at 2.00 pm with an artillery bombardment from a battery on the Immberg, and then put in an assault on the western edge of the town by one and a half battalions. After a brief skirmish the town's defenders fell back over the river, taking shelter in the vineyards on the steep slopes of the right bank. Once there they had the benefit of artillery superiority, and the Prussian guns were soon pulled back out of range, although not before they wrecked a convoy of some thirty commissariat wagons which as a consequence blocked the road leading to the east through a steep cutting.[15]

Having lost the town without putting up much of a struggle, the Württembergers now launched a series of assaults to try and retake it, possibly because the weakness of Goeben's force had now been realised. For about two and a half hours a series of attempts were made to recapture the town, but these were uncoordinated assaults, usually in battalion strength, and they invariably broke down in the face of concentrated fire from the needle guns of Wrangel's men.

As the afternoon wore on, Böcking, who commanded the troops that had taken, and now held, the town, called for support. This came in the form of a battalion of the 55th Regiment. Stoltz, its commander, led his men over the bridge with drums beating, and succeeded in taking the houses and gardens on the east bank. Other troops now waded or swam over the river to reinforce Stoltz, who was also supported by the artillery which had come up, and which engaged in a sharp artillery duel before being obliged again to retreat.

Alexander was at Gross Rinderfeld, and hearing of Wrangel's assault set off to see for himself, ordering up reinforcements including his reserve artillery, the horse artillery of the Hessian Division and finally the Austrian Combined Division. The arrival of the Austrians threatened Wrangel's right, and he brought up the Lippe Battalion, his last reserve, to meet the danger. Fortunately, however, at 6.00 pm Alexander gave the order to retreat, a decision occasioned by the Baden Division's abandonment of the position at

Prussian infantry enter Tauberbischofsheim. (Fontane)

Werbach. The Prussians were too exhausted to follow; in any case Goeben had had no intention of advancing beyond Tauberbischofsheim even though the rest of his division had come up.[16]

It had been a remarkable day. Wrangel had faced heavy odds; but bravely as the Württembergers had fought, they had been poorly led, and they had no answer to the power of the needle gun. They sustained total losses of 675 men, of whom 46 were killed and 536 wounded; the Prussians lost a total of 126 men.[17]

At Werbach the Baden Division had also enjoyed marked numerical superiority, but they made little use of it. Weltzien opened his assault by deploying first one and then a second battery which soon gained the upper hand in a duel with two batteries of Baden and one of Württemberg artillery. While this was going on he formed up his infantry in a wood running along the hills on the west bank of the Tauber. At 3.00 pm the first wave of three battalions, threading their way through the vineyards, went down the slope under heavy rifle fire. In spite of this they soon gained the line of the railway, and then took Hochhausen. The Badeners now abandoned their position on the east bank, falling back to the line of the River Welsbach which drains into the Tauber at this point. By 4.00 pm the bridge over the Tauber had been repaired, and the assault on Werbach began. Attacked on three sides, and in spite of being defended by the Badeners with great courage, the village was stormed by Weltzien's men. The Baden troops retreated up the Welsbach valley, taking further losses as they did so.[18] Unfortunately, they did not pause in their retreat until they reached Unter-Altertheim, uncovering the right flank of the troops at Tauberbischofsheim and obliging them to retreat as well. The Prussians lost a total of 71 men, and the Badeners not much more, indicating that the engagement was not especially severe.[19] As night fell, Beyer's division crossed the Tauber and relieved Weltzien's outposts.

The loss of the line of the Tauber was more serious than Alexander's rather tentative effort to hold it would suggest. The speed of the Baden withdrawal again raised the possibility of separation from the Bavarians. This point was not lost on Prince Charles, who at once ordered the abandonment of the Spessart project and the concentration of his army in the Rossbrunn area. In spite of this, the Federals were seriously exposed to the risk of defeat in detail, largely as a result of poor intelligence and their ill-considered movements. Considering that they were operating in territory where the inhabitants might be supposed to be hostile to the Prussians, the failure to find out what was going on on the other side of the hill is especially hard to understand.

33

The End of the Confederation

In the early morning of July 25 Prince Charles received at his headquarters in Remlingen a full report of the events in the front of the 8th Corps. His liaison officer's first hand account made evident to Charles the serious risk that the two corps might again be separated, so he put his troops in motion towards the 8th Corps, Stephan being ordered to Unter-Altertheim, Feder to Waldbrunn and Prince Leopold to Ober-Altertheim. These moves were entirely sensible; but the order which Charles dispatched to Alexander with Major von Massenbach at 9.00 am was certainly not, ignoring as it did the disagreeable fact that the river line had been abandoned:

> The line of the Tauber is to be held with all available force, whilst the 7th Corps is concentrating by way of Ober-Altertheim and Waldbrunn, on the Bischofsheim-Wurzburg road, for the purpose of supporting the 8th Corps.[1]

If this order meant anything, it was presumably an instruction to Alexander to retake the line of the Tauber with the same troops that had the previous day been unable to hold it. This order in fact crossed with a suggestion from Alexander that the pressure on his corps might best be relieved by a Bavarian advance on Wertheim. In bringing this proposal, Lieutenant Colonel Werner, Alexander's staff officer, was obliged also to bring the news that the 8th Corps intended going back still further, to Gerchsheim, rather than preparing for any assault in the direction of the Tauber.

Charles reiterated his previous order, and set out the true military position:

> It is only by defending the line of the Tauber at Bischofsheim that the enemy can be successfully opposed. A retreat on our part to Würzburg or Ochsenfurt is in no way necessary or justified, either by the general proportions of the forces on both sides, or by the number of those that are opposed to the 8th Corps.[2]

This of course was all perfectly true, but the advice he was giving to Alexander was much too late to be of any use. Alexander had his eyes now on the security offered by the line of the Main, and wanted to waste as little time as possible in putting the river between himself and the Prussians. As for the Wertheim project, Charles pointed out that it would only lead to a division of the Federal forces.[3]

The 8th Corps embarked on its retreat to Gerchsheim at 11.00 am, before Alexander received either of the instructions to hold the line of the Tauber. It had at least the merit of bringing the two corps closer together, leaving them well placed to launch a combined attack on Manteuffel. This was not however uppermost in his mind. His pusillanimous policy had this much logic; only an attack was going to stop Manteuffel, now that he was over the Tauber, and if Alexander was not prepared to contemplate that, the Federals were probably better off behind the Main than in front of it. But the missed

Prince Luitpold of Bavaria at the Battle of Helmstadt, drawing by Hoffmann. (Voss)

opportunities were legion; even now the Federals enjoyed a considerable advantage in numbers, and a well-planned and energetic attack might have stopped Manteuffel.

The latter was not letting the grass grow under his feet. By 10.00 am on July 25 the Army of the Main was concentrated on the east bank of the Tauber, with Flies at Urphar, Beyer at Werbach and Goeben at Tauberbischofsheim. Flies was to advance no further that day than Dertingen, covering the left flank against the Bavarians. The other two divisions were to try and cut off Alexander's retreat to Würzburg, Beyer moving to Neubrunn and then to Unter-Altertheim, while Goeben moved down the high road to Gross Rinderfeld.[4]

An hour later Beyer marched off towards Neubrunn, deploying in front of the village by 1.30 pm after driving back some Bavarian outposts. It was occupied by the advanced guard of Stephan's division, which came as a considerable surprise; the Bavarian move southwards had not been detected. A concerted attack by infantry and artillery soon chased the enemy out of Neubrunn, but Beyer was left with a problem. If he pressed on to Unter-Altertheim, he might well have a large part of the Bavarian army coming down on his left flank; and he had no reports of Goeben's progress or of the position of the 8th Corps. He concluded that he should for the moment stand his ground at Neubrunn, but soon had to change his mind. His most advanced troops came under strong pressure from Bavarian troops in the woods on the Sesselberg, a height on the road to Helmstadt. For the protection of his main body, Beyer decided to clear the Sesselberg; after a short struggle the Fusilier Battalion of the 20th Regiment threw the Bavarians off the hill, forcing them to retreat towards Helmstadt.[5]

As the Prussians advanced, they came under fire from Bavarian guns on a height east of Helmstadt, and Beyer had to bring up his own artillery to return fire. It was becoming clear to him that his intention to break off the fight and take up a defensive position was not achievable. The strength of the Bavarians in his immediate front obliged him to bring up the bulk of his force. He was now facing Prince Leopold's 3rd Division, Stephan having retreated further to the east of Helmstadt in order to concentrate for an assault, a process which occupied him for several hours, leaving Leopold facing the Prussians. The latter got no help from Prince William of Baden, whose division was the nearest unit of the 8th Corps; as usual that enigmatic commander found excellent reasons for not doing anything very much at all, this time relying on the absence of any direct order from Alexander to assist. There is no evidence that he took any steps to seek instructions; it was suggested by one contemporary historian that his conduct was quite deliberate because he believed that, after Königgrätz, 'for the remainder of the campaign he had to confine himself within the narrowest limits in the discharge of his duty.'[6] Since Charles was in overall command, though, he and his staff can scarcely escape blame for giving belated and irrelevant instructions to the 8th Corps, and no orders at all for cooperation between the two parts of the army on July 25.

Beyer was by now hotly engaged. His main body in front of Helmstadt had gradually got the better of the Bavarians there, but on his right the 32nd Regiment met increasingly strong opposition, and Manteuffel ordered up the 39th Fusilier Regiment in support at 5.30 pm. The effect was immediate, and the Bavarians fell back quickly to Waldbrunn. Once again it seemed to Beyer that he could break off the action, and he

A Bavarian skirmish line at Helmstadt, drawing by Anton Hoffmann. (Regensberg/*Mainfeldzug*)

ordered his troops to bivouac for the night. By now the division was in a position facing east near the Ziegelhutte, where most of the fighting had taken place.

To the amazement of the Prussians, however, there suddenly appeared on their left strong columns of infantry. It was not even clear at first if these were hostile, but as soon as they were identified as Bavarian the 70th and 30th Regiments changed front to meet them. The newcomers were from Stephan's division, which had passed behind Helmstadt while Leopold fought in front of the village, and were now advancing from Uettingen in an effort to retake Helmstadt. Their attack was delayed for a while because Stephan was also uncertain of the identity of the troops before him. Soon, though, his artillery came into action on the Prussian left, compelling the infantry there to take shelter in the woods. Glümer now brought up the 20th Regiment in support. Moving through the tall standing corn, they were on top of the advancing Bavarians before their approach was suspected, and attacked them with such vigour that they were forced back so quickly as to expose the Bavarian gun line. The gunners were obliged to retreat at once to Uettingen to avoid capture. From there they engaged the Prussian guns, which had taken up a position on the Lange Hohe, in a fierce artillery duel, while in the valley below the opposing infantry were engaged in a bitter struggle. As darkness fell, the Bavarians finally retreated, their losses amounting to 43 men killed, 408 wounded and 279 taken prisoner. Prussian losses were 31 killed, 285 wounded and 37 missing.[7]

While the fighting at Helmstadt was going on, Flies had advanced from Urphar to Dertingen, driving back the weak Bavarian detachments opposed to him. As the day wore on, Manteuffel ordered him to move further forward to support Beyer, but he arrived at Uettingen at 9.00 pm, too late to take part in the fighting, so went into bivouac there, patrolling towards the Bavarian position at Rossbrunn. Beyer's troops remained around Helmstadt, much further from Goeben than Manteuffel had intended, having been unable to support the advance of Goeben's division.

The latter had as a result fought an entirely independent action with the 8th Corps. Kummer had led the way along the high road, followed by Weltzien and Tresckow; Wrangel advanced on the right towards Ilmspan. Alexander had taken up a position astride the road at Gerchsheim. The Combined Division, as an advanced guard, was posted in front of the main position, on the right of which was the Baden Division, with the 2nd Württemberg Brigade in the centre and the Hessian Division on the left. The rest of the Württemberg Division was in reserve. The position, along a line of heights in front of Gerchsheim, was a strong one, and Alexander disposed of over 40,000 men to face an enemy one-quarter the size. Since the Bavarians were only about five miles away, while the Army of the Main covered an arc of some fifteen miles, it might have been supposed that Alexander would be able to hold up Manteuffel's advance for a considerable time.

This was not the kind of thought which occurred to Goeben. As soon as his advanced patrols reported the positions taken up by the Federals, at 4.00 pm he ordered Kummer to deploy for action in a wood below the heights, while Wrangel was to turn the enemy's left by advancing from Ilmspan on Gerchsheim. Kummer had available two batteries, but as soon as they emerged from the trees they were fired on at first by three and later by five enemy batteries, suffering so heavily that after forty five minutes they had to be withdrawn into the sheltering woods. Emboldened by this success, Neipperg began a heavy bombardment of the woods in which Kummer's infantry stood waiting; but when the Nassau Brigade advanced to the attack it was driven off some 400 yards short of the edge of the wood by the ferocity of the Prussian rifle fire.[8] Since neither Perglas nor Hardegg were prepared to commit their divisions to a fresh assault, on the grounds that their troops were exhausted, Alexander could do no more than to hold his position on the heights.

Soon, however, Wrangel appeared on the Federal left, and their artillery switched to this new target, whereupon Goeben ordered Kummer again to advance. The batteries that had been so roughly handled had been refitted, and this time, reinforced by an Oldenburg battery, they were able to gain artillery superiority, enabling Kummer's infantry to storm the heights, followed by Weltzien's brigade. Alexander feared for his line of retreat, threatened as it was by Wrangel's advance which had pushed back the Hessian troops and was making ground rapidly towards the high road running east from Gerchsheim, and soon made up his mind to pull back. This decision was reinforced by the spectacle of Bavarian stragglers and support services streaming back towards Würzburg in such numbers that there was a serious risk of the high road becoming clogged with traffic; this could compromise the retreat of the whole of the 8th Corps.

The intention was that an orderly withdrawal should be covered by the Hessian Division and the 2nd Württemberg Brigade. But as they fell back, the units of the 8th Corps became increasingly intermingled; some never received their orders at all. As night fell, total chaos threatened. Fortunately, though, all this was unknown to the Prussians; otherwise a brisk assault on the tail of the retreating Federals must have brought disaster. The 8th Corps was finally collected together around Kist, while the cavalry and artillery fell back towards the Main. Goeben's losses were slight, at a total of 60 men; the Federal losses were three as four times as many.[9]

The Federal army was now in considerable danger. The series of defeats which it had sustained had forced it back to a position in which even getting across the Main in one piece was going to be difficult. Behind it lay a few narrow roads, blocked by wagons, artillery and other traffic of all kinds, which led to the deep valley of the Main. The experience of the 8th Corps on July 25 had demonstrated the speed with which discipline could disintegrate in the course of a retreat under pressure. That night Charles held a council of war at Hettstadt. Given the substantial numerical advantage of the Federals, and that they could now operate as a unit, it was felt that an attack on the Army of the Main must have a good chance of success. At worst, it should facilitate an orderly retreat over the river. This determination soon wavered, though, when information came in of the retreat of the 8th Corps to Kist, and the condition in which it had been left by the day's events; and the plan was finally ditched when, before dawn on July 26, news was received that Alexander was pulling back to Würzburg itself.[10]

But Charles had to face the fact that even if he did not attack, he would still have to fight. The persistence of his oncoming enemy made that clear, and he ordered Alexander to hold the Nicolausberg, the heights opposite Würzburg, in order to cover a Bavarian retreat if that became necessary. His intention was to occupy a position on the Waldbüttelbrünn plateau and await attack there. He meant, though, to seize a number of key points to strengthen his position.

The most advanced Prussian unit was Korth's brigade, at Uettingen facing eastward. Flies, who visited Korth during the evening of July 25, concluded that his position was dangerously exposed and by 3.00 am next morning had started forward with the rest of the division to support Korth. Impatient to see for himself what was going on, Flies rode on ahead; he found that the Bavarians, pursuant to the original plan to take the offensive, were already making a forward move. He at once ordered the occupation by two battalions of the Kirchberg, one of two heights to the north of Uettingen, the other being the Ossnert. He was too late; the Bavarians were well aware of the tactical value of the heights, and elements of Hartmann's division were on the Kirchberg before the Prussians could get there. South of Uettingen the Bavarians were also advancing to occupy key positions on the Leite and the Brunschlag hills. Flies' earlier concern was entirely justified; Korth was in fact in danger of being surrounded.

As he had shown at Langensalza, Flies was always full of the offensive spirit, and the two battalions detailed to occupy the Kirchberg were at once sent forward. Storming into the vineyards at the foot of the hill, they pressed on into the woods on the hillside; although sustaining heavy casualties, they drove the Bavarians off the crest and back onto the Ossnert. Following up, they next took that hill, driving the Bavarian riflemen back on the main body of their division which had deployed on the heights beyond the Mühlbach, taking over a hundred prisoners.

To the south of Uettingen there was also heavy fighting. Bavarian artillery at Rossbrunn had opened fire on the village, setting it on fire. Freyhold's brigade was ordered to launch an assault on the heights to the south, which had been occupied by a brigade from Feder's division, and thereby to remove the threat of encirclement; such a move would also enable the Prussian artillery to deploy and respond to the enemy bombardment.

It was not an easy task. Although the Leite was the crucial position, the Brunschlag must also be taken, as it commanded the approaches to the Leite. One battalion was sent against each hill; both encountered stiff opposition. The men of the 3rd Battalion of the 36th Regiment, advancing on the Leite, 'were met by a murderous fire in front and flank,

The storming of the Ossnert at Uettingen by the Prussian 36th Line Füsilier Regiment, July 26. (Fontane)

General Friedrich Beyer, commander of Division Beyer in the Army of the Main. (Rogers)

and were shelled by a battery posted on the Vogelberg, so that the men instinctively leaned more to the right towards the Brunschlag.'[11] Freyhold, whose brigade was getting very strung out, saw that he had to take the Leite without delay. With Colonel von Thile, the commander of the 36th Regiment, he led the remaining battalion of the regiment straight forward over the exposed ground at the foot of the hill, with drums beating and bayonets fixed. The Bavarians 'concentrated a most withering fire on the battalion. The horses of both above-named officers fell, the commander of the battalion was killed and a great number of officers and men were disabled.'[12] Inspired by their officers' example the troops pressed on until they got into the shelter of a strip of low meadow. Meanwhile on the Brunschlag the other two battalions were making ground through the woods. Reinforced by the Magdeburg Fusiliers, they finally ejected the Bavarians from the woods and occupied the crest of the Brunschlag; the battery on the Vogelberg withdrew and by 7.00 am the Prussians held this hill as well.

Deployment from Uettingen had been held up by the Bavarian artillery which was located at the Rossbrunn post house; when this retreated at 6.00 am, two Prussian batteries got through the village and took up a position to the north. By 7.00 am Flies had four batteries in action against Bavarian positions around Rossbrunn, and with the exit from Uettingen now open was able to bring up further troops to support Freyhold. The arrival of three fresh battalions soon enabled him to take the Leite. To his right, further support was arriving as Beyer, attracted by the sound of heavy firing, got his division moving to lend a hand in the fighting. The Prussians had suffered heavily while storming these hills and during the hand-to-hand fighting in the woods; once the Bavarians fell back, it was their turn to be in open country, and both in retreat and when attempting to counter-attack they took heavy losses.[13]

Beyer's advance, which extended to Mädelhofen, threatened the Bavarian line of retreat, which was already under way under the cover of artillery fire from five batteries on the plateau south of Greusenheim. The Prussians maintained the pressure, advancing at 8.00 am on Greusenheim and compelling its defenders to join the retreat.

In the centre, using the woods on the Leite as cover, the Prussians reformed for an advance on Rossbrunn. Here again, resistance was slight, and by mid-morning the Prussians had taken the place and the heights to the north. On the right a mixed force from the divisions of both Flies and Beyer advanced from the Brunschlag and on Mädelhofen; the Bavarians fell back at first to the Himmelreich Wald, but the impetus of the Prussian attack soon drove them out of that wood.

Meanwhile the cavalry had also had a chance to distinguish itself. Colonel Krug von Nidda had taken a combined cavalry brigade around the Bavarian right at Greusenheim; when the enemy troops there fell back he trotted off in pursuit and reached a position about a mile from Hettstadt. From there, unseen in a little dell, he could see the enemy artillery and, behind it, the Bavarian cavalry. Emerging from cover, Krug drove back the enemy skirmishers, but was soon assailed by the cavalry. In the first clashes, a squadron each of Prussian dragoons and hussars overcame the Bavarian 6th Chevauxleger Regiment, but in their turn fell back in the face of artillery fire. Gradually, on both sides, the rest of the cavalry were drawn in. Krug had committed all his force, and had deployed König's battery of horse artillery, when an entire brigade of Bavarian cuirassiers advanced. The sheer mass of this body threatened to overcome the Prussians. König, however turned his guns on the cuirassiers 'who were advancing from several sides, with such a hail of grapeshot at a very close range that their career was checked.'[14] At that moment two squadrons of the 5th Dragoons charged the cuirassiers and with the support of the rest of the Prussian cavalry drove them back. Krug tried to follow up his success, but the Bavarian artillery and the appearance of a fresh brigade of cavalry obliged him to fall back on his guns. After a tentative advance by the Bavarian cavalry was beaten off, Krug, feeling he had done enough, withdrew behind the rest of Flies' division.

While the fighting at Rossbrunn had been going on Goeben had remained at Gerchsheim, his troops exhausted and dangerously low in ammunition. This was fortunate for the 8th Corps which, unknown to Manteuffel (though he might have guessed) was pulling back over the river, leaving the Bavarians alone on the left bank. Contemplating the heavy casualties which a further attack might incur, Manteuffel concluded that they would be sacrificed to no purpose. That afternoon he sent his troops into bivouac, Flies at Rossbrunn and Beyer at Mädelhofen, making no attempt to molest the Bavarians as they retreated across the Main partly by the bridges at Würzburg and partly by temporary bridges to the north of the city.[15]

The last major engagement of the Army of the Main had been one of the fiercest. Against superior numbers of an enemy force, that was for once allowed to make the best use of its skill and courage, the Prussians lost a total of 856 men, of whom 101 were killed, 715 wounded and 40 missing; the Bavarian losses were practically identical. Both sides were by now coming to the conclusion that further heavy fighting should be avoided if possible, but their situation did not permit any local ceasefire to be agreed without higher orders. Meanwhile, military considerations dictated that, in view of the position taken up by the Federals, Manteuffel must move forward.

Early on July 27, therefore, the Army of the Main advanced on Würzburg, with a small detachment southwards towards Heidingsfeld to cover its flank. Goeben moved on Höchberg, which he found to be unoccupied; but in advancing further Kummer's brigade came under heavy fire from the Marienberg, west of the river. As Goeben deployed, the Bavarian skirmishers fell back, and Wrangel occupied the Nicolausberg and Kummer the Hexenberg. From here it was evident that the Marienberg was strongly garrisoned and well equipped with heavy artillery.[16] The Prussian infantry was able to take up positions around it without much difficulty; but the constant Bavarian artillery fire obliged Goeben to bring up his own artillery. Between 12 noon and 1.00 pm there was a brisk artillery exchange, in which the guns in the Marienberg position were supported at long range by Federal batteries from the other side of the river. But the cover of the positions carefully chosen by the Prussian gunners and the strength of the works on the Marienberg meant that neither side was able to do much harm, although by concentrating on the citadel buildings Goeben succeeded in setting fire to the arsenal.

Further north Manteuffel had ridden off with a hussar squadron to see the enemy position for himself, coming under heavy fire from Bavarian troops over the river, which killed one of his staff. It seemed clear that a prolonged artillery duel would produce no useful result, and he ordered Goeben to break off the action, and sent the whole of his army into bivouac, Flies at Hettstadt, Beyer at Waldbüttelbrünn and Goeben at Höchberg. He established his headquarters at Eisingen. The Marienberg guns continued to fire, but the Prussians ignored them. The strength of the positions held by the opposing armies meant for the moment a virtual stalemate, although the situation of the Federals cannot be said to have been comfortable.

Strategically, that situation was rapidly deteriorating. To its rear, and now not so very far away, the advance of the Prussian II Reserve Corps was already threatening Bayreuth. Commanded by the Grand Duke of Mecklenburg-Schwerin, this corps was intended to attain a total strength of 25,000 men, but it had not reached its full complement when it set off from Leipzig on July 20 to advance deep into Bavaria. Taking advantage of the newly-repaired railway line, the advanced guard reached Plauen on July 22 and that night marched directly on Hof. There, it surprised the garrison of two companies and in a short engagement took 65 prisoners.[17] Next day the advanced guard pressed on, followed by the main body, which reached Hof on July 27. These movements obliged Charles to do something; he could not afford to sit opposite Manteuffel and await events. As a precaution, the Baden Division moved out towards Ochsenfurt to secure the crossings there, while Kitzingen was occupied. Charles' principal move, though, was to write to Manteuffel calling on him to spare Würzburg, as an open town, if fighting recommenced. He followed this up with copies of despatches he had received with news of the Prusso-Austrian armistice, proposing a week's truce. A third messenger went with despatches from the Bavarian Government announcing that an armistice had now been concluded with Prussia.

On his side Manteuffel had heard nothing. On the other hand, he reckoned that he might as well take advantage of the situation to try and get Würzburg without a fight, so his response was to point out that since it was defended by the Marienberg citadel it could not be treated as an open town, and could only be spared from attack if it was surrendered at once. He gave emphasis to this suggestion by ordering the preparation of entrenchments for the batteries to be employed in an attack, and demanded a reply by 7.00 am on July 28. This brought von der Tann to Eisingen to start negotiations, and he soon went back to the Bavarian headquarters accompanied by his opposite number, Colonel von Kraatz-Koschlau. The basis of these talks was for Würzburg to be surrendered, with the Marienberg remaining garrisoned but declared neutral. While the talks were proceeding, a cipher despatch arrived for Manteuffel. Charles broke off the discussions, and Kraatz took the despatch back to Manteuffel. Timed at 5.40 am, it read: 'Peace preliminaries with Austria signed on the 24th. Truce with Bavaria agreed to; to commence on the 2nd August. Telegram by way of Berlin, and courier *en route* since yesterday. (Signed) von Moltke.' No mention being made of an immediate ceasefire, Manteuffel sent off a telegram explaining the position; for the moment it was agreed that a *de facto* ceasefire should be observed, to be ended only on twenty four hours' notice.

Next day the weather broke; on both sides the troops went into quarters, spreading over a wide area in which to find them. The Prussians were scattered west of the Main; the Bavarians were all along the river line, and the 8th Corps largely in the Gossmansdorf-Marktbreit area. Manteuffel moved his headquarters to Marktheidenfeld, and awaited further orders which because of the unreliable communications with Nikolsburg were slow in coming. On July 30 Moltke confirmed an earlier instruction that Manteuffel should in any case occupy as much territory as possible.[19]

Meanwhile the Grand Duke had continued to advance with the II Reserve Corps, brushing aside repeated protests from the Bavarians that an armistice was now in force. Hearing that the Bavarians intended to garrison Bayreuth on July 28, he sent a company of fusiliers, in country carts, escorted by a squadron of dragoons, under Major von Loos in order to forestall them. They arrived in time to meet the first trainload of Bavarian infantry at 3.00 pm. The Bavarian commander protested; Loos agreed to a brief truce pending the Grand Duke's decision. At 9.00 pm he told the Bavarians that the truce must end and at 10.00 pm the Prussian infantry advanced by moonlight. The Bavarians fell back; next day there were further skirmishes as they tried unsuccessfully to halt the Prussian advance.[20] The Grand Duke now resolved to march directly on Nürnberg, which he entered on August 1, hoisting the Prussian flag on the old castle of the Hohenzollerns. For a scratch force, the II Reserve Corps had done rather well, marching 180 miles in twelve days, and occupying a number of famous and important cities *en route*.

Meanwhile the 8th Federal Corps had, unsurprisingly, begun to disintegrate. On July 30 Prince William of Baden sent a messenger to Manteuffel with news of direct negotiations between the Grand Duke of Baden and the King of Prussia in which, he said, it was agreed that the Baden troops could go home. Manteuffel had no orders on the point, but it was obviously sensible to speed the breakup of the 8th Corps, and he agreed to the homeward march. That night he received a message from Moltke that until August 2 he had full freedom of action, so he returned his headquarters to Eisingen and next day gave orders to his army to concentrate again in front of Würzburg. He sent Kraatz off to Charles to tell him that the truce would end at 6.00 am on August 1 unless Würzburg was at once surrendered on the terms previously discussed. To this Charles had no choice but to agree; and with the occupation of Würzburg on August 2 the campaign came to a final conclusion with the receipt of a telegram of thanks from King William to the troops of the Army of the Main for their bravery and devotion.[21]

They deserved his praise. The Official History summed up their achievement:

> At the end of this campaign Prussia was thus in actual possession of either the whole or a considerable part of the territories of all her enemies, and thereby in a position to dictate the terms of peace. This object had been attained on the western theatre of war, not by a grand decisive battle but by a series of engagements fought

> right and left. Unity of leadership and unceasing activity had counterbalanced the numerical superiority of the enemy.[22]

The military victory over the Middle States was as remarkable as it was complete. This was the last occasion in their history when they pursued an independent foreign policy and conducted independent military operations. In the event those operations were conducted with more independence than strategic sense; but the courage of their soldiers gave the separate peoples of Germany at least something to remember with pride out of an episode that marked the end of their independent history. It also marked the end of the Confederation; Sybel noted that it was the first and last war that the Diet had had to wage. He wondered 'what would have become of Germany, had she been obliged to undergo a war with France or Germany under the leadership of that institution!'[23]

Historians have paid little attention to Prussia's campaign against the Middle States, quite understandably, since it was completely overshadowed by the events in Bohemia. Nonetheless, it is not unimportant, not only for the remarkably complete victory gained by a much inferior force, but also for its influence, in its political effect, on the subsequent history of Germany. It is only necessary to speculate on the possible consequences of a Prussian defeat. It would not, of course, have affected the outcome of the decisive battles in Bohemia; Moltke was certainly right in believing that any defeats in western Germany could be made good later. But it might have influenced Franz Joseph to fight on, causing the Prussians to undertake a further campaign on the Danube, at the end of long lines of communication, against a substantially reinforced opponent.

More significantly, the shape of the political negotiations at Nikolsburg might have been much affected had Austria's German allies been able to take advantage of their pronounced numerical superiority, instead of suffering a comprehensive defeat. The importance of the campaign is to some extent indicated by Bismarck's willingness to interfere at critical moments, and by his determination to prolong it until his negotiating position had been maximised by the extent of the success of the Army of the Main. Thus the campaign is a material part of the story of 1866. With the events that had immediately preceded it, it demonstrated conclusively the inability of the Middle States to exert any effective influence on the course of events.

34

Moltke at Nikolsburg

While engaged in superintending the army's advance to the Danube and making preparations for the next phase of the war, Moltke and his staff were also closely involved with the political processes by which the war would be brought to an end. Not surprisingly, as soon as the magnitude of the victory at Königgrätz had sunk in, strong opinions began to be expressed as to what should be Prussia's demands in the subsequent peace negotiations. Moltke does not seem to have been one of those who argued particularly stridently for extreme territorial acquisitions, perhaps because he was more realistic than some of his colleagues, and perhaps because he still had a huge army to manage and the next stages of what could still be a difficult campaign to plan. Others among the military, however felt passionately on the subject, and their influence on the King's reaction to the diplomatic developments was considerable, and certainly made Bismarck's task much more difficult.

When Napoleon announced his intention to act as a mediator it gave him outwardly, albeit temporarily, the diplomatic initiative, as Bismarck at once recognised. The Minister President was entirely clear in his mind that Prussia's interests required a swift settlement. He had not finally determined what should be Prussia's objectives in the peace negotiations, and nor had William. But the latter had, immediately after Königgrätz, made a note of some points that should be aimed at; the Duchies must become Prussian, Austria's position in Germany must be curtailed, and something must be done in relation to the smaller states of North Germany.[1] In the following days Bismarck carefully developed his own policy. The attitude of the King and his generals was however becoming unhelpful. On July 9 Bismarck reported to his wife:

> We are doing well, in spite of Napoleon; if we are not extravagant in our claims and do not imagine that we have conquered the world, we shall achieve a peace that will be worth our trouble. But we are as easily intoxicated as disheartened, and it is my thankless part to pour water into the foaming wine, and to insist that we do not live alone in Europe, but with three other Powers which hate and envy us.[2]

Moltke, planning the army's further advance, noted to his wife on July 12 that he would shortly be only five marches from Vienna, but that 'after that there is little doubt but that diplomacy will be brought into play, and that will be rather unfortunate.'[3] But by now Bismarck was reaching the conclusion that the organisation of a North German Confederation under Prussian leadership would not suffice, and that there must be extensive annexations which would add three or four million inhabitants to the population of Prussia. This, of course, went down well with the military; upon hearing of it Blumenthal noted in his diary on July 15 that he was 'greatly pleased' with the news:

> The demands of Prussia are certainly a little strong, but the Emperor of the French makes no demur, and so there will be no difficulties from that quarter. Austria must and will conclude a treaty of peace, or else she is lost for ever. She certainly cannot count on her army for years to come.[4]

Bismarck's relations with the soldiers at this time were not, however, very easy. He was particularly edgy about their apparent determination to cross the Danube and take Vienna before peace negotiations got under way; on one occasion, he gave way to his annoyance by enquiring sarcastically why the army should stop in Vienna: 'Why not pursue the Austrians into Hungary and, since it would be difficult to maintain communications with the rear, go on to Constantinople, found a new Byzantium, and leave Prussia to her fate?'[5] On another occasion he expressed very strongly his disapproval of a plan to storm the Austrian fortifications at Florisdorf, a project put forward by Frederick Charles as indispensable to forcing the line of the Danube. What troubled Moltke and other military leaders was the possibility that they would be forced to agree to a premature armistice which would give the Austrians the chance to recover. The predictable failure of the Italians' campaign had already had the effect of releasing reinforcements for the northern front, and a cessation of operations would give the Austrians the chance to regroup. On July 15 Moltke reflected on this in a letter to his wife: 'There must be no such thing as an armistice! We must in the first place have some definite propositions, and these are not yet forthcoming.'[6] The fear that diplomatic activity might intervene to hamper his future operations never left him. Royal Headquarters moved to the castle of Nikolsburg on July 18, and Bismarck's confrontation with the soldiers came to a head on the following day. By now Napoleon had conceded a number of the points set out in Bismark's programme but, because Goltz, the self-willed Prussian ambassador in Paris, had not pressed them, these did not include the demand for annexations in North Germany which Bismarck had decided on. Benedetti, the French ambassador, now insisted that these terms having been accepted by the Austrians, there should now be an armistice. To accept this meant a military risk, to which the generals naturally objected; but to refuse it could provoke conflict with France, which Bismarck wanted to avoid if at all possible.

Bismarck had had a particularly violent altercation with the generals at a meeting at Czernahora on July 15. He arrived late to find William in discussion with senior advisers over the plan to capture the Florisdorf lines in front of Vienna. Frederick Charles had continued to be in favour of this; but it was reckoned that in order for the attack to succeed the heavy artillery which had been sent for would be needed, and this would not be available for a fortnight. Even then, a casualty estimate of 2,000 men was suggested. Bismarck was aghast at the prospect of such a delay, saying that 'we cannot spend fourteen days in waiting without considerably increasing the deadweight of the French arbitration.' He went on, he later claimed, to point out that the Florisdorf line could be bypassed by a move to cross the river at Pressburg, in which case the Austrians would either have to fight south of the Danube, facing east, or retreat to Hungary. After looking at a map, William agreed, and this plan was accordingly adopted, although with unconcealed reluctance on the part of the military.[7]

Moltke was less concerned about fighting the French. He was in any case in favour of crossing the Danube and his opinion on this, and the desirability of finishing off the

Austrians without more ado contributed to the hardening of William's position. As to France, Moltke displayed his confidence in his ability to fight a two front war when two years later he told Lord Clarendon, then the British Foreign Secretary, that he regretted that the opportunity to defeat France and complete German unification had not been taken in 1866. In answer to the Minister President's enquiry as to what he would do if France did take military action, Moltke told Bismarck: 'I should adopt a defensive attitude towards Austria, confining myself to the line of the Elbe, and in the meantime prosecuting the war actively against France.'[9] Bismarck did not at all like the sound of this, and it confirmed him in his view that a quick peace was essential. France, he thought, would be a tough nut to crack if forced on the defensive; if he did have to fight a two front war he would have preferred to smash Austria completely before turning on France.

The mounting assertiveness of the military and the consequent stiffening of the King's attitude depressed Bismarck still further. A meeting with a number of senior generals on July 19, presided over by the King, took place in his rooms, as he was suffering from 'a painful illness.' He described the scene in his Reminiscences:

> On this occasion I was the only civilian in uniform. I declared it to be my conviction that peace must be concluded on the Austrian terms, but remained alone in my opinion; the King supported the military majority. My nerves could not stand the strain which had been put upon them day and night: I got up in silence, walked into my adjoining bedchamber and was there overcome by a violent paroxysm of tears.[10]

The military were practically unanimous in their support for the operation to cross the Danube; Boyen, the King's Adjutant-General, noted that day that the leading units were now closing up to the river, cheerfully observing that 'its bank can be reached tomorrow; the crossing will be easy or difficult, depending on what luck we have; I count with complete confidence on the former.' He went on to reflect the military discontent with the course of the peace negotiations: 'In eight days it will be all over, if the diplomats, who attach themselves to every honourable war like bugs to a bed, don't destroy the sport for us.'[11]

But July 19 was to mark the high point of Bismarck's immediate anxiety. There soon came from Paris a report from Goltz that Napoleon accepted the annexations in North Germany, and with this, an armistice could now be agreed. The question was when. Bismarck asked Moltke if the move on Pressburg would be dangerous. As he reflected in his Reminiscences:

> So far we had not a spot upon our white waistcoat. If we were sure of a happy issue to it, we must allow the battle to be fought out, and the truce postponed by half a day; victory would naturally strengthen our hand in negotiating; otherwise it would be better to abandon the enterprise altogether.

In reply, Moltke told him that he 'considered the issue as doubtful and the operations as risky; but in war everything was hazardous.' This was hardly bullish enough for Bismarck, and he advised William that the five day truce should come into force on July 22 at noon.[12] Bismarck, in stressing to Goltz that the Prussian programme of annexations must be accepted, had been able to add a sweetener for Napoleon; he had succeeded during the course of his discussions with Moltke in persuading him to agree not to insist on a formal entry into Vienna.

The armistice was, however, only for five days, and in that time a number of matters must be sorted out if preliminaries of peace were to be agreed. One was to deal with Prussia's Italian ally. Following the defeat at Custozza, the Italian army had fallen into a state of frozen immobility, from which it took two weeks to recover. Thereafter Cialdini, his strength brought up to fourteen divisions, moved slowly forward through Venetia, taking a further two weeks to reach Vicenza. The Italians were, however, extremely unhappy about the prospect that Bismarck would conclude a separate peace, and protested very strongly. Bismarck dismissed this contemptuously, saying:

> We have neither concluded peace nor truce without the consent of Italy, but only granted a five days cessation of hostilities in order to be able to talk about both of these things. Moreover, if our troops rest for five days, that is nothing more than the Italian Army did for weeks after Custozza.[13]

Ricasoli, whose influence had substantially increased at the expense of that of La Marmora, wanted the Trentino, Friuli and Istria as well as Venetia, and wanted to deal direct with Austria rather than through France. Prince Napoleon was sent to Florence to bring the Italians round. Napoleon III was getting extremely annoyed with his clients, and remarked viciously to Metternich: 'I would ask nothing better today than that you could beat them again, chase them from the Quadrilateral and keep Venetia.'[14] He bombarded his cousin with telegrams urging the importance of a quick acceptance by

The peace negotiations at Nikolsburg. (Voss)

the Italians of the armistice; and in the end, greatly assisted by the news of Tegetthoff's stunning victory at sea off Lissa, Prince Napoleon was successful in arranging an armistice to take effect on July 25.

Even more importantly, the outline of the peace terms must be agreed. Negotiations formally began on July 23; Austrian acceptance of the prospective annexations in North Germany was obtained by an agreed statement that 'His Majesty the Emperor of Austria pledges himself to sanction the arrangements to be made in North Germany by His Majesty the King of Prussia, including territorial changes.'[15] What was more difficult for Bismarck was to get the agreement of His Majesty the King of Prussia to what those territorial changes should be. He expressed his view especially forcefully with regard to Saxony, as he explained to Karolyi:

> He regarded Beust as the special originator of the trouble which produced the war; that Saxony was the seducer, the other states, especially Electoral Hesse and Hanover, were merely the seduced, and it was unfair to let the seducer emerge quite unscathed, when Prussia would be compelled, both in order to link up her territories and to assert her rights as victor, to make territorial acquisitions at the expense of the seduced.[16]

With negotiations still incomplete on July 23, they were adjourned for two days so that the negotiators might take instructions. Bismarck took advantage of the pause to set out in a detailed paper for William the terms that Prussia should seek; his anxiety for a quick deal was fuelled by news that the Czar was talking about a Congress of the Great Powers, and was trying to persuade Britain and France to agree joint action. In his paper Bismarck stressed the dangers of delay. If the annexations proposed, albeit leaving Austrian and Saxon territory intact, could be obtained, and Austria excluded from Germany, the outcome would be far more favourable than could have been aimed at before the war began. If this result could be obtained at Nikolsburg:

> Then it would be in my most humble and respectful opinion a political mistake if we, by the attempt to gain from Austria a few more square miles of territory or a few more millions for the war indemnity, should cause the whole result to be again brought into question and exposed to the uncertain chances of a prolonged war or a negotiation from which it would be impossible to exclude foreign interference.[17]

By now Bismarck had more or less brought Moltke and the rest of the military round to his way of thinking. Moltke, at the outset of the negotiations, in which he took part, hoped that they would 'surpass all expectations.' He wrote to Mary on July 23:

> I am very strongly of opinion, however, that the results which have been already obtained should not be set in jeopardy, if that can possibly be avoided. There should be no necessity to do so, either, if only thoughts of revenge are dispensed with, and our eyes are kept fixed upon what is to our own advantage.[18]

And Blumenthal, noting in his diary on July 22 that the peace preliminaries would probably have been concluded but for the difficulties raised by the King, added after reviewing the terms proposed: 'It is wise to be content therewith, as foreign nations will not interfere, and Austria will be severed from the Confederation.'[19]

But William remained obdurate. Bismarck feared that not only would he insist on making territorial gains at the expense of Austria and Saxony but would also press for a resumption of the army's advance. His failure to break down the King's resistance, coupled with the King's rising excitement, finally got too much for Bismarck, and he abruptly left the room with thoughts of immediate resignation in his mind. The ensuing scene provided him with one of his favourite stories, which he steadily embellished over the years and which he included in his Reminiscences:

> On returning to my room I was in the mood that the thought occurred to me whether it would not be better to fall out of the open window, which was four storeys high; and I did not look round when I heard the door open, although I suspected that the person entering was the Crown Prince, whose room in the same corridor I had just passed. I felt his hand on my shoulder, while he said: "You know that I was against this war. You considered it necessary, and the responsibility for it lies on you. If you are now persuaded that our end is attained, and peace must now be concluded, I am ready to support you and defend your opinion with my father." He then repaired to the King, and came back after a short half hour, in the same calm, friendly mood, but with the words: "It has been a very difficult business, but my father has consented."[20]

William bitterly minuted on Bismarck's memorandum that if there could not be obtained

Victory celebrations in Berlin at the Brandenburg Gate, September 20. (*Illustrirte Kriegs-Chronik*)

> from the vanquished what the army and the country are entitled to expect, that is to say a heavy war-expenses indemnity from Austria as the principal enemy or quite strikingly extensive territorial acquisitions… the victor will have to swallow this bitter pill at the very gates of Vienna and let posterity be the judge.[21]

With this painful private victory won, the rest of the peace negotiations were more or less plain sailing. When they resumed, Bismarck allowed Karolyi to beat him down to forty million thalers for the war indemnity; but he refused to countenance the Austrian attempt to exclude Saxony from the North German Confederation. Thereafter, the deal was done; the preliminaries were signed by Bismarck and Karolyi, and by Degenfeld the Austrian military delegate and Moltke, on July 26; the truce was extended until August 2, when the armistice would formally take effect. Notwithstanding William's disappointment, the territorial gains were huge; in addition to Schleswig-Holstein, Prussia was to annex the Kingdom of Hanover, Electoral Hesse, the Duchy of Nassau and the city of Frankfurt.

Moltke was profoundly relieved. Although the detailed discussions over the terms of the peace treaty remained, and major international questions must be settled as well as the new arrangements in Germany, there was no longer any doubt as to the extent of Prussia's success. Soon, he could return to Berlin secure in the knowledge that the staggering victory he had won had produced correspondingly enormous political results. 'Let us thank God with full hearts,' he wrote to Mary on July 26, announcing that the preliminaries of peace had been signed.[22]

35

Conclusion

One of the most remarkable aspects of the war was the total confidence which Moltke felt not only in his own ability but in the ability of his staff and senior commanders and the fighting qualities of his army. Apart from the small-scale war of 1864, and the confused and scrappy campaigns of 1848-1850, the Prussian army had not seen action since the end of the Napoleonic wars. In that time all the other Great Powers had been engaged in major conflicts; the Austrians had had recent experience of fighting under modern conditions as recently as 1859, and they enjoyed an extremely high reputation among military experts.

It is especially noteworthy that Moltke felt able to confine himself to broad strategic directives, rarely intervening to give operational instructions. He remained in Berlin until only four days before the decisive battle, preferring to monitor the movement of three widely scattered armies from his office there, rather than to be involved in person in the early stages of the campaign. The campaign which he conducted began with a strategic decision that was bold in the extreme – to limit the forces fighting in western Germany effectively to three divisions, in order to achieve an approximate equality of force in Bohemia. In spite of Falckenstein's wilful misunderstanding of his instructions, the success of the campaign against Austria's German allies amply vindicated his view that the forces deployed there would be sufficient. In any case, even a temporary set back there would, he knew, have been recoverable after the decisive battles in Bohemia had been fought and won.

There, his military options were severely circumscribed by both political and geographical considerations. Thanks to William's insistence on postponing the start of Prussian mobilisation, Moltke was obliged to deploy his armies on a broader front than he would have chosen in order to be able to use all the available railways. As a result, the initial disposition of the Prussian army was over an arc of 275 miles, and he at once began to reduce this by bringing about a concentration towards Görlitz. What he never intended to do, however, was to concentrate them in Napoleonic style in a small area, and this was a concept which shocked not only commentators such as Friedrich Engels but also some members of Moltke's own staff. It was always his intention to seek a victory of encirclement. As things turned out, his effort to shorten his front was thwarted by fears for Upper Silesia, so that he had again to extend his left towards the Neisse. His ultimate aim was a concentration in the Gitschin area – subject, of course, to the enemy's movements. But the concept of a victory of encirclement was never fully understood by many of those who had to execute his plans. As Schlieffen observed:

> The idea of annihilating the enemy, which completely absorbed Moltke, was not fathomed by the subordinate commanders. They understood the problem before them to lie in the junction of the separated armies. In this they agreed with Moltke.

> But he wished to see the opponent within the circle of the united armies, while they were willing to leave it to the enemy to concentrate his forces where he desired.[1]

It is an important part of Moltke's achievement that he resisted the pressure to bring about a premature junction of his armies, even on the day of Königgrätz. There, his serene confidence in ultimate victory was shared by few of his anxious colleagues on the Roskosberg. He knew as they did not, that in effect the decisive battles had already been fought; Königgrätz, as Schlieffen pointed out, was the working out of the situation which these had created.[2]

Moltke's clear grasp of the strategical possibilities and his single-minded pursuit of his chosen option contrasted with the irresolute and changeable policy of his adversary. In spite of his apparent advantage of operating on interior lines, and the fact that political circumstances enabled him to reach the battle zone in better time than might have been expected, Benedek was never certain as to which of the advancing Prussian armies he should first attack. And the cool efficiency, and consistency, of the Prussian staff was not matched on the Austrian side, where Krismanic was only the worst of the unfortunate influences on Benedek's decision making.

The superiority of the higher leadership of the Prussian Army was not the only factor in its success, though it was, in the end, decisive. Immediately after Königgrätz many military commentators, bewildered by the unexpected and comprehensive defeat of the Austrians, ascribed it to the needle gun. The English newspapers in particular had carried highly-coloured accounts of its effectiveness; the *Spectator*, for instance observed that 'riflemen sent against men armed with breech loaders might almost as well carry slings or bows and arrows, for all the harm they are likely to effect.'[3]

In the *Manchester Guardian*, Engels was more thoughtful. 'This immense and rapid success could not have been obtained without such superior fire, for the Austrian army is habitually less subject to panic than most European armies.' Engels did, however, go on to pay tribute to the 'order and punctuality' of the Prussian movements and to the Prussian soldiers:

> All the world must have been surprised at the dash displayed by these young troops in each and every engagement without exception. It is all very well to say the breech loaders did it, but they are not self-acting, they want stout hearts and strong arms to carry them. The Prussians fought very often against superior numbers, and were almost everywhere the attacking party; the Austrians therefore had the choice of ground. And in attacking strong positions and barricaded towns, the advantages of the breech loader almost disappear.[4]

The point is reinforced by the remarkable fact that throughout the campaign only 1.4 million rounds of infantry ammunition were expended by the Prussian troops, an average of only seven for each combat soldier. The figures for the battle of Koniggratz are even more startling; on July 3, an average of only one round per soldier was fired.[5] The intelligent and far-sighted Stoffel, the French military attaché, put it bluntly. 'People have assigned to the weapons of the Prussian infantry the greatest share in its victories. But it is a great error. The superiority of the weapons has been only a secondary cause … the superiority of the Prussian over the Austrian army is undeniable and great in every respect. This, and the incapacity of the Austrian general were the two main causes of the Prussian victories.'[6]

In one area of materiel, the Austrian performance had come up to expectation. In part because the Prussian artillery was in a state of transition – a third of the Prussian guns were smoothbore – the results achieved appeared not to equal the effectiveness of the Austrian artillery, particularly in covering the retreat of the defeated infantry. Another factor was the incomplete development of artillery tactics. Hohenlohe was candid about the use of the artillery: 'In 1866 our artillery, on almost every occasion, entered upon the scene far too late and with far too small a number of guns.'[7] It was this failure above all which accounted for the disappointing performance, although Hohenlohe also noted that the Prussian gunners did not shoot as accurately as had been expected, and the system of replenishment of ammunition was also unsatisfactory. By 1870 the lessons of 1866 had been learned; not only were different tactics employed, but by then the Prussian army had been completely reequipped with Krupp steel guns.

Similar considerations applied to the use of cavalry during the campaign. Cavalry leaders were fascinated by the notion of cavalry being able to provide a stunningly decisive blow by the use of shock tactics; as a result the cavalry divisions had followed, rather than preceded the main body of the army, to be kept in reserve until the *moment d'appui* arrived. As a result, Moltke was obliged to observe in a paper prepared soon after Königgrätz that while the infantry had in every respect performed 'excellently', it had been inadequately supported by the artillery 'and by the cavalry as good as not at all.'[8] By 1870 these lessons, too, had been learned.

Another area in which experience proved the most effective tutor was in the supply of the troops during the campaign. By June 29 the advancing Prussians had got out of touch with their supply trains, which did not catch up until after Königgrätz, overcoming appalling traffic difficulties *en route*. Moltke summarised the reasons for this failure in a circular to army commanders on July 8. Apart from the priority naturally given to combat units, the field police who should have sorted out the problems were deployed elsewhere, causing congestion particularly in narrow defiles. Discipline generally was poor, while the supply convoys were enlarged by the addition of unsuitable and unauthorised vehicles.[9]

Nor did the performance of the railway system come up to expectation. There was complete indiscipline over the bringing forward of supplies, resulting in severe congestion and the pile up of huge quantities of supplies at the railheads. The problem was apparently compounded by Moltke's decision to bring his director of railways to the battlefield as part of the general staff, instead of leaving him in Berlin to impose some order on the system.[10] On the other hand, repairs to the railway system in Bohemia had been effected with relative ease; the only serious interruptions to the Prussian use of the Austrian rail system occurred where the line passed through the fortresses.

What was clear to all, however, was that the outcome of the war had fundamentally altered the military balance of power in Europe. Moltke may have been confident in the power of his army to see off the French as well as the Austrians; but it was only after the military world came to terms with the Prussian victory, and its consequences, that it was apparent that the Prussian army was now the most powerful military organisation in Europe, and that it need fear no enemy. The incorporation of the military forces of the North German Confederation, and the military treaties with the states of South

Germany, meant that Napoleon's moment for imposing a military solution on Germany had passed, if indeed it had ever existed.

Although obvious now, this change in the balance of power was still not entirely apparent to contemporary politicians. In Austria, a desire for revenge was understandable, although a belief that it was possible was further evidence of the incapacity of Austrian statesmen to grasp reality. Soon after the Nikolsburg negotiations were concluded, in an evident expression of his determination to stand up to Prussia in Germany notwithstanding the outcome of the war, Franz Joseph appointed Friedrich von Beust to take over the conduct of foreign affairs. Beust himself expressed surprise. In his memoirs he noted that during the closing weeks of the war, the Austrians had looked on him as an unwelcome visitor 'and the man whose energetic conduct had been praised to the skies by the Vienna papers, who had even in Prague been hailed as a "true man", was now frowned upon as the supposed promoter of the war… Vienna was glad to have a scapegoat.'[11] However much the Austrians desired revenge, though, for the moment all that they could do was to wait. The political initiative in Europe was now in the hands of one man.

And that man was no longer Napoleon III. Although he remained as much a potential menace to the peace of Europe as ever, his apparently dominant position in international power politics had been destroyed. Some observers went further; Disraeli's view was blunt:

> Napoleon is finished. He cannot wage a war against Prussia at all; quite apart from his illness, which exercises the most disadvantageous influence on his mental ability, he is so seriously threatened at home that we shall soon experience the end of the tragi-comedy of the Second Empire.[12]

Certainly Napoleon's own position had been exposed to danger by the scale of Prussia's success, and what it betokened for the future. To Lord Stanley, writing to Cowley on August 18, the prospect of further rapid change was already evident:

> I begin to suspect that the German revolution may go farther and faster than its authors intend. Bismarck wants a new German federation. Napoleon wanted an Italian federation. We know what came of that: may not the precedent be followed? In any case the southern states will not long endure exclusion: and then will be seen, whether France and Russia will tolerate a German empire. But, as I think you said in one of your letters, it is a question for '68 rather than for '66.[13]

As it turned out, it was to be a question for 1870.

Appendix I

Order of Battle, Combined Allied Army 1864

1st February 1864

Commander	Field Marshal Baron von Wrangel
Chief of Staff	Lieutenant General Vogel von Falckenstein
Senior Quartermaster	Colonel von Podbielski
General Staff Officers	Lieutenant Colonel von Schönfeld (Austrian)
	Major von Stiehle
	Captain Count von Hardenberg
	Premier Lieutenant von Gottberg
	Premier Lieutenant von Roon
Assigned to Headquarters	Lieutenant Colonel Prince Kraft zu Hohenlohe-Ingelfingen
Supernumerary	HRH Lieutenant General Crown Prince Frederick William
Attached to Staff	HRH General of Cavalry Prince Albrecht (Senior)
Temporarily attached	HRH the Grand Duke of Mecklenburg-Schwerin
	HRH General of Infantry Prince zu Hohenzollern-Sigmaringen
	Colonel the Hereditary Prince of Anhalt

ROYAL PRUSSIAN COMBINED ARMY CORPS
(I Corps Combined Army)

Commander	General of Cavalry HRH Prince Frederick Charles
Chief of Staff	Colonel von Blumenthal
Commander, Artillery	Colonel von Colomier
Commander, Engineers	Lieutenant Colonel von Kriegsheim
General Staff Officers	Major Count von Waldersee
	Major von Roos
Attached to Staff	HRH Colonel Prince Albrecht (Junior)
Temporary Headquarters Attachment	HRH Prince Charles

6TH INFANTRY DIVISION

Commander	Lieutenant General von Manstein
11th Infantry Brigade	(Major General Baron von Canstein)

Brandenburg Fusilier Regiment Nr. 35 (Colonel Elstermann von Elster)

7th Brandenburg Infantry Regiment Nr. 60
(Lieutenant Colonel von Hartmann)
12th Infantry Brigade (Major General von Roeder II)
4th Brandenburg Infantry Regiment Nr 24 (Colonel Count von Hacke)
8th Brandenburg Infantry Regiment Nr. 11 (Lieutenant Colonel von Sirthin)
3rd Foot Artillery Division, Brandenburg Artillery Brigade Nr. 3
(Lieutenant Colonel Bergmann)
3rd Howitzer Battery
3rd 6-pounder Battery
3rd 12-pounder Battery
Brandenburg Pioneer Battalion Nr. 3

13TH INFANTRY DIVISION
Commander Lieutenant General von Wintzingerode
25th Infantry Brigade (Major General von Schmidt)
1st Westphalian Infantry Regiment Nr. 13 (Colonel von Witzleben)
5th Westphalian Infantry Regiment Nr 53 (Colonel Baron von Buddenbrock)
26th Infantry Brigade (Major General von Goeben)
2nd Westphalian Infantry Regiment Nr. 15 (Colonel von Alvensleben)
6th Westphalian Infantry Regiment Nr. 55 (Colonel Stolz)
Divisional Troops
Westphalian Jäger Battalion Nr. 7 (Major von Beckedorff)
Westphalian Dragoon Regiment Nr.7 (Lieutenant Colonel von Nibbeck)
1st Foot Artillery Division, Westphalian Artillery Brigade Nr.7 (Major Grave)
1st Howitzer Battery
1st 6-pounder Battery
1st 12-pounder Battery
4th 12-pounder Battery
Westphalian Pioneer Battalion Nr. 7

COMBINED CAVALRY DIVISION
Commander Major General Count zu Münster-Meinhövel
6th Cavalry Brigade (Colonel Flies)
Ziethen Hussar Regiment, Brandenburg Nr. 3 (Colonel Count von der Goltz)
Brandenburg Cuirassier Regiment Nr.6 (Colonel HRH Duke Wilhelm of Mecklenburg-Schwerin)
1st Horse Artillery Battery, Westphalian Artillery Brigade Nr.7
13th Cavalry Brigade (Major General von Hobe)
Westphalian Hussar Regiment Nr.8 (Lieutenant Colonel von Rantzau)
Westphalian Cuirassier Regiment Nr.4 (Lieutenant Colonel von Schmidt)
2nd Horse Artillery Battery, Westphalian Artillery Brigade Nr. 7

RESERVE ARTILLERY
Commander Lieutenant Colonel von Saenger
2nd Foot Artillery Division, Brandenburg Artillery Brigade Nr. 3 (Major von Held)
2nd Howitzer Battery

2nd 6-pounder Battery
4th 6-pounder Battery
2nd 12-pounder Battery

Horse Artillery Division, Westphalian Artillery Brigade Nr. 7 (Lieutenant Colonel von Saenger)

3rd Horse Artillery Battery
4th Horse Artillery Battery
5th Horse Artillery Battery
6th Horse Artillery Battery

Ancillary Units

Munitions and Bridging Train
Ammunition Trains Nrs. 1, 2 and 3 – Westphalian Artillery Brigade Nr. 7
Ammunition Trains Nrs. 4, 5, 6, 7, 8 and 9 – Brandenburg Artillery Brigade Nr.3
Light Field Bridging Train – Guards
Pontoon Trains Nrs. 3 and 7

K. K. VI ARMY CORPS
(II Corps, Combined Army)

Commander	Lieutenant Field Marshal Baron Gablenz
Chief of Staff	Colonel Baron Vlasits
Deputy chief of Staff	Major Edler von Poppenheim
Commander Artillery	Lieutenant Colonel Weisser
Commander Engineers	Major Baron Salis-Soglio

1st Brigade (Major General Count Gondrecourt)

30th Infantry Regiment (Martini) (Colonel Baron von und zu Lilienberg)
34th Infantry Regiment (King of Prussia) (Colonel Benedek)
18th Jäger Battalion (Lieutenant Colonel von Tobias)
4-pounder Foot Battery Nr. 2,1st Artillery Regiment

2nd Brigade (Major General Dormus)

35th Infantry Regiment (Khevenhüller) (Colonel Camptner)
72nd Infantry Regiment (Ramming) (Colonel Ritter von Abele)
22nd Jäger Battalion (Lieutenant-Colonel Ritter von Siller)
4-pounder Foot Battery Nr. 3,1st Artillery Regiment

3rd Brigade (Major General Nostitz)

14th Infantry Regiment (Hessen) (Colonel Freiherr Schütte von Warensberg)
27th Infantry Regiment (King of the Belgians)
(Colonel Duke Wilhelm of Württemberg)
9th Jäger Battalion (Lieutenant Colonel Schidlach)
4-pounder Foot Battery Nr. 4,1st Artillery Regiment

4th Brigade (Major General Tomas)

6th Infantry Regiment (Coronini) (Colonel Fellner von Feldegg)
80th Infantry Regiment (Holstein) (Colonel Count Auersperg)
11th Jäger Battalion (Colonel von Schwab)
4-pounder Foot Battery Nr. 5, 1st Artillery Regiment

Cavalry Brigade
Commander — Major General Baron Dobrzhensky
- 2nd Dragoon Regiment (Windischgrätz) (Colonel Count Bellegarde)
- 9th Hussar Regiment (Liechtenstein) (Colonel Baron Baselli von Süssenberg)

Technical Troops
- 4th Company 1st Pioneer Battalion with Bridging Train Squadrons 39 and 40
- 3rd Company 1st Pioneer Battalion
- 11th Engineer Company

Corps Artillery Reserve — (Major Ritter von Neubauer)
- 8-pounder Battery Nr. 9 1st Artillery Regiment
- 8-pounder Battery Nr. 10 1st Artillery Regiment

Ancillary Units
- Field Magazine, with attached Transport Squadrons 2, 35 and 53
- Corps Distribution Depot
- Corps Reception Depot
- Corps Munitions Park, with attached Transport Squadrons 27 and 28.
- 1st Park Company, 5th Field Repair Company
- Munitions Field Depot, with detachment, 1st Park Company

ROYAL PRUSSIAN COMBINED GUARD DIVISION
(III Corps, Combined Army)

Commander — Lieutenant General von der Mülbe
Chief of Staff — Major von Alvensleben
Combined Foot Guards Brigade (Major General Count von der Goltz)
- 3rd Foot Guards Regiment (Colonel von der Groeben)
- 4th Foot Guards Regiment (Colonel von Korth)

Combined Guard Grenadier Brigade (Colonel von Bentheim)
- 3rd Guard Grenadier Regiment (Colonel von Winterfeld)
- 4th Guard Grenadier Regiment (Colonel von Oppell)

Guard Hussar Regiment (Lieutenant Colonel von Kerssenbroigk)
Guard 4-pounder Battery
3rd Guard 6-pounder Battery

Appendix II

Order of Battle, Royal Danish Army 1864

1st February 1864

Commander	Lieutenant General de Meza
Chief of Staff	Colonel Kauffmann
Deputy Chief of Staff	Captain Rosen
Naval Liaison Officer	Captain Frøhlich

1ST DIVISION

Commander — Lieutenant General Gerlach

1st Brigade (Colonel Lasson)
- 2nd Infantry Regiment (Lieutenant Colonel Dreyer)
- 22nd Infantry Regiment (Lieutenant Colonel Falkenskjold)

2nd Brigade (Major General Vogt)
- 3rd Infantry Regiment (Major Mathieson)
- 18th Infantry Regiment (Lieutenant Colonel Hirsch)

3rd Brigade (Colonel Worishoffer)
- 16th Infantry Regiment (Major Wolle)
- 17th Infantry Regiment (Colonel Bernstorff)

4th Dragoon Regiment
- 2nd Half Regiment (Major Lillienskjold)

Divisional Troops
- Divisional Artillery (Major Glahn)
  - 2nd Field Artillery Battery
  - 10th Field Artillery Battery
- 5th Engineer Company
- Divisional Magazine with Provisions Column
- Brigade Magazines

2ND DIVISION

Commander — Major General du Plat

4th Brigade (Major General Wilstere)
- 4th Infantry Regiment (Colonel Faaborg)
- 6th Infantry Regiment (Major Caroc)

5th Brigade (Colonel Harbou)
- 7th Infantry Regiment (Lieutenant Colonel Muus)
- 12th Infantry Regiment (Colonel Hein)

6th Brigade (Colonel Bülow)

5th Infantry Regiment (Major Myhre)
10th Infantry Regiment (Colonel Lange)
Guard Hussar Regiment
1st Half Regiment (Ritmester Hegermann-Lindencrone)
Divisional Troops
Divisional Artillery (Major Schoning)
7th Field Artillery Battery
9th Field Artillery Battery
1st Engineer Company
Divisional Magazine with Provisions Column
Brigade Magazines

3RD DIVISION
Commander Major General Steinmann
7th Brigade (Colonel Müller
1st Infantry Regiment (Lieutenant Colonel Beck)
11th Infantry Regiment (Major Rist)
8th Brigade (Colonel Scharffenberg)
9th Infantry Regiment (Lieutenant Colonel Tersling)
20th Infantry Regiment (Lieutenant Colonel Scholten)
19th Brigade (Lieutenant Colonel Faerch)
21st Infantry Regiment (Lieutenant Colonel Nielsen)
4th Dragoon Regiment
1st Half Regiment (Major Gerlach)
Divisional Troops
Divisional Artillery (Major Just)
11th Field Artillery Battery
12th Field Artillery Battery
2nd Engineer Company
Divisional Magazine with Provisions Column
Brigade Magazines

4TH (CAVALRY) DIVISION
Commander Lieutenant General Hegermann-Lindencrone
1st Cavalry Brigade (Major General Honnens)
3rd Dragoon Regiment (Major Brock)
5th Dragoon Regiment (Lieutenant Colonel Brock)
2nd Cavalry Brigade (Colonel Scharffenberg)
6th Dragoon Regiment (Lieutenant Colonel Bauditz)
Divisional Troops
Divisional Artillery
5th Field Artillery Battery (Captain Lonborg)
Divisional Magazine with Provisions Column
Brigade Magazines

Army Infantry Reserve (Major General Caroc)

- 8th Infantry Regiment (Colonel Hveberg)
- 15th Infantry Regiment (Lieutenant Colonel Zepelin)
- Brigade Magazine

Army Artillery

Commander	Lieutenant General Lüttichau
Divisional Troops	(Lieutenant Colonel Haxthausen)

- Reserve Artillery
- 1st Field Artillery Battery
- 6th Field Artillery Battery
- 8th Field Artillery Battery
- 13th Field Artillery Battery

Artillery Command, Dannewerke Position (Colonel Wahl)

- 1st Fortress Company
- 3rd Fortress Company
- 5th Fortress Company
- 6th Fortress Company
- Dannewerke Position Artillery Park
- Fieldpark

Appendix III

Order of Battle of the Royal Prussian Army in 1866

Commander-in-Chief	His Majesty the King
Chief of the Staff	General von Moltke
Inspector-General of Artillery	Lieutenant General von Hindersin
Inspector-General of Engineers	Lieutenant General von Wasserschleben

FIRST ARMY

Commander-in-Chief	General of Cavalry HRH Prince Frederick Charles
Chief of the Staff	Lieutenant General von Voigts-Rhetz
Quartermaster-General	Major General von Stülpnagel
Commandant of Artillery	Major General von Lengsfeld

II CORPS

General Commanding	Lieutenant General von Schmidt
Chief of the Staff	Major General von Kameke
3rd Division	Lieutenant General von Werder
5th Brigade	(Major General von Januschowsky)
2nd and 42nd Regiments[1]	
6th Brigade	Major General von Winterfeld)
15th and 54th Regiments	
Pomeranian Rifle Battalion No 2	
Blucher Hussars No 5	
Pioneer Battalion No 2	
Four Batteries	
4th Division	Lieutenant General von Herwarth
7th Brigade	(Major General von Schlabrendorff)
9th and 49th Regiments	
21st and 61st Regiments	
Pomeranian Uhlans No 4	
Four Batteries	

1 Unless noted otherwise, all Prussian Line Infantry and Guard Infantry Regiments had three battalions.

III CORPS

General Commanding — None
5th Division — Lieutenant General von Tümpling
- 9th Brigade — (Major General von Schimmelmann)
  - 8th and 48th Regiments
- 10th Brigade — (Major General von Kamiensky)
  - 12th and 18th Regiments
- 1st Brandenburg Uhlans, No. 3
- 3rd Battalion Pioneers
- Four Batteries

6th Division — Lieutenant General von Manstein
- 11th Brigade — (Major General von Gersdorff)
  - 35th and 60th Regiments
- 12th Brigade — (Major General von Kotze)
  - 24th and 64th Regiments
- Brandenburg Dragoons No 2
- 3rd Jäger Battalion
- Four Batteries

IV CORPS

General Commanding — None
7th Division — Lieutenant General von Fransecky
- 13th Brigade — (Major General von Schwarzhoff)
  - 26th and 66th Regiments
- 14th Brigade — (Major General von Gordon)
  - 27th and 67th Regiments
- 4th Pioneer Battalion
- Magdeburg Hussars
- Four Batteries

8th Division — Lieutenant General von Horn
- 15th Brigade — (Major General von Bose)
  - 31st and 71st Regiments
- 16th Brigade — (Major General von Schmidt)
  - 72nd Regiment
- 4th Jäger Battalion
- Thuringian Uhlans No 6
- Four Batteries

CAVALRY CORPS

General Commanding — General of Cavalry HRH Prince Albrecht (Snr)
1st Cavalry Division — Major General von Alvensleben
- 1st Heavy Brigade — (Major General HRH Prince Albrecht (Jnr)
  - Garde du Corps
  - Cuirassiers of the Guard
- 2nd Heavy Brigade — (Major General von Pfuel)
  - Brandenburg Cuirassiers No. 6

Magdeburg Cuirassiers No. 7	
1st Light Brigade	(Major General von Rheinbaben)
1st Dragoons of the Guard	
1st Uhlans of the Guard	
2nd Uhlans of the Guard	
Two Horse Batteries	
2nd Cavalry Division	Major General Hann von Weyhern
2nd Light Brigade	(Major General Duke William of Mecklenburg-Schwerin)
2nd Dragoons of the Guard	
Brandenburg Hussars No. 3	
2nd Brandenburg Uhlans No. 11	
3rd Light Brigade	(Major General Count von der Groeben)
Neumark Dragoons No. 3	
Thuringian Hussars No. 12	
3rd Heavy Brigade	(Major General von der Goltz)
Queen's Own Cuirassiers No. 2	
2nd Pomeranian Uhlans, No. 9	
Two Horse Batteries	
Reserve Artillery of Cavalry Corps	
One Horse Battery	
Reserve Artillery of First Army	
Sixteen Batteries	

SECOND ARMY

Commander in Chief	HRH General Crown Prince Frederick William
Chief of the Staff	Major General von Blumenthal
Quartermaster General	Major General von Stosch
Commandant of Artillery	Major General von Jacobi
Commandant of Engineers	Major General von Schweinitz

I CORPS

General Commanding	General von Bonin
Chief of Staff	Colonel von Borries
Commandant of Artillery	Colonel Knothe
Commandant of Engineers	Colonel Weber
1st Division	Lieutenant General von Grossman
1st Brigade	(Major General von Pape)
1st and 41st Regiments	
2nd Brigade	(Major General von Barnekow)
3rd and 43rd Regiments	
Lithuanian Dragoons No. 1	
1st Jäger Battalion	
Four Batteries	
2nd Division	Lieutenant General von Clausewitz
3rd Brigade	(Major General von Malotki)

4th and 44th Regiments
4th Brigade (Major General von Buddenbrock)
5th and 45th Regiments
1st Royal Hussars No. 1
1st Pioneer Battalion
Four Batteries
Reserve Brigade of Cavalry of I Corps (Colonel von Bredow)
East Prussian Cuirassiers No.3
East Prussian Uhlans No. 8
Lithuanian Uhlans No 12
One Horse Battery
Reserve Artillery of I Corps
Seven Batteries

V CORPS

General Commanding	General von Steinmetz
Chief of the Staff	Colonel von Wittich
Commandant of Artillery	Colonel von Kraewel
Commandant of Engineers	Colonel von Kleist
9th Division	Major General von Löwenfeld
17th Brigade	(Major General von Ollech)
37th and 58th Regiments	
18th Brigade	(Major General von Horn)
7th Regiment and 5th Jäger Battalion	
1st Silesian Dragoons No. 4	
Four Batteries	
10th Division	Major General von Kirchbach
19th Brigade	(Major General von Tiedemann)
6th and 46th Regiments	
20th Brigade	(Major General von Wittich)
47th and 52nd Regiments	
5th Pioneer Battalion	
West Prussian Uhlans No. 1	
Four Batteries	
Reserve Artillery of V Corps	
Seven Batteries	

VI CORPS

General Commanding	General von Mutius
Chief of the Staff	Colonel von Sperling
Commandant of Artillery	Major General Herkt
11th Division	Lieutenant General von Zastrow
21st Brigade	(Major General von Hanenfeldt)
10th and 50th Regiments	
22nd Brigade	(Major General von Hoffmann)
38th and 51st Regiments	

Silesian Pioneer Battalion
2nd Silesian Dragoons No. 8
Three Batteries

12th Division — Lieutenant General von Prondzynski
Combined Brigade — (Major General von Kranach)
22nd and 23rd Regiments (from 23rd and 24th Brigades)
2nd Silesian Hussars No. 6
6th Jäger Battalion
Two Batteries

Reserve Cavalry
1st Silesian Hussars No. 4

Reserve Artillery of VI Corps
Five Batteries

(N.B: Two Infantry Regiments of the 12th Division were detached, the 63rd to garrison Neisse, the 62nd to the command of General von Knobelsdorf, who protected Silesia at Ratibor, and to whom the Silesian Uhlans and one battery were attached. Three batteries were with General Manteuffel).

GUARD CORPS

General Commanding — Prince August of Württemberg
Chief of the Staff — Colonel von Dannenberg
Commandant of Artillery — Major General von Colomier
1st Division of the Guard — Lieutenant General Hiller von Gärtringen
1st Brigade (Colonel von Obernitz)
1st and 3rd Guard Regiments
2nd Brigade (Major General von Alvensleben)
2nd Guards and Guard Fusilier Regiment
Hussars of the Guard
Jägers of the Guard
Four Batteries

2nd Division of the Guard — Lieutenant General von Plonski
3rd Brigade (Major General von Budritzki)
Grenadiers of Kaiser Alexander and 3rd Grenadiers of the Guard
4th Brigade (Major General von Loen)
Grenadiers of Kaiser Franz, and 4th Grenadiers of the Guard
3rd Uhlans of the Guard
Sharpshooter Battalion of the Guard
Four Batteries

Reserve Artillery of Guard Corps
Five Batteries

(N.B: The 4th Regiment of the Guard was retained at Berlin and sent later to the Second Reserve Corps)

Reserve Cavalry of the Second Army

General Commanding — Major General von Hartmann

1st Line

- Cuirassier Brigade (Major General von Schoen)
  - West Prussian Cuirassiers No. 5
  - Silesian Cuirassiers No. 1

2nd Line — (Major General von Borstell)

- Light Brigade (Major General von Witzleben)
  - Posen Uhlans No. 10
  - 2nd Royal Hussars No.2
- Landwehr Brigade (Major General von Frankenberg)
  - 2nd Landwehr Hussars
  - 1st Landwehr Uhlans

Two Horse Batteries

ARMY OF THE ELBE

Commander in Chief — General von Herwarth von Bittenfeld
Chief of the Staff — Colonel von Schlotheim
Commandant of Artillery — Colonel von Rozynski

14th Division — Lieutenant General Count zu Münster-Meinhövel

- 27th Brigade (Major General von Schwarzkoppen)
  - 16th and 56th Regiments
- 28th Brigade (Major General von Hiller)
  - 17th and 57th Regiments
- Westphalian Dragoons No. 7
- 7th Jäger Battalion
- Two Companies of 7th Pioneer Battalion
- Four Batteries

15th Division — Lieutenant General von Canstein

- 29th Brigade (Major General von Stückradt)
  - 40th and 65th Regiments
- 30th Brigade (Major General von Glasenapp)
  - 28th and 68th Regiments
- Royal Hussars No. 7
- 8th Pioneer Battalion
- Four Batteries

16th Division — Lieutenant General von Etzel

- 31st Brigade (Major General von Schöler)
  - 29th and 69th Regiments
- Fusilier Brigade (Colonel Wegerer)
  - 33rd and 34th Regiments
- 8th Jäger Battalion
- Two Batteries

14th Cavalry Brigade (Major General Count Goltz)

- Westphalian Uhlans No. 5

2nd Westphalian Hussars No. 11
Reserve Cavalry Brigade (Major General von Kotze)
Rhenish Cuirassiers No. 8
Rhenish Uhlans No.7
Pomeranian Landwehr Reiter Regiment
One Horse Battery
Reserve Artillery VII Corps, six Batteries
Reserve Artillery VIII Corps, seven Batteries

I RESERVE CORPS

General Commanding Lieutenant General von der Mülbe
Landwehr Division of the Guard General von Rosenberg
1st Brigade of Guard Landwehr
1st and 2nd Guard Landwehr Regiments
2nd Brigade of Guard Landwehr
1st and 2nd Guard Grenadier Landwehr Regiments
Combined Landwehr Division General von Bentheim
1st Landwehr Brigade
9th and 21st Landwehr Regiments
2nd Landwehr Brigade
13th and 15th Landwehr Regiments
Landwehr Cavalry Division Major General Count Dohna
Six Landwehr Cavalry Regiments
Reserve Artillery Regiments
Nine Reserve Batteries

ARMY OF THE MAIN

Commander in Chief General Vogel von Falckenstein
Chief of the Staff Colonel von Kraatz-Koschlau
13th Division Lieutenant General von Goeben
25th Brigade (Major General von Kummer)
13th and 53rd Regiments
26th Brigade (Major General von Wrangel)
15th and 55th Regiments
Two Companies of 7th Pioneer Battalion
13th Cavalry Brigade
Westphalian Cuirassiers No 4
1st Westphalian Hussars No. 8
Six Batteries
Combined Division Major General von Beyer
19th, 20th, 30th, 32nd, 39th and 70th Regiments
(N.B: The 30th and 70th were detached to garrison Hesse Cassel)
2nd Rhenish Hussars, No 9
Three Batteries
Combined Division (formerly in Holstein) Major General von Manteuffel

1st Combined Brigade (Major General von Freyhold)
    25th and 36th Regiments
2nd Combined Brigade (Major General von Korth)
    11th and 59th Regiments
Cavalry Brigade (Major General von Flies)
    Rhenish Dragoons No. 5
    Magdeburg Dragoons No. 6
Two Battalions (Coburg-Gotha)
One Battalion (Lippe)
Five Fourth Battalions
9th Jäger Battalion
Three newly raised Regiments of Landwehr Cavalry
Oldenburg Hanseatic Brigade (nine Battalions, three Squadrons, two Batteries)

II RESERVE CORPS

Commander in Chief HRH the Grand Duke of Mecklenburg- Schwerin
Mecklenburg Division (five Battalions, four Squadrons, two Batteries)
Combined Prussian Division (sixteen Battalions)
Two Anhalt Battalions
Two Reserve Regiments of Landwehr Cavalry
Eight Batteries

Appendix IV

Order of Battle of the Imperial Austrian Army of the North in 1866

General in Chief	Feldzeugmeister Ritter von Benedek
Chief of the Staff	Lieutenant Field Marshal von Henikstein
Director of Artillery	Lieutenant Field Marshal Archduke William
Engineers	Colonel von Pidoll

1ST CORPS

General Commanding	General of Cavalry Count Clam Gallas
Assistant	General Count Gondrecourt
Chief of the Staff	Colonel von Litzelhofen

Commandant of Brigade (Major General Poschacher)
- 18th Field Jäger Battalion
- 30th Infantry Regiment (Martini)[1]
- 34th Infantry Regiment (King of Prussia)

Commandant of Brigade (Colonel Count Leiningen)
- 32nd Field Jäger Battalion
- 33rd Infantry Regiment (Giulay)
- 38th Infantry Regiment (Haugwitz)

Commandant of Brigade (Major General Piret)
- 29th Field Jäger Battalion
- 18th Infantry Regiment (Constantin)
- 45th Infantry Regiment (Sigismund)

Commandant of Brigade (Major General Ringelsheim)
- 26th Jäger Battalion
- 42nd Infantry Regiment (Hanover)
- 73rd Infantry Regiment (Württemberg)

To each Brigade one squadron of the Nikolaus Regiment of Hussars (No 2) and one 4-pounder Field Battery were attached

2ND CORPS

General Commanding	Lieutenant Field Marshal Count Thun-Hohenstadt
Assistant	Major General von Philippowich
Chief of the Staff	Colonel von Döpfner

Commandant of Brigade (Colonel Thom)
- 2nd Jäger Battalion

1 Unless noted otherwise, all Austrian Infantry Regiments had three battalions.

40th Infantry Regiment (Rossbach)
69th Infantry Regiment (Jellachich)
Commandant of Brigade (Major General Henriquez)
9th Field Jäger Battalion
14th Infantry Regiment (Hesse)
27th Infantry Regiment (King of the Belgians)
Commandant of Brigade (Major General von Saffran)
11th Field Jäger Battalion
64th Infantry Regiment (Saxe-Weimar)
80th Infantry Regiment (Holstein)
Commandant of Brigade (Major General Duke Württemberg)
20th Field Jäger Battalion
47th Infantry Regiment (Hartung)
57th Infantry Regiment (Mecklenburg)

To each Brigade one Squadron of the Imperial Uhlans (No. 6) and one 4-pounder Field Battery were attached

3RD CORPS

General Commanding — Lieutenant Field Marshal Archduke Ernst
Assistant — Major General von Baumgarten
Chief of Staff — Colonel von Catty

Commandant of Brigade (Major General Kalik afterwards Colonel von Abele)
22nd Field Jäger Battalion
35th Infantry Regiment (Khevenhüller)
72nd Infantry Regiment (Ramming)
(N.B. This brigade which had garrisoned Holstein on the outbreak of hostilities was attached to the 1st Corps)
Commandant of Brigade (Major General Appiano)
4th Field Jäger Battalion
46th Infantry Regiment (Meiningen)
62nd Infantry Regiment (Archduke Henry)
Commandant of Brigade (Colonel Benedek)
1st Field Jäger Battalion
52nd Infantry Regiment (Archduke Franz Karl)
78th Infantry Regiment (Sokcevics)
Commandant of Brigade (Colonel Kirchsberg)
3rd Field Jäger Battalion
44th Infantry Regiment (Archduke Albrecht)
49th Infantry Regiment (Hess)
Commandant of Brigade (Colonel Prohaska)
13th Border Infantry Regiment
4th Battalion of the 55th Regiment (Gondrecourt)
4th Battalion of the 56th Regiment (Gorizutti)
33rd Jäger Battalion
34th Jäger Battalion

To each brigade were attached one squadron of the Count Mensdorff Uhlans (No. 9) and one 4-pounder field battery

4TH CORPS

General Commanding — Lieutenant Field Marshal Count Festetics
Assistant — Major General von Mollinary
Chief of the Staff — Colonel von Görz

- Commandant of Brigade (Major General von Brandenstein)
  - 27th Field Jäger Battalion
  - 12th Infantry Regiment (Archduke William)
  - 26th Infantry Regiment (Michael)
- Commandant of Brigade (Colonel Fleischhacker)
  - 13th Field Jäger Battalion
  - 6th Infantry Regiment (Coronini)
  - 61st Infantry Regiment (Czarevitch of Russia)
- Commandant of Brigade (Colonel Poeckh)
  - 8th Field Jäger Battalion
  - 37th Infantry Regiment (Archduke Joseph)
  - 51st Infantry Regiment (Archduke Charles Ferdinand)
- Commandant of Brigade (Major General Archduke Joseph)
  - 30th Field Jäger Battalion
  - 67th Infantry Regiment (Schmerling)
  - 68th Infantry Regiment (Steininger)

To each brigade one squadron of the 7th Hussars and one 4-pounder Field Battery were attached

6TH CORPS

General Commanding — Lieutenant Field Marshal Baron Ramming
Assistant — Major General von Kochmeister
Chief of Staff — Colonel Frölich

- Commandant of Brigade (Colonel von Waldstätten)
  - 6th Field Jäger Battalion
  - 9th Infantry Regiment (Hartmann)
  - 79th Infantry Regiment (Frank)
- Commandant of Brigade (Colonel Hertwegh)
  - 25th Field Jäger Battalion
  - 41st Infantry Regiment (Kellner)
  - 56th Infantry Regiment (Gorizutti)
- Commandant of Brigade (Major General Rosenzweig)
  - 17th Field Jäger Battalion
  - 4th Infantry Regiment (Deutschmeiister)
  - 55th Infantry Regiment (Gondrecourt)
- Commandant of Brigade (Colonel Jonak)
  - 14th Field Jäger Battalion
  - 20th Infantry Regiment (Crown Prince of Prussia)
  - 60th Infantry Regiment (Wasa)

To each brigade one squadron of the 10th Uhlans and one 4-pounder Field battery were attached

8TH CORPS

General Commanding Archduke Leopold
Assistant Major General Weber
Chief of the Staff Lieutenant Colonel von Majnone

Commandant of Brigade (Colonel Fragnern)
5th Field Jäger Battalion
15th Infantry Regiment (Nassau)
77th Infantry Regiment (Tuscany)

Commandant of Brigade (Major General von Kreyssern)
31st Field Jäger Battalion
8th Infantry Regiment (Gerstner)
74th Infantry Regiment (Nobili)

Commandant of Brigade (General Count Rothkirch)
25th Infantry Regiment (Mamula)
71st Infantry Regiment (Tuscany)

Commandant of Brigade (Colonel von Roth)
24th Field Jäger Battalion
21st Infantry Regiment (Reischach)
32nd Infantry Regiment (Este)

To each brigade one squadron of the Archduke Charles's Uhlans (No. 3) and one 4-pounder Battery were attached

10TH CORPS

General Commanding Lieutenant Field Marshal von Gablenz
Assistant Baron Koller
Chief of the Staff Colonel Bourgignone

Commandant of Brigade (Colonel Mondl)
12th Field Jäger Battalion
10th Infantry Regiment (Mazuchelli)
24th Infantry Regiment (Parma)

Commandant of Brigade (Colonel Grivicics)
16th Field Jäger Battalion
2nd Infantry Regiment (Alexander)
23rd Infantry Regiment (Airoldi)

Commandant of Brigade (Major General von Knebel)
28th Field Jäger Battalion
1st Infantry Regiment (Emperor Franz Joseph)
3rd Infantry Regiment (Archduke Charles)

Commandant of Brigade (Major General Wimpffen)
13th Infantry Regiment (Bamberg)
58th Infantry Regiment (Archduke Stephen) (four battalions)

To each brigade were attached one squadron of the 1st Uhlans and on 4-pounder Field Battery

First Light Cavalry Division Major General Baron Edelsheim
- Commandant of Brigade (Colonel Appel)
  - 2nd Dragoons (Windischgrätz)
  - 9th Hussars (Liechtenstein)
- Commandant of Brigade (Colonel Wallis)
  - 1st Dragoons (Savoy)
  - 10th Hussars (King of Prussia)
- Commandant of Brigade (Colonel Fratricievies)
  - 5th Hussars (Radetzky)
  - 8th Hussars (Hesse Cassel)

Second Light Cavalry Division Major General Prince Thurn and Taxis
- Commandant of Brigade (Colonel Count Bellegarde)
  - 4th Hussars (Cseh)
  - 19th Hussars (Haller)
- Commandant of Brigade (Major General Westphalen)
  - 6th Hussars (Württemberg)
  - 11th Hussars (Palffy)

First Reserve Division of Cavalry Lieutenant Field Marshal Prince Schleswig Holstein
- Commandant of Brigade (Major General Prince Solms)
  - 4th Cuirassier Regiment (Ferdinand)
  - 6th Cuirassier Regiment (Hesse)
  - 8th Uhlans (Emperor Max)
- Commandant of Brigade (Major General Schindlöcker)
  - 9th Cuirassier Regiment (Stadion)
  - 11th Cuirassier Regiment (Emperor Franz Joseph)
  - 4th Uhlans Regiment (Emperor Franz Joseph)

Second Reserve Division of Cavalry Major General von Zaitsek
- Commandant of Brigade (Major General Boxberg)
  - 3rd Cuirassier Regiment (Saxony)
  - 7th Cuirassier Regiment (Brunswick)
  - 2nd Uhlans (Schwarzenberg)
- Commandant of Brigade (General Count Soltyk)
  - 1st Cuirassier Regiment (Emperor Franz Joseph)
  - 5th Cuirassier Regiment (Nicolas)
  - 5th Uhlans (Walmoden)

Third Reserve Division of Cavalry Major General Count Coudenhove
- Commandant of Brigade (Major General Prince Windischgrätz)
  - 2nd Cuirassier Regiment (Wrangel)
  - 8th Cuirassier Regiment (Prince Charles of Prussia)
  - 7th Uhlans (Archduke Charles Louis)
- Commandant of Brigade (Major General von Mengen)
  - 10th Cuirassier Regiment (Bavaria)
  - 12th Cuirassier Regiment (Neipperg)
  - 11th Uhlans (Alexander)

To each Cavalry brigade was attached one battery of Horse Artillery

Reserve Artillery of the Army
16 Batteries

Appendix V

Order of Battle of the Royal Saxon Army Corps in 1866

General Commanding	General Crown Prince of Saxony
Chief of Staff	Major General von Fabrice
Commander of Artillery	Major General Schmalz
1st Infantry Division	Lieutenant General von Schimpff

- 2nd Infantry Brigade (Major General von Carlowitz)
  - 5th, 6th, 7th, 8th Infantry and 2nd Rifle Battalions
- 3rd Infantry Brigade (Colonel von Hake)
  - 9th, 10th, 11th, 12th Infantry and 3rd Rifle Battalions
- Divisional Cavalry
  - Two Squadrons of 2nd and 3rd 'Reiter' Regiments
- Divisional Artillery
  - 12-pounder Battery
  - 6-pounder Battery

2nd Infantry Division — Lieutenant General von Stieglitz

- 1st Infantry Brigade (Colonel von Boxberg)
  - 1st, 2nd, 3rd, 4th Infantry and 1st Rifle Battalions
- 4th Infantry ('Leib') Brigade (Colonel von Hausen)
  - 13th, 14th, 15th, 16th Infantry and 4th Rifle Battalions
- Divisional Cavalry
  - Two Squadrons of the Guard and 1st 'Reiter' Regiments
- Divisional Artillery
  - 12-pounder Battery
  - 6-pounder Battery

Cavalry Division — Lieutenant General von Fritsch

- 1st Cavalry Brigade (Lieutenant General Prince George of Saxony)
  - Guard 'Reiter' and 1st 'Reiter' Regiments
- 2nd Cavalry Brigade (Major General von Biedermann)
  - 2nd and 3rd 'Reiter' Regiments
- 12-pounder horse Artillery Battery 'Zenker'

Reserve Artillery — Colonel Köhler

- Three 12-pounder Batteries
- Two 6-pounder Batteries

Total of Saxon Corps:
16 Battalions of Infantry; 4 Battalions of Rifles; 16 Squadrons;
58 guns; 2 Companies Pioneers

Appendix VI

Order of Battle of the Royal Hanoverian Army on June 18 1866

Commanding General	Lieutenant General von Arentschildt
Chief of Staff	Colonel Cordemann
Adjutant General	Colonel Dammers
Commander of Artillery	Major General von Stolzenberg

- 1st Brigade (Major General von dem Knesebeck)
  - Guard Regiment, 1st ('Leib') Regiment
  - Battalion of Guard Rifles
  - Queen's Hussar Regiment
  - 12-pounder Battery
- 2nd Brigade (Colonel de Vaux)
  - 2nd Infantry Regiment
  - 3rd Infantry Regiment
  - 1st Battalion of Rifles
  - Duke of Cambridge Dragoon Regiment
  - 6-pounder Battery
- 3rd Brigade (Colonel von Bülow Stolle)
  - 4th Infantry Regiment
  - 5th Infantry Regiment
  - 2nd Battalion of Rifles
  - Crown Prince Dragoon Regiment
  - 6-pounder Battery
- 4th Brigade (Major General von Bothmer)
  - 6th Infantry Regiment
  - 7th Infantry Regiment
  - 3rd Battalion Rifles
  - Guard Hussar Regiment
  - 6-pounder Battery
  - Horse Artillery Battery
- Reserve Cavalry (Lieutenant Colonel von Geyso)
  - Guard du Corps Regiment
  - Guard Cuirassier Regiment
  - Horse Artillery Battery
- Reserve Artillery (Major Hartmann)
  - 6-pounder Battery
  - 24-pounder Howitzer Battery

Total of Royal Hanoverian Army
16 Battalions of Infantry; 4 Battalions of Rifles; 24 Squadrons; 24 Guns;
Besides 10 Guns incompletely horsed

Appendix VII

Order of Battle of the Electoral Hessian Division in 1866

Commanding General	Major General von Lossberg
Chief of Staff	Major Darapsky
Commander of Artillery	Major General von Kochenhausen
1st Infantry Division	Major General von Buttlar
Guard Regiment	
1st Infantry Regiment	
Rifle Battalion	
Sharpshooter Battalion	
2nd Infantry Division	Colonel von Osterhausen
2nd Infantry Regiment	
3rd Infantry Regiment	

Cavalry Brigade (Major General von Bardeleben)

- 1st Hussar Regiment
- 2nd Hussar Regiment
- Two Squadrons of the Guard du Corps Regiment

Artillery

- One 4-pounder and three 6-pounder Batteries; besides four 6-pounder and eight 4-pounder guns not yet horsed

Total of Electoral Hessian Division
8 Battalions of Infantry; 2 Battalions of Rifles; 8 Squadrons; 16 guns and 1 Company of Pioneers
(N.B: Two Squadrons were detached to the Combined Austrian-Nassau Division)

Appendix VIII

Order of Battle of the Royal Bavarian Army in 1866

Commander in Chief — HRH Field Marshal Prince Charles of Bavaria
Chief of the Staff — Lieutenant General Baron von der Tann
Director of Field Artillery — Lieutenant General von Brodesser
1st Infantry Division — Lieutenant General Stephan
- 1st Infantry Brigade (Major General von Steinle)
  - 'Leib' and 1st Infantry Regiments and 2nd Rifle Battalion
- 2nd Infantry Brigade (Major General von Wetsch)
  - 2nd and 8th Infantry Regiments
- 3rd Regiment of Chevauxlegers
- One 6-pounder and one 12-pounder Battery

2nd Infantry Division — Lieutenant General von Feder
- 3rd Infantry Brigade (Major General Schumacher)
  - 3rd and 12th Infantry Regiments and 7th Rifle Battalion
- 4th Infantry Brigade (Major General von Hauser)
  - 7th and 10th Infantry Regiments and 3rd Rifle Battalion
- 4th Regiment of Chevauxlegers
- One 6-pounder and one 12-pounder Battery

3rd Infantry Division — Lieutenant General von Zoller
- 5th Infantry Brigade (Major General Ribeaupierre)
  - 11th and 15th Infantry Regiments and 5th Rifle Battalion
- 6th Infantry Brigade (Colonel Schweitzer)
  - 6th and 14th Infantry Regiments and 1st Rifle Battalion
- 2nd Regiment of Chevauxlegers
- One 6-pounder and one 12-pounder Battery

4th Infantry Division — Lieutenant General von Hartmann
- 7th Infantry Brigade (Major General Faust)
  - 5th and 13th Infantry Regiments and Rifle Battalion
- 8th Infantry Brigade (Major General Cella)
  - 4th and 9th Infantry Regiments and 6th Rifle Battalion

6th Regiment of Chevauxlegers
One 6-pounder and one 12-pounder Battery

Reserve Cavalry Corps

Commanding General Lieutenant General Prince Taxis

Heavy Cavalry Brigade (Major General von Rummel)
1st 2nd and 3rd Regiments of Cuirassiers
1st Light Cavalry Brigade (Major General Duke Ludwig of Bavaria)
1st and 2nd Regiments of Lancers
2nd Light Cavalry Brigade (Major General Count Pappenheim)
5th Regiment of Chevauxlegers
and 3rd Regiment of Lancers
Two 12-pounder Batteries

Artillery Reserve
Six 12-pounder and two 6-pounder Batteries

Total of Bavarian Army:
38 Battalions of Infantry; 7 Battalions of Rifles; 44 Squadrons; 144 Guns and 3 Companies of Engineers

Appendix IX

Order of Battle of the VIII Federal Corps on July 9 1866

Commander in Chief	Prince Alexander of Hesse
Chief of Staff (Württemberg)	Lieutenant General von Baur
Second Chief (Baden)	Major General Kraus
Director of Artillery (Baden)	Lieutenant General von Faber
1st Division (Württemberg)	Lieutenant General von Hardegg

1st Brigade (Major General von Baumbach)
 1st and 5th Regiments of Infantry
 and 3rd Rifle Battalion
2nd Brigade (Major General von Fischer)
 2nd and 7th Regiments of Infantry
 and 2nd Rifle Battalion
3rd Brigade (Major General Hegelmeier)
 3rd and 8th Regiments of Infantry
 and 1st Rifle Battalion
Cavalry Brigade (Major General Count von Scheler)
 1st and 4th Cavalry Regiments
(N.B: A third Regiment with the Reserve Cavalry of the Corps)

Artillery (Colonel von Leube)
 Three 6-pounder Batteries
 (N.B: Three Batteries were with the Reserve of the Corps)

2nd Division (Baden)	Lieutenant General Prince William of Baden
Commander of Infantry	Lieutenant General Waag

1st Brigade (Major General von Laroche)
 'Leib' Grenadiers Regiment 5th Infantry Regiment
 and Rifle Battalion
2nd Brigade (Colonel von Neubronn)
 2nd and 3rd Infantry Regiments
 and 2nd Fusilier Battalion
Cavalry Brigade
 Two Regiments of Dragoons
(N.B: A third Regiment with the Reserve of the Corps)

Artillery (Colonel Count Sponeck)
 Three 6-pounder Batteries
 (N.B: Two Batteries with the Reserve of the Corps)

3rd Division (Hesse-Darmstadt) Lieutenant General von Perglas
- 1st Brigade (Major General Frey)
  - 1st and 2nd Infantry Regiments
  - Company of Rifles
- 2nd Brigade (Major General von Stockhausen)
  - 3rd and 4th Infantry Regiments
  - Company of Rifles
  - Battalion of Sharpshooters
- Cavalry Brigade (Major General Prince Ludwig of Hesse)
  - One Chevauxlegers Regiment
- (N.B: A second Regiment with the Reserve of the Corps)

Artillery
- Two 6-pounder Batteries

4th (Combined) Division (Austria, Nassau, Electoral Hesse)
Lieutenant Field Marshal Count Neipperg
- Austrian Brigade (Major General von Hahn)
  - 16th Infantry Regiment (Wernhardt)
  - 4th Battalions of the 21st and 49th Regiments (Reischach and Hess)
  - 35th Field Jäger Battalion
  - 4-pounder Battery
  - (N.B: One 8-pounder Battery with the Reserve of the Corps)
- Nassau Brigade (Major General Roth)
  - 1st and 2nd Infantry Regiments and Rifle Battalion
  - Two half Batteries (6-pounder)
  - (N.B: One 6-pounder battery with the Reserve of the Corps)

Two Squadrons of Electoral Hessian Hussars

Reserves of the Corps

Cavalry — Lieutenant General von Entress (Württemberg)
- One Württemberg, one Baden and one Hessian Regiment
- One Württemberg Horse Artillery Battery

Artillery
- Two 12-pounder Batteries (Württemberg)
- One 12-pounder Battery (Hesse)
- One 6-pounder Battery (Hesse)
- One 5-pounder Battery (Nassau)
- One 6-pounder Battery (Baden)
- One 6-pounder Battery (Baden)
- One 8-pounder Battery (Austria)

Total of VIII Federal Corps:
39 Battalions of Infantry; 7½ Battalions of Rifles; 36 Squadrons; 134 Guns

Appendix X

Order of Battle of the Detachment of Major General von Flies in the Battle of Langensalza June 27 1866

General Commanding — Major General von Flies
Commander of Artillery — Major Petzel

- Advance Guard (Colonel von Fabeck)
  - Saxe Coburg Infantry Regiment (Lieutenant Colonel von Westernhagen)
    - 1st Battalion (Major von Bassewitz)
    - Fusilier Battalion (Major von Gerstein)
  - 'Merseburg' Garrison Squadron of 12th Landwehr Hussar Regiment
  - Half of a Sally Battery of the 4th Brigade
  - Third 4-pounder Battery of 6th Field Artillery Regiment
- Main Body (Colonel Baron von Hanstein)
  - 25th Regiment of Infantry
    - 1st Battalion (Major von Loebell)
    - Fusilier Battalion Major Bassenge
  - 2nd (Torgau) Battalion of 32nd Landwehr Regiment
  - 11th Regiment of Grenadiers (Colonel von Zglinitzki)
    - 1st Battalion (Lieutenant Colonel des Barres)
    - 2nd Battalion (Major von Bonin)
    - Fusilier Battalion (Major von Bausse)
  - Depôt Squadron of 10th Hussar Regiment
  - 4th Horse Artillery Battery of 7th Artillery Regiment
- Reserve (Major General von Seckendorff)
  - 1st Line (Colonel von Hellmuth) Landwehr Battalion (Aschersleben)
    - 3rd (Naumburg) Battalion of 32nd Landwehr Regiment
    - 3rd (Aschersleben) Battalion of 27th Landwehr Regiment
  - 2nd Line (Major Baron von Wintzingerode)
    - 3rd Battalion (Potsdam) 20th Landwehr Regiment (Captain von Kirschy)
    - 2nd Battalion (Treuenbrietzen) 20th Landwehr Regiment (Major Küntzel)
- 3 Companies of Depôt Battalion 71st Regiment
- 'Stendal' Garrison Squadron
- Two guns of Sally Battery of 4th Artillery Brigade
- 3rd Horse Artillery Battery of 7th Field Artillery Regiment

Appendix XI

Order of Battle of the Prussian Army of the Main (from July 20 1866)

Commander in Chief	Lieutenant General Baron von Manteuffel
Chief of the Staff	Colonel von Kraatz Koschlau
Quartermaster General	Colonel von Strantz
Commander of Artillery	Colonel von Decker
13th Infantry Division	Lieutenant General von Goeben

25th Infantry Brigade (Major General von Kummer)
53rd Infantry Regiment (Lieutenant Colonel von Manteuffel)
13th Infantry Regiment (Colonel von Gellhorn)
26th Infantry Brigade (Major General Baron von Wrangel)
55th Infantry Regiment (Colonel Stoltz)
15th Infantry Regiment (Colonel Baron von der Goltz)
Lippe Detmold Fusilier Battalion (Captain Kellner)
8th Regiment Hussars (Colonel von Rantzau)
Four batteries of 7th Field Artillery Regiment (Major von Drabich-Wächter)
Combined Reserve Brigade (Major General von Tresckow)
19th Infantry Regiment (Lieutenant Colonel von Henning)
4th Cuirassier Regiment (Colonel von Schmidt)
3rd Horse Artillery Battery of 7th Field Artillery Regiment

Total of the three Prussian Brigades: 16 battalions 9 squadrons 31 guns 1 company of Pioneers

Oldenburg Hanseatic Brigade (Major General von Weltzien)
Oldenburg Infantry Regiment (Colonel Lehmann)
Lübeck Battalion of Light Infantry (Major von Bültzingslöwen) (joined on 26th July)
Bremen Fusilier Battalion (Lieutenant Colonel Niebour)
Hamburg Infantry Regiment (Colonel Bess)
Two squadrons of Hamburg Dragoons (Major Heinsen) (joined on 29th July)
Oldenburg ' Reiter' Regiment (Colonel Beseke)
Two Oldenburg batteries (Lieutenant Colonel Rüder)

Total of Oldenburg Hanseatic Brigade: 7 battalions 5 squadrons 12guns

Total of 13th Infantry Division: 23 battalions 14 squadrons 43 guns 1 company of Pioneers

Combined Division of Major General von Beyer
- 32nd Infantry Brigade (Colonel von Woyna I) (commanding 70th Infantry Regiment)
    - 70th Infantry Regiment
    - 30th Infantry Regiment (Lieutenant Colonel von Koblinski)
- Combined Infantry Brigade (Major General von Glümer)
    - 20th Infantry Regiment (Colonel von der Wense)
    - 32nd Infantry Regiment (Colonel von Schwerin)
    - 39th Fusilier Regiment (Colonel von Woyna II)
    - 9th Hussar Regiment (Major von Cosel)
- Two squadrons of 10th Landwehr Hussar Regiment
- Three batteries
- Reserve Artillery
    - Four Reserve Batteries
- One Company Pioneers

Total of Division Beyer: 15 battalions 7 squadrons 42 guns 1 company of Pioneers (N.B: 2nd Battalion 70th Regiment and 1st Battalion 30th Regiment had been left as garrison in Cassel, and re-joined on 21st July. Two squadrons of 10th Hussars were in Frankfurt and Hanover).

Combined Division of Major General Flies
- 1st Combined Infantry Brigade (Major General von Freyhold)
    - 36th Fusilier Regiment (Colonel von Thile)
    - 25th Infantry Regiment (Colonel Baron von Hanstein)
    - 9th Rifle Battalion (Captain von Medem)
- 2nd Combined Infantry Brigade (Major General von Korth)
    - 59th Infantry Regiment (Colonel von Kessler)
    - 11th Grenadier Regiment (Colonel von Zglinitzki)
    - Saxe Coburg Gotha Infantry Regiment (Colonel von Fabeck)
- Five batteries
- Combined Cavalry Brigade (Major General von Below) (took command 30 July)
    - 5th Regiment of Dragoons (Colonel von Wedell)
    - 6th Regiment of Dragoons (Colonel Krug von Nidda)
    - 4th Horse Artillery Battery of 7th Field Artillery Regiment

Total of Division Flies: 15 battalions 8 squadrons 36 guns

Total of Army of the Maine: 53 battalions 29 squadrons 121 guns 2 companies of Pioneers

Appendix XII

Order of Battle of the Royal Italian Army in June 1866

Commander	His Majesty King Victor Emanuel II
Chief of Staff	General La Marmora
Deputy Chief of Staff	Colonel Bariola

	1st Corps
General Commanding	General Durando
Chief of Staff	Colonel Lombardini
1st Division	General Cerale

Brigade Pisa (General de Villarey)
 29th and 30th Regiments
Brigade Forli (General Dho)
 43rd and 44th Regiments
2nd and 18th Bersaglieri Battalions
Three batteries

2nd Division — General Pianelli

Brigade Siena (General Cadolino)
 31st and 32nd Regiments
Brigade Aosta (General Dallaglio)
 5th and 6th Regiments
8th and 17th Bersaglieri Battalions
Three batteries

3rd Division — General Brignone

Brigade Sardegna (General Gozzani)
 1st and 2nd Grenadier Regiments
Brigade Lombardia (General Prince Amadeo)
 3rd and 4th Grenadier Regiments
13th and 37th Bersaglieri Battalions
Three batteries

5th Division — General Sirtori

Brigade Brescia (General Villahermosa)
 19th and 20th Regiments
Brigade Valtellina (General Lopez)
 65th and 66th Regiments
3rd and 5th Bersaglieri Battalions
Three batteries

Corps Cavalry — Major General Ghilini

Aosta Lancers, Lucca Light Cavalry and Guide Regiment

Corps Artillery
Two Companies of 2nd Artillery Regiment

2nd Corps

General Commanding	Lieutenant General Cucciari
Chief of Staff	Colonel Escoffier
4th Division	General Duke of Mignano

Brigade Regina (General Carini)
9th and 10th Regiments
Brigade Ravenna (General Fioruzzi)
37th and 38th Regiments
1st and 21st Bersaglieri Battalions
Three batteries

6th Division — General Cosenza
Brigade Acqui (General Schiaffino)
27th and 18th Regiments
Brigade Livorno (General Radicatti)
33rd and 34th Regiments
15th and 20th Bersaglieri Battalions
Three batteries

10th Division — General Angioletti
Brigade Umbria (General Masi)
53rd and 54th Regiments
Brigade Abruzzi (General Peyron)
57th and 58th Regiments
24th and 31st Bersaglieri Battalions
Three batteries

19th Division — General Longoni
Brigade Calabria (General Adorni)
59th and 60th Regiments
Brigade Palermo (General Caffarelli)
67th and 68th Regiments
33rd and 40th Bersaglieri Battalions
Three batteries

Corps Cavalry — General Barral
Novara Lancers and Piacenza Hussars

Corps Artillery
One company of 2nd Artillery Regiment

3rd Corps

General Commanding	General Della Rocca
Chief of Staff	Colonel di Robilant
7th Division	General Bixio

Brigade del Re (General de Fornari)
1st and 2nd Regiments
Brigade Ferrara (General Novaro)

47th and 48th Regiments
9th and 10th Bersaglieri Battalions
Three batteries

8th Division — General Cugia
Brigade Piemonte (General Noaro)
3rd and 4th Regiments
Brigade Cagliari (General Gabet)
63rd and 64th Regiments
6th and 30th Bersaglieri Battalions
Three batteries

9th Division — General Govone
Brigade Pistoia (General Bottacco)
35th and 36th Regiments
Brigade Delle-Alpi (General Danzini)
51st and 52nd Regiments
27th and 34th Bersaglieri Battalions
Three batteries

16th Division — General Prince Umberto
Brigade Parma (General Ferrero)
49th and 50th Regiments
Combined Brigade (General de Sauget)
8th and 71st Regiments
4th and 11th Bersaglieri Battalions
Three batteries

Corps Cavalry — General Palermo
Foggia Lancers and Alexandria Light Cavalry

Corps Artillery
One company of 4th Regiment

Reserve Cavalry Division General de Sonnaz
1st Cavalry Brigade (General Soman)
Savoy and Genoa Dragoon Regiments
2nd Cavalry Brigade (General Cusani)
Nizza and Royal Piedmont Regiments

Reserve Artillery
9 batteries

4th Corps

General Commanding — General Cialdini
Chief of Staff — Major General Piola Caselli

11th Division — General Casanova
Brigade Pinerolo (General de la Roche)
13th and 14th Regiments
Brigade Modena (General Bonvicini)
41st and 42nd Regiments
10th and 26th Bersaglieri Battalions
Three batteries

12th Division General Ricotti
- Brigade Casale (General Bonardelli)
  - 11th and 12th Regiments
- Brigade Como (General Brianza)
  - 23rd and 24th Regiments
- 16th and 35th Bersaglieri Battalions
- Three batteries

13th Division General Mezza Capo
- Brigade Savona (General Pallavicini)
  - 15th and 16th Regiments
- Brigade Bologna (General Angelino)
  - 39th and 40th Regiments
- 12th and 22nd Bersaglieri Battalions
- Three batteries

14th Division General Chiabrera
- Brigade Reggio (General Druette)
  - 45th and 46th Regiments
- Brigade Marche (General Bossolo)
  - 55th and 56th Regiments
- 7th and 14th Bersaglieri Battalions
- Three batteries

15th Division General Medici
- Brigade Pavia (General Parrochia)
  - 27th and 28th Regiments
- Brigade Sicilia (General Sacchi)
  - 61st and 62nd Regiments
- 23rd and 25th Bersaglieri Battalions
- Three batteries

17th Division General Cadorna
- Brigade Napoli (General Manca)
  - 5th and 6th Grenadier Regiments
- Brigade Toscana (General Diana)
  - 7th and 8th Grenadier Regiments
- 28th and 32nd Bersaglieri Battalions
- Three batteries

18th Division General Della Chiesa
- Brigade Cremona (General Balegno)
  - 21st and 22nd Regiments
- Brigade Bergamo (General Castelli)
  - 25th and 26th Regiments
- 29th and 36th Bersaglieri Battalions
- Three batteries

20th Division General Franzini
- Combined Brigade (General Barieri)
  - 7th and 72nd Regiments
- Brigade Ancona (General Alberti)

69th and 70th Regiments
38th and 39th Bersaglieri Battalions
Three batteries
Cavalry Division
1st Brigade (General Poninski)
Milan Lancers, Montebello and Lodi Light Cavalry
2nd Brigade (General Della Forest)
Victor Emanuel Lancers, Firenze Lancers and Monferrato Light Cavalry
Corps Artillery
Two companies of 2nd and 4th Artillery Regiments
Reserve Artillery
4 batteries of 7th Artillery Regiment

Appendix XIII

Order of Battle of the Imperial Austrian Army of the South in June 1866

Commander in Chief	Field Marshal Archduke Albrecht
Chief of Staff	Major General von John
Artillery Commander	Major General von Hutschenreiter von Glinzendorf

5th Corps

General Commanding — Major General von Rodich
Chief of Staff — Colonel Gallim
Commandant of Brigade — (Colonel Bauer)
- 19th Field Jäger Battalion
- 28th Infantry Regiment (Benedek)
- 70th Infantry Regiment (Nagy)
- One battery

Commandant of Brigade — (Major General Möring)
- 21st Field Jäger Battalion
- 53rd Infantry Regiment (Archduke Leopold)
- 54th Infantry Regiment (Gruber)
- One battery

Commandant of Brigade — (Major General Piret)
- 5th Kaiser Jäger Battalion
- 50th Infantry Regiment (Grand Duke of Baden)
- 75th Infantry Regiment (Crenneville)
- One battery

Corps Cavalry
- Two squadrons of 12th Lancer Regiment

Corps Artillery
- Three batteries

7th Corps

General Commanding — Lieutenant General Maroicic
Chief of Staff — Colonel von Littrow
- Commandant of Brigade (Major General Scudier)
  - 10th Field Jäger Battalion
  - 19th Infantry Regiment (Crown Prince Rudolf)
  - 48th Infantry Regiment (Archduke Ernst)
  - One battery

Commandant of Brigade (Colonel Töpley)
- 7th Field Jäger Battalion
- 43rd Infantry Regiment (Alemann)
- 65th Infantry Regiment (Archduke Ludwig Victor)
- One battery

Commandant of Brigade (Colonel Welsersheimb)
- 3rd Kaiser Jäger Battalion
- 31st Infantry Regiment (Mecklenburg-Strelitz)
- 76th Infantry Regiment (Paumgartten)
- One battery

Corps Cavalry
- One squadron 3rd Hussar Regiment
- Corps Artillery

Corps Artillery
- Three batteries

9th Corps

General Commanding — Lieutenant General Hartung
Chief of Staff — Lieutenant Colonel von Pielsticker

Commandant of Brigade (Colonel Böck)
- 15th Field Jäger Battalion
- 63rd Infantry Regiment (King of the Netherlands)
- 66th Infantry Regiment (Tuscany)
- One battery

Commandant of Brigade (Major General Kirschberg)
- 23rd Field Jäger Battalion
- 7th Infantry Regiment (Maroicic)
- 29th Infantry Regiment (Thun)
- One battery

Commandant of Brigade (Major General Weckbecker)
- 4th Kaiser Jäger Battalion
- 5th Infantry Regiment (King of Bavaria)
- 39th Infantry Regiment (Dom Miguel)
- One battery

Corps Cavalry
- One squadron of 11th Hussar Regiment

Corps Artillery
- Three batteries

Reserve Infantry Division — Major General Rupprecht von Virtsolog
Chief of Staff — Lieutenant Colonel von Franz

Commandant of Brigade (Major General Benko)
- 37th Field Jäger Battalion
- 17th Infantry Regiment (Hohenlohe)
- 12th Frontier Infantry Regiment
- One battery

Commandant of Brigade (Colonel Prince Weimar)
36th Field Jäger Battalion
36th Infantry Regiment (Degenfeld)
4th Battalions of 7th and 76th Infantry Regiments
One battery

Army Cavalry Reserve Colonel Pulz
Commandant of Cavalry Brigade (Colonel Bujanovics)
3rd and 11th Hussars and 12th Lancers
Commandant of Cavalry Brigade (Colonel Pulz)
1st and 13th Hussars and 13th Lancers
Reserve Cavalry
16 squadrons and one battery

NOTES

Introduction

1 Quoted Peter H Peel, *British Public Opinion and the Wars of German Unification: 1864–1871* (Maryland 1981) p216
2 Professor G Craig, *Königgrätz* (London 1964) p13
3 ibid, p12
4 Field Marshal Count A von Schlieffen, *Cannae* (Fort Leavenworth, Kansas 1931) p178
5 Professor A Bucholz, *Moltke and the German Wars 1864 – 1871* (London 2001) p10
6 Quoted ibid, p11
7 Professor DJ Hughes, *Moltke on the Art of War* (Novato California 1993) pp4-5

Chapter 1: Helmuth von Moltke

1 Quoted Craig, *Königgrätz,* p39
2 Field Marshal H von Moltke, *Letters to his Mother and his Brothers,* trans C Bell and HW Fischer (London 1891), II p112
3 Field Marshal H von Moltke, *His Life and Character,* trans M Herms (London 1892) p19
4 ibid, p36
5 ibid, p20
6 A Bucholz, *Moltke, Schlieffen and Prussian War Planning,* (New York 1991) p220
7 Lieutenant Colonel FE Whitton, *Moltke,* (London 1921) p36
8 Field Marshal H von Moltke, *As a Correspondent,* trans M Herms (New York 1893) p220
9 Whitton, p37
10 Field Marshal H von Moltke, *Letters to his Wife,* (London 1896) p16
11 Moltke, *His Life and Character,* pp129-39
12 Whitton, p38
13 Moltke, *As a Correspondent,* p222
14 Field Marshal H von Moltke, *The Russians in Bulgaria and Roumelia in 1828 and 1829,* (London 1854) p256
15 Moltke, *Letters to his Wife,* (London 1854) I p283
16 Quoted Whitton, p60
17 Moltke, *Letters to his Wife,* I p211
18 Moltke, *Letters to his Mother and his Brothers,* I pp228-9
19 Moltke, *Letters to his Wife,* I p226
20 Quoted Whitton, p67
21 ibid
22 Quoted GA Craig, *The Politics of the Prussian Army,* (Oxford 1964) p151
23 GA Craig, *War, Politics and Diplomacy,* (London 1966) p92
24 M Kitchen, *A Military History of Germany,* (London 1975) p103

25 G Ritter, *The Sword and the Sceptre,* (London 1972) I p112
26 Colonel Stoffel, *Military Reports addressed to the French War Minister,* trans Capt. Home (London 1872) p87
27 Quoted Craig, *Politics of the Prussian Army,* p107

Chapter 2: Moltke and the General Staff

1 Lieutenant Colonel JD Hittle, *The Military Staff,* (Harrisburg, Pennsylvania 1949) p52
2 General P Bronsart von Schellendorff, *The Duties of the General Staff,* (London 1905) p19
3 ibid, p22
4 ibid, p23
5 ibid, p24
6 W Görlitz, *The German General Staff,* (London 1953) p36
7 A Jones, *The Art of War in the Western World,* (London 1988) p392
8 Görlitz, p53
9 Bronsart von Schellendorff, pp29-9
10 Hittle, p64
11 Bronsart von Schellendorff, p32
12 Moltke, *Letters to his Mother and Brothers,* I pp249-50
13 Moltke, *Letters to his Wife,* II p95
14 Ritter, I p193
15 Hittle, pp65-6
16 Ritter, I p187
17 Colonel JN Dupuy, *A Genius for War,* (London 1977) pp64-5
18 W McElwee, *The Art of War: Waterloo to Mons,* (London 1974) p67
19 DE Showalter, *Railroads & Rifles,* (Hamden, Connecticut 1976) p44
20 W O'Connor Morris, *Moltke,* (London 1893) p36
21 A Bucholz, *War Planning,* p42
22 Quoted Whitton, p74
23 Hughes, 235-236
24 ibid, p184
25 J Luvaas, *The Military Legacy of the Civil War,* (Lawrence, Kansas 1988) p126
26 EA Pratt, *The Rise of Rail-Power in War and Conquest,* (London 1915) p122
27 Görlitz, pp75-76
28 Whitton, p76

Chapter 3: The New Technology

1 Showalter, p33
2 Pratt, pp2-3
3 Showalter, p21
4 Showalter, p24
5 Pratt, p4
6 ibid, p5
7 Showalter, p29

8 ibid, p30
9 Whitton, p71
10 Quoted Whitton, p54
11 Showalter, p37
12 Field Marshal H von Moltke, *Essays, Speeches and Memoirs,* trans M Herms and others (London 1893) II pp173-4
13 Pratt, p10
14 Showalter, p40
15 ibid, p42
16 ibid, p44
17 Pratt, p11
18 Hughes, p108
19 Showalter, p44
20 ibid, p46
21 Hughes, p113
22 M van Creveld, *Command in War,* (Cambridge, Massachusetts 1985) p108
23 ibid
24 Showalter, p18
25 ibid, p99
26 ibid, pp96-8
27 ibid, p106
28 ibid, p111
29 ibid, p110
30 Hughes, p48
31 Showalter, *Railroads & Rifles,* p112
32 ibid, pp112-113
33 Hughes, pp48-49
34 Craig, *Königgrätz,* p30
35 Showalter, *Railroads & Rifles,* p150
36 ibid, p174

Chapter 4: Army Reform

1 P Wiegler, *William the First,* (London 1929) p85
2 Ritter, I p115
3 Craig, *Politics of the Prussian Army,* p141
4 Ritter, I p123
5 Craig, *Politics of the Prussian Army,* p143
6 Ritter I p128
7 ibid, I p184
8 Craig, *Politics of the Prussian Army,* p151
9 ibid, p155
10 Prince O von Bismarck, *Love Letters,* (London 1901) II p107
11 Ritter, I p127
12 Quoted Ritter I p305
13 Prince O von Bismarck, *Reflections & Reminiscences,* (London 1898) I p310
14 ibid, p371

Chapter 5: Strategic Planning

1 Bucholz, *War Planning,* p38
2 ibid, p39
3 Showalter, *Railroads & Rifles,* p39
4 Moltke, *Letters to his Mother & Brothers,* I pp255-6
5 Field Marshal H von Moltke, *Strategy: Its Theory & Application,* (Westport, Connecticut 1971) p99
6 Field Marshal H von Moltke, *Military Correspondence 1870-71,* ed S Wilkinson (Oxford 1923) pp1-2
7 ibid, pp3-5
8 ibid, p6
9 ibid, p8
10 Moltke, *Strategy* p7
11 ibid, p11
12 ibid, p11
13 ibid, p19
14 Field Marshal H von Moltke, *Correspondance Militaire,* (Paris n.d) IV p1
15 ibid, IV pp2-9
16 ibid, IV pp9-20
17 ibid, IV pp22-30
18 Bucholz, *War Planning,* pp42-3
19 Luvaas, p122; Bucholz, *Moltke and the German Wars,* pp72-73

Chapter 6: Schleswig-Holstein

1 Moltke, *Letters to his Wife,* I p207
2 W Carr, *Schleswig-Holstein 1815-48,* (Manchester 1963) p311
3 LD Steefel, *The Schleswig-Holstein Question,* (Cambridge, Massachusetts 1932) p57
4 Quoted Steefel, p61
5 Moltke, *Correspondance Militaire,* IV pp31-34
6 ibid, IV pp35-41
7 ibid, IV pp41-48
8 Moltke, *Letters to his Wife,* II pp119-121
9 Showalter, p44
10 ibid, p50
11 Moltke, *Correspondance Militaire,* IV pp49-55
12 ibid, IV pp61-62
13 ibid, IV pp72-73
14 ibid, IV pp75-76
15 Moltke, *Letters to his Wife,* II p121
16 Moltke, *Essays, Speeches and Memoirs,* II p162
17 H von Sybel, *The Founding of the German Empire,* (New York 1891) III p261
18 Colonel NP Jensen, *Den Anden Slesvigske Krig 1864,* (Copenhagen 1900) Appendix II; M Embree, *Bismarck's First War,* (Solihull 2006) pp368-377
19 Quoted Steefel, p165
20 Steefel, p171
21 ibid, p175

22 Moltke, *Correspondance Militaire,* IV pp107-110
23 ibid, IV pp110-111
24 ibid, IV p97
25 H Friedjung, *The Struggle for Supremacy in Germany,* trans AJP Taylor and WL McElwee (London 1935) p50
26 Craig, *Politics of the Prussian Army,* p183; Sybel p266

Chapter 7: The Dannewerk

1 Jensen, p111
2 Lieutenant Colonel F von Fischer, *Der Krieg in Schleswig und Jütland im Jahre 1864* (Vienna 1870) p111
3 ibid, p116
4 L Oliphant, *Episodes in a Life of Adventure,* (London 1888) p412
5 Jensen, p126
6 Sybel III p115
7 E Dicey, *The Schleswig-Holstein War,* (London 1864) I p84
8 Fischer, p115
9 A Gallenga, *The Invasion of Denmark,* (London 1864) I pp161-2
10 Sybel, III pp273-4
11 HR Madol, *Christian IX,* (London 1939) p163
12 Sybel, III p276
13 Quoted Craig, *Politics of the Prussian Army,* p184
14 Moltke, *Letters to his Wife,* II p122
15 Moltke, *Correspondance Militaire,* IV pp114-5
16 ibid, IV pp115-6
17 Quoted Craig, *Politics of the Prussian Army,* p185
18 Sybel, III pp293-4
19 Prince O von Bismarck, *Gesammelte Werke,* IV p328; quoted Craig, *Politics of the Prussian Army,* p185
20 Moltke, *Correspondance Militaire,* IV p117-9
21 ibid, IV pp119-121
22 Sybel, III p294
23 ibid, III p295
24 R Stadelmann, *Moltke und der Staat,* (Krefeld 1950) p138
25 Moltke, *Correspondance Militaire,* IV pp122-4
26 ibid, IV pp124-5
27 ibid, IV pp126-7
28 Quoted Craig, *Politics of the Prussian Army,* p187
29 Moltke, *Correspondance Militaire,* IV pp127-130
30 ibid, IV pp130-133

Chapter 8: Düppel

1 Sybel, III p308
2 ibid, III p309
3 Quoted Craig, *Politics of the Prussian Army,* p186
4 Moltke, *Correspondance Militaire,* IV pp135-8

5 Quoted Craig, *Politics of the Prussian Army,* p189
6 Moltke, *Correspondance Militaire,* IV pp139-140
7 ibid, IV pp141-3
8 ibid, IV pp145-9
9 ibid, IV pp150-4
10 ibid, IV pp160-1
11 Moltke, *Letters to his Wife,* II p126
12 Moltke, *Correspondance Militaire,* IV p175
13 Buchanan to Russell, F0425/77 p106
14 Dicey, I p175
15 Skinner, J *The Tale of Danish Heroism,* (London 1865) p60
16 C Lowe, *The Redoubts of Düppel* in *Battles of the Nineteenth Century,* (London n.d) p224
17 Dicey, I p274
18 Captain Fritsch-Lang, 'Notes upon the attack of the Duppel Entrenchments in March and April, 1864', *Papers on subjects connected with the Duties of the Corps of Royal Engineers,* Vol 14 (Woolwich 1865) p179
19 Prince K zu Hohenlohe-Ingelfingen, *Letters on Infantry,* trans NL Walford (London 1889) p82
20 Sybel, III p328
21 Fritsch-Lang, p184
22 Moltke, *Correspondance Militaire,* IV pp178-9
23 ibid, p181
24 ibid, pp182-3
25 ibid, pp183-4
26 Dicey, II p176
27 Fritsch-Lang, p185
28 Lieutenant Colonel JF Lewis, *Textbook of Fortification and Military Engineering,* (London 1892) II p158
29 Fritsch-Lang, p186
30 Skinner, p190
31 Lewis, *Textbook of Fortification,* I p209
32 Skinner, pp193-4
33 Dicey, II p180
34 Quoted Count E Corti, *The English Empress,* (London, 1957) p131

Chapter 9: Alsen

1 Quoted FO425/77 p159
2 Moltke, *Correspondance Militaire,* IV pp189-191
3 Russell Papers PRO30/22/15B, p53
4 ibid, p50
5 Moltke, *Correspondance Militaire,* IV pp191-2
6 ibid, IV pp192-7
7 ibid, IV p198
8 ibid, IV p199
9 ibid, IV pp202-5

10 Moltke, *Letters to his Wife,* II pp128-9
11 Moltke, *Correspondance Militaire,* IV pp205-210
12 Moltke, *Letters to his Wife,* II p129
13 Moltke, *Correspondance Militaire,* IV pp210-214
14 ibid, IV pp214-216
15 ibid, IV pp217-8
16 Quoted Craig, *Politics of the Prussian Army,* pp191-2
17 Moltke, *Letters to his Wife,* II p131
18 Moltke, *Correspondance Militaire,* IV pp218-223
19 ibid, IV pp224-6
20 ibid, IV p228n
21 ibid, IV p239
22 Moltke, *Letters to his Wife,* II p133
23 Moltke, *Correspondance Militaire,* IV pp250-252
24 Fischer, p350
25 E Denis, *La Fondation de l'Empire Allemande,* (Paris 1906) p362
26 Moltke, *Letters to his Wife,* II pp135-144;
27 Moltke, *Correspondance Militaire,* IV pp272-4
28 ibid, IV pp283-289
29 ibid, IV p294; *Letters to his Wife,* II p155
30 Moltke, *Letters to his Wife,* II p156
31 Quoted Sybel, III p420
32 Moltke, *Letters to his Wife, II p158*

Chapter 10: Mounting Tension

1 Moltke, *Strategy,* p23
2 CW Clark, *Franz Joseph and Bismarck,* (Cambridge, Massachusetts 1934) p18
3 Quoted Clark, p238
4 H Böhme (ed), *The Foundation of the German Empire,* (Oxford 1971) pp154-155
5 Moltke, *Letters to his Mother and his Brothers,* II p25
6 Sybel, IV p168
7 ibid, IV p205
8 Clark, p303
9 Moltke, *Strategy,* pp24-31
10 ibid, pp31-2
11 Sybel, IV pp320-323
12 Moltke, *Correspondance Militaire,* V pp67-74
13 Sybel, IV pp320-323
14 Sir AW Ward, *Germany 1815-1890,* (Cambridge, 1917) II p209
15 Sybel, IV p339
16 Moltke, *Correspondance Militaire,* V pp75-6
17 Sybel, IV pp354-5

Chapter 11: Mobilisation

1 Böhme, pp159-160; Clark, pp337-339 and 560-572
2 Clark, p337

3 Sybel, IV pp344-345
4 J Presland, (G Skelton), *Vae Victis,* (London 1934) p210
5 Sybel, IV p350; Clark, p345
6 Moltke, *Correspondance Militaire,* V pp92-95
7 ibid, V pp102-3
8 ibid, V pp103-106
9 ibid, V p107
10 ibid, V pp108-109
11 ibid, V pp115-117
12 Clark, p380
13 Friedjung, p132
14 Showalter, p61
15 Prussian Official History, *The Campaign of 1866 in Germany,* trans Colonel von Wright and Captain HM Hozier, (London 1872) p11
16 Moltke, *Correspondance Militaire,* V pp247-251)
17 Friedjung, p190
18 Quoted Friedjung, p190
19 Sybel, IV pp497-500
20 Moltke, *Correspondance Militaire,* p272
21 Craig, *Politics of the Prussian Army,* p195

Chapter 12: Deployment

1 Moltke, *Correspondance Militaire,* V p13
2 ibid, V pp13-14
3 ibid, V p17
4 ibid, V p18
5 ibid, V p21
6 ibid, V p48
7 ibid, V p52
8 ibid, V pp135-147
9 ibid, V pp147-157
10 ibid, V pp157-163
11 ibid, V pp165-178
12 ibid, V pp179-185
13 ibid, V pp186-189
14 ibid, V pp190-191
15 ibid, V pp200-204
16 ibid, V pp213-216
17 ibid, V pp218-220
18 ibid, V pp221-227
19 ibid, V pp228-229
20 ibid, V pp234-235
21 ibid, V p240
22 Official History, p20

Chapter 13: The Prussian Army

1 Lieutenant Colonel GJR Glünicke, *The Campaign in Bohemia 1866,* (London 1907) p22
2 F Engels, *Engels as a Military Critic,* (Manchester 1959) p123
3 Stoffel, p2
4 ibid, p3
5 Craig, *Königgrätz,* p35
6 S Wilkinson, *War and Policy,* (London 1900) pp164-165; *The Brain of an Army,* (London 1895) pp183-4
7 Craig, *Königgrätz,* p33; Prince K zu Hohenlohe-Ingelfingen, *Letters on Artillery,* trans NL Walford, (London 1890) p1
8 Craig, *Königgrätz,* p33
9 Hohenlohe, *Letters on Artillery,* pp2-16
10 W Berdrow, (ed) *The Letters of Alfred Krupp1827-1877,* (London 1930) p226
11 Field Marshal Count K von Blumenthal, *Journals for 1866 and 1870,* (London 1930) p226
12 Craig, *War Politics and Diplomacy,* p113

Chapter 14: The Austrian Army

1 GE Rothenberg, *The Army of Francis Joseph,* (West Lafayette, Indiana 1998) p31
2 ibid, pp38-9
3 ibid, p39
4 ibid, p55
5 ibid, p59
6 ibid, p59
7 ibid
8 Craig, *Königgrätz,* p21
9 Engels, p58
10 Rothenberg, p64
11 N Rich, (ed) *The Holstein Papers,*(Cambridge 1955) I p28
12 Quoted G Wawro, *The Austro-Prussian War,* (Cambridge 1996) p31
13 Presland, p210
14 Quoted Rothenburg, p68
15 Engels, pp122-123
16 Presland, p163

Chapter 15: Final Plans

1 Field Marshal H von Moltke, *Militarische Werke,* II pt 2 pp33-40; quoted Hughes p45
2 Whitton, p89
3 Moltke, *Corrrespondance Militaire,* pp247-251
4 Blumenthal, pp16-18
5 Moltke, *Correspondance Militaire,* V pp253-254
6 ibid, V pp260-262
7 Blumenthal, p21
8 Moltke, *Correspondance Militaire,* V pp268-272

9 ibid, V pp278-281
10 ibid, V pp281-282
11 Blumenthal, p26
12 Moltke, *Correspondance Militaire,* V p285
13 ibid, V pp288-290
14 ibid
15 ibid, V p312
16 Official History, p22
17 General H Bonnal, *Sadowa,* (London 1907) p41
18 Caemmerer, Lieutenant General von, *The Development of Strategical Science,* (London 1905) p186
19 Engels, p134
20 Quoted Bonnal, p62
21 Quoted Presland, p226
22 Official History, p25
23 Quoted Whitton, p100

Chapter: 16 Countdown to War

1 Peel, p204
2 Lynn M Case, *French Opinion on War and Diplomacy during the Second Empire,* (Philadelphia, Pennsylvania 1954) p198
3 ibid, p199
4 Peel, p205
5 ibid, p206
6 ibid, p212
7 ibid, p224
8 Quoted Sir H Maxwell, *The Life and Letters of the Fourth Earl of Clarendon,* (London 1913) II p322
9 R Wemyss, *Memoirs and Letters of Sir Robert Morier,* (London 1911) II p74
10 Colonel F Wellesley, (ed) *The Paris Embassy during the Second Empire,* (London 1928) p297
11 J Breuilly, *Austria, Prussia and Germany 1806-1871,* (London 2002) p102
12 ibid, p91
13 ibid, p99
14 L Gall, *Bismarck: The White Revolutionary,* (London 1986) I pp275-276
15 Quoted O Pflanze, *Bismarck and the Development of Germany,* (Princeton, New Jersey 1990) I p305

Chapter 17: Confronting the Middle States

1 Sybel, V p33
2 Moltke, *Correspondance Militaire,* V pp61-65
3 ibid, V p305-306
4 ibid, V pp308-309
5 ibid, V p309
6 ibid, V pp240-243
7 ibid, V p247-251

8 ibid, V p289
9 Sybel, V p40
10 Showalter, *Railroads and Rifles*, pp119-120
11 GLM Strauss, *Men who have made the New German Empire*, (London 1875) II p181
12 Sybel, V p354
13 Prince Hohenlohe-Schillingsfurst, *Memoirs*, (London 1906) I p149
14 Quoted Count E Corti, *The Downfall of Three Dynasties*, (London 1934) p178
15 ibid, p179

Chapter 18: Langensalza

1 Sybel, V p42
2 Official History, p37
3 Quoted Craig, *Politics of the Prussian Army*, p197
4 ibid
5 Sybel, V p44
6 ibid
7 Official History, p40
8 Sybel, V p48
9 ibid, V p52
10 Sir A Malet, *The Overthrow of the Germanic Confederation*, (London 1870) pp223-224
11 Captain WJ Wyatt, *A Political and Military History of the Hanoverian and Italian War*, (London 1868) p54
12 ibid, p55
13 Sybel, V p57; Moltke, *Correspondance Militaire*, V p421
14 Sybel, V pp58-59
15 Wyatt, p60
16 Sybel, V p64
17 ibid V p67; Moltke, *Correspondance Militaire*, V p436
18 Sybel, V p68
19 Official History, p52
20 Malet, p254
21 ibid, p256
22 Schlieffen, pp83-84

Chapter 19: The Advance into Bohemia

1 HM Hozier, *The Seven Weeks' War*, (London 1867) I p167
2 Official History, p59
3 Hozier, I p170
4 Moltke, *Correspondance Militaire*, V p319
5 Official History, p61
6 Bonnal, p57; Whitton, p105
7 Field Marshal H von Moltke, *Correspondence during the Campaign of 1866 against Austria*, ed Spenser Wilkinson (London 1915) p43
8 ibid, pp44-45

9 ibid, pp48-49
10 Moltke, *Correspondance Militaire,* V pp325-326
11 ibid, V pp326-327
12 ibid, V p329
13 ibid, V p328
14 Quoted Whitton, p121
15 General von Schlichting, *Moltke und Benedek,* (Berlin 1900), quoted Whitton, p122
16 Official History, p62
17 Blumenthal, pp32-33
18 Quoted Whitton, p107
19 Quoted Presland, p228
20 Presland, p229
21 Official History, p65
22 ibid
23 Moltke, *Correspondance Militaire,* p328
24 Blumenthal, p34
25 Quoted Official History, p66
26 ibid, p70
27 ibid, p75
28 Whitton, p125
29 ibid, p126

Chapter: 20 The Second Army in the Mountains

1 Quoted Presland, p233
2 Friedjung, p216
3 Official History, p87
4 Hozier, I p281
5 Official History, p94
6 Official History, p237
7 Presland, p237
8 Official History, p79
9 ibid, p82
10 Quoted N Malcolm, *Bohemia 1866,* (London 1912) p61
11 Quoted (from the German edition of the Official History) Bonnal, p92
12 Official History, p82
13 Blumenthal, p36
14 Official History, p105
15 ibid
16 ibid, pp113-114
17 Presland, p237
18 ibid, pp238-239
19 Friedjung, p220
20 Presland, p240
21 Glünicke, p109
22 Friedjung, p220

23 Official History, pp125-126
24 General Sir C Beauchamp Walker, *Days of a Soldier's Life,* (London 1894) p230
25 Presland, p240
26 Quoted Craig, *Königgrätz,* p81
27 Official History, p106
28 ibid, p109
29 Hohenlohe, *Letters on Artillery,* pp10-11
30 Official History, p112

Chapter 21: Gitschin

1 Official History, p98
2 ibid, p103
3 Craig, *Königgrätz,* p85
4 Official History, p103
5 Moltke, *Correspondance Militaire,* V pp330-331
6 ibid, V p331
7 ibid, V p332
8 ibid
9 Malcolm, p42
10 Official History, pp128-129
11 ibid, p129
12 Presland, p250
13 Official History, p136
14 ibid, p133
15 ibid, 135
16 Presland, p148
17 Official History, p136
18 Hozier, I p245
19 Official History, pp144-145
10 ibid, p149
21 ibid, p155
22 Presland, pp243-244
23 ibid, p245
24 ibid, p248
25 ibid, p251
26 ibid, p254
27 ibid, p255
28 ibid, pp256-257
29 ibid, p256
30 Craig, *Königgrätz,* p94
31 Official History, p156
32 Craig, *Königgrätz,* p95
33 ibid, p94
34 Bismarck, *Love-Letters,* II p177
35 Bismarck, *Reflections and Reminiscences,* II p35

Chapter 22: Contact Regained

1 Moltke, *Correspondance Militaire,* V p334
2 ibid
3 Official History, p158
4 ibid, p158
5 Moltke, *Correspondance Militaire,* V p337
6 Field Marshal H von Moltke, *The Franco-German War,* (London 1907) p414
7 Blumenthal, pp38-39
8 Bonnal, p118
9 ibid, p114
10 Presland, p260
11 ibid, p259
12 Wawro, pp208-209
13 Craig, *Königgrätz,* p104
14 Wawro, pp208-209
15 Craig, *Königgrätz,* p100
16 Official History, pp162-163
17 ibid, p163
18 ibid, pp164-165
19 Moltke, *The Franco-German War,* p414
20 Official History, p166
21 ibid, p167
22 Blumenthal, pp39-40
23 ibid, p40
24 ibid
25 Presland, p266
26 Whitton, p152
27 Bonnal, p137
28 Presland, p262
29 Official History, p168
30 Hozier, I p310

Chapter 23: The Crossing of the Bistritz

1 Official History, p174
2 ibid, p174
3 Hozier, I p315
4 Quoted Presland, p275
5 Official History, pp168-169
6 F Hoenig, *Tactics of the Future,* (London 1899) p40
7 Official History, p179
8 Hozier, I p317
9 Craig, *Königgrätz,* p108
10 Quoted ibid
11 Quoted Official History, p171
12 ibid, p184
13 ibid, p185

14 Official History, p191
15 ibid
16 Presland, p272
17 Official History, p196
18 ibid, p197
19 ibid, p199
20 Quoted Craig, *Königgrätz,* pp120-121
21 Official History, p200
22 ibid
23 ibid
24 ibid, p205
25 Craig, *Königgrätz,* p111
26 Quoted Craig, *Königgrätz,* p122

Chapter 24: Anxiety on the Roskosberg

1 Official History, pp173-174
2 ibid, p210
3 Blumenthal, p41
4 Crown Prince, *Diaries,* p36
5 Official History, p206
6 ibid, pp206-207
7 ibid, p205
8 ibid
9 Moltke, *Letters to his Wife,* II p299
10 Craig, *Königgrätz,* p122
11 Presland, p273
12 ibid, pp273-274
13 Official History, p232
14 ibid, p236
15 ibid
16 Hoenig, p41
17 Official History, p246
18 Quoted Craig, *Königgrätz,* p122
19 ibid, p133
20 Presland, p278; Craig, *Königgrätz,* p134

Chapter 25: The Taking of Chlum

1 Blumenthal, pp40-41
2 Crown Prince, *Diaries,* p37
3 ibid
4 Official History, p211
5 Craig, *Königgrätz,* p129
6 Presland, p276
7 Hohenlohe, *Letters on Artillery,* p22
8 ibid, p62
9 ibid, p63

10 ibid, pp65-66
11 Official History, p225
12 Hohenlohe, *Letters on Artillery,* p68
13 Hohenlohe, *Aus Meinem Leben,* III p289
14 Official History, p229

Chapter 26: The Advance of the Army of the Elbe

1 Official History, p236
2 Moltke, *Letters to his Wife,* II p187
3 Official History, p236
4 ibid, p239
5 ibid, p243
6 ibid, p242
7 ibid, p254; Craig, *Königgrätz,* p134
8 Official History, p248
9 Craig, *Königgrätz,* p136
10 Official History, p252
11 Hoenig, pp48-49
12 Official History, p253

Chapter 27: Rosberitz

1 Craig, *Königgrätz,* pp150-151
2 ibid, p151
3 Official History, p258
4 ibid, p261
5 Hohenlohe, *Letters on Artillery,* p69
6 Field Marshal Paul von Hindenburg, *Out of My Life,* (London 1920) p26
7 Official History, p262
8 Craig, *Königgrätz,* p161-162
9 Official History, p265
10 ibid
11 ibid, p266
12 Hoenig, pp58-9
13 ibid, p60
14 ibid, p64
15 Official History, p273

Chapter 28: Victory

1 Moltke, *Letters to his Wife,* II p300
2 Official History, p277
3 ibid, p279
4 ibid, p281
5 Craig, *Königgrätz,* p163
6 Official History, pp282-283
7 ibid, p284
8 Hoenig, p63

9 Official History, p284
10 ibid, p287
11 ibid, p288
12 Presland, pp288-289
13 Quoted Wawro, p265
14 Official History, p289
15 ibid, p290
16 ibid, p291
17 Crown Prince, *Diaries,* p44
18 Official History, p294
19 ibid, p296
20 ibid
21 Moltke, *Letters to his Wife,* II p301
22 ibid,
23 Whitton, p159
24 Crown Prince, *Diaries,* p49
25 Berdrow, p230
26 Presland, p294
27 Quoted Craig, *Königgrätz,* p175
28 Official History, pp297-298

Chapter 29: Custozza

1 Official History, p18
2 Wawro, p89
3 Count E Della Rocca, *The Autobiography of a Veteran, 1807-93,* trans J Ross (London 1899) p238
4 Moltke, *Correspondance Militaire,* V p313
5 ibid, V pp313-314
6 Wawro, p90
7 J Pocock, *Bitter Victory,* (Tiptree 2002) p44
8 Wyatt, pp176-177
9 Della Rocca, p235
10 Wawro, p93
11 CS Forester, *Victor Emmanuel II and the Union of Italy* (London 1927) pp157-158
12 Pocock, pp95-97
13 Quoted Wawro, p71
14 ibid, p72
15 Pocock, p51; Wawro, p104
16 Pocock, p56
17 ibid, p59
18 Della Rocca, p249
19 Wyatt, p220
20 ibid, p223
21 Della Rocca, pp252-254
22 Wawro, p118
23 ibid, p121

24 Wyatt, p283

Chapter 30: Advance to the Danube

1 Official History, pp300-301
2 Hohenlohe, *Aus Meinem Leben,* III pp306-307
3 ibid
4 ibid
5 Official history, p303
6 Hozier, II p90
7 Official History, p306
8 Moltke, *Letters to his Wife,* II p191
9 Moltke, *Correspondance Militaire,* V pp351-352
10 Moltke, *Letters to his Wife,* II p191
11 Hozier, II p101
12 ibid, II pp113-114
13 ibid
14 Quoted Presland, p301
15 Blumenthal, pp47-48
16 Moltke, *Correspondance Militaire,* V pp358-359
17 Hozier, II p128
18 Official History, pp324-325
19 Moltke, *Correspondance Militaire,* V pp366-367
20 Hozier, II p156; *The Times,* July 14 1866
21 Official History, p332
22 Moltke, *Correspondance Militaire,* V pp366-367
23 Blumenthal, pp49-50
24 Official History, p334
25 ibid, p338
26 Presland, p306
27 Official History, p339
28 ibid, p341
29 ibid, p345
30 Hozier, II p159
31 Moltke, *Correspondance Militaire,* V pp371-373
32 ibid, V pp375-376
33 Hozier, II p179
34 Official History, p357
35 Moltke, *Letters to his Wife,* II p195
36 Presland, p308
37 Official History, p361
38 Hozier, II p184
39 ibid
40 Official History, p365
41 ibid, p367
42 ibid, p369

43 Hozier, II p190
44 ibid, II p191
45 Official History, p373
46 Hozier, II p193
47 Official History, p373

Chapter 31: Kissingen

1 Quoted Corti, *Dynasties,* p180
2 Official History, p390
3 W Blunt, *The Dream King,* (London 1970) p53
4 Quoted Official History, p392
5 Quoted Corti, *Dynasties,* p181
6 Moltke, *Correspondance Militaire,* V p447
7 Official History, p394
8 ibid, p402
9 Hozier, II p34
10 Official History, p400
11 ibid, p403
12 Hohenlohe-Schillingsfurst I p155
13 Official History, p405
14 Malet, p274
15 G Zernin (ed), *August von Goeben in Seinem Briefen,* (Berlin 1903) p216
16 Hozier, II p41
17 Official History, p409
18 ibid, p411
19 Hozier, II p41
20 Hohenlohe-Schillingsfurst, II p157
21 Sybel, V p363
22 Official History, p413
23 Sybel, V p365
24 Official History, p417
25 ibid, pp417-418
26 ibid, p418
27 Hohenlohe-Schillingsfurst I p157
28 Blunt, p54
29 Official History, p429
30 Hozier, II p46
31 Official History, p420
32 ibid, II p421
33 ibid
34 Sybel, V p369
35 Zernin, p218

Chapter 32: The Fall of Frankfurt

1 Hozier, II p48
2 Malet, p277

3 Hozier, II p87
4 Official History, p426
5 Hozier, II p53
6 Official History, p430
7 ibid, p431
8 ibid, p432
9 Sybel, V p373
10 Official History, p436
11 ibid
12 ibid, p440
13 ibid, p441
14 ibid
15 ibid, p444
16 ibid, p447
17 ibid, p448
18 Hozier, II p67
19 Official History, p451

Chapter 33: The End of the Confederation

1 Official History, p453
2 ibid
3 ibid
4 ibid, p454
5 ibid, p455
6 Malet, p330
7 Official History, p460
8 ibid, p462
9 ibid, p464
10 ibid, p465
11 ibid, p467
12 ibid, p468
13 ibid
14 ibid, p471
15 ibid, p472
16 ibid, p474; Malet, p360
17 Official History, p478
18 Malet, p366
19 Official History, p478
20 ibid, pp479-480
22 ibid, p483
23 Sybel, V 384

Chapter 34: Moltke at Nikolsburg

1 Sybel V 254
2 Prince O von Bismarck, *Love Letters,* II p178
3 Moltke, *Letters to his Wife,* II p191

4 Blumenthal, pp51-52
5 Craig, *Politics of the Prussian Army,* p200
6 Moltke, *Letters to his Wife,* II p194
7 Bismarck, *Reflections and Reminiscences,* II p40
8 Lord Newton, *Lord Lyons: A Record of British Diplomacy,* (London n.d) pp140-141
9 Bismarck, *Reflections and Reminiscences,* II p37
10 ibid, II pp47-48
11 Quoted Craig, *Politics of the Prussian Army,* p202
12 Bismarck, *Reflections and Reminiscences,* II pp45-46
13 Sybel, V p328
14 EA Pottinger, *Napoleon III and the German Crisis, 1865-1866,* (Cambridge, Massachusetts 1968) p178
15 Sybel, V pp338-341
18 Moltke, *Letters to his Wife,* II p196
19 Blumenthal, p55
20 Bismarck, *Reflections and Reminiscences,* II pp51-52
21 Quoted Gall, I p306
22 Moltke, *Letters to his Wife,* II p196

Chapter 35: Conclusion

1 Schlieffen, p128
2 ibid, p137
3 Quoted Craig, *Königgrätz,* p184
4 Engels, pp139-140
5 M van Creveld, *Supplying War,* (Cambridge 1978) p81
6 Stoffel, pp8-9
7 Hohenlohe, *Letters on Artillery,* p6
8 Quoted Craig, *Königgrätz,* p186
9 van Creveld, p80
10 ibid, p84
11 Friedrich von Beust, *Memoirs,* (London 1887) I pp326-327
12 Quoted Friedjung, p301
13 Quoted WE Mosse, *The European Powers and the German Question,* (Cambridge 1958) p249

Bibliography

ANDERSON, EN, *The Social and Political Conflict in Prussia 1858-1864,* (London 1994)

ANDERSON, JH, *The Austro-Prussian War in Bohemia,* (London 1912)

BERDROW, W, (ed.) *The Letters of Alfred Krupp 1827-1877,* (London 1930)

BENEDETTI, V, *Ma Mission en Prusse,* (Paris 1871)

BESSER, DWF, *Sechs Wochen im Felde,* (Halle 1866)

BIGGE, W, *Feldmarschall Graf Moltke,* (Munich 1901)

BISMARCK, Prince O von, *Love Letters* (London 1901, 2 vols)

BISMARCK, Prince O von, *Reflections and Reminiscences,* (London 1898, 2 vols)

BISMARCK, Prince O von, *The Correspondence of William I and Bismarck,* (New York 1903, 2 vols)

BLUNT, W, *The Dream King: Ludwig II of Bavaria,* (London 1970)

BÖHME, H, (ed.) *The Foundation of the German Empire,* (Oxford 1971)

BLEIBTREU, C, *Langensalza: Der Mainfeldzug,* (Stuttgart n.d)

BLUMENTHAL, Field Marshal Count K von, *Journals for 1866 and 1870-71,* (London 1903)

BONNAL, General H, *Sadowa,* (London 1907)

BREUILLY, J, *Austria, Prussia and Germany, 1806-1871* (Harlow 2002)

BRIDGE, FR, *The Habsburg Monarchy,* (New York 1990)

BROPHY, JM, *Capitalism, Politics and Railroads in Prussia,* (Columbus Ohio 1998)

BRÜHL, Count Ferdinand von, *The History of the Prussian Garde du Corps during the Campaign of 1866,* trans D Rogers, (Solihull 2000)

BUCHOLZ, A, *Moltke, Schlieffen and Prussian War Planning,* (New York 1991)

BUCHOLZ, A, *Moltke and the German Wars,* (Basingstoke 2001)

CAEMMERER, Lieutenant General von, *The Development of Strategical Science,* (London 1905)

CARR, W, *Schleswig-Holstein 1815-1848,* (Manchester 1963)

CARR, W, *The Origins of the Wars of German Unification,* (London 1991)

CASE, LM, *French Opinion on War and Diplomacy during the Second Empire,* (Philadelphia 1954)

CLARK, CW, *Franz Joseph and Bismarck,* (Cambridge, Massachusetts 1934)

COOKE, Lieutenant Colonel, *The Campaign in Austria of 1866,* (Woolwich 1866)

CORTI, Count E, *The Downfall of Three Dynasties,* (London 1934)

CORTI, Count E, *The English Empress,* (London 1957)

CRAIG, GA, *Germany 1866-1945,* (Oxford 1978)

CRAIG, GA, *The Battle of Königgrätz,* (London 1964)

CRAIG, GA, *The Politics of the Prussian Army,* (Oxford 1964)

CRAIG, GA, *War, Politics and Diplomacy,* (London 1966)

CREVELD, M van, *Command in War,* (Cambridge Massachusetts 1985)

CREVELD, M van, *Supplying War,* (Cambridge 1977)

DAWSON, WH, *The German Empire 1852-1871,* (London 1919)

DELLA ROCCA, Count E, *The Autobiography of a Veteran, 1807-93,* trans J Ross (London1899)
DENIS, E, *La Fondation de l'Empire Allemand, 1852-1871,* (Paris 1906)
DENISON, Colonel GT, *A History of Cavalry,* (London 1913)
DICEY, E, *The Battlefields of 1866,* (London 1866)
DICEY, E, *The Schleswig-Holstein War,* (London 1864, 2 vols)
DUPUY, Colonel TN, *A Genius for War: The German Army and the General Staff* 1807-1945, (London 1977)
DUVAL, J, *Vers Sadowa: Étude stratégique,* (Paris 1907)
ECHARD, WE, *Napoleon III and the Concert of Europe,* (Baton Rouge 1983)
EMBREE, M, *Bismarck's First War: The Campaign in Schleswig and Jutland 1864* (Solihull 2006)
ENGELS, F, *Engels as a Military Critic,* (Manchester 1959)
FEUCHTWANGER, E, *Imperial Germany 1850-1918,* (London 2001)
FESSER, G, *1866: Königgrätz – Sadowa,* (Berlin 1994)
FISCHER, Lieutenant Colonel F von, *Der Krieg in Schleswig und Jutland im Jahre 1864,* (Vienna 1870)
FOERSTER, W, *Prinz Friedrich Karl von Preussen,* (Stuttgart 1910, 2 vols)
FONTANE, T, *Der Deutsche Krieg von 1866* (Berlin 1984, 2 vols)
FÖRSTER, S and NAGLER, J, *On the Road to Total War: The American Civil War and the German Wars of Unification 1861-1871* (Cambridge 1997)
FREDERICK, Emperor, *Diaries,* ed. M von Poschinger, (London 1902)
FRIEDRICH, Otto, *Blood and Iron. From Bismarck to Hitler: The von Moltke family's impact on German history,* (New York 1995)
FRIEDJUNG, H, *The Struggle for Supremacy in Germany 1859 – 1866,* trans AJP Taylor and W McElwee (London 1935)
FRITSCH-LANG, Captain, 'Notes upon the attack of the Duppel Entrenchments in March and April, 1864', *Papers on subjects connected with the Duties of the Corps of Royal Engineers,* Vol 14 (Woolwich 1865)
FULLER, Maj Gen JFC, *Decisive Battles of the Western World,* (London 1956)
GALL, L, *Bismarck: The White Revolutionary,* (London 1988)
GALLENGA, A, *The Invasion of Denmark,* (London 1864, 2 vols)
GLÜNICKE, Lieutenant Colonel GJR, *The Campaign in Bohemia 1866,* (London 1907)
GÖRLITZ, W, *The German General Staff,* (London 1953)
HINDENBURG, Field Marshal P von, *Out of My Life,* trans FA Hott (London 1920)
HITTLE, Lieut. Col. JD, *The Military Staff,* (Harrisburg Pennsylvania 1949)
HOHENLOHE-INGELFINGEN, Prince Kraft zu, *Aufzeichnungen aus meinem Leben 1848-1871,* (Berlin 1897, 4 vols)
HOHENLOHE-INGELFINGEN, Prince Kraft zu, *Letters on Cavalry,* trans NL Walford (London 1889)
HOHENLOHE-INGELFINGEN, Prince Kraft zu, *Letters on Artillery,* trans NL Walford (London 1890)
HOHENLOHE-INGELFINGEN, Prince Kraft zu, *Letters on Infantry,* trans NL Walford (London 1892)
HOHENLOHE-INGELFINGEN, Prince Kraft zu, *Letters on Strategy,* (London 1898)

HOHENLOHE-SCHILLINGSFURT, Prince C, *Memoirs,* (London 1906)
HÖNIG, F, *Inquiries Concerning the Tactics of the Future,* trans Capt HM Bowes (London 1899)
HOWARD, Sir M, *The Franco-Prussian War,* (London 1961)
HOWES, Colonel P, *The Catalytic Wars. A study of the development of warfare* 1860-1870, (London 1998)
HOZIER, Capt HM, *The Seven Weeks War,* (London 1867, 2 vols)
HUGHES, DJ, *Moltke on the Art of War,* (Novato California 1993)
JAHNS, M, *Feldmarschall Moltke,* (Berlin 1906)
JAMES, Lieutenant Colonel FN, *Modern Strategy,* (London 1903)
JENSEN, Colonel NP, *Den Anden Slesvigske Krig 1864* (Copenhagen 1900)
JOHNSTONE, Captain HM, *The Foundation of Strategy,* (London 1914)
JONES, A, *The Art of War in the Western World,* (London 1988)
KITCHEN, M, *A Military History of Germany from the Eighteenth Century to the present day,* (London 1975)
KOPPEN, F von, *Helmuth von Moltke,* (Glogau n.d.)
LACKEY, SW, *The Rebirth of the Habsburg Army. Friedrich Beck and the rise of the general staff,* (Westport Connecticut 1996)
LEWIS, Lieutenant Colonel JF, *Text Book of Fortification and Military Engineering,* (London 1892)
LOWE , C, 'The Redoubts of Düppel' in *Battles of the Nineteenth Century,* (London n.d)
LUVAAS, J, *The Military Legacy of the Civil War,* (Lawrence Kansas 1988)
MADOL, HR, *Christian IX,* (London 1939)
MAGUIRE, TM, *Notes on the Austro-Prussian War of 1866,* (London 1904)
MALCOLM, Lieutenant Colonel N, *Bohemia 1866,* (London 1912)
MCDONOUGH, G, *Prussia,* (London 1994)
MALET, Sir A, *The Overthrow of the Germanic Confederation by Prussia in 1866,* (London 1870)
MAUDE, Lieutenant Colonel FN, *The Evolutions of Modern Strategy,* (London 1905)
MAY, Major ES, *Guns and Cavalry,* (London 1896)
MAY, Major ES, *Field Artillery with the Other Arms,* (London 1898)
MAY, Captain J, *The History of K.u.K. Infantry Regiment Graf Khevenhüller-Metsch* Nr 35 *during the Campaign of 1866,* trans D Rogers, (Solihull 1999)
MAXWELL, Sir H, *The Life and Letters of the Fourth Earl of Clarendon,* (London 1913, 2 vols)
MCDONOUGH, G, *Prussia,* (London 1994)
MCELWEE, W *The Art of War: Waterloo to Mons,* (London 1974)
MILLER, Lieutenant Colonel F, *The Campaign of 1866 in Germany,* (London 1867)
MILLOTAT, Colonel COE, *Understanding the Prussian-German General Staff System,* (Carlisle Pennsylvania 1992)
MOLTKE, Field Marshal Count H von, *Correspondance Militaire* (Paris, 1899-1902, 5 vols)
MOLTKE, Field Marshal Count H von, *Correspondence during the Campaign of 1866 against Austria,* ed S Wilkinson, (London 1915)

MOLTKE, Field Marshal Count H von, *Essays, Speeches and Memoirs,* trans M Herms and others, (London 1893, 2 vols)

MOLTKE, Field Marshal Count H von, *His Life and Character,* trans M Herms (London 1892)

MOLTKE, Field Marshal Count H von, *Letters to his mother and brothers,* trans C Bell & HW Fischer (London 1891, 2 vols)

MOLTKE, Field Marshal Count H von, *Letters to his wife and other relatives,* (London 1896, 2 vols)

MOLTKE, Field Marshal Count H von, *Letters sur l'Orient,* (Paris 1872)

MOLTKE, Field Marshal Count H von, *Military Correspondence,* ed S Wilkinson, (Oxford 1923)

MOLTKE, Field Marshal Count H von, *Moltke as a Correspondent,* trans M Herms, (New York 1893)

MOLTKE, Field Marshal Count H von, *Strategy: Its Theory and Application,* (Westport Connecticut 1971)

MOLTKE, Field Marshal Count H von, *The Franco German war,* (London 1907)

MOSSE, WE, *The European Powers and the German Question,* (Cambridge 1958)

NASO, E von, *Moltke,* (Hamburg 1937)

NEWTON, Lord, *Lord Lyons: A Record of British Diplomacy,* (London n.d.)

NIDDA, R Krug von, *1866: Königgrätz,* (Vienna n.d)

O'CONNOR MORRIS, W, *Moltke,* (London, 1893)

OLIPHANT, L, *Episodes in a Life of Adventure or Moss from a Rolling Stone,* (London 1888)

PARET, P (ed), *Makers of Modern Strategy,* (Oxford, 1994)

PEEL, PH *British Public Opinion and the Wars of German Unification: 1864-1871,* (Maryland 1981)

PFLANZE, O, *Bismarck and the Development of Germany,* (Princeton New Jersey 1990)

PHILLIPS, Colonel G, *Text Book on Fortifications Etc,* (London 1884)

POCOCK, J, *Bitter Victory,* (Tiptree 2002)

POCOCK, J, *Langensalza 1866,* (Harrow 2002)

POTTINGER, EA, *Napoleon III and the German Crisis,* (Cambridge Massachusetts 1968)

POSCHINGER, M von (ed), *Diaries of the Emperor Frederick,* (London 1902)

PRATT, EA, *The Rise of Rail Power in War and Conquest,* (London 1915)

PRESLAND, J, (Skelton, G), *Vae Victis: the life of Ludwig von Benedek 1804-81,* (London 1934)

PRUSSIAN GENERAL STAFF, *The Campaign of 1866 in Germany,* trans Col von Wright and Capt HM Hozier, (London 1972)

REDLICH, J, *Emperor Francis Joseph,* (London 1929)

REGELE, O, *Feldzeugmeister Benedek,* (Vienna 1960)

RICH, N (ed.) *The Holstein Papers,* (Cambridge 1955)

RITTER, G, *The Sword and the Sceptre. The Problem of Militarism in Germany,* (London 1972)

RODD, R, *Frederick: Crown Prince and Emperor,* (London 1888)

ROTHENBERG, GE, *The Army of Francis Joseph,* (West Lafayette Indiana 1998)

SCHELLENDORFF, General P Bronsart von, *The Duties of the General Staff*, (London 1905)
SCHLICHTING, General von, *Moltke und Benedek*, (Berlin 1900)
SCHLIEFFEN, Field Marshal Count A von, *Cannae*, (Fort Leavenworth Kansas 1931)
SEECKT, Colonel General H von, *Moltke*, (Berlin 1938)
SHEEHAN, J *German History 1770-1866*, (Oxford 1989)
SHOWALTER, DE, *Railroads and Rifles. Soldiers, Technology and the Unification of Germany*, (Hamden Connecticut 1976)
SHOWALTER, DE, *The Wars of German Unification*, (London 2004)
SKED, A, *The Decline and Fall of the Habsburg Empire*, (London 1989)
SKINNER, J, *The Tale of Danish Heroism*, (London 1865)
STADELMANN, R, *Moltke und der Staat*, (Krefeld 1950)
STEEFEL, LD, *The Schleswig Holstein Question*, (Cambridge Massachusetts 1932)
STOFFEL, Colonel, *Military Reports addressed to the French War Minister*, trans Capt. Home (London 1872)
STOSCH, General A von, *Denkwürdigkeiten*, (Berlin 1904)
STRAUSS, GLM, *Men who have made the New German Empire*, (London 1875)
SYBEL, H von, *The Founding of the German Empire*, (New York 1891, 7 vols)
TAYLOR, AJP, *Bismarck*, (London 1955)
TAYLOR, AJP, *From Napoleon to the Second International*, (London 1993)
TAYLOR, AJP, *The Habsburg Monarchy*, (London, 1948)
TAYLOR, AJP, *The Struggle for Mastery in Europe, 1848-1918*, (Oxford 1954)
TOVEY, Lieutenant Colonel, *The Elements of Strategy*, (London 1904)
TUIDER, Dr O, *Die Preussen in Niederösterreich 1866*, (Vienna 1983)
TURNBULL, P, *Solferino: The Birth of a Nation*, (London 1985)
VERDY DU VERNOIS, General J von, *Im Hauptquartier der Zweiten Armee 1866*, (Berlin 1900)
WALKER, General Sir CP Beauchamp, *Days of a Soldier's Life*, (London 1894)
WAGNER, A, *The Campaign of Königgrätz*, (Fort Leavenworth Kansas 1889)
WARD, Sir AW, *Germany 1852-1871*, (London 1917)
WAWRO, G, *The Austro-Prussian War*, (Cambridge 1996)
WEMYSS, R *Memoirs and Letters of Sir Robert Morie*, (London 1911, 2 vols)
WHEATCOFT, A, *The Habsburgs*, (London, 1995)
WHITE, JR *The Prussian Army 1640-1871*, (London, Maryland 1996)
WHITTON, Lieutenant Colonel FE, *Moltke*, (London 1921)
WIEGLER, P, *William the First: His Life and Times*, (London 1929)
WILKINSON, S, *The Brain of an Army. A Popular Account of the German General Staff*, (London 1895)
WILKINSON, S, *War and Policy*, (London 1900)
WOOD, Field Marshal Sir E, *Achievements of Cavalry*, (London 1897)
WORMS, Baron H de, *Memoirs of Count von Beust*, (London 1887, 2 vols)
WYATT, Captain WJ, *A Political and Military History of the Hanoverian and Italian Wars*, (London 1868)
ZERNIN, *G, August von Goeben in seinen Briefen* (Berlin 1903, 2 vols)

Index

Related titles published by Helion & Company

The Franco-Prussian War 1870-71 Volume 1. The Campaign of Sedan. Helmuth von Moltke and the overthrow of the Second Empire
Quintin Barry
Paperback (ISBN 978-1-906033-45-3), eBook (ISBN 978-1-907677-58-8)

The Franco-Prussian War 1870-71 Volume 2. After Sedan. Helmuth von Moltke and the defeat of the Government of National Defence
Quintin Barry
Paperback (ISBN 978-1-906033-46-0), eBook (ISBN 978-1-907677-59-5)

The Somme 1870-71. The Winter Campaign in Picardy
Quintin Barry
Hardback (ISBN 978-1-909384-49-1)

War in the East. A Military History of the Russo-Turkish War 1877-78
Quintin Barry
Hardback (ISBN 978-1-907677-11-3)

HELION & COMPANY
26 Willow Road, Solihull, West Midlands B91 1UE, England
Telephone 0121 705 3393 Fax 0121 711 4075
Website: http://www.helion.co.uk
Twitter: @helionbooks | Visit our blog http://blog.helion.co.uk